The Villas of Pliny
from Antiquity to Posterity

Pierre de la Ruffinière du Prey

The Villas of Pliny

FROM ANTIQUITY TO POSTERITY

The University of Chicago Press   *Chicago and London*

PIERRE DE LA RUFFINIÈRE DU PREY is professor of architectural history at Queen's University in Ontario and the author of *John Soane: The Making of an Architect*, also published by the University of Chicago Press.

The University of Chicago Press, Chicago 60637
The University of Chicago Press, Ltd., London
© 1994 by The University of Chicago
All rights reserved. Published 1994
Printed in the United States of America
03 02 01 00 99 98 97 96 95 94   1 2 3 4 5
ISBN: 0-226-17300-3   (cloth)

Library of Congress Cataloging-in-Publication Data

Du Prey, Pierre de la Ruffinière.
    The villas of Pliny from antiquity to posterity / Pierre de la
Ruffinière du Prey.
        p. cm.
    Includes bibliographical references and index.
    1. Architecture, Domestic—Rome—Influence. 2. Architec-
ture, Roman—Influence. 3. Pliny, the Younger—Contributions
in architecture. I. Title.
NA324.D8   1994
728.8'0937–dc20   93-44209
                                                       CIP

This book has been supported by a grant from the National
Endowment for the Humanities, an independent federal agency.

To my teachers

past, present, and future

CONTENTS

*I*LLUSTRATIONS

PLATES
(following page 46)

FIGURES

ACKNOWLEDGMENTS

The Villas of Pliny from Antiquity to Posterity concerns designing, building, and writing about architecture. It deals to a considerable extent with literature and its relation to architects. As such it owes a great deal to the many archives, libraries, and museums that have made available books, periodicals, and manuscript material and have granted permission for them to be reproduced. These institutions, and in some cases specific persons associated with them, are listed below, arranged alphabetically by location. The various place-names alone reflect the complex scope of the research involved in this ten-year endeavor. It remains for me to add a personal note of thanks to those from so many quarters whose help made my work such a gratifying experiment in international cooperation. Annapolis: Maryland State Archives. Beltsville, Md.: National Agricultural Library. Berlin: Freie Universität; Kunstbibliothek; Schinkel Archive (Gottfried Riemann); Staatliche Museen (Marianne Fischer); Staatsbibliothek (Regina Mahlke); Technische Universität, Plansammlung der Universitätsbibliothek (Dieter Radicke). Bloomington: Lilly Library, Indiana University (Joel Silver). Cambridge: Harvard University Library. Champaign-Urbana: University of Illinois (Nancy L. Romero). Città di Castello: Biblioteca Communale (Anna Traversini); Biblioteca "Storti Guerri" (Beniamino Schivo). Clinton, N.Y.: Hamilton College Library (Frank K. Lorenz). Dresden: Sächsische Landesbibliothek. Durham, N.C.: Duke University Library (Daniel J. Rettberg). Florence: Biblioteca Medicea Laurenziana; Galleria degli Uffizi; Museo Firenze com'era. Ithaca, N.Y.: Cornell University Library (James Tyler). Kingston: Douglas Library and Interlibrary Loan (Bonnie Brooks, Pamela Thayer). London: British Architectural Library (Ruth Kamen); British Library; Royal Institute of British Architects, Drawings Collection; Sir John Soane's Museum. Madrid: Accademia di San Fernando. Montreal: Blackader Lauterman Library, McGill University (Irena Murray); Canadian Centre for Architecture (Robert Desaulniers, Robert Fortier); Université de Montréal Library. New York City: Avery Architectural Library, Columbia University; New York Botanical Garden; New York Public Library; Pierpont Morgan Library; Thomas J. Watson Library, Metropolitan Museum. Ottawa: Carleton University Library; National Library of Canada. Oxford: Ashmolean Museum (Michael Vickers); Brasenose College (Elizabeth Boardman); Lincoln College Library; Oxford Central Library. Paris: Académie d'Architecture (Mme de Vaulchier); Bibliothèque Nationale; Ecole Nationale Supérieure des Beaux-Arts (Annie Jacques); Institut de France; Institut Français d'Architecture (Susan Day).

Princeton: Marquand Library, Princeton University; Institute for Advanced Study Library (Faridah Kassim, Elliott Shore). Rome: Accademia Nazionale di San Luca; British School at Rome (Amanda Claridge); Vatican Library (Leonard Boyle). Toronto: Robarts Library, University of Toronto. Warsaw: Biblioteka Narodowa; Biblioteka Uniwersytecka; State Archives. Washington, D.C.: Dumbarton Oaks, Garden Library (John Dixon Hunt, Linda Lott).

Without the advice of contemporary architects I was privileged to meet and their generous collaboration, it would have been impossible for my study to span the period from antiquity to the present. They have assisted enormously in person or by letter, have let me interview them, and have given me permission to illustrate or quote from their works. Above all, the architects concerned have freely shared their insights, confirming my hypothesis that common ideals and practices link past, present, and future members of the profession. I salute most cordially the following: Jean-Pierre Adam, José Ignazio Aguirre, David Bell, Giorgio Benucci, David Bigelman, Jean-Pierre Braun, Ricardo Castro, Melvin Charney, Maurice Culot, Jacek Cybis, Alberto Damp, Michael Djordjevitch, Paolo Farina, Esteban Fernández, Philippe Fraisse, Jean-Claude Garcias, Michael Graves, Bernard Huet, Manual Iñiguez, Léon Krier, Phyllis Lambert, Didier Laroche, Erik Marosi, Fernando Montes, Enrique Muga, Pierre Pinon, Eugenia Salza Prina Ricotti, Serge Santelli, Thomas Gordon Smith, Justo Solsona, Manfred Sundermann, Jean-Jacques Treuttel, Jérôme Treuttel, Alberto Ustarroz, and Patrick Weber.

As this book goes to press, I would like to add a last-minute tribute to Darrell Griest, architect. I owe to his professionalism and conscientious artistry the excellent redrawings that appear as my figures 10–14, 17–18, and 24–25.

It is a pleasure to record here the names of the photographers and scholars who have assisted me in ensuring excellent-quality illustrations worthy of the artworks reproduced: Michel Boulet, J. E. Bulloz, Geremy Butler, Dominique Delaunay, Foto Grafica, George Innes, Alain Laforest, Claudia Lazzaro, Richard Margolis, Godfrey New, Tomasz Prazmowski, Hernan Sotto Lichio, Studio Littré, David Tewksbury, and Dan Wilby.

From the outset I envisioned photographs in color taken either by me or by those just mentioned as an important complement to my text. The generous subventions that have made my color plates possible deserve a few very special words. I wish to express my gratitude to the National Endowment for the Humanities in the United States for their initial grant toward underwriting the costs. For matching funds from Canada, my sincere thanks go to the Samuel and Saidye Bronfman Family Foundation and to my own university. This last mark of support coming from so close to home was all the more heartwarming, and I wish to acknowledge Dr. A. R. Eastham, Dean John M. Dixon, and Vice Principal William McLatchie at Queen's University for speeding the snowball on its downward course.

These acknowledgments would be far from complete without a glowing tribute to the many individuals who helped me by permitting access to their homes, granting interviews or permission to reproduce works of art in their collections, corresponding with me and providing documentation, assisting with travel arrangements, translating, chauffeuring, and performing a host of other invaluable acts of kindness: Richard Adams, George Alexandrovicz, Pierre-Yves Balut, T. T. Bannister, Clara Bargellini, William Beiswanger, Bettina Bergmann, Rand Carter, Douglas Chambers, John Coolidge, Joseph Connors, Arthur C. Downs, Jean-Luc and Bernadette du Prey de la Ruffinière, Sabine Eiche, Kurt Forster, Reinhard Förtsch, Ludwig Glaeser, Lee and Peter Gordon, Grzegorz Grątkowski, Delores Gutierrez, Hellmut Hager, Fritz-Eugen Keller, Margarete Kühn, Michael J. McCarthy, Alexander G. McKay, Lorenzo Mazzini, Yolanta and the late Edmond Jan Osmanczyk, Principe Castelbarco Albani, Principe Torlonia, Giovanna Pucci, Nancy Rosen, Ingrid Rowland, Marchese Giulio Sacchetti, Leon Satkowski, Marco Savelli, Charles Scarlett, Richard E. Snyder, Barbara Sulek, Roman Stachyra, Pierre Elliott Trudeau, David Watkin, and Rita Wolff.

A special group of individuals at Princeton University and the Institute for Advanced Study deserve separate mention for the encouragement and advice they gave me when this book was still in its preparatory stages: Eve Blau, Charles Burroughs, Petra Chu, Robert J. Clark, David R. Coffin, Alan Colquhoun, Slobodan Ćurčić, John V. Fleming, Alexander Grouchevoy, the late Felix Gilbert, George Gorse, Paul Siegfried Jäkel, Irving and Marilyn Lavin, William La Riche, Louis Martin, Thomas Mathews, Joseph M. Levine, Alessandra Ponte, John Pinto, Georges Teyssot, Homer Thompson, and Françoise Waquet.

In my initial research during 1982–84 I received expert assistance at the Canadian Centre for Architecture from Johanne Desilets and Jocelyn Gervais. During my 1987 stay at the Institut Français d'Architecture in Paris the organizational, diplomatic, and secretarial skills of my wife enabled me to accomplish my research objectives expeditiously. Subsequently many persons at Queen's University have aided me. Among those I would like to thank especially are the staff, the supportive students, and my indulgent colleagues in the Department of Art.

Since the preparation of the manuscript, I have been much obliged to my two readers for their helpful comments, to my editors and designer at the University of Chicago Press for the encouraging enthusiasm with which they acted upon those readers' reports, and most especially, once again, to my wife Julia for having gone over the entire text with her fine-tooth comb, eliminating mistakes, infelicities, and lack of clarity. Carol Bram kindly and most expertly read the page proofs.

This lengthy paean ends by acknowledging with loving gratitude those nearest and dearest: my wife, my son, and my daughter, who physically as well as spiritually accompanied and sustained me through the entire Plinian odyssey.

PROLOGUE

In Praise of Restitution

URING A CHILDHOOD spent in the country outside New York City, I used to be taken on periodic pilgrimages to the family dentist, Dr. Gulick, who practiced in a skyscraper high above Lower Manhattan. Those visits, despite the physical pain, were not without reward. The dental chair overlooking the Hudson River gave me a ringside seat for watching the great transatlantic liners as they entered or left the harbor guided by tugboats. As time marched on and the cavities showed no sign of stopping, I developed an additional source of distraction in the unusual local toponymy that recalled the history of the port city: Bowling Green, Conties Slip, the Battery, Wall Street, Pearl Street, Governors Island, and so forth. My mind began to conjure up vivid pictures of a New Amsterdam reborn. I visualized the wooden palisade and ditch that had given its name to the heart of the financial district. The Customs House, which I could see from Dr. Gulick's window, disappeared in favor of the old fort with the mansion of Governor Peter Stuyvesant. Broad Street would split down the middle to accommodate the canal that had once been there, so I had read, lined with crow-step gabled houses of brick imported from Holland long before the English took over and called the place New York.

My childish daydreams concocted at the dentist's reflected several things about myself and about the origins of this book. I suppose they were the first glimmerings of my interest in architectural history. Second and no less revealing, the phoenixlike resurgence of this idealized Williamsburg-on-the-Hudson provided an antidote to the grime and noise I associated with modern cities on those all-too-frequent trips to New York. Herein lay the seeds, perhaps, of a preference for the architecture of the country, which finds a distant echo in this text devoted to rural villas. Third, though I little realized it at the time, I was already happily engaged in a pursuit beloved of architects for centuries: the imaginary restitution of ideal country houses offering a pleasant escape from the daily rigors of the profession.

Restitution is a process whereby lost property can be restored, and by extension so can buildings or entire cities like Periclean Athens, imperial Rome, or the Lower Manhattan I wanted to transform into New Amsterdam. As I learned from my own thwarted experience with New York, it is rarely realized. The term restitution adroitly sidesteps the inherent ambiguities in the words reconstruction and restoration, so often loosely applied in architectural contexts that do not warrant them. Both reconstruction and restoration carry the sense of a physical act of rebuilding, either the modification of an existing structure to some former shape or an entirely new, more-or-less faithful replica rising upon old foundations. In consequence, the words restoration and reconstruction introduce an element of concreteness into a process that often goes no further than an artist's imagination, an architect's drafting table, or a child's fantasies. But restitution remains less tangible, more ambiguous, and for these reasons more appropriate to describing the intellectual pastime discussed throughout this book.

Of all the imaginary restitutions I know, none forms a more unbroken sequence from the Renaissance to the present than the one that generations of architects, archaeologists, and classicists have devoted to the lost villas of Pliny the Younger. The actual Roman country houses—reputedly situated somewhere in the Apennines, at a spot called Laurentinum on the seacoast near Ostia, and on the shores of Pliny's native Lake Como—have so far eluded discovery, despite surviving letters by their owner describing them in glowing Latin. Until archaeological excavation and precise identification take place, they will continue to hover miragelike. The villas themselves sound almost too good to be true in their combination of beautiful location, architectural refinement, horticultural ingenuity, worry-free comfort, and above all the ability to inspire, which Pliny so often sought and referred to in his writings. With no physical remains to hamper flights of the imagination, Pliny's villas become the ideal embodiment of what life in the country can mean to an artist or a client. With few restraints imposed by budget, by structural problems, or by the difficulties of a specific site, Pliny's descriptions fuel the most fanciful of restitutions. Afterward, evocations of Pliny's villas turn up in the built oeuvre of the artists who attempt them. Yet so like a will-o'-the-wisp are the villas, so vain is the effort to bring back what is irretrievably lost, that they slip through the net. There is always room for another, and perhaps better, solution.

I first became aware of the villas of Pliny in a 1966 graduate seminar conducted by David R. Coffin at Princeton University. There, among the wonderfully accessible holdings of the Marquand Library, I easily found my way to the basic bibliography, especially Helen Tanzer's pioneering book of 1924 titled *The Villas of Pliny the Younger*. In my seminar paper I concluded that the owner and the designer of the Renaissance Villa Medici at Fiesole had been inspired in their choice of hilltop situation by reading Pliny's letters—the first such imitation since antiquity. A contemporary poem sounding like Pliny supported my case, and the fortunate discovery of material revealing the later building history of the house resulted in my maiden publication, a 1969 article written in collaboration with Clara Bargellini. But despite this early interest, subsequent travels to see Palladio's villas, and the presence of a rich villa tradition in Kingston, Ontario, where I came to teach in 1971, the topic of Pliny's villas did not cross my path again for more than a decade.

In midsummer 1982 I arrived in Montreal, on a two-year leave of absence from my university, to set up study programs at the newly established Canadian Centre for Architecture. At the time the CCA's director, Phyllis Lambert, had just returned from Paris infectiously enthusiastic about an exhibition she had seen there at the Institut Français d'Architecture, devoted to the restitutions of Pliny's villas. The show and its accompanying catalog, *La Laurentine et l'invention de la villa romaine,* had been the brainchild of IFA's Maurice Culot, who came to Montreal by chance that following autumn. Then and there the decision was reached that the CCA would mount its own version of the show, which opened a year later at the Musée des Beaux-Arts de Montréal. The new title, "The Villas of Pliny and Classical Architecture in Montreal," reflected the fact that this show expanded the traveling one from Paris by including both of Pliny's major country houses, the Tuscan Villa as well as the Laurentine, and enlarged the didactic scope to consider more fully the influence the villas have exerted on classicism over the course of history. My involvement as guest curator of the exhibition established the personal contacts and set in motion the bibliographic research that has finally resulted in this book.

Among the important steps along the way were further research at the CCA in 1986, six months as a visiting scholar at IFA in 1987, and the term I spent in 1990 as a fellow at the Institute for Advanced Study in Princeton. In some respects my stay at Princeton was a return full circle to the surroundings in which my interest in Pliny had first been aroused. But on this occasion, and in a villalike setting, I profited from discussion both with former professors at the university and with my distinguished colleagues at IAS. Those discussions helped greatly to chart the course of the manuscript then being created. On the heels of these experiences, and no less fruitful in their own way, I conducted seminars on my material with graduate and undergraduate students who allowed me to test out my ideas on them and shared the freshness of their own thoughts. Further European and South American research trips in 1988 and 1991 paved the way for an intensive summer of writing and revision in 1992. For these opportunities I am much indebted to a leave fellowship and research grant from the Social Sciences and Humanities Research Council of Canada, to my supportive colleagues at the Arts and Science Research Committee of Queen's University, and to my hosts the CCA, IFA, and IAS. All three institutions offered the very sort of hospitality and stimulation that Pliny so frequently proffered to his correspondents.

At an early stage in the writing of the manuscript I decided to adopt an approach different from the chronological one employed by Helen Tanzer, or by Pierre Pinon's historical essays in the *Laurentine* exhibition catalog. These publications are readily available on library shelves, and it seemed a duplication of perfectly good effort to follow in their footsteps. Besides, a strictly chronological sequence would have obscured some of the overriding intellectual issues raised by the design of villas over the ages. As I assembled my material on the topic of Pliny's villas, these overriding themes assumed equal importance with the individual restitutions themselves. These themes touch on the relation between literature and architecture, between building and nature, and between different national schools of art. Not least of all, the pedagogical uses that literary texts like Pliny's have been put to arouses the process of emulation whereby an awareness of historical precedent provides the impetus for subsequent artistic endeavors, each rivaling and possibly improving on its predecessors. In much the same spirit Pliny himself had studied the writings of Cicero and Statius in order to create his own unique epistolary style.

Each separate restitution, of course, carries a wealth of overlapping associations that could equally well be viewed under the heading of several of my themes rather than any single one. Usually, however, I found that one characteristic or another predominated and best helped to explain the author's motivation. I have therefore grouped those Pliny restitutions that seem to have a largely archaeological bent separately from those for which Pliny's texts served as the starting point. Those that had first and foremost a pedagogical purpose form a third distinctive group, whose creators saw the alluring Pliny descriptions as a means of stimulating the at times sluggish imaginations of their students or colleagues. In all, three chapters group together the historical restitutions of the past. A fourth deals with architects of more recent times whose restitutions further exemplify emulation in action.

In organizing the chapters of this book I was mindful of the contrived literary character of Pliny's villa letters: the way they form balanced, pendant pairs; the way they move from the usual pleasantries to build up to a final flourish. In some ways I took my inspiration from Pliny's letter writing: my early chapters set out my topic; the central four develop the body of my material; the conclusion mirrors in form and content Pliny's technique of employing a climactic final passage to sum up the essence of what he loved most about each country house that he owned and himself took a hand in designing. Unlike the appetizers, main dishes, or sweetmeat course of a banquet such as Pliny served in his dining pavilions, none of my three parts should be deemed subordinate to the next. The introduction sets out the essential literary tradition that Pliny emerged from and helped to establish. His letters as a whole contributed to defining the now universally held ethos of villa life as a restful, regenerative, and artistically fruitful period of months spent in the country. But to enjoy this good life selfishly was immoral. The sense of well-being must be shared with others; it must serve as the impetus for hospitality in the broadest sense. Thus a villa, cottage, camp, or dacha, be it ever so humble, comes fully into its own once it inspires the verbal or pictorial imagery others may enjoy, even if at a distance.

The introduction specifically focuses on Pliny's literary aspirations as reflected in the two Lake Como retreats that he lovingly called "Tragedy" and "Comedy"—pet names for villas are a custom that seems to defy national boundaries or the passage of centuries. The next chapter, titled "Four Cardinal Points of a Villa," pursues the definition of villa by offering four ways of interpreting the word within the literary and architectural framework already set out. Like the different types of restitution, these categories may overlap considerably in any given example; but cumulatively, I believe, they provide a set of simple yet useful guidelines for dealing with the complex meaning of villa. Although I restrict myself to examples with a Plinian aspect, the chapter ranges widely, incidentally reflecting my own villa travels and the educational experiences that have shaped my attitude to the subject. Another example of this method of inquiry, the chapter on Pliny and the Medici, returns to take a second look at my very first article on this topic. By concentrating on a single family of Renaissance humanist art patrons and bibliophiles, I show how, over several generations, they indulged their love affair with Pliny's villas to an extent never encountered before or since. Finally, the conclusion sweeps back to consider the villa restitutions from a critical bird's-eye view. I single out those restitutions whose authors took up the pen to write as well as to draw, and who as a result seem to have penetrated closest to Pliny's innermost feelings about art, nature, and creativity as expressed through his villas and their gardens.

Readers who wish to disentangle the villa restitutions from my thematic arrangement for chronological consultation may refer to appendix 4, listing by date all of them known to Tanzer or Pinon in addition to those I have subsequently discovered. The list is as complete as it can be at this time, but it makes no claim to be all-inclusive. Conversely, neither does my text pretend to include every restitution listed in the appendix. My aim has been to select representative examples, to portray existing richness, to investigate thematic issues, and in some small measure to encourage others who will speculate in the future upon the appearance of Pliny's villas. Make no mistake, such restitutions will continue as long as the villas' physical remains elude identification—supposing they ever existed in exactly the form Pliny described. Hence my title, *The Villas of Pliny from Antiquity to Posterity,* draws attention to the ongoing nature of a phenomenally persistent architectural tradition that this book sets out to record.

"Thrums" near Glendower, Ontario   August 1993

Postscript

After my manuscript had gone to press, I received a much anticipated copy of the recent book by Reinhard Förtsch, *Archäologischer Kommentar zu den Villenbriefen des jüngeren Plinius* (Mainz am Rhein, 1993). Unfortunately it arrived too late for inclusion in my text. As its name implies, this copiously illustrated and well-researched study is archaeological in character. As I already knew from previous correspondence with the author, he has little interest per se in restitutions of Pliny's villas, either past or present. Rather, he meticulously sets out to consider a typology of Roman architectural and gardening terms as they specifically apply to Pliny's houses and their surroundings. A catalog section provides a room by room, garden space by garden space analysis of Pliny villas in combination with excavated remains that may have served as precedents. Only a few restitutions are illustrated, including several of the Tuscan Villa by Förtsch. From the point of view of completeness it is a pity I cannot reproduce them, but they show the appeal Pliny is likely to enjoy in the future.

Note on the Translations

So far as possible I have allowed foreign-language authors to speak in their own voices, especially when the passage quoted is characteristic or the phrases are well turned. In such cases I have either supplied a translation in a note or have provided in the text a brief English paraphrase to help readers grasp the meaning.

The Villas of Pliny
from Antiquity to Posterity

INTRODUCTION

Comum Tuae Meaeque Deliciae

Tell me what you are doing at Como. Como equally the object of
our delight [*Comum tuae meaeque deliciae*]! Tell me some news of that
enchanting villa [of yours]; of the gallery where it is always spring; of the plane
trees, which spread themselves most diffusively . . . are you wholly engaged
by these beauties. . . . or are you called from them, as usual, by frequent
excursions to your family affairs? Come, my friend, it is high time,
leave low and sordid cares to others and apply your mind entirely to
your studies in the deep recess of such an undisturbed retreat: let this
be your business and your recreation; your labor and your rest;
the object of your waking thoughts and of your dreams.

PLINY, *Letters*[1]

I N A PAIR of similar letters to a friend and fellow countryman, Caninus Rufus,
Pliny the Younger recommended the pleasures of study and meditation in
a villa retreat on the shores of their beloved Lake Como (bk. 1, ep. 3; bk.
2, ep. 8). Born in either A.D. 61 or A.D. 62 at the city called Novum Comum
in ancient times, Pliny knew whereof he wrote. The ancestral estates he inherited
there figure fondly in his writings. He further affirmed his attachment to Como
when he married a local woman of good family named Calpurnia. Apparently he
died before her, about A.D. 113, while on an official tour of duty in the province
of Bithynia-Pontus on the Black Sea. In the meantime the Roman statesman had
led a fairly uneventful life; his most dramatic experience was witnessing the eruption of Mount Vesuvius on 29 August A.D. 79. It claimed the life of his illustrious
uncle, the naturalist Pliny the Elder, in honor of whom he assumed the full name
Caius Plinius Caecilius Secundus. According to the younger Pliny's account, when
his uncle crossed the Bay of Naples he was left behind in the relative safety of
Misenum, reading a copy of Livy by the volcano's lurid glare (bk. 6, eps. 16, 20).
An engraving of 1751, included in the earl of Orrery's translation of Pliny's letters
quoted from above, imaginatively depicts the scene (fig. 1). It shows a messenger
bringing the teenager the terrible tidings. Characteristically, the budding litterateur
has had his nose in a book.

Although Pliny's fame rests on the elegant Latin prose of 247 personal letters
plus his official correspondence, this book focuses on the influence those writings

1. Orrery and Wale, A messenger brings Pliny the Younger the news of his uncle's death (*Letters of Pliny the Younger*, Orrery ed.)

LARII LACVS VVLGO COMENSIS DESCRIPTIO, AVCT. PAVLO IOVIO.

Excurrit Larius a Meridie in Septentrionem, pronior tamẽ in Oriente

have had upon architecture, specifically domestic architecture. During his lifetime the patrician Pliny commissioned numerous buildings, among them two villas, or country houses, on his Como estates. These he amusingly nicknamed "Tragedy" and "Comedy" in reference to their high- and low-lying situations on the lake. The location of these long-vanished structures is a continuing source of speculation among local residents. Various legends have arisen over time that have helped foster a string of villas along the lakeshore, each claiming descent from Pliny. The most architecturally outstanding gems in this misty diadem are the neighboring eighteenth-century Villa Olmo and Villa Resta-Pallavicini, just outside Como itself (pl. 1, extreme right and left, respectively). Like Pliny's ancient villas, they form an intentionally contrasting pair: the first, by Simone Cantone, is palatial but flat; the smaller second one, by Leopoldo Pollak, curves gently forward to take advantage of the view up the lake. Known as the "Rotonda" because of this central bombé feature, it occupies the approximate site of a Renaissance villa that belonged to another celebrated native of Como, Paolo Giovio (1483–1552), bishop of Nocera.

Giovio followed Pliny's advice to Caninus Rufus and retired to a life of study in the place of his birth after a distinguished career as cleric, courtier, and man of

2. Ortellius, map of Lake Como (Ortellius, *Theatrum orbis terrarum*)

letters. The analogies to Pliny do not end there. According to Giovio's posthumously published *Descriptio Larii Lacus* (1559), he planted a grove of plane trees around his house in emulation of one of Pliny's villas, although the passage quoted above referring to the establishment of Caninus Rufus was what Giovio actually had in mind. Whatever their artistic license, Giovio's book, his letters, and an anonymous contemporary description of his villa explicitly mention a grove of plane trees similar to the one that shaded Caninus Rufus when he sat beneath his colonnade.[2] Indeed, a map of Lake Como published by Abraham Ortellius in 1570 marks the site of Giovio's own villa, or *museo* (fig. 2, left), as the very spot where Pliny mentioned the grove. In physical terms, therefore, Giovio tried to embody the literary ideal of a charmed life in a villa beside Como's waters. Giovio even boasted that his study—his *museo* proper—had a balcony overhanging the lake to fish from, an advantage Pliny had also claimed. The *museo* furthermore followed the Roman custom of lining the walls with the likenesses of great literary figures, as recommended by Pliny (bk. 4, ep. 28). Although Pliny did not appear in this portrait gallery, his personality overshadowed the place as profusely as the plane trees.

Farther along Lake Como the Ortellius map pinpoints the location of an intermittently flowing freshwater spring called the Fons Plinianus (fig. 2, center of left half). Pliny certainly knew of it, because he devoted to its predictable gushes a minute description (bk. 4, ep. 30) that enlarged on the one in the *Natural History* written by his late uncle.[3] (The study of nature ran in the family.) At the precise spot where the spring spills into the lake, there still unfolds a magnificent prospect encircled by mountains. Scenes of natural beauty like these must have nurtured in the young Pliny the special love of scenery his letters so strongly convey. Whether Pliny had one of his several villas here remains moot; nevertheless, Plinian associations quickly attached themselves to the place. By about the mid-sixteenth century the so-called Villa Pliniana at Torno had been built on the site and had incorporated the famous spring into the back of its loggia (pl. 2). At the front the arcade frames a panorama preserving the aspect of relative isolation and tranquillity that must have characterized these shores in ancient Roman times. For Pliny such a natural setting gained in beauty by virtue of the architectural elements framing the scene—doorjambs, window embrasures, arches, or columns. Pliny put in writing for the first time a principle of design that villa architects have found fundamental ever since: the view through the loggia.

Pliny addressed to his boyhood friend Voconius Romanus an entire letter on the subject of their villa expansion projects, particularly those Pliny undertook on Lake Como (bk. 9, ep. 7). He joked about his buildings' relative positions above the waterline by alluding to the high-stilted or flat-soled footwear of tragedians or comedians in the ancient theater. The villa named Tragedy, he told Voconius,

occupied a ridge between two bays and consequently enjoyed panoramic views of
the type Pliny had admired at the Neapolitan seaside resort of Baiae. Ortellius
placed it far up the shore from the Villa Pliniana and directly opposite the villa
named Comedy, which sat right on the water's edge (fig. 2, left of center). Its
terrace followed the curving contour of a bay, much as Pollak's "Villa Rotonda"
does to this day—conceivably their situations are the same. The bedroom window,
within earshot of the lapping waves, served as a place to fish. What a delightful
conceit of Pliny's to equate the bed inside with being rocked to sleep in an open
boat! Yet surprisingly few of Pliny's later commentators were inspired to envision
in more concrete terms this architecture devoted to the joys of pure loafing.

An exception is Pliny's translator John Boyle (1701–62), fifth earl of Orrery
and Cork. As he rendered Pliny into English, the images of Como captivated him
as they have no other scholar before or since. Orrery's patrician background
equipped him well to interpret Pliny. For this reason I have chosen to use Orrery's
words exclusively wherever Pliny is quoted in translation. He could make telling
comparisons, for instance, between the villa at Chiswick designed by his cousin,
the architect earl of Burlington, and Pliny's villas. In 1751, just two years before
Burlington's death, Orrery brought out his two-volume *Letters of Pliny the
Younger*, copiously illustrated by the painter Samuel Wale (d. 1786). Among the
most charming of Wale's vignettes is a rare—perhaps even unique—representation
of the Comedy Villa (fig. 3). The artist chose a raking viewpoint to show off his

3. Orrery and Wale, Comedy
Villa (*Letters of Pliny the
Younger*, Orrery ed.)

command of perspective, a subject he later taught at the Royal Academy of Arts, London. A galley pulls up to the water gate of a building that looks a little like the Thames-side villa of Orrery's friend, the poet Alexander Pope. In accordance with the moral gravity of the Augustan age typified by Pope, Orrery found it necessary to censure the Como villas as "extravagant and unnecessary." But Pliny, living in the silver age of Latin writing, had said of them according to Orrery's translation, "Each . . . has particular beauties; a diversity which renders them to their master still more agreeable."[4]

The idea of retreating to the country to pursue one's literary bent is a constant refrain in Pliny's letters and those of other Latin authors. The exhortation to Caninus Rufus to adopt the life of secluded study is just one case: by no means did Pliny invent the mode of addressing a correspondent in this manner. He copied Cicero's letters not only for their epistolary style, which he admired, but also for their descriptions of villa life in the country. In a well-known instance, Cicero wrote about wishing his friend Atticus would describe his rustic shrine to the nymph Amalthea so Cicero might copy it on his own country estate at Arpinum (*Letters to Atticus*, bk. 1, ep. 16).[5] Several generations later Pliny referred to receiving just such enticing letters from Voconius, and others from his mother-in-law describing the baths in her country place at Narnia (bk. 1, ep. 4). Whatever the tradition before Pliny's time—and it may have been considerable, as these few extant prose fragments suggest—it fell to him to develop and perfect a new genre of letter. With his mouthwatering evocations of nature and the built environment, he devised what might be called the literary house and garden tour.

By Pliny's time the written description of a work of art, called *ekphrasis* by the Greeks, had become a standard literary formula, and so it continued well into the Byzantine era.[6] In general terms *ekphrasis* had focused on paintings, sculptures, interior decoration, and cityscapes. (Homer's description of Achilles' shield established a famous early precedent.) Pliny changed that once and for all by devoting lengthy passages, even whole letters, to the architecture of villas and their relation to the landscape setting. He thereby virtually invented architectural description as a separate subcategory of *ekphrasis*. His approach, moreover, differed diametrically from that of the most famous architectural writer up until then, his great predecessor Vitruvius. In *De architectura* Vitruvius emphasized such dry technical information as siting, proper foundations, drainage, structure in general, and the use of the orders of architecture in particular. Pliny adopted an entirely more sensuous—one is tempted to say impressionistic—attitude to architecture. That Vitruvius's writings escape mention in the letters probably means that Pliny was ignorant of them. He took the approach of a gifted amateur: one strong on conveying the general atmosphere of a building but weak on specifying its precise appearance. His letters, for instance, ignore structure almost totally, and rarely do they hint at even so fundamental a feature as the column. Pliny thought mainly in flat, planimetric terms, as untrained persons tend to do when attempting to design their own houses. His descriptions speak most often of simple sequences of spaces. He succeeded better when it came to garden areas, where at least the plants' botanical species automatically supply clues to shape, color, and aroma. Even so, the garden settings often sound like rooms with the ceilings left off. Pliny rendered one-dimensional what are by nature the three-dimensional arts of building and landscape architecture.

A valuable insight into Pliny's limited grasp of architectural space and mass comes in the form of a business letter he wrote to an otherwise unknown architect named Mustius (bk. 9, ep. 39). The exchange between client and architect is fairly typical of such correspondence.[7] Pliny wrote to Mustius from one of his villas concerning a rustic temple of Ceres on the property. Pliny plotted out the situation for Mustius with an accuracy befitting a surveyor. He then vaguely instructed Mustius to beautify the sacred precinct with four columns of any kind he thought suitable. An architect like Mustius or Vitruvius would never have left to chance the crucial decision on which type of column to use. The temple's appearance would depend entirely upon the system of proportions inherent in the order and would probably follow certain gender-related considerations. Almost certainly either architect would have adhered to the dictates of decorum and would have required the "matronly" Ionic order appropriate to the goddess Ceres.[8] In a way, then, the instructions to Mustius reveal Pliny's limitations as an architectural writer. He had a real gift for describing the lay of the land, yet words seemed to fail him when writing about buildings in precise terms. Perhaps, like many architectural amateurs, he simply lacked the necessary technical vocabulary. Or equally likely, Pliny may have felt it beneath his rank to delve too deeply into bricks and mortar, deferring to architects' professional knowledge in such matters.

Why, then, should we study Pliny's letters from the architectural standpoint, given their unreliability as to details or dimensions? The answer lies in the undisputed fact that Pliny's are the most telling descriptions of the Roman house to have survived from antiquity. The unaffected ease of their prose makes them extremely evocative reading even today. After all, Pliny was to the villa born. More generally speaking, the letters convey a wealth of insight into the essence of life on a country estate. As such they greatly enhance the testimony unearthed by excavations of villas. Especially valuable are the passages devoted to the gardens: until very recent times, archaeological digs tended literally to sweep away the evidence for them. No amount of scientific investigation can fully replace Pliny's graceful and natural account of the joy a landowner takes in his estates; his observance of the crops and the rotation of the seasons; his duty to his employees; and above all his sensuous delight in the odor and texture of different plant forms or the effects of the elements. His depiction of the physical setting of Roman domestic life in the country has continued to influence subsequent readers, many architects among them. This book primarily devotes itself to that wide-ranging influence and its perennial relevance over the centuries. The allure of living in a villa has not changed materially since Pliny first wrote almost exactly nineteen hundred years ago.

CHAPTER ONE

Four Cardinal Points of a Villa

APART FROM PLINY'S LETTERS describing Como, two other villa letters stand in a class by themselves. Their exceptional quality stems in part from their unusual length. Whereas most of his writings average a dozen or so sections, these comprise twenty-nine sections in the one case and forty-six in the other, making them the longest of the entire Pliny correspondence (bk. 2, ep. 17; bk. 5, ep. 6; see appendix 1 for the full texts). The other exceptional feature is their singular preoccupation with villa architecture. Nothing in Roman literature can compare with their complexity, not even the scattered references elsewhere in Pliny to such villas as those near Lake Como.

Pliny addressed the first of these two letters to a certain Gallus, perhaps Clusinius Gallus, according to some commentators.[1] The second and even longer letter names Domitius Apollinaris as its recipient. No date for either letter has been assigned with any certainty, but the early second century A.D. is probably close enough for a nonphilological study like this one. Salutations to each correspondent make clear the literary character of the exercise. The letter to Gallus opens with the purported description of a villa belonging to Pliny on the Italian coast near Ostia. The letter took the traditional form of an invitation to spend a relaxing few days in the country—Pliny himself had responded enthusiastically to such an invitation to visit Junius Mauricus at his villa near Formiae (bk. 6, ep. 14). Pliny's letter to Apollinaris, less blunt in its message, concludes by evoking as precedents the famous *ekphraseis* by Homer and by Virgil describing the armor of Achilles and of Aeneas. Just as the *Aeneid* sought to imitate Homer's passage, so Pliny implied that he sought inspiration from the Virgilian and Homeric descriptions of works of art. For Pliny the villa letter had obviously become much more than a message of welcome. He had turned it into a medium for expressing his fondness for and understanding of the allied arts of architecture and horticulture.

The letter to Gallus sets the scene believably enough at a Latian seaside spot called Laurentinum, hence the name "Laurentine Villa" that centuries of subsequent readers have attached to this property. In the letter to Apollinaris the location shifts to a spot near the source of the Tiber River in the foothills of the Apennine Mountains of Tuscany, hence the name Tuscan Villa, or *Tuscos meos*, to use Pliny's own term. Another letter mentions Tifernum (modern Città di Castello) as the nearest town (bk. 4, ep. 1). Thus the word *villa* never appears in direct connection with either place-name. The geographical location itself signified the house, and in course of time the name of its owner has become synonymous. There are in effect only one Laurentine Villa and one Tuscan Villa in the history of architecture. At the end of the letter to Gallus, however, Pliny did employ the diminutive *villula* to stand for Laurentinum, much to the confusion of later interpreters. He must have meant this as an endearment, because the house was anything but small and modest, as we will see. It was Pliny's way of playing down the size of a place noted by some recent writers for its "lavishness" and "fantastic" quality.[2]

In general the Latin word *villa* connotes a house in the country, built on a sizable plot of land and often intended by its wealthy owners as a seasonal, part-time habitation. Already in Roman Republican days the villas belonging to a single person tended to proliferate. Plutarch in his *Lives* likened the consul Lucullus to "Xerxes in a toga" because of the oriental profligacy of his expenditure on his marine establishments with their fish hatcheries. The same biographer quoted Lucullus as justifying the number of his villas with the exclamation: "Do you think me more stupid than cranes and storks that I do not change my residences with the seasons?"[3] Plutarch also recorded the famous incident of the Apollo dining room, when Cicero tried to put to a blind test the fabled epicureanism of his friend Lucullus. By a ruse, Lucullus avoided being cornered. He specified that the meal should take place in his Apollo triclinium, which he knew had the most sumptuous menu prescribed for it (Plutarch, *Life of Lucullus* 41.5–6). Cicero had little reason to play the moralist in the affair: he is credited with having eight villas of his own, including his favorite at Tusculum outside Rome, besides smaller ones on the coast. In his letters he often grumbled about his self-imposed political retirement. But if he had to be bored, he certainly chose pleasant and varied surroundings for his exile.

Like Cicero, Marcus Terrentius Varro set himself up as a judge. Whether he did so in good conscience is another matter. He too possessed country estates aplenty. That did not stop him from including in his *De re rustica* a diatribe against the senselessness of luxury villas. He wrote a mock Platonic dialogue, set it in the Villa Publica on the Roman Campus Martius, and good-humoredly named the fictive debaters Mr. Sparrow, Mr. Magpie, Mr. Peacock, and so forth (*De re rustica* 3.1.2–11). It is all reminiscent of Aristophanes' comedy *The Birds* with its jokes at the expense of architects or city planners, and it is almost as funny. But Varro's debate about the meaning of villa had a serious side. A villa is defined as a place where pleasurable relaxation (*otium*) may mix with profitable forms of husbandry (*negotium*), such as the selling of game birds. The good old agrarian days are nostalgically preferred to the palatial villas of Lucullus, which are a drain on the well-being of the state. Costly revetment in marble, such as Lucullus employed, was to be despised in favor of the plain stucco that had covered the farming villa at its inception.

By the time of Pliny, a century and a half after Varro, the opprobrium attached to luxury villas had abated, or even dissipated, so frequent had they become. Pliny circumspectly avoided boasting about the luxury of his establishments; sizable they obviously were, but not rich, to judge from his silence about ornamental painting or sculpture. Pliny let down his guard only on a couple of occasions in his description of the Tuscan Villa. He discussed an outdoor dining pavilion, or *stibadium,* where the white marble benches offset the columns of green Carystian marble imported from an island in the Aegean (see conclusion, p. 284). Earlier in the same letter he described one of the bedrooms in the villa, decorated with a marble revetment below a painted frieze of birds amid branches, speaking as if he had in mind his uncle's anecdote about the celebrated still life of grapes by Zeuxis, which live birds mistook for the real thing.[4]

In another of his letters to Caninus Rufus, Pliny criticized a former consul for doting on his villa to excess by adorning it with books and statues (bk. 3, ep. 7). Nevertheless Pliny, himself a consul, senator, and busy trial lawyer, subscribed to the time-honored custom of living in different villas at different times of the year. Those at Como stood on inherited lands, and Pliny refused to part with them at any price for sentimental reasons, even if they were not particularly profitable (bk. 7, ep. 11). He complained about having to trudge around the estates meeting tenant farmers and trying to settle their disputes, to the detriment of his literary pursuits (bk. 5, ep. 15). The Tuscan property in the hills lent itself primarily to a summer-time and autumn routine. The Laurentine Villa served for winter and spring. All this and more Pliny pointed out in two letters to the same friend, Fuscus Salinator, a fellow lawyer (bk. 9, eps. 36, 40). In the first, Pliny recounted his daily rounds in Tuscany, then in the second he went on to discuss his activities at Laurentinum. Thinking back on the letters to Caninus, Voconius, Gallus, and Apollinaris, it is obvious that Pliny liked writing pendant letters as much as he liked living in pairs of houses.[5]

Despite the unprofitable prospects at Como, Pliny's other estates did bring in some revenue. In Tuscany the principal cash crop was grapes. Letters regarding the harvest in the fall, the sale of the year's vintage, and the fairness of Pliny's dealings with middlemen show how seriously he took these matters (bk. 8, ep. 2; bk. 9, ep. 20). To Apollinaris he stressed the extensive rows of vines, but to Julius Naso he pointed out the risk of hail damage (bk. 4, ep. 6). In the next breath, however, he wrote with relief that the crop at Laurentinum had come in for him to fall back on. He alluded, seemingly tongue-in-cheek, to the figs that flourished in the sandy soil of Laurentinum's kitchen garden. But in reality the harvest he reaped came from his writing. Pliny was pretty much a gentleman farmer: neither villa could have provided for much beyond his own needs and those of his numerous servants and slaves. The question of staffing a villa brings to mind a significant omission on Pliny's part. Clearly he had slaves as well as freedmen and freed-women, but he ignores their housing except to state that it was more commodious than average. He probably considered a letter an unsuitable place to catalog his worldly goods or list his retainers. His patrician correspondents would have known such mundane details anyway from their own experience. The net effect, however, is to deny the letters the dimension of human animation. An unnatural hush hangs over the villas, except during the boisterous merrymaking at the Saturnalia, as described to Gallus.

Whatever the real statistics, the *otium/negotium* balance sheet remained an intellectual and moral goal to strive toward. Varro's writings, those of Vitruvius, and the hints in Columella's guide to property management[6] all provided the necessary background to understanding this dichotomy, but Pliny expanded enormously upon it. His analyses of the Laurentine and Tuscan villas set the ground rules for the basic definition of a villa. His writings immediately establish the main points of reference—cardinal points, as it were. They help us grasp what the villa concept meant and to some extent continues to mean, in both an architectural and a social context. The notion of cardinal points also tallies well with Pliny's own scientific method of description, which never failed to refer to the compass rose. He oriented his villas according to the prevailing winds and to the rising and setting of the sun. These constant astronomical and meteorological indicators have not changed appreciably since Pliny's day, and they have therefore added immediate comprehensibility for readers over the ages. Such fundamental considerations as orientation still lie at the heart of any intelligent client/architect discussion about the merits of a building site in the countryside. But despite this semblance of science and practicality, conclusive physical evidence of the remains of the villas has so far eluded discovery, thereby casting doubt on their true location and even their reality.

In this chapter I have selected four cardinal points to consider in depth. I shall trace them starting from Pliny's Laurentine and Tuscan villas and moving onward to others that in some way relate directly to the Plinian prototypes or that demonstrate the validity of his criteria in subsequent periods. The four cardinal points or criteria thus elucidate the basic desiderata that have motivated villa owners and designers from ancient times to the present. Each will be initially illustrated by one of the restitutions prepared by Karl Friedrich Schinkel (b. 1781) in the 1830s and published as color lithographs in the month before his death on 9 October 1841. With greater than usual artistry, Schinkel's four prints highlight these four cardinal characteristics: to see and be seen; room to breathe; openness and movement; house and garden.[7]

4. Schinkel, Laurentine Villa, perspective from the water (Schinkel, *Architektonisches Album*)

To See and to Be Seen

Pliny's letters to Gallus and Apollinaris begin with brief salutations, followed directly by descriptions of the seacoast near Ostia or the Tuscan hill country. The Laurentine Villa enjoyed a variety of prospects, including views of the Mediterranean. On the opposite side from the sandy shore where Pliny went for strolls, a rich pastureland stretched off to a backdrop of the distant low-lying Alban Hills. The general ambience is brilliantly portrayed in Schinkel's imaginary restitution of the marine villa (fig. 4). Its somewhat hazy silhouette is mirrored in the unruffled Mediterranean waters, heightening the miragelike quality of the building. A sailboat drifts by in a gentle puff of wind. Schinkel's viewpoint differs from Pliny's, which favored the entrance facade on the landward side, reached from Rome by either of two well-paved roads, the Via Ostiense or the Via Laurentina. Pliny made a point of mentioning those routes to stress the villa's relative seclusion, yet ease of access. It had a private side looking out to sea, as shown by Schinkel, and a public side facing the road. Pliny could enjoy the feeling of remoteness but still arrive at the villa after a day's work in Rome in time to spend the night. He elsewhere recommended convenience and good roads as the key characteristics to look for

when buying a country property (bk. 1, ep. 24). Villas might act as havens, but they ought not to be inaccessible or so large as to tax the energy and resources of a scholar-bureaucrat turned farmer.

On the coastline the Laurentine Villa stands out, drawing attention to itself as a work of tasteful architecture. From the public road passersby would also have enticing glimpses of it, perhaps shielded by a screen of trees. The villa hides coyly but reveals itself for the delight of its owner and his guests. In the guests it is supposed to arouse feelings of admiration tinged with envy. One cannot help coveting Pliny's possessions. In fact he concluded his letter by guessing that poor Gallus, stuck back in town, was already dying to visit the house after having only read about it. Seen in this dual sense, a villa such as the Laurentine is like a beacon by the shore that attracts attention as its prospects radiate in all directions. Lest this analogy seem restricted to the marine villa, the principle applies just as strongly to the Tuscan situation of its counterpart. There the villa nestles on the slopes of a natural amphitheater, as Pliny described it to Apollinaris. A fertile plain extends below, with the Tiber winding through it, partly navigable at this point except during the height of the summer drought. The main residence is positioned to profit from these views and from the southerly prevailing breezes. They can play in and out of the long colonnade that stretches across the entire south facade, creating a shady zone away from the glare of the midday sun. The view down into the river valley compares to a carefully composed landscape picture, according to Pliny. He added that the villa sits partway down the slope and therefore is more easily accessible than it might sound. The pristine architecture, unstained by the smoke of cities or salt from the sea air, stands out brightly for the traveler to spy from a distance against the green vineyards behind. This is no remote chalet or mountain eyrie, but a tantalizing blend of the near and the far.

Precisely this quality of the remote yet accessible seems to have inspired Andrea Palladio (1508–80) when he designed the most famous and influential villa of all time, La Rotonda (pl. 3). Not to be confused with Pollak's villa of the same name (pl. 1), this one perches on a low suburban hilltop a short distance from the north Italian town of Vicenza. The impact La Rotonda has come to exert, from its 1570 publication as a woodcut in Palladio's book to the present, owes much to the memorable quality of the graphic image itself. Palladio's *I quattro libri dell'architettura* provided an accompanying descriptive text on the page opposite the illustration. The lengthy text, unusually effusive for Palladio, reads in part:

> The site is one of the most pleasant and delightful that one could find because it is at the top of a little hill [*monticello*] with an easy ascent and is bathed on one side by the Bacchiglione, a navigable river, and on the other is surmounted by other most agreeable hills which give the aspect of a great theater; and all are cultivated and abound in most excellent fruits and the best wines.[8]

The Plinian ring to Palladio's words regarding the amphitheater of hills seems hardly coincidental. It could well mean that Palladio and his client Paolo Almerico, a cleric with an unenviable reputation for vice, had classical literary allusions in mind when placing the villa on a little knoll overlooking the bowl-shaped and vine-covered slopes of the Monti Berici (pl. 4). Palladio's text also stressed the closeness of the site to the town by river or by road. For that reason he went so far as to class the suburban villa among his palaces in the *Quattro libri*. Whatever the classification of La Rotonda, it exemplifies perfectly the first of the four cardinal points enunciated in Pliny's letters. Whether or not Almerico knew Pliny's writings, Palladio certainly did, because he mentioned them during his discussion of the villas of the ancients.

True to Palladio's written claim, the four shady porticoes of La Rotonda provide pleasingly varied views out over the landscape. The one looking west faces Monte Berico directly, that looking north the Bacchiglione's alluvial plain, that looking east a gently sloping field or vineyard; and the one looking south is steeply inclined and wooded. Originally, before the trees grew to their present height, the portico in that direction must have overlooked the full range of hills in the direction of Lonigo. Ease of access apart, these views formed the principal raison d'être for La Rotonda's being set where it is. But at the same time as they look outward, the four porticoes fulfill the other half of the "to see and to be seen" concept. They attract attention from all points of the compass. Seen from the hills above it to the west and south, the villa appears almost toylike in the valley below; its quadripartite arrangement is perfectly comprehensible, and the classical good taste of its patron is obvious to all. From the network of narrow lanes round about to the north and east, its domed profile, magnified by a raised position, could proclaim the owner's heyday in papal Rome, where he served for some years in the Vatican bureaucracy before retiring to Vicenza.[9] At La Rotonda there is no such thing as an unsightly rear facade or a bad view.

A hilltop site similar to Paolo Almerico's suggested to Karl Friedrich Schinkel an unexecuted design of 1838 for a villa in the Crimea (pl. 5). Its stunning appearance also recalls Pliny's villas, which the architect had vividly imagined just five years earlier at the behest of his patron, the crown prince of Prussia. On this later occasion Schinkel took up the pen not only to draw, but also to write to his client, the czarina Charlotte of Russia. He waxed eloquent about the location overlooking the Black Sea, a place he had never seen except in his mind's eye. Perhaps it occurred to him while composing his letter that Pliny had died on the opposite shore of that same sea centuries before. Be that as it may, Schinkel began his description as Pliny would have done, by evoking in words and pictures the situation just south of Yalta at Orianda. The architect then moved on room by room, culminating in the central temple, or valhalla, that rose above the rooftops. Appropriately

enough, the peripteral form and raised location exactly recall the design for Frederick the Great's mausoleum by Schinkel's friend and mentor, Friedrich Gilly (d.
1800). Not coincidentally, perhaps, the czarina Charlotte was Frederick the Great's
granddaughter. These Prussian reminiscences mingled with specifically Russian
ones in the courtyard immediately below.[10]

The facade of Orianda facing the water contains the principal reception rooms
and is more strictly classical in style than the rest, according to Schinkel. It even
includes Greek caryatids (pl. 6). To either side of this Crimean version of the
Porch of the Maidens, semicircular Ionic porticoes afford spectacular views out to
sea. The color lithograph printed to Schinkel's design makes it clear that the inter-
stices between the columns are filled with large sheets of plate glass—a nineteenth-
century innovation unavailable to Pliny. The anachronism notwithstanding, these
glassed-in areas refer to a passage in the letter to Gallus that Schinkel knew well
by this time. Pliny prided himself on several large windows or French doors made
of glass (*specularia*), used to shut out the bad weather but let in the light.[11] Moreover, opposite them Schinkel axially related windows for a view through the building to the inner peristyle in emulation of the arrangement at the Laurentine Villa.
By means of an almost seamless glazing technique and the alignment of the openings, Schinkel contrived to draw the eye from inside Orianda right out onto the
terrace as if no barrier existed. From this plunging vantage point, with no foreground to speak of, the sky and the water could merge imperceptibly into a common shade of Prussian blue, blurring the horizon in an almost vertiginous way.
But at the same time Orianda, on its Crimean promontory, stood out for miles
around as a perfect landmark that would have set the sailors asking what exalted
status the owners might enjoy. Transparent and natural, yet so very contrived, the
villa is never as artless as it may at first appear.

Shortly after Schinkel was preparing his Orianda design, an enterprising land
speculator in Kingston, Upper Canada (as it was then known), purchased a prime
piece of farmland, lot 22 on the western outskirts of the city. It stood about the
same distance from town as La Rotonda was from Vicenza. The owner, Charles
Hales, proceeded to develop the lower strip, conveniently bordering the King's
Highway, into a revenue-producing row of five attached houses known as Hales's
Cottages. He had them designed in 1841 by the Irish-born architect George Browne
(1811–85).[12] It seems reasonable to assume in the absence of documentary evidence
to the contrary that the same architect received the patron's next commission, for
a house named Bellevue, higher up the same slope. A slightly later date is suggested
because the house is skewed on its site in order not to directly overlook the
unsightly back view and laundry lines of the cottages (pl. 7). Instead Hales's new
house takes in an enchanting scene composed like a contemporary picturesque
painting. The foreground has a sweep of land for interest's sake, the waters of

Lake Ontario form the middle ground, and distant Wolfe Island closes off the composition on the horizon.

Soon after construction the house too became a rental property. An early tenant, the lawyer John A. Macdonald, later became a statesman like Pliny and was eventually knighted as the first prime minister of Canada. He also had a gift for writing letters. In a delightful one of 1848 to his sister he joked: "I have taken a cottage or rather, I beg its pardon, a *Villa*. . . . The house was built for a retired grocer who was resolved to have a "Eyetalian Willar."[13] Sir John attempted to mimic the plebian accent of Hales, the "grocer," and thereby poke fun at the import/export merchant's pretentiousness in wanting a villa. Elsewhere in the correspondence Sir John referred to Bellevue as Tea Caddy Castle and Pekoe Pagoda, grocery store analogies that have stuck in the popular nomenclature to this day. They still sum up nicely the fanciful and vaguely Chinese aspect of this Shangri-la marooned amid the snow.

If Browne knew Pliny's letters, he probably learned about them indirectly through such nineteenth-century pattern books as Andrew Jackson Downing's *Cottage Residences*. This publication appeared in 1842, at just the right moment for Browne to profit from it. He may well have consulted an illustrated Downing plan and elevation (design 6).[14] But the real point, which Sir John relayed from Hales's own lips, was the need for the house to stand as a hard-won symbol of its owner's aspirations to gentility. The main east-west highway, ideally positioned just below, made the villa the natural object of admiring glances from travelers. Conversely, the principal design feature of Bellevue, its Italianate and very Downingesque tower, afforded the views that the villa's name alluded to. The tower's distant antecedents are the typical fortified farmhouses of the Campagna outside Rome, so beloved of the painters Claude and Poussin, or their nineteenth-century architect imitators from John Nash to Downing. Looking even further back in history, Pliny's Laurentine and Tuscan villas both possessed towers intended mainly as viewing platforms. The Laurentine tower housed a dining room overlooking "numberless beautiful villas interspersed upon the shore," to quote from Orrery's translation. Another tower overlooked an enclosed garden surrounded by hedges and a curved exercise track. At the Tuscan property, to all appearances, the single tower mentioned must have allowed several vistas at once: up the slope to the vineyards; down into the villa's inner court; and out to the hanging gardens at the front. Quite obviously, the towers serve a dual function. They enhance views at the same time as they command attention from afar. They perfectly reflect the villa's double role in playing up the owner's status or his designer's art and in giving the inhabitants the elation of feeling they are masters and mistresses of all they survey. A conspicuous tower distills the essence of seeing and being seen. It is the very locus classicus of a villa's self-consciousness.

Room to Breathe

One of the recurrent ways Pliny characterized his villas was as places to go to for health, recreation, relaxation, and seclusion—in short, for room to breathe. He began his letter to Apollinaris on the theme of the healthful climate and refreshing altitude of his Tuscan Villa. "The heat in summer is very moderate," he wrote. "There is always some air stirring abroad. . . . To this I attribute the number of our old men." Indeed, Schinkel's Tuscan restitution takes its cue from this aspect of longevity and makes the villa appear more like a sanitorium in the high Alps than a villa in the Apennine foothills (fig. 5). Pliny's letters explain that thanks to the cool climate he could combine mental and bodily exercise. He would walk in the shade of the colonnade if it got too hot, or take constitutionals in the racecourse-shaped part of the gardens he called the hippodrome, or drive his chariot in the country, or go hunting wild game, always with a book by his side (bk. 5, ep. 18; bk. 9, ep. 36).[15] Exercise both physical and intellectual sharpens the mental faculties; peace and quiet lead to inspiration. In addition, both the Laurentine and Tuscan villas came equipped with a full set of Roman-style baths, massage rooms, and ball courts to relax and invigorate the villas' inmates. The sophisticated

5. Schinkel, Tuscan Villa, perspective (Schinkel, *Architektonisches Album*)

furnace and hypocaust meant that certain rooms adjacent to the baths would be snug enough to live in during the late autumn months. What was good enough for the owner and his guests was also good for servants. Pliny spoke in one passage about a servant valued for his recitations, whose consumption might improve if he was exposed to the better air in Tuscany (bk. 8, ep. 1).

Coupled with the recreational aspects at his Tuscan property, Pliny took full advantage of the country informality. Often in Tuscany he would shed his toga, "the Roman equivalent of the suit and necktie."[16] And Schinkel, in response, adapted his vision of the Tuscan Villa to that easygoing amorphousness compared with the blocky massing and tighter organization of his Laurentinum (fig. 4). This difference in the character of Pliny's descriptions in part explains why many more architects have chosen to visualize the Laurentine Villa than have drawn its Tuscan counterpart on paper. The one is relatively clear, in contrast to the vagueness of the other. Schinkel was one of the few to attempt both and succeed at each. He has captured supremely well the feeling of easy indolence that Pliny cultivated (bk. 2, ep. 2).

Pliny noted that in Tuscany he had elderly neighbors who sought the same healthful climate as he did. Schinkel seems to depict some of their adjacent villas on the slope above Pliny's, yet there is still no sense of crowding. The rest of the letter to Apollinaris implies a total absence of civilization by stressing the natural beauties of the landscape. Breaking into an almost rhapsodic tone, he declaims, "On every side of you are wood and wildernesses; which, together with the silence that constantly attends this diversion, are powerful incitements to study and reflection (bk. 1, ep. 6). Similarly, he expressed himself in something approaching verse when recalling Laurentinum, "O sea! O shore! Thou genuine retreat of study! How . . . you assist and enrich our invention! With what thoughts do you inspire us!" (bk. 1, ep. 9). According to these sentiments, a villa ought to be surrounded by open stretches of salubrious countryside and yet be within sight of the curling smoke from neighboring houses to ensure a desirable contact with civilization. What Pliny termed a solitary shore was not solitary at all. A neighbor's place was all that separated the Laurentine Villa from the nearby village of Vicus Augustanum. Pliny, moreover, opined that at night the twinkling lights of the other villas gave the reassuring illusion of distant cities and added to the attraction.

Perhaps the most memorable instance of Pliny's quest for solitude relates to parts of the Laurentine and Tuscan villas completely shut off from light and intrusion. At the seaside the inner sanctum took the form of a separate pavilion (*diaeta est amores mei*) where Pliny could escape the sound of the waves, the flash of lightning, or the noise of the Saturnalia (see conclusion). In Tuscany an enclosed and darkened room within the house served many of the same unusual functions. A need for tranquillity and solitude in which to write motivated Pliny initially, but surely no such elaborate architectural measures were needed. Trouble with his eyesight may have contributed to his taking these precautions. Pliny confided to Cornutus Tertullus about a worrisome temporary blindness and discussed how he used curtains and blinds to shut out the light (bk. 7, ep. 21). Contrary to what Schinkel's restitutions show, with their open colonnades and windows, Pliny may have resorted to various blinds not only to keep out the heat, but to create areas of gloomy penumbra well away from painful glare. Open yet shuttered, Pliny's villas present the first of a number of inherent contradictions.

Pliny's attitude to country living and country dwellings underwent a renaissance in the humanist writings of late fourteenth- and fifteenth-century Italy. Among the earliest exponents of these ideas, Francesco Petrarca (1304–74) practiced what he preached by ending his days at a place in the Euganean Hills renamed in his honor, Arquà Petrarca. In this retiring spot he inhabited a small house (pl. 8), placed so as to profit from the prospect of peaceful countryside whose vineyards, abundant fresh water, and breezes generally recall Pliny's Tuscan setting. As a writer, of course, Petrarch shared Pliny's need for quiet. The title of Petrarch's work of 1346, *Vita solitaria,* says all that is needed on that score. He also wrote letters of his own, apparently without knowing about Pliny's precedent. A late example, deliberately Ciceronian in flavor, was composed at Arquà and spoke of "loving solitude and quiet as much as ever . . . in the little house attractive and adequate" that he had built.[17] In this way, perhaps for the first time since antiquity, Petrarch linked the villa building type to the benefits of artistic creativity and inspiration that came from peaceful life in the countryside.

Writing before his untimely death a century after Petrarch, the precocious Michele Vieri (1469–87) implied that Pliny had by that time become the bedside reading of his fellow humanists.[18] He had a point in that the letters make a soothing way to nod off to sleep. And it certainly was the custom in the Renaissance to read from classical authors at mealtimes, on the model of Pliny during his summers in Tuscany (bk. 9, ep. 36). Federigo da Montefeltro revived such recitations at his Renaissance court in Urbino. At some time before he became marquis in 1474, he already owned a codex containing Pliny's letters.[19] The date is important because it probably places the book at the palace of Urbino during the tenure of Federigo's architect for the second construction phase, Luciano Laurana (ca. 1420–79). After his departure in 1472, Federigo's role in the design likely increased. Ludwig Heydenreich has speculated that the famous *studiolo* room in the palace is either Luciano's or Federigo's own rendition of Pliny's inner sanctum at the Laurentine Villa. There is much to say in favor of this idea. The *studiolo* answers the predilection for seclusion and study common to both statesmen. Moreover, its enclosed position lets the room be plunged into virtual darkness, like Pliny's suite. Or in an instant Federigo could fling open the doors onto an adjacent loggia (pl. 9). There, with his hands on the balustrade, he could breathe in the countryside he ruled. With a slight twist of the imagination, the view itself could be described as Laurentine by substituting the undulating hills of the Marche for the waves on the seashore.

One further point noted by Heydenreich substantiates a Plinian interpretation of the *studiolo*. Pliny's discussion of his favorite hideaway is directly preceded by the words *ipse posui*, as if to suggest that Pliny rather than a trained architect such as Mustius devised it. Similarly, the idiosyncratic quality of the *studiolo* complex cannot fail to impress today's observant visitor. The tiny rooms in this wing elicit a cramped and strangely disorganized feeling; perhaps their awkwardness derives from Federigo's whims and his dabbling in the design process. Such an interpretation would explain the bizarre planning—the way the rooms are disposed at odd angles as if to fit into the preordained envelope of external walls. As often happens when amateurs try planning their own houses, too many design features get squeezed in. Even the decoration of the *studiolo* itself, with intarsia bookcases below a frieze of classical authors, recalls the *museo* of Paolo Giovio and its Plinian precedents.[20] The connection between all three remains the need for the confines of a study combined with the equally important need for inspiration and a breath of fresh air.

In the tucked-away corner of Maryland where Whitehall stands (pl. 10), there hangs an undisturbed aura of colonial America. The house slumbers on, in defiance of the 225 years and more that separate us from its construction in 1764–65. The colonial governor Horatio Sharpe (1718–90) commissioned the house from another English immigrant, the architect William Buckland (1734–74). Sharpe named his country residence Whitehall partly for the gleaming Corinthian portico, partly in lighthearted allusion to the Whitehall in London from which he received some of his instructions and dispatches. Lightheartedness is above all the keynote of this place to escape the affairs and cares of state. Sharpe intended Whitehall for his eventual retirement, which came sooner than expected when his patron Frederick Calvert, the sixth Lord Baltimore, relieved him of his duties in 1769. Sharpe finally went to England on business in 1773, never to return. But he left behind one of the most sophisticated, though least known, of all pre-Revolutionary buildings, probably the first real villa in North America.[21]

In correspondence with his brother, the antiquarian Dr. Gregory Sharpe, Horatio used the term "small elegant lodge" to describe his new property. By this he meant something akin to what the architect Roger North had earlier defined as follows: "A villa, is quasy a lodge, for the sake of a garden, to retire to injoy and sleep, without pretence of enterteinement of many persons."[22] But Lord Baltimore's secretary and uncle preferred the Latin-derived word "villa" when writing to Sharpe about Whitehall. Since his name was Caecilius Calvert, it would not be surprising to find he knew the writings of Caius Plinius Caecilius Secundus. What-ever the case, Calvert's brother, the fifth Lord Baltimore, certainly subscribed to Robert Castell's publication of 1728 on Pliny's villas (see chap. 4). By the time Sharpe wrote to the sixth Lord Baltimore in 1767 requesting plant cuttings, fruit trees, and grapevines, Whitehall had become his "farm." Then in his subsequent letter of resignation to the same correspondent he reflected philosophically: "I shall be as happy in cultivating my Garden after resigning the Reins of Government as I have ever been since I came to America."[23] It all sounds rather like Cicero going into exile at his farm, except that Sharpe avoided the old Roman's unhappy fate of assassination.

In keeping with Pliny's use of the pet name *villula* when referring to his Laurentine Villa, Sharpe's "small elegant lodge" seems to have been primarily a plaything for amusement. The entire main block consists of a single thickness of reception rooms, centering on a magnificent hall that rises a story and a half. In the corners of the coved ceiling, carved masks of extraordinary Buckland workmanship represent the four wind gods, evoking the theme of the cardinal points. George Washington came here to a party just before Sharpe's final departure, as the future president's diary entry for 15 April 1773 attests. It has also been suggested, but without as much documentary authority, that Thomas Jefferson (1743–1826) was entertained in these same rooms during his visit to nearby Annapolis in 1766.[24] Once the guests like Washington went back to Annapolis by pinnace, the villa would regain its mysterious, less sociable side: white and remote, perceived down a long lane or seen against boxwood-bordered lawns leading up from an unspoiled expanse of Chesapeake Bay (pl. 11). The disposition is not unlike Pliny's at the Laurentine Villa. "Over against the middle portico," Pliny had similarly placed "a very handsome dining room, which projects towards the seashore; and the walls of it are gently washed by the waves of the sea." At the heart of any true villa lies a reception room with a magnificent view like Whitehall's, where good food, wine, and perhaps music mingle with the conversation of a few close friends (bk. 9, ep. 36)—"without pretence of enterteinement of many persons," as Roger North so delightfully put it.

A breathtaking landscape seen from a villa inspired some of the finest prose to come from the pen of Thomas Jefferson. Writing to his friend Maria Cosway in 1786 from his mountaintop home in Virginia, he expressed sentiments like those of Pliny centuries before: "Our own dear Monticello, where has nature spread so rich a mantle under the eye? mountains, forests, rocks, rivers. With what majesty do we there ride above the storms."[25] Pliny had commented similarly on the "many different views" from his *amores mei* pavilion at Laurentinum, where "I am never disturbed by . . . the murmurs of the sea, nor the violence of a storm, neither [by] lightning" nor thunder. The resemblances are all the more explicable considering that these very words come from the Orrery edition of Pliny that Jefferson owned in addition to an earlier translation by Robert Castell.[26] Moreover, as we have already seen, Jefferson's first love among architectural writers, Andrea Palladio, had expressed himself in similar high-flown prose when describing the Villa Rotonda on its delightful *monticello*. Jefferson owned *I quattro libri dell'architettura*, which he called "the Bible," and from which he may well have derived the name of his own Monticello.[27]

Jefferson's words quoted above strongly connote the meditative detachment sought by statesmen eager to escape their worries. He wrote Maria Cosway from an elevated plateau, looking down on what he called "the workhouse of nature." He surveyed the world from a distance, just as he had physically surveyed the uncharted wilderness as a young man. Moving his theodolite from one mountain benchmark to another to get the best visibility, he acquired his affection for high places and the detachment they provide. A literal gulf separates Monticello from low-lying Whitehall in Tidewater Maryland. In later years, so legend has it, Jefferson would use his elevated position to observe the ongoing construction of his beloved University of Virginia through a telescope. Maybe Pliny would have traded his native Italy, which even in Roman times had begun to look built-up, for these wide-open expanses of western Virginia frontier.

Palladio and Pliny conspired to express what Monticello stood for. They also helped to fashion the architecture of the house itself, though in a less direct way (pl. 12). It cannot be said that Monticello is strictly neo-Palladian or neoclassical; the sources of inspiration are far too complex for that. Monticello has one of the most fascinating building histories of any home, largely because of its gifted amateur architect-designer. Indeed, it has amateurish features—the cramped stairways, for example, or the dome room with its difficult access and the quirky laborsaving devices Jefferson invented. In a way, however, Jefferson's additive and rule-of-thumb approach would have been congenial to Pliny, whose favorite pavilion at the Laurentine Villa was an afterthought. And Pliny described certain innovations of his own, such as the system of shutters to keep out the glare. At Tuscany he had a dining room serviced by a private staircase reminiscent of the dumbwaiter Jefferson used to keep guests and servants out of each other's way. It has been suggested that, apart from many other influences on Jefferson, the unusual semisubterranean service corridors linking Monticello's main block with the wings stem directly from the cryptoporticus at Laurentinum that Pliny mentions.[28] Above all, Monticello exemplifies the exceptional integration with its site that marks much great architecture. The wooden dome echoes the crest of the mountain it sits on. In an ideal villa, therefore, a just proportion must be observed between the realms of art and nature. The one should be admirable for its artifice, while still allowing communion with the other. The villa seeks isolation, yet it is a perfect product of civilization.

Openness and Movement

Readers through the centuries have puzzled over Pliny's vague use of architectural terminology. Rarely did he specify the internal decoration or architectural framework except as already noted about the Tuscan Villa, in the painted room next to a small inner courtyard planted with four plane trees. On one point, however, he allowed no ambiguity. At every step along the way of his literary house tours, he referred his correspondents to the orientation of the principal rooms: whether they enjoyed the prevailing winds; whether they were suited to winter or summer use; whether they were secluded or noisy. Extending this principle, Pliny singled out the views from his villas, as when he stated that the bowl-shaped hills at Tuscany resembled a beautiful painting: "You would be much delighted, were you to take a prospect of this place . . . as you could scarce believe you were looking upon a real country, but a landscape painting drawn with all the beauties imaginable." In Pliny's mind, no rigid barrier existed between the real and built worlds; on the contrary, everything aimed at reducing that artificial division by any architectural means possible.[29]

Pliny's villas created a sense of openness and movement. The colonnades, cryptoporticus, and enfilades of rooms through which in his imagination he guided Gallus and Apollinaris encouraged leisurely strolling from space to space. Schinkel's restitution of the Laurentine plan (fig. 6) suggests the complicated series of movements necessary in passing through the galleries, loggias, pergolas, and bow-fronted rooms, all proclaiming an openness to the surrounding countryside. But the various twists and turns are harmonized by Schinkel's use of a sinuous line to link them all in a single movement. Outdoor terraces and promenades in the gardens further blur the distinction between interior and exterior. The door and window surrounds themselves frame views of the seashore so as to reinforce the association between real views and the painted ones Pliny mentions. Earlier in the first century Statius had resorted to such framing devices in his poem extolling the delightful views from the Neapolitan marine villa of Pollius Felix—a happy man indeed, as his name suggests. From the Capo di Massa promontory he enjoyed the silhouettes of Cape Sorrento and Cape Miseno appearing through different windows, like the scenic lookout points along the modern Amalfi Drive as it twists its way along this same coast. Pliny could relate to Statius's description, having spent some of his youth at Misenum across the bay. He said that his three-sided Laurentine dining triclinium, like Pollius's, dominated three different expanses of the sea.[30]

This selfsame Laurentine triclinium stood in the path of the occasional southwest gale, which at times sent the salt spray beating against the walls. An adjacent group of rooms, by contrast, protected from the wind in the lee of the house, formed a kind of solarium ideal for winter. The cryptoporticus in the garden Pliny

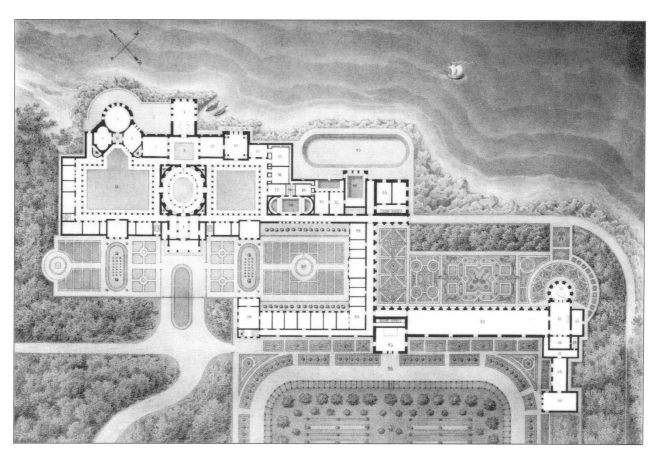

6. Schinkel, Laurentine Villa, plan (Schinkel, *Architektonisches Album*)

devised so as to keep off the southwesters by means of shuttered windows. But by opening them in calm weather, he could "have a thorough draft of the west wind, which prevents all bad effects arising from the stagnation of unwholesome air." No less importantly at the Tuscan Villa, the free movement of air figured right from the beginning of the letter to Apollinaris. The thermal system of downdrafts prevalent in the mountains creates convection currents, giving rise to refreshing gusts. In the middle of one wing of the villa the text describes a perfect dining gazebo, open to the "wholesome air" from the Apennines. These frequent references to winds, vistas, and crisscrossing axes demonstrate how vital Pliny considered them to the success of a villa. Proper alignment to distant landmarks, to prevailing breezes, and to the rising or setting sun dictates the overall form a villa must take. Obviously it must be more supple than rigid to pliantly comply with so many overlapping climatic and picturesque considerations.

The onrushing, wavelike motion of Pliny's prose, captured nicely by Schinkel's Laurentine plan, hardly gives the reader time to catch his breath. Pliny professed unawareness of the conceptual difficulty his letters pose. They must be followed very closely so as not to lose the thread leading one through a virtual labyrinth of interior and exterior spaces. At one point Pliny did apologize to Apollinaris for the length of his letter, but he went right on to add yet another digression to an already protracted text. He likened his letter to a long walk—in fact the longest in his entire oeuvre—in the course of which the reader could pause and sit down, scroll in hand. (The digressions are like the marble benches Pliny thoughtfully provided in his own garden *stibadium.*) The sauntering, meandering quality of Pliny's villas made for difficult reading, particularly in the prearchaeological age when people understood Roman domestic buildings less well than they do today. The same apparently aimless drifting, however, suggests a flexibility of planning to the would-be emulator who takes Pliny at his word. Pliny reflected well the sprawling—at times almost incoherent—Roman villas designed during the period of the Flavian emperors he served.

In a way somewhat analogous to Pliny and the Roman emperors, Agostino Chigi (1466–1520) served as financial adviser during the reign of two great Renaissance builder-popes: Julius II della Rovere and Leo X Medici. It was Agostino who decided to move his banking operations from his native Siena to Rome in a bid to secure an international clientele. He thereby bought his way out of the merchant class, and his labors were rewarded when his great-grandnephew became the Chigi pope Alexander VII. Coinciding with the death of Agostino's father in 1505 and his own rise to head of the firm, he purchased a suburban building site on the banks of the Tiber with the hilly vineyards of Trastevere behind it. According to Christoph Frommel, the situation would have recalled to Agostino the Tuscan Villa of Pliny. More recent researches into Chigi's art patronage have added weight to Frommel's rather tenuous geographic association.[31] Specifically, Agostino's self-mythologizing took a very Tuscan turn at the hands of his articulate hangers-on. These eulogizers simply redrew the map of Italy so the southern border of Tuscany (more properly ancient Etruria) would fall precisely on the Tiber's northern shore. By means of this geographic sleight of hand they could write of Agostino's future villa:

> Magnanimous Chigi built his
> Palace, a Tuscan himself, right on Tuscan soil;
> So that the god [Jove] himself, whenever he came from the heavens
> Might find another heaven ready to hand on earth.[32]

Let us remember that Pliny was not above self-flattery, as when he replied to a letter describing a rival villa by turning it into a compliment to his own in Tuscany (bk. 5, ep. 18).

In a spirit of chauvinism, Agostino hired his compatriot Baldassare Peruzzi (1481–1536) as the architect for the Villa Farnesina. The actual construction did not begin until two or three years after the land purchase, and it was almost complete by 1510. For the next decade Agostino used the villa as a sort of corporate reception center. The dinner parties he gave there for his papal clients have become legendary.[33] Their sumptuousness, leavened with a touch of bawdy humor, seems thoroughly in keeping with Agostino's character as a rough diamond. Despite a certain personal crudeness, his villa must rank as one of the most innovative and cultivated of its day, not least on account of its openness coupled with the element of movement (pl. 13). Peruzzi achieved this by adopting for the villa a U-shaped plan that literally embraces the garden parterres and invites movement out from the house toward the terrace or vice versa. The Villa Farnesina's exterior, once richly figured in a painting technique known as *terretta,* set a new standard of elegance. Here the villa building type finally returned to Rome, the scene of so many of its early associations stretching back to Varro. For several hundred years to come the villa would remain the ne plus ultra of status symbols—a barometer of the rising and falling fortunes of papal families and their favorite artists. In a twist of fate, papal *nipoti,* bureaucrats, and bankers simply replaced the senators and dictators of ancient Rome. Luxurious villas again were pawns in a renewed round of exiles and the inevitable sequestering of property that followed.

Peruzzi's previous villa for the Chigi family a short distance southwest of Siena provided the model for the Farnesina. At least as early as January 1500 Agostino mentions a villa on the site as belonging to his father; and since its name, "Le Volte," meant vaults, it implied a still earlier structure of some sort.[34] Peruzzi's name has been connected with it on account of the marked resemblance between the Farnesina and the two projecting wings at Le Volte, dated 1505 in a Latin inscription that refers to the house as a *refugium.* But in the light of new documents, these wings must be Peruzzian additions to an already inhabited structure or structures. Indeed, the front and back portions of Villa Le Volte convey two quite different impressions of scale and probably of architectural intention. If the hypothetical two-phase building history is correct, it appears to be a matter of coincidence rather than design that the completed building came to resemble a traditional Roman porticus villa with projecting corner blocks.[35] Nevertheless, by the time of the Farnesina's construction, Peruzzi had profited from the experience at Le Volte, and his artistry had matured.

The U-shaped configuration of the Farnesina is among the most open the Renaissance produced. Its other claims to fame include the Peruzzi outbuildings in the gardens, which extended the architectural sphere to a now-lost riverside banqueting pavilion where Agostino entertained in truly Lucullan style. His repasts featured costly place settings on which were served exotic dishes such as giant sturgeon, byzantine eels, and parrots' tongues—this last item on the menu surely intended as a humorous talking point.[36] Pliny, with his demeanor of moderation in all things, would certainly have censured such showy excess. His letters never mention extravagant meals except once when he questions the good taste of certain lascivious entertainments around the dinner table (bk. 9, ep. 17). Whether Peruzzi's pavilion reflected a knowledge of Pliny must remain moot. But at least two Peruzzi drawings in the Uffizi for garden layouts indicate a sophisticated design sense, and one of them shows a garden feature in the form of a hippodrome (U453A recto, U580A recto).

The crowning touch to Agostino's Farnesina gardens came in 1514 when he commissioned from Raphael a now half-destroyed stable block and guesthouse fronting the street. Here Agostino staged a banquet for Leo X, who did not realize where he was eating until the horses were revealed in their stalls hidden behind tapestries. Previously Raphael had contributed his celebrated *Galatea* fresco to the downstairs of the main villa, reached by the equally brilliant frescoed open loggia in the center of the garden facade. The artists employed inside tried in every way to reinforce the notion that the villa spilled over into the outdoors. The climax occurred about 1515 in the upstairs room called the Sala dei Prospettive, where Peruzzi turned his talents to painting. His trompe l'oeil columns and fictive loggias seem to open out to views in the same manner as those doors and windows that Pliny describes as framing a picture. In the Farnesina, of course, the landscapes are painted and the breezes are an illusion. According to a time-honored anecdote, one of the Peruzzi landscapes contains a view of the Farnesina itself. To a former scene painter like Peruzzi, this architectural play within a play would have been a congenial conceit. The playful punning humor would not have been lost on the practical joker in Agostino Chigi.[37]

What Peruzzi began in terms of openness and movement, Palladio continued to develop at La Rotonda (pl. 3) and Vincenzo Scamozzi (1548–1616) capitalized on at the Villa Rocca Pisani. The Scamozzi villa of 1576 took its name from a former Pisani stronghold on the site in the Monti Berici, no more than a dozen miles from La Rotonda. The one can almost be seen from the other, so exposed is the Villa Rocca Pisani on its bald hilltop (pl. 14). For its altitude alone it ranks high on any list of Renaissance villas. In date it followed quickly on the heels of La Rotonda and owes much to Palladio's conception. To add to the similarities, in their final form the two domes resemble one another closely because Scamozzi completed and altered Palladio's building after his death in 1580.[38] Nevertheless, to categorize Scamozzi as an imitator, let alone a desecrater, of Palladio would do him a grave injustice. The Villa Rocca Pisani has a character of its own, fine and almost ethereal. It is so open, so insubstantial, that despite its cubic mass it gives the impression it might blow away.

Scamozzi included the Rocca Pisani in his *Idea dell'architettura universale* (Venice, 1615), along with an imaginary restitution of the Laurentine Villa, the first ever to be brought out in print (fig. 50). The circular Laurentine courtyard influenced Scamozzi's plan for the Rocca as much as Palladio's La Rotonda did. In any event a strong case can be made for Scamozzi's reliance on Pliny's writings. As a book, the *Idea* is construed in a very different way than *I quattro libri dell'architettura*. Where Palladio provided hardly a single date for his works and embellished their appearance in his woodcuts, Scamozzi strove to avoid any ambiguity. The description of the Pisani villa, the character of its owner Count Vettor, the reason for the commission, the plan, the elevation, the location, the orientation, and the construction technique all come across crystal clear. And clarity is certainly the word for the Rocca. In phrases that recall the letter to Apollinaris, Scamozzi noted that from the villa high above the plain, on a clear day uninterrupted views extended as far as the distant Alps. He went on to state that the quality of the air and the limpid light were what had motivated the client to build his future vacation home here. As was implicit with La Rotonda, the Rocca's radially symmetrical plan and its dome explicitly echo the underlying pure forms of nature and of geometry.[39]

Besides permitting views from the front steps or from the large Serliana openings on the other three sides, the Rocca Pisani's axial organization promotes cross-ventilation. Wide corridors leading back along four major routes converge in a round domed room open to the sky through an oculus (pl. 15). Here in the center, the crisscrossing axes transfix the visitor, creating the sensation of a man-made Scamozzian universe. The bone-white dome above suggests the terrestrial globe or, better still, a giant cranium—like being inside the skull of the architect. In all the Renaissance, Scamozzi comes closest to evoking Pliny's concept of the villa as a glorified breezeway where one can circulate as freely as the wind. Indeed the house, which surely was never heavily furnished, is virtually empty and devoid of distracting painted decoration. In its echoing, almost naked, state it invites balletic movement through its spaces and darting glances at the views that open up at every architectural pore.[40]

Pliny is no stranger to California-born architect Thomas Gordon Smith (b. 1948). In 1980, as a recently returned scholar from the American Academy in Rome, Smith actually built the first houses in modern times inspired by the Laurentine and Tuscan villas. Neither bears any relation to the seaside or hilltop situation of the originals; they resemble two gaily painted bungalows occupying lots side by side on a perfectly flat suburban street in Livermore, California.[41] Not content to let his Plinian vision fall prey to the changing tastes of successive owners, Smith decided in 1981 to design an antique-style house for himself (pl. 16). Illustrated here as it reached completion in spring 1983, its location at first had little to recommend it. The skinny lot is four times as deep as it is wide. The villa stands amid fairly ordinary houses in Richmond near Berkeley, where Smith was teaching in the school of architecture. To redeem the banality of his surroundings, he named the house Richmond Hill after the poem about Richmond upon Thames by the

seventeenth-century writer Thomas d'Urfey.[42] Artfully selected camera angles enhance the villa look by avoiding the neighbors' chain-link fences and dodging
telephone wires. An aura of Italy comes across especially well under sunny California skies, when the cast shadows have an almost Mediterranean depth, or at night
when the adjacent dwellings fade into obscurity and Richmond Hill stands out
with illusory monumentality.

Richmond Hill set out to achieve grandeur and openness on a budget of
$95,000—a mere drop in the bucket for Pliny, Agostino Chigi, or Vettor Pisani.
The young Smith salvaged massive Tuscan columns from a demolished sanitorium
and covered the ordinary frame-and-plaster walls with Texas limestone coursed in
imitation of Roman *opus quadratum.* The columns create a vine-covered pergola
effect while acting as a carport. Underneath, in the equivalent of Pliny's elliptical
gestatio, children can race their tricycles in safety. Then at the sides and the back
a seemingly random fenestration pattern with large areas of glazing lets in the light
from every direction. Smith's cunning insertion of mezzanines, like those Scamozzi
used for the Rocca Pisani, creates several interesting internal and external changes
of level. In this way Smith provided five rooms and usable attic space amounting
to nearly 1,600 square feet.

In terms of internal movement, the living room at the back of the house (pl.
17) fuses two kidney-shaped spaces into one, in the manner of Smith's favorite
Roman baroque architect, Francesco Borromini. The twin ellipses move the gaze
sideways out a pair of corner windows and over a sea of suburban rooftops to a
distant glimpse of San Francisco Bay. The decor evokes Pompeian Third Style wall
paintings. The frieze depicting birds could come straight out of Pliny's letter to
Apollinaris. All this takes place in a claustrophobically cramped area. Smith pushes
everything to the brink: reminiscences of Tuscan farmhouses, Pliny the Younger's
pergolas and enfilades, Pliny the Elder's Pompeii before the eruption, and so forth.
It is like a habitable history book of architecture. What does it really achieve? A
love of sun, shade, vegetation, views, breezes, freedom of movement, and the
artistic will to synthesize all these transcends any triteness the historical references
may connote.

House and Garden

According to Roger North, quoted earlier, a villa exists "for the sake of a
garden." His statement implies an interdependence between the villa and the
landscape garden surrounding it. Time and again the letters of Pliny to Gallus and
Apollinaris bear out this close relationship. Pliny provided his correspondents with
ample details about his plantings, specifying them far more fully than the architecture of his villas. At Laurentinum, for example, the relatively sandy and arid soil
supported only some fig and mulberry trees, and a few vines around the approach

drive. Hedges of box were interspersed with the even hardier rosemary bush, whose name alludes to its original marine habitat. Rosemary also is useful in cooking. Pliny in fact alluded to a kitchen garden, but he failed to say what grew in it. All this makes a pleasant and sweet-smelling enough picture, though not nearly as elaborate as Schinkel made it out to be (fig. 6). He played up the Laurentine garden lest it pale by comparison with the greater profusion of detail in his Tuscan Villa plan (fig. 7).

The top of Schinkel's Tuscan plan, here turned upside down to avoid confusion, corresponds to the north, where a principal access route to the villa descends through sloping vineyards. The bottom of the plan corresponds to the south-facing elevation shown in Schinkel's perspective view (fig. 5). In the southernmost part of the foreground, to speak in the same highly pictorial terms Schinkel employed, lies a sea of soft acanthus waving in the breeze. Perhaps Pliny resorted to this watery analogy in landlocked Tuscany when he missed the shoreline at Laurentinum.[43] The acanthus bed extended into the fields, where Schinkel's foliate borders encroach

7. Schinkel, Tuscan Villa, plan (Schinkel, *Architektonisches Album*)

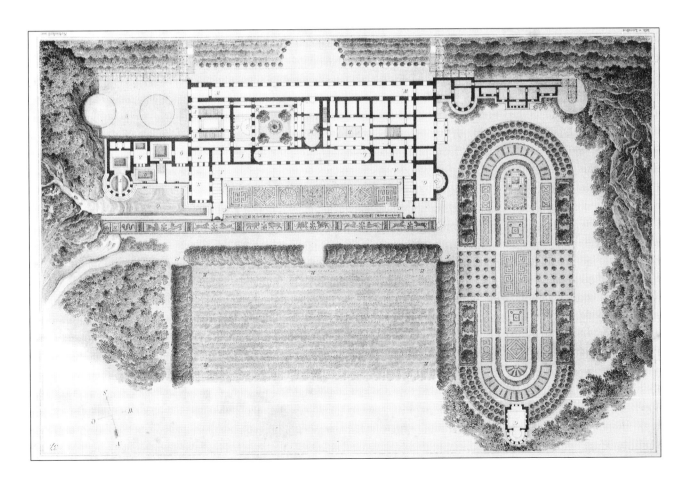

upon the more tamed area, hinting at a wilder part of the estate. A pergola, like a long, vaulted tunnel of green, encloses the acanthus and represents the walkway (*ambulatio*). Here is an interesting instance of the garden as an inducement to healthy physical exercise—not in the sense of Pliny's pulling weeds, of course, but in the sense of his walking a considerable distance in his grounds as a constitutional. In addition, there was a driveway shaped like a racecourse (*in modem circi*) and a riding paddock, as we will see presently.

To return to Pliny's perambulation without getting out of step, the middle area contains the southern terrace, elaborately laid out with topiaries in the shapes of various animals. Passing on into the breezy colonnade of the loggia, a courtyard lies ahead, clearly distinguishable because of its four plane trees. These same trees abound in the most spectacular section of the garden, off to the right. Pliny described it as a hippodrome, or riding ground, constructed entirely from plants. The plane trees delineate the sides of the ellipse, with festoons of ivy draped between them and box or laurel hedges filling in the gaps below. The ends of the ellipse, however, introduce a deeper shade of green because of the cypress groves planted there. Pliny's horticultural knowledge and his painterly eye together create a varied spectrum of colors that jumps from the pages of the letter to Apollinaris. Even Schinkel's fertile imagination had difficulty coping with Pliny's next remarks—that the lawn of this paddock was somehow interspersed with box hedges spelling out the names of Pliny and the topiary artist. Then come box shrubs cut into obelisks, more letters of the alphabet, and—in the middle—a small wilderness garden in imitation of nature's half acre. It is all reminiscent of the profusion of shapes down the central *spina* of a Roman racecourse.

One feature that emerges clearly from Pliny's verdant version of the Circus Maximus is the architectonic quality of the tonsured geometric forms (Pliny used the word *tonsis*) and the roomlike spaces they imply. Pliny described all this just as he would have done for an interior suite.[44] Not content with this complex verbal picture, Pliny added a final glorious touch at one end of the hippodrome in the dining pavilion he called his *stibadium*. As with the analogous *amores mei* pavilion at the Laurentine Villa, Pliny and Schinkel saved some of their greatest words and images for this (see conclusion and fig. 182). Water from fountains flowed through and around the little structure, creating natural air-conditioning. Presumably the canal system hooked up with the one servicing an additional structure near at hand, which Pliny mentioned and Schinkel showed on an axis with the *stibadium*. This little building served as a bedchamber. From a shaded recess tucked away within it, Pliny's couch looked out over the gardens as though from an open-air glade, with only a vault of foliage for a roof. On this tantalizing note Pliny interrupted his letter, feigning fear that he might be boring his correspondent. No wonder

Pliny concluded his letter to Apollinaris by saying that he preferred his Tuscan Villa to all the others except the Laurentine.

When Italian Renaissance humanists found their way to the letters written to Gallus and Apollinaris, the discovery promoted at least as much interest in gardens as in architecture. After all, without Pliny there would have been virtually no visible evidence on how the ancient Romans had perfected the art of horticulture. Pliny's vivid language let anyone familiar with roses, box, and rosemary easily visualize the garden settings. The architectural descriptions, by comparison, remained hard to grasp precisely because their terminology was unfamiliar. The Florentine architect Bartolomeo Ammannati (1511–92), who specialized in gardens and waterworks, would naturally have found much to inspire him in Pliny's writings. In common with his near contemporary Palladio, however, Ammannati expressed his familiarity with Pliny indirectly, by taking up the pen. Never mentioning Pliny by name, Ammannati nevertheless couched in very Plinian terms a letter he sent to a Paduan friend and client on 2 May 1555.[45] The recipient, Marco Benevides, received a lengthy account of the Villa Giulia and its gardens on the outskirts of Rome, which Pope Julius III del Monte had pushed to near completion that same year, the year of his death. Step by step, space by space, Ammannati led his reader through the whole complex—and complex it is in both senses of the word. It is complicated not simply in spatial terms, but also on account of its tangled building history.

A special brand of Tuscan chauvinism, already encountered in the discussion of Agostino Chigi, resurfaces two generations later at the Villa Giulia. Before becoming pope in 1550, Cardinal Giovanni Maria del Monte gathered around him three central Italian artists: Giacomo Barozzi da Vignola (1507–73), Giorgio Vasari (1511–74), and Ammannati. Before taking charge of the Villa Giulia project in 1551, Vasari had landscaped a farmstead or *gran coltivazione* on the slopes near the future pontiff's native town of Monte San Savino in Tuscany. Then Vasari's exact contemporary and frequent collaborator Ammannati arrived on the scene. Third, the Bolognese Vignola had had entrusted to his capable hands the engineering aspects. The pope had met him in that capacity while acting as papal legate to Bologna. Vasari readily acknowledged Vignola for having completed the main villa building, but he reserved to himself credit for the overall design, with a little advice from his friend Michelangelo Buonarotti. So the Villa Giulia is really a four- rather than three-sided artistic puzzle.[46]

To return to Ammannati's letter, it conveys a good picture of the Villa Giulia in all its complicated parts. The text mentions first the main villa building on which Vignola principally worked. The stern, rusticated entrance facade proclaims a country atmosphere. But it hides the unexpected delight of an elegant semicircular court facade (pl. 18), whose form suggests the cavea of an antique theater.

Indeed, Ammannati's letter resorts to theatrical terminology to describe the facade and the large courtyard it overlooks. Given the fondness for amateur theatricals in the papal courts of this period, performances may have been held in this part of the Villa Giulia. Almost immediately another change of scene takes place, when the first courtyard suddenly gives way to a lower one reached by two curving staircases. The paved floor at the bottom has protective railings around a sunken nymphaeum fed by the waters of the Acqua Vergine spring, famous for its therapeutic powers since antiquity. Tucked away virtually out of sight is the pope's private bathing area, where Julius could disport himself and gain some relief from the gout he suffered like a martyr.

Despite some later alterations and some points of Ammannati's letter that continue in dispute, the picture it paints of the villa in the last days of Pope Julius has served as the basis for a fairly reliable restitution drawing by the late Turpin Bannister (pl. 19). It takes as its vantage point the level of the *giardino secreto* behind the second courtyard. There birds in aviaries sang amid the scent of the orange trees counted among 36,000 plant specimens reputedly purchased for the project. Level upon level, surprise after surprise unfolds before the viewer's astonished eyes. Not least surprising, the second court is shown as less stony than it is today. Renaissance prints and Ammannati's letter concur that the courtyard was planted with "quattro plantani." So precise a reference to the exact number and species of the trees must surely relate to the four plane trees in Pliny's courtyard adjacent to the fresco-painted room in the Tuscan Villa.[47] Was the Villa Giulia, like the Farnesina, intended as some sort of *imitatio* of Pliny's villa? If so, which of the three designers was the mastermind behind it?

The answer to the second question is probably Vasari, because of both his greater erudition and his prior role in the Monte San Savino garden, geographically close to the reputed site of Pliny's Tuscan property. In his life of Fra Giocondo, Vasari revealed his acquaintance with Pliny's letters when he referred to their rediscovery. He also knew about the 1508 printed edition by Aldus Manutius and the critical writings on Pliny by the French classical scholar Guillaume Budé (known among philologists as Budaeus).[48] But Vasari's knowledge of Pliny by no means excludes Ammannati from the picture. The letter to Benevides argues for Ammannati's having absorbed Plinian ideas from Vasari, if he had not already done so when working with Girolamo Genga in the 1530s on the Villa Imperiale near Pesaro.[49] According to one Ammannati scholar, the story does not end at the Villa Giulia either. Ammannati went on to design the Palazzo Pitti in Florence, with its attendant Boboli Gardens. Its central elliptical area could refer directly to Pliny's Tuscan Villa, and by extension to Grand Duke Cosimo de' Medici's rebirth of the Tuscan state.[50]

In common with the Renaissance *studiolo* at Urbino, the Villa Giulia emulates

Pliny in an unsystematic way. Specific elements taken from the letters blend with elements dictated by the client. Pope Julius III certainly had no lack of personal whims. His well-earned reputation for flightiness may in part account for the extreme idiosyncrasy of his villa. Anecdotes about Julius disporting himself seminude at his villa—like Pliny without his toga—probably contain a good deal of malicious exaggeration encapsulating a grain of truth. They have given rise to John Coolidge's colorful description of him as "the last pope to . . . gorge, to gamble, and to sunbathe naked amid the pagan splendors of his own suburban villa": a real-life Silenus figure among his marble statues of nymphs.[51] As with Agostino Chigi's Farnesina, great sophistication in the architecture and gardens went hand in hand with the coarse personal habits of the pope, notably a passion for onions. Some of the villa's eccentricities, like the sunken bath to ease Julius's gout, may relate directly to the pontiff's indigestion. Pliny's hydrotherapeutic provisions at the Laurentine and Tuscan villas come readily to mind. Above all, however, the pope's self-indulgent hedonism, unexcelled since Pliny's day, explains the Villa Giulia's sequence of courtyards and water gardens.

What of the possible Plinian interests of Vignola, the third of the architects working at the Villa Giulia? His later works merit investigation, especially since they include several elaborate gardens, notably those at the central Italian villas of the Farnese at Caprarola and Giovanni Francesco Gambara at Bagnaia, over the hill. Vignola's authorship of the Villa Lante at Bagnaia, as it is now called, hinges on the interpretation of a letter from his employer Cardinal Alessandro Farnese to Cardinal Gambara regarding the loan of the architect's services for some unspecified work in September 1568.[52] The friendly spirit of information sharing among brother cardinals and neighbors made practical sense. At Caprarola, Vignola had encountered the challenge of building on a steeply sloping site and had overcome it on so vast a scale that the Farnese complex is generally referred to as a palazzo or *regia* rather than a villa. Moreover, Vignola's experience with canalizing springs for waterworks on the one side of Monte Sant'Angelo could serve Cardinal Gambara on the other. Work under a supervising architect pushed ahead at Bagnaia, advancing to near completion by 1574, but not quite reaching it.

From the outset the design at Bagnaia called for two pavilions, or casinos, sharing a common terrace about midway between upper and lower levels of the garden (pl. 20). During Gambara's lifetime only one pavilion was built and inhabited. A subsequent owner carried out the second (that on the left), finally fulfilling Gambara's intentions almost half a century later. Pliny's delight in pairs of villas is worth bearing in mind as a possible source of inspiration for Gambara and Vignola. Twin buildings situated on a terrace are something of a Vignola hallmark and a strong point in favor of attributing the Villa Lante to him. His well-documented Orti Farnesiani of earlier in the decade features just such an arrangement. In the

case of these Farnese pleasure gardens on the Palatine Hill, the structures act as
open belvederes from which to admire the ruins of the Forum Romanum. To an
only slightly lesser extent the Bagnaia gardens take precedence over the buildings,
which in any event are blocky pillbox affairs of no great distinction. They become,
in the words of David Coffin, mere "garden ornaments";[53] others on the same
terrace included colonnaded grottoes on the lower level with colonnaded aviaries
positioned above. To describe them, the marginalia of seventeeth-century engravings and drawings of the estate employ the Latin term *hypoporticus,* a word Pliny
never used, though this does not diminish his possible influence.

In an analogous position along the embankment wall of the next terrace higher
up ran a pair of similar colonnaded passageways, single-story this time and called
porticus deambulatoriae. The aviaries already referred to might well derive from
the ornithon that Varro described as ornamenting his villa at Reate. But the porticoes strongly recall those mentioned in Pliny's letters. To strengthen the link further, this terrace has cool waters from Monte Sant'Angelo running down the middle
of it and constantly refilling a long, tablelike trough in which to chill bottles of the
local vintage (pl. 21). (Elsewhere on the property there formerly stood a fountain
with Bacchus and four inebriated companions astride large wine barrels; and at
La Rotonda the drain cover in the floor of the central room depicts the head of a
faun with grape leaves in his hair.) Commentators agree that the table fountain is
without precedent except in Pliny's description of his Tuscan dining pavilion. This
stibadium had Carystian marble corner columns supporting a pergola that shaded
the reclining diners, who sailed little boat-shaped sweetmeat dishes back and forth
across the watery surface. As the number of servants needed decreased so the
intimacy increased. What an unforgettable image of lazy living![54]

At the Villa Lante the upper terraces were less dark, green, and secluded
before the grove of large plane trees on the hillside grew to full maturity. Originally
the terrace with the table fountain provided a more open picnic ground for alfresco
parties centered on a cold buffet. With chilled wine in hand, or seated on the
balustrade with a good book, one could see an enchanting view down to the lowest
terrace and the silhouette of Bagnaia's rooftops. Perhaps coincidentally, the central
motif at this level also resembles a table—a round one this time. Boats containing
jets of water rather than sweetmeats float on the surface of the four ponds that
surround the island in the middle, probably emulating an ancient naumachia rather
than Pliny's *stibadium.* Whatever the exact levels of meaning—surely as many as
there are terraces at the Villa Lante—the whole presents a consummate Renaissance integration of house and garden along the lines specified by Pliny.

Of all the attempts to recapture the essence of Pliny's villa gardens, none can
surpass those that Schinkel executed for members of the Prussian royal family on

the outskirts of Berlin in the 1820s and 1830s. The earliest of this series of villas is the one built for Prince Karl at Klein Glienicke (pl. 22) on the bank of the river Havel where it broadens into the Jungfern See. The main building, called the casino, got under way in 1824. Schinkel collaborated on the design with Karl's elder brother, Crown Prince Friedrich Wilhelm. The heir to the throne, an amateur of the arts at least as talented as Jefferson or Federigo da Montefeltro, felt the same love for architecture as a distraction from affairs of state. His passion for Mediterranean culture, which he shared with Schinkel, was reinforced when the architect returned to Germany from a trip to Italy in 1824, imbued with the classical scenes he had witnessed. The result was Glienicke, much more a true Italianate villa glistening in the sunshine than a Prussian schloss.[55]

Schinkel and his royal patrons consulted the genius of the place, which at Glienicke consisted of a delicious spot at the point where the main road from Berlin crosses over the Havel to the Potsdam side. The presence of water and the possibility of arriving by boat suggested a final form not unlike the Laurentine Villa restitution produced almost a decade later, except slightly higher on the embankment. An artistic impulse on Schinkel's part, related to yet separate from the restitution of Pliny's villas, thus informed and helped shape that process. Especially similar are the integration of the villa with gardens, the blockiness of the built forms, the play of reflections on the water, and the general feeling of horizontality. At Glienicke the horizontality results in large part from the way the garden elements extend the house laterally by means of vine pergolas. The pergola as a motif fuses plant and built materials in obvious emulation of the way a villa at its best integrates with its natural environment. In much the same spirit of integration, a pergola was added to Glienicke by Schinkel's frequent collaborator and pupil, Ludwig Persius (1803–45).[56] Some distance inland from the casino he erected a treillage-work roof carried aloft by a single caryatid over a curving bench that purports to be a Plinian *stibadium*. From under its canopy of leaves Prince Karl's view once stretched as far as the Charlottenhof Villa where his brother, the crown prince, had previously planned a *stibadium* of his own in fulfillment of his and Schinkel's Plinian dreams (fig. 181). Thus the power of a mere literary description connected the two royal siblings not only to each other across physical space but through the dimension of time back to Pliny.

CHAPTER TWO

The Medici and Pliny

A S SOON AS PLINY'S NINE BOOKS of personal correspondence began to circulate in public about A.D. 100, the process of rewriting and corrupting them began. The law of human error soon took charge to the extent that what pass for Pliny's letters are undoubtedly only a distorted version of what he originally wrote. Despite the inevitable mistakes and all the knotty philological problems that have ensued, the sheer existence of these texts remains remarkable. Their survival owes a great deal, no doubt, to the tireless efforts of medieval scribes working away in monastic scriptoria. Once again it is a question of writing, in this case the physical act of recopying what Pliny had put down in the first place. The monks laboriously transcribed Pliny by hand, replacing each old manuscript as it wore out, not so much because they cared what Pliny wrote about architecture as because they appreciated the specialized vocabulary he sometimes employed, his elegant turns of phrase, and the insights he provided into ancient Roman life in general.[1]

The preserved medieval manuscripts of Pliny belong to several "families" of texts all produced about the same time. One widely circulated compendium available before 1419 comprised a hundred letters culminating with the one to Apollinaris—a fact that underscores its significance. In that year, however, Guarino Veronese found in the chapter library of Verona cathedral a now-lost manuscript of all nine books of letters, which he proceeded to copy. This was the origin of the various Pliny editions that have come down over the past four centuries. Some would attribute it to pure coincidence that Guarino's discovery occurred at almost exactly the same time as that of a copy of Vitruvius, found by the humanist scholar Poggio Bracciolini in the Saint Gall monastic library in Switzerland. Another explanation for the twin discoveries so close in date is that Poggio and Guarino had been attuned to seek out such material by a rising neoantique aesthetic promulgated the previous century by such proto-Renaissance thinkers as Petrarch. Thanks to them, Pliny's writings found a wider acceptance in the quattrocento—at least that is one conclusion to be drawn from the hundred or so manuscripts dating from that century alone, each testifying to the author's popularity.[2] The advent of printing, of course, increased his readership.

Among quattrocento philologists, the architect Fra Giocondo stood out from the rest. He not only found a Pliny manuscript in Paris, as we saw in the previous chapter, but also found a Vitruvius manuscript at Ghent and included information

from it in his 1511 printed edition of *De architectura*. A knowledge of Vitruvius
and Pliny can similarly be proved for the architect Leon Battista Alberti (1404–72).
The case can be argued more circumstantially for his near contemporary Michelozzo di Bartolommeo (1396–1472). By the 1440s Michelozzo had become the
favored architect of Cosimo de' Medici (1389–1464), merchant banker and unoffi-
cial ruler of Florence. Their association culminated with the building of the Palazzo
Medici in 1444. Michelozzo remained in the family's employ until his definitive
departure in 1462 to work as chief fortifications engineer for the city of Dubrovnik
on the Adriatic coast.[3] Among his other notable domestic structures for the Medici,
Michelozzo carried out their villa at Fiesole overlooking Florence, initiated at the
moment of the invention of printing by movable type. In its own way the *all'antica*
Villa Medici made as significant a contribution to the domestic architecture of the
Renaissance as contemporary innovations did for book production.

On the hill at Fiesole, Cosimo de' Medici purchased a property called Belcanto
on the slope facing south, overlooking Florence and the whole Arno river valley.[4]
On this challenging site Cosimo's architect built a villa for his client's younger son,
Giovanni di Cosimo de' Medici (1421–63). The attribution to Michelozzo rests
solely on the authoritative life of the architect by Giorgio Vasari, whose opinion
always commands respect in instances like this where no earlier documentation
has come to light. Vasari discussed Fiesole in the context of Michelozzo's other
villas for the Medici but singled it out as

> another magnificent and honored palace at Fiesole, the foundations being dug in the
> side of the hill at a great expense, but not without great advantage, since in that lower
> part he made vaults, cellars, stables, butteries, and other fine and useful rooms. . . . in
> this building Michelozzo displayed his full worth in architecture because the building,
> besides what I have said, was so well constructed that although it is on the slope, it
> has never stirred a hair's breadth.[5]

Hewn out of the living rock, the Villa Medici had yet another advantage in addition
to the long list provided by Vasari. Its own crater became the source of its materials;
the quarries at Fiesole had produced excellent building stone for centuries.

In characteristic fashion a letter carries on the villa's story. It is a letter written
in the autumn of 1455 by the humanist Bartolomeo Scala (1430–97) to his mentor,
the philosopher Francesco Filelfo. It reports to the recipient that Scala had just
paid a visit that same afternoon to their mutual friend Giovanni de' Medici at
Fiesole, where he found him "rusticating, absorbed in his building." In the course
of their conversation a Filelfo missive and poem previously received came up.
Giovanni promised he would reply, but in the meantime he sent the message viva
voce that he wished some obscurities in his readings of Petrarch explained—an
appropriate enough author to come to mind in the setting of a country retreat.[6]
On the assumption that this precious piece of evidence refers to the Villa Medici

and not to some other building project, it securely places its inception near the middle of the decade. In any event work probably halted about the time of the death of Giovanni's son Cosimino in the autumn of 1459, at which point Giovanni is said to have lost heart. Apart from the date of construction, the Scala letter sheds light on the question of patronage at the Villa Medici. The text strongly implies that Giovanni personally initiated and supervised the building with family backing but not under parental control, an inference that has to be considered in detail later on, once the original appearance of the villa has been established. Finally, the letter conveys the impression of Giovanni as a humanistically inclined patron, an impression further supported by the "Dialogue of Consolation" Scala addressed to the bereft Cosimo after Giovanni's death.[7]

No surviving fifteenth-century document better portrays Giovanni de' Medici than a warm tribute written by the architect Antonio Averlino (ca. 1400–ca. 1465) at a time when Giovanni already lay dead and flattery could not avail the writer to the same degree. The Florentine Averlino, known by his Greek pseudonym Filarete, penned his words of praise in the twenty-fifth and last book of his manuscript *Treatise on Architecture*, written in the period that separated his own death from Giovanni's. Without obsequiousness he praised Giovanni for his "gentle soul" and his love of the arts.[8] And it is as a lover of the arts that Giovanni emerges briefly from the shadow of Cosimo. Filarete's remarks are confirmed by scattered references to Giovanni's patronage that take the form of dedications in illuminated manuscripts of great beauty that he commissioned and that in some cases still occupy the shelves of the ancestral Bibliotheca Medicea Laurentina in Florence. This evidence of Giovanni's artistic pursuits first came to light when the eighteenth-century Medici historian William Roscoe put to use the scrupulous earlier researches of the great bibliographer Bandini, onetime librarian of the Laurentian collection.

Angelo Maria Bandini's cataloging efforts in the Medici Library had revealed a series of codices with associations to Giovanni, some of them precisely dated in the mid-1450s when the Villa Medici was under construction. According to a delightful rhyming passage in a letter to Giovanni of 31 August 1457, he possessed a fine Cicero, a Lactantius, a Virgil, a superb Flavius Josephus, and among other texts, Columella's *De re rustica*, which would have provided food for thought at a villa.[9] The same singsong shelflist goes on to mention the Catullus and Tibullus manuscript, datable to 1457 from the colophon, and a copy of Pliny's letters, which Bandini could not connect to any specific codex by means of secure inscriptions. But Bandini relied too heavily on documentary evidence to the exclusion of stylistic considerations. A manuscript edition of Pliny's letters in the Laurentian Library (Plut. 47, cod. 31), richly illuminated with Medici mottoes and heraldic insignia, gives every indication of having been prepared for the same client as the Josephus

(Plut. 66, cod. 9) or the Silvius Italicus dated 1457 (Plut. 37, cod. 16). The interest of the Pliny, moreover, extends into the philological sphere. It is one of the few early manuscripts to describe the Laurentine Villa's courtyard as shaped like a letter *D,* the now generally preferred reading of the obscure passage in question.

Filarete's praise of Giovanni continued when he singled out the collections the Medici had amassed of books, antique gemstones, and musical instruments. (Vasari's life of Michelozzo seems to echo Filarete when it refers to a library and a separate music room at the Villa Medici.) More to the point, perhaps, Filarete discussed the Villa Medici itself in an interesting light. He called it a "luogho . . . per refuggierio," in other words, Giovanni's retreat where "he could go when he wished to take the country air." This statement gains additional credence when compared with the main biographical fact known about Giovanni: his reputation for youthful dissipation and his subsequent chronic ill health. As early as 1438 his mother was inquiring about her seventeen-year-old son's kidney complaint. From then on hardly a year went by that Giovanni did not take the waters at some spa like Bagno di Petriolo.[10] So the "country air" Filarete referred to may have had a direct bearing on a patron known for a recurrent health problem, someone perhaps inclined to read with special interest Pliny's claim that his Tuscan Villa promoted good health for himself and his entire household (bk. 8, ep. 1). In this sense the villa at Fiesole may rank as the first recorded *station climatique* of modern times.

Additional evidence for regarding the Villa Medici at Fiesole as a special place, not only out of the mainstream of villa building for its date but eccentric even within the oeuvre of Michelozzo, turns up in a witty contemporary anecdote. The anecdote, in a collection of *facezie e motti* by Teodoro degli Angeli, records a reputed discussion between Cosimo and Giovanni. The pragmatist Cosimo supposedly said that his son's love of the expansive view at Fiesole was not worth the expenditure, because the land itself was not fertile. Cosimo preferred his own Michelozzo-designed villa in the lush valley at Cafaggiolo. When Giovanni asked how his father could enjoy living on a flat plain the reply was that at least there everything Cosimo saw belonged to him: "Cio che tu vedi di quivi è tu."[11] By implication the anecdote highlights the fact that constructing on the heights of Fiesole was regarded as something of an engineering marvel in contemporary technological terms, a point to which Vasari's life of Michelozzo subsequently returned.[12]

Two quattrocento paintings and a cinquecento tapestry testify to the fame of the Villa Medici in its heyday. The earliest of these works of art is a fresco painted by Domenico Ghirlandaio between 1481 and 1490 as part of his cycle decorating the choir of Santa Maria Novella in Florence (fig. 8). By including the villa in the remote top right of the *Adoration of the Lamb,* the artist paid an oblique compliment to his client, Giovanni Tornabuoni, maternal uncle of Lorenzo de' Medici

8. Ghirlandaio, Villa Medici, Fiesole, detail of the ca. 1490 fresco *Adoration of the Lamb,* Santa Maria Novella, Florence

(1449–92), who by this time had inherited the Fiesole property. Out in the street the actual villa on its slope would have been easily visible to the naked eye, but inside the church the painted representation might only have caused a smile among Giovanni Tornabuoni and his circle, so far out of sight is it on the tall north wall. Protected from the light, the colors have remained vivid: a whitish gray for the villa and red for the roof, set amid a vernal green landscape against a slightly overcast sky. Seen from the floor of the choir the perspective works best. The earthworks and terracing Vasari admired loom more majestically from this vantage point than when the angles have been corrected by the lens of the camera. Higher up, the buildings that look down on the villa belong to the convent of San Girolamo, one of Giovanni de' Medici's good works. Ghirlandaio's difficulty arose when he tried to depict the access road that seems to wind up to the villa, disappears behind a conveniently placed hillock in the middle ground, and then pops up again at the top.

The *Annunciation to the Virgin,* a panel altarpiece by Biagio d'Antonio, includes an almost identical view of the Villa Medici in the background, prominently positioned directly above the lilies the archangel is presenting to the Madonna. In the painting Biagio improved on the perspective technique of Ghirlandaio, with whom he sometimes worked. As a result the lower terrace with its plantings can be better distinguished from the upper terrace on the level of the main eastern loggia of the villa.[13] In fact the only *all'antica* feature of the villa as depicted is the eastern loggia arcade. The fresco shows it with four arches. The panel picture, slightly later and hence perhaps less reliable, depicts only three arches, placed to the left in violation of Renaissance norms of bilateral symmetry. But the paintings both agree in showing a simple, compact, grayish cube of a house that would have stood out like something of a sore thumb when newly built on its empty hillside.

The last work of art dates from 1571–72 and was probably inspired by the earlier paintings. It belongs to the series of five tapestries commissioned by Grand Duke Cosimo de' Medici to commemorate the exploits of his great namesake and to hang in the Palazzo Vecchio in the room that also bears Cosimo's name. They were woven in the Medici tapestry works from cartoons by the Flemish artist Jan van der Straet (known as Stradano). One of the scenes has recently been brought to light in Siena and was included in the Council of Europe's 1980 exhibition in Florence on the patronage of the Medici.[14] It depicts Cosimo il Vecchio seated in a Savonarola chair contemplating a model of the monastery of the Badia at Fiesole, whose construction he paid for. In the background at some considerable distance, thickly woven and on a small scale, stands the Villa Medici, appearing much as it does today from the beautiful Badia. (Was Cosimo's placement of the Badia meant in some sense to upstage his son's contemporary works at San Girolamo and at the villa?) Thus the tapestry shows that the Villa Medici, over a hundred years after its completion, still attracted the attention of painters and designers by virtue of its innovative quality and its prominent position on the unbuilt-up slopes at Fiesole. Artists focused on it as if with the aid of Galileo's as yet uninvented telescope. At no point in its long history has the Villa Medici at Fiesole been safe from prying eyes. No doubt the retiring Petrarch, one of Giovanni de' Medici's preferred authors, would have gasped in horror to find that wayside rest stops and even inns had sprung up to accommodate travelers who wanted to gawk at villas and their inhabitants.[15]

The proportions of the Villa Medici no longer accord with the appearance recorded by the painters and tapestry weavers. Before the First World War the art historian Bernhard Patzak had already assembled a good deal of documentary evidence on the villa, together with the few visual sources known to him. Bothered by the villa's length in proportion to its height, he hypothesized that the house had been radically altered at some point. He deduced from the engravings in Giuseppe Zocchi's *Vedute delle ville e altri luoghi della Toscana* (Florence, 1744) that the building's original three stories had diminished to two by the date of Zocchi's publication (fig. 9). But the quattrocento paintings unknown to Patzak prove that he erred in his conclusions. When comparing Zocchi's views with photographs of the villa from below, Patzak had failed to take into account that the high position of the villa tends to make it look taller than it really is. Patzak's uneasiness about the proportions, however, proves to have been founded on astute observation. Alterations had in fact occurred in the eighteenth century, but they took place slightly later than he had speculated and were of a different order.

The Medici disposed of the villa at Fiesole in 1671 for 4,000 scudi. After that it changed hands numerous times before being acquired in 1772 by Margaret, Lady

9. Zocchi, Villa Medici, Fiesole, detail of a drawing for plate 39 of the 1744 book *Vedute delle ville e altri luoghi della Toscana* (Pierpont Morgan Library, New York City, 1952, 30:39)

Plate 1. Borgovico near Como, Villas Resta-Pallavicini and Olmo facing Lake Como

Plate 2. Torno, Villa Pliniana, view of Lake Como from the loggia

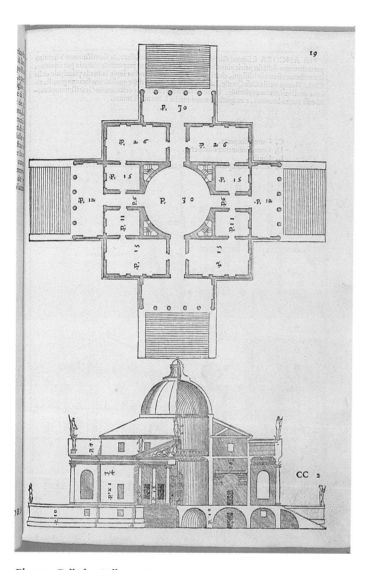

Plate 3. Palladio, Villa La Rotonda, plan, elevation, and section (Palladio, *Quattro libri dell'architettura*)

Plate 4. Vicenza, Villa La Rotonda, view from the west portico

Plate 5. Schinkel, Orianda Villa, perspective looking out to the Crimean Sea (Schinkel, *Entwurf zu dem Kaiserlichen Palast Orianda in der Krimm*)

Plate 6. Schinkel, Orianda Villa, perspective of the terrace (Schinkel, *Entwurf zu dem Kaiserlichen Palast Orianda in der Krimm*)

Plate 7. Kingston, Bellevue,
west facade

Plate 8. Arquà Petrarca, House of Petrarch, east facade

Plate 9. Urbino, Palazzo Ducale, view from the *studiolo* balcony

Plate 10. Whitehall, south facade

Plate 11. Whitehall, view from south portico

Plate 12. Monticello, west facade

Plate 13. Rome, Villa Farnesina, west facade

Plate 14. Lonigo, Villa Rocca
Pisani, south and west facades

Plate 15. Lonigo, Villa Rocca
Pisani, interior of the rotunda

Plate 16. Richmond, Richmond Hill House, south and west facades

Plate 17. Richmond, Richmond Hill House, interior of the living room

Plate 18. Rome, Villa Giulia,
west facade

Plate 19. Rome, Villa Giulia,
restitution of the west facade
and gardens by Turpin Bannister (T. T. Bannister collection, Rochester, N.Y.)

Plate 20. Bagnaia, Villa Lante, pavilions and gardens from the west

Plate 21. Bagnaia, Villa Lante, table fountain

Plate 22. Berlin, Schloss Glienicke, west facade from the
water

Plate 23. Fiesole, Villa Medici, view from the east loo[k]
ing down the *viale*

Plate 24. Fiesole, Villa Medici, east facade

Plate 25. Fiesole, Villa Medici, east and south facades from lower terrace garden

Plate 26. Fiesole, Villa Medici, west facade

Plate 27. Fiesole, Villa Medici, east facade and upper terrace gardens

Plate 28. Poggio a Caiano,
Villa Medici, south and west
facades

Plate 29. Poggio a Caiano,
Villa Medici, loggia in south
facade

Orford, who was the widow of Robert Walpole, earl of Orford and elder brother of Horace Walpole, the celebrated letter writer, novelist, and amateur architect.[16] Knowing of Horace's architectural interests and kinship to Lady Orford, his correspondent Sir Horace Mann, the British consul at Florence, took pains to report on her activities in his chatty letters. In no uncertain terms Mann revealed to Walpole on 13 April 1776 that "your sister Countess some years ago converted the long lease of a villa on the hill at Fiesole into a purchase since when she has made great alterations to the house and has done all she could to make it accessible in a coach which it never was before."[17] The editor of Vasari's lives of the artists, Gaetano Milanesi, added in a footnote the information that Lady Orford had employed the architect Nicolò Maria Gaspare Paoletti (1727–1813). Milanesi specifically credited him with the present avenue from the east, lined with magnificent rows of cypress (pl. 23).[18] Against this somber massing of dark green, the alluring white villa in the distance stands out crystalline and pure.

In the eighteenth century the twisting and narrow Via Vecchia Fiesolana was almost as convoluted as depicted by Ghirlandaio, and it remains so to this day. Although Mann described Lady Orford as uncommonly vigorous for her age, she must have found the access to her villa too tortuous. She therefore created a *viale,* or carriage drive, linking the house to the new Via Fiesolana on a gentle downward slope. At the same time, as Mann noted, she had Paoletti make changes to the villa itself—changes she enjoyed only briefly before her death in 1781. After that the villa passed into and out of English hands throughout much of the nineteenth and early twentieth centuries, ending up with Lady Sybil Cutting-Scott-Lubbock. About 1915 her second husband, the art historian Geoffrey Scott, began collaborating on the villa with Cecil Pinsent (1884–1963), a landscape architect with an extensive practice among the expatriate British in Tuscany. In the years during and just after the First World War, Scott and Pinsent created the existing garden layout at the Villa Medici and were responsible for installing the red lacquer paneling inside the library.[19] Perhaps in that very room, within sight of Florence and enjoying the smell of the wisteria arbor or tubbed lemon trees (pl. 24), Scott wrote the 1924 epilogue to his book *The Architecture of Humanism.* Careful records kept by Pinsent show that he hardly changed the house at all structurally, though he could see that changes had taken place earlier. And so the villa continued virtually unaltered until the 1987 restoration of the exterior stucco at the expense of the present owners, who have treasured the house since acquiring it in 1959. The architect for the restoration, Giorgio Benucci of Florence, has skillfully returned the buff-colored, slightly shimmering coat of intonaco to the way it appeared in the quattrocento. He has thereby intensified the dichotomy between the soft vegetation of the upper and lower terraced gardens (pl. 25), partly of Scott and Pinsent's arranging, and the Michelozzo villa's faceted cubic mass.

Looking back over its history, marked by so many different owners, the Villa Medici at Fiesole has resisted major alterations except for those of Lady Orford and Paoletti. Superficially the present east or garden facade looks much as it did in the Ghirlandaio fresco (cf. fig. 8 and pl. 24). Old photos taken before the restoration, however, reveal that the fourth arch of the loggia as shown by Ghirlandaio really existed but had been blocked up, leaving telltale marks in the plaster. Pinsent also found column shafts embedded in the existing piers, which would correspond to the more slender quattrocento appearance. To reopen the missing archway, of course, would destroy the present symmetry of the facade and draw further attention to the long, low proportions that Patzak found so atypical of the 1450s. But if the imagination strips away the last bay on the north or right end of the facade, at the same time reopening the arch on the left, then everything falls into place and Patzak's problem is resolved as if by magic (fig. 10). Can it be as simple as that? The answer is probably no, but because insufficient photographic records were kept when the stucco was removed in 1987, a hypothetical reconstruction diagram based on Benucci's measured survey will have to suffice. At the very least the diagram demonstrates how easily Lady Orford's architect could have made a room out of the last bay of the loggia and created an entirely new section on the opposite end without losing symmetry. In fact, he could achieve even truer classical balance by having the composition center on a void archway rather than on a solid Michelozzo column.

10. (*Below*) Fiesole, Villa Medici, east elevation. Dotted lines and hatching indicate hypothetical restoration (line drawing after Benucci)

11. (*Opposite, top*) Fiesole, Villa Medici, plans of principal floor. Dotted lines and hatching indicate hypothetical restoration according to first and second versions (line drawing after Benucci)

12. (*Opposite, bottom*) Fiesole, Villa Medici, plans of upper floor. Dotted lines and hatching indicate hypothetical restoration according to first and second versions (line drawing after Benucci)

Street

N

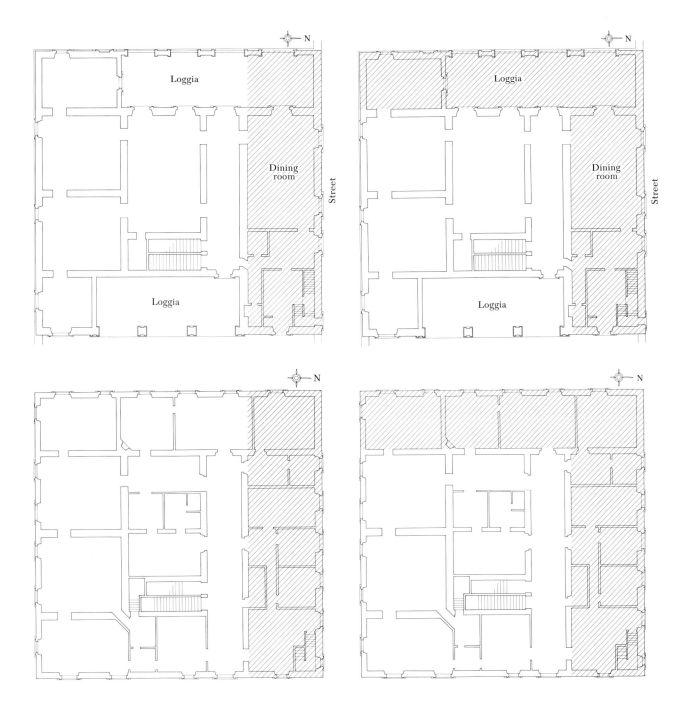

Until Benucci carried out his complete and reliable survey in preparation for the restoration, it was never possible to assess the repercussions of the shortened east facade upon the interior disposition (figs. 11 and 12).[20] Although some of the plans' measurements are approximate, the right-hand wall of the central corridor on both floors is certainly thick enough to have acted as the principal load-bearing exterior surface on that side. Conjecturally, to eliminate everything lying to the right or north of this wall would simply remove two rooms on the main floor. The kitchen in the southeast corner is no loss; it would surely have been relegated to the extensive Renaissance basements in any event. And the adjacent dining room, to judge from its present interior decor, could date entirely from the eighteenth-century remodeling. Its windows directly overhang the busy Via Vecchia Fiesolana. To dine in a villa within spitting distance of the public road makes nonsense of the concept of "room to breathe." Turning to the bedrooms directly above, the partitions between the various chambers facing north are demonstrably thinner in construction than those elsewhere on the same story. Had poor Giovanni de' Medici placed his sickbed in any of these spaces, he would never have had a moment's respite from the noises below, reverberating off the stony street. It would have defeated the healthful and peaceful ethos he sought in the villa.

These same complaints occurred to Giovanni's occasional correspondent Leon Battista Alberti, who voiced them as early as 1450 in his book *De re aedificatoria*.[21] Of course Alberti had downtown Florence in mind when he complained about being awakened by carts in the street and the swearing of their drivers. But the same applies to the Villa Medici, which occupies a notorious hairpin bend where cursing motorists try to squeeze past one another. More fascinating still, Alberti's proposed remedy caused him to make one of his rare references to Pliny. "Take the advice of Pliny the Younger in one of his letters," wrote Alberti, who then went on to describe the *amores mei* pavilion at Laurentinum and the way a corridor or dead space had served Pliny as a sound and light barrier.[22] In accordance with Alberti, removing the existing northern sections of the Villa Medici would place the ample east-west corridor on both floors in just the right position to insulate the house from street noises. It would also continue to provide good back-to-front access and ventilation in the manner of a Venetian palace corridor, or *androne*, an analogy Patzak made long ago. Furthermore, assuming roughly the present disposition of house to public road, a garden wall on the site of the present north facade would provide greater spaciousness around the villa, with more openness and less constricted movement. The Alberti and Pliny associations seem to fit the Villa Medici like a glove.

Having carried the hypothetical reconstruction of the original Villa Medici this far, consider the implications for the west-facing facade. A thick slice would have to be cut off the north end, reducing the present loggia from four bays to three

Street

N

13. Fiesole, Villa Medici, west elevation. Dotted lines and hatching indicate hypothetical restoration according to first version (line drawing after Benucci)

(fig. 13). Indeed, the somewhat indistinct Zocchi preparatory drawing in the Morgan Library (cf. fig. 9) does indicate three large arched openings along the piano nobile level. The present-day elevation therefore approximates what Zocchi saw about 1740. On plan, however, the bedroom story, with its four awkwardly reached chambers separated by thin partitions, hints that an important intermediary stage had intervened. Below on the main floor an open loggia occupies the entire width except for a small sitting room in the southwest corner. A similar room on the basement level (fig. 14) abuts the unusually placed chapel. Like a public church rather than a place of private worship, it occupies the entire rest of that floor and opens onto the western forecourt.[23] (Note that the chapel's length stops short at just the point where the proposed northern section would have been added by Paoletti.)

One piece of corroborating physical evidence to emerge from the replastering of the villa concerns this western facade. Before the masons covered up the traces and it was too late to document them photographically, Benucci found blocked-up *bifora* windows on the level of the bedchambers. What he saw was almost certainly the remains of the open arcuated *upper* loggia clearly visible in a Telemaco Buonaiuti aquatint (fig. 15) illustration in his *Una giornata d'istruzione a Fiesole* (Florence, 1826). Since no such arches appear in the Zocchi drawing, the upper loggia would

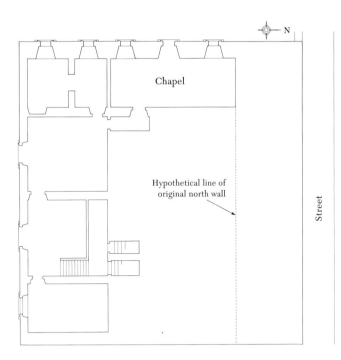

Chapel

Hypothetical line of
original north wall

N

Street

14. Fiesole, Villa Medici,
plan of basement floor. Dotted lines and hatching indicate hypothetical restoration
(line drawing after Benucci)

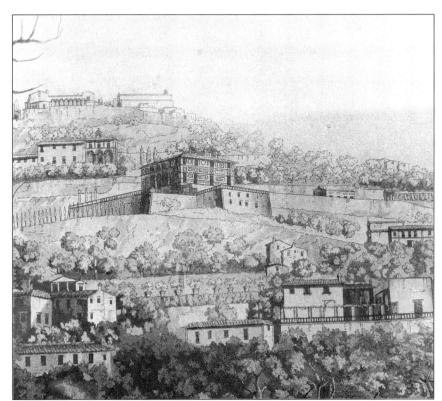

15. Buonaiuti, Villa Medici,
Fiesole, south and west facades from an aquatint in
the 1826 book *Una giornata
d'istruzione a Fiesole*

probably be Paoletti's doing. The closing in and subdividing of this loggia would account for the flimsy partitions and awkward planning just referred to. But the double loggia does encourage admiring the views and taking advantage of the breezes. It also breaks the glare and intense heat of the western sun, which otherwise could have baked the occupants as in an oven.

In the late nineteenth century Carl von Stegmann and Heinrich von Geymüller had already expressed reservations about the western loggia, saying they thought it was of later date.[24] To remove it altogether poses problems as well as enticing possibilities. It would probably entail removing the entire western facade on all three existing levels: chapel, loggia, bedchambers, and all. After such radical surgery excising an entire L-shaped section from the north and west sides, a drastically reduced villa would emerge. One of the attractions to this curtailment proposal is that the villa thus diminished in size forms an almost perfect square of 60 feet, or 19 meters on a side—which is to say the ratio of 1:1, or the musical interval of the octave. This is the kind of simple, harmonious ratio that Renaissance architects like Alberti and Michelozzo preferred to employ.[25] In conversation Architetto Benucci raised a further point in favor of this hypothesis. If the Florentine quattrocento measurement of the braccio is calculated at 1.17 meters, that would make the house according to this proposal almost exactly 16 braccia (18.72 meters) on a side; a lovely round number, the square of 4. The figure has a certain Albertian logic, not to mention all the anthropocentric connotations of a system of measure based on the braccio, or arm's length. In any event the east and west facades, if reconstructed to their proposed quattrocento size, would have that width; it is only the depth of the villa that would remain in question.

As matters stand, the southern and western sides of the Villa Medici best preserve the flavor of the Michelozzo original (pls. 25 and 26). When seen from the south, especially looking upward, the various buttressed earthworks progressively mount the hillside in the same manner that impressed the architect's contemporaries. The western terrace would have been occupied by a self-contained garden not unlike the one that projects at the back of the slightly later Palazzo Piccolomini at Pienza. In Lady Orford's day Paoletti transformed this into an entrance from the Via Vecchia Fiesolana. Before that the only means of access was from below, by internal stairs through the lower service block occupying its own southern bulwark quite separate from the western one. This route finally deposited the visitor on the paved southern terrace contiguous with the western one framed by an arched gate at the end. Just above this point, at the southwestern corner where the two facades meet, there is set into the masonry a sculpted stemma, or shield, missing its heraldic insignia but in other respects apparently of quattrocento date (pl. 26, right). Assuming it occupies its original situation, it tends to confirm the southwest corner as a part of the original Michelozzo structure.

On the southern terrace, directly opposite the exit from the service block, stands the splendidly preserved doorframe at the original point of entry into the villa (pl. 25). Indoors the barrel-vaulted staircase leading up shows every sign of occupying its original location. Proof of alterations to its form, however, exists in a cupboard off the stair landing, which has hidden in its north wall an original corbel from the ceiling support system. The staircase ascends to the barrel-vaulted corridor of the main floor, then doubles back to reach the flat-ceilinged corridor on the level of the bedrooms. Here doorframes have inscribed upon them at a later date the names of famous persons associated with the villa, such as the Medici pope Leo X and the poet Poliziano, of whom more presently. In fact, throughout the villa the decorative program celebrates through painting and sculpture the glorious early days of Medici occupancy. Turning to the right instead of ascending, the visitor reaches the eastern loggia and garden (pl. 27) that would have been the most private parts of the villa. Before Paoletti's *viale* turned it into a busily traf-ficked forecourt, the eastern terrace would have provided the widest panorama and the coolest, most secluded spot, ideal for strolling, drinking in the view, and poetizing about it.

In conclusion, then, the Villa Medici as conjecturally restored in these various counterprojects ceases to be a rather grand mansion and assumes instead the character of a relatively compact country house for part-time habitation. According to the anecdote referred to earlier, Giovanni de' Medici justified the expense involved on account of the coolness and the view provided by the high altitude. These intentions are not diminished by reducing the physical size of the house as proposed here. On the contrary, in a sense the villa grows in stature by becoming the smaller abode of a humanist philosopher. Indeed, the Villa Medici's pristine clarity and simple yet satisfying proportions seem to exemplify the ancients' belief in moderation as the just measure of all things. A quattrocento Greek inscription in the house bears out this interpretation. It reads:

ΤΕΡΜΑ ΟΡΑΝ ΒΙΟΤΟΙΟ
ΜΕΤΡΟΝ ΑΡΙΣΤΟΝ

In other words, "To see the end of life is the best measure of destiny."[26] Such a philosophical purpose for Fiesole emerges from the dialogue between Giovanni and Cosimo referred to above. Cosimo's Cafaggiolo house in the rich fields of the Mugello region stands for *negotium,* or the profit to be derived from cultivating the land. Giovanni's Fiesole home on its stony site represents *otium* in that it is not intended for profit, except in the intellectual or artistic sense. The fruits har-vested from Fiesole's soil would be primarily philosophical discourse, music mak-ing, reading, and writing. Pliny made this same point about his Laurentinum, where the best crops he reaped were his studies (bk. 4, ep. 6). In all likelihood, as others have persuasively suggested before, the Villa Medici at Fiesole is the first true villa of the Renaissance in the Plinian sense.[27]

Lorenzo de' Medici (1449–92), the nephew of Giovanni, probably knew his uncle's villa as a youngster. Eventually he came to inherit it sometime after his aunt Ginevra's death, or maybe sooner.[28] Certainly by 1478 he resided at Fiesole, because in April of that year he gave a party attended by the Pazzi conspirators, who originally planned to carry out their assassination plot at the villa. Lorenzo frequented the Villa Medici for short periods to confer with the members of his humanist circle installed there. The chief ornament of the Fiesole branch was Angelo Poliziano (1454–94). During his time as poet in residence, at some point in the early or mid-1480s, Poliziano wrote a significant letter to a friend, addressing it from Fiesole. The recipient was Marsilio Ficino, sweltering down in the valley at another Medici property, the Careggi Villa, where he fulfilled the same scholar-in-residence function as his fellow humanist, Poliziano. The Latin letter ends:

> When you are incommoded with the heat of the season in your retreat at Careggi, you will perhaps think the shelter of Fiesole not undeserving your notice. Seated between the sloping sides of the mountain we have here water in abundance and being constantly refreshed with moderate winds find little inconvenience from the glare of the sun. As you approach the house [*villula*] it seems embosomed in the wood, but when you reach it you find it commands a full prospect of the city. Populous as the vicinity is, yet I can enjoy the solitude so gratifying to my disposition.[29]

There is intentional emulation of Pliny's literary style in this letter, especially in the Poliziano passage echoing the description of the moderate winds wafting over the Tuscan Villa. The general similarities are further confirmed by Poliziano's use of *villula,* the same diminutive Pliny employed near the end of his letter to Gallus. In Poliziano's case, moreover, the term was doubly apt because the original Michelozzo building had few pretensions to grandeur. What had probably started out with Plinian reminiscences on the part of Giovanni, Michelozzo, and even Alberti in the 1450s had remained current with the next generation of inhabitants, who reinforced the allusions.

With a final flourish, Poliziano concluded his letter to Ficino much as Pliny had ended his to Gallus, with an open invitation to attend a picnic and wine tasting. Outdoor dinner parties such as Pliny gave in his *stibadium* must have increased at Fiesole as its fame spread.[30] Perhaps the little open pavilion seen off to the right end of the lower terrace in both quattrocento paintings served for such entertainments—a retreat away from the retreat. A subsequent Ficino letter of 1488 suggests he took Poliziano's bait and visited Fiesole. He evoked the hilltop scene after a personal tour of inspection and went on to imagine an ideal villa on a spot corresponding to that of the Villa Medici. In words that recall Pliny's and Poliziano's, but also those of Palladio and Jefferson, Ficino wrote: "We saw beneath us all

Florence—fields, houses and, in the middle, over the Arno, mist, and on the other side, steep mountains. We imagined a house placed on the slopes of the hill in such a manner as to . . . allow it to receive breezes when the weather is warm."[31]

In due course Lorenzo's affections shifted away from both Cafaggiolo, where he had spent much of his childhood, and Fiesole, where he liked to entertain, to the little hillock at Poggio a Caiano. He purchased it and some surrounding farms in 1474–75, moved in two years later, and about 1485 had started to build anew. Work stopped in 1492, not to be resumed until 1513 (pl. 28). At Lorenzo's death a semicomplete villa occupied the site, which in every way differed from the twin homes of his youth, yet amalgamated references to them. Poggio a Caiano mixes the well-watered lushness of Cafaggiolo with a hilltop location only slightly less panoramic than Fiesole's, but with easier access. The humanist writings of Michele Vieri elucidate the choice of this pastoral setting. Having written of his fondness for Pliny's letters, as we have already seen, he again took up the pen to describe Poggio a Caiano. Not surprisingly, he chose the epistolary mode reminiscent of Pliny. After commenting on the elevated situation, he drew attention to the excellent road from Florence, the fields, the streams, the mulberry bushes, and so forth. He clarified that at this point, shortly before he died in 1487, only the foundations of the future villa existed. He nevertheless visualized the mansion as if it stood, and he mentioned the attendant model dairy that Lorenzo had recently completed.[32] Here Lorenzo hoped to combine his passions for falconry, gentleman farming, book collecting, and poetizing. Such a multiplicity of functions on such a grand physical scale far outstrips the earlier and humbler Michelozzo prototype villas for the Medici.

The sumptuous pedimented central loggia sums up the confident new spirit at Poggio a Caiano (pl. 29). Its architect, Giuliano da Sangallo (1445–1516), emphasized classicism by picking up where Michelozzo had left off at Fiesole with his plainer arcade (cf. pl. 27). Sangallo's elements are much more blatantly *all'antica*. The elaborate Ionic columns, ornamented barrel vault, and sheer size bespeak a greater daring in the revival of antique forms. From what Vieri and others say, the entrance loggia with its pediment would have been in place by 1492, distinguishing it as the first temple-fronted domestic structure of the Renaissance—the direct antecedent of Palladio's Villa La Rotonda (cf. pl. 3).[33] Above all, the classical pediment points to Alberti's influence almost two decades after he may have acted in the same capacity at Fiesole. It is said that Lorenzo kept close watch on the progress of *De re aedificatoria* as the Florentine editio princeps came off the press chapter by chapter in 1485. In book 4 he would have noted the section on temple fronts in domestic architecture.[34] According to Alberti, the classical fastigium motif imparted to villa architecture a quasi-public, even sacred connotation. This agrees with the symbolism of the loggia's blue-and-white ceramic frieze. Apart from its dynastic and political undertones, it allegorizes enlightened Medici rule and patron-age by referring to the Ambra, the poetic name for Poggio a Caiano, as a hill of the Muses in whose secular temple Lorenzo serves as Apollo's chief priest.

In a series of poems, one of which is titled *Ambra,* Angelo Poliziano descended from the Olympian heights of Fiesole, where he set the *Rusticus* verses, to sing the praises of Poggio a Caiano in the plain below. The first lines of the *Ambra,* given in the original Latin for maximum significance, take a hortatory tone:

> Macte opibus, macte ingenio, mea gloria Laurens
> Gloria musarum Laurens! montesque propinquos
> Perfodis, et longo suspensos excipis arcu,
> Praegelidas ducturus aquas, qua prata supinum
> Lata videt podium, riguis uberrima lymphis[35]

They exhort Lorenzo to raise his voice in song to which the hills, the river, and even the villa's arched "podium" will resound. Steeped in Pliny as his *Rusticus* proves him to have been, surely Poliziano noticed the coincidental resemblance between the Latinized form of his patron's name, Laurens, and the possessive adjective Pliny used in describing the Laurentine Villa as *his* "Laurens." Such a punning allusion would not have been lost on Lorenzo, the second generation of the Medici apparently infatuated with Pliny.

In many other respects Poggio a Caiano represents a new and quite personal blend of the poetic tradition rooted in bucolic pursuits down on the farm, and the more high-flown ideal of studious contemplation entirely removed from manual labor. The contrast occurs strikingly about a mile from the villa and within direct sight of it. There Lorenzo established a *cascina* for his herd of prize cattle, housed around a courtyard in a moated model farm complex, unusual for its early date.[36] The *cascina* also functions as a painterly *repoussoir* device, in that its low profile leads the eye back to the higher outline of the main house, etched against a distant ridge where the Medici Villa Artimino ultimately came to be built in the next century. When Bartolomeo Ammannati set Artimino on an exposed plateau, it overlooked Poggio a Caiano in more senses than one. Seicento Artimino with its central loggia, raised podium, and sparse fenestration is intentionally a mock quattrocento villa. The owner was the same Grand Duke Cosimo who had commis-sioned the Stradano tapestry cycle to glorify past Medici deeds. In fact, Poggio a Caiano had thrown down a sort of architectural gauntlet that Artimino rather belatedly picked up.[37] At an earlier date Lorenzo's own middle son, Giovanni, to become Pope Leo X in 1513, carried into a third generation Medici ideas of patron-age. With his vastly increased wealth and ambition, he finished off his father's incomplete Poggio a Caiano. He then went on to fulfill the family's long-standing dream of building a grand *all'antica* villa inspired to some considerable degree by the writings of Pliny. The Medici's love of Pliny and their pride in their own history became a family obsession.

Giovanni de' Medici (1475–1521) received much of his early education in the setting of the family's villas at Cafaggiolo, Fiesole, and later Poggio a Caiano. He inherited the Medici love for villa life, which went so naturally with their love of classical literature and their mania for book collecting. In 1508, while still a cardinal, Giovanni acquired, in somewhat questionable circumstances, a doubly rare manuscript formerly in the monastic library at Corbie. Bound as a single codex, it contained a copy of the *Annals* of Tacitus and an early Pliny. Like his bibliophile great uncle and his father Lorenzo, after whom the family library is named, Giovanni surrounded himself with men of letters such as Filippo Beroaldo the Younger (1472–1518). Starting in 1514, Filippo acted both as Giovanni's private secretary and as acquisitions librarian, and therefore he must have known both Corbie manuscripts. He prepared the Tacitus for publication in 1515, and his cousin, the elder Beroaldo, had previously brought out the seventh and best-known quattrocento printed edition of Pliny at Bologna in 1498. A knowledge of Pliny seems to have run in the Beroaldo family.

The bibliophile pope's involvement with the Pliny manuscript in his possession did not remain passive. He actively encouraged its use, a fact referred to by Giovanni Maria Cataneo in the illustrated 1518 edition he produced of Pliny's letters, as a worthy successor to his larger and copiously annotated Venice editions of 1506 and 1510. (The editio princeps by Lodovico Carbo had appeared in the same city as far back as 1471.) Meanwhile, the first elegant Aldus Manutius editions had come off the Venetian presses in 1502, followed by numerous reprints. Included among those is the 1515 Florentine edition, which makes reference to Pope Leo X on its title page.[38] In themselves these early editions of Pliny provide a history in microcosm of the emergence of the printed book from the manuscript tradition (fig. 16). The one edition improves upon the legibility of the next, as can be seen by comparing the texts reproduced here, each of them open to the same key passage from the letter to Gallus, in which the shape of the Laurentine courtyard is compared to the letter *O*. In the end the book evolved much as it still exists today: the dated title page replaces the colophon; clear chapter headings divide the text; consecutive pagination in arabic numbers takes over from roman numerals arranged by gathering; and so forth. By 1518, at all events, the Latin letters circulated in no fewer than twenty-three printed versions, the bulk of them post-1500. Thereafter a period of almost seventy years followed, at least in Italy, during which the market for Plinys slacked off. Looked at another way, then, it could be said that the cardinalate and papacy of Giovanni de' Medici corresponds with a major wave in the proliferation of Pliny through the medium of the printed page. As it happens, 1518 is also a benchmark year in the history of restitutions of Pliny's villas.

16. (*Opposite and pages 60, 61*) Composite of five fourteenth- and early fifteenth-century Italian printed editions of Pliny's letters, all open to the same passage in the letter to Gallus: (*a*) Naples, 1476, Iunianus Maius; (*b*) Venice, 1492, Ioannes Vercellius; (*c*) Bologna, 1498, Phillipus Beroaldus; (*d*) Milan, 1518, Ioannes Maria Cataneus; (*e*) Venice, 1518, Aldus Manutius

O τεα

mediato corridin

admissux

Canediuin

Nubilarius long I ꝓpᷓ
ad arcendã nubila unbra
ꝫ plunas

amphora .ī testudo

haspeda

protestzio +

protestrion

Saca ad balneandi
apter

baptisterui

Aspendá
:testudo

Villa usibus capax nõ suptuosa tutela:cuius iprimã pte atri
um frugi:neqȝ tm sordidũ deīde porticus in o. litteræ simi
litudinē circũactæ:qbus puula:sed festiua area īclũdit ;egre
giũ hoc aduersus tēpestates receptaculũ:Nã specularibus a ē
multo magis iminētibus tectis muniũt .Est cõtra mediasta
nediũ hilare:mox tricliniũ satis pulchrũ quod ī littus excur
rit:ac siqn africo mari ipulsũ est fractis iã & nouissis flucti
bus leuiter abluit:ũdiqȝ ualuas & fenestras nõ minores ual
uis hēt:atqȝ ita a lateribus:a frõte q̄si tria maria pspectat:a
tergo cañediũ:porticũ areã porticũ rursus:mox atriũ siluas
et lõgiquos respicit mõtes:huius a leua retractius paulo cu
biculũ est aplũ:deinde aliud minus quod altera fenestra ad
mittit orientē :occidētē altera retinet:hæc & subiacēs mare
lõgius qdē:sed securius ituet:huius cubiculi et illius triclinii
obiectu īclũdit ãgulus:q purissimũ solē cõtinet et accēdit
hoc hybernaculũ:hoc etiã gymnasiũ meorȝ ēsibi omēs uēti
silent exceptis q̄ nubilũ īducũt:& serenũ ãq̄ usũ loci eripi
unt:adnectit ãgulo cubiculũ ī haspida curuatũ:quod ãbitũ
solis fenestris oibus seqtur:parieti eius ī bebliothecæ spem
armariũ īsertũ ē:qp nõ legēdos libros:sed lectitandos capit
adheret dormitoriũ mēbrũ & transitu iteriacētē:q suspen
sus & sublatus cõceptũ uaporē salubri tēperamento huc il
lucqȝ digerit & ministrat:reliq̄ pars lateris huius seruorȝ li
bertorȝqȝ usibus detinet :Plerisqȝ tã mũdis ut accipere ho
spites possint.Et ex alio latere cubiculũ est politissimũ:deīde
uel cubiculũ grãde:uel modica coenatio q̄ plurio solet plu
rio mari lucet:post hãc cubitulũ cũ pceriore altitudie æstiuũ
munimētis hiberniũ. Est eni subductũ oibus uētis:huic cu
biculo aliud cõi & pceriori pariete iũgitur:ide balnea cella
frigidaria spaciosa & effusa:Cuius in cõtrariis parietibus
duo baptisteria uelut eiecta sinuantur:abunde capacia.Sin

a

to decimo lapide:Hostiensis ab undecimo relinquēda est. Vtrinq̃
excipit iter aliqua ex p̃te arenosum iũctispaulo grauius & longius
equo breue & molle:uaria hic atq̃ inde facies: Nã mõ occurrenti-
bus siluis uia coarctat:modo latissimis pratis diffundif & patescit
multi greges ouiũ:multa ibi equoꝶ bouq̃ armenta:quæ mõtibus
hyeme depulsa herbis & tēpore uerno nitescũt.uilla usibus capax
Nõ sũptuosa tutela:cuius in prima p̃te atriũ frugi nec tamē sordi-
dũ:deinde porticus in.O.litteræ similitudinē circũactæ:q̃bus paruula sed festiua area icludit:egregiũ aduersum tēpestates recepta-
culũ:nã specularibus ac mũlto magis iminentibus tectis muniũt.
Est cõtra medias cauediũ hilare:mox tricliniũ satis pulchrũ: quod
in littus excurrit:ac si quando Africo mare ipulsum est fractis iam
& nouissimis fluctibus leuiter adluitur. Vndiq̃ ualuas & fenestras
nõ minores ualuis habet:atq̃ itæ a lateribus a fronte quasi tria ma
ria p̃spectat:A tergo cauediũ:porticũ:areã : porticum rursus:mox
atrium siluas & longinquos respicit mõtes:huius a læua retractius
paulo cubiculũ est ãplum: Deinde aliud minus : q̃d altera fenestra
admittit orientē:occidētē altera retinet.hæc & subiacēs mare lõgi
us q̃dē sed securius ituef:huius cubiculi & illius triclinii obiectu
icludif ãgulus:q̃ purissimũ sole cõtiet & accēdit:hoc hibernaculũ
hoc ēt gymnasiũ meoꝶ est.ibi oēs silēt uēti exceptis q̃ nũbilũ idu
cũt:& serenũ ateq̃ usũ loci eripiũt.Adnectif ãgulo cubiculũ i aspi
da curuatũ:q̃d ãbitũ solis fenestris oĩbus seq̃t.parieti eius in bibli
othecæ specie armariũ insertũ est:q̃ nõ legēdos libros:sed lectitan
dos capit:adhæret dormitoriũ mēbꝶ & transitu iteriacente: q̃ su-
spensus & sublatus cõceptũ uapore salubri tēpamēto huc illucq̃
digerit & ministrat.jreliqua pars lateris huius seruoꝶ libertoruq̃
usibus detinef plerisq̃ tã mũdis:ut accipe hospites possint. ex alio
latere cubiculũ est politissimũ:deide uel cubiculũ grãde uel modi
ca cœnatio:quæ plurimo sole plurio mari lucet.Post hãc cubiculũ
cũ procestrio:altitudine æstiuum:munimēto hibernũ.Est enim sub
ductũ oĩbus uentis:Huic cubiculo aliud & procestriõ cõmuni parie
te iũgunt:inde balinei cella frigidaria spaciosa & effusa:cuius i cõ
trariis parietibus duo baptisteria uelut eiecta sinuanf abũde capa
cia:sin mare i pxio cogites:adiacet unctuariũ:hypocaustũ: adiacet
propigeõ balinei:Mox duæ cellæ magis elegantes q̃ sumptuosæ. co
hæret calida piscina mirifice:ex qua natantes mare aspiciunt:Nec
procul spæristerion:quod calidissimo soli inclinato iam die occur-

ta ibi equõrum bouímq̃ armēta:quæ montíbꝰ hye
me depulsa herbis & tepore uerno nitescunt. Villa
usibus capax/non sumptuosa tutella:Cuius in prima parte atrium frugi:nec tamen sordidum: deinde porticus i.O.litteræ similitudinem circumactæ:
quibus paruula sed festiua area includitur:egregi-
um aduersus tempestates recœptaculum.Nam specularibus ac multo magis iminentibus tectis muni
unt.Est cõtra medias cauædium hilare:mox tricli
nium satis pulchrum / quod in littus excurrit . ac si
quãdo Africo mare impulsum est fractis iam & no
uissimis fluctibus leuiter adluitur:undiq̃ ualuas at
q̃ fenestras non minores ualuis habet : atque ita a
lateribus a frõte q̃si tria maria p̃spectat:a tergo ca
uædium /porticum/aream / porticum rursus / mox
atrium/siluas/& longinquos respicit montes.Hu-
ius a læua retractius paulo cubiculum est amplum:
deinde aliud minus quod altera fenestra admittit
orientem/occidētem altera retinet.hæc mare & sub
iacens longius quidem/sed securius intuetur : huius & illius obiectu includitur angulus/qui purissi-
mum solem continet & accēdit/hoc hibernaculum:
hoc ēt gymnasium meoꝶ ē:ibi omnes silét uenti ex
ceptis qui nubilum inducunt/& serenum antequã
usum loci eripiunt:adnectitur angulo cubiculum
in absida curuatum:quod ambitum solis fenestris
omnibus seq̃t:parieti eius in bibliothecæ specié ar-

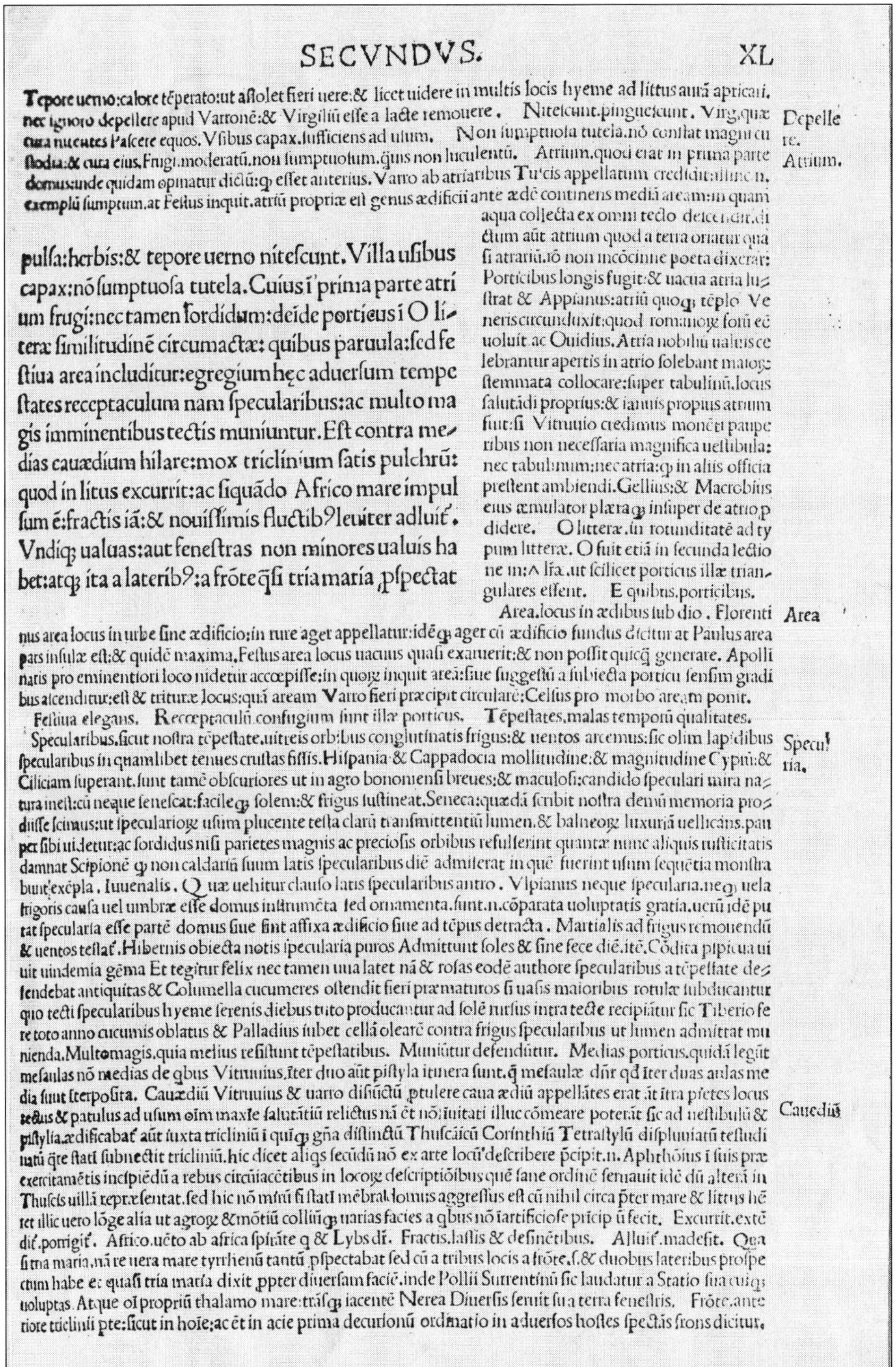

Tepore uerno:calore téperato:ut aſolet fieri uere:& licet uidere in multis locis hyeme ad littus aurā apricā. nec ignoro depellere apud Varroné:& Virgiliū eſſe a lacte remouere. Niteſcunt.pingueſcunt. Virg.quæ cura nucentes Paſcere equos. Vſibus capax.ſufficiens ad ultum. Non ſumptuoſa tutela.nó conſtat magnî cuſtodia.& cura eius.Frugi.moderatū.non ſumptuotum.q̄us non luculentū. Atrium.quod erat in prima parte domus:unde quidam opinatur dictū:q̄ eſſet anterius. Varro ab atriaribus Turcis appellatum credidit:illinc n. exemplū ſumptum.at Feſtus inquit.atriū propriæ eſt genus ædificii ante ædē continens mediā aream:in quam

[marginal gloss: Depelle re. Atrium.]

pulſa:herbis:& tepore uerno niteſcunt. Villa uſibus capax:nó ſumptuoſa tutela.Cuius í prima parte atri um frugi:nec tamen ſordidum:deide porticus í O li teræ ſimilitudiné circumactæ: quibus paruula:ſed fe ſtiua area includitur:egregium hęc aduerſum tempe ſtates receptaculum nam ſpecularibus:ac multo ma gis imminentibus tectis muniuntur. Eſt contra me dias cauædium hilare:mox triclinium ſatis pulchrū: quod in litus excurrit:ac ſiquādo Africo mare impul ſum é:fractis iā:& nouiſſimis fluctib9 leuiter adluit. Vndiq3 ualuas:aut feneſtras non minores ualuis ha bet:atq3 ita a laterib9:a frote q̄ſi tria maria ,pſpectat

aqua collecta ex omni tecto deterret.di ctium aūt atrium quod a terra oriatur qua ſi atraria.iò non incōcinne poeta dixerat: Porticibus longis fugit:& uacua atria lu ſtrat & Appianus:atriū quoq3 tēplo Ve neris circunduxit:quod romanoҙ ſoli eē uoluit.ac Ouidius.Atria nobiliū ualuis ce lebrantur apertis in atrio ſolebant maioҙ ſtemmata collocare:ſuper tabulinū.locus ſalutādi proprius:& ianuis propius atriū fuit:ſi Vitruuio credimus monēt paupe ribus non neceſſaria magnifica ueſtibula: nec tabulinum:nec atria:q̄ in aliis officia preſtent ambiendi.Gellius.& Macrobius eius æmulator plæraq3 inſuper de atrio de didere. O litteræ.in rotunditate ad ty pum litteræ. O ſuit etiã in ſecunda lectio ne in:Λ lſa.ut ſcilicet porticus illæ trian gulares eſſent. E quibus.porricibus.

[marginal gloss: Area]

Area.locus in ædibus ſub dio. Florenti nus area locus in urbe ſine ædificio:in rure ager appellatur:idē q3 ager cū ædificio fundus dicitur at Paulus area pars inſulæ eſt:& quidē maxima.Feſtus area locus uacuus quaſi exaruerit:& non poſſit quicq̄ generare. Apolli natis pro eminentiori loco nidetur accœpiſſe:in quoq3 inquit area:ſiue ſuggeſti a ſubiecta porticu ſenſim gradi bus aſcenditur:eſt & trituræ locus:quī aream Varro fieri præcipit circulare:Celſus pro morbo aream ponit. Feſtiua elegans. Recceptaculū configium ſunt illæ porticus. Tēpeſtates.malas temporū qualitates.

[marginal gloss: Specularia.]

Specularibus.ſicut noſtra tēpeſtate.uitreis orbibus conglutinatis frigus:& uentos arcemus:ſic olim lapidibus ſpecularibus in quamlibet tenues cruſtas fiſſis.Hiſpania.& Cappadocia mollitudine:& magnitudine Cypri:& Ciliciam ſuperant.ſunt tamē obſcuriores ut in agro bononienſi breues:& maculoſi:candido ſpeculari mira na tura ineſt:cū neque ſeneſcat:facileq3 ſolem:& frigus ſuſtineat.Seneca:quædā ſcribit noſtra demū memoria pro diſſe ſcimus:ut ſpeculariæq3 uſum plucente teſta clarū trāſmittentiū lumen.& balneoҙ luxuria uellicans.pan per ſibi uidetur:ac ſordidus niſi parietes magnis ac precioſis orbibus refulſerint quanta` nunc aliquis ruſticitatis damnat Scipioné q̄ non caldariū ſuum latis ſpecularibus diē admiterat in quē fuerint uſum ſequētia monſtra bunt:exēpla. Iuuenalis. Quæ uehitur clauſo latis ſpecularibus antro. Vlpianus neque ſpecularia.neq3 uela frigoris cauſa uel umbræ eſſe domus inſtrumēta ſed ornamenta.ſunt.n.cōparata uoluptatis gratia.uerū idē pu tat ſpecularia eſſe parté domus ſiue ſint affixa ædificio ſiue ad tēpus detracta.Martialis ad frigus remouendū & uentos teſtat.Hibernis obiecta notis ſpecularia puros Admittunt ſoles & ſine fece diē.itē.Cōdita pīpicua ui uit uindemia gēma Et tegitur felix nec tamen uua latet nā & roſas eodē authore ſpecularibus a tēpeſtate de fendebat antiquitas & Columella cucumeres oſtendit fieri præmaturos ſi uaſis maioribus rotulæ ſubducantur quo tecti ſpecularibus hyeme ſerenis diebus tuto producantur ad ſolé rurſus intra tecte recipiātur ſic Tiberio fe re toto anno cucumis oblatus & Palladius iubet cellā oleareē contra frigus ſpecularibus ut lumen admittat mu nienda.Multomagis.quia melius reſiſtunt tēpeſtatibus. Muniūtur defendūtur. Medias porticus.quidā legit meſulas nó medias de q̄bus Vitruuius.īter duo aūt piſtyla itinera ſunt.q̄ meſaulæ dr̄ qd iter duas anlas me dia ſunt ſterpoſita. Cauædiū Vitruuius & uarro diſiūctū ,ptulere caua ædiū appellátes erat .it ītra pretes locus tectus & patulus ad uſum oīm maxē ſalutātiū relictus nā ēt nó:inuitati illuc cōmeare poterāt ſic ad neſtibulū & piſtylia.ædificabat aūt iuxta triclinia í q̄iq3 gña diſtinctū Thuſcaicū Corinthiū Tetraſtylū diſpluuiatū teſtudi nati q̄te ſtati ſubnectit triclinia.hic dicet aliq̄s ſecūdā nó ex arte locū deſcribere ,ncipit.n. Aphthōius í ſuis præ exercitamētis incipiēdū a rebus circūiacētibus in locoq3 deſcriptiōibus quē ſane ordiné ſeruauit idē dū alterā in Thuſcis uilla reptæſentat.ſed hic nó mſū ſi ſtatī mēbra domus aggreſſus eſt cū nihil circa ,pter mare & littus ha bet illic uero lōge alia ut agroҙ &mōtiū colliūq̄ uarias facies.q̄s nó ſartificioſe pricip ũ fecit. Excurrit.extē dīt.porrigit. Affico.uēto ab africa ſpirāte q̄ & Lybs dr̄. Fractis.laſſis & deſinētibus. Alluit.madeſit. Qea ſitna maria.nā te uera mare tyrrhenū tantū ,pſpectabat ſed cū a tribus locis a frōte.ſ.& duobus lateribus proſpe ctum habeāt:quaſi tria maria dixit.,ppter diuerſam faciē.inde Pollii Surrentinū ſic laudatur a Statio ſua cuiq3 uoluptas.Atque oī propriū thalamo mare:trāſq3 iacentē Nerea Diuerſis ſeruit ſua terra feneſtris. Frōte.antē riore triclinii pte:ſicut in hoie:ac ēt in acie prima decurionū ordinatio in aduerſos hoſtes ſpectās frons dicitur.

[marginal gloss: Cauædiū]

[label: d]

[marginal handwritten notes: mulſa / ſeruula]

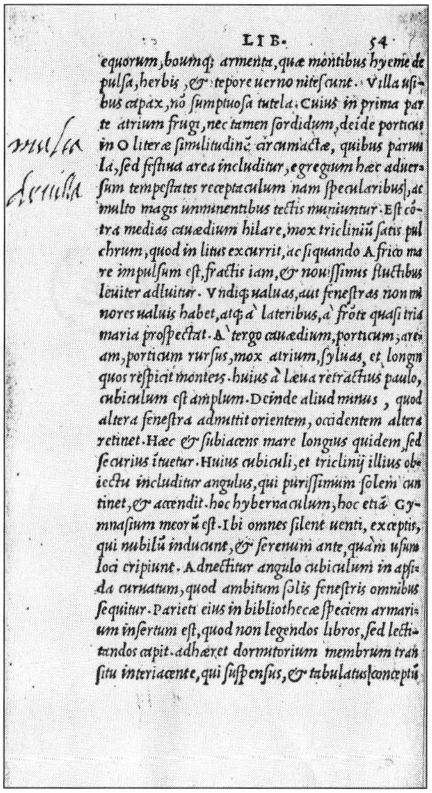

equorum, boumq3 armenta, quæ mōtibus hyeme de pulſa, herbis, & tepore uerno niteſcunt. Villa uſi bus capax, nó ſumptuoſa tutela. Cuius in prima par te atrium frugi, nec tamen ſordidum, deide porticus in O literæ ſimilitudiné circumactæ, quibus parnŭ Lā, ſed feſtiua area includitur, egregium hæc aduer ſum tempeſtates receptaculum nam ſpecularibus, ac multo magis unminentibus tectis muniuntur. Eſt cō tra medias cauædium hilare, mox tricliniū ſatis pul chrum, quod in litus excurrit, ac ſiquando A frico ma re impulſum eſt, fractis iam, & nouiſſimis fluctibus leuiter adluitur. Vndiq3 ualuas, aut feneſtras non mi nores ualuis habet, atq3 a` lateribus, a` frōte quaſi tria maria proſpectat. A` tergo cauædium, porticum, atri am, porticum rurſus, mox atrium, ſyluas, et longin quos reſpicit montes.huius a` Leua retractius paulo, cubiculum eſt amplum.Deinde aliud minus, quod altera feneſtra admittit orientem, occidentem altera retinet.Hæc & ſubiacens mare longius quidem ſed ſecurius ituetur.Huius cubiculi, et triclinij illius obi iectu includitur angulus, qui puriſſimum ſolem cōn tinet, & accendit.hoc hybernaculum, hoc etã Gy naſium meorū eſt.Ibi omnes ſilent uenti, exceptis, qui nubilū inducunt, & ſerenuin ante quàm uſum loci eripiunt.Adneſtitur angulo cubiculum in apſi da curuatum, quod ambitum ſolis feneſtris omnibus ſequitur.Parieti eius in bibliothecæ ſpeciem armari um inſertum eſt, quod non legendos libros, ſed lecti tandos capit.adhæret dormitorium membrum tran ſitu interiacente, qui ſuſpenſus, & tabulatus concæptū

[label: e]

The year 1518 coincided with the initiation of a stupendous new villa on Monte Mario to the northwest of the Vatican, unlike anything Rome had seen since imperial times. Intended to house the papal nephew Cardinal Giulio de' Medici (1478–1534) in great style, it has gained renown as the Villa Madama, named after a subsequent owner. Giulio, éminence grise and understudy of Leo X, is well known from his portrayal standing behind the pontiff in the celebrated portrait by Raphael (1483–1520). Characteristically, the pope is shown with an illuminated manuscript open before him. Giulio for his part availed himself of the architectural services of Raphael. Overextended though Raphael already was in the last year or so of his life, he undertook to write the cardinal a long and complicated letter about a great country house project. It described the villa as if it already existed, in the same fashion Poliziano and Michele Vieri had employed when writing about Poggio a Caiano. To an even greater degree, however, Raphael's prose is pure Pliny pastiche. It begins with the orientation and approach roads to the house and proceeds to describe the house and gardens with such words as *dyetha, xysto, clyptoportico,* and *hypodramo,* snatched right out of Pliny and often misspelled.[39] Throughout there are constant references to the winds and the cardinal points of the compass. The climax of the plan is the round courtyard in the center (*cortile tondo*) modeled on the one at Laurentinum. Depending on the manuscript tradition followed, Pliny's courtyard was construed in the shape of either an *O* or a *D*. On this fine point of philology Leo X's own Corbie manuscript was imperfect and uninformative. By that date, as I noted above, numerous printed editions existed, but only one, brought out in Rome in 1490 by Pomponius Laetus, availed itself of the *D* interpretation based on the Laurentian Library manuscript or on an even earlier version in the San Marco monastic library in Florence.[40] Raphael could easily have referred to the printed Cataneo, Aldine, or Beroaldo edition for inspiration.

In effect, Raphael sought far more than the loose adaptations of Pliny at Fiesole or at Poggio a Caiano, both villas well known to his Medici clients Pope Leo and Cardinal Giulio. Raphael intended a proper full-scale reconstruction insofar as lay within the knowledge of his age and the means at his disposal—in this case an almost inexhaustible supply of Medici and papal money.[41] He would transform the long-standing Medici dream of a Plinian villa into reality. In the same spirit of hubris, he chose a site that presented enormous technical difficulties but offered corresponding attractions. The platform for the villa, part natural and part man-made, occupies a spot within easy distance of the Ponte Molle over the Tiber, on a ledge fairly high up the slopes of Monte Mario. This setting might well have brought back to the pope scenes of his youth, especially at Fiesole. It has been remarked that the landscape here has a positively Tuscan look.[42] The ledge in question runs on roughly an east-west axis from its entrance at the front (pl. 30) out to a long terraced garden not unlike the one at Fiesole in general disposition (cf. pl. 27). In addition to the obvious references to the Tuscan Villa, Raphael's letter adds Laurentine Villa features such as the large central courtyard, intended to form a full circle. Lengthy passages by Raphael explain the gradual ascent of the hill to either of two entrances. The reference is probably to the old Roman Via Cassia and Via Flaminia, which pass close to Monte Mario, just as Pliny emphasized that his Laurentine Villa could be reached by two main roads. In this way the Villa Madama was admirably situated as a suburban retreat for the Medici within easy distance of Rome, or as a place where Cardinal Giulio could dispense hospitality to visiting dignitaries in his capacity as papal chief of protocol.[43]

In a way that recalls Vasari's later description of the Villa Medici at Fiesole, Raphael's letter to Giulio de' Medici stresses the advantages of a multistory dwelling built into a hillside. The lower level of both buildings was used for storage, served as cellars, and kept the kitchen cool by its semisubterranean construction. In addition, the Villa Madama's waterworks would have serviced elaborate antique-style baths at this level and huge stables with gravity-fed watering troughs for a small army of horses. The only surviving vestiges of all this are in the area of the terrace beneath the high embankment wall supporting the upper or hanging garden (pl. 31). Here Raphael mentioned the fishpond, which still faintly echoes the provisions of certain ancient Romans, notably the millionaire sybarite Lucullus. Raphael mentioned the existence of a vast hippodrome nearby (never built), with cryptoporticus at the top and more stabling along one side. Raphael's letter jumps confusingly all over the villa's plan, making Pliny's text look restrained and coherent by comparison. But that is beside the point. Raphael's exuberance, his tendency to exaggerate, conveys the same impression of novelty, complexity, audacity, and extreme optimism that characterizes the art of the High Renaissance in which he had such a formative hand.

Were it not for the huge fragment of the Villa Madama left standing and eight related sheets of architectural projects extant in the Uffizi collection, Raphael's letter might be dismissed as pure fiction. The drawings, however, raise complicated questions of their own, because none of them unequivocally comes from the pen of Raphael. Are they datable to before his death, or to afterward when his former associates, the Sangallo family, continued his ideas until work on the villa ceased about 1527? Scholarly opinion remains sharply divided on this question.[44] On two important points there is some agreement. First, the drawings themselves belong to various members of the Sangallo clan, such as Antonio the Younger, Battista, or Giovanfrancesco, all of them related to the builder of Poggio a Caiano. They drew them either on their own initiative or following lost original schemes by Raphael. Second, one anomalous drawing (U1054A) everyone accepts as pre-1520, though it has not received the close attention it deserves (fig. 17). Whatever its

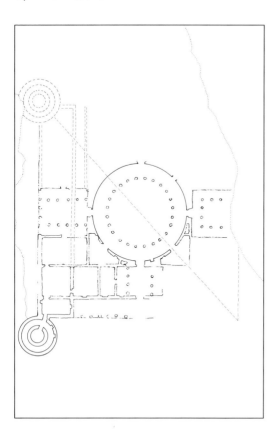

17. Raphael and the Sangallos, preparatory plan, Villa Madama, Rome. Broken lines indicate scored lines on the drawing; dotted lines indicate edge of the paper before conservation (line drawing after U1054A)

oddities, the evidence it provides may prove crucial. The recto of this sheet—in reality hardly more than a scrap of badly crumpled paper—shows an ideal, perfectly square structure with deep columnar vestibules on three if not all four sides. This is one of several features to reappear subsequently; another is the central round courtyard, derived from the Laurentine Villa; a third is the corner tower.

When observed in a raking light, U1054A reveals that the artist, after first using a stylus to score the paper, subsequently colored in most but not all of the lines with sepia ink. The uncolored grooves, though readily visible to the naked eye, do not show up on photographs. The schematic redrawing illustrated here shows all the lines, inked over or not, for the first time and extends the information contained on the sheet up into its top left corner. What emerges is a perfectly balanced plan centering on the vestibule with *two* symmetrically placed corner towers, not one, just as they appear in designs for the Villa Madama such as U273A. That particular sheet, not illustrated here, carries the misspelled word *dieta* on one of the towers and points to a connection with Pliny's letters.[45] These observations tend to strengthen the case for regarding U1054A as a relatively modest early stage in the planning of a Pliny-inspired villa about 1518–19. Later it would be superseded by much grander schemes, written or drawn either after the death of

THE MEDICI AND PLINY 65

Raphael or just before. The imaginary restitutions that followed this tentative start increased its size but consequently lost some of the foursquare compactness that harks back to the quattrocento Villa Medici at Fiesole. Although U1054A is generally regarded as being in the hand of the younger Sangallo, the drawing may well represent Raphael's original scheme for the Villa Madama.

To make matters more interesting, the verso of U1054A bears an extremely difficult to read but significant inscription that has been deciphered as follows:

> Colunela
> la villa sia partita in tre parte
> in urbana
> rustica
> fruttuaria[46]

Despite their architectural relevance, these intriguing words have not received further commentary in the literature on the Villa Madama. They allude directly to a passage on villas in the writings of Lucius Junius Moderatus Columella (bk. 1, chap. 6) in which the author listed the three subdivisions of an ancient farmstead in Latin as the *urbana* or manor house, the *rustica* or farmhouse, and the *fructuaria* or storehouse. The inscription on the verso helps explain the plan on the recto as an unusual archaizing attempt at architectural restitution based on literary sources—in this case Columella's *De re rustica* rather than Pliny's letters. But the rediscovery and publication of Columella and Pliny took place in circumstances so similar that the story is worth retelling briefly.

A copy of Columella's writings came into Italy early in the quattrocento with the famous bibliophile Poggio Bracciolini. Before he died in 1459, he sold another copy to Giovanni di Cosimo de' Medici. This manuscript joined several others on the shelves of the Medici family library, including a more crucial one that belonged to Giovanni's brother Piero.[47] As already seen, the Medici assisted a circle of scholars responsible for editing and disseminating knowledge of rediscovered classical texts like the Columella. The elder Beroaldo's edition of Pliny in the 1490s coincided with the Columella he published in conjunction with the writings of other so-called agronomes. His nephew became a trusted Medici adviser, as already seen, and in 1516 served as the Vatican librarian, or *prefetto,* during Leo's papacy. Assuming that the pope or Cardinal Giulio did not do so in person, the younger Beroaldo would have been ideally placed to steer the designer of U1054A to the right reading desk or cupboard, where the Columella manuscripts and incunables may have sat side by side with the Plinys.[48] The younger Beroaldo's death on 30 August 1518 overlaps just slightly the earliest dates associated with the Villa Madama project. And though it could be pure chance, Raphael's letter describing the villa considerably singles out a special room for the members of the Medici secretariat such as Beroaldo.

To recapitulate, U1054A has some definite connection with two other drawings in the same collection, U273A and U314A, both of which demonstrably attempt to reproduce on paper the plan of Pliny's Laurentine Villa. Both are attributed to various members of the Sangallo clan. Drawing U314A is the more distinguished of the pair in both design and draftsmanship (fig. 18). Badly damaged and therefore illustrated here in a clearer redrawing, it retains much of the visionary quality of U1054A. This can be observed in the exaggerated number and virtuosic character of the staircases in proportion to the livable space. It is also the more overtly Plinian of the two, with its round courtyard, although the rectangular one in U273A might be a response to Leo X's Corbie manuscript of Pliny, which left the shape indeterminate. All three drawings feature round towers—Pliny referred to two at Laurentinum overlooking the strand. The Raphael letter explains that glass windows all around (like Pliny's *specularia*), would make an ideal winter apartment commanding a view of its own little secret garden. The pendant tower at the

18. Raphael and the San-gallos, preparatory plan, Villa Madama, Rome (composite line drawing of U314A, U1356A, U916A after Coffin)

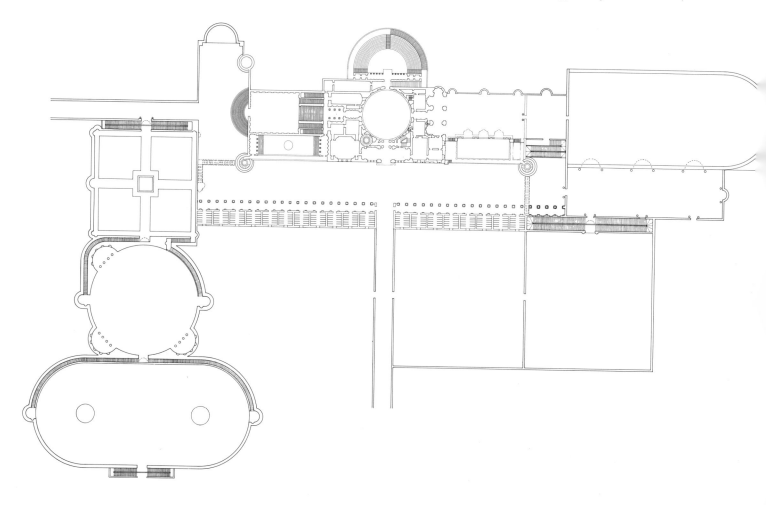

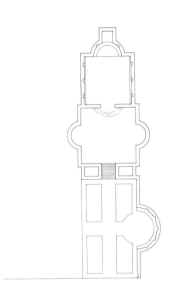

opposite end of the lengthy terrace would contain a chapel. With a view to possible surprise attack, the third tower is for defense. Seen from a distance, the letter says, the three towers would convey a fortified air. In complete contrast, however, the hillside behind the circular courtyard has built into it an open-air semicircular theater in the manner of the ancients, with elaborate provision made for the performance of classical dramas. Immediately, Pope Julius III's Villa Giulia comes to mind (cf. pl. 19). There may be a sense in which the later villa, across the Tiber valley but within sight of Monte Mario, acknowledged its predecessor with a kind of reverential bow, just as Pliny's Tragedy and Comedy villas echoed each other across Lake Como.[49]

Of all the Uffizi drawings for the Villa Madama, U314A resembles most closely the main part of the house as it survives, trimmed of its most eccentric features such as the theater. No sign exists of the towers. The elaborate means of access ended up simply as a sloping drive, thus obviating all the impractical and overly abundant staircases. The stabling dwindled to nothing from the preposterous four hundred stalls specified in Raphael's letter. But to get an inkling of Raphael's original conception it is only necessary to look again at the open loggia from the garden side (pl. 31). The splendid painted vaults within and giant pilasters without convey a grandeur truly worthy of antiquity. They reflect the height of splendor the house had reached by 1527, the year it was damaged during the sack of Rome as a helpless Giulio de' Medici, by that time Pope Clement VII, watched it burn from afar.[50] Though the villa was repaired after the fire damage, the pope's death finally brought construction to a halt in 1534. Despite all the vicissitudes then and later, nothing detracts from the Villa Madama's position as one of the grandest conceptions produced in Rome before the High Renaissance bubble burst.

By chance, not by design, the courtyard in its present truncated form (pl. 30) resembles the *D*-shaped atrium that modern philologists believe formed the entrance of the Laurentine Villa. Perhaps in the end the semicircle better suited shrinking Medici resources and resolve. To get a sense of the intended circular form, the best place to look is somewhere else: the palace of Charles V at Granada in Spain, begun the year after the burning of the Villa Madama. At Granada the two-story circular courtyard has a tunnel-vaulted colonnade below and a flat-ceilinged one above. Ironically, Charles V was the perpetrator of the sack of Rome, and it was his soldiers who pillaged the Villa Madama, thereby destroying the thing he apparently loved. (Could the copy at Granada be construed as an architectural act of atonement for the damage to the original at Rome?) The earliest drawing for the palace conserved in the Madrid archives dates from 1528. The Toledan architect in charge, Pedro Machuca (1485?–1558), had studied with Raphael in Rome before returning to Spain in 1520, so he could have absorbed the Villa Madama schemes right at the source. The coincidences continue. Baldassare Castiglione, the papal nuncio to Spain at the time of the palace's construction, possessed a copy of Raphael's letter to Cardinal de' Medici. Castiglione might form an additional link between Pliny, Raphael, and the Granada building works of Emperor Charles. In a final twist of fate, Charles's illegitimate daughter Margherita is the "Madama" who married Giulio de' Medici's heir Alessandro and after whom the villa is now named.[51]

In succeeding centuries, as the Villa Madama slowly declined into desuetude and delapidation, it exerted increasing appeal as a place of pilgrimage among student architects eager to preserve a record of it. Their visits and the visual documents they have left behind form a rich legacy documenting the building's history at various stages—too rich for consideration in detail here.[52] The work of the students, predominantly from France and Britain, culminates in that of a brilliant Canadian, Ernest Cormier (1885–1980), who united the theoretical Beaux-Arts French approach with the more pragmatic measured surveys of the English. Born in Montreal, where he graduated from the Polytechnique, Cormier attended the atelier Pascal at the Paris Ecole des Beaux-Arts in the six years leading up to the outbreak of the First World War. Unlike other French-speaking predecessors in Paris, Cormier was ineligible for a coveted Prix de Rome because of his citizenship. As a Canadian, however, he competed for and won the Henry Jarvis Studentship sponsored by the Royal Institute of British Architects in London. This enabled him to spend the better part of the next two years, 1914–16, attached to the British School at Rome. The fulfillment of the syllabus for the Jarvis Prize is what launched Cormier's Villa Madama studies.[53]

Two-thirds of the way through his stay at Rome, Cormier addressed a letter and a progress report to the honorable secretary of the British School. Drafts of these documents, both dated 1 July 1916, are preserved in the Cormier Archive at the Canadian Centre for Architecture in Montreal. In them Cormier revealed the hardships he labored against. He found it increasingly hard, he said, to accomplish the requirements of the Jarvis Prize without the advantage of what he called "companions" or the "milieu" necessary for proper "emulation," because so many men had been mobilized in the war effort.[54] In other words, he lacked the partnership that had helped such previous teams at the Villa Madama as the Frenchmen Percier and Fontaine or the Englishmen John Soane and Thomas Hardwick. Despite these difficulties, Cormier's list of drawings in progress on the major project he called "a scheme for the restoration and completion of the Villa Madama" represents no small achievement. The restoration part of the project involved an exact survey of the site, more precise than any before. This would be possible, Cormier explained, "Thanks to Mr. Bergès, now proprietor of Villa Madama," who provided "use of scaffolding for the measurement of the existing constructions," available for the first time since Raphael's pupils had dismantled their own painting platform in the 1520s.

Fortunately for Cormier, he had an unrivaled opportunity to study the Villa Madama close up because his stay in Rome coincided with a turning point in the villa's history. After the death of the last hereditary owner in 1894, its decline accelerated at an alarming rate. Just at this nadir in its fortunes, a French engineer named Maurice Bergès and his Italian-born wife stepped in to save the situation by acquiring the structure. This took place in December 1912—not without some local protest over the sale to a foreigner. By spring of the next year, Bergès had retained the services of Pio Piacentini (1848–1928) as architect for the restoration. The drawings he prepared in April secured the necessary permission for alterations by late November 1913. When Cormier reached Rome in January 1915 work had already started, with Piacentini in charge. Then, after his abrupt resignation, it continued under the headstrong personal supervision of Bergès himself. To Cormier and to the director of the British School, Thomas Ashby, the restoration of the Villa Madama presented a once in a lifetime chance. Open access to a historical monument already full of scaffolding provided the perfect conditions for an accurate measured survey. Cormier set to work sketching almost immediately. The surviving set of his fourteen preparatory drawings must fall more or less within the dates 27 February and 4 March 1915 inscribed on two of them.[55]

According to Cormier's progress report sent the summer before his impending departure at Christmas 1916, he aimed to finish a full set of line drawings based on his survey sketches. These in turn generated a set of ink-and-wash elevations and sections, some with evocative landscape views of Monte Mario in the background. With two notable exceptions these drawings survive only in the form of black-and-white snapshots.[56] A delicately colored group that does exist comprises five renderings both large and small of the ornamental stucco work of the loggia. Clearly the decorative aspects of the villa appealed to Cormier. At an early date he manifested an interest in ceiling as well as floor decoration, which in later years characterizes some of his best work as a practicing architect. A second group comprises three watercolors painted in the villa's gardens. They emphasize the architect's love of combining fountains, foliage, and architecture, especially on a hillside. Information of this quality and quantity ranks Cormier's Villa Madama measured survey among the most extensive of the many that had been executed by others, mostly students like himself, captivated by the Villa Madama's alluring mastery of site and eager to emulate its embodiment of the relaxing delights of villeggiatura. Throughout his career Cormier maintained his sensuous taste for Italy: the sound of splashing water, the refreshing sight and smell of greenery, and the coolness of marble to the touch.

As revealing in its own way as any of his other studies is a mammoth semifinished Cormier plan purporting to show the "completion" of the Villa Madama (fig. 19). This plan belongs to an entirely different intellectual tradition, one that at-

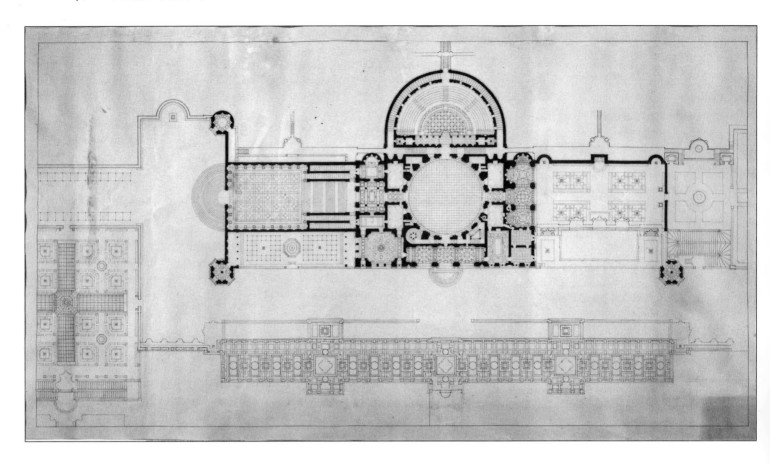

19. Cormier, Villa Madama,
Rome, plan after U314A but
indicating actual loggia and
existing or proposed floor and
ceiling patterns (CCA, AR01:
BL-06)

tempts to restitute the villa from the drawings in the Uffizi rather than to restore
its appearance based on a measured survey. Cormier's starting point was surely
the similar plan illustrated in a book of Roman studies from the 1790s by Percier
and Fontaine, of which Cormier owned a reprint edition.[57] But the differences
from Percier and Fontaine are as significant as the similarities. Whereas they had
copied U314A in Florence (fig. 18), Cormier followed another course of action.
He tried to superimpose on the Uffizi outlines his own measured survey, in addition
to elements such as the flooring and parterre patterns that came from his own
artistic imagination. Apart from Percier and Fontaine, Cormier knew the work of
many other predecessors at the Villa Madama. Sheaves of historical notes by Cormier, show that he had familiarized himself with Vasari's and others' lives of Raphael, had read the recent studies by the Italian Carlo Pontani, the Englishman
Lewis Gruner, and above all the Germans Heinrich von Geymüller and T. Hoff-
man.[58] Cormier based a good deal of his garden layout on von Geymüller's interpretation of the Uffizi drawings. The emphasis on landscape architecture was moreover
reinforced by Cormier's contemporary readings in the garden histories of Pierre

Planat, Gustave Meyer, and Georges Riat. Some of the passages Cormier quoted referred to the villa gardens of Pliny, particularly the hippodrome-shaped one in Tuscany.[59] So it is conceivable that Cormier, unaided by other sources, drew his own conclusions about Pliny's influence on Raphael and the Medici.

In addition to the normal textual references, Cormier resorted to up-to-date copying methods for his visual sources. Special paper allowed him to trace from Pontani's mid-nineteenth-century survey and from von Geymüller's *Raffaello Sanzio studiato come architetto,* published in Milan in 1884. Cormier also had numerous photostats and lantern slides made from the plates in that book. Besides all this, Cormier ordered from a Paris firm a set of four photographs of Emile Bénard's restitution of the Villa Madama, which had previously appeared as plates in Hector d'Espouy's *Fragments d'architecture du Moyen Age et de la Renaissance.* Henri-Jean-Emile Bénard (grand prix 1867) produced a whole series of drawings of the villa in 1871 during the time he was a recipient of the Prix de Rome.[60] He studied the villa in minute detail and also consulted the Sangallo drawings as Percier and Fontaine had done. Then he tried to harmonize everything into one grand, extravagant vision of the Villa Madama as it might have looked (fig. 20). His drawing of the plan, when compared with Cormier's, demonstrates the similarity of their theoretical stance and synthetic approach. Both sought through a study of history to recreate an artistic state of mind from the past at a particular point in time that would encourage emulation and still leave room for the exercise of their own invention. The final result in each case would probably have flabbergasted Raphael. Even the Sangallos might have been a bit taken aback, despite the reputation they earned at Saint Peter's for an unbridled megalomania that often lost sight of the original parti. The Villa Madama as conceived by Ernest Cormier, with its topiary, parterres, pergolas, stucco work, and tiled flooring, became a pure figment of his romantic artistry—an early twentieth-century amalgam of all that he had read, the previous studies he had admired, and the sense impressions he had absorbed among the pines and fountains of Rome.

Fittingly, when Cormier came to design a house for himself in Montreal in 1930, memories of the Villa Madama came flooding back to inspire him (pl. 32). The site encourages Roman recollections because it occupies the flanks of Mount Royal, the equivalent of Monte Mario, and dominates the skyline below. The avenue des Pins borders the top of the property, from which the house descends steeply in terraced stages, corresponding to three main internal levels. The piano nobile with the principal reception rooms sits at the top, and the balcony and windows looking south from here enjoy the broadest views, extending as far as the distant Adirondack Mountains on a clear day. At this level the restrained but very elegant stucco ceilings, marble columns, spiral staircase, and terrazzo flooring all subtly echo the Villa Madama. On the garden level down below, Cormier devised

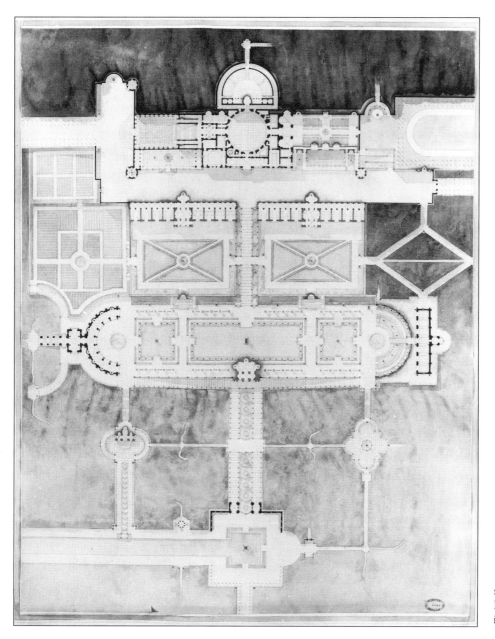

20. Bénard, Villa Madama,
Rome, plan after U314A but
indicating actual loggia (EBA)

the layout of the plantings in rectangular beds, an evocation in miniature of the Raphael terrace he had painted in watercolors while a student in Rome. The Villa Madama had imbued him with a love of gardens and hillside situations that he retained for a lifetime and that influenced some of his greatest masterpieces. When the stairs inside his house became too much for the elderly Cormier, he vacated the property. In 1982 it had the good fortune to come into the hands of Pierre Elliott Trudeau, who meticulously restored it as a home for himself after retiring from public office. Here all the threads join with a final twist: Cormier, the Medici, Pliny, and finally Trudeau, another statesman. The resonances are not lost on Trudeau, who knows the Villa Madama from personal experience, having stayed there as a guest of the Italian government.[61]

CHAPTER THREE

Ruins and Restitutions

ABROAD ALLUVIAL PLAIN of the river Tiber passes beside Città di Castello, known in Roman times as Tifernum Tiberinum. This ancient Umbrian city on the border with Tuscany sits in a virtual bowl of the Apennines with a fine view of them in all directions. The resemblance of such landscapes to the one described by Pliny near his Tuscan Villa intrigued the Renaissance once it had rediscovered his letters. The possibilities for speculation about the villa's location were alluring and all too numerous. Somewhere in those nearby hills would have existed Pliny's fabled Tusci, according to what he wrote to his father-in-law, Calpurnius Fabatus (bk. 4, ep. 1), and to Apollinaris. In recognition of Pliny's strong association with the place, rivaled only by that of Como far to the north, the local high school bears his name. In the immediate vicinity of the school, moreover, the Biblioteca Comunale of Città di Castello owns a fascinating manuscript "Discrizione" relating to the Tuscan Villa, compiled by the priest and Castellane native Francesco Ignazio Lazzari (1633–1717). His lengthy late seventeenth-century attempt to position and describe the Tuscan Villa follows in date the Pliny-inspired restitution of 1615 by Scamozzi (see chap. 4), but it is still the second earliest to survive, owing to the disappearance of the drawing by the architect/monk Giovanni Ambrogio Magenta, about which little is known besides its existence and authorship.[1]

The misfortune that befell Magenta's drawing almost repeated itself with Lazzari's scholarly legacy. Though scattered to the winds, it can fortunately be patched back together at last now that the dispersed bits and pieces have come to light. The numerous fragments consist of the Città di Castello manuscript, an earlier version of it that has found its way to the Dumbarton Oaks Garden Library, and two extremely rare little books. All these documents in turn point to Lazzari as the author of an anonymous drawing that has ended up in a private New York City collection (fig. 21). The drawing is a remarkable object on account of its large size (20⅝″ high × 50½″ wide) and also its conceptual complexity for so early a date, well before the age of scientific archaeology. The two books, each no bigger than a file card, include the *Vita di S. Crescentiano martire e protettore di Città di Castello,* which provides a firm chronological point of departure because of its date of publication in 1709. It was written by Lazzari's fellow cleric Alessandro Certini, who alluded in it to a Lazzari restitution drawing.[2] Lazzari himself mentioned Pliny's Tuscan Villa in his own tiny book of 1693, *Serie de' vescovi e breve notizia . . .*

21. Lazzari, Tuscan Villa, plan, elevations, and perspectives (private collection, New York City)

di Città di Castello, a chronicle of the local bishops. But the printed passage itself is too short and vague to determine whether the book preceded or followed the two Lazzari manuscripts and the drawing alluded to above. In this respect the two signed manuscripts help with the chronology because both refer back to the *Serie*—whether to the printed version or the manuscript, also preserved in the city, is unfortunately unclear. All in all, a date in the late 1680s or early 1690s before the printing of the *Serie* seems indicated. Internal evidence in the manuscript, such as the mention of Bernini's colonnades at Saint Peter's, places the manuscript no earlier than 1669, when the famous piazza in front of the Vatican reached completion.[3]

Before proceeding to associate the author of the manuscripts with the author of the restitution drawing, I should first say something about the virtually unknown Francesco Ignazio Lazzari. Again Certini comes to the rescue, this time in his capacity as genealogist. Certini undertook a genealogical survey of the thirty-three most prominent Castellane families, including the Lazzari. He lists the son of Nicola and Lucrezia, one Francesco Ignazio, as having trained for the priesthood and having shown his literary ability as early as 1669 by writing the first of a series of liturgical pieces and sacred dramas. Certini went on to note Lazzari's talent at painting, perspective drawing, and architecture. Presumably, therefore, he had had some artistic training while studying at Rome, whose baroque monuments he certainly knew well, because he referred to them here and there in his "Discrizione." Likewise, his writings are sprinkled with references to classical texts. Besides

Pliny he mentioned Vitruvius and also Palladio, which tends to establish him as a member in good standing of the local Accademia degli Illuminati, much as Palladio was a member of Vicenza's Accademia Olimpica. Lazzari died at Città di Castello on 16 October 1717 at the advanced age of eighty-three and is buried there.[4]

Apart from reiterating Certini's documentation, the nineteenth-century history by the bishop Giovanni Muzi of Città di Castello could find little to add about Lazzari. Muzi did state that Lazzari had designed the funeral catefalque for Bishop Sebastiani in 1689, about the same time as he contributed to the completion of the cathedral by building the balustraded staircase on the north facade.[5] Lazzari never alluded to these artistic achievements in his writings except on page 139 of his *Serie*, when he claimed the great Bramante Lazzari as a distant forebear. The cathedral staircase may be a far cry from Bramante's innovative one in the Belvedere courtyard, but Lazzari undoubtedly had some facility with pen and wash. His two manuscript "Discrizione" contain numerous rather scratchy sketches of existing villas. Faulty "rushing" perspective technique and general amateurishness aside, they convey a certain feeling of assurance. All these qualities carry over to the anonymous restitution drawing of Pliny's Tuscan Villa. Stylistic affinities are not the only basis for suggesting a connection. The manuscript texts often refer to a plan, elevation, and aerial view prepared in conjunction with them. Furthermore, the *Serie*, the manuscripts, and the marginalia on the drawing all concur in locating the Tuscan Villa at a place known as Pliniano, corrupted into the vernacular "Pitigliano" or "Pittigliano." With so much circumstantial evidence, the conclusion seems almost inescapable that no one other than Lazzari could have designed the restitution drawing illustrated here.[6]

The subsequent wanderings of the drawing merit a brief digression in their own right. Apparently the restitution's existence was first made known by the 1931 Florentine Mostra del Giardino exhibition, which cataloged it as the work of an unidentified seventeenth-century hand without so much as hinting at the provenance or the lender. Until that time, at least, the drawing had obviously remained on Italian soil, together with the two manuscript texts from which it has subsequently suffered a double separation.[7] The first occurred when one of the texts migrated to the United States as early as the 1950s. At that time Mildred Bliss, founder of the Dumbarton Oaks Garden Library, placed her bookplate inside the vellum folder that now contains the manuscript. Following this the drawing, after having disappeared from sight, turned up for sale on the Paris art market in 1983. Five years later it had also crossed the Atlantic, only to be acquired by a private collector, thanks to whose generosity it could finally be studied and properly photographed for the first time in 1990.[8] Each of the two manuscripts already mentioned consists of a three-part scholarly preamble intended to establish the verisimilitude of the restitution. To begin with, Lazzari's texts sought by elimination to narrow down the field of possible sites for Pliny's villa, an honor seemingly contended for by every hillside around. First he summarized the local history literature on the subject and found it rife with the chauvinistic bias of the various authors. He then somehow worked into his argument a running commentary on the best villas in his area of Umbria. In a region not especially rich in examples, he singled out for illustration such Renaissance structures as the Castello Bufalini at San Giustino and the splendid Villa Graziani at Celalba. None of the locations, however, matched Lazzari's criteria for the Pliny villa. In the end his choice fell two miles to the east of Celalba at a place called Colle Plinio, near Pitigliano. A crucial passage referring to the seventeenth-century Villa Brozzi-Cappelletti reads: "Lascio per ultimo Colle [Plinio] Villa continguo a Pitigliano. . . . Ed in detto sito . . . , ritrovando tutte le condizioni descritte da Plinio nella sua Villa io mi fermo . . . che il Palagio, Portico, o Residenza magnifica de Plinio fosse dove e di presente la sud:ᵃ Villa del Cav:ʳᵒ Girolamo Brozzi."[9] Despite deference to local traditions and hearsay, or "la commune oppinione de Paesani, e concittadini," as he put it, Lazzari relied most upon the "qualche pezzo di muro . . . varri pezzi de Pietre, o marmi fini" he could examine lying around in plain evidence. Perhaps it is this reliance on archaeological evidence that makes Lazzari's manuscripts so remarkable. He provided a virtual catalog of all the recent finds he knew of—Plinian ruins, Latin inscriptions, the chance discovery of underground chambers, and even two statues of Priapus, all recorded with considerable care.[10] Alas, what was easy to see in his day is more difficult of access now. Short of government expropriation, the firmly closed gates of the Villa Brozzi-Cappelletti will continue to bar the way to further scientific excavation at Colle Plinio.

The two concluding sections of the Lazzari manuscripts provide a word-by-word architectural and horticultural analysis of the letter to Apollinaris. These forty-two numbered subheadings and their explanatory texts correspond very closely to the densely packed information in the long marginalia accompanying the right-hand third of the restitution. The drawing, in fact, consists of three sheets of paper joined into a single oblong, about the size of a large corporate desktop. The welter of data crammed in betrays a somewhat provincial enthusiasm for erudition at the expense of artistic presentation. But from the historical standpoint the advantages of this provincialism outweigh the unattractiveness. Simply put, by working in a virtual vacuum and without benefit of emulation, Lazzari invented single-handedly the idea of a restitution devoted to the Tuscan Villa. Putting aside Michelozzo, Raphael, and the Sangallos, he is the first known architect ever to undertake such a thing on paper. What motivated Lazzari to such a considerable task? Probably it was a mixture of archaeological fervor, a little academic art education, though not all that much, and civic pride. Lazzari literally produced a Castellane architectural triptych. Cloth binding around the edges, creases down the fold lines, and loose threads where ribbons might have been suggest it could be closed up like an altarpiece or portfolio to protect it when not in use. In spite of these precautions it has suffered considerably from water damage and abrasion at some point during its three hundred years of existence, making it a stained, but no less precious, vestige of its former self.

The left-hand "panel" of Lazzari's drawing shows the plan of a strange quadrangular main building around an open court linked by causeways to corner towers. These causeways interconnect with terraces and very low wings to form a larger square around the inner one. To the front and sides extend elaborate gardens. Amid the parterres at the rear sit two separate buildings, one rectangular and the other behind it semicircular. At the front of the site an enclosure wall curving forward in the reverse direction is pierced by three gates specified in the seventh numbered subheading of the two Lazzari manuscripts. The eighth subheading goes on to pinpoint the inspiration as the garden wall of the Palazzo Vitelli at the Porta San Egidio in Città di Castello. Lazzari had drawn it for inclusion in his manuscripts. In this way visually and textually he made links between Roman gardening and that of his contemporary Umbria insofar as it reflected those ancient practices. The side portals align with two oblong areas called hippodromes on the numbered legend at the bottom of the right-hand "panel." (In this instance number 31 of the legend agrees exactly with subheading 31 in the manuscripts, more proof that the same person devised them all.)

Turning to the central "panel" (fig. 22), Lazzari's typical tipped perspective clarifies the Tuscan Villa layout when seen in conjunction with the plan. The garden in the foreground has espaliered trees arranged in arbors, and alongside them run box hedges so tall that round-headed niches cut into them accommodate full-sized statues. The parterres in the garden at the rear have lower borders of hedge, clipped in circular patterns to make room for a pair of fountains and a pair of gazebos flanking the several-story *palazzina,* big enough to be a villa in its own right. Farther back still, the composition culminates with the drafty semicircular baths—hot, cold, and tepid—under a triple arrangement of open cupolas. On the same level as the baths, balustrades extending to the left and right have topiary animals sitting on top and more parterres behind. At this point the manuscripts take over by listing all kinds of kitchens, granaries, and servants' quarters. These are unspecified in the letter to Apollinaris, but Lazzari assured his readers that they were necessary to life in a villa (subheadings 17 and 22). Thus by slow and steady degrees Lazzari swelled Pliny's Tuscan Villa to gargantuan proportions.

The full extent of Lazzari's Tuscan Villa is revealed only in the third, or right-hand, "panel" of his restitution. In this case better command of aerial perspective permits the eye to soar over the garden wall, forecourt, main building, *palazzina,* and baths before coming to rest on Pliny's dining pavilion at the top of a hill in

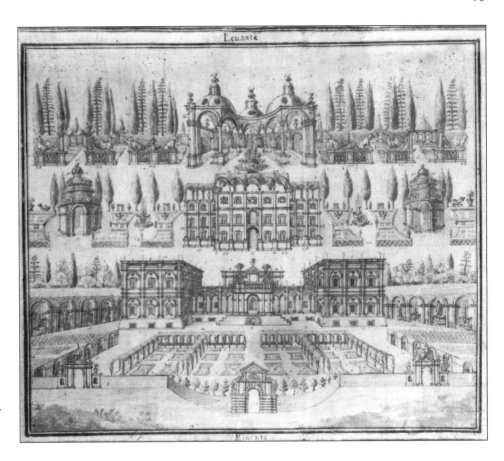

Levante

Ponente

22. Lazzari, Tuscan Villa, detail of central panel (private collection, New York City)

the background (see fig. 178). Lazzari speculated that this structure should be several stories tall, a kind of belvedere as much as a *stibadium*. His local pride caused him to think in grandiose terms. To him Pliny's is no ordinary country house but *sua magnifica villa*, as subheading 20 of the manuscripts puts it. It looks as if a convex series of staircase treads leading up to the pavilion may actually be a *catena d'acqua*, or artificial waterfall like the one by Vignola at Bagnaia (pl. 20), or like Giacomo del Duca's at the casino in the grounds of the Palazzo Farnese at Caprarola. Lazzari's megalomania results in an ever expanding synthesis of these Renaissance planning ideas with Latin sources on the villa—Varro and Vitruvius in addition to Pliny. Apart from developing a composite set of ideal buildings, Lazzari ransacked the rich horticultural traditions of his day for ideas on gardens. Had it ever been erected, his garden villa would surely have exceeded Pliny's in scale. It would have rivaled, in a somewhat ungainly way, the outstanding central Italian examples of the previous century mentioned above. Nothing in all Umbria would have held a candle to Lazzari's conception.

Francesco Ignazio Lazzari had one distinct advantage over all other admirers of the Tuscan Villa in his own era and for two centuries to come. He knew the local landscape intimately. Although his restitution by no means reproduces the actual landscape at Colle Plinio as it now appears, it evokes the scene in general terms. Lush flatlands ascend from the Tiber bed and rise gradually to vine-covered slopes, just as Pliny had described them in Roman times. From there the altitude increases more rapidly to the remote hamlet of Valdimonte, overshadowed by Monte Giove—at 694 meters the tallest peak around. A mountain torrent with a small cataract plunges down from the heights, constantly watering Colle Plinio and nearby Pitigliano. At a point about midway between these two communities a view opens up to the opposing range of Apennines to the south, spread out more or less like an amphitheater, as Pliny had stated. Modern archaeologists claim not to have known much about Lazzari's speculations, but the fact remains that they started excavating in 1975 very near the spot Lazzari had pinpointed long before. With amazing precision Lazzari focused in on these same fields near the church of Santa Fiora and on a copse encircling the Villa Brozzi-Cappelletti.[11]

In the absence of final excavation reports, preliminary ones together with periodical articles and newspaper clippings fill in the progress of the archaeological work carried out at Colle Plinio. By the end of the first three campaigns (1972, 1977, 1979) it had already become clear to the archaeologists that they had unearthed the winery of the *pars fructuaria* belonging to a sizable latifundium of late Republican date. Among the significant finds were some inscriptions referring to a Marcus Granius Marcellus, proconsul of Bithnia and a maternal relative of Pliny's. More-over, terra-cotta roof-tile shards bore the imprint of a seal (or *bollo laterizo*) with the initials C.P.C.S. Here at last seemed conclusive proof that the excavators had uncovered lands that had passed to Caius Plinius Caecilius Secundus by inheritance. Six subsequent digs were conducted from 1984 to 1989 by Laura Bonomi Ponsi and others. They have confirmed the information and enlarged the scope of the excavation site to several hundred meters square on either side of the road between Pitigliano and Colle Plinio, close to the bridge over the Valdimonte stream. At the end of the penultimate season, a section of terra-cotta drainpipe stamped with Pliny's *bollo* came to light, proving that the winery and small attached bathing complex had been built or altered by him (fig. 23).

Since 1989 all attention has shifted to the walled Cappelletti estate, which archaeologists now surmise is the site of the main Tuscan Villa. Whether the next logical step occurs remains a matter of conjecture. Should the Villa Brozzi-Cappelletti and its handsome landscaped grounds be expropriated and dug up to prove the hypothesis that Pliny's house lies beneath? On the face of it the evidence supporting such drastic action is insufficient. Of course it would be fascinating to finally put Pliny's letter to the test, but what if the remains found did not live up

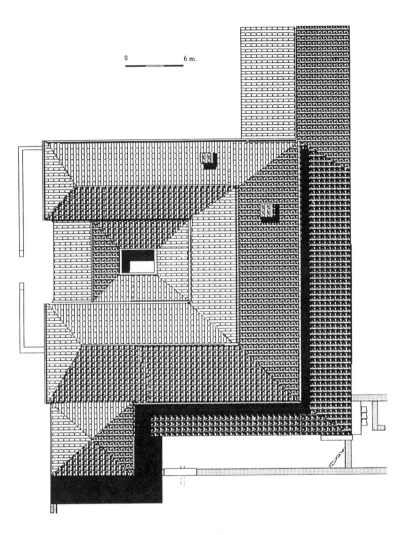

0   6 m.

23. Colle Plinio, plan of the
roofing of Pliny's winery (line
drawing after Braconi)

to the expectations of Lazzari or his modern successors in the Soprintendenza
Archeologica dell'Umbria? Worse still, what if damaging excavations turned up
nothing?[12] The arguments waver back and forth between those advocating excavation and others wishing to exercise restraint. Certain architect emulators might go
so far as to say it would be better to leave well enough alone. The archaeological
facts, whether flattering to Pliny or not, might lessen the compelling fascination
that the Tuscan Villa has exerted upon the imagination of architects from Lazzari's
day right down to the present.

As just noted, a strong tradition of regionalism has led Italian antiquarians to
associate places in their immediate locale with memorable passages in ancient
literature, such as those relating to the villas of Pliny. What Giovio had written
about Como (introduction) and Lazzari about Città di Castello also applied in due

course to the supposed location of the Laurentine Villa on the seacoast near Ostia in ancient Latium. Inasmuch as Latium incorporated most of the seacoast within easy reach of the archaeologically minded popes in Rome, it is surprising that an expedition to locate the Laurentine Villa did not take place until 1712. Before that such seventeenth-century geographers as Philipp Cluver and Lucas Holsten had simply hazarded guesses about the location of Pliny's villa.[13] Unaccountably, even the great Jesuit polymath Athanasius Kircher passed over the matter in silence in his book *Latium,* published at Amsterdam in 1671. Could Kircher, who slightly later attempted imaginary restitutions of the Tower of Babel and Noah's Ark, have reserved Pliny for some future work? If so, he made no such allusions. But the eighteenth century filled the relatively blank page on the Laurentine Villa with voluminous writings.

In 1712 Dr. Giovanni Maria Lancisi (1634–1720) addressed a letter to a fellow naturalist from a famous seaside villa near Ostia that had been frescoed early in the previous century by Cortona for the aristocratic Sacchetti brothers. The location of the villa at Castel Fusano is in the heart of a pinetum that the Sacchetti planted, according to Lancisi, and that stretches southward along the coast as well as for a considerable distance inland. The flat and relatively arid landscape could hardly differ more from the lush one at Colle Plinio, yet Pliny relished precisely this sort of change of scene. Of course many things about the topography had changed since he wrote, including the groves of pines. Lancisi speculated that the coastline had altered fundamentally and as a result the area had changed from the healthy place it had been in Pliny's time to one with a reputation for pestilence. This turns out to have been the primary raison d'être for Lancisi's presence at the villa. As a physician he specialized in the diagnosis of these diseases and their treatment with medicinal plants that could be collected in the low-lying marshlands. Lancisi was staying at Castel Fusano as the guest of Fra Marcello Sacchetti (1644–1720), descendant of the original owners.[14] Their lack of interest in Pliny turned into a passion for him on the part of Fra Marcello, knight of Malta and amateur archaeologist. And improbable though it may sound, the only eyewitness account of his Laurentine excavations as recorded by Lancisi lies hidden between the covers of a scholarly book on mushrooms.[15]

Sometime before the spring of 1712 when Lancisi wrote from Castel Fusano, a villa site had been excavated by Marcello Sacchetti on the family property at a place known as Piastra. Lancisi alluded to the dig in a jovial letter that had much more to say about the delights of philosophical discussion in a villa setting and the joys of botanical discovery. In a much longer letter of two years later, written to Marcello Sacchetti from Rome, Lancisi kept up the bantering tone intended to recall quite specifically Pliny's epistolary style. Lancisi noted, for instance, that his earlier observations of the excavated ruins at the villa had occurred during a country house party, whose noise reminded him of the Saturnalia festivities Pliny described to Gallus as taking place near that very spot. Perhaps this explains the unhelpful haziness of Lancisi's remarks. According to him he saw a series of rooms, courts, and tower foundations constructed in opus reticulatum, with mosaic floors and some fragmentary ornamentation in Numidian and Alexandrian marble. He went on to add that Sacchetti had prepared a plan of the ruins.[16] Its information would no doubt supplement Lancisi's vague verbal description. Unfortunately the plan itself has so far not turned up, either in the Sacchetti archives or in the Vatican Library. But the Jesuit antiquarian Father Giuseppe Rocco Volpi, writing a generation later, insisted that he knew two copies of the drawing of the site: one in the Vatican, another in the private collection of Cardinal Alessandro Furietti.[17] No one has reported seeing the documents since. Lancisi added one tantalizing piece of information when he mentioned the existence of an earlier Laurentine restitution prepared by the Bolognese architect and general of the Barnabite order, Giovanni Ambrogio Magenta (1565–1635).[18] Without his realizing it, Lancisi's discussing Sacchetti and Magenta in the same breath had established the battle lines between two opposing camps of those wishing to convey an impression of Pliny's villa on paper. There would be those like the architect Magenta who worked purely from the imagination and treated the letter to Gallus as a challenge to their artistry. Then there would be others like Fra Marcello Sacchetti who represented a new breed of more archaeologically minded scholars intent on finding ruins that they could somehow or other match up with Pliny's description. Far from going away, this dichotomy persists. As with the present excavations at Colle Plinio, much the same dilemma applies on the Ostian coast today.[19]

At times history has a capricious tendency to turn back on itself. The earliest attempt at discovering Pliny's Laurentine Villa corresponds closely with the most recent one, even though 271 years separate them. After so many hypotheses based on the same letter to Gallus, the architect-archaeologist Eugenia Salza Prina Ricotti decided in 1983 to put to the test her own imaginary restitution inspired by her fondness for Pliny's letter (fig. 24). In the blazing heat of August that year, she investigated a site known as the Villa Magna, or delle Grotte di Piastra, which she now proposes as the Laurentine Villa's ruins. Her suggested location is close to but different from those put forward earlier in this century by the archaeologists Rodolfo Lanciani and Antonio Collini. It also cannot be very far from where Marcello Sacchetti dug in his own backyard—in fact the sites may be the very same, though Ricotti does not think so.[20] Unlike the Colle Plinio excavation, however, the element of certainty is missing because the inscriptions that have turned up this time date from a generation after Pliny's death.[21] In fairness to Ricotti's three strenuous summer excavation campaigns (1983–85), they have demonstrated conclusively that what she calls the *litus plinianus* was a prime stretch of gold coast

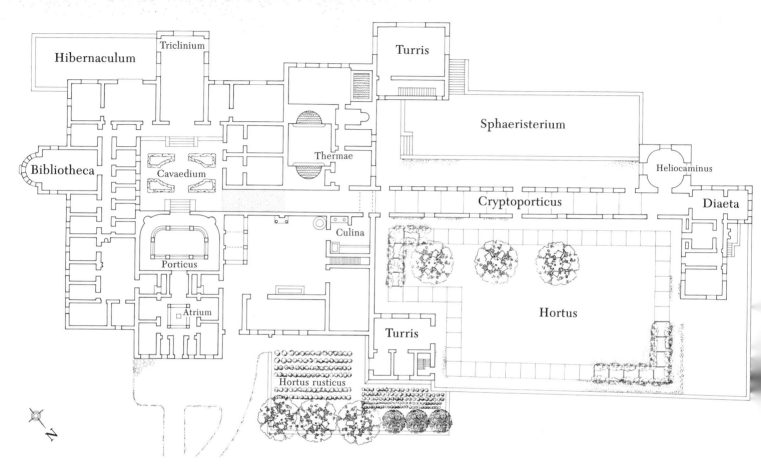

Hibernaculum

Triclinium

Turris

Sphaeristerium

Bibliotheca

Cavaedium

Thermae

Heliocaminus

Cryptoporticus

Diaeta

Culina

Porticus

Hortus

Atrium

Turris

Hortus rusticus

N

real estate in antiquity. The shorefront properties changed hands frequently and changed architecturally as well, in accordance with successive owners' whims. Sacchetti, Lanciani, Collini, and now Ricotti prove that the beach was virtually littered with villas cheek by jowl, built before, during, and after Pliny's lifetime. This detritus of the ages has piled up like so much flotsam and jetsam on the strand. It would be a stroke of luck to single out any one site as indisputably Pliny's. Add to this the destructive effects of previous excavations and the erosion by the sea over the centuries.

In her excavation report (fig. 25), Ricotti attributes her failure to find the main triclinium to action by the waves. But earlier Lancisi, Lanciani, and Thomas Ashby had used the argument of a progressive silting up to support their candidates for the Laurentine site.[22] Another interesting outcome of Ricotti's investigations is the similarity between her initial imaginary restitution, based on a reading of Pliny (fig. 24), and the restitution subsequently based on the excavation reports (fig. 26). Notably, the atrium and *D*-shaped portico are close in both drawings, although the

24. Ricotti, Laurentine Villa, plan (line drawing after Ricotti)

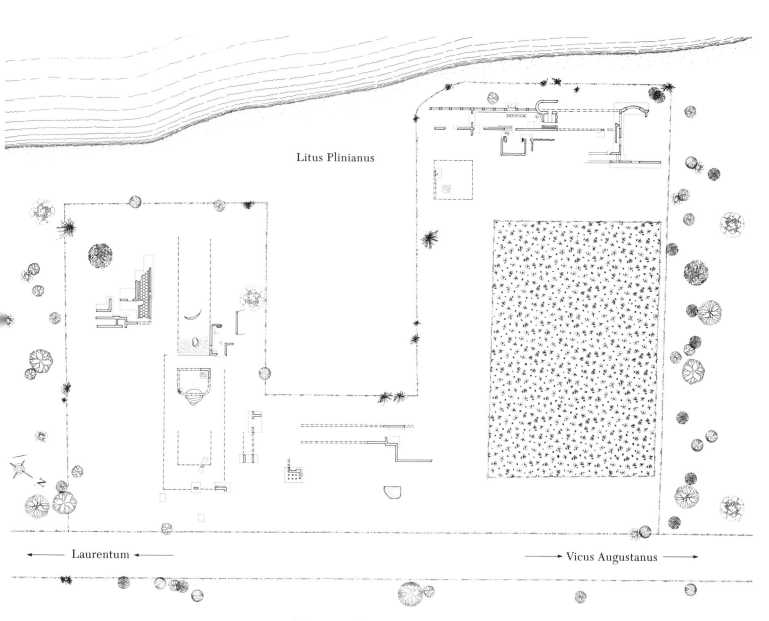

Litus Plinianus

← Laurentum ←   → Vicus Augustanus →

25. Grotte di Piastra, plan of the excavations (line drawing after Ricotti, "Il Laurentino: Scavi del 1985")

test pits of the area dug in 1984 did not uncover enough to establish the basic outlines with certainty. In this regard, Ricotti aligns herself with others who were first trained in architecture and then turned their attention to archaeology. She feels strongly that only certain planning solutions are workable. She favors the practical knowledge of an architect like Canina (cf. fig. 30) over the purely archaeological approach of a Lanciani—the same Lanciani who had confidently written in 1909: "I am, I believe, the only living archaeologist who can claim the privilege of having entered Pliny's house and walked over its floors."[23] Ricotti also reveals how evidence, scientifically arrived at but not always incontrovertible, has a habit of

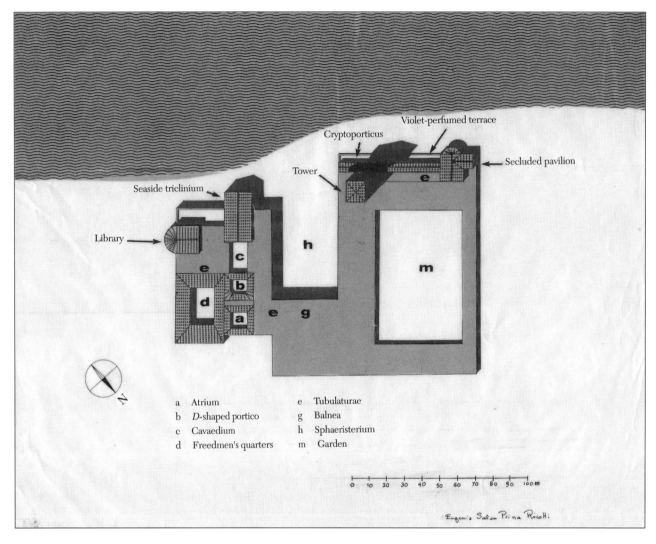

Violet-perfumed terrace

Cryptoporticus

Secluded pavilion

Tower

Seaside triclinium

Library

e

h

c

b

d

a

e

g

m

N

a   Atrium   e   Tubulaturae
b   *D*-shaped portico   g   Balnea
c   Cavaedium   h   Sphaeristerium
d   Freedmen's quarters   m   Garden

0   10   20   30   40   50   60   70   80   90   100 m

Eugenia Salza Prina Ricotti

26. Ricotti, Laurentine Villa, plan including evidence from the excavations (collection of the artist)

fulfilling wished-for a priori conclusions. Although she resists stating outright that she has finally located the Laurentine Villa, all her inclinations lean in that direction. So with evident regret she has had to conclude that, until more funds for additional excavation become available, unresolved questions rule out a final answer.[24]

At a time in the early 1790s when signs of the Sacchetti excavation might still have been discernible, a party of three men set out from Rome to the seacoast to find them. Since they had failed to locate a copy of Sacchetti's plan, the search seemed doomed from the start, akin to hunting for a specific pebble on a beach. This international trio comprised Silvestre Perez (1767–1825), a Spanish architect; Charles-Louis Petit-Radel (1756–1836), a French Roman Catholic priest with a penchant for archaeology;[25] and his Mexican counterpart, the former Jesuit Pedro

José Marquez (1741–1820). Marquez was the eldest and the longest established in Rome, where he worked as a librarian at the Biblioteca Casanatense, supplementing his income by turning out books at a great rate. The most unusual are his pioneering publications on the Aztecs of his own native country, from which he had been exiled. But he had also written four books on aspects of classical architecture: one in 1795 on Roman domestic buildings; another in 1796 titled *Delle ville di Plinio il giovane;* a third in 1803 about the Doric order; and a fourth in 1812 on the Villa of Maecenas at Tivoli.[26] With each new title—most of them published by the Salomoni Press—he took every opportunity to congratulate himself on his previous studies, as though to boost his sales.

Marquez's slim and rare volume on the villas of Pliny begins with an account of the expedition he and his companions undertook to the coast near Castel Fusano. In the end they found what seemed more or less to agree with Lancisi's published account of the remains. Petit-Radel unearthed an inscription or two, and then the party returned to Rome. (In the case of the Tuscan Villa, Marquez never visited the site at all but relied on the authority of unnamed persons in Città di Castello with whom he had corresponded—so much for archaeological methodology.)[27] On the historiographic front, however, the librarian Marquez fared somewhat better by at least mentioning earlier efforts, although he took much of his information directly from the secondhand account by Volpi.[28] That much having been acknowledged, Marquez paid no attention whatever to previous restitutions, in an attempt, as he put it on page 6, to get back to *il nudo testo di Plinio.* The real motivation, however, may have had more to do with his wish to make the villas book a sequel to his general study of the previous year. In other words, he wanted to harmonize his translation of Vitruvius on Roman domestic architecture, to which he makes frequent self-congratulatory references, with Pliny's much more detailed, but less organized, observations. For all this apparently rational synthesis, Marquez followed traditional interpretations, sometimes despite the evidence before his eyes. He chose to consult the authoritative Amsterdam 1734 edition of Pliny by Paul Daniel Longolius, for instance, one of the very few since the Renaissance to accept the letter *D* as best describing the Laurentine Villa's courtyard. But Marquez took exception to this and reverted to the generally favored *O* configuration of previous restitutions on the grounds that it was more pleasing in form.[29] He obviously wavered from strict adherence to precedent whenever it suited him, pleading the argument that practice often diverges from theory. Overall, Marquez oscillated between extremes of laxness in method and arbitrary rigidity.

As might be expected from the remarks above, Marquez's villa plans have an angular, jerky look, as though composed of disconnected dots and dashes (figs. 27 and 28). This impression is reinforced in the Laurentine plan by the unusual and thoroughgoing asymmetry, which applies to the entire disposition as well as the lay-

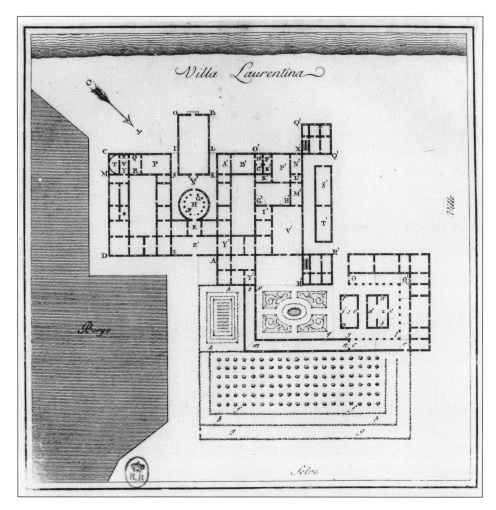

27. Marquez, Laurentine Villa, plan (Marquez, *Ville di Plinio*)

out of the architecture. At first sight water appears to surround the house on two sides. The wavy lines at the top representing the Mediterranean, however, should not be confused with the straight hatching on the left that delineates the city limits of a nearby town, meeting Pliny's grounds along a jagged perimeter. Off on the right, the plan indicates the presence of adjacent villas in a deliberate attempt to echo Pliny and remove his Laurentine Villa from the tabula rasa of semi-isolation where it had been placed by all previous restitutions except Castell's (see chap. 4). Marquez chopped up the Laurentine site by contending that the neighborhood impinged on the villa. Pliny's villa had little room to breathe, sandwiched between the village and other villas. In his own words to Apollinaris, as translated by Marquez, he likened the situation to *un prospetto di molte città*. In line with that, Marquez stressed that the proliferation of villas in antiquity made them almost commonplace.[30] Marquez had begun suburbanizing the Laurentine Villa.

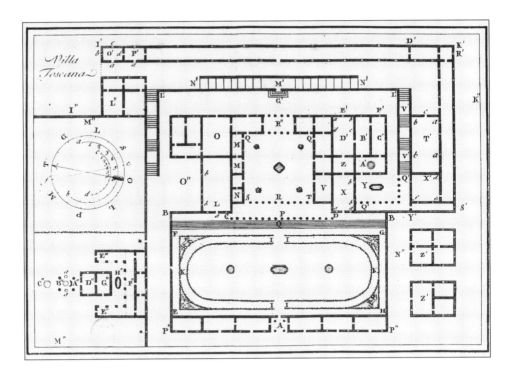

28. Marquez, Tuscan Villa, plan (Marquez, *Ville di Plinio*)

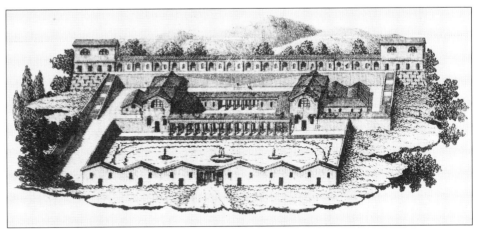

29. Marquez, Tuscan Villa, vignette (Marquez, *Ville di Plinio*)

Despite the amateurish appearance of the plans in Marquez's book, Silvestre Perez must have helped to prepare them. Some of the tricks of presentation he used in his own student drawings as a pensioner of the Spanish academy in Rome are recalled in the engaging vignette of the Tuscan Villa (fig. 29). It is shown as if served up on a large sloping platter with sprigs of vegetation spilling over the edge.[31] The vignette does not entirely agree with the corresponding plan, which calls for even more asymmetrically disposed rooms along the edges than appear in the aerial view. A series of distinct enclosed spaces centers on a courtyard with a portico of seventeen Doric columns—a significant choice of order, as will be clear in a moment. The villa's various levels cascade down the slope to the hippodrome, screened from the outside by low service buildings. At the top of the complex, a curious elongated structure stretching between two tower blocks answers to Pliny's requirement that the cryptoporticus look down the valley and up over the vineyards at the same time. The author visualized Pliny's villa as spreading out over a hillside at a place in Umbria called Meltina. (Although he had seen neither it nor Celalba himself, he assured his readers that the latter was not nearly high enough in altitude.) Despite the innovative asymmetry, the planning in general terms is deficient. It resembles a warren of small chambers with no controlling rationale. Marquez was forced into this position by adhering too closely to Pliny's description of the peculiarities of each room. Marquez delighted in the *stibadium,* for example, which he differentiated from the normal, less private triclinium. By placing it at the front of the plan (it does not figure in the vignette), he contended that the inhabitants could enjoy the view as well as the food. He visualized and spelled out every comfort as though he had a prospective client in mind.[32]

A fascination with the specificity of the site linked Marquez with the aristocratic dedicatee of his book, Don José Nicolás de Azara (1731–1804), the Spanish ambassador to the Holy See. The dedication referred to Azara's helpful remarks on the topography around Laurentinum and mentioned the grandee's great interest in the Maecenas Villa and the origins of the Doric order, both topics on which Marquez subsequently published. Azara is also known to have supported his countryman Silvestre Perez. In addition to his possible involvement with the Pliny book, the young architect devoted a project to the Maecenas Villa while studying at Rome. This establishes another strong connection between Azara, Perez, and Marquez.[33] In fact the Marquez restitutions so closely mirror Azara's interests in villas, the orders, and ancient topography that the *ricco padrone* of Roman times whom Marquez imagined inhabiting them might easily have passed for Azara, a statesman and lover of the arts like Pliny.[34] If Marquez anticipated a villa revival under the aegis of Don José, he had a big disappointment in store. Two years after the publication of *Delle ville di Plinio il giovane,* Azara left Rome never to return. Marquez departed for Mexico in 1816 to enjoy brief celebrity at home as a noted antiquarian and astronomer before passing into eclipse.

In the annals of Italian Pliny projects, stretching from Raphael in the Renaissance to Ricotti today, Luigi Canina's name should stand out more than it does. In his own day, Canina (1795–1856) received international recognition, but only recently has he been rediscovered as an unsung hero of "architectural classicism of the first half of the nineteenth century."[35] Because he produced so little as a practicing architect, most major histories of the profession overlook his contribution. Moreover, his nonspecialist training has caused contemporary archaeologists to deny him credit as a pioneering confrere. As an architect-archaeologist he falls into a kind of limbo, occupying neither one well-defined niche nor the other. But in reality he ought to be considered on the same footing as his distinguished predecessors Giovanni Battista Piranesi and Giuseppe Valadier, who combined talents similar to his: they built, they excavated, they restored, and they published their lavishly illustrated findings.

In terms of book production alone, Canina deserves attention: for he established his own prolific publishing house, just as Piranesi had done before him. Far from being in any sense a homespun affair, Canina's press turned out weighty and sumptuous tomes in all sorts of variant editions that make them a bibliographer's nightmare. As demand required, Canina would reissue his volumes with slightly different titles and dates. To make matters more complex, he had several ambitious projects in the works at once. With production protracted over decades, they make any precise chronology difficult. The range of subject matter is also staggeringly encyclopedic, far too vast for any one person in the nineteenth century to have encompassed, let alone excavated in person. Yet as a compendium of archaeological information—some original, much received from elsewhere—Canina's accomplishment is outstanding even in an age given to vast projects. In comparison, the output of Marquez, remarkable through it was for the previous generation, seems puny and cheaply produced.

Canina arrived from Piedmont to study in Rome in 1818 and quickly launched himself into a triple career as restorer, garden building designer, and archaeological investigator. In the last of these capacities he published the bulk of his literary output, culminating in his truly monumental *Architettura antica descritta e dimonstrata coi monumenti* (Rome, 1830–44). In it he divided up the ancient world according to three distinctive styles: Egyptian, Greek, and Roman,[36] and to each category he devoted an immensely thick volume of plates. The engravings contained in these atlases total no fewer than 648, an achievement of Herculean, even Piranesian, proportions. But the difference between Canina and Piranesi lay in the former's less chauvinistic and more rational method. Canina gave theoretical considerations, a historical overview, and analysis by building type. In the category of Roman domestic structures, for instance, he focused on marine villas as among the most notable the Romans had invented. Hence, from his point of view the literary information Pliny provided was invaluable. Canina simply stated that the villas along the coast near Rome were too poorly preserved to permit anything but a restitution based on literary evidence.[37]

Working from the Laurentine Villa description, in 1840 Canina prepared his beautifully executed restitution plan (fig. 30). A lengthy section of text prefaces Canina's plate. It is not what one expects from an archaeologist building a case on inscriptions, excavation reports, or rigorously established architectural precedents.

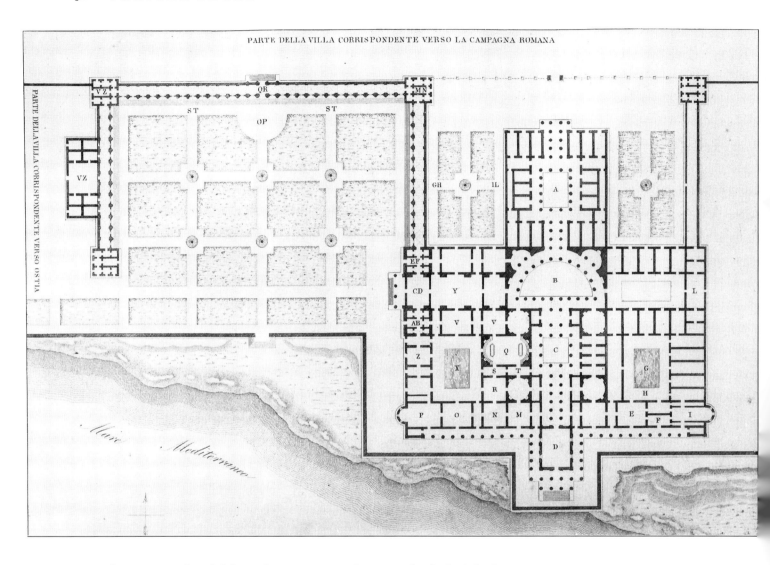

30. Canina, Laurentine Villa, plan (Canina, *Architettura romana*)

Instead Canina used a philological argument, on the strength of which he became the first in Italy to suggest a *D*-shaped courtyard for the Laurentine structure. He cites no precendent for such a radical departure from the norm. (Ricotti uses the so-called Villa of the Discobolus as her justification.) Canina's text bluntly asserts that had Pliny wished to describe a circle he would have written the word *rotondo*. From this point on, all pretense at scholarly dissection of the text disappears. What follows is an uncritical, warmly evocative, and sympathetic paraphrase of Pliny's words to Gallus. Canina evoked the sights, smells, sounds, and caressing breezes as perhaps only a native Italian could. His poetic interpretation smoothes over the textual rough spots that had plagued and preoccupied previous restitutions. Whereas Marquez struggled to understand the villa's practical inner workings and therefore produced a somewhat awkward result, Canina's is suave by contrast. He seems to have been in control of archaeological information and the classical language of architecture to the extent of almost flying in its face.

Canina's prose floats mellifluously over the many interpretive snags that arise from a reading of the seventeenth epistle of Pliny's book 2. A similar feeling of effortlessness carries over to the conception of the villa, which conveys an unprecedented sense of assurance, whatever its faults on an archaeological scale of truth. It is a big, majestic place, densely packed with columns—123 not counting applied shafts. No wonder Lanciani, writing at the beginning of this century, chastised Canina's as "an immense structure fit for an emperor or for a financial magnate."[38] Almost perfect bilateral symmetry prevails here, in distinction to such examples as Hadrian's villa at Tivoli or Cicero's near Frascati, both dealt with later in Canina's book.[39] To some extent, then, Canina knowingly ignored archaeological evidence to achieve an ideal villa in keeping with the idyllic tone of Pliny's letter.

Along the imaginary shoreline Canina's burin cut walled embankments, whose hard edges contrast with the irregular topographical strata marking the height above sea level. The outlying pavilion to the left, attached to the villa by an exceedingly long cryptoporticus on three sides of a square, maintains the same unyielding rectilinear geometry. The pavilion would have been a chore to reach at the best of times. In bad weather the visitor would be inconvenienced by having to pass through the private apartments clustered at two of the walkway's corners. All together this is not an especially supple plan, and it suggests Canina's limitations in original architectural design. Nevertheless, he conceived on a grand scale, as is apparent from a perspective view of the villa not published until 1856, the year of his death (fig. 31). Hardly had the ink dried on his *Architettura romana* than Canina

31. Canina, Laurentine Villa, perspective (Canina, *Architettura romana*)

embarked in 1848 on his equally monumental six-volume *Gli edifici di Roma antica.* The final two volumes appeared in 1856, one of text and another of plates. They concerned the architecture of the Campagna around Rome and returned to the theme of the Laurentine Villa. Canina discussed Pliny's letter and related it anew to his plan published in the 1840s.[40] (Marquez was not the only author on Pliny's villas who was interested in boosting sales of his other writings.) In Canina's later publication he printed his perspective view "dalla parte del mare." Seen in elevation Canina's villa appears less hard edged. Tall, spindly columns and painted wall decoration give the building a feeling of soft fabric. In fact, several cloth canopies and a velarium, or rooftop awning, hang from the villa's upper stories. In this way Canina imparted some of the whimsy of the "theatrical style" Pompeian wall paintings he had admired. For once, then, archaeological truth coincided with the imaginative, fanciful yearnings of the age, thus overcoming the dilemma of the nineteenth-century architect-archaeologist. A constant inner tussle was waged over which should prevail: the evocative spirit of Pliny's writings or the information increasingly revealed by excavators.[41]

In the interval between his two books, Canina may have been influenced by the works of Haudebourt and Schinkel, which used similar devices of Roman galleys and the viewpoint taken from the sea to magnify the Laurentine Villa (cf. figs. 32 and 4). Louis-Pierre Haudebourt (1788–1849) was Canina's senior by seven years. The Frenchman arrived in Rome earlier than Canina and spent the politically turbulent period 1815–16 there. While in Rome he favored Renaissance buildings, as had his mentor, Charles Percier. Upon Haudebourt's return from Italy he published in 1818 a book on the Palazzo Massimo alle Colonne, anticipating by two decades the celebrated views of it by another Percier pupil, Paul-Marie Letarouilly.[42] A second, more unusual work, *Le Laurentin maison de campagne de Pline le jeune,* published in Paris in 1838, revealed another side of Haudebourt's student days in Italy. It related to his love of literature, his aspirations as an author, and his quest for Pliny's Laurentine Villa. This book's combination of advanced archaeology with prevalent French romanticism makes it a revealing portrait of its writer and the age in which he wrote.

In almost schizophrenic fashion, Haudebourt split his book into two distinct parts. The first forms the matter-of-fact archaeological backbone, while the second part clothes this skeletal framework with colorful literary raiment. The first section, consisting of a brief preface and *avant propos,* deals with the state of the archaeological literature on the Laurentine Villa. It is followed by a mostly factual account of Haudebourt's two-day pilgrimage to the site one October day early in the century. But about midway through the mood rapidly changes to one of total reverie, as we will see in greater detail shortly. To return to the beginning, the text either ignores or casts in doubt all preceding restitutions, most recently that of Marquez,

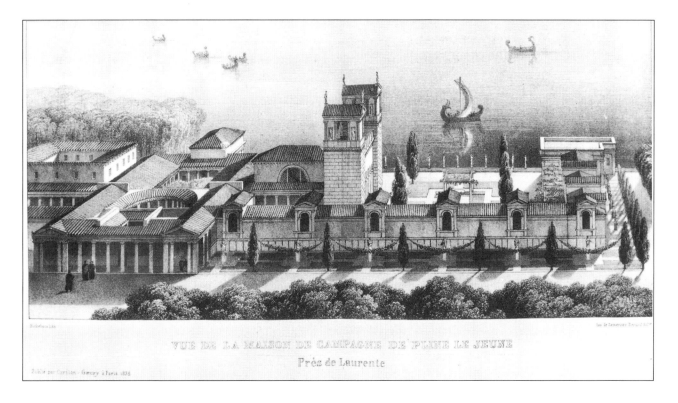

VUE DE LA MAISON DE CAMPAGNE DE PLINE LE JEUNE

Prés de Laurente

32. Haudebourt, Laurentine Villa, perspective (Haudebourt, *Laurentin*)

by citing the opinion of the archaeologist Désiré Raoul-Rochette that no one had convincingly pinned down the Pliny description. The reason given was that the recent excavation of Pompeii by Raoul-Rochette and by François Mazois had revolutionized knowledge of Roman domestic buildings. Haudebourt himself conducted Pompeian studies similar to and only slightly later than Mazois's of the years 1809–11, and the two must have met subsequently in Rome.[43]

Haudebourt's visit to Laurentinum differed markedly from the earlier expeditions by collectors of botanical specimens or scavengers of antique artifacts. His bent was more purely archaeological than theirs. Finally to stand amid what he believed were the ruins of the Laurentine Villa brought both intellectual satisfaction and emotional resignation: the passage of time and the various digs had turned the site into a hopeless mess. Since the time of Marcello Sacchetti the new owner of the property, Prince Agostino Chigi, had carried out further excavations in 1802. These continued sporadically until 1819, so evidence of fresh digging must have greeted Haudebourt.[44] He sadly concluded that serious scientific excavation and restitution would be, to use his own word, *infructueuse*. Far from discouraging him, this simply opened the floodgates of imagination in the second part of his book. The result is a curious mixture of fact and fiction.

According to the story as told by Haudebourt, the hiker returns to Rome and collapses in exhaustion. In a dream sequence a servant of Pliny's presents him with an invitation to visit the Laurentine Villa, which he accepts. Once there, he is taken on a tour of the house of Pliny in person, accompanied by the architect Mustius. The imagery comes straight from Dante's visit to the underworld with Virgil as his guide. At this point the descriptive language becomes more rich and colorful, in the manner of François-René de Chateaubriand, the romantic novelist whose writings are admiringly cited.[45] Suddenly Haudebourt awakens, and the anecdote continues in the same vein as when the composer Giuseppe Tartini is roused from a nightmare and can faintly remember the theme of the *Devil's Sonata*. First Pliny, then Dante, then Chateaubriand and Tartini; the literary allusions pile up. But Haudebourt is still not done. He discovers that, like the Greek philosopher Odesius, he has transcribed the whole episode in his sleep—the only instance of automatic writing in the entire villas of Pliny literature.[46]

Haudebourt's bird's-eye perspective of the Laurentine Villa looks as though borne on *l'aile des songes,* which the author says dreamily transported him back to the time of Pliny. The place is not particularly large if the human figures in front of it convey an accurate sense of scale. In fact Haudebourt, unlike Canina, made a specific point of stressing smallness as a means of emphasizing Pliny's modest demeanor and avoidance of the conspicuous luxury indulged in by many of his contemporaries. Starting on the left of the entrance portico and ending up on the right, Mustius and Pliny walked with Haudebourt from room to room, tracing out an elaborate paraphrase of the letter to Gallus. The formula allowed Haudebourt the opportunity for dialogue and the chance to display his knowledge of archaeology and the classics. But he flipped from the first to the third person too often to be fully convincing. To draw his guides artificially into discussion, Haudebourt made himself into a provincial ignoramus from Gaul, unfamiliar with Roman living habits.[47] The technique derives from Mazois once again, this time on the literary rather than the archaeological side. Mazois embellished an 1819 archaeology book with an imaginary palace on the Coelian Hill belonging to a fictional Roman millionaire named Marcus Scaurus. Mazois described it by casting himself in the guise of Merovir, a Germanic visitor, who supposedly wrote a series of letters home. His admiration for the classical epistolary tradition of Pliny turned into a *roman épistolaire* of the romantic period.[48]

By the stratagem of a guided tour, Haudebourt entered into the minutiae of Roman domestic arrangements until they almost overshadow his grasp of the villa as a whole. This perhaps accounts for the cramped quality of the plan published in *Le Laurentin* (fig. 33). Nevertheless, certain revolutionary features emerge. One is the complete asymmetry previously hinted at by Marquez; another is the courtyard in the shape of a *D*, an idea Canina adopted two years later, perhaps inspired by Haudebourt. Both authors resort to a philological argument, but the Frenchman

33. (*Opposite*) Haudebourt, Laurentine Villa, plan (Haudebourt, *Laurentin*)

34. (*Opposite*) Haudebourt, Laurentine Villa, interior of atrium (Haudebourt, *Laurentin*)

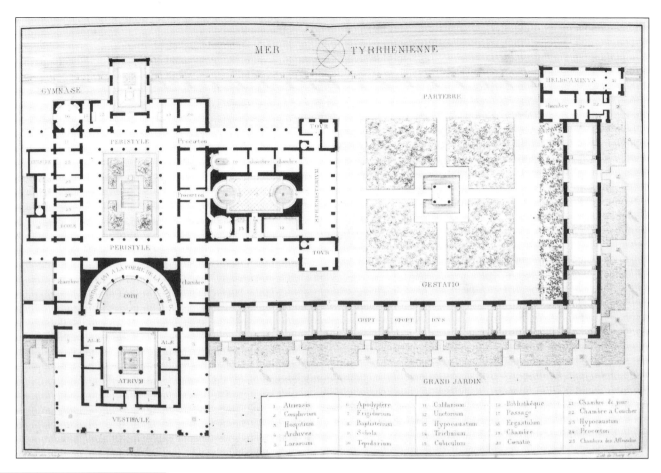

goes further by evoking the authority of his countryman Louis de Sacy (1654–1727). De Sacy's by then respected French translation of Pliny's letters, first printed in 1699 and reprinted many times, made the point that the *O* configuration would not have needed clarification by reference to the alphabet.[49]

Haudebourt's genial host, Pliny, stands at the door ready to lead his guest through the *D*-shaped courtyard to the peristyle garden and the main triclinium beyond. Presumably it is Pliny, then, who is shown striding about in the illustration of the atrium interior (fig. 34). Not unlike the plan, the room, with its plethora of Pompeian-style wall decorations, conveys a cluttered impression. To return to the walking tour, Pliny pauses in the circular library to refer to his codices, whose storage he carefully explains (fig. 33, top left). He then lets Mustius take over the visit to the left-hand range of apartments, including the slaves' quarters, kitchens, and latrines—none of them mentioned in the letter to Gallus. A rather lengthy discourse on the evils of Roman slavery gives Haudebourt the chance to reveal a social consciousness worthy of Victor Schoelcher, the contemporary French abolitionist. Once more Haudebourt lets his mask slip by confusing past with present mores.

Haudebourt's text is most unusual of all in the attention it pays to the apartment of Pliny's third wife, Calpurnia, which provides the occasion for an interesting and novel discussion of the role of women in ancient Roman society. Although she does not figure at all in the letter to Gallus, Calpurnia does make brief appearances in other epistles as a charming woman of great accomplishment in musical composition (bk. 4, ep. 19; bk. 6, ep. 4; bk. 7, ep. 5). Based on the first of these references and on a study of Pompeian wall paintings, Haudebourt delves expansively into Calpurnia's virtues in his discussion of the women's quarters. After he first meets her there in his guise as the fictional Gaul, he encounters her again at an imaginary banquet held atop one of the twin towers. She holds her own at dinner-table conversation in company with her husband and his author friends Suetonius and Tacitus. She then proceeds to entertain the assembled company with her musical setting of some verses by Pliny: "Then Calpurnia, instructed by Love alone, the most skillful of all teachers, modestly rose, took a lyre, and sang the verses of Pliny."[50] To Haudebourt she represents the epitome of modesty, natural graces, simplicity, and beauty.

A romantic love story may account for some of Haudebourt's effusive prose on the subject of Calpurnia. In 1807 Hortense-Victoire Lescot, a twenty-two-year-old prodigy of painting, reached Rome with her teacher Guillaume Lethière, who had come to take over the directorship of the French academy in the city. She remained for at least the next seven years, during which she met Haudebourt. The two married back in France at the end of the decade. Surely in retrospect, if not at the actual time he saw Laurentinum, Haudebourt took Mlle Lescot as his model for Calpurnia. Later, as Mme Haudebourt-Lescot, her fame as *femme peintre* far exceeded that of her husband, who built very little. To her may belong some of the painterly quality of Haudebourt's restitution, and her speciality in genre pictures is reflected in the delightful Pompeian-style vignettes that precede the opening of each chapter of *Le Laurentin*. If this is so, then, it is not the last such husband and wife team to turn their attention to Pliny (cf. pl. 33).[51]

After Calpurnia's musical performance, Pliny leads the diners down from the tower to take a walk in the cryptoporticus. (This long gallery intercepted by little gabled pavilions not coincidentally adapts the design of the Chapelle Expiatoire in Paris by Percier.) Rounding a bend, the party reaches Pliny's favorite *amores mei* apartment, where its architect, Mustius, stands waiting to join the group. The design of this key feature is hardly inspiring but, by culminating the tour at *les délices*, Haudebourt makes the point that a trained architect had been the designer and emphatically not Pliny, as other interpreters thought. *Le Laurentin* ends up glorifying the architectural profession as much as it does Pliny's villa. Mustius steps

out of the shadows onto center stage. Before leaving for a tour of the gardens
Pliny proudly takes Haudebourt aside and, as if revealing to him a state secret,
shows off his inner sanctum hidden within. The end comes with a doubly witty
literary parody complimentary to Mustius's powers of design. The dry theorems of
Vitruvius are couched in Ciceronian turns of phrase, much to everyone's amusement and to the credit of Mustius. Laughter resounds; a cock crows; Haudebourt
awakens; and the book stops abruptly with no real conclusion. True, it has provided
a great jeu d'esprit, but what has it really said of substance about architecture past
or present? The book is as intangible as a dream, which is not inappropriate
considering the will-o'-the-wisp quality of Pliny's Laurentine Villa itself.

Fourteen years after Haudebourt's book, another one came out with a very
similar title, *Le Laurentin maison de campagne de Pline le consul.* On more than
one score it closely resembles the restitution by Haudebourt, as does the life of
its author, Jules-Frédéric Bouchet (1799–1860). Bouchet had also studied at the
Ecole des Beaux-Arts in Paris, or the Ecole Royale des Beaux-Arts as it was then
known. He won a second prize in the grand prix competition of 1822 for an opera
house.[52] He tried for the first prize again in 1824 without success, and his subsequent achievements as a practicing architect are as negligible as those of Haudebourt. Bouchet nevertheless proceeded to Rome, where his stay coincided with
that of Désiré Raoul-Rochette, whose publication on Pompeii has already been
mentioned. The two compatriots collaborated on this work and on another of 1837
for which Bouchet is perhaps best known, *La Villa Pia des jardins du Vatican
architecture de Pirro Ligorio.* For each book Raoul-Rochette provided the text and
Bouchet the enticing perspective illustrations staffed with figures in appropriate
period costumes. To turn over the pages is to step three-dimensionally into another
world.

Bouchet exhibited his Laurentine Villa restitution for the first time in the
1850 Paris Salon, and three years later he exhibited a Tuscan Villa plan, which
unfortunately seems to have vanished.[53] In between those dates he published *Le
Laurentin* when poor Haudebourt was hardly cold in his grave. Bouchet's entire
book, from its title until the last of its superb plates, must be considered largely
an act of artistic piracy. This applies especially to the brief and disjointed text,
several long passages of which Bouchet took straight from Haudebourt.[54] Bouchet
was no aspiring poet, nor had he much original intellect when left on his own. It
is not even clear that he visited the Laurentine Villa site. What then possessed
him to produce a rival publication to Haudebourt's? Quite possibly Bouchet's work
on the casino of Pope Pius IV in the Vatican gardens put him in mind of the *casin
des délices* Haudebourt had referred to in Pliny's grounds and indeed had likened
to the Casino Pio. (Ligorio himself may have been inspired by Pliny when he
attached twin pavilions to an oval area, which may recall a hippodrome or *gestatio*

as described to Gallus and Apollinaris.)[55] The final evidence of Bouchet's capitulation to Haudebourt occurs in the ground plan of the villa (cf. figs. 35 and 33). It basically enlarges—and in that sense improves on—the earlier restitution, with some slight modifications to the seaward-facing facade and to the straighter configuration of the cryptoporticus and *amores mei* pavilion. Why bother with Bouchet, then? Despite his derivativeness, he furthered the Laurentine restitution process on three counts—one illustrative, another critical, and a third methodological—each of which I will examine in turn.

Any weakness of perspective or scale in Haudebourt's illustrations disappears from the adaptations produced by the consummate artistry of Bouchet. The view into the Laurentine atrium (fig. 36), for instance, could bear comparison with the background of a painting by Couture or Alma-Tadema showing the decadence of the Roman Empire or the frenzied last days of Pompeii. Bouchet was an architectural artist, a perspectivist who exhibited at the Paris Salon alongside painters such as those just mentioned. In effect his restitution drawings were fanciful, painterly

35. Bouchet, Laurentine Villa, plan (Bouchet, *Laurentin*)

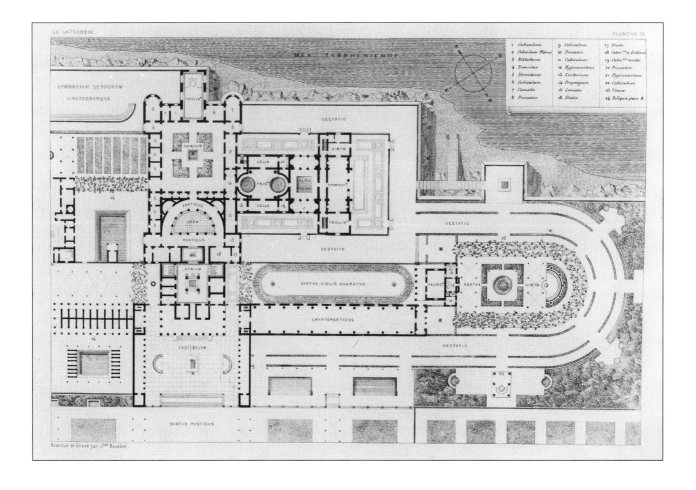

36. Bouchet, Laurentine Villa, interior of atrium (Bouchet, *Laurentin*)

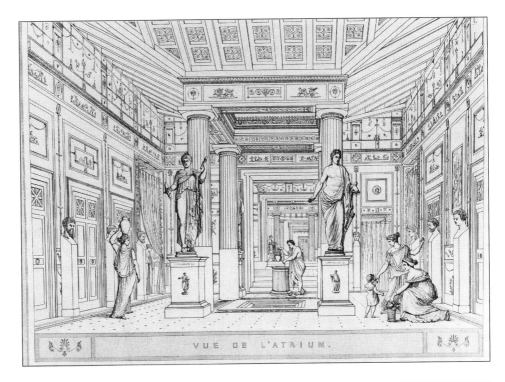

VUE DE L'ATRIUM.

37. Bouchet, Laurentine Villa, perspective (Bouchet, *Laurentin*)

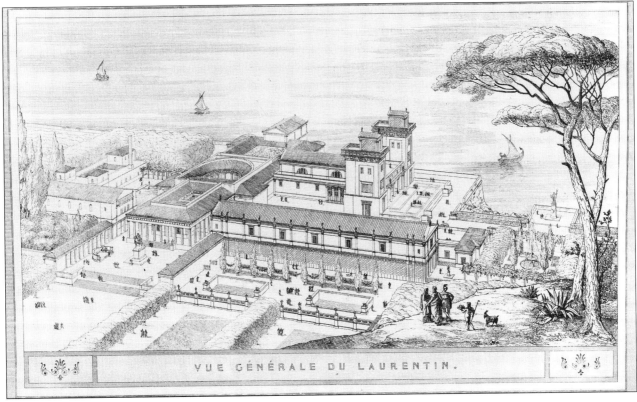

VUE GÉNÉRALE DU LAURENTIN.

visions of ancient Rome with a veneer of archaeological accuracy. Salon viewers must have been astonished by the virtuosity of his aerial perspective of the villa (fig. 37) just as modern architects are today. His conception certainly left an impression on Luxembourg-born painter Rita Wolff, who chose to emulate Bouchet's setting in 1982 when she depicted her husband Léon Krier's Laurentine Villa glimpsed from under the shade of two umbrella pines (pl. 33). She shows Krier's restitution as if seen from a hairpin bend on a Mediterranean coastal highway, while offshore islands hover in a metaphysical wild blue yonder, intensifying the villa's ethereal nature.

Bouchet's short text accompanying his illustrations and Pliny's letter makes one critical point a good deal more forcefully than had hitherto been done. The author distinguished clearly between the scientific archaeological excavations of his own age and the erudite speculations of Latinists of the previous century (see chap. 4). In his inelegant if earthy way Bouchet wrote: "Vingt metres cubes de poussière enlevés . . . ont plus apprit tout à coup sur l'architecture domestique des anciens . . . , que toutes les ingénieuses théories des antiquaires spéculatifs."[56] He pressed the point by stating that no amateurs without true training in the art of architecture or a grounding in archaeological excavation could make any serious contribution to the study of ancient architecture. These categorical statements echo Haudebourt's earlier implications about the professionalism of Mustius, but they do so more pointedly. A hardening of positions has occurred in less than a generation. Lurking behind Bouchet's statements, however, is something slightly more ominous. His vaunting of the artist's sole right to interpret antiquity and his somewhat strident denunciation of past restitutions hid a lack of self-confidence. To compensate for his own sense of inferiority, he criticized the contributions of others.

To be fair to Bouchet, however, he carried his comparisons to new methodological heights. Except for the recently deceased Haudebourt, to whom Bouchet remained deferential for obvious reasons, he tried to evolve a more rational basis for the interpretation and critique of restitutions. Typically, he succeeded better with images than with words. He devoted the first two plates in *Le Laurentin* to an assembly of five previous Laurentine plans, all reduced to the same scale and rendered in an identical manner. Their relative virtues as restitutions have been or will be considered here and in subsequent chapters. But the point is that Bouchet for the first time applied to Pliny's villas the academically approved method of the *parallèle,* so called because the French systematized it into a rigorous method of comparative presentation.[57] As a product of the French academic educational system, Bouchet quite naturally applied the *parallèle* technique to the ongoing debate over the Laurentine Villa restitution. The ground plans marching across Bouchet's printed pages graphically reveal the steady chronological development toward greater asymmetry and the change in configuration of the central courtyard from *O* to *D*. From the precedent set by Bouchet stems the comparative method of such modern Pliny commentators as Helen Tanzer and especially Pierre Pinon (fig. 38), the most recent critic to employ the system while studying this topic.

38. Composite *parallèle* of early Laurentine Villa plans (line drawing after Pinon and Culot, *Laurentine*)

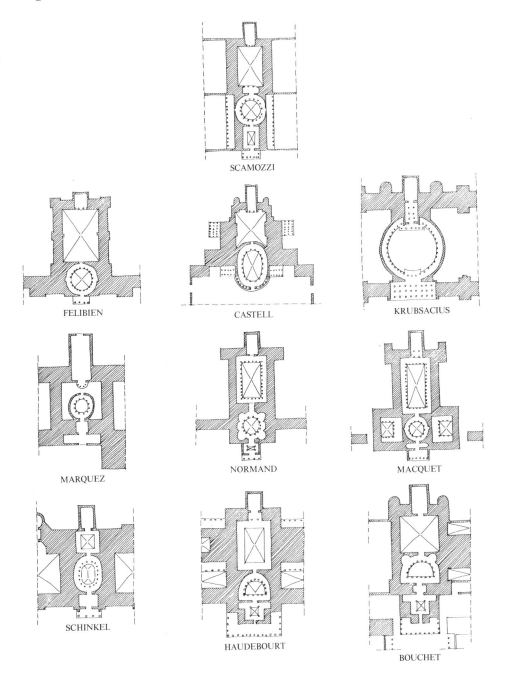

Johann Joachim Winckelmann (1717–68) was the father of the German school of art history, and some would argue the father of the discipline as a whole. Among his voluminous works, written in an impressive array of languages, Winckelmann made passing reference to the villas of Pliny. But like most of what he wrote, his words had far-reaching influence on subsequent generations, notably on the architect-archaeologist Aloys Ludwig Hirt (1759–1837), who tried to pick up the thread of Winckelmann's investigations. The published correspondence of Winckelmann, known to Hirt, proves that the older historian contemplated a serious study of the Laurentine Villa that various factors, ending with his violent death, prevented him from undertaking. In the last year of his life he wrote about this to his friend the Frenchman Charles-Louis Clérisseau (1721–1820). Normally Clérisseau had the knack of being at the right place at the right time to assist at the birth of neoclassicism, but not in this instance. He had recently left for the south of France after many years' residence in Rome. Winckelmann lamented that the departure forestalled his own plan to revisit the Laurentine site, about which he said to Clérisseau, "Vous auriez pu m'aider beaucoup."[58] H. Jansen, a contemporary of Winckelmann's and the first editor of his letters, claimed that the great man had in mind his own restitution of Pliny's villa that would repudiate all previous attempts. Perhaps a glimmer of what it might have resembled appears in a grandiose restitution of a Roman imperial residence sent by Clérisseau to the empress Catherine of Russia in 1774. The scheme relies heavily on the Latin nomenclature Pliny employed to describe room types, yet it blows the whole thing up to flatter the vanity of the empress.[59] Like the Laurentine scheme it may distantly reflect, it too came to naught.

When the various bits of Winckelmann's knowledge about the Laurentine Villa are assembled, they turn out to be extensive. In 1761 he learned from his frequent Swiss correspondent Leonhard Usteri about the Dresden architect Friedrich August Krubsacius's Laurentine Villa restitution just published in Leipzig the previous year—news traveled remarkably fast in neoclassical scholarly circles (see chap. 4). In his reply to Usteri he asked how someone could publish a book on the Laurentine Villa without ever having visited the site.[60] Winckelmann's rather gruff dismissal of the new book he had not even seen typifies the way his own extensive writings downplayed literary sources when recent archaeological evidence from Pompeii or Torre Paterno could be substituted. Thus, when writing slightly later to G. L. Bianconi, Winckelmann noted a recent find at Torre Paterno of terra-cottas that "si crede della villa di Plinio, Laurentum." Similarly, his majesterial *Geschichte der Kunst des Altertums*, first published in 1764, mentions a marble head found near Ostia that was supposed to come from Pliny's nearby villa.[61]

Perhaps the most influential factor for Winckelmann's intellectual development was the patronage of Cardinal Alessandro Albani. In this respect it is worth

remembering that Magenta's Laurentine restitution had been in the private collection of the Albani pope Clement XI, uncle of Winckelmann's Roman patron.
As with the Medici, it may well be that the Albanis had an obsession with Pliny's
villas and that a wish to please an employer, as much as readings of Pliny, could
have aroused Winckelmann's special interest in Laurentinum. The neoantique associations surrounding Cardinal Albani's celebrated villa on the outskirts of Rome
(pl. 34) strengthen a hypothetical link between its owner, Pliny, and ultimately
Winckelmann. Work on it done to the designs of Carlo Marchionni (1702–86) had
advanced rather far by 1755 when Winckelmann arrived on the Roman scene, so
there can be no question of his influence at the inception. As for Marchionni, his
numerous and quite beautiful drawings for the villa provide no hint of any connection with Pliny.[62] Yet his contemporaries distinctly saw the Villa Albani in Plinian
terms, especially the garden building of 1762 called the "coffeehouse," situated on
an axis with the main house seen off to its left here. A semicircular portico and
elaborate parterres separate the main villa from the "coffeehouse." A better example of the symbiotic relationship between villa and garden would be hard to
find.

Magnan's 1779 guide to Rome refers to the main axis of the Villa Albani with
the Latin name *diaeta*, the same word Raphael had used in his letter to Cardinal
Giulio de' Medici. Two foreign contemporaries of Magnan, one French and the
other German, go further and describe Albani's villa as a modern counterpart to
Pliny's Laurentine Villa. Although most eighteenth-century guidebook writers are
notoriously derivative and inaccurate, the German traveler Johann Jacob Volkmann
stands in a class apart. For one thing, Volkmann knew Winckelmann and corresponded with him on matters relating to the Villa Albani. In addition, in reading
his book *Historisch-kritische Nachrichten von Italien . . .* it becomes clear that he
was unusually well informed about Pliny's villas. They come up in discussion on the
pages he devoted to the coast near Ostia.[63] In a lengthy footnote he demonstrated a
complete knowledge of the restitutions of the Laurentine and Tuscan villas published up to that date. His description of the Villa Albani in Plinian terms therefore
carries greater weight than it otherwise might. The impression he conveys is confirmed by a special timeless quality pervading the place. As if by magic, modern
hubbub ceases inside the high perimeter walls.

Although urban sprawl has engulfed the Villa Albani, the view on a fine day
still stretches off to the Alban Hills, the same bluish backdrop that Pliny mentioned
seeing from his Laurentine property. That not far down the same Ostian shore the
Albani had a villa at Anzio, enlarged by Marchionni in these years, means that the
cardinal and his circle did not have far to look for reminiscences of Pliny almost
wherever they went. The positively Plinian ambience Winckelmann enjoyed at
Anzio certainly seems to have made its mark on him. From the Albani Villa he

wrote to a friend in 1767 describing his blissful routine of scholarly writing inter-spersed with long constitutionals on the beach.[64] The letter ecstatically describes the "blissful" place and concludes "Dieses ist der Ort meiner Seligkeit." The rest of the text reads exactly like a day in the life of Pliny as described in a pendant pair of letters to Fuscus Salinator (bk. 9, eps. 36, 40), the first devoted to Laurenti-num, the second to summertime in Tuscany.

Aloys Ludwig Hirt arrived in Rome in 1782 to begin a stay of nearly a decade and a half, during which he supported himself by guiding fellow Germans around the sights, such as the Villa Albani. In this respect and others we may safely assume that he emulated his predecessor, Winckelmann, with whom he shared humble origins and a provincial education, despite which they both reached Rome by sheer self-determination. Winckelmann, of course, won acclaim for his aesthetic philosophy. As for Hirt, he is an all-but-forgotten figure of neoclassicism,[65] having based his theories almost slavishly on Winckelmann's three developmental stages: birth, flowering, and decline. Even Hirt's two best-known books, *Die Baukunst nach den Grundsätzen der Alten* (Berlin, 1809) and *Die Geschichte der Baukunst bei den Alten* (Berlin, 1821–27), have suspiciously Winckelmann-like titles. In all probability, then, Hirt saw himself as providing the architectural counterpart to Winckelmann's writings, principally devoted to the arts of painting and sculpture. This holds especially true of Winckelmann's scattered published references to Pliny's Laurentine Villa in his letters and his *Geschichte,* as already mentioned, but also in his main architectural work, the 1762 *Anmerkungen über die Baukunst der Alten.*[66]

Hirt's *Die Geschichte der Baukunst bei den Alten* organizes ancient architec-ture according to building types and includes a discussion of Pliny's villas in the section on dwellings. This served simply as the excuse for a highly speculative digression about Pliny as a public figure, from which he emerges as an exemplar for the Age of Reason. Pliny, like Cicero, embodies the man of taste who chooses deliberately to build for delight rather than ostentation. He could choose from any of the favored watering places of ancient villeggiatura, but he selects the relatively obscure spots dear to him. Pliny's preference for retirement sounds like Frederick the Great's at Sans Souci. This analogy has its source in historical fact. Hirt had conceived a monument to the Prussian monarch's memory in 1797 in the form of a peripteral temple.[67] His unsuccessful entry into the domain of monumental architecture seems to have convinced Hirt to apply his impressive knowledge to writing and teaching about ancient art—he designed little and built less. He held lectureships at Berlin's Akademie der Wissenschaften und Künste (1796) and in the Bauakademie once it was established in 1799. His students there included Karl Friedrich Schinkel.

Although Hirt knew about earlier restitutions of Pliny's villas, he refused to

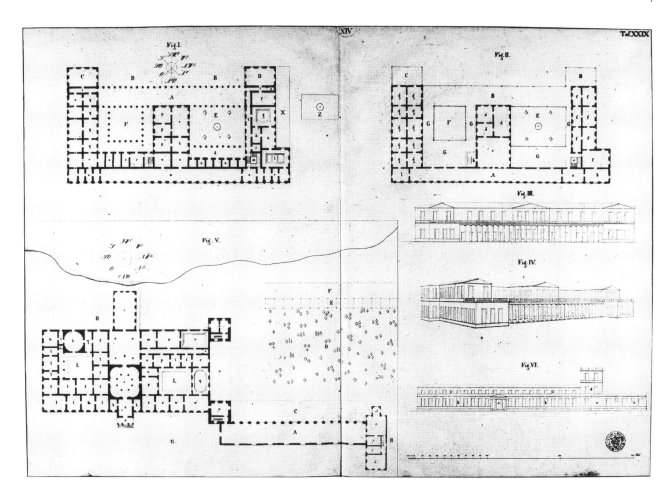

39. Hirt, Laurentine and Tuscan villas, plans and elevations (Hirt, *Die Geschichte der Baukunst*)

comment on them, following the lead of Marquez, whom he may have known in Rome. Hirt went back to the source by producing his own translation of the Pliny villa letters and interpolating the original Latin in cases where technical terms remained in dispute. One should make up one's own mind as much as possible, according to Hirt, and avoid preconceived notions. Despite this, Hirt's Laurentine plan closely resembles Félibien's earlier scheme (fig. 39, lower left; cf. fig. 54). In keeping with Marquez's ideas, however, Hirt strengthened the asymmetrical aspect of the layout with towers awkwardly appended at one end (fig. 39, lower right). If his colorless renditions are anything to judge by, his gifts as a designer were far from outstanding. In the linear manner fostered by J. N. L. Durand (cf. fig. 88)— whose Ecole Polytechnique curriculum Hirt also favored—the Laurentine plan and elevation lack any dynamism either of massing or of presentation. They are as dry as the Laurentine soil, with its groves of fig and mulberry trees shown by Hirt on the engraving. Yet Hirt was not as lacking in imagination as his plate might suggest. He waxed eloquent about the villas' ambience and described from personal experience the oppressive heat of the Roman Campagna during the dog days. He reasoned that the Laurentine Villa was principally for use in the autumn and winter months when the Tuscan Villa could not easily be reached.[68]

In a similar way, Hirt rhapsodized in prose about the freshness of the air and *schöne Aussichten* to be enjoyed at Pliny's Tuscan Villa. Somehow he could not instill any of this enthusiasm into the rather rigid *E*-shaped plan he settled on. With Hirt the power of words had trouble conveying itself to the drafting board. Perhaps he erred in so stressing Pliny's sobriety and reserve that it left his design little room to maneuver. Hirt's single stroke of invention came when he provided for Tuscany a balustraded terracelike viewing platform along the entire facade. In keeping with Durand's doctrine of plainness, and in harmony with the geographical setting, the Tuscan order was used throughout supporting saltire grillwork that united the three prongs of the *E*. Unfortunately, Hirt's style of representation again excludes the element of the gardens, although his text quickly points out that they influenced subsequent developments at least as much as the architecture. He thought the displays of topiary work at the Tuscan Villa a bit excessive and felt other plants should be substituted. But Pliny's hippodrome garden won his unconditional admiration for its form and its connotations of healthful gymnastics.[69] Hirt's emphasis on the hippodrome must surely explain its subsequent revival among the Prussian court gardeners less than a decade after his book appeared (see conclusion). No less influential, his careful translation of Pliny, and presumably his spirited expositions in the classroom, drew the Laurentine and Tuscan villas to the attention of a brilliant rising generation of students, most notably Schinkel.[70]

As I already mentioned, Hirt taught the young Schinkel not only inside the classroom but outside it by example. Both he and Schinkel's other mentor, the young and brilliant Friedrich Gilly, briefly held the same professorship at the Berlin Bauakademie until the latter's death in 1800 at twenty-eight years of age. And both contributed competing designs for the Frederick the Great mausoleum. Gilly's remained so firmly implanted in Schinkel's imagination that it reemerged almost unaltered many years later as the distinctive central motif in the Orianda Villa project (pl. 5). The lasting impression made on Schinkel by Gilly's visionary, cloud-capped mausoleum was matched by the weight of Hirt's classical learning and wealth of Italian experiences. The same two strands of Schinkel's artistic makeup—the romantic and the rational—help to explain his Tuscan and Laurentine villa restitutions published in September 1841, accompanied by Hirt's previously published translations of the letters to Gallus and Apollinaris. An editorial note disclaims any other connection with Hirt's previous work, and in the strict artistic sense there is none.[71]

Compared with Hirt, Schinkel produced far more painterly and appealing

Laurentine and Tuscan restitutions. Hirt had led the way, however, and Schinkel deferred to his firsthand acquaintance with Roman remains and classical languages. Eventually Schinkel would close the gap between his teacher and himself when he took his own Grand Tour to Italy in 1803–4. Curiously enough, Schinkel's fragmentary record of this trip largely avoids mention of the antique in favor of the medieval. He especially admired the way the Italian Middle Ages had used discarded classical elements in new architectural combinations. He thereby revealed his love not so much of classicism itself as of the piecemeal way the tradition had carried on over the course of history. For example, there is no indication whatever that while in Italy he went in search of the Pliny villa sites he might have heard Hirt discourse on. What impressed Schinkel the most, so he told David Gilly in a letter near the end of the trip, was the total range of historical architecture rather than antique remains so well hashed over by his predecessors. Schinkel said he wanted to return buildings to the original context from which the likes of Hirt had isolated them.[72] In that way their approaches differed radically. Hirt's belief in some abstract archaeological truth led to a denuded look. In contrast, Schinkel's less dispassionate admiration of Italy shines through strongly in the picturesque settings of the Pliny villa restitutions he began preparing shortly after the appearance of those in Hirt's book. But in another sense, contact with the monuments on Italian soil proved no less fundamental in each case. Winckelmann, Marquez, Hirt, and now Schinkel all express a special conviction denied to architects who never set foot on that hallowed ground.

Given Schinkel's predilection for the painterly interpretation of a villa in the landscape, it is not surprising that he found his way to the Pliny restitutions of Marquez. A drawing in the Schinkel Archive proves the architect somehow came upon a copy of the Mexican's hard-to-find little book and sketched the vignette of the Tuscan Villa in its mountainous setting, along with its plan and that of its Laurentine counterpart (fig. 40). The vignette's modest contribution to Pliny villa imagery (fig. 29) paved the way for Schinkel's more bold, less sober approach. From the Renaissance on, architects and archaeologists, great like Schinkel or obscure like Marquez, have turned to Pliny's letters as a source of refreshment. Schinkel shared his thirst for them with his client Crown Prince Friedrich Wilhelm of Prussia. Their common admiration prompted a scheme for an antique-style villa to ornament the pleasure grounds of the royal palace at Potsdam. Some of the drawings for the unexecuted twin-domed project, including an alluring perspective showing it encircled with terraces and pergolas, date from 1833 (fig. 41). The same date appears on one of the related drawings in the Pliny suite.[73] A year earlier, as we will see (chap. 5), a Schinkel pupil named Wilhelm Stier had produced his own set of Laurentine and Tuscan restitutions for use in the classroom. The vintage year for Pliny in Berlin was 1832–33.

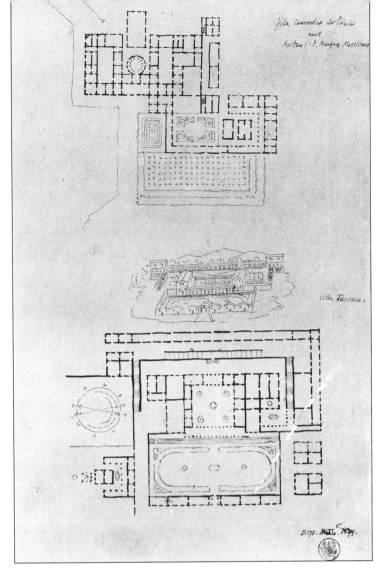

40. Schinkel, Laurentine and Tuscan villas, plans and a perspective after Marquez (SA, S.175 M.XL.ᶜ, no. 74)

41. Schinkel, antique villa design, perspective (SA, S.144 XXXIV, no. 36)

42. Schinkel, Tuscan Villa, perspective (SA, S.175 M.XL.ᶜ, no. 70)

Regardless of the influence Marquez, Hirt, and Stier may have had on Schinkel, his breathtaking pencil version of the Tuscan Villa (fig. 42) owes its originality to the way it returns to and so beautifully sums up Pliny's words to Apollinaris: "Imagine to yourself an amphitheater of immense circumference. . . . A wide-extended plain is surrounded by mountains. . . . My house, although built at the foot of a hill, has a view as if it stood upon the brow. The ascent is so gradual and easy that you find yourself on the top almost before you perceive yourself ascending. Behind it, but at a distance, is the Apennine mountain range." How deftly Schinkel's pencil has captured the essence of this villa: remote yet accessible; ostentatious yet primarily designed to profit from the view; set among little farmhouses and vineyards, yet with plenty of room to breathe; a structure, to be sure, yet embraced by nature. As an unabashed exponent of romantic classicism, Schinkel emphasized the craggy background and the shaggy foreground more than Marquez. In a similar fashion, Schinkel's manicured garden is encroached on by untamed nature and by the serried rows of vines from which Pliny made his wine. Under the influence of such a heady vision, it is hard not to forget all precedents and regard the designer as without peer.

As distinctly seen in the pencil drawing—later turned into a blurrier colored version and the 1841 lithograph—a stream cascades down the mountainside to the left, much as indeed occurs at Colle Plinio. The water enters a large basin directly in front of the thermal baths attached to the villa.[74] From this point a lower Ionic colonnade stretches off to the east and is surmounted by a smaller loggia (probably

Corinthian), also facing out over the topiary and trelliswork below. In other respects the original and later versions differ hardly at all; not so the plan, the preliminary version of which provides both the ground floor and the upper floor layout on a single sheet (cf. figs. 43 and 7).[75] The somewhat boxy lines recall superficially the Marquez scheme placed upside down, but within these rectilinear outlines Schinkel inserted a great many curvilinear rooms, especially in the wings to either side of the main body of the house. Then, off at the far end of the site, the gardens ripple outward in a series of concentric ellipses forming the hippodrome beloved by Pliny, admired by Hirt, and emulated by Schinkel at Charlottenhof in 1836. Schinkel chose not to interpret it as an actual racecourse for horseback riding, though Pliny claimed that of an afternoon he took rides in a chariot (bk. 9, ep. 36). Instead, under Schinkel's guidance the hippodrome becomes a depression in the landscape banked up the sides with trees and flowers of the type Pliny specified. Down the central greensward Schinkel disposed a summerhouse and the *stibadium*, which seem largely to have escaped the notice of his predecessors but become such a highlight of his restitution (see conclusion).

In the final suite of lithographs, the second-story plan of Schinkel's Tuscan Villa restitution reappears at the bottom of a separate plate. Above it a cross section cuts through the short axis of the house (fig. 44). The sloping site, far more precipitous than Lazzari's, provides views in all directions. The barrel-vaulted upper chamber on the second story overlooks the vineyards at the back, the pergolas below at the front, and the foliage in the open courtyard to one side. A window cunningly frames the top of each of the four plane trees in Schinkel's breezy conception. No one before him and few since had taken the trouble really to think through the amenities of such a place both inside and out. The same delights, however, do strike a similar chord many years later with a compatriot, Manfred Sundermann. He began to reflect on the Tuscan Villa in 1983 during a fellowship he held at the Villa Massimo, the German Academy in Rome. In the library there copies of the works of Schinkel and Hirt inspired him.[76] During the autumn he worked on a series of atmospheric pen-and-ink or black charcoal sketches. Through the medium of these sketches he imagined the pleasures of almost every nook and cranny of the villa's various spaces. Early in the new year he prepared measured drawings, including various cross sections not unlike Schinkel's at first glance, and a daring isometric projection (figs. 45 and 46). But first impressions can be deceptive. Sundermann clearly set out to differentiate himself from Schinkel. Where Schinkel had devised an open form, Sundermann's is closed behind fortified walls. Where Schinkel's layout had been relatively symmetrical and relaxed, Sundermann's is complicated and cramped. The hippodrome, for example, looks almost the same in each case, but Sundermann tightly packs his in without the slightest hint of greenery. He has gained in archaeological truth at the expense of openness and movement.

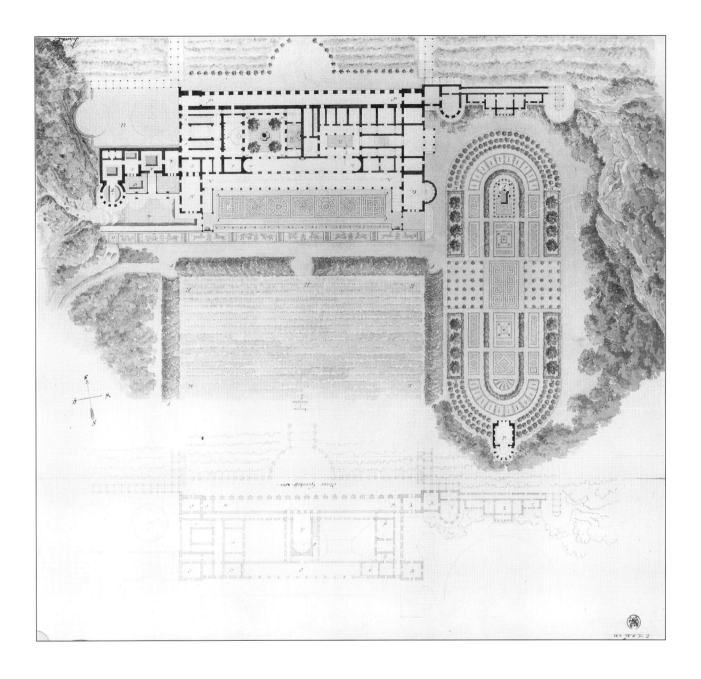

43. Schinkel, Tuscan Villa, plans of principal and upper floors (SA, S.175 M.XL.ᶜ, no. 83). The plan is here turned upside down to avoid confusion.

Compared with the Tuscan plan, Schinkel's preparatory version for the Laurentine Villa is if anything finer drawn and more informative (fig. 47; cf. fig. 6).[77] The sprawling extent reaches almost palatial dimensions; its generous use of the site gives the impression of exceeding most previous restitutions in size. The complicated layout suggests a series of intricate movements a visitor must make to pass from space to space. Everywhere galleries, loggias, terraces, pergolas, and bombé-fronted projections proclaim an openness to the surrounding gardens and distant

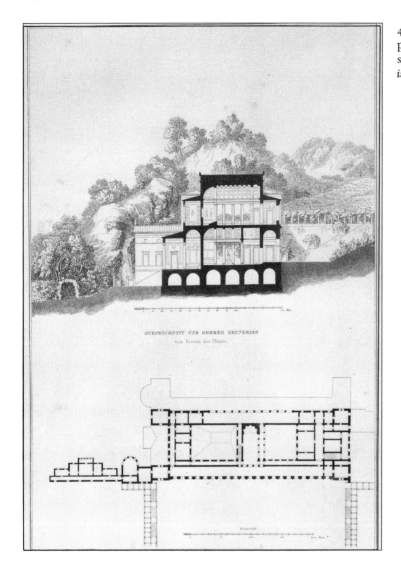

44. Schinkel, Tuscan Villa, plan of upper floor and cross section (Schinkel, *Architektonisches Album*)

vistas. In the flowing pattern of rooms, certain pools or eddies distinguish themselves from the rest; the main courtyard is an example. For it Schinkel persisted in using a form that was circular, or more precisely ovoid, and soon to become outmoded. The central axial arrangement, however, constitutes one of the few recognizably conventional parts of the Schinkel design. From here on it evolves in a more and more original, more and more curvilinear fashion. The library wing to the left, for instance, adapts the shape of an eighteenth-century casino, or *rendez-vous de chasse*.[78] Castell's restitution (fig. 58) provided the only precedent for this library arrangement, but his repetitive symmetricality was replaced by the almost complete asymmetry of Schinkel's plan as a whole. Way off at the other, or right-

45. Sundermann, Tuscan Villa, cross sections and vignettes (collection of the artist)

Der Turm im Südwesten

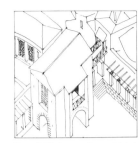

Das Schlafgemach am Teich

Die beiden Pavillons an der Reitbahn

Ideenskizze

Der Weg zur Wandelhalle

Ideenskizze

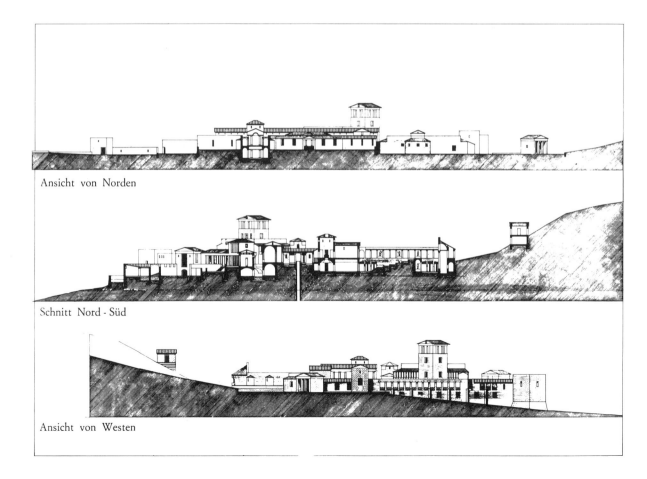

Ansicht von Norden

Schnitt Nord - Süd

Ansicht von Westen

Die Therme

Der Sportplatz

Die grosse Freitreppe

46. Sundermann, Tuscan Villa, aerial perspective and vignettes (collection of the artist)

Nordostecke des Platanenhofes

Ideenskizze

Der Platanenhof

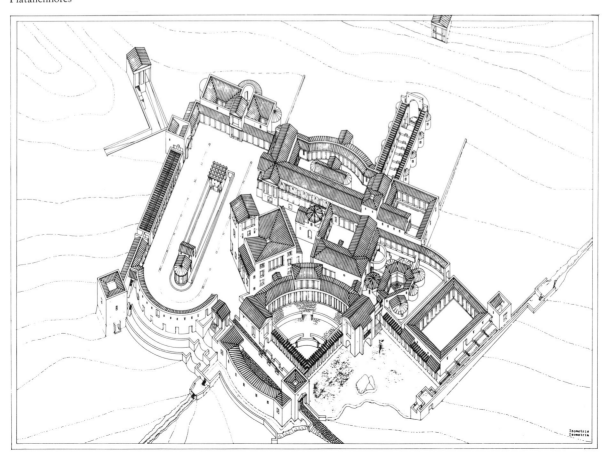

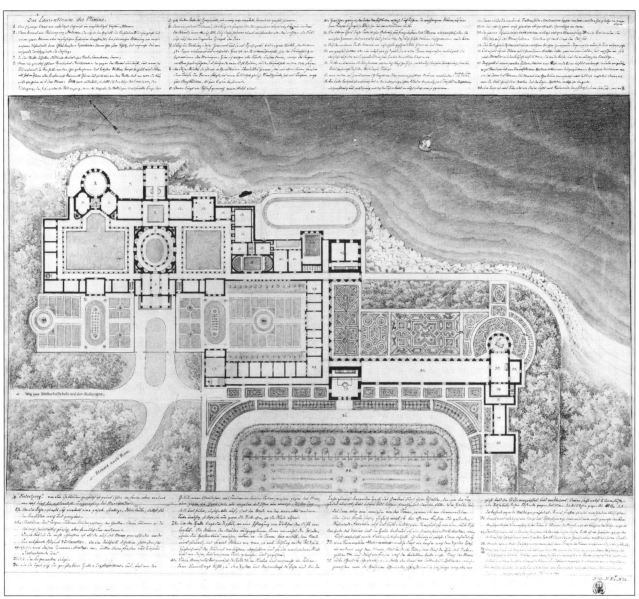

47. Schinkel, Laurentine Villa, plan (SA, S.175 M.XL.ᶜ, no. 72)

hand, extremity of the site Schinkel located the cryptoporticus leading to the *amores mei* cluster of rooms. Schinkel created out of it a locus of architectural interest whose reverberations created a ripple effect on the rest of the villa. Circles from the seawall and curvaceous flower beds eddy around it like a rock in the middle of a millrace. The architecture matches and does justice to Pliny's text because of Schinkel's sensitive reading. His grasp of the literary high points of the letter to Gallus is what makes his exercise at restitution seem so unaffected and so effortless.

Laurentinum des Plinius vom Meere gesehen.

48. Schinkel, Laurentine
Villa, perspective from the
water (SA, S.175 M.XL.ᶜ,
no. 86)

The tempestuous, almost Alpine scenery of the Tuscan Villa set among high peaks changes diametrically in Schinkel's preparatory ink and gray wash drawing elevation of the Laurentine Villa's seaward side (fig. 48; cf. fig. 4).[79] Here Schinkel stressed placidity. The wind hardly ruffles the mirror-smooth sea, which reflects the long, low-lying Laurentine outline. Reality and mirage merge in Schinkel's sensitive drawing on paper much as they probably did when Pliny wrote his original scroll. Schinkel sensed that the letters to Gallus and Apollinaris acted as an artificial pair of pendant villa portraits: one flat, the other hilly; one calm, the other windy; one sprawling, the other relatively compact; one for winter, the other for summer; and so on. No one before Schinkel had thought of stressing the aspect from the sea—not even Pliny. He had emphasized the architectural aspect from the entrance side, and yet unconsciously his best descriptive prose is reserved for the stretch of beach, which he spoke of as the source of his inspiration, his *museion* (bk. 1, ep. 9). The Schinkel view explores the implicit self-consciousness of the Laurentine Villa, its wish to be seen. Through its doors and windows the Mediterranean appears in view; but more important, the waters reflect its proportions, enhancing them when admired from afar. Pleasing variety characterizes the elevation centering on a pair of towers, not dissimilar to those Haudebourt would use but better integrated than his. From this angle Schinkel's masterstroke of design becomes clear in the way he took the two study areas, the library and the *amores mei* pavilion, accentuated them with curves, and pushed them to the two ends of the site. Practically speaking, to function properly the study areas would have to be removed from the noisier, more heavily trafficked parts of the villa. With a perspicacity rare in any Pliny restitution, Schinkel penetrated to the inner logic and underlying organization of the at times rambling letter to Gallus.

The Puerto Rican-born architect David Bigelman (b. 1943), currently teaching at the Paris-Belleville School of Architecture, was obviously inspired by Schinkel when he came to design his own 1982 response to the Laurentine restitution (fig. 49). In the cubic simplicity of Schinkel's classicism, however, Bigelman found the way of expressing his own preference for the simple brickwork masses of the early Christian churches he had studied in Rome while preparing his design.[80] All that Schinkel blurred and made soft becomes more hard edged in the Bigelman rendition, not least because of the stark pen-and-ink medium he employed. Even the reflections in the water have a sharply etched quality. He, like Schinkel, seems to attain an antique-looking architecture without really limiting himself to the classical language of architecture in the strict sense. Both architects' schemes use the orders sparingly, but that does not detract from the basically balanced proportions and calm rhythms of the villas' massing. Bigelman managed in this way to draw together architectural strands as seemingly diverse as imperial Roman, early Christian, and what looks like a basilica from the era of Charlemagne. He shares with Schinkel a nonexclusive and reductionist view of architecture. And like Schinkel too, he favors writing, studying, and book collecting, the same quiet pastimes they share with Pliny (see also chap. 6 and conclusion). A philosophical kinship links the three.

49. Bigelman, Laurentine Villa, perspective from the water (collection of the artist)

FACIES·GEO
METRICA·ILLIVS
VILLAE·QVAE·MA
RIS·RESPICIT
EQ·D·BIGELMAN
ANNO·POST·MCMLXXXI
1982·FECIT

CHAPTER FOUR

From Words to Images

ALTHOUGH VINCENZO SCAMOZZI (1552–1616) brought out *L'idea dell'architettura universale* in December 1615, preparations for the book went back at least to 1602, when one of the woodcut illustrations is dated, and probably a decade earlier. Scamozzi planned *L'idea* as his architectural last will and testament. His timing was good; he died in his adopted city of Venice just six months after publication. *L'idea* succeeded better than he hoped in establishing his fame as a theorist, if not a practicing architect. With rare exceptions (pls. 14 and 15), his buildings have been criticized as derivative of Palladio or as overly cerebral. His writings have fared slightly better, but they reflect too much of the aggressive and egotistical nature of their author to be truly likable. In keeping with its author's boastful character, *L'idea* set out to supersede Palladio's *I quattro libri dell'architettura*. Scamozzi had two volumes printed, not one; he originally intended ten or twelve books rather than Palladio's four. Scamozzi sought more international coverage by drawing on his impressions from travel abroad. Finally, when it came to antiquity, Scamozzi was not content until he had surpassed his rival's restitution of the private house of the Greeks (bk. 2, chap. 11) by proliferating additional types: Vitruvian, Roman, Senatorial, and Plinian. All these tactics of aggrandizement lent credence to the treatise's pretensions to universality.[1]

By the word *idea* in its title, Scamozzi's treatise refers to neo-Platonism. According to this philosophical tradition, there existed an abstract hierarchy of ideal concepts reaching far beyond the simple relativism that Scamozzi would have imputed to Palladio. Scamozzi found the key to the immutable system in the orders of architecture and the mathematically regulated scheme of proportions they connoted. A common denominator like the diameter of a column shaft could determine the entire form of a building according to systematically increasing multiples. Such a logic, though it risked inflexibility, might appear divine to someone like Scamozzi. It is not altogether surprising, therefore, that he preferred villas, which posed fewer contextual problems than other building types. A town house, for instance, would have to take into account the homes of the neighbors so as not to arouse their envy. But a home removed from such proximity might indulge in pure delight for delight's sake. A villa can afford to revel in its desirability. It occupies a sort of rural no-man's-land outside the realm of practical, citified considerations. It lends itself to superlatives, which suited Scamozzi well. It can be scrutinized from many points of view, like a concept in Plato's philosophy.

Scamozzi devoted a whole prefatory section of his second book to discussing the antecedents of the villa building type, both ancient and modern. In that way he could display his considerable knowledge of classical sources, his erudition as a Latinist, and his breadth of experience. In the next book he augmented the examples taken from antiquity with a select group of his own structures. The Scamozzi buildings are more austere than Palladio's, yet paradoxically more down to earth in the way they take into account all manner of utilitarian aspects. They consider access routes, landscape, orientation, prevailing winds, service areas, and private as well as more public interior spaces. Yet at the same time they have a certain sameness that suggests no special relationship to all the particular circumstances of their situation as meticulously laid out by Scamozzi. In other words, they lack the subtlety, the dynamism, almost the elasticity that characterize the villas of Palladio in response to their sites. Much the same criticism of sameness applies to Scamozzi's parade of restitutions based on classical precedents. Notable among them is his Laurentine Villa restitution, the very first to be published by an architect (fig. 50). Say what you will, being first undeniably has its virtues.

The Scamozzi text accompanying this landmark woodcut is singularly awkward in style, enlivened here and there by flashes of the braggadoccio that irked such near contemporaries as Inigo Jones—an artist not noted for his own modesty.[2] The section on the Laurentine Villa begins by reiterating the time-honored reasons for villeggiatura, with special emphasis on the healthful benefits of country air. Then Scamozzi gave a brief résumé of Pliny's letter to Gallus, noting that it was the best surviving account of the suburban villa type still popular in his own day. At the outset he established the basic module as a ten- or twelve-foot intercolumniation. All subsequent dimensions of the villa fell neatly into place as a result. Pliny never went into the measurements of his houses, but it is clear Scamozzi had read him with care, even to the extent of noting so small a detail as the translucent stone used in the Laurentine windows (*Idea,* pt. 2, bk. 7, chap. 4). Scamozzi followed Pliny room by room, brushing aside obscure passages as if they were crystal clear. Without too much justification, he simplified the landscaping by differentiating between an ornamental garden (*horti delitiosi*) and a more rustic one (*horti rusticali*). The views of and from these gardens and the prospects out to sea receive special praise.[3] But neither the views nor the gardens are easily localized, because no legend or numbering system links the text to the extremely schematic woodcut illustration.

Apart from the triclinium that projects outward at the bottom of Scamozzi's plan, its most striking feature by far is the round courtyard. (The compass rose inscribed right in the center forms no part of the architecture, of course, but it typifies Scamozzi's concern with orientation.) Probably Scamozzi consulted one of the Venetian editions of the letter to Gallus, either that by Giovanni Maria Cataneo

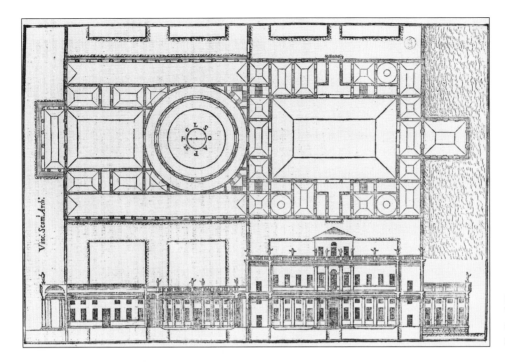

50. Scamozzi, Laurentine
Villa, plan and cross section
(Scamozzi, *Idea dell'archi-
tettura*)

or perhaps the one by Aldus Manutius. Both subscribed to the notion that Pliny
had in mind the letter *O* when referring to the shape of his portico, rather than
the *D* favored by most modern critical editions. Scamozzi's acceptance of this
erroneous transcription by some medieval scribe led to a chain reaction among
Laurentine Villa restitutions for the next two centuries. Yet Scamozzi had no special
preference for the circle, as the rest of his rigidly rectilinear plan demonstrates.
Could it be that he had the Villa Madama in mind as a prototype? The guess does
not fall altogether wide of the mark. During the year and a half he spent in Rome
about 1580, Scamozzi visited the villa on the Monte Mario. In fact *L'idea* refers
to it twice, once in the list of modern monuments to emulate and a second time
in more detail under the heading of forecourts to villas.[4] But it is clear from his
comments that he thought the semicircular, or *D*-shaped, courtyard was what
Raphael intended. Inadvertently Scamozzi strayed in the right direction with respect to the probable appearance of the Laurentine Villa.

Perhaps the tallness of Scamozzi's Laurentine Villa distinguishes it most from
Palladio's low-lying villa restitution based on Vitruvius (bk. 2, chap. 16), or from
Scamozzi's variant, for that matter (pt. 1, bk. 3, chap. 15). The Palladio passage
only mentions Pliny's letters in passing, and Scamozzi too set Pliny's Laurentinum
somewhat apart because it belonged to a class of luxury villas abhorred by ancient
moralists. In Scamozzi's mind as in Vitruvius's, some opprobrium remained
attached to the villas of the rich and decadent. Yet Scamozzi was irresistibly at-

tracted to such houses. He could not help admiring their splendors *con grandissima meraviglia*. Nor could he refrain from retelling the Plutarch story of how Lucullus had his Apollo dining triclinium set up with a menu to match its splendor. At so appetizing a thought Scamozzi's mouth watered, but he soon checked himself by blaming the excessively indulgent style of life in a villa.[5] Nevertheless, his restitution of the Laurentine Villa reflected its owner's station through mounting height. The giant columns of its portico and its round court led back to an even larger rectangular court lined with superposed orders of architecture crowned by a rooftop pavilion, corresponding to the towers where Pliny dined alfresco.

Scamozzi's own buildings betray a similar preoccupation with height. His Villa Rocca Pisani, already mentioned (see chap. 1), occupies a hilltop high above Lonigo. The suburban home he built for the Verlato family dominates the tiny community of Villaverla. And in the wing he added to the piazza of Saint Mark's in Venice, Scamozzi felt entitled to dwarf Sansovino's adjacent library building by adding on an extra story. The Laurentine Villa restitution shares in this tendency to aggrandizement by means of roof architecture. In keeping with most other restitutions, it echoes its designer's style more than the essence of Pliny's letter.[6] The design is neither an ideal polemic diagram nor a usable prototype for the would-be villa builder. It seems to epitomize the dryness of the master's late work as opposed to the self-assurance he manifested at the Rocca Pisani before the death of Palladio. Scamozzi may be one of those architects who, by outliving the competition, lived too long. But he did exploit more fully than anyone before him, even Pirro Ligorio or his followers, the idea of an imaginary reconstruction on paper of a lost building. All future writers publishing on the subject of Pliny's villas owe a debt to Scamozzi, especially the Frenchmen Jean-François Félibien des Avaux and François Mazois, who paid him the homage of reprinting his 1615 Laurentine text in 1699 and in 1819.[7] Surely such international attention would have piqued the vanity of the author of *L'idea dell'architettura universale*.

One of the most lastingly influential French institutions on the world scene was founded by Louis XIV in 1671 as the Académie Royale d'Architecture. Since then it has undergone many internal reorganizations and changes of name, but in one form or another it has survived to this day, proving itself hardier than the monarchy that created it. This French model imposed upon the fine arts adherence to an agreed-upon set of rules, in opposition to the more freewheeling approach of the Italians in the age of Scamozzi. True, they had been the first to resuscitate the old Greek institution of an academy for teaching art, but they lacked the Gallic love of order and organization that fostered a state-controlled arts establishment. Its main purpose was to regulate and standardize the means of artistic production in a way dear to the mercantilist heart of Colbert, Louis's chief adviser in such matters. Apart from the Académie's teaching function, it provided an important forum for discussion among its practitioner members, all elected for life. It acted as a clearinghouse for current ideas, new technologies, advanced artistic theories, and artistic history as well. A key player in this unfolding dialogue, the perpetual secretary, kept the minutes or *procès verbaux* of the meetings and could influence the course of debate. For this sensitive position Louis XIV chose high-ranking civil servants, paid by and loyal to the Crown, who were often recruited from the minor nobility such as the Félibien family, sieurs des Avaux.

André Félibien des Avaux (1619–95) represented the first generation of his family in the service of the Bourbon arts administration. He is best known for his *Entretiens . . .* , a series of lives of the painters along the lines of the one written by Vasari in the previous century. From 1669 onward he served as historiographer of the *bâtiments du roi,* dominated in these same years by another family, the Mansarts. He was also a member of the newly created Académie des Inscriptions et Belles Lettres. These twin positions reveal the talents of historian and litterateur that André brought to his most taxing of jobs, the perpetual secretaryship. In the next generation his son, Jean-François Félibien des Avaux (ca. 1656–1733), inherited these responsibilities. Both Félibiens lived up to their title of *secrétaire perpetuelle* by enjoying quarter-century reigns, as did their successors Abbé Camus, Sedaine, and later Quatremère de Quincy. As a sequel to his father's *Entretiens,* the younger Félibien wrote a counterpart covering the lives of architects. Titled *Receuil historique de la vie et des ouvrages des plus célèbres architectes,* it first appeared in 1687.[8] Its text ranged from antiquity and the Judeo-Christian period— his primary interests—to the architecture of the Middle Ages and later times. In the section on antiquity, Pliny's villa descriptions were compared not unfavorably to the better-known writings of Vitruvius. Moreover, Pliny's letters permitted the younger Félibien to resurrect the otherwise unknown personality of Mustius, mentioned as the architect of a temple dedicated to Ceres, probably situated on Pliny's Tuscan estate (bk. 9, ep. 39).[9]

In the six years following the *Recueil*'s publication, Félibien's curiosity developed to the point that Pliny's villas formed the entire subject of his next book. It is best understood as an expression of Félibien's talents as a Latinist attached to the Académie des Inscriptions and as an antiquarian who became the keeper of Louis XIV's antiquities collection. The younger Félibien, then, was an architectural amateur in the best seventeenth-century sense of the word: he loved the art form without ever having practiced it. He found Pliny's villa descriptions *fort belles,* and that was justification enough for studying them. The first concrete evidence of his Pliny project came in 1692. It took the form of engraved Tuscan and Laurentine villa restitutions illustrating the writings of his mentor, Claude Le Peletier (1630–1711), successor to the great Colbert at the royal finance ministry. Le Peletier and Félibien therefore shared similar backgrounds in the civil service as well as a consuming passion for classical scholarship. (It must have surely occurred to them that their careers in government ran a course parallel to that of Pliny.) In his spare time the classicist-bureaucrat Le Peletier brought out a charming compilation of Latin texts on horticulture that he titled *Comes rusticus.* Some though not all copies of the first 1692 edition contain Félibien's engravings, six in all. They form extra illustrations tipped into the book at the front and the back in no particular order and without being referred to in the printed text.[10] Whoever instigated this strange compilation, two things emerge clearly: the plates themselves represent the first state of those reissued by Félibien with only minor modifications; in the book where they later appear, Félibien's preface gives credit to Le Peletier as his patron and as the inspiration of his scholarly endeavors.

After the appearance of *Comes rusticus,* Félibien must have continued hard at work preparing his commentary on the Latin letters, altering his engraved plates, and then presenting his Laurentine material at two meetings of the Académie Royale d'Architecture for the academicians' approbation. He accompanied his oral presentation, as he did his book, with a highly unfavorable critique of Scamozzi.[11] In effect he put Scamozzi on trial. In all fairness, Félibien provided the full Italian text from *L'idea* alongside a French translation within which key Latin technical terms were italicized for subsequent definition in detail. Scamozzi's woodcut was engraved for inclusion in Félibien's book. But Félibien dismissed the plan and especially the elevation as "peu assujetti," or poorly related, "à la description que Pline a faite" and as reflecting the taste of the Renaissance author rather than the Roman one.[12] Of course Félibien was right, but he cast the first stone at his own peril. Ever afterward in the great Pliny debate it would be common practice to disparage the work of one's immediate predecessors. Félibien started off the vicious cycle and in due course suffered the same punishment he meted out to Scamozzi.

Félibien titled his book *Les plans et les descriptions de deux des plus belles maisons de campagne de Pline le consul . . . .* He brought it out in the last year of the century in Paris, although the printing had been finished the previous autumn, according to a permission to publish dated 1698. Far from bringing to a close Pliny studies in the baroque age, it really announced a new era. Besides reprinting Scamozzi's discussion, the 167 pages include a French translation of *both* the letter to Gallus and the letter to Apollinaris, arranged in parallel columns beside the texts given in the original Latin. More important still, there are lengthy explanations of the reasoning behind Félibien's restitutions as well as additional commentary. These so-called *remarques* take Scamozzi's show of erudition as a challenge to go much further. Although the Italian realized that Pliny owned villas elsewhere than at Laurentinum, he neglected to comment on any of them. Not so Félibien, who, as a direct outgrowth of his earlier interest in Mustius, introduced almost all of Pliny's letters that have a bearing on architecture, whether about villas or about public works projects in Bythnia. Based on this almost encyclopedic compilation of material, Félibien could begin to speculate intelligently about Pliny's means, goals, and taste. Finally, there are the plates themselves to consider. They are engraved with a numerical system that corresponds to numbered legends printed alongside, like the marginalia attached to the Tuscan restitution by Lazzari. It is these engravings, three of the Laurentine Villa and three of the Tuscan, that deserve the most attention (figs. 51–54 and 176–77).

Taken as a group, the Félibien restitutions herald the French academic preoccupation with the rules of planning, which eventually culminated in the teachings of the Ecole des Beaux-Arts in the next century (see figs. 89–94). In quite a

51. Félibien, Tuscan Villa, site plan (Félibien, *Plans*)

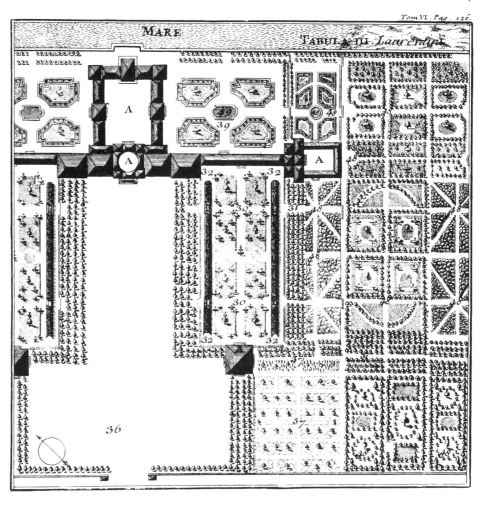

52. Félibien, Laurentine Villa, site plan (Félibien, *Plans*)

plausible way, Félibien explained his exclusive use of plans on the grounds that Pliny had hardly mentioned the external appearance of his houses.[13] But the reasoning went deeper. The distinction of plan from elevation—made right in the title of his book—hints at Félibien's differentiation between appearances and their underlying logical causes. As such his approach embodies the mathematical clarity and geometric precision of a Cartesian proposition dear to the French from the mid-seventeenth century onward. This certainly holds true for the balanced, symmetrical impression conveyed by the architecture and landscape gardening depicted in his plates. Félibien's quincuncial arrangement around his Tuscan Villa (fig. 51), for example, suggests that even the trees and shrubs are drawn up in regimented rows, like soldiers on parade before their monarch. If the Laurentine site plan (fig. 52) looks asymmetrical, it is a false impression. For want of space Félibien had to suppress a long wing on the left that would have mirrored the one

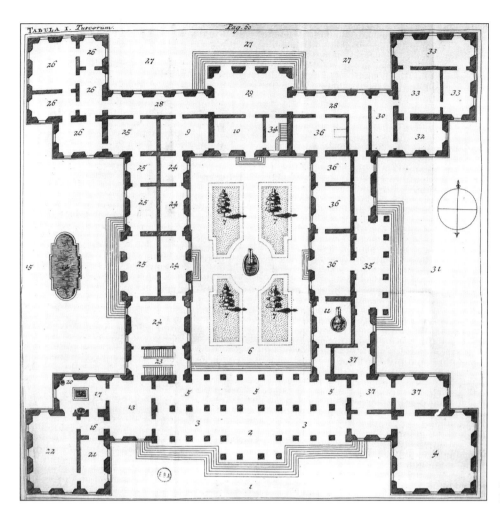

53. Félibien, Tuscan Villa,
plan (Félibien, *Plans*)

on the right. Presumably the missing section would have housed the service areas
and slaves' quarters, which the text remarks on as absent from the letter to Gallus.
All in all, the plans succeed best as intricate two-dimensional patterns. That they
lack three-dimensionality may be attributed to Félibien's intellectual position vis-à-
vis planning and greater fidelity to Pliny's letters. It is also true, however, that it
suited him to ignore the elevations, which would have more readily revealed him
as a nonpracticing architect.

On an axis with the center of the Laurentine wings and situated directly below
them is a pair of pavilions, to one of which Félibien devoted a separate plan (fig.
176), numbered plate 2 or 3 depending on the edition consulted.[14] The layout of
the plantings all around is particularly reminiscent of the manner popularized by
the contemporary royal gardener André Le Nôtre. The engraver's burin makes the
little lollipop trees seem to stand upright against the background, a graphic tech-

nique that may have influenced the much more recent restitution by the Italian Paolo Farina (fig. 133). A similar detailed plate relates to the Tuscan Villa, at the spot on the top left numbered 43, where Pliny's *stibadium* would have stood. It and the correspondingly detailed plan for Laurentinum, just mentioned, will be considered separately later (see conclusion). As for the actual ground floor arrangements of the main houses, the Tuscan one (fig. 53) with projecting corners resembles Serlio's plan for the mid-sixteenth-century château of Ancy-le-Franc, itself derived from the villas at Poggio Reale and Poggio a Caiano, discussed in chapter 2. The rooms are grouped either *en appartement* or *en enfilade,* according to the preferred French taste of Félibien's time. And the Laurentine Villa restitution (fig. 54), with its rectangular courtyard separating the circular one from the triclinium jutting out to sea, bears a striking overall resemblance to the much maligned arrangement by Scamozzi.[15] Félibien found it easier to criticize others than to break with ingrained cultural traditions and invent new solutions. His schemes are as unmistakably French baroque as he could make them.

Félibien concluded his *remarques* and his book by recording some antique inscriptions that related to Pliny. This brings back to mind that Félibien *fils* suc-

54. Félibien, Laurentine Villa, plan (Félibien, *Plans*)

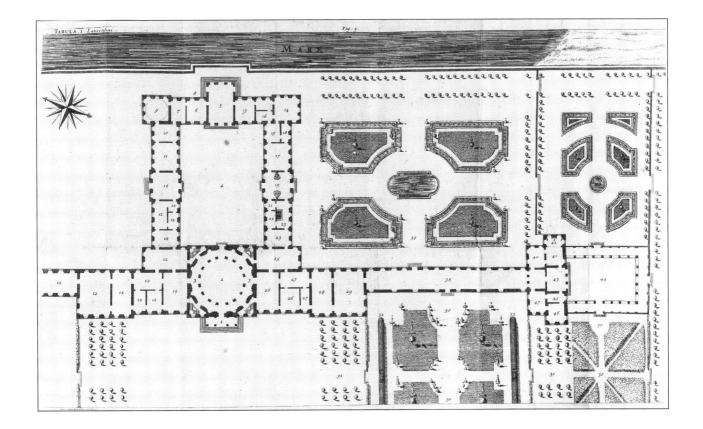

ceeded his father as a member of the Académie des Inscriptions et Belles Lettres. The task set this *petite académie*—as contemporary pundits named it—was to advise the Crown on matters related to inscriptions ancient and modern. By extension the learned society concerned itself with numismatics, with the philology of classical languages, with archaeology, and with the art of translation. In the capacity of translator and philologist, Félibien had cause to pride himself on his erudition. In his preface he warned readers against the outmoded school of translation that would stress the elegant style of Pliny's Latin letters and thus sacrifice their architectural content. The modern Pliny translator would strive for a critical method based on the assumption that the hardest words in any text provide the key to understanding. Félibien thus betrayed his elitism and occasional pedantry, but he mitigated it by an earnest desire to explore the newly emerging science of linguistics.[16]

Where did Félibien stand in the battle then being waged between the "ancients" and the "moderns"? The simple answer is that the younger Félibien stepped into the elder's historiographic and theoretical shoes. The *Entretiens* served its author's son as a model for his own *Recueil* in more ways than one. The *Entretiens* stressed that the "ancients" had "enjoyed the liberty of choosing and adjusting things as they wished . . . [so] why should we today depend so slavishly on their views?"[17] Phrases like that set the tone for Jean-François's preference for the "modern" point of view, despite the Plinian subject matter of his later book. He keenly saw the need for new laws—*les règles* is one of his leitmotivs—but the rules were not the unchangeable, universal ones that Scamozzi had tried to establish. Looking back at Pliny's writings and comparing them with his own, Félibien could not help seeing language as an evolutionary process. Similarly, he stressed that architecture responded to climatic, topographical, and societal changes and never remained the same for all times or all places.[18] Hence he arrived at the reason for the number of Pliny's villas, their responsiveness to different locations—compact at Tuscany, spread out in Laurentinum—and their various rooms laid out according to the seasons. The ideal academician, in Félibien's view, would learn from these patterns of the past without becoming stifled creatively. Later academies gave the French one a reputation for stagnant thinking it did not deserve at the outset.

Clearly Félibien sought some measure of artistic freedom of expression within the bounds permitted by the classical tradition. At the same time it proved hard for this scholar and chronicler to put aside the scruples of his academic background. He stood at the threshold of Pliny's villas, not fully daring to let his imagination cross over. He needed the backbone of fixed rules, yet he wanted to apply them flexibly. This paradoxical state of mind may help to explain the ambivalent, unresolved quality of his restitutions. Their apparent rationalism and rigidity mask a half-suppressed desire for abandon and luxury revealed in the preponderance of curving herbaceous areas bordering the sober and static architecture. Félibien's encyclopedic grasp of Pliny as statesman, builder, and letter writer contrasts with the fearfulness of an amateur finding excuses to sidestep the real issue of redesigning Pliny's villas from the ground up. Ultimately he fell victim to his own timidity. Just twenty years after the publication of his book, the many volumes of Bernard de Montfaucon's *Antiquité expliquée . . .* began appearing. Extending the encyclopedic principle, it explained and tried to illustrate every imaginable facet of life in ancient times. The section devoted to country houses translated Pliny's letters afresh, and Félibien's restitutions came under fire. Damning with faint praise, Montfaucon ruefully concluded, "Il y a réussi autant qu'on le peut en des matières si obscures."[19]

It is hard to imagine that only a generation passed between Félibien's restitutions and the utterly different ones of Pliny's villas published by Robert Castell in 1728, the year of his death. Félibien's *Plans* had been a normal octavo volume; Castell's *The Villas of the Ancients Illustrated* stands too tall for most bookshelves. Félibien used Pliny to illustrate an exception to the Vitruvian rules of classical architecture; Castell placed Pliny's writings alongside those of his contemporaries in an attempt to exemplify the importance of rules among the ancients. Félibien's villas adhered to the French preference for near-perfect bilateral symmetry in the architecture and gardens; Castell's restitutions, taken as a whole, abandoned these set geometric principles in favor of greater freedom, especially in the garden designs. They unleashed a wild profusion of forms that served as the basis for the English landscape garden, so opposed in form to the French (fig. 55). Had Castell known of Félibien's approach in the 1720s, he would probably not have approved of it. By this time, however, the Frenchman had risen to become a respectable academician, whereas his English counterpart had died of smallpox amid the utmost squalor in the Fleet debtors' prison. Yet for all this they had much in common, especially their passionate love of the Latin language and their pursuit of the elusive joys of interpreting Pliny's villas on paper.

Perhaps the single most striking thing about the little-known Castell was his phenomenal erudition in an age that had no shortage of classical scholars. In addition to Pliny's letters, Castell set out to master *all* the relevant classical sources, including Vitruvius and the authors known collectively as the agronomes. For Castell, first things came first. Without preamble, except for a dedication and short preface, *The Villas of the Ancients* plunges right into the Latin letter to Gallus, annotating obscure words and printing right beside it Castell's English version. (His translation predates by decades the first comprehensive one of 1746 by William Melmoth.) Then and only then come the explanatory remarks. The same sequence repeats itself for the letter to Apollinaris. Castell's arrangement puts the emphasis squarely on the original texts. In between them a long excursus tries to harmonize

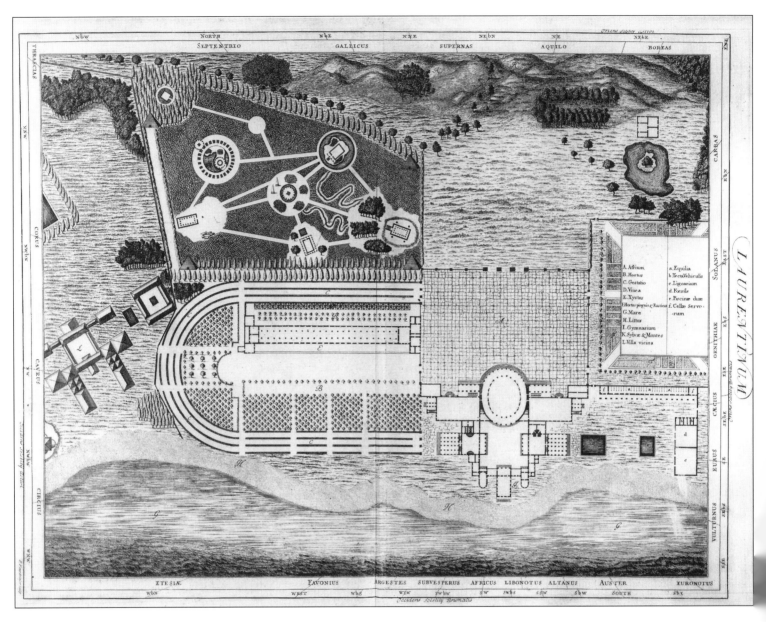

the two letters with other relevant villa writings by Marcus Terentius Varro, Colu-mella, and Vitruvius. In fact it was the lack of commentary on country houses by Vitruvius that supposedly diverted Castell from his initial objective of translating the Latin author's *De architectura*.[20] But a pauper's grave claimed Castell before he could return to fulfill his first ambition. His villa book remains his only monument.

Right in his unpaginated dedication, Castell set out to characterize Pliny's writings as "founded on the rules of the ancients," and the rest of the book proceeds

55. Castell, Laurentine Villa, site plan (Castell, *Villas of the Ancients*)

to demonstrate it. Almost every subsequent scholarly note harps on the idea that Pliny adhered to a set of fixed rules, even though it may not be apparent. In effect Castell used the same basic evidence as Félibien to prove exactly the opposite. Castell did so without ignoring the differences between the principles stated by Vitruvius and the villas built by Pliny. He simply overcame the discrepancies by establishing the Laurentine and Tuscan houses as suited to winter or summer habitation. In that sense, he claimed, they obeyed a set of rules that Vitruvius had neglected to mention. According to Castell, every peculiarity about the villas could be accounted for either climatically or chronologically. At times he forced the climatic argument to extremes, as when he contradicted himself by referring to the heat of day or the need for cool shade at Laurentinum, which supposedly Pliny occupied only in winter.[21] In the orientation of the Tuscan Villa, Castell explained away the apparent divergence from Vitruvian rules by an elaborate, none too convincing discussion of Roman sundials or water clocks. He then brought to bear a chronological consideration according to which "the length of time betwixt Vitruvius and Pliny had so far altered customs, that there seems to be but a little resemblance of the more ancient building in either of his villas."[22] By these scholarly arguments Castell managed to retain his unshakable faith in the necessity of universally applicable rules. Contrary to the illustrative evidence, *he* sided with the "ancients," while Félibien held the "moderns" position.

The Villas of the Ancients excels at compiling classical literary sources to form one grand, more or less harmonious scheme of things. Throughout Castell's explanatory remarks, but especially in part 2, devoted to the agronomes Varro and Columella, he attempted to integrate everything known about villas. The result can best be appreciated in his amazingly complex site plans. For example, the entire right-hand side of the Laurentine plate lays out stabling and slaves' quarters on the authority of Vitruvius, though Pliny hardly mentioned them. (The left-hand side anticipates Marquez by indicating the position of a neighboring villa; cf. fig. 27). Along the upper border of the estate Castel organized the *hortus pinguis et rusticus* into an enclosure with strange pyramidal corner pavilions. This garden, hosting no fewer than three peripteral temples and three tholoi, has been called "a zoo of antique delights."[23] The real menagerie is situated around the borders of the Tuscan Villa (fig. 56). It boasts a deer park, an apiary, a *cochleare* for raising snails, and a *gliarium* to breed dormice, which the Romans considered delicacies, as Castell gleefully informed his readers. No hint of any of this exists in Pliny's letters, and Castell knew it. When straying to Apicus's Roman cookery manual, for example, he would use lowercase letters of the alphabet in his legend to make the distinction clear between Plinian and non-Plinian information. It goes to show how a scrupulous method can lead to estate maps that would have astonished Pliny, as they continue to astonish today.

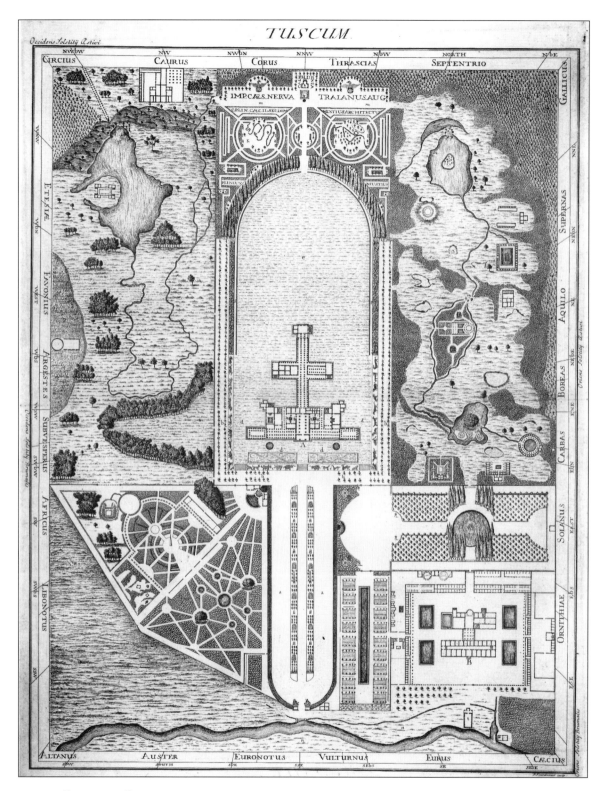

56. Castell, Tuscan Villa, site plan (Castell, *Villas of the Ancients*)

On two additional plans, not reproduced here, Castell continued to display his arcane knowledge by citing sources on rabbit hutches, fish hatcheries, pheasantries, sheepfolds, kennels, and so forth. Nor did he forget houses for the animal keepers, gardeners, or farmhands, since Castell tried to imagine the full complement of farm buildings attendant on the house of the villa owner. Basing himself principally on Columella and Varro, or alternatively on Vitruvius and Palladius, he came up with schemes for farmsteads complete down to the most menial details. As such, Castell's book had the added interest of being one of the first in the literature to deal with the farm as an architectural building type worthy of consideration. At considerable expense, he had the gifted engraver Fourdrinier do a separate plan and cross section representing Varro's aviary, or ornithon.[24] There was nothing parsimonious or half-hearted about Castell's approach. At the end of this second section came a fold-out plate (fig. 57) that spread out a grandiose vision inspired by Varro's idea of a villa and its environs—his fantastic ornithon is shown at the bottom left. According to Varro, the Latin military word *cohors* applied to the arrangement of villas, and it meant precision along the lines of a Roman encampment. Here Varro and Castell sacrificed at the altar of efficiency the freer type of organization implied by Pliny's letters.

57. Castell, Varro's villa, site plan (Castell, *Villas of the Ancients*)

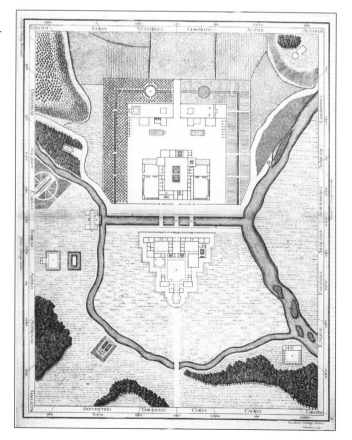

Some of this quality of organizational rigor spills over to the bottom right of the Tuscan Villa site plan (fig. 56). Castell included a farmstead there on a modified Vitruvian model, although Pliny never referred to one. Pliny's letters hardly deign to discuss the harvest, the money it brought in, or the tedious round of visits with tenant farmers that he obviously detested as a diversion from his literary pursuits (bk. 9, ep. 15). As with the Laurentine Villa, templelike structures litter the Tuscan landscape. At the extreme bottom, Castell thoughtfully included the one to Ceres rebuilt by Mustius—Félibien surely would have approved of such a nice touch. The whole engraving, occupying a double-page spread of folio size for each villa, conveys an impression of bewildering richness. Castell's concoctions have parted company with Pliny. They owe less to him and more to Castell's own imagination, fired by a vast knowledge of the classical world in all its domestic details. Like many a work of imaginative genius, it borders on the excessive and even the slightly mad.

The genial impression created by Castell's site plans does not entirely carry over to the elevations and floor plans that proliferate throughout his book—no fewer than seven of these occur, which suggests that the author was gilding the Plinian lily. Of the two villa schemes, the Laurentine is the fuller and more successful (five plates vs. two for the Tuscan). Castell noted that Pliny had been "not so particular" in his description of the Tuscan house and gardens,[25] so the book opens with a ground-floor plan of Laurentinum (fig. 58). For the central entrance portico

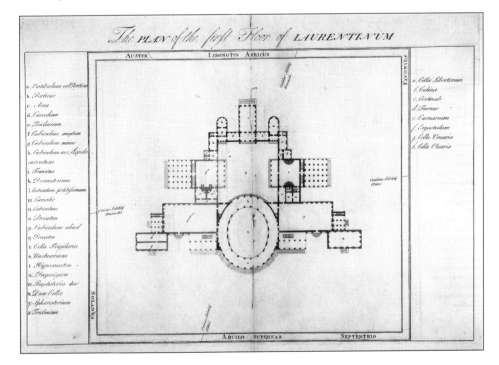

58. Castell, Laurentine Villa, plan (Castell, *Villas of the Ancients*)

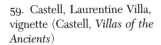

and the area behind it, Castell chose an oval rather than a circle. He justified this by referring to Roman inscriptions, which he claimed tended to favor an ovoid shape for the letter *O*. (His extensive footnotes to this passage perfectly characterize his out-of-the-ordinary knowledge in areas as diverse as epigraphy, geometry, and astronomy.)[26] The entrance portico curves outward, as is seen in a small and somewhat crude vignette showing this facade with the Mediterranean behind it (fig. 59). The bulging, saucer-domed central pavilion thus created is far ahead of its time. It foretells neoclassical performances half a century later, such as William Newton's (cf. fig. 62). It also shows Castell's unevenness in that the portico's startling giant order nestles between towers of the most banal design imaginable. Similarly, the elevation of the Doric cryptoporticus has the monotony of a barracks or a stable (fig. 60).

Castell repeated the curving wall masses of the Laurentine Villa in two rooms projecting out to either side of the rectangular triclinium on the seafront. By this he intended to evoke what Pliny described as the *cubiculum in apsida curvatum,* with bookcases lining its rounded end in an arc following the sun's path. Here Pliny had his browsing library to curl up with on a stormy winter's day. Félibien had shown it with a domed ceiling, but Castell, without benefit of the Frenchman's architectural background, hit upon a quite obvious outward-curving solution that took the Latin at face value for the first time. Most likely he had in mind such recent country mansions as Blenheim and Castle Howard, still very much the talk of London. Each as originally designed featured curved projections; at Blenheim one example is occupied by a bookroom. Or he may have drawn his inspiration from Jacobean and Elizabethan "prodigy houses," with their great multistory oriel windows.[27] Whatever the sources, so natural and elegant was Castell's design breakthrough that similar solutions occurred spontaneously to later architects, among them Bouchet (fig. 35) and Krubsacius (fig. 101), neither of whom apparently had seen *The Villas of the Ancients* beforehand.

If the Laurentine Villa restitution by Castell embodies a certain elegance, his

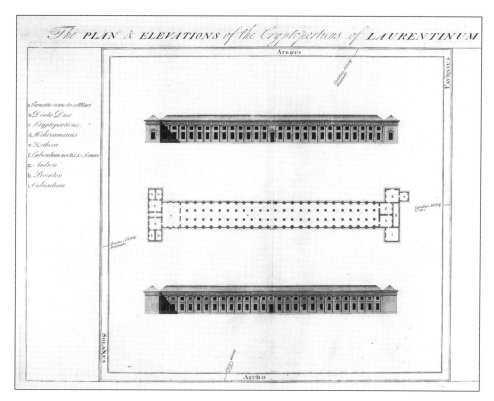

60. Castell, Laurentine Villa, plan and elevation of the cryptoporticus (Castell, *Villas of the Ancients*)

Tuscan Villa plan illustrates his shortcomings as a designer (fig. 61). With wings shooting off at right angles from a seemingly endless central hallway, it has the excruciating length of a modern airport terminal. Most designers avoid cruciform houses, with good reason; Castell blundered right in. His Tuscan Villa would have inflicted a daily crucifixion on its inhabitants. Instinctively, practicing architects must have realized Castell's impracticality—not a single member of the profession subscribed to his book! It is perhaps equally significant, however, that Castell's restitutions have found favor with Latinists from William Melmoth to Christian Ludwig Stieglitz, Nicolaus Eligius Lemaire, and Helen Tanzer.[28] Castell speaks to them with his lucid prose, his carefully reasoned etymological arguments, his epigraphic sources, and his dispassionately nonderogatory textual glosses. At the same time, this evenhandedness toward his predecessors—his obvious lack of egotistical malice—leads to a certain vacuousness that carries over to the architectural designs.

Who then was this remarkable Robert Castell? Clearly he had received an excellent classical education. He may have been the young man of gentle birth, born at "Dedford" (Deptford?) in Kent, who matriculated at Lincoln College,

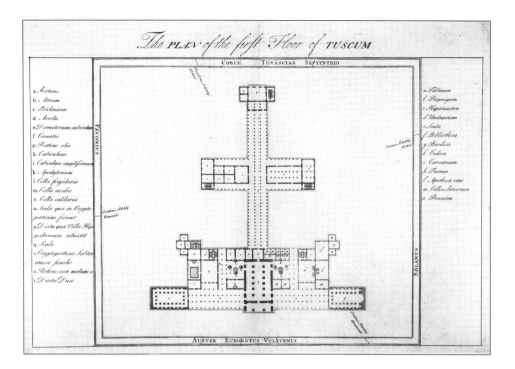

61. Castell, Tuscan Villa, plan (Castell, *Villas of the Ancients*)

Oxford, in 1711 at age sixteen. In that event he would have been about thirty-three years old at the time of his death.[29] He died on 12 December 1728—not 1729 as once thought—a victim of smallpox contracted in one of the dependencies of the Fleet prison where the disease raged. The previous June he had been committed to jail for debts, probably incurred because of the lavishness of his publication on Pliny and the translation of Vitruvius that he also had in the works. It would be ironic if he were a distant kinsman of Edmund Castell (1606–85), the scholar of Semitic languages, who shared the dubious distinction of having fallen into debt and having briefly gone to jail on account of his publishing ventures. As one of Robert's creditors put it, "Mr. Castell, surely your luck is worse than anybody's."[30] Castell's luck had indeed run out. Born "to a competent estate," he left "his affairs in the greatest confusion," leaving a destitute widow and numerous small children "in the utmost distress."[31]

A number of influential persons, including some of the 116 subscribers to *The Villas of the Ancients*, tried to come to Castell's aid. Among them was the celebrated James Oglethorpe (1696–1785), a member of Parliament at the time and already active in prison reform. Oglethorpe visited Castell during his last days but was unable to effect his release. In 1729 Oglethorpe brought the whole Castell scandal before the House of Commons, as a result of which a trial of the infamous warden of the Fleet took place. According to the evidence submitted at the trial, other Castell friends included the painter John Vanderbank (ca. 1694–1739), who visited him in confinement to no avail, and Thomas, earl of Londonderry, who hoped to spirit him abroad. Finally there is the matter of Richard Boyle, earl of Burlington (1694–1753), to whom Castell dedicated his book. It has particularly puzzled Castell's and Burlington's admirers that the earl did not exert his power to free his dedicator. *The Villas of the Ancients* must have won his approval as early as 1727, the date borne on some of the engraver G. King's ornamental vignettes. There is, however, no evidence that Burlington underwrote the publication. Burlington probably knew of Castell's reputation for mismanaging his affairs and decided to keep his distance when he learned of the whole messy business. Still, some ill-defined connection links the unfortunate Castell with Lord Burlington's circle.

Castell's buildings may look bizarre compared with the staid ones of the architect earl, but the Laurentine and Tuscan gardens have a lot in common with Burlington's experiments, commenced in 1725 at his own Chiswick Villa.[32] In accordance with Castell's overall thesis, the Laurentine garden had a distinctly seasonal appearance. At the seaside winter villa, the sandy soil and time of year suggested to Castell a relatively sparse vegetation of shrubs and stunted fig or mulberry trees (fig. 55). Only the *hortus pinguis et rusticus*, protected behind its windbreak of cypresses, hints at verdure. A more formal *hortus* closer to the seashore ends in a curve within the larger semielliptical *gestatio*. Placed on an axis with the villa, it resembles the curved exedra in clipped box hedge similarly situated within sight of Lord Burlington's principal reception room at Chiswick. Both gardens seen on plan also have the same strange mixture of geometrically shaped areas and other, less regular sections intersected by straight and squiggly paths. Castell had an interesting justification for these abrupt shifts of horticultural character. He said the first villa gardens had tried to make the best they could of the existing soil and topography of their location. This "rough manner," as Castell called it, did not appeal to more orderly tastes, so a second style, devised "by the rule and the line," came into being. Finally, a mixture of the two types took place so that both some accidental variety and some regularity could squeeze into a small area for maximum effect.

Castell called the third state of gardening "artful confusion." He likened it to "the present manner of designing [gardens] in China . . . where, though the parts are disposed with the greatest art, the irregularity is still preserved . . . [and] where there is no appearance of that skill which is made use of."[33] His statement appears oddly anachronistic. It is the only instance in the entire book of a contemporary, nonclassical reference. Such an atypical and out-of-context interjection has been put forward by some garden historians as evidence of a connection with Lord Burlington's gardening. They believe that the Chiswick library possessed a copy of the Chinese garden views that Father Matteo Ripa had engraved during his years as a missionary attached to the imperial court at Peking (1711–23). After his departure from Asia, he landed in England in 1724 and spent a month there. At that time he was received at court and became something of a celebrity. Ripa's plates, thirty-six in all, show the winding paths, asymmetrical collections of buildings, lopsided clumps of vegetation, and irregular bodies of water that typified Chinese pleasure grounds. These ensembles acted as a three-dimensional philosophical expression—a sort of Confucianism without confusion. Castell introduced into his villa master plans exactly this same conflation of meandering walkways, serpentine streams, artificial hillocks, and hermetic temples set in druidical copses. Furthermore, Ripa's and Castell's engravings in the hands of William Kent, Burlington's garden adviser at Chiswick, could have led to the mixed approach the French rightly call *le jardin anglo-chinois.* At Chiswick, at Alexander Pope's Twickenham Villa, and later elsewhere, William Kent developed the English landscape garden, perhaps Britain's greatest single contribution to the arts in eighteenth-century Europe.[34]

Castell's Tuscan Villa site plan (fig. 56) sums up his gardening theories, at the same time introducing a note of summertime luxuriance and autumnal abundance. The major features, the pair of hippodrome-shaped areas to the front and back, treat the villa building as though it were a chariot within a racecourse. The *gestatio* at the front with a central *spina,* decorated with pillars and obelisks in topiary work, was intended by Castell to evoke a real Roman hippodrome.[35] Coming into the curve at the far upper end, spiky cypress trees abound, just as Pliny had written. Beyond them the axially related *stibadium,* or "summerhouse" as Castell called it, is a reminder of the preferred season for inhabiting the villa in the Apennines. Behind the cypresses are box hedges arranged to spell out the names of Pliny, his wife Calpurnia, Mustius the architect, and the emperor Trajan—a natural topos in topiary. Three other areas coincide with Castell's three main styles of gardening, already mentioned. Starting clockwise at the bottom left, the first is the regular geometric type, organized around *ronds-points,* with parterres and *pattes d'oie* formed by allées. Castell consciously acknowledged his debt to French garden terminology, fashionable in his time as it still is today.[36] Then moving up the hillside is an area of unaffected garden in the "rough manner." Natural rolling countryside has plantings of trees in small hursts set around an irregular body of water and a sinuous rivulet. The informal meadow, or *pratulum,* situated in a circular plot below the name of the emperor Nero cut out in box, would fall into this same category. But the corresponding circular plot on the right side, and the rest of the garden from there on clockwise, would correspond to the *ruris imitatio* described in the letter to Pliny and likened by Castell to the Chinese technique.

To counterbalance the impression of Castell as a scholar completely steeped in classicism, a final instance of his Latinism at work reveals another side of his personality. Castell noted that at both villas Pliny mentioned soft footpaths to walk on.[37] On the strength of that, and perhaps misconstruing somewhat the letter to Calvisius Rufus (bk. 3, ep. 1), Castell visualized Pliny naked and running barefoot over the sandy soil at the seaside, or tripping along the mossy acanthus paths in Tuscany without his sandals. This little glimpse of the private side of a Roman villa, with Pliny doffing his clothes, goes to show how the constraints of living in Castell's Augustan age might chafe. Not unlike Félibien, Castell felt a little hemmed in by the laws passed down from the ancients, which had to be obeyed. He discovered exceptions to those rules and sought a way either to rationalize them or to introduce some of the newfound freedom into his designs. The stately measured rhythms of Plinian architecture were therefore reserved for the stately home and were mixed with a more wayward, even chaotic, note of abandon in the gardens. If Pliny the statesman saw the villa as a realm of relaxation from the bonds of polite behavior in town, he was not alone: Castell sought to introduce something of the same sort. In the same spirit, William Kent once whimsically depicted his patron Lord Burlington on a walk in the grounds of Chiswick with an irreverent pet dog beside him lifting its leg to urinate on its master.

Castell's book had considerable impact on the successful reception of Plinian gardening ideas after his lifetime. The June 1733 issue of the magazine *Practical Husbandman and Planter's Guide,* edited by Stephen Switzer, included an "Inquiry into the Villas of the Ancients" that drew heavily on Castell.[38] Later, at the end of the century, a posthumously published article by Thomas Wright (1711–86) took the form of a letter describing his *villula* at Byer's Green in County Durham (see appendix 3). Improbable though it may sound, it actually existed on a lilliputian scale, though it has long since vanished. Some of its charm no doubt derived from the literary as well as the architectural side. Wright's tongue-in-cheek mimicry of Pliny and of Castell reached a hilarious climax when the author boasted that his nearest neighbor was a hundred yards away! Just a few years later, however, Castell emerged into the horticultural mainstream and out of the rarefied world of antiquarians and Latinists. John Claudius Loudon, that great popularizer with a Latin middle name, reproduced some of Castell's plans in miniature in his April 1830 *Garden Magazine,* and later in the second, or 1834, edition of his *Encyclopedia of Gardening.*[39] Any immortality that Castell gained came as a result of the wide circulation of books on gardening in the nineteenth century. His speculations received attention and approbation until doubts were raised as a result of methodical excavations of Roman villa gardens.

The true heir to Castell's literary and scholarly legacy was the obscure London-born architect William Newton (1735–90). On the paternal side he claimed kinship with Sir Isaac Newton. On the maternal side he was descended from the Reverend

Humphrey Ditton, a mathematician of repute who taught at Christ's Hospital, where young William received his classical education. After graduation in 1750, the success his relatives had enjoyed continued to elude him. Without distinguishing himself, he worked in several architectural offices and entered several competitions: those for the Royal Exchange, Dublin (1769); Saint Alphage, London Wall (1774); Saint Mary's Battersea (1775); and Saint Luke's Asylum for Poor Lunatics (1777). Meanwhile, Newton had briefly visited Italy in 1766–67, an advantage he had over Castell, who never made the Grand Tour as far as is known.[40] Then Newton picked up literally where Castell had left off by publishing a translation of Vitruvius—the first half of *De architectura,* to be more exact. Thus ended at long last the campaign to translate into English the canonical trilogy of great architectural treatises: Palladio (1715–20), Alberti (1726), and finally Vitruvius (1771). Add to that Castell's work on Pliny, and all the basic texts on the villa stood in readiness for the villa revival in the last quarter of the eighteenth century in Britain.

Newton's first volume of *The Architecture of M. Vitruvius Pollio* displays to advantage his almost complete knowledge of the various printed editions available, besides various unpublished manuscripts that the translator had consulted in the British Museum.[41] The energies he failed to employ on the building site he simply channeled into becoming the perfect bookworm. Newton also knew about the attempted translation by his predecessor, Castell. And he had special reason to refer to Castell's work on Pliny when he tackled the second volume on Vitruvius, the one containing the most passages on domestic architecture. Demonstrating to the public his progress on the project, Newton exhibited drawings based on Vitruvius's description of the Roman town house and the "villa pseudo urbana." These imaginary restitutions appeared in the exhibitions of the Royal Academy and the Society of Artists in 1776 and 1777, respectively.[42] The drawings eventually became illustrations to the second volume of Newton's book, but it did not appear in print until 1791, in a reedition of the entire ten books prepared and engraved by James Newton, William's brother and literary executor. One plate is of special interest (fig. 62). At the 1777 exhibition it had the title "an idea of the urbana (or master's) part of an ancient Roman villa; formed according to the description of the classic writers." By 1791 the caption had been reduced to read "villa pseudo urbana." The apparent homogeneity of the design belies the fact that William Newton arrived at it by a synthetic process akin to Castell's, in which various sources were combined.

The plate in question shows a sprawling, symmetrically disposed plan and elevation of a large villa. The elevation depicts a downward-sloping site at the front and a split-level arrangement. In this case a preliminary drawing by Newton survives, badly torn along the fold but still faintly legible (fig. 63). The plan in the main agrees closely with the engraved version, but the difficult-to-read notes amplify the

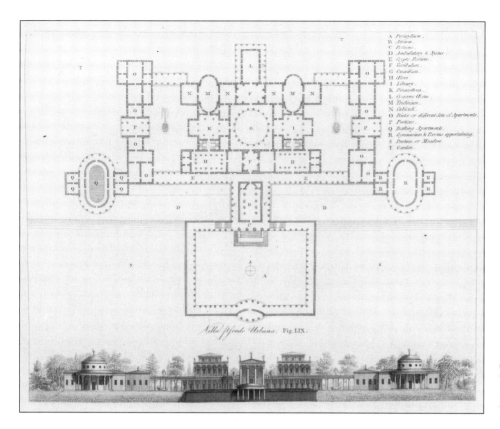

The following legend appears within the figure:

A Peristylium.
B Atrium.
C Porticus.
D Ambulatory & Xystus.
E Crypto Porticus.
F Vestibulum.
G Cavædium.
H Œcus.
I Library.
K Pinacotheca.
L Cænare Ræ.
M Triclinium.
N Cubicula.
O Diœta or different Sets of Apartments.
P Porticus.
Q Bathing Apartments.
R Gymnasium & Rooms appertaining.
S Pratum or Meadow.
T Garden.

Villa Pseudo Urbana. Fig. LIX.

62. Newton, "villa pseudo urbana," plan and elevation (Newton, *Architecture of M. Vitruvius Pollio*, 1791)

thought process behind the final solution.[43] Although the inscription at the bottom center reads "Villa Urbana," the lines at the top right end with the abbreviation "Pli." and refer to fig and mulberry trees and a *gestatio.* Obviously Newton had been reading Pliny as well as Vitruvius. On the lower slopes the words *pratum* and *xystus* appear. Fainter still, the sketch plan hints at fountains in the villa courtyards—the central one is shown as round in the engraving and is too damaged to make out for certain in the drawing. Finally, far up near the top of the sheet, Newton indicated a hippodrome and a theater. Newton's justification for this reliance on Pliny's letters emerges in the printed text accompanying the engraving:

> Vitruvius has only treated of the apartments and conveniences of the husbandry part of villas, and not of the master's dwelling, . . . or pseudo urbana. . . . The description he gives . . . is not definite enough to authorize any one particular disposition, and . . . [my] design is only offered as one mode of distribution conforming to the description of Vitruvius and other ancient authors as nearly as has occurred to me.[44]

Vitruvius had been scrutinized and found wanting by Newton, who by inference turned to other authors including Pliny, as the surviving sketch plan proves.

Like Castell, or like James Stuart, whose *Antiquities of Athens* Newton edited,

63. Newton, Laurentine Villa, sketch plan (RIBA, K9/1[6])

the author's erudition emerged principally in copious footnotes, liberally sprinkled with abbreviated references—the more in Latin, the better. In one such note Newton referred to the authority of Pliny the Younger's "description of his villa at Laurentinum" and proceeded to cite in Latin the passage about the *porticus in O litterae similitudinem.*[45] This is Newton's principal reference to Pliny—others occur fleetingly elsewhere—but behind it stand hitherto unstudied restitutions of both the Laurentine and Tuscan villas carried out in sketch form sometime during the mid-1770s. Rough though the sketches are, they convey the distinct impression that Newton remembered his Latin declensions and his Pliny well.

Newton's Laurentine Villa (fig. 64) generally favors the bilateral symmetry seen in Castell's and also seems to borrow from him the curving projections at each extremity of the facade facing the seashore. (The same motif reappears in a slightly different position in the later Newton engraving; fig. 62.) The novel part, insofar as the smudgy pencil sketch reveals it, occurs on the left end behind the "elliptical cubiculum" in a cluster of chambers set aside for "freedmen & servants." Nothing on the right-hand side corresponds symmetrically with it. Castell had avoided the problem of asymmetry by placing the mundane aspects of villa management off in his *villa rustica*. Newton also planned a *villa rustica* with large slaves' quarters, which appeared as his plate 60. Some of the same practical thinking obviously spilled over to the Laurentine Villa, making it a less conventional design. Two major axes crisscrossed through it: the first down the middle of the site linked a sequence of column-lined halls; the second ran at right angles and culminated in the baths on the west and the slaves' quarters on the east. A difficult-to-interrelate plan on the verso of this same sheet refers to the cryptoporticus/*sphaeristerium* complex. An inscription suggests that its position might be staggered in front of the rest of the villa to improve the views. Such flexible planning has little in common with Castell's approach but anticipates that of Marquez by twenty years.

All these inherent tendencies rise unmistakably to the surface in the Tuscan Villa. Crude though the sketch may look (fig. 65), it shows the first decidedly asymmetrical Pliny villa since antiquity. This restitution therefore is probably the closest for its date to true classical principles of villa design. The long north-south axis begins at the bottom of the sheet amid "fields" and reaches "vineyards" at the top. The verso in this case reveals only that the "slope" figured in Newton's thinking. The main architectural spaces stretch out in a sequence arranged *en enfilade* with a few columns here and there. Then off to the right extends an *L*-shaped wing consisting of a cryptoporticus, the hippodrome, and finally the rapidly sketched-in *stibadium* with its bedroom apartment. There is no point in making any exaggerated claims about Newton's artistry. His unimaginative, schematically drawn room shapes would suit his contemporary Saint Luke's Lunatic Asylum design just as well as a retreat for a Roman statesman. In his equanimity, at least, he treated the mad and the super rich almost the same.

Asymmetry is not so surprising in the light of Newton's emphasis on setting apart the private and more public zones of a villa. At Laurentinum he placed the elliptical library at one end; in Tuscany the *stibadium* stood way off to the side. These spaces obviously struck Newton as important. In contrast to Castell, who planned for public show, Newton concerned himself more with the villas as sym-

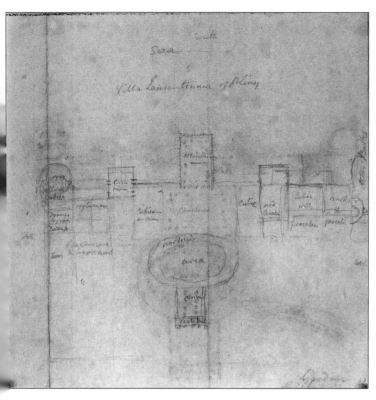

64. Newton, Laurentine Villa, sketch plan (RIBA, K9/1[14])

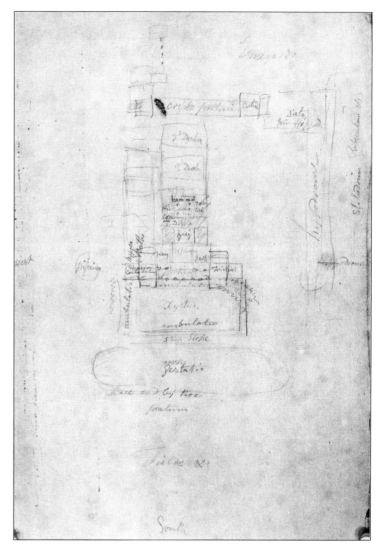

65. Newton, Tuscan Villa, sketch plan (RIBA, K9/1[16])

bolic of the need to retire for study and meditation. Reflecting this train of thought, Newton praised Vitruvius as an architect-scholar who, because of his high principles, had failed to succeed in the building profession. With considerable personal warmth Newton wrote:

> We also learn that then, as in our days, persons unfounded and ignorant in the art assumed the name of architects, and have obtained more employment and encouragement than those who were well skilled in their profession. This will probably ever be the case. For the habits of study by which knowledge is acquired, and perhaps the turn of mind and diffidence which, as Vitruvius says, generally accompanies men of sensibility and merit, unfits them for dealing with . . . the necessary steps to success.[46]

Surely this passage reflects Newton's own experience and frustrated hope. Somewhat uncritically, perhaps, he came to confuse his personality with that of Vitruvius. Had not success in the worldly sense eluded them both, and could not the one architect find comfort in the immortality the other had achieved as a writer rather than a builder? Similarly, the studious rather than the worldly side of Pliny struck a responsive chord. Newton found his refuge not in a villa but in the British Museum, poring over dictionaries, manuscripts, and variant editions. He preferred puzzling over an obscure Latin technical term to measuring rods of brickwork or juggling shillings and pence.

Count Stanislas Kostka Potocki (1757–1821) can claim the honor of being the most unusual of those who conceived restitutions of Pliny's villas.[47] He embodied in one person the Polish Winckelmann—an expression he himself concocted for a book title—and the Lord Burlington of his country. For a long time his fellow Poles have honored him as a patriot, political thinker, agronomist, art patron, historian, linguist, antiquarian, and distinguished amateur architect. But outside his native land he remains simply the dashing young man in his famous life-size equestrian portrait by Jacques-Louis David. First exhibited at the 1781 Paris Salon, it then hung in the Potocki family portrait gallery at Wilanów as a trophy of Stanislas Kostka's 1779–80 Grand Tour of Italy. During that trip, in addition to the David, he commissioned many other works of art, including a series of restitution drawings of Pliny's Laurentine Villa.[48]

In the absence of the original travel diaries, either lost in World War II or previously stolen, the circumstances surrounding Potocki's costly effort to recapture Laurentinum on paper remain unsure. Whatever is known comes from summaries of the missing documents and Potocki's own reminiscences written shortly after 1800 and certainly no later than 1820. Despite the lapse of a generation, his twenty-four-page manuscript titled "Notes et Idées sur la Ville de Pline" vividly depicts almost the exact moment when the idea of a restitution struck him. From the manuscript it becomes clear that for Potocki, as for Hirt, the initial inspiration came from Winckelmann's *Geschichte der Kunst des Altertums*. At least that is the book Potocki obliquely referred to when he wrote about the ruins from which, according to Winckelmann, "one removed precious marbles, beautiful mosaics, and some busts of the greatest beauty." He then went on in his fluent but faulty French to recount his personal impressions of the Laurentine site as follows:

La maison decrite par Pline tire son nom du Laurentium, lieu habité et embeli par les Romains, dont il ne reste aujourd'hui que de faibles traces. Une chetive taverne nomé S. Lorenzo, occupe une partie de l'emplacement de l'ancient Laurentium. Non loin de la sur les dependences de la Ville Sacchetti l'on decourvrit en 1714 les ruines de la Villa de Pline, sur les quels l'emplacement des lieux leurs etendues et l'accord commun de plus scavants antiquaires ne laissent aucun doute. . . . Elle etait assise sur les bords de la mare mediterreine . . . (dont les accroissements successives des sables l'ont éloigne à six cent pas) dans le terrain du *Latium*. . . . Ces ruines [ont] été entierement neglige . . . et se trouvent sous tere pour la seconde fois. Ce qui en exite . . . est plus tot fait pour manquer l'emplacement de cete maison que pour donner la moindre idée. La beaute de la situation et de les environs tant vanté par Pline, n'est plus reconnaisable.[49]

With a copy of Winckelmann in hand, or accompanied by an informative guide, Potocki had tracked the letter to Gallus back to the landlocked Ostian site, occupied by a miserable tavern and barely recognizable as Pliny's villa. Standing in the presence of those nostalgic ruins, unearthed in 1714 but covered over again, Potocki had the idea of undertaking a restitution—the most extensive ever in number of finished drawings.

The factual description Potocki left of the untidy mess he saw at Laurentinum admits of few illusions compared with the highly colored and romantic yarns spun by Haudebourt and subsequently by Wilhelm Stier (chap. 5). Nor does the Pole's manuscript leave any room to imagine that he actually conducted an archaeological dig on the site, as some of his compatriots would have liked to understand. After the introductory remarks quoted above, Potocki wrote a perfectly straightforward word-by-word analysis of the Latin letter in the manner of Castell. This section took up most of the day or so he spent writing the manuscript. Before abruptly ending it, as if interrupted in midthought, the author reserved a few general remarks for archaeology and art theory subtitled "Idées sur les quels le plan de la maison de Pline a été dirige." In them he made brief but amusingly astute assessments of the previous literature on the subject by Scamozzi, Félibien, and even Marquez. With considerable insight Potocki characterized the Frenchman's restitution as a château, the Italian's as a villa on the banks of the Brenta, and the Mexican's as in "le goust corrompue" of the previous century. (No attempt was made to disguise the retrospective nature of the commentary written sometime after 1800.) Not surprisingly, he preferred his own to theirs because they had tried too hard to outsmart the ancients.[50]

The marked differences among restitutions Potocki noted caused him to think for himself. He wrote: "Various systems have pretended to submit the creative genius of the Greeks, as well as the grandeur and daring of the Romans, to a set of fixed rules. . . . But all the research of the most learned antiquaries in this regard seem to me the vain efforts of people who grope through the dark shadows that veil antiquity. . . . It is as senseless to pretend to fix the form of our own houses as it is those of the ancients."[51] Thus speaks a person whose visits to the ruins of Laurentinum, Pompeii, and Herculaneum had turned him against the rules that "*scavants antiquaires*," as he called them, had tried to impose on the physical remains. In a somewhat evasive way he never exactly spelled out his own solution, but reading between the lines it appears to have been assimilative and synthetic. He valued the ruins no less than the literary evidence that so much reveals the tenor of the times. According to Potocki, "Cete maniere de devoiler l'antiquité quelque imparfaite qu'elle puisse etre m'a parue la plus sure et la plus simple."[52] His is the outcry of an intelligent amateur against the self-styled experts, an appeal for freedom from the constraints of rigid theories—and freedom from domination is what Polish history of that period is all about.

Whether or not Potocki ever intended his *petit ouvrage* on Pliny for publication, much the same spirit of rebellion against authority subsequently saw its way into print in a significant if little-known art historical treatise by him titled *The Art of the Ancients, or Polish Winckelmann.*[53] As its name indicates, it is a rendition *and* critique of Winckelmann's history of ancient art *in Polish,* thus advocating freedom from reliance on foreign art terms. Although it recognizes Winckelmann's methodological contribution, it is critical of his domineering arbitrariness and his misinterpretation of classical sources such as Pliny the Elder, excerpts from whose writings fill the last of the book's four volumes. Ironically, the writings of Pliny's nephew hardly enter the discussion at all. It is almost as if Potocki had forgotten about them in the thirty-five years since they had preoccupied him to the extent of having the Laurentine Villa drawn in exhaustive detail. Whatever else may be said about the merits of his theories on archaeology and architecture, they single him out as an independent thinker with a profound knowledge of art. Here was an intellect perfectly capable of conceiving a Laurentine restitution, yet without the artistic skill to execute it unassisted.

Along with David's portrait, other Potocki property from Wilanów that made its way to the Polish state included two portfolios bulging with drawings. Tags stuck on the binding label them "Villa de Pline le jeune, di^{tt} Laurentina," and "Interieure de la Villa de Pline le jeune par Brenna" (WAF. 67 and 68, in the National Library of Warsaw graphic collection). Other tags pasted inside the meter-high covers tell the interesting provenance of the drawings. In his own hand Stanislas Kostka Potocki described the first group as: "Drawings of the villa of Pliny according to his own description. There were thirty-two of them but a draftsman removed nine. In the plan one followed the facts as given by Pliny. As for the ornament, one tried to put together all the best examples that Roman architecture of that period had to offer by way of models." A second tag in a hand identified as that of Potocki's son Alexander enlarges on the information by stating that the work was carried out for his father "during his visit to Rome in 1778 [date changed from 1777] and under the direction of Count Potocki by Polish and Italian artists. They [the drawings] number thirty-four. It is to be regretted that the drawings of beautiful capitals and bases of all the orders of architecture have been stolen and that only one of them remains . . . by Joseph Manocchi [Giuseppe Manocchi (1731–82)]." Finally, on the inside cover of the second portfolio Potocki wrote:

> Vincent Brenna aujourd'hui Architecte de l'Empereur de Russie, milionaire a ce que l'on dit, m'a volé plusieurs de ces dessins en quitant la pologne. . . . Pour prix apparament de l'avoir tiré de la misere a Rome de lui avoir enseigné le peut d'Architecture qu'il sait, de l'avoir fait voyager, de l'avoir bien place en Pologne enfin de l'avoir reccommandé à l'Empereur Paule pour lors Grand Duc.

Tales of collaborations gone sour, such as Potocki and Brenna's, are unfortunately not uncommon in the age of international neoclassicism. But Brenna's thievery, double-dealing, and desertion of his benefactor Potocki for the future czar Paul seem the unkindest cuts of all.

Some of the Laurentine drawings went on exhibition for the first time in 1933, and since then they have been seen in public only twice. Their wider recognition therefore is due to the tireless efforts of a single art historian: the late Stanislas Lorentz.[54] By repeating the same basic information in numerous publications, he brought the drawings to international attention. After his initial analysis of the portfolios' contents, however, they never again received systematic study. Even the basic tool of a proper catalog is missing. As a result, no clear picture emerges on so fundamental a matter as the number of drawings related to the Laurentine project. Is it all thirty-five at present accounted for, thirty-four as Alexander Potocki contended, twenty-eight according to Lorentz, or only twenty-three, as I will suggest here based on Stanislas Kostka Potocki's enumeration? Before the restitution can be assessed as a whole, one must try to establish a chronology and a provisional attribution by different styles of draftsmanship. Only then can one proceed with a drawing-by-drawing analysis of what truly relates to Pliny's villa.

Potocki spent considerable time in Italy during his early manhood. From 1772 to 1774 he studied at Turin Academy under the architectural tutelage of F. Bonvalli. He returned to Italy in 1775 and again in 1776, though almost no record exists of these brief stays. Then in 1779–80 he took along his wife, Alexandra, and his sister-in-law, Isabella Potocki, née Lubomirska. The highlights of their trip—Venice, Rome, and the Bay of Naples—can be gleaned from a booklet filled with topographical sketches and running lists of expenses all mixed in together.[55] In addition, the loose-leaf booklet of sketches titled "Idées d'architecture 1779" illustrates Potocki's fascination with architecture at the same time as it shows his limitations as a draftsman. It contains a plethora of typical neoclassical dream schemes—a triumphal bridge, a garden casino, a Palladian-style villa, several centralized churches, and so forth—none of them dated, particularly well drawn, or very original in design. Potocki did not lack imagination, but he found the help he needed from trained artists like the Roman-based Florentine architect Vincenzo

Brenna (1745–1820). They may well have known each other before the 1779–80 Grand Tour, as Alexander Potocki implied in his note on the provenance of the portfolios. That might also account for the presence in the Potocki collection of drawings by Brenna dated 1776.[56] About the time of Potocki's return to Warsaw, Brenna joined him there for a stay of three years before departing for Russia in 1783. While in Poland, Brenna prepared two alternative competition entries for a Temple of Divine Providence intended for construction at Ujazdów. Brenna's drawings, now in the Warsaw University Library drawings cabinet (Zb. Król. T. 193 nos. 36–44), in certain respects fall short of the artistic excellence of the Pliny drawings in the Biblioteka Narodowa. This comparison lends credence to Alexander Potocki's statement that his father employed several artists, Italian as well as expatriate Polish. Stanislas Lorentz had suggested in 1946 that one of the other artists could have been the painter Francesco Smuglewicz (1745–1807), an Italophile Pole living in Rome. Such an explanation might account for the exquisite, painterly quality of a gem among the Potocki Pliny drawings depicting a relatively minor round room in the Laurentine Villa (pl. 35). Talent has been lavished on this interior, from the precise underdrawing in pen and ink to the superlative rendering in the French wash technique to convey the proper impression of rotundity. Three-legged torchères, watercolored to resemble bronze, belch smoke realistically. With consummate skill the artist shows an embracing statuary group. This sheet and several others like it to be discussed shortly rise above the neoclassical norm by any standard. They surpass in quality most of the other drawings in the portfolio, not to mention those Brenna produced in Warsaw.

Despite its undeniable importance to the entire suite of Pliny drawings, the main site plan has a certain woodenness, heightened by the unimaginative arrangement and depiction of the trees in straight little rows (fig. 66). In this respect the gardens resemble those conceived by Félibien, but they lack his flair. The long facades with their pairs of bombé projections could lead to the deduction that someone had taken a peep at Castell's Laurentine plan, except that Potocki made no mention whatever of the Englishman. It seems more likely that the Polish/Italian plan—with scale bars in *palmi romani* as well as *braccia polacche*—struck out pretty much on its own, whether for better or for worse. A good indication is the peculiar arrangement in the grounds of a long, narrow cryptoporticus connecting two extraordinary pavilions. The pavilion on the left near the seashore is slightly irregular in plan; the one across from it centers on a room in the shape of a double ax-head. Nothing like this had been attempted before, nor would it ever occur again, thank goodness. Potocki's manuscript complained that other restitutions had erred through too much ingenuity; his own gratuitously complex planning could be accused of the same thing. Take the impractical means of access to the podium, for instance. To show off skill, three sides of the podium have staircases of totally

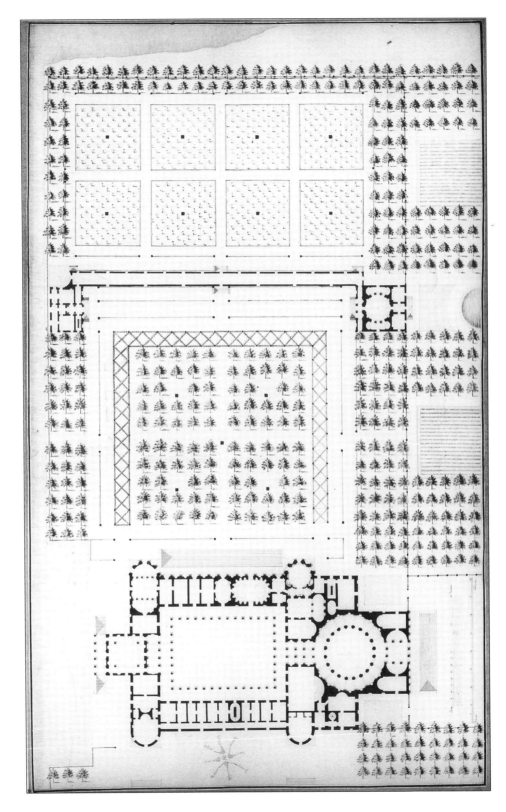

66. Potocki, Laurentine Villa, site plan (BNW, WAF 67, J. Rys. 4.999)

different widths and types. The fourth side, facing the bottom margin, has a steep drop with no stairs at all!

Within the villa's walls, variety for variety's sake also reigns supreme. Eccentric interior spaces cluster around a banal enough pair of courtyards, the first O-shaped, the second rectangular. The rotunda room, previously mentioned, occupies the top right corner, and it exemplifies the predominantly curvilinear quality of the planning. There are rooms with bombé projections, rooms with semicircular apses, rooms with apsidal ends, rooms with projections like a single ax-head, and rooms of oval form, one of them containing twin oval bathtubs. But what looks repetitious and slightly silly on plan is less so when seen in a cross section taken on the long axis of the villa (fig. 67). Here a rather lively silhouette is created by the pair of towers rising above the saucer domes of the bombé rooms and the quadriga riding atop the roofline on the seaward side. In this case a typical eighteenth-century preponderance of columns replaces the previously noted preponderance of curves. There are columnar porches at the front and the back, an engaged colonnade in the first courtyard, a peristyle in the second, and freestanding columnar screens in just about every imaginable place near the main triclinium.

Of the interiors, the triclinium received special attention from the Potocki team of collaborators, who provided a pair of drawings of the floor and ceiling, in each of which the position of the room-dividing columns is shown. The flooring pattern (fig. 68) is a brilliant contrivance in terms of design and drawing. It depicts the flooring of two rooms at once: that of the triclinium itself (lower half), and that of the apsidal room adjacent to it (upper half). Whoever drew this design had a great sense for geometric pattern and for the rich colors of marbles or terracotta—in this instance perhaps Brenna was the draftsman. The ceiling pattern, by

67. Potocki, Laurentine Villa, cross section (BNW, WAF 67, J. Rys. 5.001)

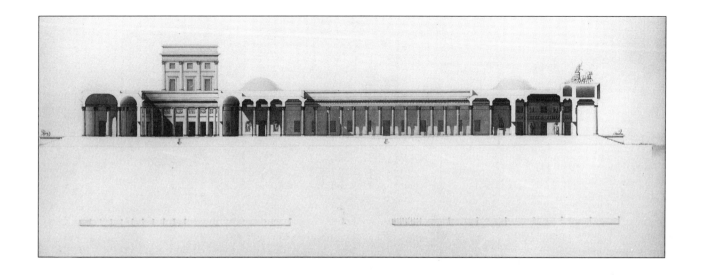

68. Potocki, Laurentine Villa,
flooring plans of triclinium
and room adjacent (BNW,
WAF 68, J. Rys. 5.032)

69. Potocki, Laurentine Villa,
ceiling of triclinium (BNW,
WAF 67, J. Rys. 5.006)

comparison (fig. 69), shows unexceptional powers of design but brilliant artistry, seen in the softness of touch in the central mythological scene. Could the painter Smuglewicz be at work here? In sharp contrast to the two previous drawings, the cross section of the same room (fig. 70) displays a perfectly ordinary conception, notwithstanding the *rosso antico* Corinthian columns arranged in screens at either end. So the three drawings just considered pose severe problems of attribution. The difficulty is compounded because of the conventions of architectural representation: the use of compass, ruler, and a minimal amount of freehand work. The draftsmanly evidence suggests that a number of different artistic hands may have been involved, and the history of architectural collaborations like Potocki's bears this out. In a project of this nature a whole team of draftsmen might conceivably be employed. This in no way diminishes the merit of so extensive a set of drawings. On the contrary, they are reproduced here in full because of their completeness,

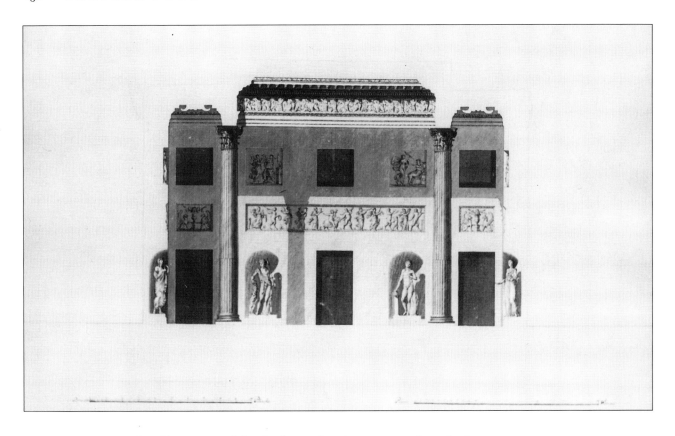

70. Potocki, Laurentine Villa, cross section of triclinium (BNW, WAF 67, J. Rys. 5.008)

their hitherto partial publication, and the freshness they have retained inside their protective portfolio.

In addition to the six drawings already considered, another seventeen dispersed throughout the two portfolios relate to the Laurentine Villa restitution. Most of them represent interiors or plans, but an initial group records the exterior appearance of the villa, facade by facade. Starting with the entrance elevation, the sheet has the peculiarity of an attached flap, here seen in the up position (fig. 71). As it is manipulated back and forth, the central saucer dome between the two tower blocks appears and disappears. Neither version entirely avoids the clash between the low-lying type of villa known from antiquity and Pliny's stipulation that his Laurentine Villa had twin towers. The wider dichotomy between Roman public and private architecture—that is, between modesty and magnificence—underlies the conflict. It concerned Potocki, who wrote about it in his manuscript "Notes." His collaborators recognized it by introducing into their design the superposed orders of architecture, though Pliny never mentioned a single column at Laurentinum, let alone two different types. Not content with their Corinthian/composite superposition, they specified an Ionic order on the facade facing the sea (fig. 72). They drew attention to it by setting it amid otherwise astylar and virtually win-

71. Potocki, Laurentine Villa, elevation of the entrance facade with flap in up position (BNW, WAF 67, J. Rys. 5.002)

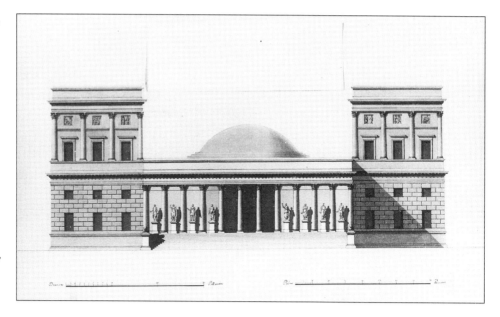

72. Potocki, Laurentine Villa, elevation of the water facade (BNW, WAF 67, J. Rys. 5.003)

dowless expanses of wall. They thus sacrificed common sense in their determination to represent the orders one by one. What possible logic could excuse a virtually blind facade on the side of the house with the best views?

Continuing in the same vein, Potocki and his collaborators employed the Roman Doric for the main garden facade (fig. 73). In this elevation details drawn to a larger scale at the bottom left and right provide more specific information about the columnar treatment. And finally, to round out the series, the last facade of the house is shown without any order at all (fig. 74). Smooth rustication replaces columns. Thus a complete circumvention of this Laurentine Villa serves the pur

73. Potocki, Laurentine Villa, elevation and details of the garden facade (BNW, WAF 67, J. Rys. 5.004)

74. Potocki, Laurentine Villa, elevation and details of the rusticated facade (BNW, WAF 67, J. Rys. 5.005)

pose of educating the viewer in the use of the orders of architecture. The conclusion seems inescapable that some didactic purpose in addition to pure restitution motivated the Laurentine series. Alexander Potocki's note on the first portfolio cover implies as much by mentioning that it once contained an extensive group of detailed drawings devoted specifically to the orders. The only one not removed by Brenna is signed and dated by Giuseppe Manocchi in 1777. It shows the capital and cornice of the Jupiter Stator temple in Rome and resembles other "mass produced" drawings that Manocchi supplied to grand tourists or traveling student architects.[57] It is not reproduced here because it has nothing specifically to do with Pliny, but it and others like it would have increased the heterogeneous aspect of the portfolios. Much the same heterogeneity applies to the appearance of the elevations themselves, with their illogical and deliberate shifts of character from facade to facade. What the elevations gain in textbooklike comprehensiveness they of course lose in design homogeneity. Nothing really matches anything else.

A ground plan of the main house (fig. 75) agrees with the site plan in every respect (cf. fig. 66) and draws attention to the interiors, drawings of which far outnumber the exterior elevations. These statistics, mute in themselves, neverthe-

75. Potocki, Laurentine Villa, plan (BNW, WAF 67, J. Rys. 5.000)

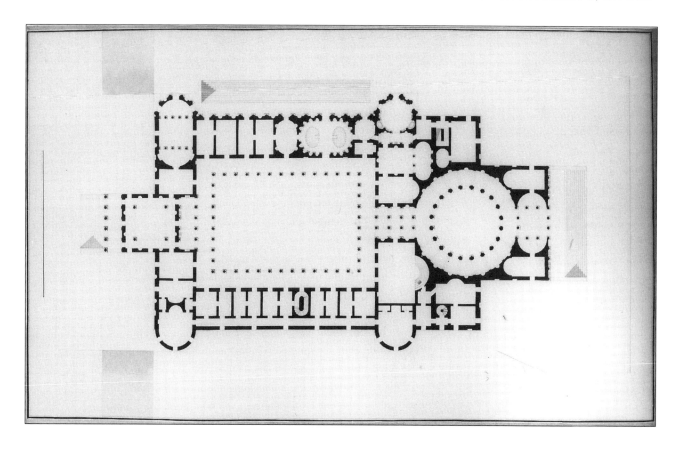

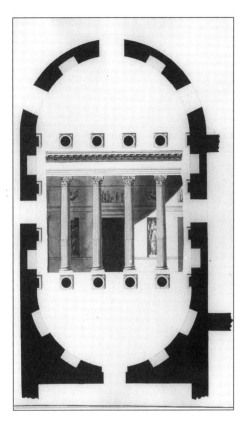

76. Potocki, Laurentine Villa, plan and elevation of room with apsidal end (BNW, WAF 67, J. Rys. 5.007)

less have a bearing on Potocki's outlook. It seems clear from his manuscript "Notes" that the interiors of ancient Roman houses concerned him particularly. He saw one of his main accomplishments as having contributed to a better understanding of the domestic life of the Romans. The rooms do not seem to have been arranged in any particular order, but for this discussion I will follow the actual sequence in the portfolios as far as possible. Thus for no apparent reason the room with the columnar screens shown on the top left of the plan receives consideration first. Two separate drawings are devoted to it. The first, numbered 9 at the bottom, is a ground plan in the center of which a nicely rendered elevation shows its Corinthian order and the alcove behind (fig. 76). Following it in the portfolio, but not numbered 10, is a cross section along the longitudinal axis of this room (fig. 77). Obviously, some relatively recent cataloger of the portfolio realized the relation between this drawing and its mate and, with the best of intentions, switched around the original placement of the loose sheets. (Stylistically this sectional drawing with its streaky yellow watercolor technique now looks a bit *hors de série*.) It is not unusual to find that the earlier and later numbering systems on the sheets do not follow the same sequence. Nor is that the only area of disagreement. The raised

77. Potocki, Laurentine Villa, cross section of the room with apsidal end (BNW, WAF 67, J. Rys. 5.008)

barrel vault of the central ceiling shown in the cross section does not appear at all in the related elevation (cf. fig. 72).

Next in order comes the large elliptical bath with two sunken tubs in the middle of the floor and an elaborate composite order around the walls (fig. 78). Potocki's "Notes" marveled especially at the imperial baths, which he regarded as the greatest proof of Roman magnificence.[58] On the corresponding ground plan, numbered 10, what receives attention this time is a doorframe incorporating the image of a well-known bas-relief of a spread eagle from the church of Santi Apostoli in Rome (fig. 79). A separate sheet of flooring patterns (fig. 80) gives that of the bath above and that of what seems to be the rotunda room below. The rotunda, in turn, merits a ground plan of its own (fig. 81) to go along with the flooring pattern and the stunning interior previously discussed (cf. pl. 35). Once again there is a detail, and it suggests that the frieze from the Temple of Antoninus and Faustina in Rome served as the model. Previous drawings had similarly singled out the Vitruvian scroll as a stringcourse motif (cf. fig. 73), or a sculpted *capo di bove* frieze based on the one at the Caecilia Metella tomb just outside Rome (cf. fig. 74). So Potocki's Laurentine restitution doubles as a compendium of approved classical motifs, blown up for closer inspection of large-scale details. The villa seems to have been assembled piecemeal by designers who found their ideas by flipping through a book of engravings, a collection of drawings, or loose Piranesi prints. This additive method of designing agrees exactly with the one Potocki

78. Potocki, Laurentine Villa, cross section of the baths (BNW, WAF 67, J. Rys. 5.010)

79. Potocki, Laurentine
Villa, plan and elevation
detail of baths (BNW,
WAF 67, J. Rys. 5.009)

80. Potocki, Laurentine Villa,
flooring plans of the baths
and round room (BNW,
WAF 68, J. Rys. 5.034)

81. Potocki, Laurentine Villa,
plan and elevation detail of
round room (BNW, WAF 67,
J. Rys. 5.011)

advocated in his manuscript written several decades later. He stated that he had taken inspiration from the Roman baths, the Pantheon, the Colosseum, the temples in the Forum Romanum, and the ornamental interiors excavated around the Bay of Naples or at the Baths of Titus in Rome. "C'est ainsi," he wrote, "that by assembling the finest remains of Roman architecture, and by embellishing the villa of Pliny with them, I believe I have done justice to the pure taste of the century of Trajan and to that of one of the great men who illuminated that age."[59]

Presumably the Roman baths and the archaeological remains excavated around Naples provided Potocki with the inspiration for the unusual room shapes of which he was apparently so enamored. The most eccentric of them all took a form analogous to either a handle and ax-head or a cork in a bottleneck. The Potocki team produced a plan of just such a room in the villa (fig. 82) and included it on the right half of one of their ingenious combined flooring patterns (fig. 83). The left half relates to the double-ax-head room in an outlying garden pavilion, of which there exists a separate plan and elevation (fig. 84). Externally it resembles a highminded version of something that Claude-Nicolas Ledoux or François-Joseph Bélanger might have designed for a French royal mistress or an exotic dancer. Potocki must have taken considerable pride in this piece of design, because his team produced three plans of it in all. The third focuses on the double-ax-head room itself with its Corinthian pilasters matching in type and height the order on the outside (fig. 85)—an all too rare instance of congruence within Potocki's Laurentine restitution. Not coincidentally, perhaps, the compact proportions and general look of the pavilion recur in the summerhouse begun in 1780 by Szymon Zug at Natolin outside Warsaw. Brenna got the job of decorating the inside on the recommendation of Potocki, a kindness he repaid by absconding with some of his

82. (*Below, left*) Potocki, Laurentine Villa, plan and elevation details of single-ax-head room (BNW, WAF 67, J. Rys. 5.017)

83. (*Below, right*) Potocki, Laurentine Villa, flooring plans of single- and double-ax-head rooms (BNW, WAF 68, J. Rys. 5.033)

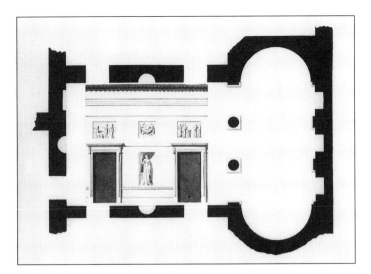

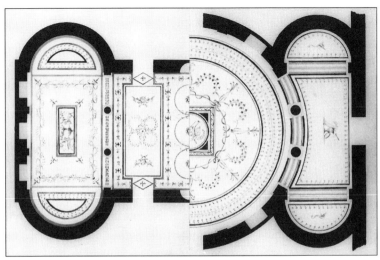

84. Potocki, Laurentine Villa, plan and elevation of pavilion with double-ax-head room (BNW, WAF 67, J. Rys. 5.020)

85. Potocki, Laurentine Villa, plan and elevation detail of double-ax-head room (BNW, WAF 67, J. Rys. 5.021)

patron's drawings. But in the end Potocki had a kind of bittersweet revenge. In 1808 he and his lifelong architectural collaborator Chrystian Piotr Aigner completely remodeled Natolin, sweeping away all of Brenna's interiors.[60]

A rusticated cryptoporticus connects the two garden pavilions in Potocki's restitution. The complex drawing of it (fig. 86), combining a plan and elevation with cross sections, shares with the rest a banality of exterior design in contrast to lavish interior decoration. The painted decoration is of the grotesque type popular in antiquity and fashionable again after its rediscovery in the Renaissance. In the eighteenth century Charles-Louis Clérisseau and his pupils, the Scottish Adam brothers, revived the vogue for this light and colorful repertoire of decorative motifs. Most of Potocki's Laurentine interiors, with their heavy, architectonic character, lagged stolidly behind the prevalent fashion in the 1770s. The cryptoporticus, however, is an exception to the rule, although not the only one among the thirty-five surviving drawings. In fact, there are a number of others[61]—the very ones most often exhibited and reproduced in connection with Potocki's Laurentine Villa.

86. Potocki, Laurentine Villa, plan, elevation, and cross sections of cryptoporticus (BNW, WAF 67, J. Rys. 5.024)

87. Potocki, Laurentine Villa, plan and elevation of the water facade of pavilion with *heliocaminus* (BNW, WAF 67, J. Rys. 5.022)

Ironically, not a single one fits with any part of the Laurentine scheme whatever. According to my analysis, all eight drawings in this group relate to a bombé-fronted pavilion design that in many ways complements the Pliny project. Undoubtedly produced by the same hands about the same time, it is nonetheless alien to the Laurentine restitution. Together with three disparate sheets that cannot be linked to either scheme,[62] this reduces the total number of drawings demonstrably connected with the Laurentine Villa to twenty-three, just as Potocki claimed.

One final drawing of the twenty-three remains for consideration (fig. 87). It is a curious plan and elevation of the second of Pliny's outlying pavilions, the one closest to the sea. Its asymmetry, so atypical of this restitution, derives from a

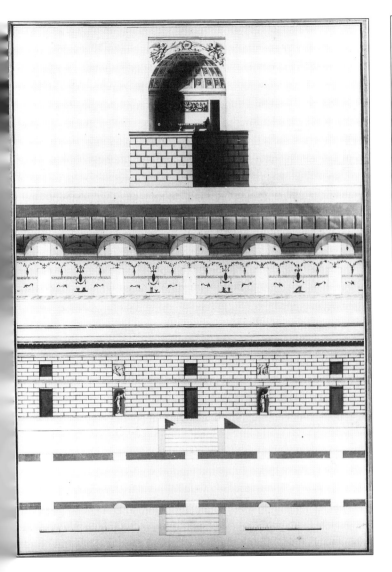

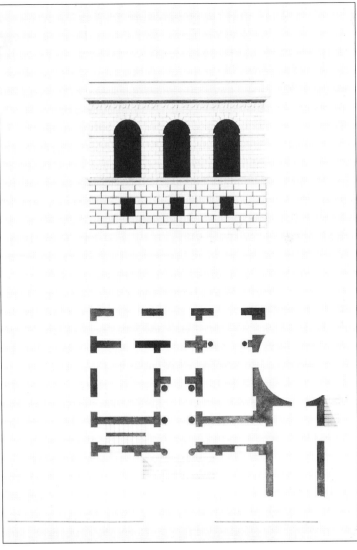

socketlike semicircular projection standing open as if a wing had been wrenched off. This must be the *heliocaminus,* or solarium, about which Potocki made some interesting remarks in his "Notes." He explained that a *heliocaminus* had been pointed out to him among some ruins on the road from Rome to Tivoli by "Monsieur Orlandi scavant Antiquaire." According to what he told Potocki, it was "a type of semicircular vaulted niche arranged in such a way as to keep off the burning sun and to provide shelter from strong winds."[63] The name of this Italian antiquary and the date of his encounter with Potocki are uncertain. But surely the event must precede the Laurentine Villa restitution, because Potocki faithfully included Orlandi's ideas in his plan. Of what significance is this incident? It further goes to show that Potocki himself masterminded the design of the Laurentine Villa restitution that he paid others to draw. Indebted to architects, artists, and antiquaries though he undoubtedly was, he may now rightly take chief credit as the instigator of what ranks as one of the most remarkable Pliny restitutions of them all. Had his words and images appeared in print, as it seems likely Potocki intended, the impact on international neoclassicism might have been considerable.[64] In keeping with the grand procession of earlier schemes reviewed in this chapter, Potocki's sought to reconcile the ancients with the moderns by resolving the eternal dilemma of artistic convention as opposed to artistic freedom.

CHAPTER FIVE

Lectures and Exhibitions

FOR THE BETTER PART of the eighteenth century, the French Académie Royale d'Architecture observed in the breach its prior claims on Pliny, dating back to the days of the younger Félibien des Avaux (chap. 4). During that one hundred years, the institution shifted away from the clublike atmosphere in which Félibien had debated the merits of Scamozzi's Pliny restitution before a chosen few. It became instead the foremost school for teaching architecture to young people. The transformation was almost entirely due to a second-rate architect who happened to be a first-rate pedagogue: Jacques-François Blondel (1705–74). Despite having an uncle who had risen in the profession to become an academician, Blondel did not attain the same distinction until 1755. His professional peers initially regarded him as something of a renegade because, without academy blessing, in 1743 he had set up a rival private school, the Ecole des Arts, on the rue de la Harpe in Paris. The para-academic course of studies he taught there soon achieved the outstanding reputation it deserved. A string of his distinguished early graduates such as William Chambers, Marie-Joseph Peyre, Etienne-Louis Boullée, and Claude-Nicolas Ledoux testified to what they had learned from their teacher. Blondel's appointment to the architecture professorship at the academy in 1762 must have seemed a foregone conclusion.

Blondel was the first truly distinguished theoretician to occupy the architectural chair at the academy since its first occupant, François Blondel. Like his earlier namesake, Blondel published his academic lectures as a *Cours d'architecture* (Paris, 1771–77). In the first volume he revealed the secret of his success at the Ecole des Arts, the same tactic he instituted almost immediately upon assuming his duties at the academy. It consisted of staging an almost unremitting series of competitions called *prix d'émulation*. In effect these *prix d'émulation* served as exercises in the proper characterization, or *caractère*, necessary to differentiate one building from another according to its use. He simultaneously hammered away at the concept of *caractère* in his lectures to the students. Practical exercises at the drafting board thus reinforced the lessons heard in the classroom.

Every month a problem would be set in the form of a written *programme*, spelling out the detailed requirements for that month's *prix d'émulation*. The subject matter might cover almost any building type; the students never knew in advance, so the anticipation kept them on pins and needles. The drawings they produced were then exhibited before a jury of academicians and judged for the first prize, a silver medal. This increasing pressure on students toughened them up for the similar but more protracted Grand Prix de Rome competition, consisting of a gold medal awarded annually. (Haudebourt and Bouchet both tried unsuccessfully for this prize.) With the gold medal came the even more dazzling prospect of a chance at a royal scholarship to Rome. Blondel's system mastered the psychology of surprise, secrecy, ambition to excel, and the intimidation attendant on open scrutiny of the final designs by the leaders of the profession. No wonder the Grand Prix de Rome established itself as the premier and most redoubtable architectural competition the Western world has so far devised.[1]

Blondel's *Cours d'architecture* makes no reference to Pliny the Younger, but in retrospect it seems inevitable that in their quest for subject matter the *prix d'émulation* would eventually come around to the villa restitution theme. As will be seen, this finally took place in the *concours d'émulation* of November 1818, just at the point when the Académie des Beaux-Arts handed over many of its teaching functions to the separate Ecole des Beaux-Arts. Antoine-Laurent-Thomas Vaudoyer (1756–1846) masterminded the *programme* of 1818, after temporarily stepping in to replace the recently deceased professor Léon Dufourny.[2] The pedagogue in Vaudoyer spotted the innate possibilities of transforming a Pliny letter into a ready-made academic set piece, complete down to the smallest detail. Probably the notion came to Vaudoyer from several sources. One might have been his ruminating over the writings of Félibien, whose role as secretary Vaudoyer came to fill in the newly founded Ecole. But the connection to Blondel emerges as equally important, because Vaudoyer had studied at the Académie Royale with Julien-David Leroy, the archaeologist-professor who succeeded Blondel and expanded on his historicist and rationalist theories. Leroy's ideas as assimilated by Vaudoyer are best reflected in the work of another former Leroy student, Jean-Nicolas-Louis Durand (1760–1834).

Durand referred back to his teacher's history lessons in his own architectural lectures at the newly established Ecole Polytechnique, the state-run engineering school. In 1799, four years after his appointment as professor, he began publishing his unusual lecture diagrams under the title *Recueil et parallèle des édifices de tout genre, anciens et modernes . . . dessinés sur une même échelle*.[3] Plate 44 is typical of his remarkably innovative if spare-looking approach to architectural representation. The plate also has a direct bearing on the villas of Pliny, to which Durand was the first since Félibien to turn attention in the French academic context (fig. 88). On the perfectly neutral background, Durand grouped together plans and cross sections of Roman houses according to such authorities as Vitruvius, Palladio, and Scamozzi. In graphic terms, he based himself on Leroy's ideas as first displayed in a booklet of 1764 titled *Histoire de la disposition et des formes différentes que les Chrétiens ont données à leurs temples depuis le règne de Constantin le Grand*

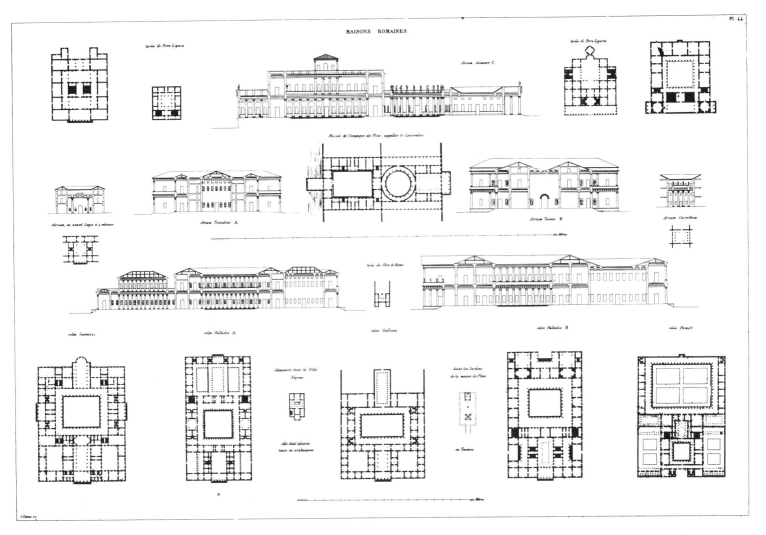

88. Durand, *parallèle* of roman houses (Durand, *Recueil et parallèle des édifices de tout genres*)

jusqu'à nous . . . . This publication had placed the ground plans of numerous religious structures side by side on a single plate so as to compare them at a glance. Durand followed suit and further elaborated the aspect of uniform scale by adopting a dry presentation that would not impede the eye in quickly scanning the page. Thus schematized and reduced almost to the size of postage stamps, the diverse images had a certain rationale and homogeneity imposed on them.

At the top center of his plate Durand included the plan and section of the Laurentine Villa after Scamozzi. Slightly to the right of bottom center, so tiny as almost to be missed, Durand added the plan of the Tuscan Villa's *stibadium* after Félibien (fig. 177). Strange as it may seem, the text accompanying the Durand plate makes no reference to these historical sources, as if the viewer had heard it all before. In a sense this was precisely the case, considering that Durand's initial audience consisted in large part of his students at the *Polytechnique*.[4] From the beginning, Durand intended them to consult the *Recueil* alongside his lectures, which began appearing in print in 1802 as *Précis des leçons d'architecture . . . .* The text of the one has cross-references to the images in the other. A first volume of the *Précis* deals with basic building blocks of architecture and general rules of composition. The second volume starts with public buildings and then turns to private residences, moving down the social scale from the palatial town house to the rustic farm. Toward the end of this volume comes a particularly lengthy section on villas; lengthy in part because of the sections of Pliny letters to Gallus and Apollinaris quoted in translation.

Durand preceded the excerpts he took from Pliny's correspondence with observations about the peace and quiet of a villa that have an almost Plinian ring: "S'il est quelque lieu où l'on puisse se flatter de trouver le bonheur," he wrote, "c'est incontestablement dans une maison de campagne agréablement située, loin du tracas des affaires, du tumulte des villes, des vices inséparables des sociétés trop nombreuses." Then on the next page he went on to provide his explanation for including such extensive quotations: "Pliny's descriptions of his Laurentine and Tuscan houses are the only literary monuments that can make us understand the spirit in which the country houses of the ancients were composed; but these rich remnants are well suited to guide us in the composition of our own country houses." Durand practiced what he preached from the podium. He favored country houses above other built forms in his small but significant oeuvre. Several compact villas he designed in the vicinity of Paris have the desirable *caractère* of "simplicity" that he implied he had learned from a study of their counterparts in antiquity.[5]

To return to the Académie des Beaux-Arts in 1818, Vaudoyer and Durand knew one another as fellow students and admirers of Leroy.[6] Vaudoyer could have heard Durand's Polytechnique lectures or read them in print by the time he proposed the restitution of Pliny's Laurentine Villa as the subject for a *prix d'émulation* in November of that year. His précis of the letter to Gallus indicates a sharp editorial eye and an equally sharp red pencil. Using words very similar to Durand's, Vaudoyer stripped away Pliny's horticultural information. The garden descriptions that had so impressed Félibien and had given his restitution its special charm were systematically expunged in an attempt to render the letter more architectural—and less atmospheric. In effect, the Vaudoyer *programme* became the verbal counterpart of Durand's bone-dry illustrations. In so doing Vaudoyer missed many of Pliny's nuances. For example, Vaudoyer ascribed the villa to Mustius, thereby ignoring any role the client might have played in its design. After taking these liberties with the form and meaning of the Pliny text, Vaudoyer's written *programme* continues by noting the scale for students' use, listing the four drawings they must produce, and prescribing a 150-meter dimension for the circular courtyard—Pliny had specified no size. It affirms the total absence of archaeological remains and suggests that the students treat this as a challenge to exercise their imaginations based on a literary description. The *programme* goes on to hint strongly at bilateral symmetry by suggesting that a matching wing for the accommodation of the villa's offices should balance the cryptoporticus. In a situation like this, the potential candidates ignored any such hints at their peril. Of the twenty contestants, the projects of only a handful can be verified by surviving drawings. In every case, however, the designs are perfectly symmetrical.[7]

According to Vaudoyer's manuscript records of 1819, the same year the Ecole des Beaux-Arts got its definitive name, the jury met on 4 January to see the contestants' drawings and pass on them. It took three ballots among the twenty-four voting academicians to award first prize to the project of Achille Normand, a pupil of Charles Percier. At this point in the meeting the jury decided to award two more prizes, since the November 1818 *prix d'émulation* had been the last of the year and medals were left over. After two or more ballots a second prize went to another Percier pupil, Pascal Lepage. It would have been a clean sweep for the Percier atelier had not the professor Louis-Pierre Baltard broken a deadlocked vote in favor of Amable Macquet instead of another Percier student named Jacob. Amazingly enough, after nearly 1,800 years Pliny's letter could still inspire this kind of creative activity and passionate debate in academic circles at Europe's leading arts institution. Nor did the matter rest behind closed doors as had happened at the academy in the previous century. With a view to wider dissemination, Baltard and Vaudoyer jointly published prizewinning projects covering the years 1808–31 and included among them the Laurentine restitutions of Macquet and Normand. Lepage was somehow overlooked.[8]

The third-prize winner Amable Macquet (1790–1865), a pupil of Delespine, delivered a cautious restitution plan, reproduced here in the form illustrated by Baltard and Vaudoyer in 1834 (fig. 89). It takes few risks. It lays out the whole villa and includes the surrounding gardens in answer to Vaudoyer's invitation to redesign them according to the students' own tastes. (For this reason the letter to Gallus suited Vaudoyer's purposes best, because it called for a perfectly flat site of the academically preferred type.) The proportions are good between the parts and the whole, which is strictly symmetrical, in accordance with the wishes implied in the *programme*. On plan, at least, it obeys the same academic conventions that had governed Vaudoyer and Percier when they placed first and second in the 1783 Grand Prix competition. It would not be at all out of character for a student of the Ecole like Macquet to look at what the judges of his scheme had themselves produced in the past, in the hope of currying favor. Of the three medalists he stuck the closest to Félibien's restitution, which, along with Scamozzi's, was mentioned in the preamble to the Vaudoyer *programme*. This guarded and retrospective attitude

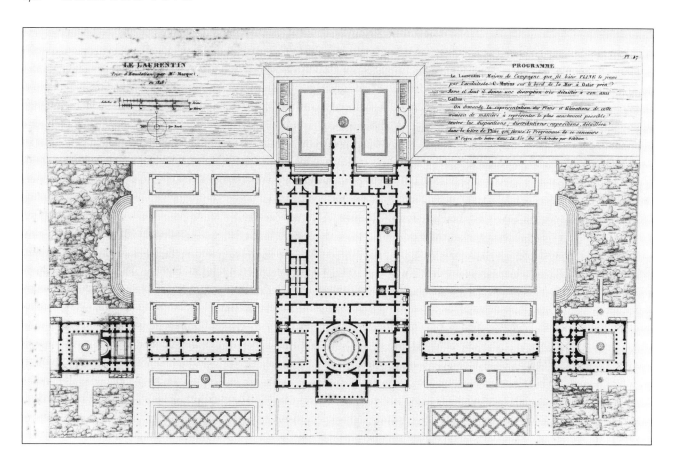

89. Macquet, Laurentine Villa, plan (Vaudoyer and Baltard, *Grands prix d'architecture*)

on the part of Beaux-Arts teaching has received the harshest treatment at the hands of its many critics. Considering that Macquet was twenty-eight at the time and the eldest of the three medalists, he produced an uninspiring if typically grand-scale performance.

Several further considerations reduced Macquet's chances at the first prize. The front and back elevations (fig. 90) feature corner and central blocks that project jarringly from the otherwise unrelieved surfaces of the facades. If the designs of the winner and runner-up are any indication, the judges had a preference for curved forms over the rectangular ones Macquet used exclusively except in the O-shaped courtyard. The cross section through the Laurentine Villa (fig. 91) resembles a typical Pompeian house of the sort that interested Haudebourt and Mazois about the same time (cf. fig. 34). Here Macquet displayed the highly controlled draftsmanship carried out in the painstaking French wash technique to create the impression of advance and recession by means of cast shadows. But nasty ink spots on the bottom left of the section and right in the middle of the

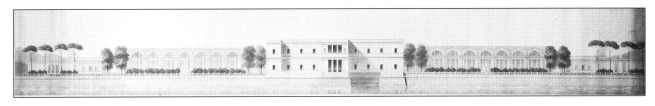

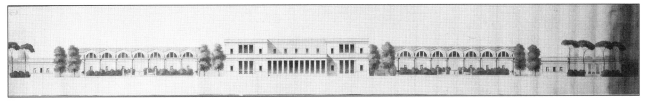

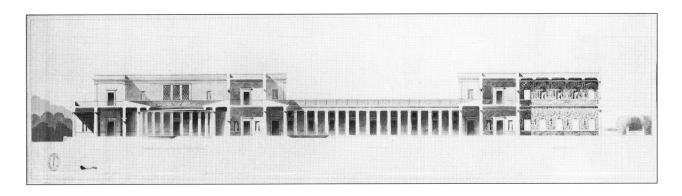

90. (*top two views*) Macquet, Laurentine Villa, elevations of entrance and water facades (EBA)

91. (*above*) Macquet, Laurentine Villa, cross section (EVA)

plan spoil the sought-after flawless appearance, suggesting last-minute haste to make the competition deadline—the moment of the charette dreaded by generations of Ecole students and their present-day counterparts. All this must have detracted from Macquet's chances in the eyes of the jury.[9] Contrary to what they might have predicted, however, he went on to distinguish himself as a practicing architect beyond either of the other winners. Distinction at the Ecole did not always predict a brilliant career outside its rarefied setting.

Pascal Lepage (1792–1869), runner-up in the November 1818 *prix d'émulation*, got himself promoted to first-class status in the Ecole on the strength of his performance. He never distinguished himself further academically, but went into public service as a government architect in the Paris area. Although he built less than Macquet, he escaped banishment from the artistic capital—still a bête noire among practitioners in France to this day (see chap. 6). Lepage's Laurentine Villa restitution has a charming delicacy lacking in the others. The villa's height diminishes progressively from the imposing entrance facade (fig. 92, bottom) through the central courtyard and down to a relatively simple elevation facing the rocky shoreline (fig. 92, top right). Greater interaction between natural and architectural ele-

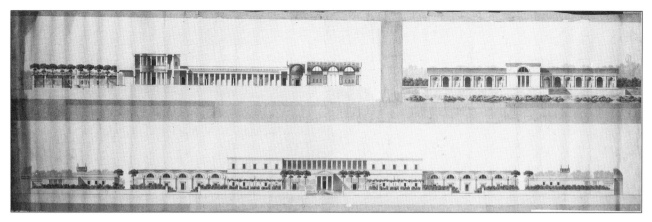

92. Lepage, Laurentine Villa, elevations of entrance and water facades, and cross section (EBA)

93. Normand, Laurentine Villa, elevation of water facade and cross section (EBA)

ments is expressed by numerous plants and small trees (fig. 92, top left). For all the plan's breadth, the house occupies only about a third of the entire surface (pl. 36). The overall *H* configuration of the villa departs most from the Félibien proto-type. Within the generally rectangular confines of the walls the room spaces are richly articulated. Nevertheless, there is an immature overreliance on all manner of indentations that give the plan a pinched look. Having to negotiate so many rooms with partitions *en enfilade* would be like passing through one bottleneck after another. Lepage's plan shared this penchant for axial planning and for colum-nar screens with the Laurentine restitution of Potocki (fig. 66).

The amplitude and spatial complexity of the Laurentine Villa by Achille Normand (1802–60) are rather remarkable coming from a sixteen-year-old (pl. 37). What may explain the plan's virtuosity is that the designer was from a family of architects. His father, Charles, produced the well-known *Nouveau parallèle des ordres* in Paris the same year that his son won the first prize. Earlier he had engraved for Durand the plate with the Scamozzi and Félibien restitutions (cf. fig. 88). So in a sense young Normand had a head start in the race for the *prix d'émulation*. Whereas Lepage's central courtyard had tentatively dared to break with the perfect circle, Normand's boldly carved out four deep, diagonally placed exedras. Two more exedras occur in the fountain-filled grounds. Moreover, the main triclinium thrusts out to sea, with curving flights of steps leading down to the water's edge (fig. 93, top). The other contestants had used thermal windows, but only Normand achieved their harmonious integration with the axial planning and spatial majesty that also belonged by rights to the Roman baths (fig. 93, bottom). The skyline works the opposite way from Lepage's by rising as the building moves back toward the seafront. Normand lowered the entrance facade to allow a view of the dramatically scooped-out rear wall of the central court, thus announcing from afar the underlying curves that repeat themselves throughout his building (fig. 94). The meticulous draftsmanship here, precise down to the depiction of the individual roof tiles, simply proves that the Ecole rated presentation almost as highly as ingenious planning and composition. The prodigy Normand subsequently tried twice for the Grand Prix without achieving it, and he eventually settled down to a career in government service. He built relatively little. Within its narrow frame of reference the Ecole could spot such a budding genius, but it could not always foster—and could sometimes stifle—the other special qualities needed for distinction: determination, originality, and willingness to experiment.

Leroy, Durand, Vaudoyer, Percier, Baltard, Normand—all these names conjure up the picture of Beaux-Arts classicism at the early peak of its unchallenged supremacy. The name of Pliny must now be added to the list as a sort of fellow traveler. His letters provided academically minded architects with additional ammunition to defend their concept of what good architecture should be: balanced, symmetrical, evenly proportioned, harmonious inside and out, suited to its use, beautifully drawn, understated in design yet vast in scale. Above all, architecture

94. Normand, Laurentine Villa, elevation of entrance facade (EBA)

would occupy some Platonic plateau of the imagination devoid of problems. Flat, calm, unruffled by wind or weather, it would take on an ideal dimension. As seen in 1818, however, a definite sameness occurred in the end products of the three winners. Not only did they emulate the precedent of Félibien, but they echoed each other's work. It is as if the walls of the cubicles separating the students were transparent.

As the nineteenth century progressed in France, the restitutions of Haudebourt and Bouchet show a flexibility missing from the *concours d'émulation*.[10] Their flurry of renewed publication of Pliny no doubt had a bearing on his next appearance in the Ecole des Beaux-Arts lecture room. It took place in 1864 under the unlikely aegis of the professor of art history, Eugène-Emmanuel Viollet-le-Duc (1814–79), who turned Pliny to very different ends than had his predecessors. Viollet-le-Duc's controversial and short-lived professorship at the Ecole came about as a result of the proposed reforms of 1862 undertaken by the arts administrators of the Second Empire. Things got off to a bad start because he was an outsider—that is, not a former student of the institution—and hence deemed unsympathetic to its traditions. In 1857 he had set up an independent atelier in which he delivered a series of *entretiens,* as he called them, which became the basis for his course of lectures at the Ecole seven years later. The first four came out in print in 1858; others, ten in all, followed in 1863 and constituted the first volume of his *Entretiens sur l'architecture.*[11] In his survey stretching from prehistoric times to his own day, Viollet-le-Duc devoted the fifth lecture to comparison between the public and domestic buildings of the ancients. The letters of Pliny contribute their part, almost to the same extent as with Durand. Although they are quoted less fully, the analysis of them is more probing. With words that echo Durand's, Viollet-le-Duc called the letter to Gallus "un des monuments le plus curieux qui existent." In contrast to the monumental structures of Roman antiquity, Pliny's letters, he observed, make no reference whatever to symmetry. In fact they preclude it by emphasizing orientation, the juxtaposition of rooms, and the opening up of vistas. They do not even mention the orders or interior decoration, which played right into the hands of Viollet-le-Duc's structurally and technologically based analysis of architecture, so totally opposed to Durand's interpretation.[12]

Viollet-le-Duc went on to state that in domestic architecture the Romans sought release from the formality of the public sphere and above all craved the good hygiene, ventilation, heating, and sanitation that a free-flowing plan could provide far better than some set of rules, or *formules de convention,* as he described them. He ridiculed with great effect the rigid rationalism and unyielding Platonism of his predecessors at the Ecole by implying that theirs was an antiquity decked out in the wigs and high-heeled shoes of the court of Louis XIV. (Pliny, who had named his Como villas after footwear, would have appreciated the analogy.) True antiquity, Viollet-le-Duc said, had a thoroughly practical side oriented to creature comfort. This is not to say that he overlooked the poetic side of Pliny. He quoted at length from the "charming" description of the Laurentine Villa and mentioned the Tuscan Villa on account of its delightful gardens. He saw the way the two formed a contrasting pair, each in tune with its particular setting rather than obedient to some immutable law. Then he singled out for special note the *amores mei* pavilion as "le lieu préféré par Pline." Here the sentiments of another architectural outsider, William Newton, come to mind. Like him, Viollet-le-Duc concentrated his attention on the *cabinet de travail* and the closed-off room for naps. In that sense, perhaps, he had penetrated closer to the core of Pliny's studious philosophy than most. Viollet-le-Duc concluded that the *amores mei* supported his diatribe against the ancients' supposed love of symmetry: "Pline n'est pas si fou que de songer à la symétrie en tout ceci, et de se gêner chez lui pour montrer des façades régulières aux passants."[13]

Violett-le-Duc had written "I love study, I hate noise" in response to the acrimonious debate surrounding his *Entretiens*. But he could not easily escape to some villa to avoid the verbal attacks of his detractors in the Ecole. They swore to disrupt the delivery of his lectures, and they succeeded. Ironically, they swore their oath against Viollet-le-Duc on a copy of Durand—the academic Bible—little realizing that the two lecturers had in common their admiration of Pliny.[14] Two of the ringleaders, Julien Guadet (1834–1908) and Jean-Louis Pascal (1837–1920), went on to distinguish themselves at the Ecole. Guadet became a professor and published his collected lectures in four volumes under the title *Eléments et théorie de l'architecture* (Paris, 1901–4). They replaced Durand's *Précis* in popularity and influence. Pascal became the patron of the most prestigious atelier of his day and a kind of living legend by the time of his death. The combined force of their personalities cannot be overestimated.

A typical if little-known case in support of such an assertion would be the Canadian architect Ernest Cormier, who had progressed through the Ecole before departing for a triumphant two years at the British School at Rome (chap. 2). Cormier owned and avidly studied Guadet's *Eléments* while enrolled in the Pascal atelier from 1909 to 1913. A *diplômé* of the Ecole in 1917, he returned to his native city of Montreal directly after the First World War. In 1925 he assumed the duties of architecture professor at Montreal's Ecole Polytechnique engineering school, from which he eventually retired after thirty-one years' successful teaching. The books he had a habit of distributing to students as prizes included copies of the *Eléments,* but also of Auguste Choisy's two-volume *Histoire de l'architecture* (Paris, 1899).[15] Choisy's many publications distinguish him as a disciple of Viollet-le-Duc's structuralist approach to architectural aesthetics and history. In Cormier, therefore, the two enemy camps of French architectural theory somehow find a peaceful resolution.

When dealing with Roman villas, Auguste Choisy introduced the topic of Pliny's villas from the *Entretiens,* but in a cursory manner. Unlike his mentor Viollet-le-Duc, he demurred at delving into Pliny because he felt the subject more appropriate to archaeologists than architects.[16] This volte-face did not discourage Cormier, who went about incorporating the Pliny villas into his lectures regardless. His mimeographed outlines survive, and although intended for spontaneous expostulation from the rostrum, they make two points quite clear: they reek of Guadet and Pascal, and like many a lecturer's yellowed notes, they remained impervious to change or improvement over the long duration of their annual delivery. A slide list indicates that Cormier projected an image of the Laurentine and Tuscan villas one after the other. The slides themselves seem to have disappeared from his otherwise amazingly complete archive. But an early pencil note makes possible almost certain identification of at least the Laurentine restitution that Cormier referred to.[17] In his forward-looking way, he chose one of the most up-to-date he could find—that of the German archaeologist Hermann Winnefeld, published in 1891 and still regarded as a reliable restitution.[18] Since the Winnefeld article in question proposes both Laurentine and Tuscan restitutions at once, it is likely that these images are the ones Cormier's students saw on the screen (fig. 95). The plans spoke for themselves. Despite their diagrammatic and lifeless quality, they showed relatively small, mostly asymmetrical villa buildings of no particular architectural distinction. In a way the vindication of Viollet-le-Duc over Durand was now complete. Certainly Winnefeld's archaeologically inspired scheme differs greatly from those entered in the 1818 *concours d'émulation.* In the final analysis, however, it is Pliny's perennial appeal to French-speaking lecturers from 1800 until 1956 that stands out as truly remarkable.

Meanwhile, in 1769 the Royal Academy of Arts came into existence across the English Channel, nearly a century later than its French sister institutions. Jacques-François Blondel's former pupil William Chambers (1723–96) established the personal link between the Paris and London academies—he served simultaneously as a corresponding member of the Académie Royale d'Architecture and as founding secretary of its British counterpart. As the Francophone and Francophile architectural tutor to George III, Chambers stood in the perfect position to influence the formation of the Academy, secure it a royal charter, and put a French stamp on it. Chambers notwithstanding, several major differences did occur in the structure and teaching practices adopted in London as opposed to Paris. For one thing, the British artists did not believe in separating the arts or the sexes. The original forty men and women members included painters, sculptors, and architects. Teaching the young remained central to their mandate, but the system of gold and silver medals changed considerably. The gold-medal competitions—the equivalent of the Parisian Grand Prix—took place biennially, and silver medals

95. Winnefeld, Laurentine and Tuscan villas, plans (*continued overleaf; line drawing from Winnefeld, "Tusci und Laurentinum des jüngeren Plinius"*)

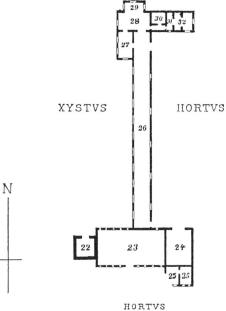

XYSTVS   HORTVS

HORTVS

RVSTICVS

N

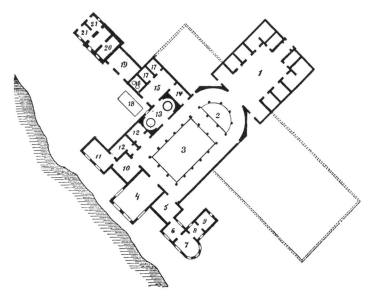

1. Atrium.
2. Area.
3. Cavaedium.
4. Triclinium.
5. Cubiculum amplum.
6. Cubiculum minus.
7. Cubiculum in hapsida curvatum.
8. Transitus.
9. Dormitorium membrum.
10. Cubiculum politissimum.
11. Cubiculum grande.
12. Cubiculum cum procoetone.
13. Cella frigidaria.
14. Unctorium.
15. Hypocauston.
16. Propnigeon.
17. Cellae.
18. Piscina.
19. Sphaeristerium.
20. Turris.
21. Diaetae duo.
22. Turris.
23. Apotheca.
24. Triclinium.
25. Diaetae duo.
26. Cryptoporticus.
27. Heliocaminus.
28. Cubiculum.
29. Zotheca.
30. Cubiculum noctis.
31. Hypocauston.
32. Procoeton et cubiculum.

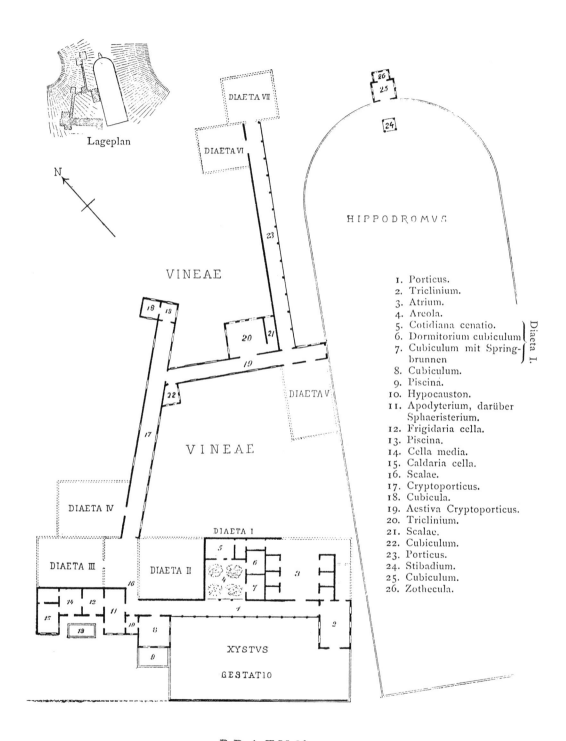

Lageplan

N

DIAETA VII

DIAETA VI

HIPPODROMVS

VINEAE

18 | 19

20 | 21

19

DIAETA V

22

17

VINEAE

DIAETA IV

DIAETA I

DIAETA III

DIAETA II

16

14 | 12

15

13

11

10

8

9

XYSTVS

GESTATIO

PRATVM

1. Porticus.
2. Triclinium.
3. Atrium.
4. Areola.
5. Cotidiana cenatio.
6. Dormitorium cubiculum
7. Cubiculum mit Spring-
   brunnen
8. Cubiculum.
9. Piscina.
10. Hypocauston.
11. Apodyterium, darüber
    Sphaeristerium.
12. Frigidaria cella.
13. Piscina.
14. Cella media.
15. Caldaria cella.
16. Scalae.
17. Cryptoporticus.
18. Cubicula.
19. Aestiva Cryptoporticus.
20. Triclinium.
21. Scalae.
22. Cubiculum.
23. Porticus.
24. Stibadium.
25. Cubiculum.
26. Zothecula.

Diaeta I.

alternated with them every other year, a practice that varied greatly from Blondel's monthly system of *concours d'émulation*. What differentiated the Royal Academy most from the Académie Royale d'Architecture, however, was the exhibition of student work before the art-loving public rather than just a jury of academicians. In this respect the English modeled themselves on the distinct but related biennial exhibitions, or salons, of the Académie Royale de Peinture et de Sculpture. In London the affair became annual, and an enormously successful moneymaking venture at that. Cash receipts netted from admissions and catalog sales rendered the Royal Academy financially independent of king and state to an extent undreamed of among the French.

On the walls of the third, or 1771, annual spring exhibition in London hung the recent work of Edward Stevens (1744–75), a gifted former apprentice of Chambers who had been elected one of the Academy's first associate members the year before. He exhibited a plan and entrance elevation for what the catalog describes as "the (Roman Villa) Laurentinum of Pliny the Consul, as described in the epistle to his friend Gallus."[19] As far as is known this is the first restitution of a Pliny villa ever put on public display. Unfortunately, it passed unnoticed in the popular London press, which in any event prejudicially favored reporting on paintings and sculptures as being more newsworthy. Because Stevens died four years later at Rome without ever publishing his designs, this one languishes in the same obscurity as the Pliny restitutions by Lazzari and Potocki. Even more than theirs, however, his deserves not to be overlooked (pl. 38). On grounds of originality alone it ranks high. The design's strict symmetry is commonplace enough in academic circles, but within that framework it displays an unrealistic and idealistic quality that lies at the root of restitution at its best.[20] Stevens's choice of Laurentinum freed his imagination to soar.

Stevens created a long colonnaded and pedimented facade with end towers all tinted tan to indicate the degree of projection in front of the bluish background structure, yet richer in silhouette. The circular shape of his central superstructure has led to some question of its derivativeness from Scamozzi (cf. fig. 50), to which it is indebted only in a general way. Additional confusion arises because the drawing reproduced here is a copy by the students of John Soane (1753–1837) from a Stevens original now presumed lost.[21] Without the survival of any preliminary sketches, memorabilia relating to Stevens, or his drawings themselves, it is hard to fully understand his design. The elevation simply shows a circular courtyard well within the tradition of Scamozzi and Robert Castell. William Newton's similar drawing exhibited at the rival Society of Artists show in 1777 surely took its cue in part from Stevens (cf. fig. 62). Another visitor to the 1771 exhibition of Stevens's work could have been Soane, by this time a probational student at the Royal Academy. Although not a Chambers pupil, he became his protégé in the mid-1770s and owed to him the much prized Rome scholarship of 1778. From Chambers he learned of Stevens's death in Rome and his burial in the Protestant cemetery outside the city walls. He knew these details because Chambers gave him a copy of the letter of travel advice he had sent to Stevens four years earlier. Soane cherished that letter as a memento of his Grand Tour. Similarly, he preserved a record of Stevens's Laurentine Villa and eventually incorporated it into his own Royal Academy lectures.[22]

When it came Soane's turn to become Royal Academy professor in 1806, he laboriously copied out the manuscript lectures he had heard from his predecessor, Thomas Sandby (1721–98), the first to occupy the architectural chair. Soane himself had been required to attend Sandby's first full course of six lectures in 1770–71. In the fifth lecture Sandby displayed to his listeners what he described as a "Plan of Pliny's Villa at Laurentinum" and the elevation to match.[23] He barely commented on the restitution except to say that the elevation showed only one side of a perfectly symmetrical building. Could it be that Stevens had prepared the illustrations for Sandby's use in 1771, or alternatively for his own mentor Chambers, who had substituted for Sandby during his indisposition the previous season? Certainly Sandby requested drawings for the lecture series from other Chambers pupils, so why not these from Stevens?[24] According to this reconstruction of the events, then, Soane would have borrowed the lectures and their illustrations from Sandby's heirs in 1806, minus the Laurentine plan whose disappearance Soane lamented to his audiences. By this time the circumstances had become sufficiently clouded in Soane's mind that he could not remember the details in one early version of the lectures; in another he claimed the Laurentine restitution had been produced in Rome in 1774 instead of three years earlier.[25] Memory plays tricks, and the true sequence of events may never be known. In all probability, however, the Stevens restitution originated in a request from Sandby as professor. If this is so, Stevens's restitution would have done triple duty: once on public view at an exhibition, and twice more in front of the student audiences of Soane and of Sandby.

Soane's own fascination with Pliny, instigated first by Sandby's lectures and Stevens's restitution, did not abate over the intervening years. Soane returned to London from Rome in 1780, and among his earliest architectural book purchases was the copy of Castell's book that he signed and dated on the flyleaf in that year. Soon thereafter he came to own Orrery's translation of Pliny's letters, as well as those of de Sacy, Melmoth, and Henley, besides a 1724 Oxford edition in Latin.[26] When it came to book collecting on a favorite topic, Soane rarely resorted to half measures. He urged his student audiences to familiarize themselves with Pliny in order to learn from the letters. All this does not mean he unswervingly admired either Pliny or Stevens. Of the Laurentine and Tuscan properties he said that the "modern style" of his own day "leaves the Gardens of the Ancients . . . from what we know of them completely in the back Ground [i.e., outmoded]." About Stevens's restitution he cautioned his audiences with the words, "Though entitled to great praise it abounds with anachronisms and has but little of the Character of the Architecture of the age in which this building was erected." He concluded his analysis of Stevens and Pliny on this bemused note:

> This villa . . . he calls his *villula,* or little villa. . . . If such be the designation of a Roman villa, wherein between forty and fifty rooms for different purposes have been enumerated and many parts left totally undescribed; if the word "villula" is really to be [so] understood . . . what ideas are we to form of the magnitude, expense, and magnificence of . . . villas which we are told contained rooms for every purpose of splendor and convenience?[27]

This hint of irony reflects Soane's wariness of restitutions based on literary sources. He never produced one of his own.

Almost without interruption—and with little variation—Soane repeated his course of lectures at the Royal Academy in Somerset House from 1806 until his death. Certain distant reverberations continued to be heard when Charles Robert Cockerell (1788–1863) took over the duties. He delivered his first series of lectures in 1841 in the new setting of the Academy headquarters on Trafalgar Square. It is by no means sure that he had heard Soane in the old days, though he probably did. Among numerous similarities, however, the fourth speech delivered in the 1843 course contained a long passage paraphrasing Pliny's letter to Gallus. According to the verbatim report given in the *Athenaeum* magazine, the professor had dismissed as unreliable all the restitutions of Pliny's villas carried out before the excavations at Pompeii. Then he proceeded to a room-by-room tour of Laurentinum with the aid of "his own restoration . . . in which, though he differed in some points from his accomplished friend Monsieur Haudebourt . . . yet he strongly recommended it to the student, on account of the great research and taste shown in the composition."[28] Reading between the lines, it appears that Cockerell's Laurentine Villa restitution with its *D*-shaped courtyard resembled Haudebourt's about as much as Bouchet's later would (cf. figs. 32 and 37). What a pity the actual Cockerell drawing has disappeared, because he had a reputation for dazzling his audience with almost theatrical performances. Sandby had started the trend with a show-stopping climax to his last lecture in the form of a sixteen-foot-long original design for a "bridge of magnificence." Years later Soane could still remember being impressed by it as a student. When it came his turn to lecture, he had his office assistants prepare a remarkable set of so-called diagrams, better than Cormier's lantern slides because Soane's were vividly colored and no projector bulb ever blew out. Cockerell went one step further by taking a leaf out of Durand's system of the *parallèle.* He held forth standing in front of a vast and complex architectural backdrop illustrating sixty-three wonders of the world side by side.[29]

Cockerell brought to the Royal Academy lectures a vivacity and a cosmopolitan scholarship lacking throughout the previous seventy years. Gone were the doggerel verses Sandby had introduced to revive flagging audience attention; gone also was Soane's extreme reluctance to comment on "living artists," as the Royal Academy regulations referred to them. In place of boredom or bland noncontroversiality, Cockerell substituted a verve that reportedly kept his listeners on the edges of their seats and once led to an outburst of spontaneous applause—unheard of in most classrooms. In contrast to Soane, he kept up interest precisely by mentioning such contemporaries as Haudebourt, Schinkel, and Canina.[30] The plain truth is that Cockerell loved speaking in public and probably relied on the inspiration of the moment that comes from oral delivery. He had difficulty writing readable prose—hence his inability to settle on a final text and his reluctance to have it published. His voluminous and now scattered lecture notes testify to their author's brilliance and also his lack of self-discipline. Season after season he compiled entirely new talks until in the end they constituted a bewilderingly long and dauntingly complex meditation on architecture. Within this panorama—as broad and beguiling as one of Cockerell's diagrams stretching across the entire lecture room—Pliny's Laurentine Villa contributed its small but not insignificant part.[31]

Cockerell's student audiences reciprocated his enthusiasm by their devotion to his memory. Three of them succeeded him in the professorship: Sydney Smirke from 1860 to 1865; Edward Middleton Barry from 1874 to 1880; and George Edmund Street, who died in 1881 in the midst of his inaugural course of lectures. They all esteemed Cockerell's contribution highly, but of the three only Smirke remained an unrepentant classicist and Italophile. Born in 1797, his memory stretched back as far as the lectures of Soane, "that in some ways remarkable man," as he told his listeners. Then, in an aside that was probably a flashback to the days of Soane and Cockerell, Smirke mentioned Pliny's Laurentine cryptoporticus, not that it would have meant much to his Gothic Revivalist students in the 1860s.[32] The most glowing tribute to Cockerell, however, came from another student who "hung upon his utterances" and "sat at his feet." This was George Aitchison (1825–1910), who followed Street in the professorship in 1887 and remained ensconced until 1905. During this long incumbency the *Builder* magazine carried an account of a lecture he delivered on 30 January 1890 titled "Pliny the Younger's Laurentine and Tuscan Villas."[33] Aitchison repeated Cockerell's admiration for Haudebourt, and he broadened the discussion by illustrating Marquez's and Bouchet's Laurentine restitutions as well as Castell's plans of the Laurentine and the Tuscan villas. Aitchison produced no new restitution of his own; those creative wells seem to have run dry after Cockerell.

Aitchison in his modest way kept the memory of Pliny's villas alive long enough for them to come to the attention of another future Royal Academy professor,

Albert E. Richardson (1880–1964). Born in London, Richardson was apprenticed to Victor Page in 1895 and received his training in the same city where Aitchison regularly spoke. Richardson apparently sat in the audience.[34] After 1911, when the various professorships at the Royal Academy completely lapsed, Richardson assumed the revived architectural chair in 1947 and continued until 1961. Writing in 1913, Richardson seemed to prophesy a return to certain academic standards when he wrote: "We have witnessed of late . . . a return to a closer appreciation of classical architecture . . . in the leading schools." That statement appeared in an article titled "Laurentinum: The Winter Villa of C. Plinius Caecilius Secundus."[35] It provided no new restitution, echoed Aitchison's preference for Bouchet's, and more or less corroborated his opinion that "there is such an absence of method and such vagueness that any attempt to restore . . . is merely an exercise of the imagination."[36] Despite Richardson's realization that Bouchet's too was a "purely imaginary version of Roman architecture . . . viewed through French spectacles," he nevertheless concluded: "In these illustrations is depicted that sense of intellectual superiority which is always apparent in the archaeological restorations undertaken by imaginative Frenchmen." He went on to propose that "if such a subject as the one now under discussion were to be set, in addition to a thesis for examination purposes, the student would have plenty of scope for imagination . . . [upon which] the finest architectural results depend."[37] Richardson enunciated more clearly than anyone the admiration for French academic teaching that Soane, Cockerell, Smirke, and Aitchison had only hinted at. This praise comes as no great surprise during the height of Edwardian enthusiasm for Beaux-Arts classicism under Reginald Blomfield, Royal Academy professor from 1905 to 1910. (Blomfield significantly prefaced his published lectures—*The Mistress Art* [London, 1908]—with a quotation from Jacques-François Blondel.) But Richardson's recipe for a renewal of Plinian restitution goes much further and is prescient of events that did not take place until the 1980s (see chap. 6).

A near contemporary of Richardson's, Clifford Fanshawe Pember (1881–1955), provides an unexpectedly brilliant, almost Technicolor, conclusion to the English episode in Plinian restitution. Pember is chiefly remembered in the literature for a 1947 article in the *Illustrated London News* titled "The Country House of a Roman Man of Letters: The Lost Villa of the Younger Pliny."[38] Pember wrote that his inspiration had been a request from Mrs. Robert Mortimer of Oxford, a personal friend and a classicist, to make a model of the Laurentine Villa "as if for the setting of a film." Pember complied, working at a scale of one-eighth inch to one foot and using all kinds of bits and pieces that came to hand—roots, twigs, paper, cardboard, varnish, and paint. The model (fig. 96) subsequently went on display in the Ashmolean Museum at Oxford, where it continues to delight a second generation of undergraduates and visitors of all ages. What the article leaves unreported are

96. Pember, Laurentine Villa, model (AMO)

Pember's unique qualifications for the job, except to note that he had training as an architect. Further ties with Oxford come to light in a fact-filled obituary in the local newspaper noting that he died there on the seventy-fifth anniversary of his birth. The obituary goes on to state that a relative had been the vice-chancellor of the university, and that Pember himself had graduated from Brasenose College in 1900.[39]

These clues lead to the Brasenose College archives and to a letter from Pember's father that adds some valuable biographical details. When Pember went down from Oxford, he entered the office of the distinguished London architect Basil Champneys for three years. Some short time after he ended this apprenticeship, Pember set out for Canada, where he had entered into practice by 1909, and it appears he remained there until shortly after the First World War.[40] In light of this it is conceivable that, like Richardson, he had heard Aitchison lecture on Pliny long before he set out to make his three-dimensional restitution at Mrs. Mortimer's request. And what an engaging little structure he produced! A mass of trees and grapevines, cunningly fashioned out of tiny pieces of green paper attached to stems, screen the cruciform villa on one side. On the other is a porous-looking rocky shoreline reminiscent of the Isle of Capri. The model glistens with varnish and mirrors to give the illusion of the gleam of sunlight on the ocean or at the bottom of a freshwater well. Holes cut in the red roof tiles expose to view painted interiors and give a glimpse down through a transparent material to the swimming bath's mosaic-lined floor. A flickering animation is further conveyed by the numerous human figures. Though not big enough to be truly realistic, these men and women—none taller than three-eighths of an inch—recline on couches, play ball in the *sphaeristerium,* and dive naked off the rocky ledges. They add a liveliness and theatricality to this Pliny restitution, the most colorful of them all until very recent times (cf. pl. 45).

Benefiting from the hindsight provided by Pember's obituary, it is now clear that his model demonstrates skilled stagecraft. His obituary states plainly what his article on Pliny quoted above only hinted at. He abandoned architecture in Toronto for the Hollywood back lots, where he collaborated with the movie director D. W. Griffith on such films as *Way Down East* (1920). Seen in this light, his Laurentine Villa scale model could almost be for the set of a movie epic on the declining days of the Roman Empire.[41] In a more scholarly context, Pember's model came to the attention of Betty de Lisle Radice in 1961, and she based a plan on it for inclusion in her translation of Pliny's letters, still the most widely read in English. By this indirect route, the restitution of an architect turned set designer has gained a certain immortality among current students of Pliny. Perhaps in the long run the most significant point is that Pember represents the end product of an unbroken chain of public utterances, published designs, and exhibited drawings that dates back to Sandby, Soane, Stevens, and the rest. They each contributed to establishing and maintaining in academic circles a consciousness of the villas of Pliny that has never entirely died away. In itself this continuity says something crucial about the way ideas—in this case an architectural idea—become firmly lodged in a culture and are uprooted only with the greatest difficulty.

Two years after Stevens's Laurentine Villa was seen in public, the second restitution ever exhibited went on display at the Akademie der Bildenden Künste, founded at Dresden in 1764 by the elector of Saxony. Like the Royal Academy to which Stevens belonged, the Dresden Academy grouped together representatives of the fine arts, including the Dresden-born architect Friedrich August Krubsacius (1718–89). He served as the first professor at the same time as he occupied the post of *Hofbaumeister* in the elector's household. In fulfillment of the Dresden Academy's teaching role, it soon had a building of its own in which lectures could take place and professors and students could live. Once a year the lecture rooms were cleared to make space for exhibiting academicians' and students' work. By tradition, the two-week exhibitions opened on 5 March, the name day of the royal founder, Frederick Augustus III and of his namesake Krubsacius.[42] Accordingly, on 5 March 1773 Krubsacius and his students submitted drawings of the Tuscan Villa. The Laurentine Villa restitution followed exactly three years later. They look almost as fresh as when they first went on display, and what is no less remarkable they escaped unscathed from the firestorm that engulfed Dresden in 1945, destroying almost all of Krubsacius's built oeuvre. As previously with Stevens, there is a distinct possibility that these drawings were prepared with the additional purpose of illustrating the architecture lectures. Unfortunately the evidence in the Sächsische Landesbibliothek remains inconclusive. Krubsacius certainly lectured, but if his notes do still exist, they have become separated from the drawings.[43]

The origin of Krubsacius's Pliny villa restitutions stretches back to the 1760s and maybe even further to 1755–56, when he went to Paris on his *Wanderjahre.* This preference for Paris over Rome reflects the French background of his first teacher, the court architect Zacharias Longuelune, who had been brought to Dresden in 1715 by the elector Augustus the Strong. In Paris, Krubsacius could have seen and purchased the published restitutions of Félibien and Scamozzi. It is also possible that he had been alerted to them beforehand by Johann Matthias Gesner's 1739 Leipzig edition of Pliny. Krubsacius subsequently made use of this version of the Latin letters, and it may be how he learned of the existence of Castell's *Villas of the Ancients,* a book he never actually saw. These various publications could have planted the idea of restitution in his mind before he left Paris. He returned to Dresden in time to see it devastated by fire in the Seven Years War.[44] The reconstruction got off to a slow start, giving Krubsacius plenty of leisure to indulge his already pronounced penchant for critical and theoretical writing. Imaginary restitution and physical reconstruction were both very much on his mind at the time. In fact, an impassioned portrayal of the horrors of war in a burning city forms the opening paragraphs of an article he wrote that translates and comments on Pliny's letter to Gallus. It appeared in an influential Leipzig periodical with the characteristic Enlightenment name *Das Neueste aus der Anmuthigen Gelehrsamkeit.*[45] The June 1760 article was quickly reissued as a separate booklet by the same Leipzig printing house of B. C. Breitkopf. The press run must have been very limited, judging from the extreme rarity of the book version. This fact, coupled with the relative isolation of Saxony and the use of gothic type, further restricted accessibility to a small circle.[46] Nevertheless, in Rome the omnivorous Winckelmann soon got word of the publication, as we have already seen (chap. 3).

Krubsacius illustrated his Laurentine essay with two crude engraved plates for whose appearance he apologized in a postscript on the last page (figs. 97 and 98).

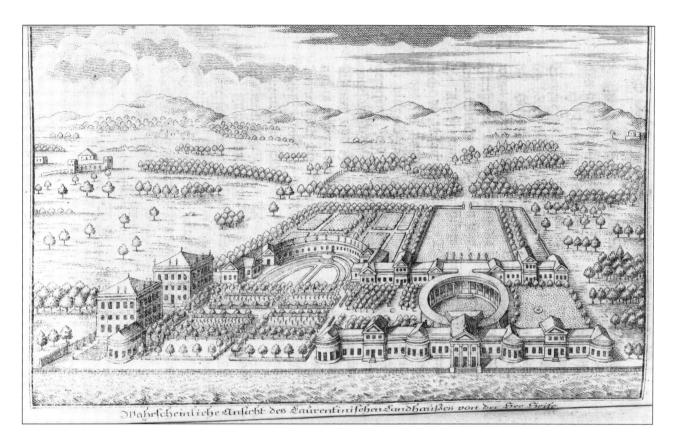

97. Krubsacius, Laurentine Villa, aerial perspective (Krubsacius, "Wahrscheinlicher Entwurf . . . Laurens")

The numbering system on the plan corresponds to the original and translated Pliny texts and is further elaborated in annotations. Disappointingly, these notes sidestep textual, let alone architectural, controversy. Krubsacius avoided passing judgment on either Félibien or Scamozzi by merely noting that their interpretations differed too much from one another for both to be correct. The Dresden design tries to blend the best ingredients of the Parisian and Venetian schemes while eliminating their imperfections. On one hand, the sprawling and lopsided arrangement of the site plan follows Félibien's suggestion of an asymmetrical wing projecting into the gardens (cf. fig. 52). On the other hand, Krubsacius's circular courtyard was derived straight from Scamozzi. But Krubsacius tried to fudge the doughnut-shaped configuration by slipping in vaguely *D*-shaped porticoes in the areas numbered 2 on the plan to make it accord better with Gesner's interpretation of the letter to Gallus. Here was another instance of Krubsacius wanting to have his cake and eat it too.

Without having seen Castell's book, Krubsacius nevertheless provided bow-fronted rooms similar to his along the sea facade, as well as numerous subsidiary rooms, shown with hatched lines by the engraver, which Pliny never mentioned but which his later interpreters like Castell believed ought to be there. Despite

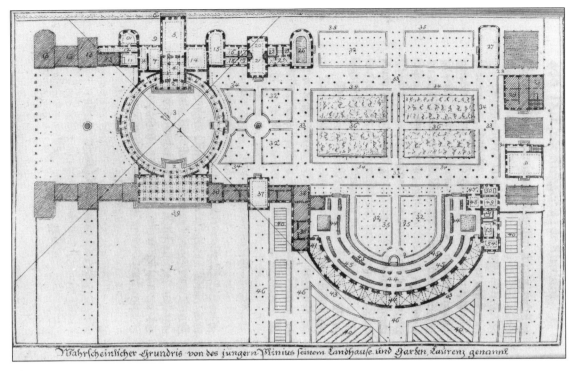

Wahrscheinlicher Grundris von des jungern Plinius seinem Landhause und Garten Laurenz genannt

Krubsacius's eclectic approach to the elements of the Laurentine plan, the final mixture looks very smooth. The villa moves gracefully from space to space, just as Pliny's sentence structure ambles along, so to speak, when describing room after room. Krubsacius's early training in Latin allowed him to understand the rhythm of Pliny's prose and then to link it architecturally to the circulation pattern of Pliny's home. In this regard Krubsacius's greatest insight was to trace the origins of his low-lying and meandering solution back to Pliny's own day. He intelligently surmised that the preferred domestic layout of rooms all on one level, known from other descriptions of buildings in Pliny's Rome, would have influenced the consul's personal villa.[47] The only exception to this rule are the multistory blocks seen on the extreme left in the engraved aerial view of Laurentinum. The one nearer the shore overshadows the *sphaeristerium* at its feet, and the other dwarfs the *amores mei* pavilion at the end of the curving cryptoporticus.

Krubsacius's exhibition drawings for Dresden, which are still preserved there, were mentioned by his late nineteenth-century biographer Paul Schumann.[48] Lost to sight after the Second World War, they have now been rediscovered. The two surviving sheets from the Laurentine set consist of a neatly written out page of Latin and German Pliny texts, dated 5 March 1776, and a splendidly colored ground plan signed by a draftsman named F. A. Fischer (pl. 39). Perhaps other drawings once accompanied them, but if so they have since been dispersed and are presumed lost. In the sixteen years separating the engraved and the exhibited versions of the Laurentine Villa, Krubsacius took the opportunity of elaborating

98. Krubsacius, Laurentine Villa, plan (Krubsacius, "Wahrscheinlicher Entwurf . . . Laurens")

upon the garden layout and improving the house plan, especially along the central axis. The entrance portico is deeper and at the same time more interesting in the way the columns to either side break forward to greet the visitor approaching the villa. Within, the courtyard and inner portico now have a less hybrid form and are shaped more like the "diamond horseshoe" in an elegant opera house. Still further in, the atrium has been expanded from a four-columned hall into a larger affair with a peristyle. Perhaps Krubsacius intended this room to be open-air; it is hard to say for sure without corresponding elevations or sections. Overall, the elements used are better integrated and less hastily concocted.

Using the same Leipzig periodical devoted to the arts and belles lettres, Krubsacius issued a second article in November 1762.[49] He began on a self-congratulatory note by stating that the favorable reception of his earlier article had encouraged him to write this one. Then, shifting his tack dramatically, he launched into an ironic attack against the proponents of the primitive hut theory. In a veiled allusion to Abbé Marc-Antoine Laugier, Krubsacius implied that such a primitivist would probably prefer straw houses, or *Leim und Strohhütten,* to the memory of Pliny's magnificent villas, which had withstood the test of time. In an equally ironic vein, he poked fun at archaeological reconstructions that came up with nonsensical, windowless structures as if to suggest that the Romans could see in the dark. (Perhaps Winckelmann's criticism of his Laurentine restitution had come to his ears in Dresden and this was his revenge.) In remarks that uncannily predict February 1945, Krubsacius defied archaeologists to reconstruct his burned-out city of Dresden from the smoldering ruins without benefit of accounts such as Pliny's. Throughout his theoretical writing there run these threads of wry humor and prophetic imagery that redeem the otherwise conventional drift of his aesthetic criticism.

After all his boastful rhetoric and facetious comments at the expense of others, Krubsacius's own engraved Tuscan plan comes as an anticlimax (fig. 99). At best it is barely comprehensible. Krubsacius showed everything all at once and failed to represent the sloping nature of the site, with its gardens on a lower level at the front and terraces higher up at the back. The resulting tangle of the horticultural and the architectural reads like Félibien's Tuscan plan, which Krubsacius had been quick to malign at the beginning of the article. Fortunately, he got a chance to improve on the results when his publisher brought out the Tuscan article the next year in booklet form.[50] The only changes to the text are a reworded title page and pages renumbered consecutively from 5 to 64. To the initial unpaginated section he added a new illustration, of far better quality than the earlier ones (fig. 100). It depicts a breathtaking aerial view that in large measure clarifies the confusing Tuscan Villa ground plan. Now the fan-shaped arrangement of topiary work really appears to spill down the hillside, while the villa building itself—as much open

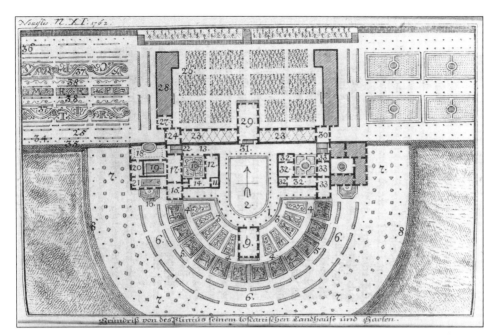

Grundriß von des Plinius seinem toscanischen Landhause und Garten.

99. Krubsacius, Tuscan Villa, plan (Krubsacius, "Wahrscheinlicher Entwurf . . . Landhause und Garten in der toscanischen Gegend")

100. Krubsacius, Tuscan Villa, aerial perspective (Krubsacius, *Wahrscheinlicher Entwurf . . . Landhause und Garten in der toscanischen Gegend*)

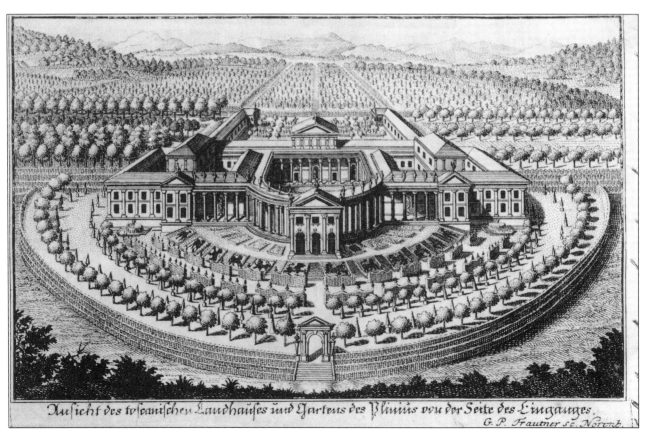

Ausicht des toscanischen Landhauses und Gartens des Plinius von der Seite des Einganges.

G. P. Frautner sc. Norimb.

colonnade as solid architecture—moves upward, culminating in a templelike series of pediments. With the benefit of a better engraver, Krubsacius clearly could convey the novelty of his design. Unlike previous Tuscan restitutions, this one called for unparalleled openness in concept, a harmonious relation to its surroundings, and an unprecedented split-level conception. Lazzari's is the only one to approach it, and his wild profusion of forms has been replaced with restrained elegance. One thing the two do share, however, is almost total obscurity. Because it seems that the surviving copies of Krubsacius's booklet can be numbered on the fingers of one hand, if that, the aerial view has never before been reproduced.

Eleven years later, in time for the 1773 Dresden exhibition, Krubsacius had overcome his problems of presentation by taking a simple step. On two separate sheets he disengaged the upper- and lower-level plans of the Tuscan Villa. The lower-level plan is dated 5 March and again bears the signature of Krubsacius's assistant F. A. Fischer (figs. 101 and 102). The upper-level plan is signed by another, less adept draftsman named J. G. Schwender. More particularly, the drawings gave Krubsacius the opportunity to revise his thinking about the two central triclinia. To the lower one he gave the avant-garde look of a peripteral temple in the antique manner. To the upper one he assigned the inner subdivisions typical of a Roman basilica. He also articulated the garden areas much more fully. The left-hand upper

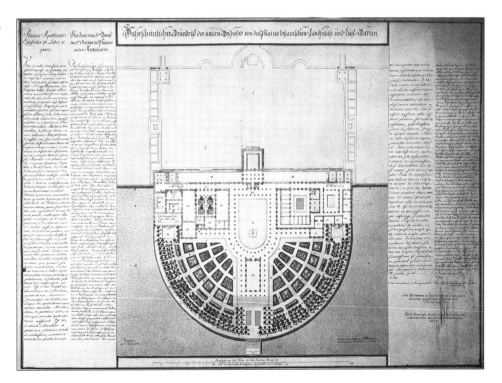

101. Krubsacius, Tuscan Villa, plan of lower level (SL, Forma max. qu. 2, Archaeol. 177, no. 1)

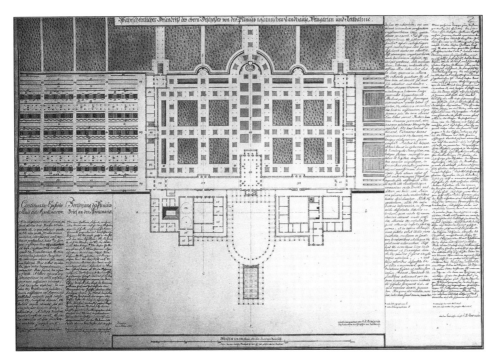

102. Krubsacius, Tuscan Villa, plan of upper level (SL, Forma max. qu. 2, Archaeol. 177, no. 2)

terrace, seen as if from above, reads like an open book with the names of Pliny, Ovid, Homer, and Socrates spelled out in shrubbery. Castell's Tuscan restitution had attempted just such a topos in topiary without exploiting nearly so well the possibilities for a literary joke. On the lower plan Krubsacius adopted Félibien's "pop-up" technique (cf. fig. 53) to make the four plane trees stand out better in relation to their courtyard, and he used it elsewhere with good effect on the sloping portion of the garden. Flat beds in the shape of animals answered the same purpose as the more sculptural treatment Lazzari gave to the passage by Pliny describing his bestiary in box ("bestiarum effigies invicem adversas buxus inscripsit").

The full sweep and majesty of the Tuscan Villas as envisioned by Krubsacius is seen best in the remaining two drawings: an unsigned sheet of elevations (pl. 40), and Schwender's various cross sections (pl. 41). His view from the side in the middle of the second sheet shows the lower triclinium as though it were a hexastyle freestanding temple. Here then is more proof of how far Krubsacius was willing to go in his pursuit of the antique. The cross section immediately below is instructive in revealing that the room is lined on the inside with two-story pilasters of the same height and order as the columns in the nearby courtyard. This thoroughgoing congruence of elements conveying the logic and the laws of antiquity makes the scheme one of the forgotten masterpieces of neoclassicism. Moreover, and to an extent not seen before, Krubsacius achieved a successful differentiation of the villa's massing without sacrificing the lay of the land. For instance, the lower-level gardens fan out apronlike to meet the surrounding landscape in perfect realization of the house and garden theme Pliny had advocated. Midway up the slope the several pediments at different levels stack up behind one another to create the impression of a sanctuary sacred to the god of repose. Higher still (pl. 40, bottom), a three-sided Doric service court with low pedimented buildings does not impede the sense of openness to the vineyards beyond. Thus the imaginary visitor to Krubsacius's Tuscan Villa would arrive in a relatively plain courtyard at the top of the site. Then by degrees as the slope descends the architecture increases in richness, progressing from Doric to Corinthian. The drawings, with their frequent use of pink poché, even hint at underlying structure and permit glimpses into rooms decorated with Pompeian-style wall decoration—another case of neoclassical exactitude insofar as Krubsacius could master it.

The Tuscan Villa of Krubsacius as exhibited at Dresden Academy in 1773 is so much more detailed than the engravings that it constitutes a new addition to the known restitutions based on the letter to Apollinaris. It gives one reason to pause before discounting its author as a nonentity or his milieu in Dresden as an artistic backwater where patronage was slack and people had time to kill. Artists in Dresden in the second half of the eighteenth century kept surprisingly abreast of trends in other art centers by means of frequent book reviews and informed articles like those by Krubsacius. This well-read and discriminating audience was catered to by such periodicals as *Das Neueste aus der Anmuthigen Gelehrsamkeit* (1751–62) and its successor the *Neue Bibliothek der Schönen Wissenschaften und der Freien Künste* (1765–1806). Beginning in 1766 the *Neue Bibliothek* carried a review of the annual exhibition at Dresden Academy. For a while there were even separate, unusually detailed, reviews on the architectural exhibitions.[51] But because they cease before the Pliny restitution drawings went on display, it is only possible to guess at contemporary reactions to these stunning works of art on paper. It seems fair to state, however, that the painstaking work by Krubsacius and his draftsmen—tantamount to a decade-long obsession with architectural restitution—reflects the intellectual ferment being generated among the young artists by their architecture professor. Krubsacius continued lecturing up to a few years before his death. He kept alive at Dresden the thrill of discovering Pliny, the joys of restitution, and the challenge of emulating the work of distinguished predecessors. He may even have had some influence on his German successors Hirt, Schinkel, and Stier.

In a scene familiar to readers of Potocki, Marquez, and especially Haudebourt, some foreign visitors to Italy set out on an excursion from Rome to Ostia in the July heat of 1826. The party included the Prussian-born architect Wilhelm Stier (1799–1856). A student of Sachs in Berlin from 1815 to 1817, Stier reached Paris on his Grand Tour in 1821 and spent a year there just as Krubsacius had done.

Then he set off for Rome. Nearing the end of his five-year stay abroad, he and some friends agreed to a quail-shooting party in the pine forest near Castel Fusano, and Stier took along his notepad just as Pliny used to do on such hunting expeditions (bk. 1, ep. 6). Stier recorded his impressions for posterity in his one contribution to literature, the *Hesperische Blätter,* aptly named to recall the garden of the Hesperides. This is a strange, almost random collection of bits and pieces: part factual travel diary, part artistic pilgrimage tale, and part fictional series of romantic novellas inspired by the lives of the Roman High Renaissance painters. The section "Der Ausflug nach Ostia," for example, tells quite factually of staying at Signor Amadeo's inn, perhaps the successor to the tavern mentioned by Potocki and frequented by Haudebourt. On one outing to Torre Paterno, Stier is shocked out of his reverie by a companion's shouting out in a heavy German accent their arrival at Laurentinum: "Ecco Signor Architetto il verissimo luogo del Laurentino di Plinio."[52] Stier in effect remarked upon seeing some ruined walls—nothing more. His text reverts immediately to describing the beautiful scenery on the journey up to Ariccia.

Returning to Berlin in 1828, Stier began to teach in the Bauschule and to display his drawings at various exhibitions. The first of these were in Berlin and Leipzig in 1842. For those occasions he prepared what is perhaps his most exquisite artistic statement: a watercolor restitution of the Laurentine Villa, set against a line of blue hills and a *bel sereno* sky (fig. 103). It sums up Stier's attitude and artistry better than does his flowery prose.[53] Significantly, he chose for his perspective drawing an offshore vantage point similar to the one Schinkel had drawn in the early 1830s and that Stier copied at some point between then and its publication in 1841 (fig. 104). In contrast to Schinkel's crystalline clarity, Stier indulged in a soft, painterly atmosphere that suggests the hazy, hot morning when he saw the Laurentine landscape for the first and only time. He preferred a diagonal view to Schinkel's head-on elevation, and thus Stier's villa takes on greater apparent dimensions, further magnified by the moisture in the sea air. The size of the house provides a foil for the dramatic background of tall mountains and foothills, in the midst of which can be discerned the unmistakable silhouette of Ariccia, where Stier went on the same excursion in 1826. So Stier's image, like his writing, blends fact and fiction. Its artistic roots are no less heterogeneous. The sketchy, impressionistic technique of the watercolor intentionally recalls the Pompeian-style wall paintings contemporary with Pliny, yet the pilasters of the frame have a neo-Renaissance look in keeping with the subjects that had inspired several of Stier's novellas.

Regardless of the sources, Stier's watercolor says a great deal about his own personality as poetic dreamer, in contrast to the busy Schinkel. Yet both exemplify the important influence of the Italian experience on their work back in Berlin. At

103. (*Top*) Stier, Laurentine
Villa, perspective (TUB,
7230)

104. (*Above*) Stier, Laurentine Villa, perspective from
the water after Schinkel
(TUB, 7231)

any rate that was the astute observation of an anonymous reviewer of the 1842 Leipzig architectural exhibition when he compared Schinkel with Stier.[54] They also shared the same dedication as teacher-architects, frequently working side by side at the Berlin Bauschule, which later changed its name to the Bauakademie. Stier's son and pupil, Hubert, commented that devotion to the classroom had prevented his father's success as a practicing architect. On paper, at least, he had a prolific output, though it was no match for Schinkel's. Stier left behind a whole series of architectural restitutions and unsuccessful competition entries that Hubert, in an act of filial tribute, began publishing early in 1867. Called *Architektonische Erfindungen*—architectural inventions—they never progressed beyond the first two fascicles dealing with the Laurentine and Tuscan villas. As with Krubsacius, the scarcity of copies indicates a tiny press run and slight demand.

The term *Erfindungen* alludes to Stier's key pedagogical principle, whereby creative projects inspired student inventiveness.[55] The elder Stier's advanced course was even called *Klasse für die Erfindungen.* It challenged the students' imagination with such problems as the verbal descriptions of Pliny to Gallus and Apollinaris. Like Durand and Cockerell, Stier mixed in a dynamic and visually challenging dimension with the lessons in theory, history, and archaeology.[56] But as happened to some degree with Cockerell, the academic environment lulled Stier's mind into a state far removed from the pressing concerns and harsh realities of the profession as practiced day to day. Stier lavished care and attention on his restitutions, yet he was lackadaisical about preparing them for publication. He left that nasty job to his heirs. His laxness in meeting competition deadlines also reflects his refusal to compromise his standards simply to win a prize. In his own words as paraphrased by Hubert: "After the long time in which I tried to discover the right principles in the art of building . . . I have attempted to clarify for myself fixed points of view and, so to speak, wholeheartedly to incorporate them into architectural inventions."[57] For Stier *Erfindungen* had become the be-all and end-all; he threw himself into it body and soul.

According to Hubert Stier's account, his father embarked on both the Laurentine and Tuscan restitutions about 1830, presumably in conjunction with the advanced lecture course he was preparing. The younger Stier went to some pains to stress that only then did Stier and Schinkel compare notes and find out that they had both been independently working along the same lines.[58] This sounds like almost too much of a happy coincidence in a relatively close-knit artistic community like Berlin's. Whatever the case, Stier soon dropped the Tuscan Villa to concentrate on the Laurentine. He went to the lengths of taking lessons so he could engrave the designs himself, which he began doing in 1832, as the inscription states on the plan illustrated here (fig. 105). If correct, this dating rules out the possible influence of the 1818 *prix d'émulation* drawings, not out in print until two years later. But it

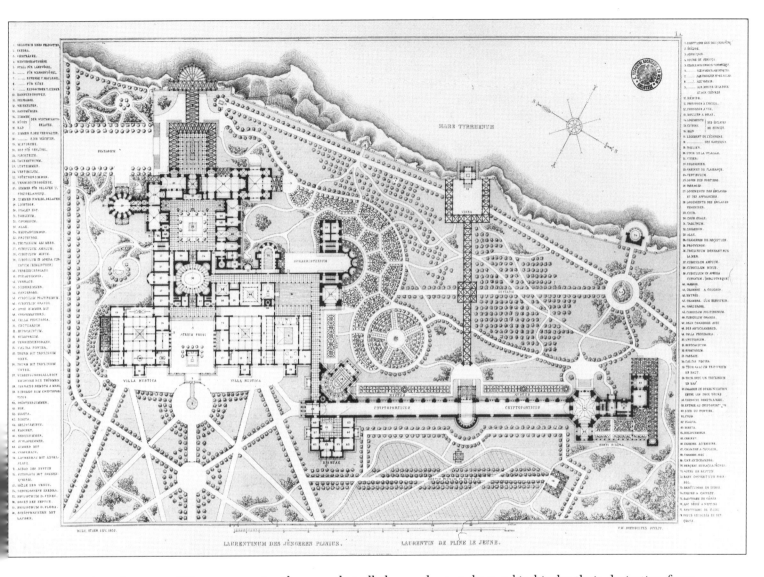

105. Stier, Laurentine Villa, plan (Stier, *Architektonische Erfindungen*)

remains the case that all these schemes share a kinship by their derivation from Félibien's (cf. fig. 52). The basic Frenchness of Stier's plan is less apparent because he embroidered on it to such an amazing extent. Significantly, perhaps, he chose French as the second language for his seventy-eight legend entries running down both sides of his elephantine plan (50 cm high × 80 cm long). The largest of all the restitutions in format, Stier's seven separately bound Laurentine plates make up their own atlas volume, which it takes considerable effort to lift.

As already stated, Stier's, Schinkel's, and Félibien's Laurentine plans all agree in according a circular or oval shape to the first courtyard. On that score they are out of step with the latest thinking soon to be voiced by Haudebourt, Canina, and

Cockerell. The main outlines of Stier's work, however, soon become submerged in a proliferation of grape arbors that surround the main house on the garden side. These arbors tend to blur the transition from architecture to nature. The principal entrance front, labeled the *atrium frugi,* Stier insisted on engulfing with two flanking service courts, despite Pliny's silence on the matter. Then in the angle between the right-hand service court and the long cryptoporticus, Stier developed a dense agglomeration of spaces, using as a pretext the Pliny passage that called for a dining room remote from the sound of pounding waves. Finally, the shoreline is positively littered with separate structures and platforms jutting out to sea, uncalled for by Pliny. One critic has recently seen Stier's plan as "fantastical" and "colossal." But she also cites a Stier letter of 1834 suggesting that he sought a practical outlet for his talents and pined for a more fertile artistic climate. He was willing to go as far south as the Crimea if necessary. This nostalgia reveals a distinct split in Stier. At the height of his infatuation with the Laurentine restitution, he had nagging doubts about spending the rest of his career in Berlin fabricating dream schemes nobody cared to implement.[59]

Stier's torn emotions and divided loyalties—theory versus practice, north versus south—come across strongly in the eclectic quality of the ten elevations and cross sections he prepared for his Laurentine Villa (figs. 106–15). He was almost profligate in the profusion of these pencil-and-wash drawings, so finely controlled that they look as meticulous as the seven copperplates that later regrouped them. The ten sheets, now housed in the Stier archives, convey better than the engravings the breadth of his vision, the depth of his commitment, and the wealth of his detail. That much said, the initial impression of the exterior is one of an enormous, heterogeneous mass, smothered in vines and bristling with towerlike superstructures, statues, acroteria, or potted trees standing on rooftop terraces. This agglomeration of elements does not disguise the overall banality of design in the front or side elevations (figs. 106–8). The last of these, the *sphaeristerium* facade, makes an interesting and rich composition in its own right, but its top-heaviness looks out of place with respect to the rest of the villa. Here the sumptuous detailing reaches a neo-Renaissance fever pitch. Surely Raphael or his client Cardinal Giulio de' Medici would have felt more at home here than Pliny (chap. 2).

Terms such as fantastic, eclectic, and colossal spring quickly to mind when regarding Stier's Laurentine Villa, yet they do him a disservice. Contrary to what the unbridled love of ornament and nervous fussiness suggests, Stier had carefully thought the whole thing through from the practical and archaeological points of view. This conclusion inescapably arises from an elaborately detailed manuscript "Erläuterung," written by Stier in January 1841 to elucidate his Laurentine restitution before it went on exhibition the next year. By the time Hubert Stier got around to publishing his late father's text, it had become enlarged in some places and

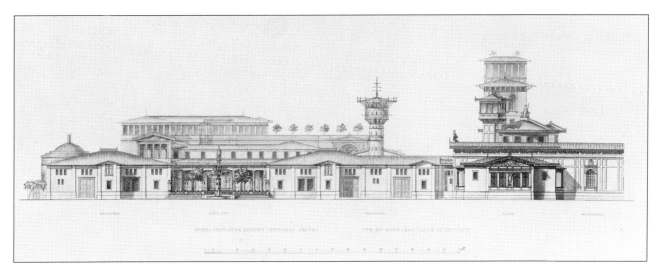

106. Stier, Laurentine Villa,
elevation of entrance facade
(TUB, 7228)

107. Stier, Laurentine Villa,
elevation of side facade
(TUB, 7227)

108. Stier, Laurentine Villa,
elevation of *sphaeristerium*
(TUB, 7226)

shortened in others to form the basis of the *Architektonische Erfindungen.*[60] To read the original version is to realize that Stier's words are occasionally better than his images. He had pictured the Laurentine Villa so vividly that for him it had become a living reality. He knew it down to the minutest detail. In the *villa rustica* service court, for instance, he assigned to the various spaces the functions of a Roman farmhouse known from archaeological investigation: winery, granary, oil press, slaves' quarters, stables, chicken coops, and a projecting pigeon loft that resembles a lighthouse from a distance (figs. 106, 111, 115). Stier paid special attention to the netting of wild birds and to aviaries such as those mentioned by Varro.[61] All in all, no one since Robert Castell had shown such knowledge of the working side of a farmstead in ancient times. But Stier went to zoological lengths when he stated that the animals ought to have stalls painted with decorations to remind them of the reeds, trees, or grasses of their natural habitat.

Inside the main house Stier went from room to room, revealing an extensive grasp of all aspects of the domestic arrangements as they existed in Pliny's time. Stier stipulated everything from the various floor coverings to the different roofing systems, and much else in between.[62] Where his artistry and erudition shone most brightly was in describing the sumptuous decorations he envisioned. The house itself received special attention in four areas. Besides the main range along the central axis (fig. 109), these included the less frequently concentrated on library, *sphaeristerium,* and dining room out of earshot of the sea. The library occupies an oval, virtually freestanding structure at one extremity of the villa (fig. 110). A choragic tripod crowns the roof as if to mark this as a writer's abode. According to the accompanying text, a sun clock alludes to the passage of time, and the cabinets are surmounted by the busts of eminent authors, as Pliny noted was the practice among fellow villa owners (bk. 4, ep. 28). In the *cubiculum amplum* adjacent to the left, the rear wall with a triple-arched motif is meant to recall a Trajanic triumphal arch out of respect for Pliny's emperor. Farther along to the left at the other extremity of the villa, Stier equipped the main reception room with a musicians' gallery at one end and a small stage at the other, even though Pliny disliked the often lewd spectacles put on by his contemporaries (bk. 1, ep. 15). The gymnast in Stier responded to Pliny's own ball court. The decorative program Stier described consisted of an Olympic hall of fame with wrestlers gripping each other in various holds, and statues in athletic poses. A separate elevation and section (figs. 112 and 113) reveal the so-called *cenatio rimota a mari* in all its barbaric splendor. Elaborate in shape, covered in costly materials, it has its own musicians' gallery supported by caryatids representing Apollo and the Muses. This highlights the fact that Apollo as deity of inspiration is the Laurentine Villa's titular god. He presides over the *cenatio,* and the cryptoporticus is designated as a *museum* full of the

109. (*Opposite, top*) Stier, Laurentine Villa, cross section on main axis (TUB, 7220)

110. (*Opposite, middle*) Stier, Laurentine Villa, cross section on axis of library (TUB, 7221)

111. (*Opposite, bottom*) Stier, Laurentine Villa, cross section on axis of baths (TUB, 7222)

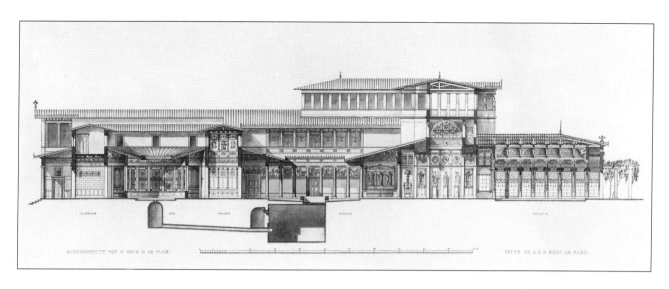

DURCHSCHNITT VON A NACH B IM PLAN.   COUPE DE A À B DANS LE PLAN.

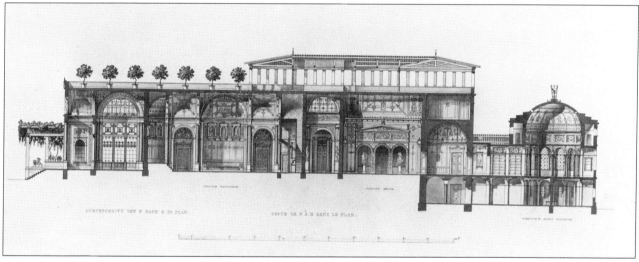

DURCHSCHNITT VON E NACH F IM PLAN.   COUPE DE E À F DANS LE PLAN.

DURCHSCHNITT VON G NACH H IM PLAN.   COUPE DE G À H DANS LE PLAN.

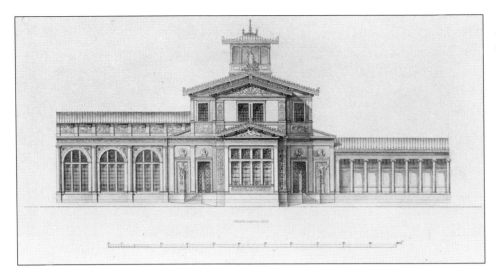

112. Stier, Laurentine Villa, elevation of *cenatio rimota a mari* (TUB, 7225)

113. Stier, Laurentine Villa, cross section of *cenatio rimota a mari* (TUB, 7224)

statues of poets and philosophers, as well as copies of the Apollo Belvedere, the Venus Anadyomene, and the three Graces.[63]

If the Laurentine Villa is the abode of a poet, then its garden must be equally poetic, according to Stier. He devoted a long section of his manuscript to the garden and the buildings within it, all of them concocted out of his own imagination without benefit from Pliny. Temples to various deities abound. Stier got carried away by the ability of his prose to enrich the villa's simple pleasures to excess. Burnished bronze, gleaming marble, snow-white statues, mythological paintings, and now all manner of plants add up to a staggering assault on the senses.[64] Stier used words to evoke the sights and smells his monochrome drawing technique could not convey. In this regard one passage twice repeated the word *Phantasie* to describe the quality of Laurentinum. In the first instance it commented on the element of fantasy ancient painters employed in their works. In the second instance it referred particularly to the writings of Pliny. Clearly Stier recognized the far-fetched and at times overblown quality of the letter to Gallus and took inspiration from it.[65]

Stier labored for nearly a quarter century at conveying the Laurentine restitution to paper. He depicted it with a poet's ecstasy, a painter's palette, a sculptor's eye for texture, and a gardener's green thumb, yet he never entirely lost an architect's practicality. In the end his students may have concluded that their teacher had so identified with Pliny as to breathe the same antique air. His lack of perspective comes to the fore in one final drawing with which he tried to distinguish himself from Schinkel and the others. Of all rooms to emphasize, his choice fell on the *heliocaminus* (fig. 114). Stier gave it an intricate plan and huge size, out of all proportion to its importance in the letter to Gallus. He even covered it with a fancy roof, though it was obvious from its Latin name that in some way it had to receive direct sunshine. Something of this same failure to distinguish the wood from the trees, and consequently to become tied up in details, recurs in the equally extraordinary Tuscan Villa restitution.

A year after Stier's Laurentine Villa went on display in the Leipzig exhibition, the similar exhibition of 1843 at Bamberg contained his drawings of the Tuscan Villa.[66] The genesis of this lesser-known Stier restitution is otherwise unclear, except that Hubert Stier claimed it was also begun in the 1830s. The finished pencil-and-wash drawings, including those for Bamberg, never progressed any fur-

114. Stier, Laurentine Villa, elevation of *amores mei* pavilion (TUB, 7229)

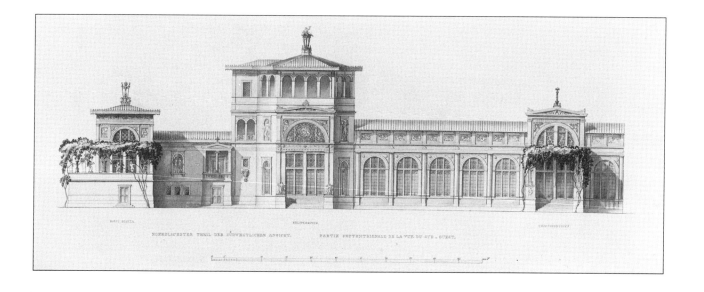

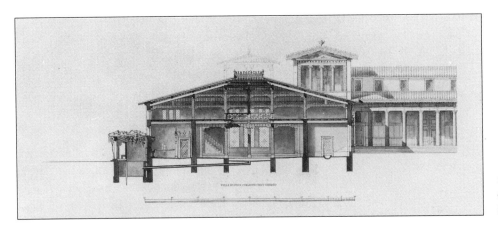

115. Stier, Laurentine Villa, cross section of *villa rustica* (TUB, 7223)

ther, and Hubert had them engraved in 1866 for publication two years later.[67] But if the Laurentine Villa had closer personal associations with Wilhelm Stier's student days in Italy, the Tuscan Villa has a freer, fresher, and less belabored look. For his part, Hubert liked it more and thought it showed how his father had profited from the experience of drawing the other villa. Perhaps he echoed his parent's preferences. Who better able to do so than a son and amanuensis?[68] Yet the younger Stier's printed "Erläuterung" of 1868 expressed the sentiments dryly when compared with the "Ansichten," which preceded them into print and are written in the florid language typical of his father. These "Ansichten" explain the design principles behind both villas, and they prepare the reader for a Tuscan restitution that is anything but dry (fig. 116).

The similarities between the perspective views of Stier's Laurentine and Tuscan villas reflect his lack of familiarity with the actual site in the Apennines compared with Lazzari's (cf. fig. 21). The German nevertheless evoked the hilly terrain well in the disposition of his many levels and hanging gardens that mount the slopes tier upon tier. He genuinely appreciated the Italian love of landscape, noting in the "Ansichten" that Italians always chose the best spots with the most commanding views.[69] This time, moreover, he did not clutter the approach to the villa with service courts. He placed them more discretely off to the side. In this way the Tuscan Villa, despite its farming function, takes on an almost urban look, as if Stier visualized those astonishing acropolis restitutions sent home as envois from abroad by students of the Ecole des Beaux-Arts. Perhaps Stier had the Tuscan perspective in mind when he quoted Seneca in the "Ansichten" to the effect that Roman country houses at times pretentiously resembled whole cities.[70] Lest the tiered aspect of the house seem chaotic, another Stier preparatory drawing clarifies the situation (fig. 117). It is a plan taken at the level of the rooftops of the main villa, showing the higher parts backing up into the hillside. A long cryptoporticus overlooks a massive columnar triclinium with two circular spaces attached to it

116. Stier, Tuscan Villa, perspective (TUB, 7219)

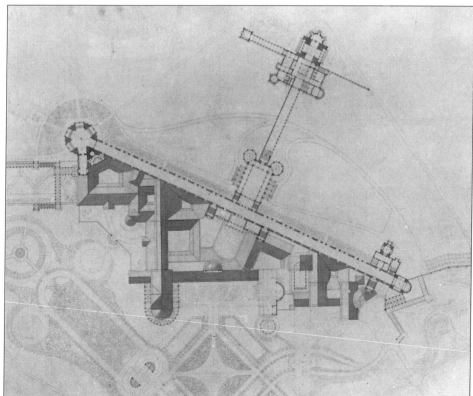

117. Stier, Tuscan Villa, plan
of upper level (TUB, 7217)

satellite fashion. From there a long, narrow gallery extends to connect with a *Gartenhaus* floating off at some distance from the villa. If in Castell's Tuscan restitution the planning of airports comes to mind, then in Stier's case the analogy ought to be to space stations.

Stier created a captivating exterior appearance, but he tried to argue that its visual appeal was secondary to its functional logic. Everything external derived directly from internal needs. He and his son stressed on several occasions that

118. Stier, Tuscan Villa, plan of lower level (Stier, *Architektonische Erfindungen*)

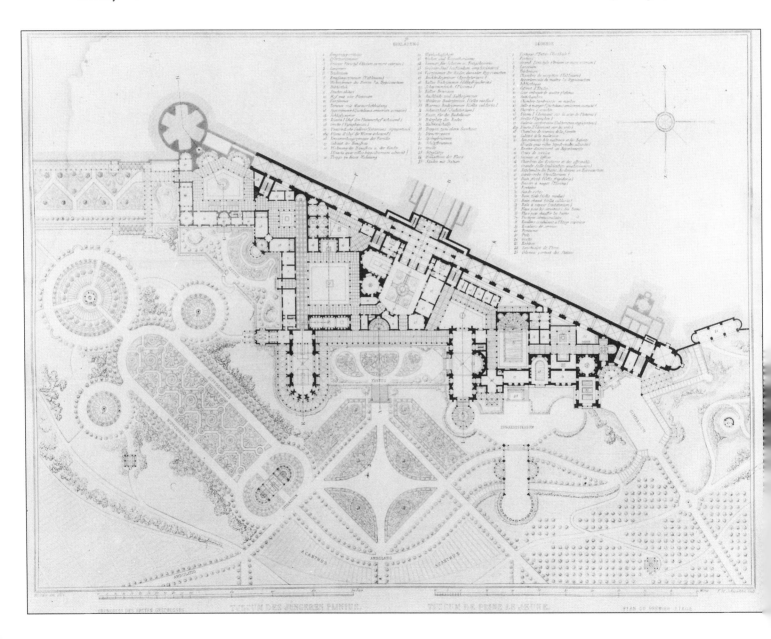

Pliny's letter to Apollinaris left out many mundane requirements in order to avoid sounding like a catalog of rooms and their functions.[71] Pliny's sin of omission gave Stier all the freedom he wanted in organizing the villa. He chose to do so around functional units, each with its separate courtyards, as at Pompeii. There were slaves' quarters, a farm court, a court for the baths, a court for visitors, a court for the master, and so forth. On the published plan of the main villa (fig. 118) these areas correspond to the courts, moving from the right to the extreme left.[72] And to make matters more logical and plausible, the cryptoporticus touches on each courtyard, connecting them like a giant communications corridor. Thus it could be argued that Stier had an essentially functionalist attitude to the planning of the Tuscan Villa, in distinction to Pliny. The hillside gardens rather than the architecture preoccupied the letter writer. For Stier the opposite holds true, and he thus blatantly contradicted his ancient literary source. In another instance of this he included apartments for occupancy in the winter, despite the seasonal nature of the house as stressed by Pliny. The treatment of the *stibadium* also alters Pliny's intent in the interest of smoother internal function. In the letter to Apollinaris the garden pavilion had to wait until the climax at the end. In Stier's plan it is indistinguishable from the *Gartenhaus* complex at the top of the site. Its function as a place of repose is duplicated by a study space within the villa overlooking the hippodrome-shaped garden, which contains its own duplicate *stibadium*.[73]

Pompeian and Renaissance-style interior decorations figure in Stier's sectional studies of the villa, in both the preparatory and the engraved states (figs. 119 and 120). One of the six published engravings shows the *Gartenhaus* above and the Schinkelesque courtyard with the four plane trees below (cf. fig. 44). It was in the neighborhood of this courtyard that Pliny gave his fullest account of an interior, notwithstanding that the letter to Apollinaris is generally less detailed. Where, then, are the paintings of birds and foliage that Pliny specifically mentioned? Stier decided to replace them with decoration more to his own taste and of his own devising. Stier once again overlooked the information Pliny provided. On the lower level he organized an immense hypostyle hall as a setting for a statue personifying the source of the Tiber. Above it supposedly are hanging gardens and a statue of Poseidon on the roof—a strange choice of god for a landlocked villa. Toward the right extends a triclinium as big as the hall below, and still farther on an exedra full of the busts of statesmen and members of the local gentry.[74] Surely there must be some reason for so many flights of fancy on Stier's part and so many departures from the authority of Pliny.

Toward the beginning of his "Ansichten" Stier gave his reasons for interpreting the villas in the way he did. He was not going to provide a factual, let alone archaeological, restitution, because those qualities did not characterize the letters of Pliny. Indeed, Stier wanted to achieve a work of art, something that would be

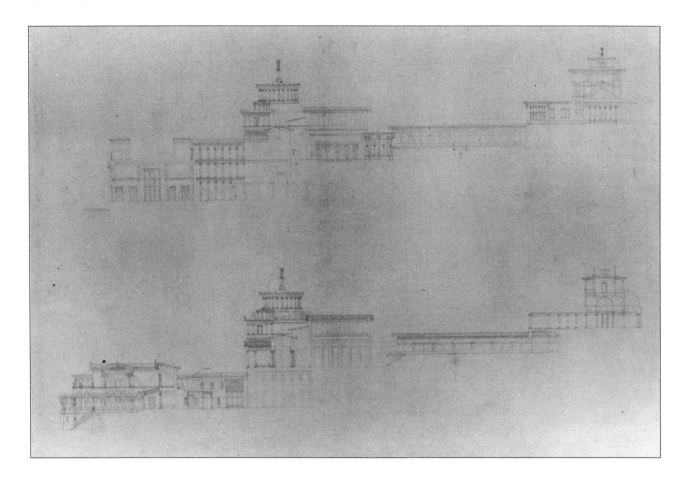

of value to students and fellow artists. Therefore he saw no contradiction in departing from Pliny. The Latin letters simply taught a set of literary rules. Stier
would develop an architectural set of his own. Chief among them would be his
conviction—repeated several times—that the ancients designed their villas from
the inside out.[75] In contrast to the Durand school of thought, he found that symmetry had been imposed upon the ancients to an extent they never subscribed to
themselves. Therefore whatever might be dismissed in their buildings as a wayward
Spiel der Phantasie was in reality nothing of the sort. It exemplified a carefully
thought out response characterized by freedom from constraint (*ungebundener
Freiheit*), a certain looseness (*Unabhängigkeit*), and a rational lack of orderliness,
supposing such a thing to exist.[76] Here was Stier's breakthrough—his *Erfindung*
to end all discoveries—the fruit of so much reflection on Pliny. Bending the rules
had been the order of the day at Laurentinum and Tuscany, so it would serve as
the guiding principle in all of Stier's work.

On several occasions Stier suggested that his work on Pliny could apply to his

119. Stier, Tuscan Villa, elevation of side facade and cross
section (TUB, 7218)

120. Stier, Tuscan Villa, cross sections (Stier, *Architektonische Erfindungen*)

own times. Human needs had not changed all that much, he observed, cultural differences apart. And though Pliny had little to offer nineteenth-century technology, he nevertheless conveyed a good idea of artistic thought in Roman times. If putting those ideas before the public in the form of lectures and drawings for exhibition had shed light on the principles of art, then Stier felt his years of labor had not been wasted.[77] In the loneliness of Stier's solitary quest, in his uncompromising devotion to an ideal, in his dedication to his students, and in his appeal for artistic freedom, despite the obscurity that has been his reward, there exist qualities that society has increasingly prized in the century and a half since his death.

CHAPTER SIX

The Joys of Emulation

THE NOTION OF a *concours* or competition based on Pliny's Laurentine Villa did not exactly sweep like wildfire through other European schools of architecture after its inception at the Ecole des Beaux-Arts in 1818 (see chap. 5). The earliest concrete evidence that this Parisian idea had caught on—or was being emulated—comes in the form of two mid-nineteenth-century Plinian restitution schemes submitted to and preserved by the Accademia di San Luca in Rome (figs. 121–25). Its competitions, of which the most famous was the Concorso Clementino, held regularly from 1702 onward, anticipated the French system of Grand Prix and *prix d'émulation*.[1] Clearly the drawings in question relate to one of these frequent *saggi scolastici*, or *concorsi*, held by the Italian academy. Both sets of drawings are anonymous and undated because the identifying inscriptions or numerals have been partly cut off. In the absence of complete documentation, therefore, the style of the two anonymous Italian schemes, in conjunction with certain historiographic considerations, narrows down the chronological field of their production. And contrary to what the literature has implied, the two do not necessarily belong to the same contest held in the same year. Their inscriptions read quite differently, which, had they been produced at the same time, would certainly have contravened the *programme* and therefore have ruled one of them hors concours. In the dog-eat-dog world of the nineteenth-century academic jury, the slightest infringement of the competition guidelines frequently disqualified projects.[2]

When setting out the detailed *programme* in 1818 the French judges had followed the precedent of Félibien (fig. 54), and not surprisingly so had the winning competitors, at least in their plans (cf. fig. 89, pls. 36 and 37). In this regard the various solutions suggest that the contestants had some foreknowledge of one another's work. Naturally their similarity to each other and their derivativeness from Félibien raise questions about true originality. But any accusation of plagiarism misses the point and in large part mistakes the intent of the process. The entire academic system rests on the principle of emulation as a means of exhorting contestants to equal or excel the example set by others. Had not Paris emulated the competitive method established at Rome, and conversely had not the Accademia di San Luca in turn followed the precedent set by the Ecole in 1818? It all worked on the premise that there was nothing entirely new under the sun, but that students could still aspire to improve on the classical tradition.

121. (*Opposite, top*) Anonymous Italian, Laurentine Villa, aerial perspective, cross sections, and details (ASL, 2290)

122. (*Opposite, bottom*) Anonymous Italian, Laurentine Villa, plan and elevation of entrance facade (ASL, 2289)

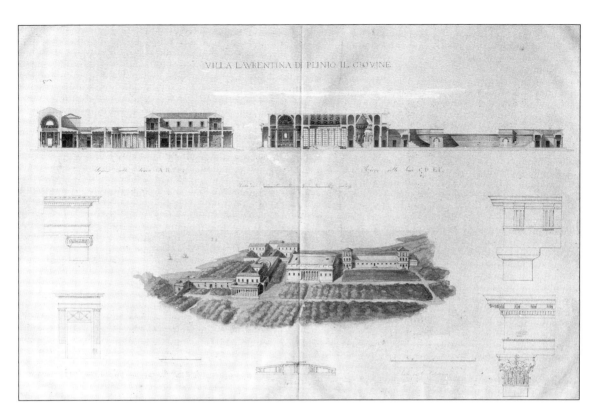

VILLA LAVRENTINA DI PLINIO IL GIOVINE

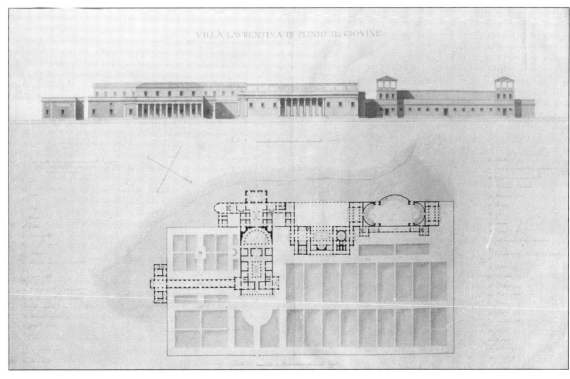

VILLA LAVRENTINA DI PLINIO IL GIOVINE

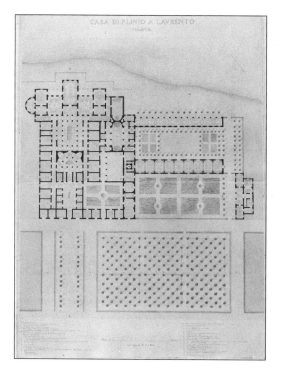

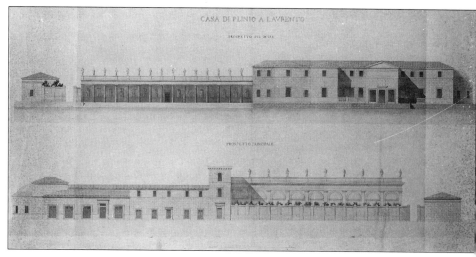

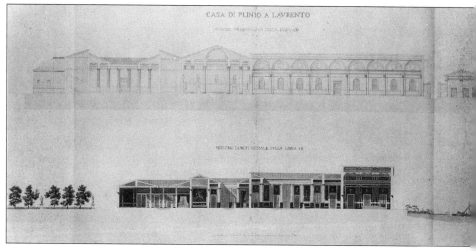

123. (*Above*) Anonymous Italian, Laurentine Villa, plan (ASL, 2291)

124. (*Above, right*) Anonymous Italian, Laurentine Villa, elevation of water and side facades (ASL, 2292)

125. (*Right*) Anonymous Italian, Laurentine Villa, cross sections (ASL, 2293)

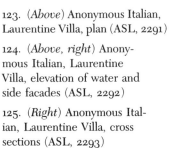

Returning to the two different Italian Laurentine restitutions, the one calls itself a *villa,* the other a *casa.* The first bears the full title "Villa Laurentina di Plinio il giovane" and consists of two drawings of identical dimensions (figs. 121 and 122). One sheet has a cross section, a crudely drawn bird's-eye view, and various details including the design of a capital in a new dolphin order of architecture in keeping with the seaside situation. The second sheet combines an elevation drawn to one scale and a plan drawn to another. Because of its *D*-shaped courtyard the plan almost certainly derived from the restitutions of Haudebourt (1838), or more likely for nationalistic reasons from that published by Canina in Rome in 1840. Despite a number of deliberate inversions in the plan to throw one off the scent, the connection to Canina and therefore a date in the 1840s or 1850s seems

Plate 30. Rome, Villa Madama, east facade

Plate 31. Rome, Villa Madama, west facade

Plate 32. Montreal, Cormier-
Trudeau house, west facade

Plate 33. Rita Wolff after
Léon Krier, Laurentine Villa,
perspective (collection of the
artist)

Plate 34. Rome, Villa Albani,
gardens and south facade

Plate 35. Potocki, Laurentine
Villa, round room elevation
(BNW, WAF 67, J. Rys. 5.012)

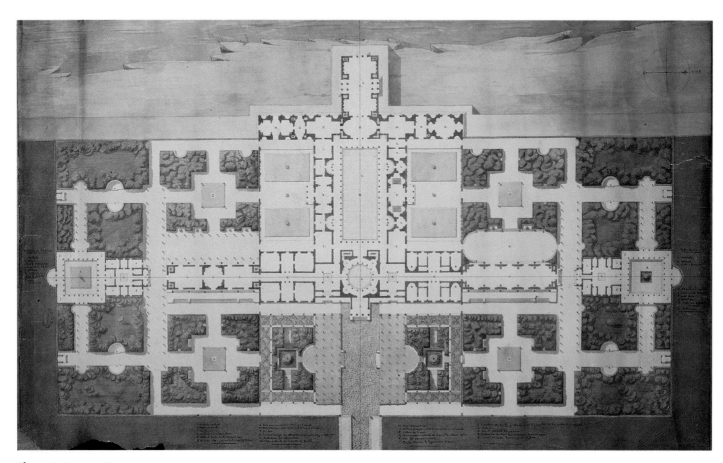

Plate 36. Lepage, Laurentine
Villa, plan (EBA)

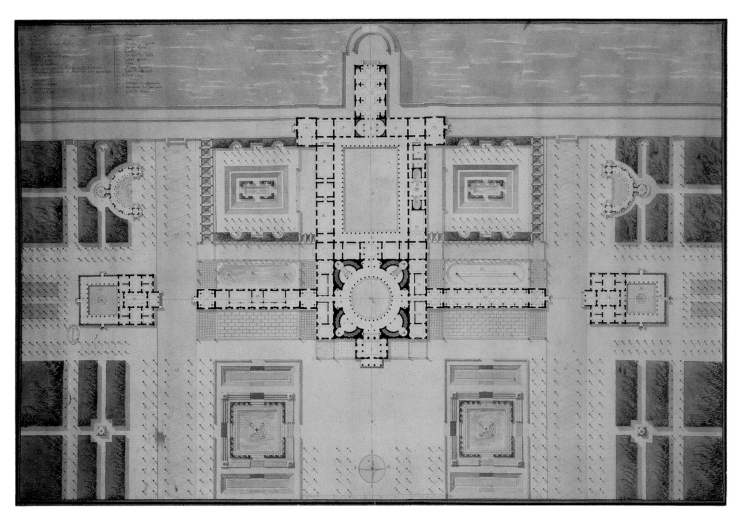

Plate 37. Normand, Laurentine Villa, plan (EBA)

Plate 38. Stevens, Laurentine
Villa, elevation (SM, drawer
22, set 6, item 13)

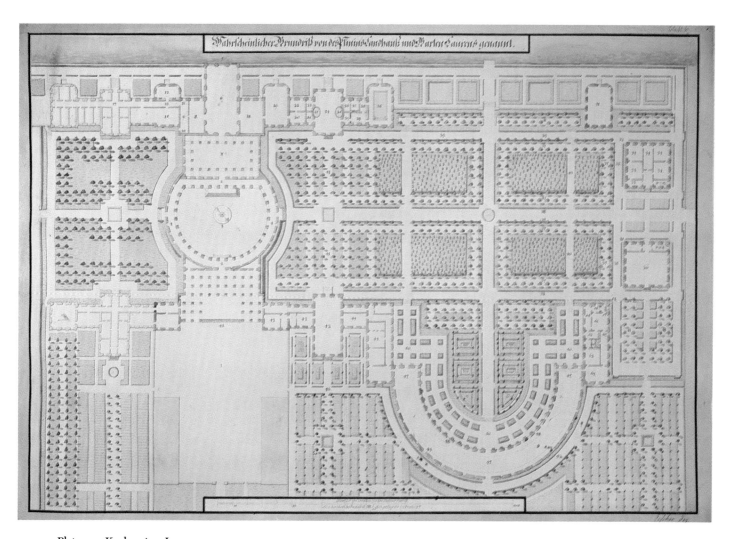

Plate 39. Krubsacius, Laurentine Villa, plan (SL, Forma max. qu. 2, Archaeol. 177, no. 6)

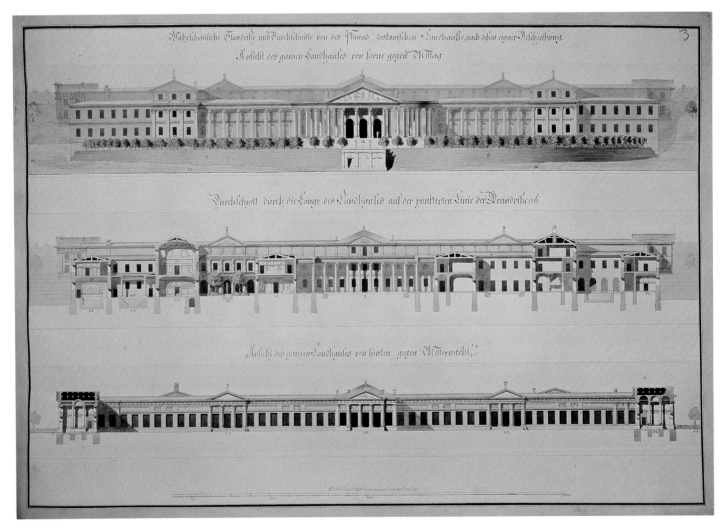

Plate 40. Krubsacius, Tuscan Villa, elevations of forecourt and garden facades, cross section through plane tree courtyard (SL, Forma max. qu. 2, Archaeol. 177, no. 3)

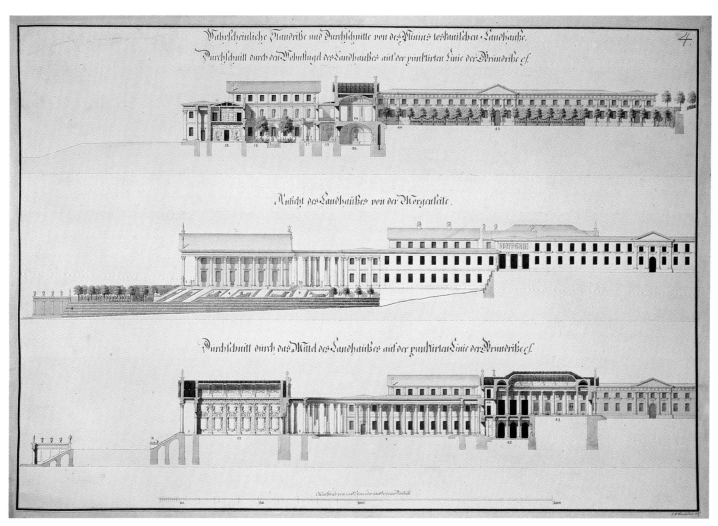

Plate 41. Krubsacius, Tuscan
Villa, side elevation and cross
sections through triclinium
and plane tree courtyard (SL,
Forma max. qu. 2, Archaeol.
177, no. 4)

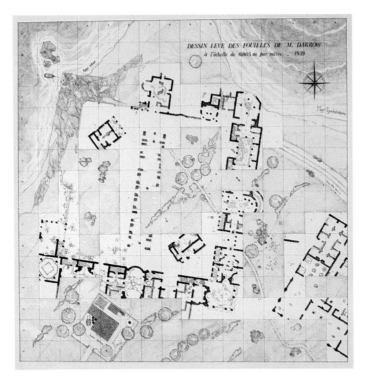

Plate 42. Fraisse and Braun, Laurentine Villa, excavation plan of Mr. Darrow's dig (collection of the artists)

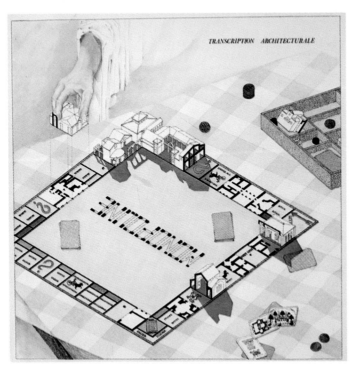

Plate 43. Fraisse and Braun, Laurentine Villa, Monopo-Pline board game (collection of the artists)

LA VILLA LAVRENTINE DE PLINE LE JEVNE

Plate 44. Weber and Laroche, Laurentine Villa, plans, elevations, cross sections, and aerial perspective (collection of the artists)

Plate 45. Montes, Laurentine Villa, model (collection of the artist)

Plate 46. Buenos Aires, Argentine Color Television Headquarters, south facade

Plate 47. Pamplona, Cordobilla Restaurant, view in
courtyard

ILS ONT FINI LA VILLA.

L'ARCHITECTURE EST FORMÉE PAR UN GROUPE DIVERS DE VOLUMES PURES, DE CRISTAL," VOLUMES PURES SOUS LA LUMIÈRE," QUI
CONTIENNENT CES VIEILLES RUINES, AUJOURD'HUI EN PARTIE RECONSTRUITES, QUE J'AI HÉRITÉ DE MES ANCÊTRES.—
LES CAISSES, EN BRIQUES DE VERRE, SONT LE CONTINENT DE MES ANTIQUITÉS, LESQUELLES PARAISSENT FLOTTER DANS
UN ESPACE DE LUMIÈRE DIFFUSE OU TOUT À L'AIR LE PLUS ADMIRABLE ET MAGIQUE.
JE PARCOURS LA VILLE EN RELISANT LE TEXTE DE PLINE, ET JE RECONSTRUIS PLUSIEURS DE SES MÉSSAGES,
TANDIS QUE D'AUTRES RESTENT LIVRÉS À L'IMAGINATION DE MES ARCHITECTES, QUI M'ONT CONVAINCU DE L'INPORTANCE
DE PLACER LES VOLUMES PRINCIPAUX SELON DES AXES NON ORTHOGONELS, POUR CRÉER AINSI DES TENSIONS ET
ET PROVOQUER DE DIFFÉRENTES PERSPECTIVES.
J'AIME LA GALERIE POSTÉRIEURE, LONGUE ET AVEC DES COLONNES, QUI AUGMENTENT LEURS DIAMÈTRE AU FUR
ET À MESURE QUE J'AVANCE, M'OBLIGEANT À LES ESQUIVER, ET PRESQUE À ME GLISSER ENTRE ELLES ET LE
MUR, CE MUR QUI NOUS PROTÈGE DU VENT DU NORD, COMME JADIS, COMME TOUJOURS.
LE SOLEIL BRILLE ET PRODUIT UN EFFET RÉVERBÉRANT SUR LES MURS DE VERRE, ET DANS L'AIR LES REFLET
DESSINENT DES TRACES DE LUMIÈRE. FINALEMENT, MA PETIT MAISON, PLACÉE SUR UN PLATEFORME ET ENTOURÉE
ENTIÈREMENT PAR DES MURS DE CRISTAL TRANSPARENT, D'OÙ JE JOUIS, EN OBSERVANT LA MOBILITÉ IMMOBILE DE LA
MER ET LE JARDIN DE VIOLETTES. PLINIO

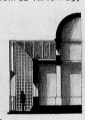

LA VILLE DE PLINE

ARQ. J. SOLSONA / ARQ. DAMP ARQ. FERNANDEZ

Plate 48. Solsona, Laurentine
Villa, aerial perspective and
cross sections (collection of
the artist)

especially likely (cf. fig. 30, looking at it upside down). Compared with Canina's villa, however, the cramped quarters and awkward changes of direction in this restitution betray its student designer's basic weakness. Gallus would have had to zigzag his way crablike to get from the left extremity of the sprawling complex to the huge *sphaeristerium* at the other end. Nor would his disorientation lessen when looking from the outside. He might easily have taken the main entrance to be the porticoed bathroom door in the center of the elevation.

The restitution titled "Casa di Plinio a Laurento" seems to belong to a different and later artistic era. The plan itself (fig. 123), though by no means ample, is not as cluttered as the mosaic flooring pattern shown in every room makes it appear. For compact, orderly organization it ranks on a par with the French designs of earlier in the century, but its garden layout is if anything even less imaginative than theirs. Much the same applies to the elevations, except for their studied asymmetry and the introduction of a castellated neomedieval tower, all of which contribute to the feeling of a later date, say the 1860s (fig. 124). The impression is strengthened by the similarity of the seaside suite of rooms to those proposed by Bouchet in 1852 (cf. fig. 35). Where this design does excel is in the colorful cross section taken from the sober atrium through to the sumptuous triclinium beyond (fig. 125). The wall decoration looks as archaeologically advanced as any of the reconstructed Pompeian rooms actually produced in the nineteenth century.[3] It almost presages the scientific accuracy of as recent a restitution as Jean-Pierre Adam's (fig. 127). Its expertness suggests a gifted student whose name and dates might emerge with more systematic research in the archives of the Accademia di San Luca. Once under way, such an investigation could be extended to other academies right across Europe, with the likely result that more unknown Plinian restitutions would turn up in dusty storerooms or on the pages of long forgotten academic registers.

What might apply to Europe certainly applies in North America, as was discovered long ago by Helen Tanzer, a professor of Latin at Hunter and Brooklyn Colleges. The research she conducted for her pioneering study of 1924 on the villas of Pliny utilized the rich holdings of the Avery Architectural Library at Columbia University. There she also found two unpublished student Laurentine restitutions in the archives of the school of architecture: the one signed by J. W. Loring, the other by a certain J. G. S. Junior, dated 3 December 1864. The pair of them are so similar that they must belong to the same academic exercise during the Civil War period. Like Tanzer, both certainly profited from the resources at the Avery Library in the way they adapted Bouchet's or Haudebourt's arrangements, giving them a slight asymmetrical twist in the process. Neither has much artistic significance except insofar as they herald the interest in Pliny's villas that has swept architecture schools in Canada and the United States during the 1980s and 1990s.

This recent resurgence can be attributed once again to the rapid dissemination of ideas from France, in this case from the Paris exhibition catalog of 1982 titled *La Laurentine.* In response to *La Laurentine,* recent design studios or competitions on a Plinian theme have been staged at McGill University by Ricardo Castro, at Princeton University by Michael Graves, at Syracuse University by Bruce Coleman, at the University of Toronto by Michael Djordjevitch, and at Rensselaer Polytechnic Institute by David Bell. Probably the North American list could go on, whereas the reception in Europe where it all began has been far less enthusiastic, as we will see.[4]

The resurgence of interest appears all the more remarkable in light of the sharp decline in the practice of restitution by architectural students worldwide. The decline reached its nadir in the late 1970s, at the very moment the Laurentine exhibition in Paris was conceived and launched. Nowhere had it sunk lower in esteem than in France, where such academic exercises had first risen to prominence. No longer did the Ecole des Beaux-Arts stage competitions on such themes. Nor did it require anymore that its Grand Prix winners send home envois, those more or less fanciful mixtures of imaginative restoration with archaeological fact.[5] Symptomatically, the Ecole as such had ceased to exist in 1968. The student uprisings that had brought about its fall caused a reorganization and decentralization of French university life in all disciplines, including the fine arts. In the process the Ecole lost much of its preeminence to schools of architecture dotted about at universities in the French provinces. After the demise of the Ecole, historians naturally turned their attention to an institution that had died just short of its three hundredth anniversary. One of these historians is Pierre Pinon (b. 1945), trained as an architect during this turbulent period. He attended the Académie de France à Rome, the branch of the Ecole housed in the magnificent Villa Medici on the Pincian Hill, well known to Mazois, Haudebourt, and Bouchet. In those conducive surroundings Pinon's attention turned to restitutions of the Roman house leading up to the early excavations at Pompeii.[6]

The writings of Palladio, Scamozzi, Marquez, and Mazois formed four obvious points of convergence between typological investigations of the house on the one hand and the villa on the other. At the Villa Medici, moreover, the aura of envois and *concours* still hangs about the place. So Pinon quite naturally began extending his researches in the direction of the villas of Pliny. The Accademia di San Luca with its student restitutions of the Laurentine Villa was also near at hand. These factors, and others no doubt, conspired to put Pinon in mind to restage an academic *concours d'émulation* modeled on the Laurentine competition held at the Ecole in 1818. His opportunity to do so arose in the context of a colloquium titled "Présence de l'architecture et de l'urbanisme romains" organized by the Classics Department of the University of Tours. By the late spring of 1981 he and Raymond

Chevallier, a professor at Tours and subsequent contributor to *La Laurentine*, had agreed to participate, together with a number of distinguished archaeologists, architects, and Latinists.[7] The Académie d'Architecture offered to host the two-day colloquium on 12–13 December 1981 at its headquarters on the place des Vosges in Paris.

Meanwhile Pinon had enlisted the collaboration of Maurice Culot (b. 1943), whom he knew from having published in his magazine *Archives d'Architecture Moderne*. In addition to Culot's duties as editor, he also headed the Archives Department of the Institut Français d'Architecture, which had just been founded in 1981 to rejuvenate French architecture. Between them Pinon and Culot began to put into action the idea of reviving a Laurentine *concours d'émulation*. It seems clear from the documents preserved at IFA that Pinon originally had conceived of some nice drawings to serve as a sort of backdrop to the colloquium. His thoughts initially turned to a pair of architect/archaeologist collaborators of his, Philippe Fraisse (b. 1949) and Jean-Pierre Braun (b. 1946), a fellow alumnus of the Villa Medici. Fraisse and Braun, in turn, worked closely with the Paris team of Treuttel, Garcias, and Treuttel and the Strasbourg team of Weber and Laroche, all of whom became involved by this means in what now had grown into a competition among friends and sympathizers. No gold medals would be handed out, of course, because the competitors were established architects rather than students. But the intangible rewards were, as they always have been in a *concours d'émulation*, matching wits with one's peers on a congenial subject: a villa where money is no object. Culot, however, had a grander vision, and he soon prevailed in turning the affair from what Braun characterized as something lighthearted and *familiale* into an international gathering.[8]

In the end Pinon and Culot had attracted thirteen architects or teams of architects from around the world to display their work in progress at the colloquium and then to submit their final version to a major exhibition accompanied by a printed catalog. The expanded show opened on 25 May 1982 in the converted orangery of the stately old Paris town house the Institut Français d'Architecture occupies on the rue de Tournon. In many ways this daring gambit by the new institution turned out to be a sort of swan song. Nothing as complex or innovative has subsequently graced the Institut's gallery tucked away at the bottom of its romantic and rather neglected garden. Although Pinon and Culot could not have fully realized the implications, Giscard d'Estaing's recent loss at the polls cast doubt on IFA's right-of-center mandate in the eyes of the new Mitterrand government. In 1981–82, however, IFA's reversal in fortunes still lay in the future, and all augured well for the exhibition. It subsequently embarked on an ambitious traveling schedule. It first reopened in the Kunstverein at Freiburg im Breisgau and then went on to the Ecole Polytechnique Fédèrale at Lausanne. Its closing engagement from

13 October to 11 December 1983 was at the Musée des Beaux-Arts de Montréal, where the Canadian Centre for Architecture cosponsored it under my guest curatorship.

For the final venue the original material from Paris was trimmed down in some respects but augmented by certain Tuscan Villa restitutions from the past, photographs of classical architecture or town planning in Montreal, and work by living local artists. To reflect the enlarged scope, the exhibition title was changed to "The Villas of Pliny and Classical Architecture in Montreal." Hence also, Montreal architect-artist Melvin Charney (b. 1935) was commissioned to create a new installation for the show centered on his two-part "construction" titled "Pliny on My Mind" (fig. 126). Crowning the top of a flight of stairs, the pedimented, templelike section suggested several things at once: a Quebec shack, the polemical primitive hut propounded by Abbé Laugier, the wooden form work of modern construction techniques, and the Freemasons' triangle, evocative of the temple at Jerusalem. All these overlapping levels of meaning, which singly and collectively fascinate the creative imagination of Charney, make this construction one of his strongest artistic statements to date.[9]

At the same time as "Pliny on My Mind" set the theme of the entire exhibition, it established an interrelation among the three sections—historical, local, and con-

126. Charney, "Pliny on My Mind No. 1 and No. 2," wood construction (Phyllis Lambert collection, Montreal)

temporary—the walls of each painted in a slightly different shade of what the designer called "Pliny green." The color was inspired by the one used in the gallery at IFA, which in itself is an instance of the emulation that was the overriding concern of the show. Charney's construction defined certain lines of sight without obstructing them. The visitor could trace visually the interconnections from section to section and could follow up instances of emulation in action. Small clusters of objects with explanatory panels formed eddies off the mainstream or pointed the attentive viewer onward. The cumulative effect stressed the way architects have learned from one another and from Pliny over the ages. Sometimes the stacking up of ideas suggested the image of architects standing on one another's shoulders to form a human pyramid.

With one accord the name of Jean-Pierre Adam (b. 1937) came to the lips of every participant in the *concours d'émulation* as the architect who best represented the traditional, archaeological approach to a Laurentine restitution. Among his fellow architect-archaeologists he is regarded as the leader of their small, highly

127. Adam, Laurentine Villa, aerial perspective and cross section (collection of the artist)

specialized, branch of the profession, and the competition organizers saw him as an obvious and key person to include. A licensed architect since 1965, a graduate of the archaeology program at the Ecole Pratique des Hautes Etudes, and the veteran of numerous excavation campaigns at home and abroad, Adam is currently attached to the Centre National de la Recherche Scientifique as head of the Paris bureau of its Service d'Architecture Antique. From his office high up in the medieval Tour du Village at the Château de Vincennes, he oversees excavations and improvements to archaeological sites all over France. His publications range from a scholarly work on Greek fortifications that grew out of his thesis and a manual on the arts and crafts in antiquity, profusely illustrated with his own line drawings, to a book for children titled *La Méditerranée*. And in a more recent work Adam returned to the theme of restitution by turning his artistry to the probable appearance of the Seven Wonders of the Ancient World as described in the words of Philo of Byzantium. Adam tempers the scholarly side of his personality with a popular side, revealed in the liveliness and wit of his drawings, which seem to bring the past back to life, as any good restitution should.

Accordingly, on 22 July 1981, Pinon and Culot sent Adam the same basic letter of invitation they sent other prospective participants. It proposed as the deadline for submission of restitution drawings the 12 December opening of the colloquium, and it enclosed a copy of Pliny's letter together with a suggested scale, maximum length of any accompanying written document, and so forth. It provided, in effect, the essential information of a standard *programme*. In addition, Pinon and Culot offered an honorarium to help defray costs. They included a bibliography of previous restitutions, with photocopies of those by Bouchet, Haudebourt, and others. An outline of the proposed exhibition catalog accompanied a list of the persons invited to compete, comprising Adam and eighteen others, not all of whom accepted in the end. But Adam said yes on the twenty-ninth of that month and congratulated the organizers. "Bravo pour l'idée," he wrote in a short postscript conveying the relish with which he anticipated the "jeu de Pline," as the organizers described it in the statement of intent they attached to their letter. Their provocative words, "Pline, toujours jeune, attend son prochain concours, c'est la pérennité du classicisme qui est en cause," were not lost on Jean-Pierre Adam.[10]

The two large, impressive drawings Adam prepared for the December exhibition of Laurentine restitutions consist of an aerial perspective and a plan together with their related cross sections (figs. 127 and 128). They nicely illustrate his basic premise that the ancient Romans often ignored symmetry in their domestic architecture. He now considers this one of the chief virtues of his restitution in comparison with the others'. He stresses that he worked in relative isolation and therefore had little idea in advance of their preference for grandeur of conception and often for a quite predictable regularity and axiality. Aesthetically admirable as such

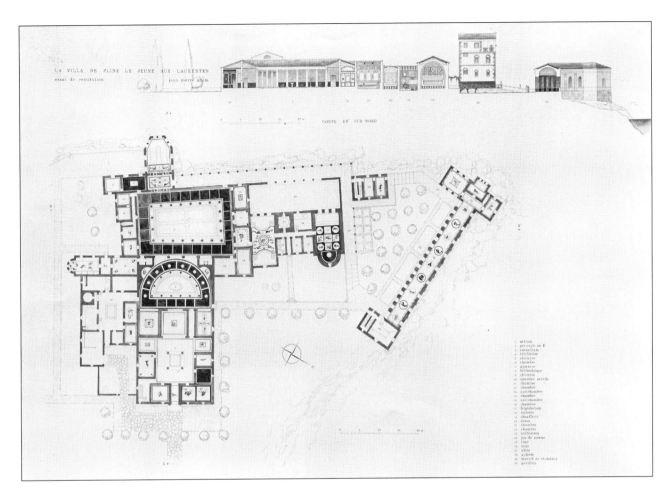

128. Adam, Laurentine Villa, plan and cross section (collection of the artist)

attempts may be, he regards them as classicizing rather than accurately classical.[11] From his wealth of archaeological experience he asserts that the Romans favored an informal layout, and they shifted axes frequently to suit their purposes or in response to the lay of the land. In just such a way the upper or rear portion of Adam's Laurentine Villa is skewed in relation to the front so as to follow the irregular shoreline. At the same time he insists on a basic core of three principal rooms arranged in sequence: atrium, *D*-shaped peristyle court, and *cavaedium*. He bases this progression on the floor plans of Pompeian houses he knows so well. Adam has made something of a speciality of Pompeii, not just in strict archaeological terms but also in reports on the deterioration of the physical fabric of the ruins, especially after the 1962 earthquake. He and his wife, furthermore, collaborated on a documentary film, *Construire et vivre à Pompéi*, into which they wove evidence of Adam's belief in the continuity of ancient craft traditions down to the present. To see this film, to hear its director speak about Pompeii in his impassioned way, is almost to believe that he personally had lived in the city at its height, had experienced its every corner, had survived its cataclysmic demise, had witnessed its excavations—in fact was Pompeii incarnate. Much the same conviction carries over to his Laurentine Villa.

In the absence of the ruins of Pliny's Laurentinum, Adam himself would admit that the houses of Pompeii, and even its suburban villas, can provide only a tentative analogy to work from. As if in recognition of this, Adam interrupted a learned interview liberally spinkled with Pompeian prototypes to interject that Pliny's *D*-shaped courtyard must have been rare, otherwise the letter would have passed over it in silence. It is hard to justify how Adam can see the Laurentine Villa as so typical yet in some ways unique. Adam also insists that, Pliny's literary artifice aside, the villa really existed. Yet somewhat contradictorily once again, he remarks that the letter constitutes an ideal "brief" such as a client might address to an architect. Adam remains adamant that Pliny could not have been his own designer. Yet he notes the many idiosyncratic features about the villa, such as the absence of farm buildings, Pliny's failure to allude to the elevations, and the "Trianon"-like nature of the *amores mei* pavilion. Despite all this, he feels confident that the Laurentine Villa must have resembled rather closely his own version of it. He is not the only one to think so. The archaeologist Pierre-Yves Balut (b. 1948) supports Adam's restitution in his controversial critical essay accompanying the published catalog. Balut, moreover, correctly detects the nostalgia in Adam's brightly colored restitution, harking back to a nineteenth-century realism when architecture and archaeology coexisted at the Ecole in such apparent harmony.[12]

Adam likes to stress the modernity of ancient Roman sanitary arrangements. His Laurentine bathing complex, for instance, occupies the entire central portion of the plan and the cross section above it. Yet he maintains that its size is not out of proportion with a rich patrician villa of this type. The sybaritic overtones of the Latin letter to Gallus extend beyond the baths to encompass the whole establishment. To Adam's mind the prose chiefly stresses the quality of *agrément*, that is to say, pleasure and delight. A squash court opens off the baths, overlooking a shady seaside terrace. Large, sweet-smelling beds of violets run parallel to the cryptoporticus at the far right, while on the other side servants' quarters accommodate the battalions of gardeners, gatekeepers, and caretakers necessary to keep such a place in order, according to Adam. In spite of himself, Adam sees a modern dream house: exotic, appealing, Mediterranean in flavor like the Villa Kerylos that Emile-Emmanuel Pontremoli actually built for the classicist Theodore Reinach on the Côte d'Azur at the turn of the century.[13] Other participants in the *concours* were less familair with antiquity than Adam or too cynical about its "delights" to reap the sensual pleasure he did in reading Pliny's letter and conveying its message so skillfully.

The brief essay Adam prepared to accompany his Laurentine drawings emphasizes two main features of Roman domestic architecture. The first, the quality of *fantaisie,* has already been analyzed with reference to the plan. The second characteristic, *couleur,* emerges in the aerial perspective and its related cross section. Not since Potocki's restitution and the anonymous Italian ones has so much attention focused on the rooms with their painted Pompeian-style decoration. Adam asserts their vivacity of color, the absence of furniture that might tone down their brightness, the polish of their surfaces, and so forth. Adam clearly designs from the inside out. This explains some of the unintentional awkwardness, such as the proportions of the insignificant-looking main triclinium jutting out to sea. The evocation of various materials and plant life cannot entirely disguise the inadequacy of planning. The bravura comes from the brilliant draftsmanship, his command of perspective, and the deftly lifelike flights of gulls or pigeons—birds are a sort of Jean-Pierre Adam leitmotiv. He seems to see Pompeii through their eyes, wheeling overhead, able to look down on every detail.

Adam concludes his text with the cautious caveat that his *essai de restitution* must be regarded as "a free interpretation . . . realized without any archaeological testimony, the interest of which resides in . . . the pleasure of expressing by means of drawing all that the text is unable to supply."[14] Realizing the problem posed by a villa that has disappeared without a trace, Adam nevertheless gave the competition organizers what they expected from him: a proper archaeological restitution emulating the envois done by the French *pensionnaires* of the past, but this time without a shred of physical evidence to go on. The restitution carries conviction owing to its designer's acknowledged cultivation, his extensive exposure to classical remains, and his intimate knowledge of Pompeii in particular. But it also owes its great charm to the almost caricature-like drawing style. Some of this whimsical quality must puzzle Adam's admirers among the archaeologists. It is as if his French Alsatian background played off against his Italian maternal influence, balancing the scholarly with the highly artistic, the serious with the flamboyant.

At the time Philippe Fraisse and Jean-Pierre Braun accepted the invitation to the *concours d'émulation,* they were both in Greece working as architect-archaeologists on the Delos excavation sponsored by the Ecole Française d'Archéologie at Athens.[15] They continue to work on joint projects and won an honorable mention at the competition for the new Paris opera on the place de la Bastille. They actively collaborate on a *certificat d'études* program in architecture and archaeology in which they give their students such problems as restituting the mausoleum at Halicarnassus or the temple at Jerusalem, in which endeavors they are often assisted by Pierre-Yves Balut of the Institut d'Art and the Strasbourg team of Weber and Laroche. As recently as June 1987 they all assembled again in the appropriate surroundings of the Ecole des Beaux-Arts, together with Pierre Pinon and me for a day-long round-table discussion devoted to a reconsideration of restitutions, including their own based on Pliny. Braun in conversation notes that most of his other collaborators are teachers, like himself, as well as practicing architects. He for one teaches at the Paris-Belleville School of Architecture and also works with a Paris firm called Triptyque. Of the other competitors in the Laurentine *concours,* however, he and his immediate associates make the most use of the practices of restitution and emulation. For this reason I will consider them all together as one of several groups among the participants in the *concours.*

With the possible exception of Krier, Fraisse and Braun were the candidates to come first to the *concours* organizers' minds and to have added the most at the initial planning stages. Once they found out that Adam had also been asked, they determined that their best course of action was to go to the diametrically opposite pole. Working in feverish haste, in less than a week they produced three drawings accompanied by a laconic and ironic explanatory text. They also knew by this time that the professional cartoonist Jacques Martin (b. 1933) would not participate, and so they decided to emulate his example by introducing a bit of their own humor into a process they felt should remain friendly and relaxed.[16] Martin, of course, is the creator and illustrator of Alix, the blond, blue-eyed hero of a series of comic book adventures set in the ancient Roman world. Martin's many devotees include Léon Krier, who dedicated his restitution to Martin in the hope that he would one day set an Alix episode at the Laurentine Villa. In the end Krier's wish came true, up to a point. Martin could not join in the competition, but he made his presence felt by contributing to the exhibition a life-size cut-out figure of Alix cradling Krier's Laurentine Villa in his arms as if it were a model.[17]

Fraisse and Braun title their essay "Un seul texte n'a jamais permis une restitu-tion définitive." In the short paragraph that follows they reiterate their belief that no definitive restitution can be based on one text. They cast doubt on Adam's analogical method of approaching the Laurentine problem by creating their own imaginary dig undertaken in 1939 by a fictitious archaeologist, "Mr. Darrow" (pl. 42). Their drawing shows a headland projecting into the sea at the top, and at the bottom a farmyard called the *rustico calpurnia* in joking allusion to Pliny's wife. The olive grove between has been staked out with a typical archaeological grid, within which the outlines of the large Laurentine Villa and its dependencies have come to light. Without any real Laurentine remains to go on, Fraisse and Braun supplied their own as the essential first step in any dig. The consequent checker-board subdivision of the grove, together with Pinon and Culot's exhortation to enter into the *jeu de Pline,* put Fraisse and Braun in mind of a board game. The third and last of their drawings (pl. 43) shows a new *jeu de société* they have named "MonopoPline." (In a rash moment they even thought of marketing the idea commercially.) Familiar Monopoly property names such as Boardwalk and Marvin Gardens become transformed into Latin descriptive terms taken from Pliny's letter. The square perimeter of the board itself corresponds to the villa courtyard unearthed by Mr. Darrow. Random elements of the Laurentine Villa replace the familiar green houses and red hotels of Monopoly. An unlucky throw of the dice may land a player on Chance!

In its own zany way "MonopoPline" makes a perfectly logical point. According to Braun, it implies that an architect-archaeologist with no physical traces to go on is working in a vacuum and inevitably must dip into the Chance cards. Some of the Chance cards are placed face up to show a confusing assortment of antique architectural monuments for emulation—all the way from Djemila in Algeria to Rome. Or a wild card may require a player to move *un coup rétro, un coup post,* to quote from the rules of the game, alluding wittily to reactionary and postmodern architectural trends.[18] This love of gamesmanship and wordplay formed an undercurrent to the entire *concours,* influenced a number of the entries, and spilled over to enliven the critical reception of the exhibition. Praise for Fraisse and Braun came from the normally caustic Balut, who admittedly knows these contestants better than most of the others. And when the Laurentine show was remounted in Montreal, Mr. Darrow's mock excavation inspired children to rearrange Pliny's doors, walls, and windows on a giant-sized map of Laurentinum placed on the floor like a carpet.[19] On the more theoretical side, Fraisse and Braun wanted their game to illustrate the way architects' minds work on the evidence from an excavation. The ghostly hand moving the pieces about on their imaginary board is the hand of the architect who gives *vie et corps* to the substructures the archaeologist unearths. In the process of supplying these missing elements, architects assemble a composite picture based on their knowledge from other sites. But the element of chance, and of possible error, remains a risk. Those who miss the point must return to the beginning at Go.

Both Didier Laroche (b. 1956) and Patrick Weber (b. 1952) teach and practice architecture at Strasbourg. The youngest team of participants in the *concours d'émulation,* they were also among the last to be invited. Both had been to Greece at various times in their early twenties, attached to different archaeological digs.[20] This was their connection to Fraisse, who also works in eastern France and who put them in touch with Culot. Laroche and Weber accepted his invitation. As they first saw it, the Laurentine competition might have degenerated into a fogyish exercise or a *jeu passéiste.* In conversation, as well as in the brief manifesto accompanying their several drawings, the young men stressed their initial reluctance to enter into an experiment in emulation so foreign to normal practice—"très en marge de la production courante," as they put it. But in the end they were won over to the idea, which they now consider to have been of fundamental importance to their work. They admit, in retrospect, that their assessment of the mission of the Institut Français d'Architecture was clouded by the anti-IFA political rhetoric of 1981–82.

Against the rising tide of Mitterrand's socialists, Maurice Culot mustered an all-out, last-ditch assault on public taste in the form of the Laurentine competition. For Weber and Laroche the high-water mark of this sandbagging attempt came on the occasion of the *jour de Pline* that took place on 25 May 1982. The crowning events were a gala lecture at the Sorbonne, a party held in the garden of IFA's headquarters, and the inauguration of the exhibition "La Laurentine" in the adjacent gallery space. Four main groups attended. Laroche and Weber belonged to the architect-archaeologists, most of whom knew each other already, as we have seen. Another group revolved around Fernando Montes, of whom I will say more later. A third group knew Bernard Huet and were collaborators of his. Finally, there were the cohorts of Maurice Culot. It was certainly a moment of triumph for him; since then his point of view has increasingly alienated him and IFA from the mainstream of French and world architectural thought. With the benefit of hindsight, Culot's fight now appears a rear-guard action, and his credibility has been seriously eroded as a result of championing in the pages of *Archives d'Architecture Moderne* such traditionalists as Quinlan Terry, Christian Langlois, and Abdel Wahed el-Wakil. Yet as Weber and Laroche remark with some wistfulness, Culot has the ability to bring people together and to engender debate, as when he invited the historian and critic Balut to write a controversial essay on the Laurentine projects, a decision Culot may subsequently have regretted.[21]

Balut's critique, with its knack for the pithy put-down, characterizes Weber and Laroche's submission as pompous, brilliant, "mais . . . soigneusement schizoïde" (pl. 44). It was an opinion the designers willingly accepted when questioned about it. Like the other architect-archaeologists, they felt it imperative to differentiate themselves from Adam. And in the sense that to emulate is also to excel, they almost achieved their goal in terms of sheer size; their main drawing exceeds Adam's, the largest in the exhibition, in breadth if not in height. They also steered away from what they call Adam's *villa plausible*. But as Balut observes, they fall between two stools. Their plan per se is all too plausible once it is isolated from the rest of the complex composition. Part of the raison d'être for that complexity, in fact, was to gratuitously reshuffle the same deck of cards played by Fraisse and Braun. Weber and Laroche have confused ingenious representation with real substance. The result is a cunningly multilayered representation, flawed with a schizophrenic split, as Balut himself terms it. As their manifesto states, they set out to immerse themselves in archaeological and literal interpretations of the letter. Only then did they turn to drawing as a means of distinguishing their project from the rest. Perhaps, they now conclude in the light of Balut's remarks, they should have reversed their order of procedure.[22]

According to what Weber and Laroche said in a tape-recorded interview, their main drawing was intended above all as an *exercise de dessein* in emulation of the best nineteenth-century draftsmanship. Their printed text, moreover, evokes such great names of the Ecole des Beaux-Arts as Hector-Marie d'Espouy (Grand Prix 1884). Their enthusiasm for the Ecole must be understood against the background of the very positive response among architects to the 1981 "Pompéi" exhibition guest-curated by Pinon in Paris. In his catalog he illustrated meticulous restitution *envois* sent back by the *pensionnaires* abroad. A careful dissection of the Weber and Laroche drawing shows the virtuosic way, for example, that cross sections serve the double purpose of vertical borders to the sheet. An aerial site plan showing the roofscape from above occupies the bottom right corner. Moving toward the center are the two halves of the plan, split apart for no apparent reason except effect. Then in the gap created in the middle the villa's front elevation is shown below, and dwarfing it above is the profile of the Arch of Trajan at Timgad set against a blue Algerian sky. The designers remark on the chance resemblance between the curved shapes and proportions of the arch and their villa. Finally the Timgad frieze, which runs along the top border, becomes a brightly colored postmodern comic strip consisting of different vignettes of Laurentinum. The plethora of visual stimuli presented here is carried off with conscious technical showmanship and panache. The contestants conclude their printed statement by dwelling on the sensuous pleasure of drawing with a good thick pencil on smooth paper. They write: "Mais enfin, et surtout, le dessin au crayon gras sur panet tendre, sans prétention polémique et sans autre alibi que l'inestimable plaisir pris à son exécution raffinée."

The Treuttel, Garcias, and Treuttel team jokingly refer to themselves as a three-man cottage industry, or "petite entreprise familiale à but culturo-lucratif."[23] The impression is confirmed by the cramped but homey Paris studio in which they work side by side. The eldest of the three, Jean-Claude Garcias (b. 1940), is a brother-in-law of the two Treuttels. He is a critic and historian as well as an architect. The elder Treuttel, the architect Jean-Jacques (b. 1943), is a Parisian by birth, as is his brother Jérôme (b. 1945), who has a background in engineering. All three teach: Garcias at Paris-Vincennes, the elder and younger Treuttels at Nantes and Clermont-Ferrand Universities, respectively. When the Laurentine *concours* was first announced they began working in association with Braun, but then they decided to submit their own entry. Faced with Jean-Pierre Adam's restitution, which they regarded as reflecting bourgeois values, and Braun's tongue-in-cheek humor, they decided to take another direction that had served them well in previous competitions they have entered since 1979. They would deconstruct Pliny's letter to Gallus in search of its hidden subtext. They also determined to counteract the unwritten bias of the Laurentine *programme* that, in their words, called for "a beautiful villa and a happy society to be restituted."[24]

The drawing labeled *Tabula Prima* (fig. 129) is a conventional enough design, especially when compared with the Weber and Laroche entry just seen. Directly underneath the Latin lettering of the inscription, Treuttel, Garcias, and Treuttel arranged two cross sections through a simple-looking villa. The singularly plain and low-lying dwelling for the master to all appearances employs the rustic Tuscan order, while the service courts beyond are either altogether astylar or support their roofs and sheltered walkways by what look like primitive tree-trunk columns. The ground plan confirms the impression that for all its elegance the villa occupies only roughly half the area of a large agricultural establishment of the sort imagined earlier by Castell or Stier (cf. figs. 57 and 105). This distinct switch of emphasis from luxury villa to working farm is the means by which the three Parisian designers want to draw attention to their critical contention that the landscape according to Pliny "est un paysage sans paysans: C'est à dire sans esclaves." They detect in Pliny's omission of any mention of slavery an unenunciated pronouncement: the *otium*, or leisure, of the Roman statesmen depended entirely upon the produce of his latifundia, harvested by the sweat of the slaves' brows. Thus the first drawing establishes a polemical argument that Pliny passed over a whole side of his villa because he thought it too banal to mention. There is nothing really new about what Treuttel, Garcias, and Treuttel have concluded, though it is interesting that they are among the only writers in the Pliny literature to acknowledge Viollet-le-Duc's contribution (see chap. 5), while differing totally from his vision of Laurentinum as a paternalistic paradise. In their eagerness to castigate Pliny, they overlook the correspondence that depicts him as a person who cared for his slaves' health and for the well-being of those who worked the land generally. It suited their purpose to jump to the conclusion that he stood for an exploitative age overdue for a slaves' revolt led by another Spartacus.[25]

The second Treuttel, Garcias, and Treuttel drawing (fig. 130) more overtly states their stance as arbiters of public conscience and critics of the latest architectural fadism. Pliny's villa becomes the whipping boy for folly past and present. And the image of the whip is not out of place in this context. The whole significance of the upper register of the drawing relates to the pleasures of *otium* and its counterpart in the utter drudgery of the slaves' lives. Four vignettes on the left conjure up pictures of slothful and overindulgent relaxation. The four contrasting ones on the right depict flagellation, incarceration, and crucifixion as the frequent lot of Roman slaves. These line drawings resemble those by Jean-Pierre Adam illustrating his manuals on the arts and crafts of the ancient world. Indeed, the three designers stress the importance of the history of techniques in preference to

INSTITVTIO GALLICA ARCHITEC-
TVRAE: LVDVS AEMVLATIONIS

RESTITVTIO CONSVLIS CAII PLINII LAVRENTINAE VILLAE
TABVLA PRIMA

INVENERVNT DELINAVERVNTQVE
TREVTTEL GARCIAS TREVTTEL

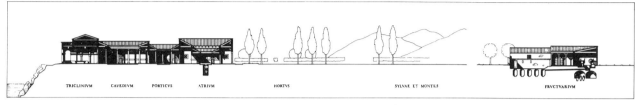

TRICLINIVM   CAVEDIVM   PORTICVS   ATRIVM   HORTVS   SYLVAE ET MONTES   FRVCTVARIVM

HELIOCAMINVS   CRYPTOPORTICVS   SPHAERISTERIVM   BALNEI   ATRIVM   VILLA RVSTICA   ERGASTVLVM   HORREA

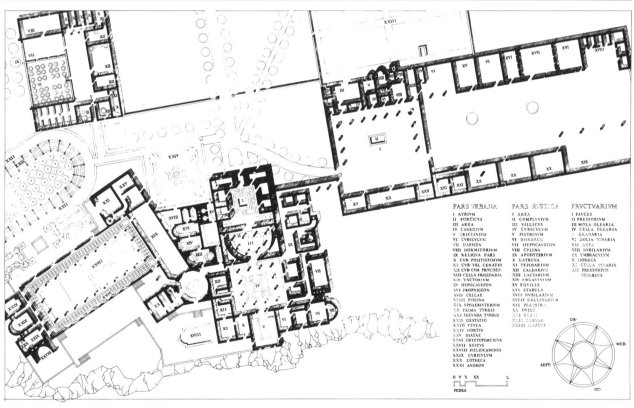

PARS VRBANA

I ATRIVM
II PORTICVS
III AREA
IV CAVEDIVM
V TRICLINIVM
VI CVBICVLVM
VII HAPSIDA
VIII DORMITORIVM
IX RELIQVA PARS
X CVB· POLITISSIMVM
XI CVB· VEL CENATIO
XII CVB·CVM PROCOET·
XIII CELLA FRIGIDARIA
XIV VNCTORIVM
XV HYPOCAVSTON
XVI PROPNIGEON
XVII CELLAE
XVIII PISCINA
XIX SPHAERISTERIVM
XX PRIMA TVRRIS
XXI SECVNDA TVRRIS
XXII GESTATIO
XXIII VINEA
XXIV HORTVS
XXV DIAETA
XXVI CRYPTOPORTICVS
XXVII XYSTVS
XXVIII HELIOCAMINVS
XXIX CVBICVLVM
XXX ZOTHECA
XXXI ANDRON

PARS RVSTICA

I AREA
II COMPLVVIVM
III VILLICVS
IV CVBICVLVM
V PISTRINVM
VI HORREVM
VII HYPOCAVSTON
VIII CVLINA
IX APODYTERIVM
X LATRINA
XI TEPIDARIVM
XII CALDARIVM
XIII LACTARIVM
XIV ERGASTVLVM
XV EQVILIA
XVI STABVLA
XVII NVBILARIVM
XVIII GALLINARIVM
XIX PLAVSTRA
XX OVILE
XXI STATI
XXII SERVAE
XXIII HORTVS

FRVCTVARIVM

I FAVCES
II PRESSORIVM
III MOLA OLEARIA
IV CELLA OLEARIA
V GRANARIA
VI DOLIA VINARIA
VII AREA
VIII NVBILARIVM
IX VMBRACVLVM
X HORREA
XI CELLA VINARIA
XII PRESSORIVM
VINARIVM

OR·
MER·
SEPT·
OC·

O   V   X   XX   L
|__|__|__|_____|
PEDES

129. Treuttel, Garcias, and
Treuttel, Laurentine Villa,
plan and cross sections (collection of the artists)

OTIVM DOMINORVM ANNO LXXXII

SALTORES

PISCINA

TRICLINIVM

LECTICA

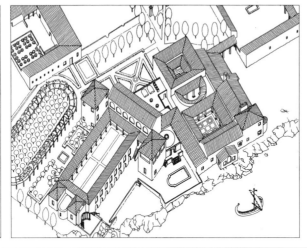

LABOR SERVORVM ANNO LXXXII

ERGASTVLVM

STIMVLI MATERIALES

SEMINATORES

PANIFEX

OTIVM CVM DIGNITATE: LABOR CVM FLAGELLO

CE PROJET VEUT MONTRER D'UNE PART QUE L'ARCHITECTURE NOBLE DE L'ANTIQUE, CELLE DES MAITRES, N'A PU SE FORMER QU'AVEC ET CONTRE L'ARCHITECTURE IGNOBLE, CELLE DES ESCLAVES; DE L'AUTRE QUE LA REACTUALISATION DE L'ANTIQUE, SOUS SES FORMES RENAISSANTE, NEOCLASSIQUE OU POST-MODERNE, S'EPUISE NECESSAIREMENT EN PASTICHE DES LORS QU'ELLE FAIT L'IMPASSE SUR LES TECHNIQUES ET LA SPHERE DU TRAVAIL.

L'APPARENTE PERENNITE DES ESPACES CONSACRES AUX PLAISIRS DE LA CLASSE DE LOISIR SEMBLE S'OPPOSER RADICALEMENT AUX BOULEVERSEMENTS SUBIS PAR LES ESPACES VOUES AU TRAVAIL. MAIS EN FAIT LES LIEUX DE LA JOUISSANCE ET DE L'EFFORT SE MODIFIENT PARALLELEMENT. LES ESPA-

CES DE L'HEDONISME NE SONT PAS PLUS FIGES QUE LES LOCAUX SERVANTS OU SERVILES DONT ILS DEPENDENT.

NOUS RESTITUONS DONC LA VILLA DU MAITRE DE L'AN 82 EN ELARGISSANT LA DESCRIPTION DE PLINE PAR DES COMMUNS ET SERVITUDES. NOUS DONNONS L'EQUIVALENT DU DOMAINE DU LAURENTIN EN 1982. L'HEDONISME PATRONAL S'Y DEPLOIE DANS UN CADRE ECLECTIQUE ET FRIVOLE. MAIN-D'OEUVRE ET PRODUCTION Y SONT LOGEES DANS UN CADRE FONCTIONNEL ISSU DE LA VULGARISATION DU MOUVEMENT MODERNE.

EN HOMMAGE AUX MOSAISTES ROMAINS, A E.E. VIOLLET LE DUC, F. GAFFIOT, ET SPARTACUS.
NOUS REMERCIONS D. HOCKNEY, LE C.S.T.B., J. MARTIN, ET LE MINISTERE DE L'AGRICULTURE.

HEDONISME D'AUJOURD'HUI

INVITEES

A BIGGER SPLASH

LIVING ROOM POST MODERNE

BELLE AMERICAINE

VILLA POST-MODERNE EN 1982

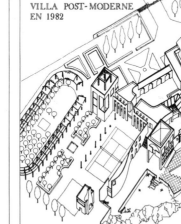

SALARIAT D'AUJOURD'HUI

LOGEMENTS DES SALARIES AGRICOLES

STIMULANT MATERIEL

BATTERIE DE POULETS

ELEVAGE DE VEAUX

130. Treuttel, Garcias, and Treuttel, Laurentine Villa and Villa Post-moderne, aerial perspectives and vignettes (collection of the artists)

the history of high-style architecture. They believe one depends on the other. It is this interdependence that their aerial restitution shows. The villa has the farming structures clustered closely around it, just as the eight vignettes cluster around the top central panel. The vignettes provide slices of real life and are, by the way, part of a didactic technique that the three architects use in other competitions where restitution plays no part. In a 1987 French government-sponsored contest for the design of a hospice for the terminally ill, Treuttel, Garcias, and Treuttel used vignettes to drive home the central but unstated point of such a place: people there usually die.

Restitution serves the Treuttel, Garcias, and Treuttel team not so much as an end in itself but as a kind of emulation in reverse. It acts as a springboard to lampoon the latest foolishness in architecture (*le style le plus criant*) and the most flagrant social injustices of the day. Therefore they resist the use of restitution in their classrooms, despite the success it brought them in the *concours d'émulation.* Part of that success results from the shock they intended when the eye moves down from their antique restitution of A.D. 82 to the bottom third of the second drawing, occupied by their pastiche postmodern villa of 1982. Emulation is present in their cunning and punning bird's-eye view of the villa in the manner of Le Corbusier. The three designers have resorted to such familiar Le Corbusier tricks as showing a speedy coupé parked in front of the four-car garage at the right. The plunging view down onto rooftop terraces deliberately recalls the aerial perspectives of his Villa Savoye, or his "Villa Steinus à Garchus," as the designers called the Villa Stein at Garches in a hilariously informal interview. As for Pliny's *villa rusticus,* it becomes an American factory farm in the Midwest. As seen in the four vignettes on the right, furthermore, hired hands are banished to distant and soulless *unités d'habitation,* and Pliny's chickens turn into battery hens. Over on the left four other vignettes make fun of what the designers regard as the hedonism of modern bourgeois life. The villa takes on the aspect of a Hollywood nightmare home as seen through the eyes of artist David Hockney, whose inspiration, along with that of Viollet-le-Duc and Jacques Martin, is acknowledged on the drawing. The vignette of the atrium/living room suggests the Miami Beach modernism of Morris Lapidus in the 1950s, as do the swept-back fins of the *Belle Américaine* Cadillac sitting beside it. What a different Eden Roc than the one imagined by Jean-Pierre Adam! But it is a tribute to their artistry that despite their biting social commentary they could not bring themselves to produce a truly vulgar villa.

Fernando Montes (b. 1939) speaks with some disdain when thinking back to the Laurentine Villa he prepared in collaboration with some other architects in his office. Yet say what he will, he had a real hand in launching the *concours d'émulation* among a group of participants who might not otherwise have heard about the competition. And though he dismisses the *remaniement moderne* of classicism as a fad of the early eighties, he recognizes that his Laurentine restitution was part of an ongoing process in his artistic life. This is certainly true of a socioliterary approach he likes to employ in his extensive Paris-based practice and teaching career. A native of Chile, educated at the school of architecture in Santiago, Montes pursued his studies in Germany and France and completed his training at the Ecole des Beaux-Arts. In and around Paris his work includes developments in such suburbs as Cergy-Pontoise, and more recently on the avenue Mozart in the metropolis and the avenue Victor Hugo in Vincennes. All these projects exploit his literary bent, which served him well in interpreting Pliny. He grew to like Pliny because he provided a complete, almost cinematographic *scénario,* to use Montes's word. As Montes said in heavily accented French during an interview: "J'essaie par tous les moyens toujours . . . de soustituer quelque chose qui est ressemblant à un scénario." In the case of Pliny, the *scénario* evoked the perennially recurrent values of pleasure, relaxation, open spaces, and enjoyment of natural surroundings. Montes sees Pliny as relating to the contemporary workforce in a positive way, in contrast to Treuttel, Garcias, and Treuttel. According to Montes, the contemporary worker with a month's paid vacation each year can think of spending it at a seaside resort. This somewhat startling association of ideas between antiquity and the welfare state of modern Europe inspired Montes to produce one of the most colorful and diverse of all thirteen Laurentine Villa restitutions.[26]

Montes began his Laurentine restitution, it seems, by composing in his mind a sort of mental letter of his own—really more of a meditation, richly embellished with literary names such as Molière, Shakespeare, Baudelaire, Alain Robbe-Grillet, Italo Calvino, and Georges Pérec. In these rambling notes, published in the catalog *La Laurentine,* Montes states that it does not matter in the least whether Pliny's villa existed in reality or only as a figment of the imagination. That the letter to Gallus survives is what counts, together with the enormous influence it has had. Montes illustrated his text with four line drawings, of which one, a masterly aerial perspective, is reproduced here (fig. 131). Seen from above like this the villa initially looks neo-Roman, but closer inspection reveals its modernity. To either side of the large triclinium with its twin docks he arranged double rows of cubicles like changing rooms at a beach resort. The analogy is not fortuitous, because just to the right stands a swimming pool with a high diving board and towers for lifeguards, which replaces the normal Roman thermal complex. The *gestatio* has been transformed into a running track. All of this is quite intentional, as the second part of Montes's printed *scénario* explains.[27]

With a rather ironic modern twist, Montes recasts Pliny as a down-on-his-luck Breton lord of the manor who can no longer keep up the family estate on the coast of Finistère. So Pliny sells off to a resort developer the towerlike main core (*amores mei,* Montes rightly calls it). The private house is soon changed into a sort of Club

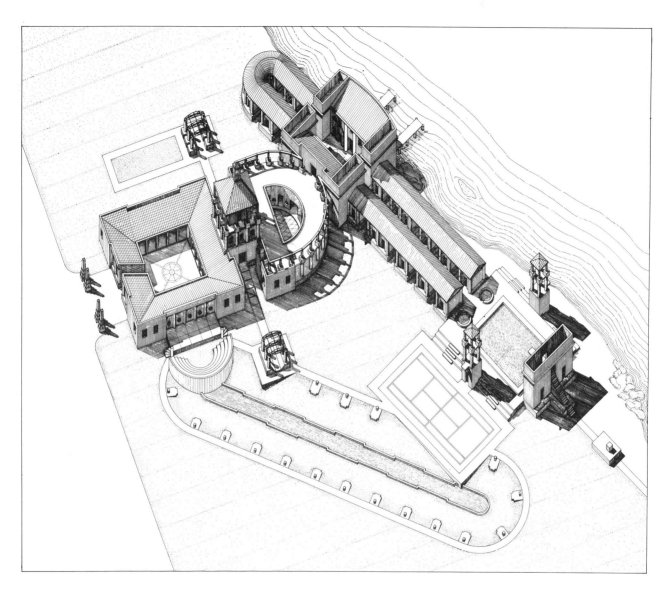

131. Montes, Laurentine Villa, aerial perspective (collection of the artist)

Med on the Atlantic, with all the aforementioned recreational facilities and a host more. The whole preposterous story ends on a seriocomic note, with poor Pliny accepting the invitation to return to the villa as its resident activities director. Like many a stately home, Pliny's turns into a profit-making fun fair for the masses.[28] Then, just to stress the absurdity, Montes had a scale model built and painted all in shocking blues and pinks with mirrors inserted for the reflective surfaces of the water, similar to the effect created by Pember (pl. 45; cf. figs. 96 and 183). Montes likes to use models in his work whenever possible. The day he was interviewed, models were being photographed in the courtyard of his atelier off the rue Richer.

A model for Montes has almost as much importance as a building, which after all may never get built. This reveals his dedicated pursuit of art for art's sake. He took the Laurentine exhibition so much to heart that in the final days before the opening he augmented his submission with eight striking gouache paintings of the villa seen from various angles. Produced in a last-minute flurry, the paintings do not exactly correspond to the model or the previous drawings. They are the end product of an almost boundless enthusiasm for the project, and they contribute to making the submission one of the biggest.

Hindsight makes Montes want to downplay his involvement with the Laurentine *concours* or its significance. But shortly after he was interviewed, history proved him wrong. In the summer of 1987 he became a participant in another *concours d'émulation,* this one in conjunction with a new Paris exhibition, itself inspired by the Laurentine *concours.* Its organizer, Jean Dethier of the Centre Georges Pompidoux, met with Maurice Culot and Léon Krier at the Café Procope in Paris in late May of that year to enlist their collaboration in setting up his competition by invitation. When the show "Château Bordeaux" opened some sixteen months later, Krier did not take part. But through Culot's assistance Dethier had lined up two former Laurentine contestants; the team of Ustarroz and Iñiguez from Spain, and Montes. The *programme* on this occasion required the half dozen participating architects to design a new winery around the existing Château Pichon-Longueville in the vineyards of the Médoc region. Montes responded with a scheme whose appearance recalls Le Corbusier, but its planning comes right out of his Laurentine Villa. The *cuvier,* or main fermentation room, resembles Pliny's triclinium in shape and positioning. It overlooks a sea of grapevines arranged in neat, wavelike rows. With typical impetuosity, Montes added to his entry a freer, more personal interpretation of a complete modern château situated on the water and even closer in inspiration to his Laurentine Villa. In both schemes Montes tried in vain to evolve a *scénario* related to the lay of the land in the Bordeaux area. But no colorful literary figure like Pliny came to Montes's rescue, and in consequence neither château nor winery can match the rich visual and textual imagery of his Laurentine Villa.[29]

Justo Solsona (b. 1931), one of Argentina's most prominent contemporary architects, is a founding partner of the large Buenos Aires firm of Manteola, Sanchez Gomez, Santos, and Solsona (MSGSS). In 1981, during a visit to Europe, Solsona met his friend and fellow South American Fernando Montes. From him Solsona learned of the *concours* being organized by IFA and decided to participate. He enlisted the help of two assistants, Esteban Fernández and Alberto Damp, at the time recently graduated from the University of Buenos Aires school of architecture, the alma mater of Solsona and all the other principals of his firm. After the formal invitations had been issued, Solsona had the dual distinction of being the last to enter the lists and of being the most senior architect to do so. This accounts for his submission's polish, the result of years of experience at MSGSS building every imaginable kind of commission, from private homes to skyscrapers to entire seaside resorts and the headquarters for the Argentinian color television network. At the same time, of course, he worked with the disadvantage of great physical distance from the other competitors and consequently the inability to share directly with them in the process of emulation. His mixture of experience and isolation explains why his Laurentine restitution is so fascinatingly out of touch with the others, and so much in touch with his own Latin American practice.[30]

The point of departure for Solsona, his parti in effect, took the form of a fictitious letter from a latter-day descendant of Pliny's, amounting to a brief discourse on the history and poetry of architecture. In it Solsona and his collaborators speak through Pliny to describe a recently finished villa that incorporates the ruins of the ancestral home. The text begins by alluding to Le Corbusier's famous definition of architecture as "le jeu savant, correct, et magnifique des volumes assemblés sous la lumière."[31] Solsona's geometric volumes caught in the light are crystalline glass-block containers encasing the ruins of the Laurentine Villa. The plan and elevations (fig. 132) visually extend the range of deliberate references to the pantheon of modern master builders. Reminiscences creep in of the villas or skyscrapers of Mies van der Rohe, of the glass blocks pioneered by Bruno Taut in his 1914 Werkbund pavilion, and of the container/contained dichotomy raised by the Italian rationalist architect Aldo Rossi when he visited Buenos Aires in 1978 at Solsona's invitation. Perhaps, too, there is a touch of Schinkel in the curvaceous seawall so prominently featured in Solsona's plan (cf. fig. 6). Montes had sent Solsona a copy of the German's restitution. Be it understood also that Damp and Fernández contributed their own ideas and enthusiasms to the design process. In the week or so they devoted to the Pliny scheme, Fernández did much of the actual planning and Damp was the draftsman. When they saw the drawings again on the lecture screen in 1988 they urged Solsona, who was also in the audience, to take up the Laurentine Villa and improve on it. He resisted the suggestion, saying that the restitution had been an amusing diversion of the moment, a *fantasia*, to use his own expression.

To a certain extent Solsona saw the academic quality of the Laurentine exercise in its true light. He approached it as a jeu d'esprit in the manner of his friend Montes. But Solsona rooted himself in a literary rather than a cinematographic tradition. In the open planning and transparent walls of the structures assembled on the site, he played with the words *vivo* (to live) and *vives* (to see). In other words, to live is to be exposed to the light and to see clearly. Exactly this preoccupation reappears in Solsona's work as an architect and secondarily as a man of letters (see conclusion). In his own office on the Avenida Florida, the interior partitions

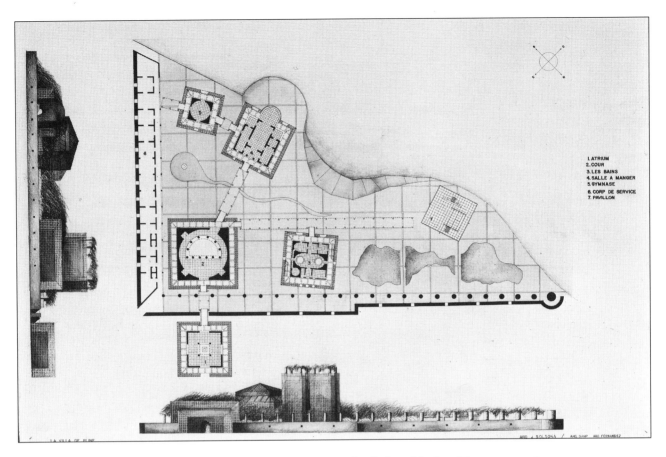

1. ATRIUM
2. COUR
3. LES BAINS
4. SALLE A MANGER
5. GYMNASE
6. CORP DE SERVICE
7. PAVILLON

around the inner conference room are largely constructed of glass blocks. The exterior of the building has large expanses of plate glass, except on the west-facing side on account of the intense heat of Argentinian summers. Solsona simply transferred to the restitution his fondness for light-suffused interiors and floating interior partitions somewhat disengaged from the outer glass skin. Each of his Laurentine buildings possesses these qualities individually. Collectively they drift somewhat aimlessly on the paper, squared up to indicate an all-marble plaza. If the Ostian seacoast is replaced by the undulating banks of the river La Plata, then the resemblance becomes all the more striking to the plaza around Solsona's 1977–78 headquarters for the Argentinian color television network (pl. 46). In Buenos Aires four separate rectangles house individual studios anchored to a vast platform—almost an antique *basis villa*. As built, the sinuous outer edge of the platform, perhaps intended to evoke the La Plata's muddy banks or the Laurentine strand, faces out over a children's adventure playground and reflecting pool.

The construction of the television building and the design of Solsona's restitution coincided with the height of the Argentinian military dictatorship. At that

132. Solsona, Laurentine Villa, plan, elevations of entrance and side facades (collection of the artist)

period Solsona and other members dismissed from the faculty of architecture founded a private school of their own, La Escuelita, so that teaching could continue. To incite emulation in the curriculum he established, Solsona included written texts as Wilhelm Stier had previously done (chap. 5). For Solsona, "architectural education *is* emulation." So when confronted with the Laurentine *programme* based on Pliny's letter, Solsona found the whole idea very congenial to what he had been practicing in the classroom. But the moment was short-lived. Everything depended on the small size and congeniality of La Escuelita. In 1983 Solsona was reinstated in his professorship and resumed teaching in what he describes as the "factorylike" environment of the university. It is not uncommon for him to drive out to the forlorn suburban campus and confront as many as six hundred students in a single lecture room. With such numbers he can no longer combine in a meaningful pedagogical way his twin interests in literature and architecture. He has had regretfully to abandon lessons that the *concours d'émulation* could teach. He still leaves behind him an outstanding Laurentine restitution, in the sense that it stood out so notably from the thirteen others because of its designer's isolation and self-reliance. This self-reliance and removal from the postmodern debate— Aldo Rossi and rational architecture notwithstanding—brought a freshness of vision to the whole procedure. Whether or not the IFA organizers knew quite what to make of Solsona's entry, he had managed to integrate the spirit of emulation engendered by Pliny's letter with the twentieth-century mainstream modernism to which he strongly adheres.

Another friend of Montes's who also made a late entry into the December 1981 *concours d'émulation* was the Milanese architect Paolo Farina (b. 1949). At that point in his career full-time teaching duties at the Milan Polytechnic had not yet curtailed his participation in such international events as the 1980 Venice Biennale and the 1981 Salon d'Automne in Paris. About the time of the Salon, Montes told Farina that the Laurentine *concours* was in preparation, and in due course an official invitation arrived. After an intensive month's work, Farina had finished his submission, which consisted of a plan and an aerial perspective, on which he then based a somewhat garish cardboard model (figs. 133 and 134). Taken all together, these three works of art reflect Farina's chief concerns of the moment: his recent study of the patchwork growth of cities like Milan; his ongoing dedication to historic preservation; his emulation of great masters from the history of architecture; and his apparently newfound love of restitution, which has had far-reaching consequences for his later development.[32]

Starting with Farina's interest in cities, it is worth noting that in June 1981 he and architect–art historian Paolo Portoghesi had planned the installation for "In labirinto," an exhibition in Milan. Out of this show and a lifelong passion for his birthplace grew Farina's approach to the analysis of Milan as though it were a

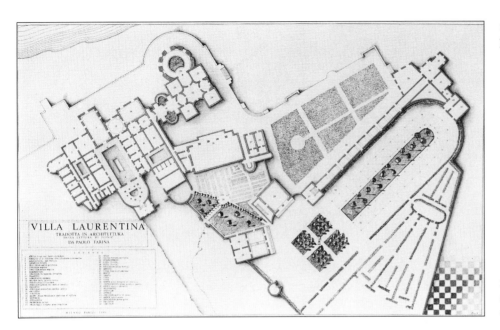

133. Farina, Laurentine Villa, plan (collection of the artist)

134. Farina, Laurentine Villa, aerial perspective (collection of the artist)

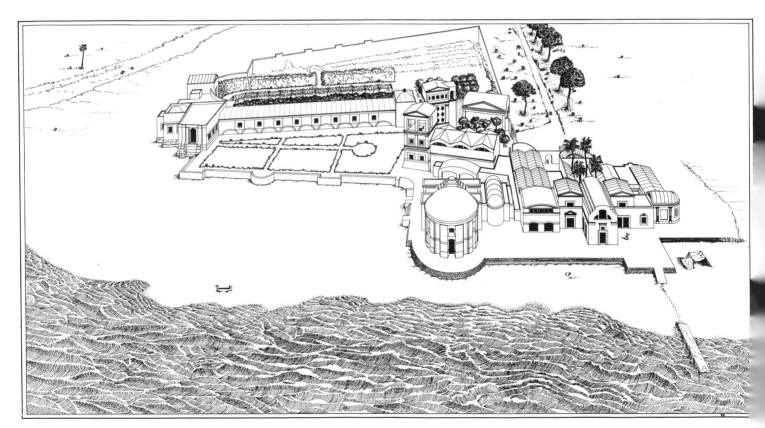

VILLA LAURENTINA
TRADOTTA IN ARCHITETTURA
DALLA LETTERA DI PLINIO
DA PAOLO FARINA

giant game board or jigsaw puzzle—he later called it "puzzle city" in an article on the same subject.[33] In allusion to this concept, Farina drew in a checkerboard jutting out from the right corner of the Laurentine Villa ground plan. So hastily added were the finishing touches in the last days as the deadline drew near that they are not reproduced in the official photograph in *La Laurentine.* The catalog does contain Farina's accompanying text, originally titled "Il 'jeu de Pline' continua." According to Farina's interpretation, Pliny's letter is the opening move on the board. In the course of history the game has been played by a series of rules, the chief one being never to reveal the real villa. The letter continues to elicit as much passionate interest as it does simply because this is a game at which every player turns up a winner.[34] Going a step further, the cut-up appearance of Farina's site plan, especially in the disjointed area of the gardens, suggests almost random growth over time. A *patte d'oie* of hedges abuts the hippodrome garden, ending in a quincuncial placement of little trees with a statue of Pliny in the middle. Toward the center of the plan all kinds of plantings converge, much as built-up urban blocks might do in a city. Fitting the pieces of the puzzle together becomes part of the fun for Farina and for the viewer. Farina understands Pliny's villa as a metaphor for megalopolis.

From a historical standpoint, Farina's restitution is no less a puzzle; in fact it is a salad of architectural delights tossed with a pinch of irony. Farina studied the letter to Gallus at the same time as he studied some of the previous restitutions. He combines elements from Canina's plan and from Félibien's garden layout. From the Frenchman he takes the idea of a symmetrical disposition, which he then deliberately twists around, all the while retaining the eighteenth-century feel of the little trees with their cast shadows (cf. figs. 30 and 51). Past and present fuse all the more in the cunningly drawn aerial perspective view of the villa. The flat and sandy stretch of Ostian coastline, dotted with palms and umbrella pines, becomes a field on which to display the major epochs of architectural history that interest Farina. In the bottom right corner, for instance, is a primitive tent, evocative of the origins of architecture. On the far left side the buttresses protruding from the little pavilion copy the base of the Temple of Solomon as engraved by Fischer von Erlach in 1721. The cryptoporticus alongside is meant to recall the Roman Milvian Bridge. The garden immediately behind, with its one end curved like an ancient theater, is modeled on the Villa Giulia and the Villa Madama situated not far from that bridge. A tower full of portholes refers, of course, to the Tomb of the Baker at Rome's Porta Maggiore. The baths echo those of Diocletian in plan, whereas in elevation they recall the Church of San Carlo alle Quattro Fontane by Borromini. Farina reeled off in conversation the mixture of these historical references. The critic Pierre-Yves Balut calls it an architectural medley and adds a few more sources of his own, thus outdoing the architect at his own game. Balut exclaims: "Pauvre client qui se verrait affublé d'un tel centon architectural."[35] It is obvious what Farina meant in his interview when he said of his ironic architectural quotations, "Je me suis amusé à créer des citations un peu ironiques."

Since entering into practice, Farina has turned his attention to the preservation and creative adaptation of historical monuments in Italy. For this reason, and with the Laurentine *concours* recently behind him, he responded positively to the 1985 Venice Biennale's call for another competition on the theme of restitution. One of several possible projects involved restoring the semiabandoned Villa Farsetti at Santa Maria di Sala near Padua.[36] Farina opted for taking the eighteenth-century structure of Abbate Filippo Farsetti as the starting point for his own *nuovo forum*. The house and its adjacent parish church become the nucleus for a large cultural center, linked by elliptical vestibules to an open-air theater at the back and a new wing of rooms. A number of features of the ground plan and the whole idea of emulating an old villa in the design of a new one relate back to the Laurentine project. More recently still, Farina designed a six-hundred-seat auditorium in Milan that would rise on a vacant lot but would blend in with the architecture of a convent courtyard next door and emulate the distinctive Milanese feature of the *galleria*. These instances, and others more recent still, show that the Plinian exercise of 1981 has continuing relevance for Farina even though, like Montes, he tries to distance restitution from his normal practice in the office. This polemical distinction seems to lose any real validity when one considers the oeuvre Farina has actually constructed.

In the various small Milanese commissions Farina has received for apartments and an architectural bookshop named Archivolto, he displays a gift for manipulating interior spaces. Owing to the exigencies of cramped city sites, these spaces are paradoxically cut up to resemble an urban street pattern, as if one were crossing busy intersections rather than interior corridors or other rooms. To add to the effect, Farina employs oversized elements taken from the vocabulary of facades in the classical style. He simply turns the exteriors in upon themselves. History forms the bond between his practical and theoretical concerns, no matter how much he may say that he never thought of associating them. In his teaching of students, for example, it is clear that what he prefers to call *refondation* is really emulation. What else is his study of such typologies as the *galleria*, the villa, and the growth of urban street patterns than another way of stating the obvious fact that all architecture is based on built forms of the past?[37]

A third group in the *concours d'émulation* centered on Bernard Huet (b. 1936) just as the architect-archaeologists had revolved around Pinon. Although only Huet's name appears on the 22 July 1981 call for submissions, the final list of participants includes his collaborators David Bigelman and Serge Santelli. In 1975 these three banded together as the group called TAU, which stands for *théorie, architecture, urbanisme.* Huet played the role of Athos to the other two musketeers, all three of whom teach or have taught at the Paris-Belleville school of architecture along with Jean-Pierre Braun. But Huet has the broadest background. In the 1950s he left Vietnam, the country of his birth, to continue his education at Toulon and then at the Ecole des Beaux-Arts in Paris before its dissolution. Out of the ashes, Huet helped to create the Unité Pédagogique d'Architecture no. 8 at Belleville.[38] In the meantime he has attended Farina's alma mater in Milan to study under E. N. Rogers, and he earned his master of architecture degree after two years (1963–65) at the University of Pennsylvania as a pupil of Louis Kahn.

According to the lengthy text by Huet accompanying his two drawings of the Laurentine Villa, he was immediately captivated by the sensuous pleasure in architecture and horticulture expressed by Pliny's letter. As the Latin text moved through the house and its grounds, it conveyed a feeling for wind, sand, stars, and vegetation that awakened in Huet memories of his extensive youthful travels to classical sites. This emphasis on "the total pleasure that architecture gives" resembles Jean-Pierre Adam's, but it is almost the only thing they share, even though they are virtually the same age and produced two of the most convincing and masterly schemes out of the entire thirteen submitted. In contrast to Adam the archaeologist, Huet takes an architectural historian's perspective by insisting that the more classical remains emerge, the more each villa seems to defy the idea of any existing norm at all. He also disagrees with the concept of the modernity of the Romans as maintained by Adam. To Huet it is a question of entirely different, exotic, and esoteric mentalities: "aussi lointaine, incompréhensible et exotique que la pensée chinoise ou arabe."[39]

The historian in Huet reveals itself in his carefully researched pronouncements on the restitutions from the past. His text is the only one of the thirteen to take any direct cognizance of the long tradition stretching back before 1981. Almost a third of what he has written recounts the evolution of the Laurentine theme all the way from the Villa Madama to Bouchet's restitution, which he facetiously likens to the Villa Kerylos, perhaps, or to a similar "riche villa hongroise à l'italienne située sur la Côte d'Azur." Each age adds its own interpretation, he asserts, but he refrains from calling the procedure a game as Farina and a number of others did. For Huet, on the contrary, the exercise is "serious . . . scholarly, and difficult." His seriousness on the printed page, however, did not exclude a bitter side when he was interviewed five years later, at which time the sting had not entirely gone from the lash of Balut's critique. Balut states that despite Huet's correct approach, the architect demonstrates a total inability to come to grips with the villa: "He is the one who has most explicitly shown that . . . caught by the ghosts of the history of architecture and of the present architectural mode, he could only talk, without really being able to act." Obviously some of the scornful fire Huet had trained on Bouchet was returned at him.[40]

In his interview Huet recalled that he was engaged on the Laurentine Villa restitution for a relatively short time, at the end of which he produced four black-and-white line drawings, assisted by two Belgian students of Culot's named Michel Leloup and Marc Heene (fig. 135). Huet supervised the work from beginning to end and had the initial inspiration. It came to him as the result of a recent trip back to Pompeii. What struck him most was the Romans' compositional system, which he characterized as *les figures et les assemblages de figures.* His villa recollects ancient ones he admired on that trip, but it goes beyond that to become an exercise in the assemblage of different ideal concepts, or *figures,* that will blend together well. He had confronted this hidden system when contemplating North African Arab architecture, having in mind a commission for the house of a friend in Tunisia. His reflections on this theme brought him to the conclusion that the Arab and Roman builders had similar principles. They built additively and at the same time coherently, though in a different sense from the strict symmetry and axiality understood by the Ecole in the nineteenth century. He went on to add that, despite the fundamentally foreign turn of the ancient mind, the modern architect has the sensitivity to enter into the real planning issues that have faced the Mediterranean world from time immemorial. To prove his point he recalled in conversation the fragmentary impression conveyed by a Piranesi print of the Roman Campus Martius that used to hang in Louis Kahn's office in Philadelphia. As his master might have done, Huet decided to "fragment" his Laurentine Villa, in the firm belief that the Romans, or the Arabs, would have done exactly the same thing unconsciously. For them, as for Huet, "the compositional axis," and "the visual axis" have nothing to do with each other.

From the projecting jetty in the foreground of his impressive aerial perspective up to the service court at the top of the drawing, a lack of right angles and an additive quality prevail. Huet says he set out to design with the *mentality* rather than the manner of an ancient Roman. To a considerable extent his design shows the extreme difficulty in achieving what he claims he wanted to do. He seeks to achieve a "fragmentary composition," at the same time using all the ingenuity needed to make everything work together under the guise of effortlessness. Huet thus adopted the opposite procedure from his architect-archaeologist friends, for whom the ruins, once unearthed, are the only basis for any correct restitution.[41] Quite the contrary, he seeks to *cover up* the traces of a highly analytic design process that he wishes to make appear quite natural and intuitive. He succeeds only up to a point. The twistings and turnings of the various masses, the labyrinthine quality of the plan, and the cramped spaces all seem contrived. Perhaps he is at his

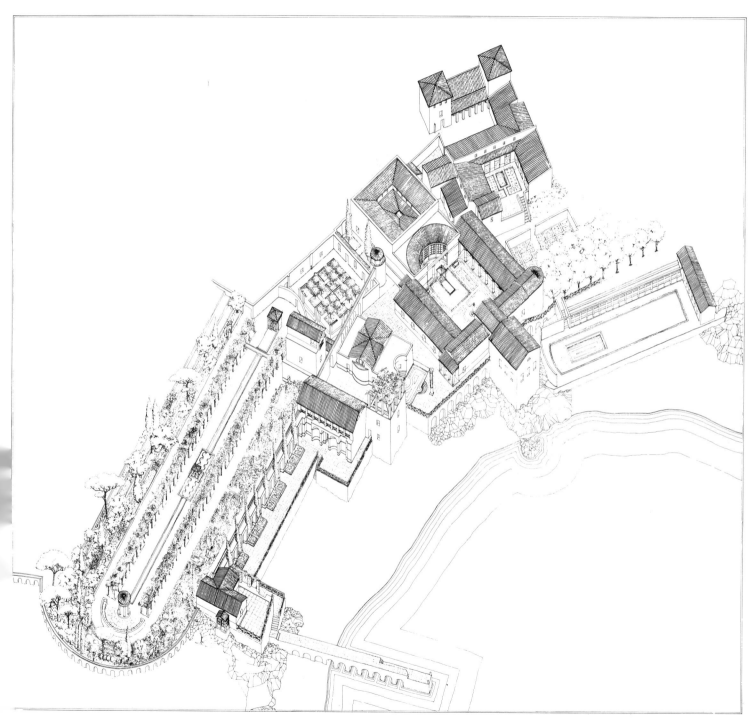

135. Huet, Laurentine Villa,
aerial perspective (collection
of the artist)

best in that integration of natural and architectural forms—that sheer delight—that initially attracted him to Pliny's prose. This aspect comes across beautifully in the various open spaces: the Schinkelesque *gestatio;* the enclosed orchard and vegetable garden; the seaside and rooftop terraces; the flagged courtyards with their refreshing watercourses. The cross section (fig. 136) conveys the feeling of integration well and noticeably resembles Schinkel's Tuscan Villa (cf. fig. 44). Huet similarly imagines a site sloping steeply downward: vegetation and balustraded terraces spill down a hillside. In distinct contrast to Farina's uninspiring site, flat as a pancake, Huet comes up with a more variegated landscape. The austere black-and-white drawings, however, seem to cry out for a touch of green.

In 1987 Huet engaged in a project involving the actual reconstruction of a monument back to a lost stage in its existence. In commemoration of the bicentenary of the French Revolution, the mayor of Paris, Jacques Chirac, the political archrival of President Mitterrand, commissioned a restoration of Claude-Nicolas Ledoux's Parisian customhouse, the Barrière de la Villette. Intended as a reply to Mitterrand's *"grands projets,"* it was very much in Huet's mind at the time he was interviewed about his previous involvement in the Laurentine *concours d'émulation*. He said that he intended the new work, inaugurated on schedule in 1989, to be an unobtrusive restitution. In his understanding that word connotes a modern-day response to the spirit of a certain place as it has evolved over a whole span of time

136. Huet, Laurentine Villa, cross section (collection of the artist)

rather than at a given period. To that end Huet takes away the early twentieth-century park that surrounded the customhouse and returns it to the closer relationship to the street it would have had in Ledoux's day. What would a customhouse be, after all, without roads leading directly up to and away from it? Then Huet proceeds to restore the planting system around the Canal de l'Ourcq, built later than the Ledoux era but not entirely out of sympathy with it. Huet's new allées of trees line up in front and then gently arch behind the *barrière* to partly hide an elevated stretch of Fulgence Bienvenue's Paris Metro that rumbles by overhead. Far from seeking to treat it as an early twentieth-century intrusion, however, Huet imitates the style when adding some big stone pylons and other street furniture. Finally, he erects long colonnades in a stylized type of Doric that is entirely his own invention but that he believes blends in with his predecessors' work. Just as he would wish his Laurentine Villa to appear properly Plinian, so too he hopes that people will see the entire project at La Villette as a "dialogue" between historical architecture and contemporary expression sensitive to the past.[42]

Bernard Huet's Laurentine restitution received special recognition from Pinon and Culot, who placed it second after Krier's in their printed catalog. In stark contrast, the restitution by Huet's younger colleague at TAU, Serge Santelli (b. 1948?), was slipped in on the last page with no accompanying text and no fanfare. Santelli readily admits that he is not pleased with the two drawings that constitute the sum total of his contribution (fig. 137). He says that in retrospect he regards the *concours d'émulation* as a lost opportunity in terms of his own career, especially as a teacher. In principle he responds well to the idea of working from a written *programme* and would resort to the device more often with his students at Paris-Belleville had he the opportunity and they the dedication. Like his former collaborators Huet and Bigelman, for whom the seventeenth-century text by Bernard Palissy describing an imaginary garden holds a continuing fascination, Santelli has another restitution up his sleeve. For him it is the descriptions of the lost palace of El Bedi at Marrakech in Morocco. Santelli has made a special study of French colonial and Arab architecture in North Africa. Some of his best-known built work also occurs in that part of the world.[43]

In 1981 Santelli became engaged on the design of a seaside apartment-hotel complex called Résidences Andalouses at Sousse on the Tunisian coast. In recognition of this achievement he received the Aga Khan Prize in 1983. Not surprisingly, a considerable amount of cultural overlap exists between this built work and the imaginary Laurentine restitution. Both feature a blocky configuration with prominent towers in the manner of North African vernacular forms, which admittedly have nothing to do with Pliny. Both carry over the squarish geometry to the internal courtyards, enlivened with Nabeul tile work in the Tunisian case. As for the sequence of rooms from the Laurentine atrium to the triclinium, it seems to derive

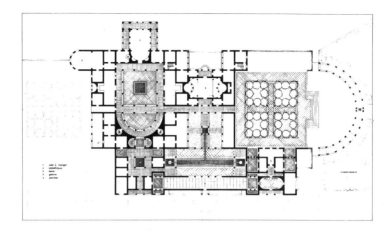

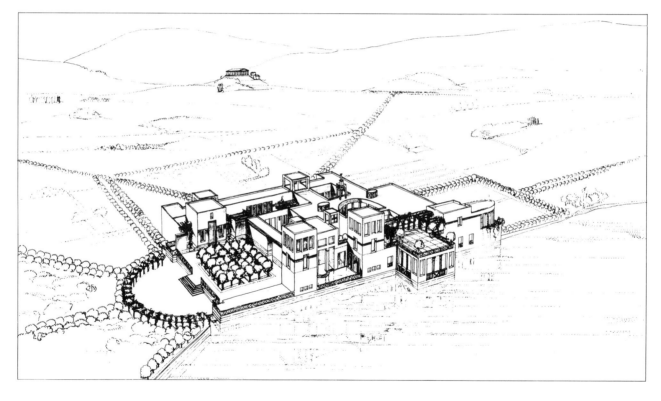

closely from Huet's scheme, whose progress Santelli could keep an eye on since his office at the time occupied a room adjacent to Huet's in the neoclassical Galerie Vivienne off the rue de la Banque. In fact Santelli's only real concession to the antique spirit of Pliny's letter is the inclusion of various Roman roads and a peripteral temple on a distant hilltop. Balut latched on to these feeble attempts with savage glee because they revealed to him Santelli's ignorance of archaeology. In

137. Santelli, Laurentine Villa, plan and aerial perspective (collection of the artist)

the words of Balut, "Why bother to have searched for the antiquity of Pliny if it was to arrive at such a result?"[44] Such criticisms by Pierre-Yves Balut seemed particularly aimed at the three former members of TAU. They did not take kindly to his bantering. "L'affair Balut," as the quarrel became known among the participants, turned into something of a cause célèbre, along the lines of Viollet-le-Duc's clash with the Ecole, mentioned in the preceding chapter.

Huet, Santelli, and Bigelman launched their own defense against Balut in a letter of 21 October 1982 to Maurice Culot. They threatened that unless he removed Balut's offending paragraphs from *La Laurentine,* or gave them the chance to respond in a new edition of the catalog, they would withdraw their work from the traveling exhibition. Culot smoothed matters over with an astute reply of 5 November inviting the architects to submit written responses within six weeks for an addendum to the catalog. As Culot probably expected, he heard nothing further on the matter. It nevertheless cast a pall over relations between the incensed architects and Balut, who felt outnumbered and on the defensive. He dismisses the complaints against him as those of an egotistical or *nombriliste* profession and claims that the entire competition was a flash in the pan.[45] But Santelli provided a less emotional perspective when looking back on the events in conversation in 1990. According to him, the exhibition had arisen at a moment of political interregnum when architects had a chance to express their more or less latent interest in history and archaeology, an interest Balut shared. His barbs were really intended to goad on the process, but the change in regimes nipped the movement in the bud, and his criticisms unintentionally added insult to injury. In any event, the matter soon went on to a bigger political arena in which Mitterrand's socialists identified themselves with a brand of modernism that favored technology and what Santelli referred to as the *beau geste* pet projects of the president of France. "L'affaire Balut" can be viewed either as a tempest in a teapot or, in a more sinister sense, as an advancing storm that eventually overshadowed the Laurentine *concours*'s significance in Europe.

The studio apartment of David Bigelman on the rue Rodier in Paris reflects the personality of its inhabiter-designer. It has a restrained neoclassical air reinforced by the Empire antiques and the library full of rare architectural books, which are the fruits of Bigelman's forays into auction houses and flea markets. Bigelman's tastes as scholar, bibliophile, bargain hunter, grand tourist, and confirmed classicist are also apparent in his Laurentine restitution. All of this, with a touch of tongue-in-cheek humor, expresses itself clearly in a letter to Maurice Culot accompanying the drawings. Born in Havana in 1943, the son of American expatriates, Bigelman was educated as an architect there and at the Catholic University of Washington, D.C., before going to Europe in 1971. He has taught architecture ever since at Paris-Belleville, except for a brief visiting professorship at the

University of Pennsylvania where Huet had preceded him. With Huet and Santelli, Bigelman participated in numerous mass housing and urbanization projects in the late 1970s and early 1980s as part of TAU. This contemporary work seems strangely distant from the Laurentine Villa and less in step with a person who obviously loves to surround himself with things of beauty from the past.[46]

The original draft of the letter to Culot mentioned above exists in a small clothbound sketchbook of Bigelman's now in the Canadian Centre for Architecture. The dateline, though heavily crossed out by the author in the process of revising it for publication, appears to read "janvier Paris [1982]." That would place it later than the submission of the drawings to the *concours* in the preceding December and at about the same time as Solsona was composing his fictitious letter in far-off Argentina (see conclusion). The writer takes as his point of departure the premise that Pliny's epistolary exercise addressed to Gallus is to a large extent fantastic. Without knowing it, perhaps, Bigelman echoes the dreamlike sequence Haudebourt invented over a century earlier (see chap. 3) by conjuring up an imaginary bargain-hunting trip he supposedly took to the Roman flea market at the Porta Portese. In one of the stalls there he discovers a rusty metal tube containing what he realizes are the original drawings for the Laurentine Villa. He bargains the dealer's price down to 10,000 lire and then rushes off to get the money. By the time he returns, stall, dealer, and tube have vanished into thin air! In this way Bigelman has perceptively grasped the miragelike contents of Pliny's letter. Truth and falsehood, dream and reality, antiques and fakes—these are the themes underlying David Bigelman's letter.[47]

On the verso of the letter's last page, Bigelman hastily sketches a barely recognizable version of the plan that he identifies as that of Bernard Huet—an instance of emulation in action. As previously seen with Santelli's restitution, Huet had an influence on the other two members of TAU. In the case of Bigelman, it is not so much a matter of the internal planning as the conscious asymmetry of overall layout that the younger architect emulates in the work of his older colleague. Bigelman acknowledges that Huet had the idea first, as well as the invitation to join in the *concours*. But Bigelman takes the procedure further by specifying in his letter to Culot three distinct stages in the construction of Laurentinum that would account for its rambling appearance. On this score Bigelman devises another story—this time a three-part tale relating to the essence of the villa. The first phase, according to Bigelman, predates Pliny's ownership and consists of an existing building that he inherited to the north of the new structure. The second phase calls for a trained architect to design Pliny's enlargements. He would have employed an architect in the circle of Apollodorus of Damascus, the favorite designer of Pliny's master the emperor Trajan. And in the third stage, to be considered in detail in the conclusion to this book, Pliny himself takes on a design role.

The earliest of the Bigelman plans at the beginning of his sketchbooks call for a *U*-shaped villa; in the center, and as an apparent afterthought, a separate structure is added on an oblique angle at the bottom (fig. 138). At a slightly later stage, so it seems, the plan tries to conform to the shoreline by taking on a more serpentine form, though the obliquely situated wing remains in place (fig. 139). Finally, the wing in question swings around forty-five degrees to the left, and the large court-yard where it now sits has exedras on the sides similar to those on Trajan's Forum in Rome designed by Apollodorus (fig. 140). This arrangement closely resembles the final one as exhibited in December 1981 (fig. 141). The main difference is in the outlying pavilions and courtyards, but the draftsmanship lacks the nervous vitality found in the sketch stage, where the road from Ostia to Terracina slashes

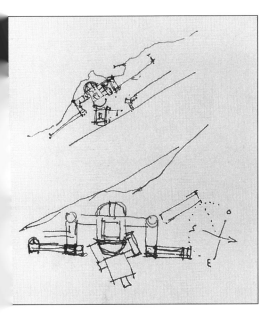

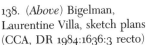

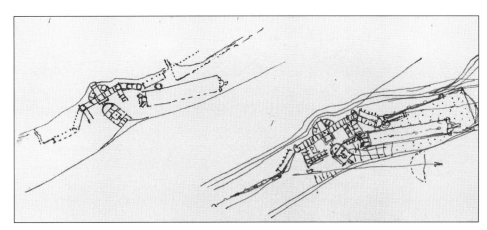

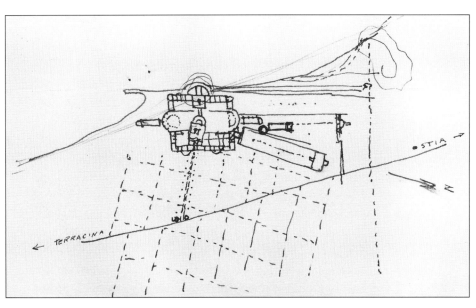

138. (*Above*) Bigelman, Laurentine Villa, sketch plans (CCA, DR 1984:1636:3 recto)

139. (*Above, right*) Bigelman, Laurentine Villa, sketch plans (CCA, DR 1984:1636:12 recto)

140. (*Right*) Bigelman, Laurentine Villa, sketch site plan (CCA, DR 1984:1636:15 recto)

across a checkerboard arrangement of meadows running in the opposite direction. As with so many of the other participants considered thus far—Adam, Montes, Farina, and Huet of course—everything is at an odd angle to everything else. Bigelman takes the tendency almost to excess.

In the letter to Culot, Bigelman refers to the pre-Plinian villa as being identifiable with a tower marked on the plan with a hard-to-decipher Roman numeral I and situated between the main villa and the *gestatio* of hippodrome shape. The *turris*, as Bigelman describes it, pops up on an early sketchbook page alongside a version of the full plan (fig. 142). Four separate drawings study the tower in elevation and on plan. The form is basically that of a triangle with three rectangular wings projecting from it. On the following sketchbook page the elevation with rooftop dining room takes shape, and the words adjacent to a plan hint at its source as "SS. Andrea. Barbara et Silvia al Celio" (fig. 143). In conversation Bigelman points out that this inscription refers to the early Christian chapels so named beside San Gregorio Magno in Rome. It is his way of displaying his intimate knowledge of Rome, both pagan and Christian, and his preference for the plain brickwork masses of early churches. A slightly later, hastily drawn, aerial perspective zooms in on the now simplified tower, lacking its two side wings but displaying its expanses of roof and the little portico at the front facing out onto the *gestatio* (fig. 144). A similar mixture of historical periods infuses the villa plan as a whole. In his letter Bigelman refers to the late antique Villa of Maxentius near San Sebastiano fuori le Mura as his general inspiration. His buttressed embankment wall along the shore supposedly derives from the antique villa that once stood by the Tiber's banks in the vicinity of the Farnesina. By thus metaphorically digging downward in a search for material to emulate, Bigelman treats his restitution as though it were a giant Roman excavation with layer upon layer of architectural detritus.

Bigelman's eclectic picking and choosing becomes abundantly clear in the *calque*, or transfer version, of his aerial perspective of the Laurentine Villa. The *calques,* more starkly than the muted original versions later disposed of to the Canadian Centre for Architecture (figs. 145 and 49), suggest that the general viewpoint and reflections in the water emulate Schinkel. The low-lying Schinkelesque silhouette spreads out to each side of a centrally placed tower. To the right is the main villa, and on the left-hand extremity Bigelman positions the *amores mei* pavilion. Adjacent to it and a little to the right looms a raised building, or *pulvinar*, and the indoor *sphaeristerium,* looking for all the world like an early Christian church. The west or entrance tower with the Serliana opening at the top goes further still by referring specifically to the palace of Theodoric at Ravenna. Bigelman calls it *un clocher carolingien* in the unedited version of the letter to Culot.[48] Another passage specifies that the eastern *pulvinar* recalls a martyrium. It is almost as if Bigelman were imagining what Diocletian's marine villa at Split might have

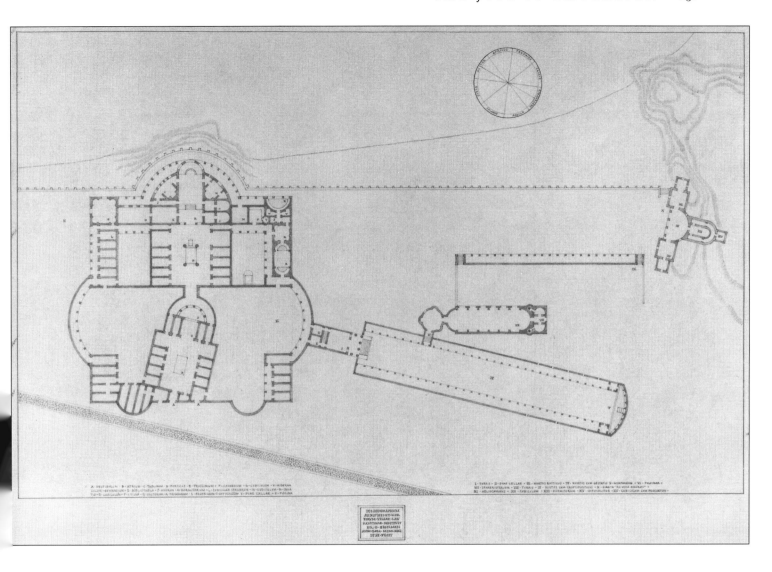

141. Bigelman, Laurentine Villa, plan (CCA, DR 1984: 1639)

looked like had Charlemagne reoccupied and embellished it five centuries after construction. Bigelman's understanding of restitution in this respect greatly resembles Huet's.

In concluding his letter Bigelman promises that the interior views he is at work on will soon be ready. A dozen or so of them occupy the beginning and end of his sketchbook, and at least one went into the Laurentine exhibition catalog (fig. 146). Bigelman is understandably proud of it and retains a copy in his personal collection. He explained when interviewed that the figure of the person seated in the *apsida curvatum* of the library looking out to sea came from a drawing by John Flaxman, the nineteenth-century illustrator of Homer—yet another instance of deliberate

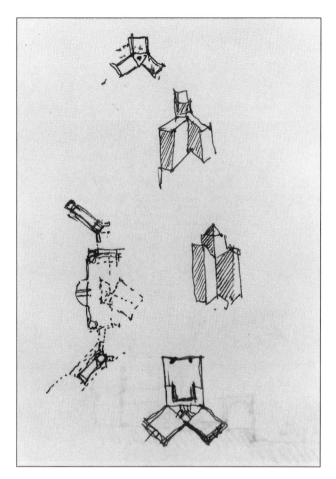

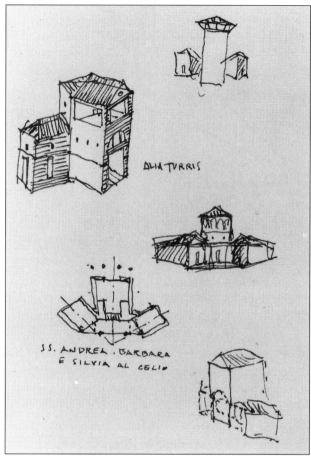

142. (*Above*) Bigelman,
Laurentine Villa, sketch plans
and elevations of tower
(CCA, DR 1984:1636:5 verso)

143. (*Above, right*) Bigelman,
Laurentine Villa, sketches of
tower and plan of Santi Andrea, Barbara, and Silvia in
Rome (CCA, DR 1984:1636:6
recto)

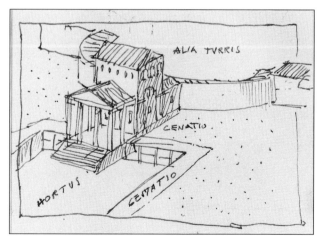

144. Bigelman, Laurentine
Villa, sketch of tower (CCA,
DR 1984:1636:19)

INTEGRA · ET · EXACTA
DESIGNATIO · AEDIFICII
ET · HORTORVM · VILLAE
LAVRENTINAE · RESTITVIT
F·R · P·I·601525211
ANNO · D·O·M · MCMLXXXI
IPSE · FECIT

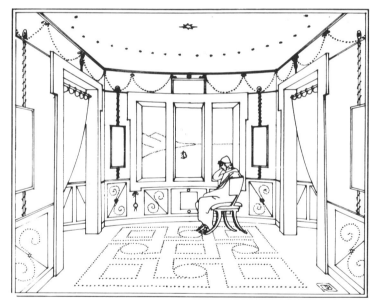

CVBICVLVM IN HAPSIDA CVRVATVM

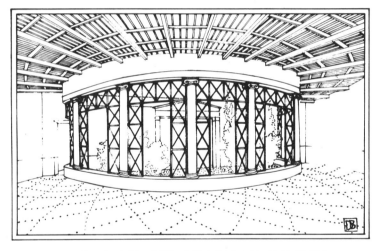

PORTICVS IM 'D' ... SPECVLARIBVS ... MVNIVNTVR

145. (*Top*) Bigelman, Laurentine Villa, aerial perspective (collection of the artist)

146. (*Above, left*) Bigelman, Laurentine Villa, interior of library (CCA, DR 1984:1637)

147. (*Above, right*) Bigelman, Laurentine Villa, interior of *D*-shaped courtyard (CCA, DR 1984:1634)

historical footnoting by Bigelman. A second interior, even more accomplished in terms of perspective, shows the *D*-shaped court (fig. 147), but it never went on display and therefore has never before been published. It shares a certain similarity with the garish gouache paintings by Montes, who also went on elaborating his restitution right up to the very end. The two Bigelman interiors make a pleasant pair, rather like some of Pliny's letters: the one curves inward, the other curves out of the picture plane. A third and final perspective also never went on display, and it concentrates on the *amores mei* pavilion, Bigelman's pride and joy as it was Pliny's (cf. fig. 186).

In the autumn of 1983, while teaching at the University of Pennsylvania school of architecture, Bigelman found that his students there were far more receptive to the practice of restitution than those at Paris-Belleville. It was at this point that he picked up an idea mentioned to him earlier by Barnard Huet as a possible subject for restitution. Somehow Huet had found his way to the *Récepte véritable,* a book written in 1563 by the French Huguenot artist Bernard Palissy. Inspired by the imagery and language of Psalm 104, Pallisy described a delectable garden that he imagined near Saintes, where in fact he had the faience atelier that made him famous as a ceramicist. In the manner of Pliny's letters, or of Francesco Colonna's *Hypnerotomachia Poliphili* (Venice, 1499), Palissy's text wanders through complex green spaces in the midst of which a building advertises his wares by its ceramic-lined rooms. Bigelman tried to apply to this description the same method he had employed with Pliny, but with less convincing results. Discouraged with what he and the students had achieved, he abandoned the half-finished restitution. He claims his present students cannot be bothered with the studious discipline required for such an endeavor. It would have no relevance to them, he says, living as they do in the shadow of the pretentious architectural undertakings of the Mitterrand government. Bigelman feels himself out of sympathy with that world around him and so retreats into the past. The quality of reverie, which has been one of the great appeals of Pliny's writings over the ages, obviously provides Bigelman with an escape to an ideal studious life.[49]

Standard histories tend to overlook the impact of the Roman Empire on Spain. For two young Spanish architects, however, the classical tradition remains a vital force. It lives on in the vernacular styles of their hometown of Pamplona in Navarre, and they find evidence of it in their adopted city of San Sebastián in the Basque country. Their names are Manuel Iñiguez (b. 1948) and Alberto Ustarroz (b. 1948). To them the Roman legacy is the legacy of fine brickwork, plain arches, exposed carpentry, and the simple cylindrical column shafts or square masonry piers found in the Basque farmhouses, or *l'etchéa.* The inspiration guiding their rediscovery of the classical roots of the Iberian vernacular has been provided by Miguel Garay, the leading light in the San Sebastián school of architecture where they all teach.

Garay, moreover, enjoys amicable relations with Maurice Culot, whose close personal associates form the fourth group of contestants. In fact it was initially Garay and his partner José Linazasoro to whom Culot wrote about participating in the *concours d'émulation*. Neither submitted an entry in the end, leaving it up to Iñiguez and Ustarroz to represent Spain in the competition.[50]

Iñiguez and Ustarroz have piled the loft they inhabit in Pamplona to the rafters with the voluminous output of twenty years of collaboration—much of it still on paper. They carry out all the work themselves, and so strong is their partnership that it proves very difficult to tell their contributions apart. Their curricula vitae are almost identical except that they graduated from the architecture school at Pamplona a year apart. They constitute an indefatigable two-man team comparable to Treuttel, Garcias, and Treuttel, and on everything they undertake they lavish untold love and care. Their Cordobilla Restaurant, for example, in the rolling countryside outside Pamplona, was completed just before their Laurentine submission. (Cordobilla refers to the god of fire, an appropriate choice for a grill specializing in charcoal-cooked meats.) The architects advised on almost all aspects of the design, including the decorative tile work inside, the furniture, crockery, and flatware. In addition, a number of points link this earlier essay in restitution (pl. 47) with the villa design. For one thing, they restored the ruins of a tower existing on the site for the owner-restaurateur's residence and placed the dining room around a peristyle court at the base. For another, their tower recalls the retreat homes designed in these same years by Krier, whose work they greatly admire. And in a further gesture of emulation, the observatory platform at the top pays homage to one of the designers' favorite buildings: Villanueva's neoclassical Madrid Observatory.[51]

For their Laurentine restitution, Iñiguez and Ustarroz produced a plethora of drawings, fourteen in all, mostly black and white, but several delicately colored. These drawings include plans at two levels (fig. 148), an overall aerial view (fig. 149), and several perspectives, interiors, cross sections, and elevations—in short far more finished drawings than any of the other submissions to the *concours*. Only about half of the material could be exhibited at IFA in May 1982 owing to lack of space. But such overzealousness is typical of the architects' dedication and their occasional lack of practicality. An apologetic letter from them on 12 January makes clear that they were so engrossed in the project that they missed the deadline altogether for the December 1981 preliminary show of work at the Académie d'Architecture. Despite all that effort the result is a long, low-lying, and not especially original villa project. It stretches from a rocky promontory housing the *heliocaminus* under an observatorylike dome to tiered open-air bleachers at the other extremity. This seating faces the designers' "Vitruvian theater," a feature nowhere mentioned in Pliny's description. Nor is this the only instance of an obvious contra-

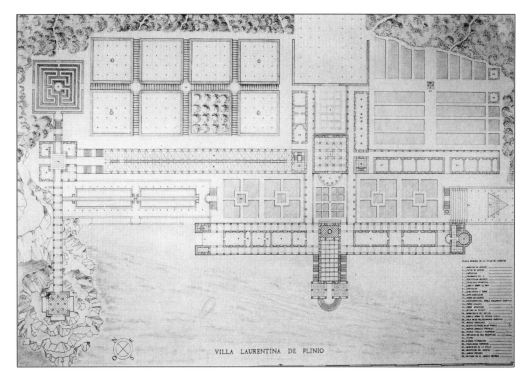

148. Ustarroz and Iñiguez, Laurentine Villa, plan (collection of the artists)

VILLA LAURENTINA DE PLINIO

149. Ustarroz and Iñiguez, Laurentine Villa, aerial perspective (collection of the artists)

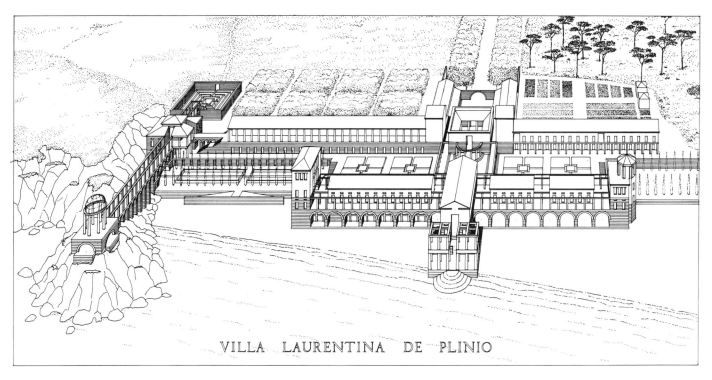

VILLA LAURENTINA DE PLINIO

diction of the text. The *amores mei* pavilion is artificially distanced from the *helio-caminus* simply to indulge a fondness for long, Schinkelesque pergolas. Vitruvius, Schinkel, Villanueva: all these heroes from the architectural past crowd the Laurentine Villa, much as busts of ancestors might have done in Pliny's day.

Generally speaking the Spaniards' restitution, its low seaside location notwithstanding, has marked similarities to Raphael's Villa Madama with its theater and terraced formal gardens. Especially similar is the provision of sunken baths and a nymphaeum shown on the left-hand side of the plan at basement level (fig. 150). Iñiguez and Ustarroz certainly admire the Villa Madama, because they mentioned it several times in their interviews. But unlike the startling sequence of Renaissance spaces (pl. 31), those by the Spaniards have a certain predictability. Compared with Bigelman's, for instance, the *D*-shaped courtyard looks weakly integrated with the overall design. Obviously such key elements of Pliny's description interest the designers far less than the sweeping panoramas they wish to create with their galleries and esplanades along the seafront. The text accompanying the drawings emphasizes the Spanish love of promenading that they claim, with some justification, was also dear to Pliny. In all fairness, the view of the courtyard is a splendid piece of perspective drawing (fig. 151), and it, more than any other view of the villa, stresses the connections to the recently completed Cordobilla. Even more exceptional, however, is the perspective taken from the terrace with the caryatid (fig. 152). This happy piece of invention neatly sums up the designers' many affiliations: the debt to their beloved Schinkel (cf. pl. 7); the exposed woodwork typical of Krier; the openness to vistas, breezes, and promenades; and the Latin inscription intended to take the mind back to the original text. "For us," say Iñiguez and Ustarroz, "the game of Pliny begins with an analysis of the text."[52]

In their essay the Spaniards interpret Pliny's text in much the same elemental way as did Adam and Huet. The sea, the sun, the seasons, the vegetation, the entire location are supposedly central to their way of thinking, as at the ancient Roman villas of Tivoli and Split. But in contrast to these fine sentiments, the glancing viewpoint of the Iñiguez and Ustarroz perspectives (fig. 153) tends to emphasize length and stoniness at the expense of all those other considerations. The visitor's eye constantly glides along great expanses of wall, interspersed here and there with meager foliage, usually spiky cypresses. (It is hard for a tree to get much more architectonic than the cypress.) The drawing of the central promenade resembles a sun-baked urban street scene despite the sensuality of the written text. With some justification, therefore, Balut refers to an institutional quality better suited to a *caserne,* or *un terrible collège,* than to a villa.[53] His second barb hit closer to the mark than he could have imagined. On the heels of the Laurentine project the architects received the abortive commission for a college of education and philosophy at the University of San Sebastián. They labored on it fruitlessly

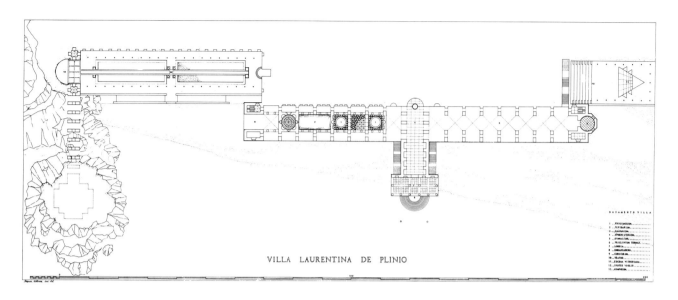

VILLA LAURENTINA DE PLINIO

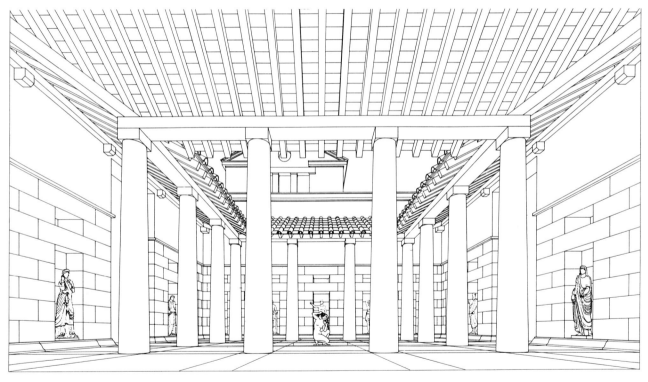

150. (*Top*) Ustarroz and Iñiguez, Laurentine Villa, plan
of basement floor (collection
of the artists)

151. (*Above*) Ustarroz and Iñiguez, Laurentine Villa, interior of courtyard (collection
of the artists)

152. Ustarroz and Iñiguez, Laurentine Villa, perspective of terrace (collection of the artists)

153. Ustarroz and Iñiguez, Laurentine Villa, perspective from theater (collection of the artists)

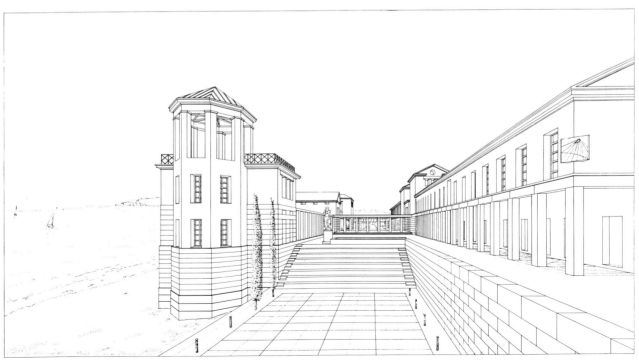

for three full years until the mid-1980s, and they transferred to it many of the Laurentine Villa's hard masonry surfaces, antiseptic plazas, and interminable colonnades, conveying a slightly sterile feeling. Working in 1986–87 on a much smaller, more human scale at a medical center on the outskirts of Lesaka, they succeed far better in implementing some of these ideas.[54]

The respect in which the Laurentine Villa is most significant to the work of Iñiguez and Ustarroz has to do with their careers as tireless and dedicated teachers. Over more than a decade and a half they have devoted themselves to their students at San Sebastián and more recently at the University of Miami. They state outright that the *concours* taught them about "the pure poetry of architecture," and that it helped them to sort out their own ideas on emulation. Restitution as a means to emulation subsequently has become very important in their classroom projects and in their extensive class field trips to monuments at home and abroad. In general they emphasize emulation within the broad classical tradition to the virtual exclusion of early twentieth-century masters after Peter Behrens and before Léon Krier. They therefore take an extreme position among architects searching for universally acceptable examples to follow. They refuse to be swayed by the latest neomodernist or deconstructionist fads, preferring instead classical and regional vernacular models. They steadfastly practice what they teach, sometimes to the frustration of their students and colleagues, who find it hard to limit themselves to so exclusive a form of emulation. Perhaps the 1989 Château Bordeaux competition highlights as well as anything both sides of this issue of exclusivity. The competition entry of tradition-bound Iñiguez and Ustarroz is certainly no more and perhaps slightly less cliché-ridden than Montes's neo-Corbusian one. They took as their inspiration the nineteenth-century Château Pichon-Longueville. They cunningly transform its round corner towers into appropriately barrel-like shapes for the outside of their new winery.[55]

Manfred Sundermann (b. 1949) is almost the same age as Iñiguez and Ustarroz. Like them he carries out his work unassisted, and he shares their admiration for Krier, another outsider. Sundermann's association with Krier dates back a long way, to 1975. At that time the young Sundermann attended the Architectural Association in London, where Krier taught and was in contact with Sundermann's previous associates at the Technical University in Aachen. At the AA Sundermann helped with the exhibition "Rational Architecture: The Architecture of the City," which involved Krier and members of the Aachen group. It was through this connection with Krier that Sundermann later received an invitation to join in the Laurentine *concours d'émulation*. Sundermann even exchanged ideas with Krier during their preparation of restitution drawings. This is the closest thing to a real collaboration in the entire Laurentine exhibition except for the close working relationship between the various members of TAU. But the exchange of ideas slowed Sundermann down, so he says, and he blames it for his missing the mid-December 1981 deadline for the *concours*. He finally submitted finished drawings on 30 January 1982, in time for the exhibition. One of the last to enter the *concours*, he is also one of the last to relinquish the theme of Pliny's villas.[56]

In common with a number of other competitors, Sundermann took as his parti a literal reading of the letter to Gallus. Speaking about it later, he reflects that "Pliny writes with his senses; his hands and his feet." What Sundermann means by this is that Pliny expressed a tactile feel for architecture and walked his reader through the villa, thereby evoking an architecture of movement. Sundermann attributes to Pliny's perambulation technique the fact that neither he nor Pliny ever really stopped in their tracks to take stock of what the villa looked like as a whole.[57] Sundermann took several pages to perceptively rephrase Pliny's train of thought, and three drawings to work it all out on paper. Only then did it intuitively dawn on him that the lesson he had learned had very little to do with what he had written or drawn and a lot more to do with a text hidden between the lines to Gallus. He began to question whether Pliny's inspired, sensual words could really be reflected in the conventional and uninspired plan that Sundermann had produced (fig. 154). His grave self-doubts were only confirmed by Balut's comments about the plan's excellent "vocabulary" but total lack of "grammatical" structure.[58] Afterward Sundermann returned to the plan, and only then did he discover traces of what he interprets as his true artistic volition unconsciously overriding his second-guessing of Krier or his studied references to history.

Sundermann draws attention to a disjointed line indicating a perimeter wall around the Laurentine plan. He now regards this as almost a form of automatic writing with which he subconsciously spelled out a fundamental statement regarding architecture in general, the architecture of the Romans versus that of the Greeks, and the architecture of Pliny's Laurentinum. Interpreted from this point of view, the Sundermann scheme takes on a more interesting aspect. Which came to Sundermann first, the concept of the wall or the spaces it enclosed? The probability is that, as he now speculates, the sense of enclosure, or pivacy, dominated his thinking at the outset. In reaction to what he regarded as the "perfect positioning" but "chaotic exterior" of Krier's villa, Sundermann opted for the reverse, a pleasing outline on a less interesting site. As he became more familiar with Krier's restitution, however, he increasingly compromised his personal vision, which failed to translate to the villa within the wall. (These over-the-shoulder glances at Krier's work indicate the depth of Sundermann's admiration at the same time as his restless desire for greater artistic freedom.) His allegiance to Krier divides his aerial perspective almost evenly in two halves, front and back (fig. 155; cf. fig. 160). Sundermann's own scraggly wall protecting the property on the landward side makes no sense in juxtaposition with the perfectly formal character of the jetties

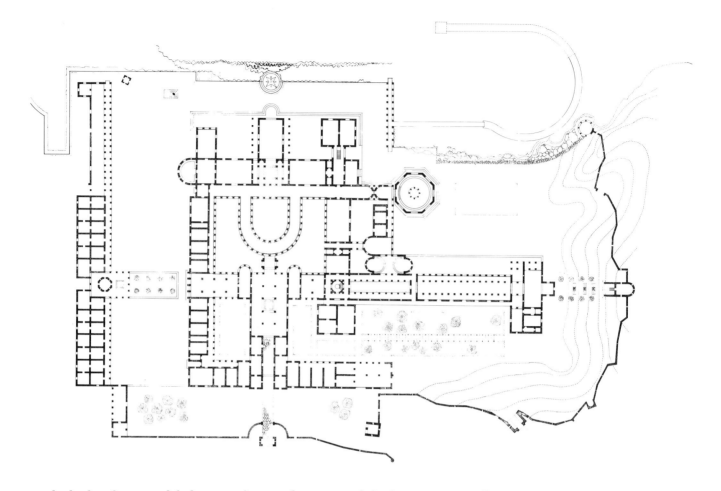

154. Sundermann, Laurentine Villa, plan (collection of the artist)

on the harbor front, modeled on Krier's. But whereas Krier's harbor remains small, Sundermann's tends toward the overblown and flaccid. In comparison, his sparsely perforated wall emphasizes blankness and inhospitality. One half hints at Pliny's Laurentine Villa as a vacation resort, the other half suggests a fortified place of last resort.

During an interview six years after the Laurentine *concours,* Sundermann continued to discuss his restitution and his ambivalent feelings about it. With characteristic dedication and earnestness, he had also continued to work on the scheme itself over that same period. He has improved the presentation of his original drawings and has recorded in a whole set of new pen-and-ink sketches how he imagines Pliny and his friends would use the villa, almost as a movie director might do.[59] Much of the impetus for this rededication to the task, and the more leisurely atmosphere in which to pursue it, came about as a result of an invitation to spend 1983–84 at the German Academy in Rome. In the conducive setting of the Villa Massimo, Sundermann set himself the logical goal of attempting

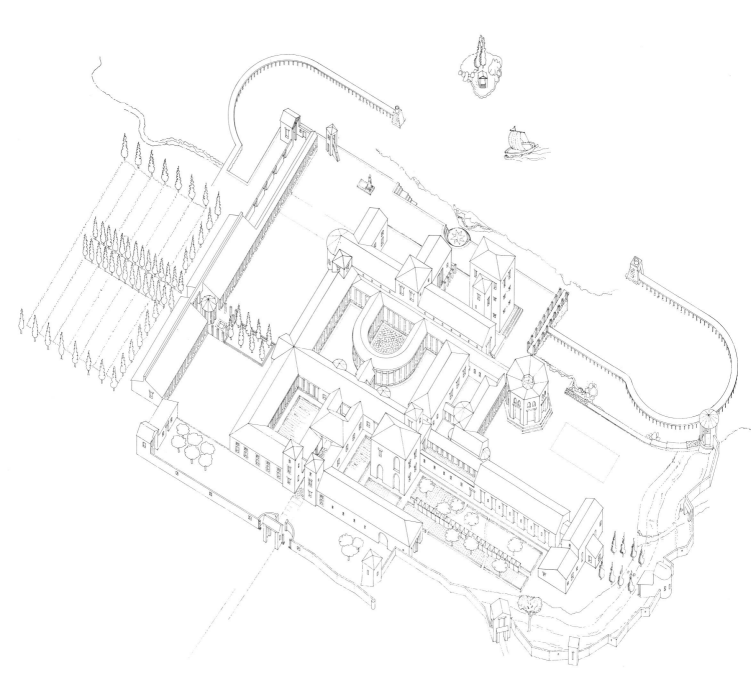

155. Sundermann, Lauren-
tine Villa, aerial perspective
(collection of the artist)

a restitution of the Tuscan Villa (cf. figs. 45 and 46). He says he felt the need for a different type of challenge—"a hilly one," as he puts it. He finished the restitution drawings in January 1984, just two years after his Laurentine set. This time he accompanied them with a series of rough sketches, which he claims gave him far greater freedom to explore his ideas by focusing his attention on the individual parts rather than the whole. He took full advantage of them to experiment with interior space, which was the biggest lesson he had belatedly learned from the Laurentine Villa. Moreover, the sketches gave immediate satisfaction to the artist in Sundermann. They add up to a multisided picture rather than the flat representation of a building that he will probably never see erected. In the words of his own published statement: "Bilder sind frei und nicht an eine bestimmte Darstellungs-form gefesselt."[60]

As laid out in the Villa Massimo yearbook and in the subsequent exhibition catalog of a show at Kassel, Sundermann's drawings are layered up the page like strata in an archaeological dig. The preliminary sketches form a continuous band across the top of the finished drawings and constitute a sequence of peeps at the villa similar to the vignettes provided by Montes or by Treuttel, Garcias, and Treuttel. The pen-and-ink sketches convey a kinetic energy to such areas as the courtyard with the plane trees. Line drawings blow up individual details such as the horseshoe-shaped baths complex, over which Sundermann labored hard, though the architect himself makes no special claims for their artistic merit. He admits they may be hasty in execution, but they represent his fascination with the whole procedure for dealing with the problems of restitution. Whatever his personal reservations, the Tuscan design clearly is an improvement over the Laurentine in sophistication and complexity. The sparsely punctuated enclosure wall remains a preoccupation, but its relation to what lies within is much tighter. Dense spatial clusters follow one another in almost bewildering succession, closely packed within the wall. Labyrinthine passages connect one eccentrically shaped courtyard after the other. In contrast to the Laurentine Villa, in this case the design and Pliny's letter have parted company, allowing the design to float freely. Except for the baths, the plane trees, and the *stibadium* garden, the description written to Apollinaris bears little direct connection to Sundermann's tour de force in spatial exploration. He answers this criticism by observing that he is a designer, not an archaeologist or even an art historian.

When Sundermann says of himself, "I learned more [from restitution] than I did throughout my earlier architectural studies," he seems to be speaking in the past tense. It is as if he had transcended restitution and the inherent classicism underlying Krier's approach. Sundermann now looks upon his onetime idol as a person who had become stuck, even if brilliantly so, in a preindustrial viewpoint. He blames Krier for boxing himself in, for being too rational and not emotional enough. Nevertheless, Sundermann learned much from Krier, not least the distinction between the classical, defined in Sundermann's words as a "superbly well done solution," and the vernacular, which is a faint reflection of the ideal. Sundermann's present aim, now that he has returned to his native Münster, is to express the vernacular of the region without losing sight of the universality that Krier tries to achieve in all he does. Only time will tell whether Sundermann can maintain the happy balance between the general and the very specific, or how far emulation and restitution will remain meaningful concepts to him.[61]

In the mid-1970s issue after issue of the magazine *Archives d'Architecture Moderne* brought to public attention for the first time a largely self-trained and unknown Luxembourg architect named Léon Krier (b. 1946). Maurice Culot, the editor of what was one of the most influential architectural periodicals of its day, championed Krier's now internationally famous theoretical writings and drawings devoted to the reconstruction of the European city.[62] This rather unusual author-editor relationship still flourished in 1981 when Culot took up the post of director of the Archives Department at IFA. His first major exhibition there was bound to spotlight Krier. The Pinon and Culot catalog *La Laurentine et l'invention de la villa romaine* gave pride of place to Krier's restitution by putting it first among the thirteen in the competition. Krier merited the honor by having thrown himself energetically into the *concours d'émulation,* with brilliant results. Before he was done, preliminary designs filled the better part of four sketchbooks, a ream of tracing paper, and loose pieces of office stationery. He also drew the often-reproduced finished suite of thirteen perspective views of his Laurentine Villa. In addition, he prepared scale drawings for an ethereal model that captivated the many visitors to the Laurentine exhibition. All told, some 160 sheets of paper record the progress of the design step by step over nearly six months of unremitting toil.[63] As a crowning touch Krier's wife and frequent collaborator, the artist Rita Wolff, was inspired by her husband's drawings to paint a delicious view of the villa, which has taken its rightful place as one of the most memorable images in the entire Laurentine iconography (pl. 33). How can so remarkable an archive be succinctly summarized? The answer may lie in a relatively cursory investigation of the better-known finished drawings, followed by a more detailed analysis of some of the unpublished sketches that preceded them.

Krier's love of what he calles *reconstruction* is well expressed in a revealing essay published as a preface to his drawings. Its title, "L'amour des ruines ou les ruines de d'amour," alludes to an amateur archaeologist friend of the architect's who has a passion for visiting and recording the ruins of antiquity. By contrast, Krier expresses his preference for the architect-archaeologists of the past, who illustrated their histories with vivid pictures showing the same ruins as if restored to their pristine state. He knows their names by heart, and he adds to them the name of Jacques Martin, the comic book creator of Alix, as a present-day representative of the breed. Their world of rebuilt ancient towns and villas thrills Krier; the tumbledown, dusty remains his friend likes leave a dry taste in his mouth and a sense of sadness. His predilection for antiquity restored to its peak of perfection reveals a childlike sense of wonder akin to Jean-Pierre Adam's. And some of that childlike spirit comes across in the feathery lightness of Krier's drawings, with their occasional humorous touches. Make no mistake, however, Krier takes this art of archaeologically based restitution extremely seriously. In his imagination he clearly sees fabled sites rising upon their old foundations like Williamsburg or Quebec City, for which he expresses great fondness. He walks their streets, discourses with their philosophers, and strolls through their marbled halls. He sees in them the future path of architecture. "The fragment only gains its value," he writes, "according to the extent to which it serves to reconstruct the whole."[64]

At the same time, Krier fears that the dread hand of archaeology can put a damper on the architect's imagination. He readily admits, for instance, that the flat coastal area around Ostia, probable site of Laurentinum, does not inspire him at all. On the contrary, its gas stations, marinas, and cheap pizzarias profoundly dismay him by confirming, as they do, all that he deems demeaning about "modernist" civilization.[65] So after careful consideration of the letter to Pliny, and after concluding that the Laurentine Villa could not have really existed in the form described, Krier elevates it on a peninsular site connected to the Italian shore by a narrow neck of land. The imaginary site as he visualized it in an aerial perspective dated 21 September 1981 (fig. 156) relies much more on his personal experiences than it does on Pliny's. In 1980 Krier and Rita Wolff wintered at the town of Sperlonga on the Mediterranean coast between Naples and Terracina. A rocky promontory occupied by the Torre Truglia forms the principal feature of the landscape and resembles the headland Krier drew three months after the official announcement of the concours d'émulation. Pliny's villa had nothing to fear from brigands, but the villa that Krier visualizes does. The "barbarians" or "pirates," as Krier called them in a postcard he sent me from Sperlonga, are his way of describing modernists who have invaded hallowed ancient sites with their steel and concrete. Their prideful insensitivity on the one hand is matched by a terrible creative timidity on the other. They are too timid to reconstruct, let alone to build anew in the spirit of the old.[66]

Two more of the final drawings, another aerial perspective dated 10 December 1981, and the same view seen in axonometric projection, finished that Christmas (fig. 157), convey the extreme complexity of Krier's design. The headland bears a dense agglomeration of structures huddled together like so many seabirds. This cluster is what Krier means when he writes that he has imagined a "villa-ge." He plays with the etymological similarity of two words to draw attention to the civic

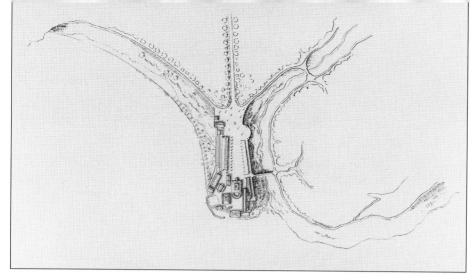

156. Krier, Laurentine Villa,
site plan (CCA, DR 1985:
292)

157. Krier, Laurentine Villa,
cutaway aerial perspective
(CCA, DR 1985:295)

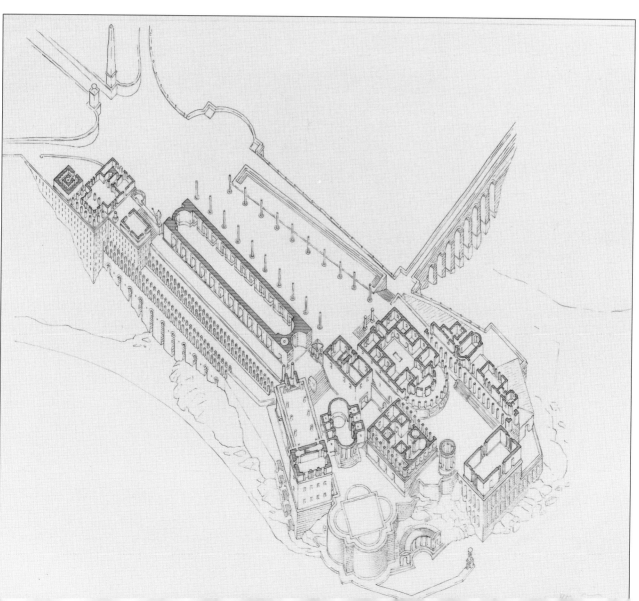

158. Krier, Laurentine Villa,
perspective of forecourt
(CCA, DR 1985:297)

159. Krier, Laurentine Villa,
plan, cross sections, and
aerial perspective of atrium
(CCA, DR 1985:304)

nature of the Laurentine Villa as he sees it. He endows it with all the necessary elements of a city in microcosm—open public places and intricately shaped private spaces. Paved Roman roads converge on the villa from the narrow neck of land and reach it over a viaduct across the deep ravine to the right (similar to the one running through his hometown of Luxembourg). By any of these landward approaches, the visitor arrives in a forumlike forecourt, which risks being arid in the manner of the archaeologists Krier criticizes in his essay. But he substitutes for the conventional urban street furniture of lampposts and bollards two neat rows of luxuriant palm trees, their tops amusingly lopped off in the cutaway view.

In Krier's forecourt (fig. 158) a terrace encourages vistas down into the ravine and off to an alluring prospect of the sea dotted with the distant profile of three islands resembling Zannone, Ponza, and Palmarola off the shore at Sperlonga. Framing the perspective on the other side, the cryptoporticus stretches the length of the miniature piazza until it halts in front of a tall masonry tower with the exposed timber work so characteristic of Krier at the top. The palm trees funnel the visitor's attention back to the atrium. By any account this central building preoccupied Krier the most, because he devoted more preliminary sketches to it than to any other part of the restitution, as we will see. He also devoted to it a drawing of its own in the final suite (fig. 159), indicating how pleased he was with its beauty of proportions and graceful form. In the completed version he particularly liked the combination of square impluvium courtyard at the front and D-shaped portico curving out at the back. He dates the sheet 10 October 1981, earlier than any other but one in the finished group. He elsewhere refers to that same day as the significant moment of transition between the initial and final phases of the designing.[67]

Moving his attention to the more private side of the Laurentine Villa, Krier continues to manifest the ability to imagine and represent a complicated grouping of structures from almost any vantage point. In one case (fig. 160) he depicts hanging gardens, pergolas, and potted lemon trees seen from the low perspective of someone doing the crawl—Alix in the adventure comics of Jacques Martin often ends up swimming to save his life. Here all three towers come plainly into view: the one beside the atrium with the flapping awnings typical of Krier; the one at the tip of the headland with its no less characteristic projecting platforms; the unusual one over on the far left with holes for carrier pigeons. These towers fascinated Krier in the earlier phases of the design process, as we will see shortly, and indeed have been a preoccupation of long standing. On this same side of the building he also visualizes Pliny on the terrace beneath the cryptoporticus about to greet a friend (fig. 161). At that very moment a mischievous cat is upsetting a vase. The next drawing in the suite shows the view from the opposite direction and, cartoon fashion, portrays the sequel to the incident. The broken vase lies in

160. Krier, Laurentine Villa,
perspective from sea (CCA,
DR 1985:300)

161. Krier, Laurentine Villa,
perspective of terrace (CCA,
DR 1985:303)

pieces on the flagstones, and the human figures have disappeared behind a fluttering curtain, presumably in pursuit of the cat. This is as close as Krier ever lets himself get to emulating Martin's illustrative techniques.[68]

On New Year's Day 1982, if an inscription is precise, Krier drew the villa in a bird's-eye view that later inspired Rita Wolff's painting in punning emulation of Jules-Frédéric Bouchet (fig. 162; cf. fig. 37 and pl. 33). The pen-and-ink draftsmanship captures more successfully than in other instances the freshness and vivacity of Krier's preliminary sketches. In this wonderfully deft evocation of the scene, Krier swoops in on the dream villa, the dream village, the dream acropolis. The nervous calligraphy convincingly conveys his deep conviction that the classical tradition, far from being dead, has a vibrant contribution to make to the present. The act of physically building such a villa would constitute nothing short of a catharsis for debased modern craftsmanship, out of which would arise, phoenixlike, *un artisanat de qualité*.[69] And he firmly maintains against his many critics that with present-day material and technological resources craftsmanship of the sort would not be impossible. He identifies so closely with this Laurentine dream that he believes in its universal appeal for all people, at all times and in all places. Confronted with such intellectual fervor, such artistic conviction in every pen stroke, such rigor conveyed softly with such a deft touch, his ideas gain plausibility. His drawings'

162. Krier, Laurentine Villa, aerial perspective (CCA, DR 1985:296)

command of their artistic medium simply sweep aside opposition by their power to make a forceful, controversial statement seem easy and palatable.

In "L'amour des ruines" Krier recalls ruefully that when he set out on his career the idea of making a beautiful drawing in the classical manner provoked such scorn that he almost turned archaeologist. But he realized in time that his imagination could never submit to the scientific constraints imposed by the dig and the grid. While awaiting the ultimate test of his work, which will be the act of reconstruction, he submits to drawing restitutions in which the trained eye of the artist imaginatively intervenes to supply the missing elements of Pliny's text. Accordingly, when Krier first learned about the *concours d'émulation,* he set to work diligently reading the letter to Gallus in French and in Latin. A pink file among his papers shows that he followed up the typed list of historical restitutions from IFA by adding their British Architectural Library call numbers. In the same pink file is a piece of blotting paper to which, as Krier explained in conversation, he attached little cutouts corresponding to individual Laurentine room shapes (fig. 163). The cutouts with tape on the back could be stuck down or moved around at will. Through frequent recombinations Krier arrived at the conclusion that Pliny's description could not work as a continuous sequence of rooms, perhaps because some later scribe had left out a vital piece of information. Krier's blotting-paper exercise furnished him with an insight that freed his imagination. It encouraged him to let each Plinian room "float about" on the peninsular site, forming a loosely knit cluster unseen in previous restitutions. He made the villa a "villa-ge" by bursting it apart into a series of separate buildings.

An undated sketchbook that Krier says he used during June and July 1981 contains ten site plans of Laurentinum in which the architect tried out different situations and orientations for the "villa-ge" of structures he had previously experimented with on blotting paper. One of the solutions already settled on a peninsular site jutting out from the Italian mainland (fig. 164). Although the width of the villa buildings somewhat exceeds the final version, the overall lines resemble one another closely. As often happens in such cases, however, the designer backs away from this initial intuitive insight. The process starts taking place in a second sketchbook of the same type, this one begun at London on 10 August and completed at Paris on 29 September, according to the informative title page. Mixed in with material relating to Krier's contemporary Tegel project for Berlin are twenty-nine page sides of sketches for the Laurentine Villa. Among the site plans near the beginning, Krier repeats the central atrium block in much the same form as in the earlier sketchbook, but with elaborate vineyards and kitchen gardens occupying the fatter peninsula (fig. 165). Then, only slightly later in the book, more fundamental changes begin to occur. In a third site plan (fig. 166) the shape and size of the atrium are dramatically transformed by the addition of two large courtyards spread-

163. Krier, Laurentine Villa,
blotting-paper sketches (collection of the artist)

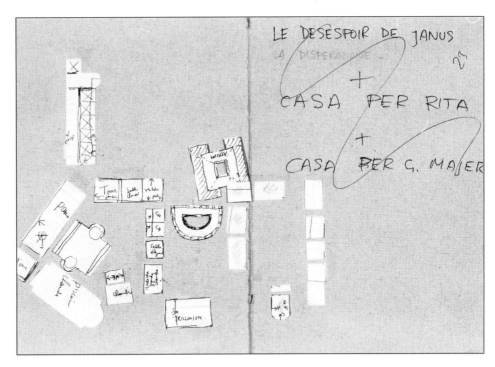

Inside the sketch: LE DESESPOIR DE JANUS / CASA PER RITA / CASA PER G. MAJER / TRICLINIUM

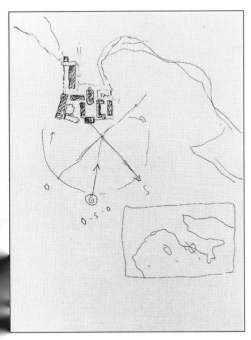

164. Krier, Laurentine Villa,
sketch site plan (collection of
the artist)

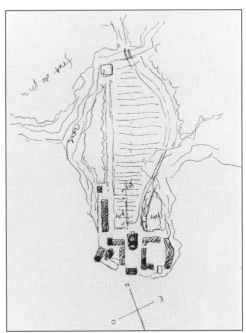

165. Krier, Laurentine Villa,
sketch site plan (collection of
the artist)

166. Krier, Laurentine Villa,
sketch plan and elevation (collection of the artist)

ing out laterally to each side. The intervening days had brought about a departure
from the initial parti. No designer undertakes such a thing lightly, and they usually
think better of it afterward; such was the case with Krier.

About the time Krier changed the plan of his Laurentine atrium, he departed
from London for Helsinki on 18 August. By the twenty-third he was already vaca-
tioning at Frebbenby on the Åland Islands in the Finnish archipelago. But Krier's
hands are rarely idle, and thoughts of Laurentinum were ever present. That same
day he dated a new site plan of the villa, quite similar to the previous monochrome
one except delicately colored green and pale salmon (fig. 167). At that same vacation spot the same day he produced an unusually soft bird's-eye view in pencil
corresponding to the plan (fig. 168). In the hazy distance lie three islands that
might be those remembered from the days at Sperlonga or just as easily others
inspired by the Baltic. In the foreground he shows the broad, very formal-looking
atrium partly blocking from sight the triclinium in the middle ground. With its
row of three distinctive sunken Serliana openings this dining pavilion derives from
the well-known Palladio design for the Villa Pojana upon which the garden facade
of Lord Burlington's Chiswick Villa was subsequently based. (Such direct historical
references are infrequent with Krier.) The distinctively urban quality of this Laurentine restitution carries over even more strongly to the courtyard between the
triclinium and the back of the atrium, where it curves out in a semicircular portico.
Using his French translation of Pliny somewhat freely, Krier describes the courtyard as "assez élégante fort gaie" (fig. 169). Sight lines indicate the vistas from this
miniature acropolis. The sea would appear only in fleeting glimpses between the
quasi-public buildings, which, as in the Athenian agora, never quite touch each
other. Enclosure and a sense of release enter into a dialogue of their own, analogous
to the give and take between Plato and his pupils during their conversations in the
Athenian Stoa Poikile.[70]

Krier could rationalize the intentional Platonic overtones of his Laurentine
restitution with the argument that Pliny's demeanor of moderation in all things
derives from the Platonic ideal of the philosopher-king. According to the Platonic
dialogue *The Republic,* this individual is altruistic and artistically cultivated on the
model of Pericles, the enlightened tyrant of Athens during the lifetime of Plato's
teacher Socrates. Through the words of Socrates as recorded in *The Republic,*
Plato concludes that the ideal city, or polis, will function best when a philosopher-
ruler oversees the well-being of all the citizens, just as Pliny in the private sphere
oversees his properties, his slaves, and the rest of his household. These three
notions of the landowner as paterfamilias, of the philosopher-king, and of the
well-tempered city as metaphor for the human soul extend from the classical
thought of Plato to Léon Krier's personal philosophy. Plato's ideas have been
influential on Krier as filtered through Hannah Arendt's book *The Human Condi-*

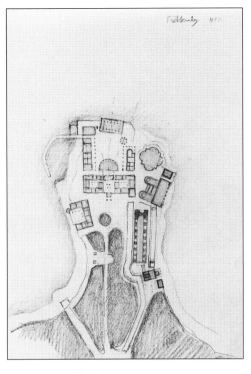

167. (*Above*) Krier, Laurentine Villa, sketch site plan
(collection of the artist)

168. (*Above, right*) Krier,
Laurentine Villa, sketch aerial
perspective (collection of the
artist)

169. (*Right*) Krier, Laurentine Villa, sketch cross section
of atrium and perspective of
it from courtyard behind (collection of the artist)

tion, which he tells me is the "pillar" of his thinking. This book discusses the pure devotion of Greeks like Plato to the democratic bustle of the agora and contrasts it with the Roman statesmen's attempts to blend the life in the public sphere (*res publica*) with the contemplative life (*res privata*) in that most introspective of spaces, the private home. Arendt might as well have used the word villa.[71] Although Krier derives his Platonism partly from Arendt, he nonetheless departs from her by conflating public and private aspects in the Laurentine Villa. In other words, the villa becomes a polis in miniature. Krier intends the villa-polis to express the Platonic eidos of ideal Beauty through its architecture, and of ideal Justice in its harmonious balance of open and closed spaces, the formal and the informal, the classical and the vernacular.

In keeping with his philosophy of order, balance, and moderation, Krier eventually abandoned the monumental atrium he favored at Frebbenby for another solution adopted in a slightly larger blue-bound notebook, this one commenced at Bargemon on the Côte d'Azur on 8 October 1981. Krier made a volte-face by returning to the reduced size of his original parti. He simply exploded away the side courtyards and went back to a simpler and more compact rectangular format with the *D*-shaped portico, now wrapped right around the building from the back to the front (fig. 170). The form hardly varies in the final version, dated just two days after the sketchbook was begun (cf. fig. 159). He elaborates upon it slightly with the eventual addition to the rooftop corners of what he calls *vases médicis* (fig. 171). The sketch version in this case figures among the forty-one relating to the Laurentine Villa drawn on loose pieces of tracing paper or office stationery. Both it and the other atrium sketch are, however, accomplished works of art in their own right, not faltering first tries. They display the same draftsmanlike vivacity and ability to visualize in three dimensions that Krier's admirers and opponents alike recognize in the finished version. Perhaps it is on account of this amazing consistency that no critics until now have recognized the months of careful preparation and the weighing of different options that lie behind the final drawings.

In the foreword to a recent book titled *New Classicism* Krier has written: "The great periods of architecture are like different stations in a planet's revolution. The Sun of universal ideas illuminates the architectural planet. . . . The classical is closest to the universal while still being a characteristic of the material world. The true cabinet-maker is inspired by the idea of the . . . table . . . the lesser one is influenced by this . . . or that particular table."[72] By making an analogy to furniture, an analogy of the type Plato loved, Krier evokes the concept of the eidos, or "universal idea," and applies it to historical architecture. He demonstrates his point with a diagram showing the progress of architecture as it orbits elliptically around the "sun" of classical values. (Plato would definitely have preferred a circle instead of an oval.) The carefully studied atrium would illustrate the dictum that the closer

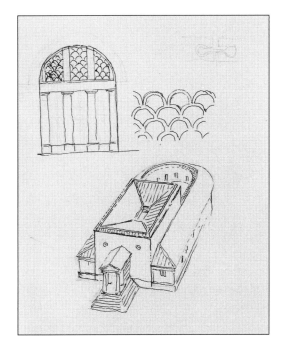

170. Krier, Laurentine Villa, perspective of atrium (collection of the artist)

171. Krier, Laurentine Villa, sketch of atrium and tower (collection of the artist)

the building is to the sun, the truer its architecture. As a proposition it has all the elegant simplicity of a Euclidean theorem. And there are moments when Krier, standing at a blackboard with chalk in hand, resembles some ancient Greek philosopher drawing figures in the sand.

The tracing-paper sketch of the atrium is significant for another reason. Beside it rises the faint silhouette of one of Krier's three Laurentine towers. Krier devoted to them a series of studies second in number only to those of the atrium and no less crucial to his conception of the villa as metaphor. According to his perception, the artist is an inspired individual who thrives on communion with nature at the same time as on relative isolation from the world. Krier had previously expressed the view in a group of tower retreats for himself, or with fellow artists such as Rita Wolff and Massimo Scolari in mind.[73] Now Krier discovered that his own quest for peace and quiet had existed in Pliny's need for retirement at his villa. Krier's identification of the tower with artistic inspiration manifests itself in a set of drawings concentrating on the "big tower," all found on a single page in the fourth and last of the Laurentine blue notebooks. The three sketches include the view of the "villa-ge" that Pliny or Krier would enjoy from the top of the tower (fig. 172). A breathtaking panorama like this seems to connote the artist's capacity to rise above the polis and, by means of this detachment, to understand the needs of the just society. On the left side of the sketches, moreover, is the third tower, quite unlike the others in external appearance. Krier in a jesting moment likened this *columbar-ium* for carrier pigeons to a modern statesman's communications center and made a separate study of it (fig. 173). (Pliny never mentioned anything of the sort, according to the *index verborum* of his writings.) As shown, the *columbarium* detaches itself and blasts away rocketlike above the earthly realm of the villa—again this sense of explosion. Krier's otherworldly conception is further borne out by the ghostly all-white plaster model he had prepared. It also hovers out of reach, like the Platonic eidos of the Good or the Beautiful.

173. Krier, Laurentine Villa, sketches of *columbarium* (collection of the artist)

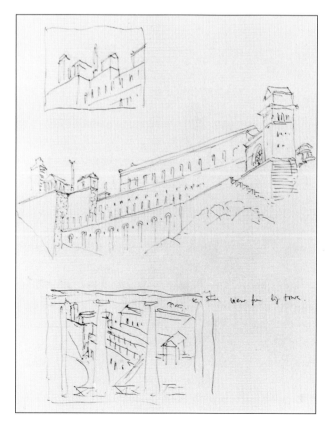

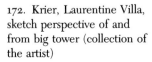
172. Krier, Laurentine Villa, sketch perspective of and from big tower (collection of the artist)

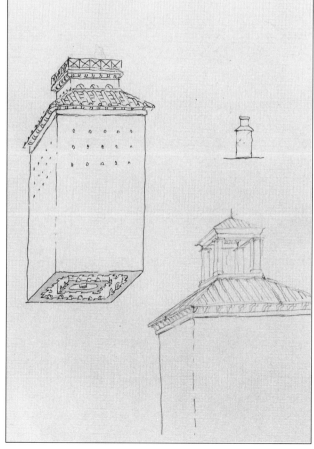

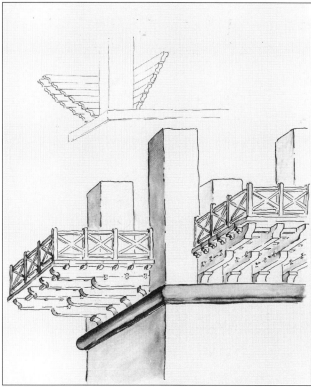

174. (*Above*) Krier, Laurentine Villa, sketches of towers (collection of the artist)

175. (*Above, right*) Krier, Laurentine Villa, sketch of carpentry work supports of tower platform (collection of the artist)

A study of Krier's Laurentine tower sketches reveals another useful point in understanding the implicit duality of his villa: part eidos of beauty, part polis. Whereas the buildings around the atrium form an urban agora embodying the classical tradition through their use of the orders, the towers do not. They are astylar, and more revealing still, their superstructures utilize a considerable amount of woodwork instead of masonry. Three sketches of towers from the last Laurentine blue notebook epitomize this aspect (fig. 174). Projecting from them are wooden viewing or painting platforms, hinting that here artists endeavor to search for the eidos. In yet another sketch, this one touched with a bit of blue-gray wash (fig. 175), Krier exposes the carpentry to reveal the gaunt timbers as though in a bombed-out building. Significantly in this regard, Krier proudly pointed out in an interview some years ago that his maternal ancestors were master carpenters from the Tirol who came to Luxembourg to rebuild the roof of Saint Willibrod at Echternach, the very place where Krier attended the Lycée Classique.[74] Could it be that these references to woodwork in the sketchbooks are a sort of secret signature, like the carpenters' and masons' marks familiar to students of medieval buildings? Whatever the case, the prominent use of wood refers to the vernacular tradition that Krier sees as emerging out of the classical tradition of architecture yet distinct from it.

Krier's restitution, if taken in the sense of an opposition of the towers to the atrium, expresses a pair of contrasting though not incompatible architectural principles: it is classical and at the same time incorporates vernacular building practices; it relies on highly crafted stonework, yet the rougher texture of wooden beams also plays a part. How do these different ideas and qualities blend as well as they do? The answer, according to Krier, comes from his firm belief that all buildings derive from the same universal source and that the vernacular has embedded within it the imprint of the eternal classical. To him it is all a question of degree, and emphatically not of kind. The classical may be a goal beyond the grasp of most, but the vernacular, if properly recognized, belongs to everyone and thus could redeem much of the degeneration Krier finds around him in the modern built environment. Moreover, Krier's Laurentine Villa nobly states the belief that a reconciliation is possible between the pressing demands of the polis, on the one hand, and the detachment necessary to pursue the eidos, on the other. The urban agglomeration around the Laurentine atrium stands for the city. The towers rising above the tumult and possessed of room to breathe are places to oversee the city's concerns and seek artistic solutions to them.

CONCLUSION

Amores Mei

THROUGHOUT THE PRECEDING CHAPTERS, an array of Pliny restitutions have been lined up in various combinations: some amateur, others professional; some large, others small; some practical, others for pedagogical purposes; some by major architects, others by those so insignificant as almost to have dropped out of sight. But at no point so far have any of them been singled out as essentially closer to Pliny's original inspiration, and in that sense better or at least truer to his spirit. As far as it lies within my abilities, the time of reckoning has now come to establish some useful criterion for the patient reader who has just completed the long peregrination from Pliny to posterity. I hope these concluding remarks may serve as a gauge of the many schemes already considered, those inadvertently overlooked, those still to come, or those that otherwise may yet come to light.

The criterion proposed here has the advantage that it derives directly from Pliny's letters themselves. It consists of reading the letters from Pliny's literary standpoint. It suggests that the same sensitive approach taken to his writings can apply to the architectural interpretations of them. This may, in retrospect, seem obvious to the point of triteness. Yet the strange fact remains that few literary critics have remarked upon it, nor have many of those who have studied Pliny and tried to convey his imagery to their visionary villas. They have all failed to make the simple observation that his letters have a beginning, a middle, and an end, as any good piece of epistolary prose should. And just as the introduction to this book served as a kind of greeting and the body of the work dealt with the meaty part of the letters devoted to the villas themselves, so the conclusion must focus on the end of those same letters.

The letters both to Gallus and to Apollinaris, having spent most of their text describing the "big house," end up by considering an outlying building in the villa gardens. Recall for a moment the culminating passages Pliny wrote to his two friends. The letter to Gallus spoke of a suite of rooms at the head of a garden cryptoporticus at Laurentinum. Pliny described it lovingly as "diaeta est amores mei, re vera amores: ipse posui." Translators have rendered the key words as "my favorite rooms," *mes délices, meine Lust,* and Orrery called them "my delight . . . my mistress." To one degree or another the Latinists have also caught the clear implication from Pliny's phrase *ipse posui,* that he had a personal hand in the design of this part of the Laurentine Villa. Certain architects when setting about their restitutions have regarded this as an indication of Pliny's meddling and have chosen to downplay any role he might have had in enlarging the villa. In so doing they have missed the point and therefore the entire climactic section of the letter. Similarly, when writing about the Tuscan Villa, Pliny told Apollinaris that among the places he referred to as *amori meo* he particularly doted upon a secluded *stibadium,* or dining pavilion. Here too he stated that "I was willing to indulge myself in the description of what I love; for I am particularly fond of places which I have either laid out by myself or have finished when begun by others." These then were Pliny's favorite haunts, or the *amores mei* referred to in the title of this conclusion.

Pliny's favorite haunts share certain characteristics that further enhance their idiosyncratic nature. Each incorporates some enclosed and easily darkened space, a sort of inner sanctum far from the commotion of the "big house." The letters are quite specific about the blinds, vine trellises, or other contrivances used to screen out the light and heat of the day, in the interest of coolness as well as darkness. In sharp contrast to the open and hospitable tone of the rest of the letters, these passages describe areas of the villa that sound like secluded retreats within a retreat; places exclusively set aside for Pliny to enjoy alone or in the company of a few intimates. As his translator the earl of Orrery put it so well, "No summons to the bar, no clients at my gate" would disturb Pliny's repose.[1] Pliny the overworked lawyer, magistrate, and statesman found in these villas within a villa the relaxation, peace, and quiet he needed for his literary pursuits. As such, each little structure and its surrounding garden provides insights into the secretive life of the artist by drawing attention to the oddity of the place and the reclusiveness of its occupant.

At Laurentinum, Pliny described how the separate *amores mei* pavilion with its adjacent sunroom, or *heliocaminus,* had a self-contained apartment principally intended as a study. According to the text, the bedchamber has attached to it a room for an attendant or secretary who can take dictation or bring writing materials at any time of the day or night. Deeper inside, somewhere in the middle of the little suite of rooms, a special space (*cubiculum noctis et somni*) is so contrived that it can completely shut out sights and sounds, even the pounding of the waves on the nearby seashore. During the Saturnalia festivities when the household members had the freedom to celebrate into the wee hours, Pliny could leave them to their riotous merrymaking, so he said, and retire undisturbed. This strongly hints at an artistic temperament known among other authors who need almost complete quiet and isolation for writing, and who get cranky when the least thing disturbs their train of thought.

In an age of faint illumination from oil lamps, Pliny's provision of complete darkness sounds peculiar. Nor is this the only reference in the letters to an absence

of light. In addition to a windowless room at each villa, the Laurentine cryptoporticus had a system of blinds designed to cut down the glare and create a kind of
penumbra. Adjacent to the Tuscan *stibadium* stood another enclosed area for
after-dinner naps, or perhaps for working sessions if the inspiration to write seized
Pliny in the midst of the garden. Such provisions for retirement bring to mind the
comparable so-called Teatro Marittimo in the emperor Hadrian's villa at Tivoli.
Cut off and encircled by a small moat, it strongly suggests the idea of seclusion
even in the absence of surviving literary evidence. The reverse applies to Pliny's
more modest-sized villas. In their case the ruins are missing, but the evocative
words of the author himself linger to help conjure up a picture of hostility to
intrusion.[2]

A possible contributing factor to Pliny's search for solitude and darkness may
have been his poor eyesight. In a letter to Cornutus Tertullus (bk. 7, ep. 21),
mentioned earlier, Pliny complains that he had to rule out reading and writing
except by dictation, owing to temporary blindness. His journey from one villa to
another consequently had to take place in an enclosed litter that he compared to
his own curtained bedroom. At the villa—it is unclear which one is being referred
to—the venetian blinds in the cryptoporticus had to be half closed to diminish any
glare that might further inflame his swollen eyes. (The perceptive Orrery took this
to mean the Laurentine Villa, and he saw Pliny as something of an invalid, if not
exactly a hypochondriac.)[3] These precautions, coupled with careful diet and bathing, seem to have worked wonders. The symptoms abated, judging from the absence of any further mention of the health problem in other letters. Only once
more does an oblique reference to blindness occur when Pliny (bk. 8, ep. 1)
laments to a correspondent that ill health had deprived him of Encolpius, his
trusted *lector,* or reader, on whom he relied so much. But Pliny was not unique
in having a personal reader, so no inferences regarding failing eyesight can be
made. It therefore does not seem prudent to attribute the peculiarities of Pliny's
garden pavilions to partial blindness just on the strength of a reference or two in
the letters. The oddness of the darkened chambers at Laurentinum and in Tuscany,
however, remains a puzzle. Were they motivated by health consciousness, they
would not be the only feature of villa architecture so dictated. For instance, the
daily regime of physical exercise and relaxation Pliny prescribed for himself necessi-
tated the *gestatio,* the hippodrome, and the baths complex. So perhaps the darkened spaces, curtains, folding doors, and venetian blinds he went to some pains to
single out and take personal credit for may have been for some therapeutic purpose.
Certainly they captured the attention of some who have admired the architecture
of Pliny's villas, especially designers with a studious, literary turn of mind.

Good Latinist that he was, Jean-François Félibien des Avaux considered Pliny's
letters with great care, hoping to interpret correctly their every implied change of

direction. For Félibien the only solution to his own interpretation based on the letter to Gallus consisted in long wings and remote pavilions. Their proliferation exceeds any earlier restitution and just about any since their engraving in the 1690s. The site plan (fig. 52), being deliberately cut off at the left margin, leaves to the viewer's imagination whether yet more buildings ought to exist beyond the bounds of the copperplate in order to balance the *amores mei* pavilion on the right-hand extremity. Then at the bottom of the plate, to either side of a formal forecourt, Félibien placed a pair of entry pavilions adding further retreats within the grounds, much like the contemporary Grand Trianon at Versailles or the even earlier château at Marly. In this way Félibien fragmented the villa into a multiplicity of smaller outlying parts, as if to suggest they were the ones most favored by Pliny's text. To one of these little ancillary buildings Félibien even devoted a separate engraving, the only known architect other than Stier to have done so. Félibien, like Stier, fabricated an entire structure inland, or *rimota a mari,* to use Pliny's description (fig. 176; cf. fig. 112). The central dining chamber is augmented by two individual suites of rooms in which, perhaps, diners could sleep off the meals served here, like courtiers after the repasts at the court of Louis XIV.

In the case of the Tuscan Villa site plan (fig. 51) Félibien made explicit his rejection of perfect bilateral symmetry in the layout of the grounds. At the far end of one off-center allée, he situated Pliny's *stibadium* and the bedchamber that went with it. Then, by pivoting the whole thing to make it more easily comprehensible, he produced a separate ground plan of the area (fig. 177). Within a hedge of shaped trees or bushes—a kind of living fence—he inserted the *stibadium* proper with its basin, its couches for eating, and the four corner columns carrying some sort of canopy above. (A dotted line running underneath and out the other side indicates the canalization of the waterworks.) Next came a fountain in a circular pool, and finally the sleeping pavilion with the bedstead, set all the way in the back but in line of sight of the delightful contrivances outdoors. Similar to Pliny's movements from one delightful space to another, Félibien took the occasion to step outside the polite confines of his academic milieu and indulge in some of the ancient Romans' sensuousness. He said that "the Romans knew how to make their country houses delightful, if that word may be permitted, by contriving to get the most advantages from the situation where their buildings were located, by choosing the most healthful orientation possible, and by catering to the sort of voluptuousness that reasonable men enjoy from an extremely temperate climate."[4] Carefully chosen expressions such as *délices* and *volupté* reflect the extreme yet still *sage* pleasure with which Félibien contemplated the *stibadium* complex in Pliny's Tuscan Villa garden. From these words and the engraved images accompanying them there wafts the ineffable atmosphere of a *fête champêtre* as depicted by the painter Antoine Watteau, a near contemporary of Félibien.

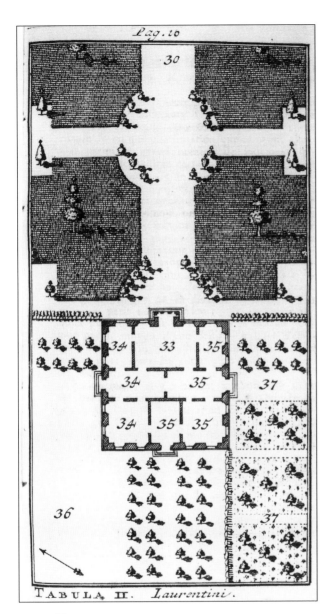

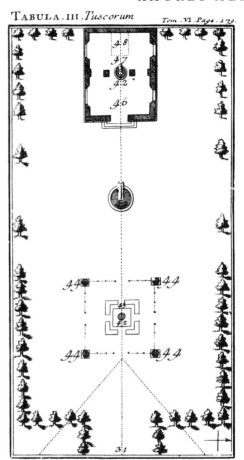

176. Félibien, Laurentine
Villa, plan of pavilion in forecourt (Félibien, *Plans*)

177. Félibien, Tuscan Villa,
plan of *stibadium* (Félibien,
Plans)

Although in each case Félibien heard the climactic crescendo in Pliny's prose,
he did not quite dare to plunge headlong into the sensuousness of the letters. He
asserted, for example, that he had inadequate textual information to assess the
appearance of the villa elevations, and only just enough to rough out the simplest
and most undifferentiated of garden treatments. His response to Pliny's rich, occasionally wild, profusion of horticultural images took the all too predictable form of
geometric parterres, flower beds arranged in broderie patterns, and allées travers-
ing denser boskets. It could all have occupied a level plain as flat as a drill ground.

No such formalistic interpretations characterize the almost exactly contemporary restitution of Francesco Ignazio Lazzari (figs. 21 and 22), who knew from personal experience the corrugated landscape of Tuscany that Pliny wrote about. The right-hand panel of Lazzari's late seventeenth-century *Tuscan Villa* (fig. 178) shows the horizon with a line of low hillocks, the central one incorporating terraces gently ascending the sloping villa garden. Down the middle runs an artificial cascade, or

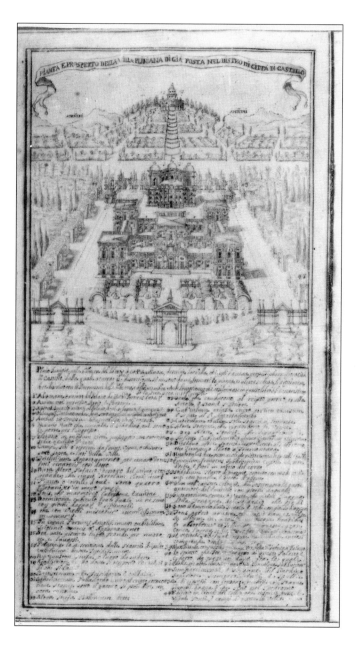

178. Lazzari, *Tuscan Villa*, aerial perspective showing *stibadium* (private collection, New York City)

so it appears, composed of curving steplike stages. At the very top, amid a grove of tall trees, stands the *stibadium,* fancifully crowning the whole Lazzari composition. Just as the description of it forms the culmination of Pliny's letter to Apollinaris, Lazzari's accompanying manuscript texts expand upon the Pliny passage in several lengthy paragraphs that build up in much the same way as the conclusion of the letter. He devoted more words to this one feature than to any other single part of the villa.

Lazzari envisioned the *stibadium* proper as a form of outdoor area on the hemicyclical plan of a *teatro,* to quote from the description given in the legend of the drawing. He covered it with a two-tiered dome supported by Carystian marble columns in order to create a spot for elegant al fresco dinner parties. As for Pliny's adjacent bedroom suite, it has swollen into a *palazzo ornato di marmi* or a *palazzetto,* words Lazzari used more or less interchangeably. The fluidity of his prose mirrors that of his pen-and-wash draftsmanship, though he ran into problems depicting what he had in mind. Indistinct at the best of times, the damp-stained drawing has now turned the color of café au lait and poses even more difficulties in deciphering. Despite ambiguities, it is nevertheless evident that Lazzari intended the *stibadium* as the crowning touch to his whole restitution, much as it functioned in Pliny's text. Lazzari designed its strange yet compellingly "theatrical" silhouette as if to stand out against a cloudless Umbrian sky, of the kind so often painted by Perugino. According to Lazzari, the building consisted of many rooms, ran up several stories in height, and warded off the sun's rays with a vine pergola instead of a true domed roof. Part arbor, part architecture, it dominates the rest of the villa lying in the valley below.[5]

As befits a translator of Pliny, John earl of Orrery and Cork knew Pliny's letters better than most who have undertaken restitutions of the Laurentine and Tuscan villas. The "Life of Pliny" that prefaces his translations and the "Observations" that follow each letter for the edification of his son drew that young man's attention to the most salient points. (Another English aristocrat, Lord Chesterfield, may subsequently have drawn inspiration from Orrery's technique.) Orrery thus remarked on the architectural letters in general: "You will find, Charles, that Pliny had several country houses. . . . [and] I imagine you will be delighted with a little garden apartment adjoining to his gallery, and built by himself. He mentions it with ecstasy. . . . And tells us that he . . . found himself not only enclosed in sweetness and solitude, but perfectly defended from all kinds of interruptions."[6] As Orrery's observations later put it: "The soul of Pliny . . . formed for studious privacy" imbued his letters with a spiritual message that far exceeded in importance any strictly factual information they might reveal about his building endeavors. Orrery then went on to extol the virtues of the Laurentine *amores mei* pavilion, saying: "He raised this additional building, at the end of his gallery, as an asylum to his studies and a sanctuary to his speculations; he speaks of his favorite edifice in the rapturous style of a lover." At this juncture, as if in unison with Pliny, Orrery's text itself breaks into verse:

> Here is my heart, here fix'd my soul's delight
> Here the calm chamber of forgetful night
> Freed from domestic noise, and public strife
> I drink oblivion of an anxious life.

And in conclusion—just to drive home the point—Orrery likened the delights of Laurentinum to those his cousin, Lord Burlington, enjoyed at Chiswick Villa.[7]

Orrery's observations on the letter to Apollinaris continued in much the same amorous vein. "A more enamoured description cannot be given of a place," he wrote with respect to the Tuscan Villa. "Here again," he continued, "the lover dwells upon the charms of his mistress; he views in rapture every feature." Indeed, Pliny preferred Tuscany over Laurentinum for many of the same reasons that endeared to Orrery his country house at Marston, in the depths of the West Country. "To the studious mind," said Orrery, "no retirement can be too private; no solitude too obscure: and therefore the greater the distance from the metropolis, the more complete will be the scene of tranquility."[8] Concerning the *stibadium* in particular, Orrery called it "the most beautiful and most expensive summer house in Pliny's garden," though he thought the boats of sweetmeats too contrived for his taste, and English taste in general.[9] Despite these chauvinistic reservations, Orrery had the artist Samuel Wale design an engraved vignette of the *stibadium* that is one of the rare illustrations of it ever to have been prepared (fig. 179). Wale's stylized rococo cartouche perfectly frames a scene infused by the energy of the selfsame plant forms. Creepers entwine the Carystian marble columns, and the fountain in front plays against a backdrop of cut shrubbery. Clearly the artist and translator shared their captivation with Pliny's evocative words, in defiance of the passage of centuries. The astute way Orrery, albeit an amateur, understood Pliny's innermost feelings and design aims has been ignored far too long in the scholarly literature. He should take his rightful place among those who have penetrated nearest to the heart of Pliny's architectural letters.

In the discussion of the Tuscan property, as in the previous one devoted to the Como villas, Orrery noted that the exact geographical locations had been hypothetically pinpointed in Abraham Ortellius's *Theatrum orbis terrarum* (fig. 2). In the light of this topographical knowledge and Orrery's obvious kinship with Pliny's life and letters, it is all the more puzzling that he felt no motivation whatever to seek out the actual villa sites during his 1754–55 Grand Tour to Italy. Strange though it may seem, the epistolary travelogue Orrery wrote, posthumously published in 1774 as *Letters from Italy . . .*, carries not a single reference to Pliny's villas. Yet Orrery had passed close to Como on his outbound journey and had spent the better part of an entire year in Florence, from where he could easily have traveled to Umbria. Perhaps such a literal-minded piece of detective work did not suit Orrery's detached hauteur. He explained away any lack of thoroughness on his part by commenting: "Time has destroyed all remains of . . . these houses; and, to speak ingenuously, it is impossible to rebuild them exactly, even upon paper." In the final analysis Orrery, for all his insights, preferred to retain his illusions about Pliny's architecture rather than have them spoiled by the harsh reality of an overgrown or otherwise unappealing site.[10] In some curious way he felt he had so imbibed the spirit of Pliny that he could ignore the evidence to avoid being disappointed by it.

Echoing Orrery's statements, Karl Friedrich Schinkel was most inspired by the fanciful and intimate spaces in the Laurentine and Tuscan villa gardens. Schinkel's imaginary restitutions, and the actual buildings he evolved jointly with them, revealed his understanding of Pliny's innermost aspirations for artistic fulfillment in an inspiring ambience. As we saw earlier in the discussion of Schinkel's Laurentine

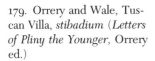

179. Orrery and Wale, Tuscan Villa, *stibadium* (*Letters of Pliny the Younger*, Orrery ed.)

plan (figs. 6 and 47), he produced a seductively symphonic orchestration of curves, culminating in the *amores mei* pavilion on the right. It features a circular room set off amid semicircular flower beds behind a curving seawall. In this way Schinkel accorded special treatment to Pliny's favorite suite rather than simply leaving it undifferentiated as so many other restitutions had done. For example, the French- man Haudebourt in his book about Laurentinum had built up anticipation for the pavilion in the dream sequence, only to disappoint his readers by designing some- thing banal compared with the much stronger Schinkel solution (cf. figs. 47 and 32). Moreover, Schinkel went beyond all his predecessors except Orrery by carrying out his ideas for Pliny's Tuscan *stibadium*—a fantastic contrivance to be sure, but not so much as to be completely inconceivable archaeologically.[11] In fact, this most extraordinary feature captured Schinkel's imagination so strongly that he transferred it almost literally from the ancient Latin text into his garden designs. The result was one of the most exceptional garden ensembles the nineteenth century ever produced, and the closest anyone has come to physically recon- structing a Plinian villa.

Throughout the period 1826–28 when Schinkel designed and then began con- struction of the Charlottenhof Villa at Potsdam, a rectangular plot of land remained outside the Prussian royal enclave. Eventually Crown Prince Friedrich Wilhelm secured this additional piece of land. It proved large enough for the insertion of a 150-meter hippodrome garden refulgent with the same Plinian overtones as the adjacent villa.[12] The planning stages did not take place until 1835, and the actual planting was done in 1836. The whole had more or less reached completion from the horticultural point of view by the time a colored map showing it appeared three years later (fig. 180). (The map nicknames Charlottenhof "Siam" to underscore its Shangri-la aspect.) Although Peter Joseph Lenné took nominal responsibility for the park landscaping from the time of his appointment as court gardener in 1828, Schinkel clearly masterminded the hippodrome area.[13] Not only did he leave a description of it that distinctly recalls Pliny's wording, but he also prepared a sectional drawing for inclusion as a lithograph in his *Sammlung architektonischer Entwürfe* (fig. 181). Schinkel's pen-and-wash drawing delineates the sides of the hippodrome rising tier upon tier like the seats around an antique racecourse. At each ascending step are plantings of different flowering shrubs and trees: lilac, linden, chestnut, fir, and pyramidal poplars. The central rectangular area is laid out as an open greensward for country dances to be performed in front of what Schinkel called the "Stibadium, wie es Plinius nennt."[14] He wrote this warmly evocative passage about the *stibadium* and the nearby summerhouse in such a way as to demonstrate how fully he was imbued with Pliny. He imagined the little structures as if already in existence, with the sound of splashing water inviting slumber—a comforting thought to an overworked *Oberbaudirektor*.

180. (*Opposite, top*) Potsdam, Charlottenhof, 1835 map of villa and gardens

181. (*Opposite, bottom*) Schin- kel, Tuscan Villa, cross sec- tion of *stibadium* (SA, S.144 M.XXXIV, no. 32)

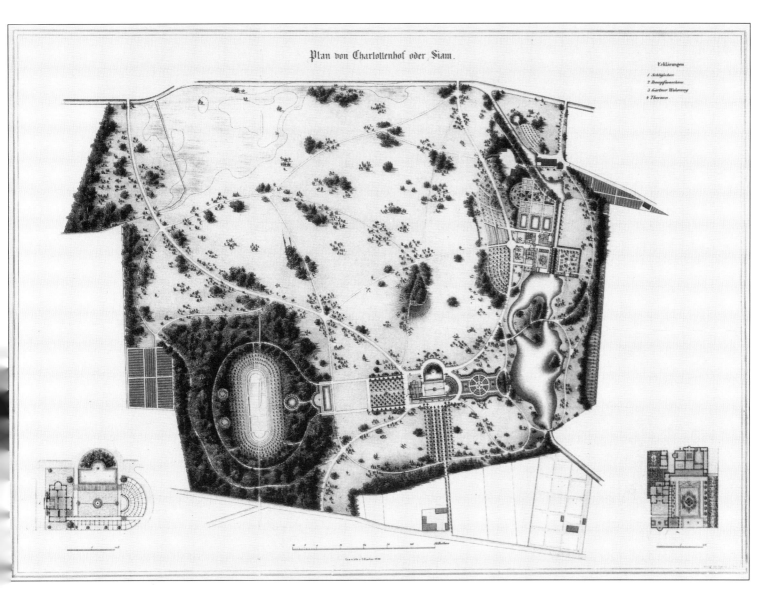

Plan von Charlottenhof oder Siam.

Erklärungen
1. Schlösschen
2. Dampfmaschine
3. Gärtner Wohnung
4. Thermen

Realizing that most previous restitutions such as Hirt's and Krubsacius's had inexplicably overlooked the *stibadium,* Schinkel's 1833 scheme devoted a separate drawing to it that eventually became the basis for a color lithograph of 1841 all in Prussian blue (fig. 182).[15] This one structure, which Pliny had saved mentioning to Apollinaris until the end, summed up for Schinkel the element of fantasy implicit throughout the Latin garden description. Both architect and royal client literally drank in its evocation of sunny Italy, memories of which they ·shared with Pliny because of their Grand Tours. No doubt the *stibadium* reminded them of vineyard-covered slopes of Tuscany, where they might have spent a carefree afternoon with a good bottle of the local vintage. In a similar way Pliny could lie in his *stibadium* while delicacies floated by on the waters of the fountain basin. His dinner guests could sail sweetmeats back and forth across this oversized lazy Susan. According to Schinkel's conception, not carried out until 1843 after his death, a vine pergola

182. Schinkel, Tuscan Villa, plan of *stibadium,* perspective, and details (Schinkel, *Architektonisches Album*)

formed a canopy overhead so one could almost reach up and pluck grapes while in the reclining position. What decadence, what frivolity, but what joy!

With true dramatic flair Clifford Pember approached the letter to Gallus in the same manner as his many set designs during the 1930s and early 1940s (fig. 96). Based on his reading of the Latin text he prepared a colorful scale model, which had a distinct advantage over his sets for black-and-white movies. In his 1947 article for the *Illustrated London News* he had the model photographed against painted backdrops to give the illusion of cloudscapes and the distant horizon of the Tyrrhenian Sea off the Ostian coast. (His obituary credits him with having invented in 1932 a rear projection device for creating just such effects.) In addition, he went right to the heart of the matter instead of postponing it to the end as Pliny had done in his letter to Gallus. Pember started off his discussion of the Laurentine Villa by immediately stressing Pliny's "carefully conceived plans for affording himself opportunity to escape the ever increasing demands of his public life."[16] Much as a cinematographer might do, Pember then zoomed in on the *amores mei* pavilion, devoting to it the principal part of his relatively short account of the villa. On the opposite page side a diagram identifies the pavilion set off discreetly at one end as the *amores mei* (fig. 183; cf. fig. 96). Labels clearly position the *heliocaminus*, the *cubiculum*, and the *zotheca*, which is large enough to contain a couch for siestas. According to the magazine text, the couch would appear alluringly screened from sight by a pair of glazed doors of tracery work. Pember was no classical scholar and had not practiced architecture for decades, yet he intuitively grasped the sensuous delights that lay at the very core of the Laurentine Villa.

Pember conjured up in his imagination an uncannily clear picture of the *amores mei* pavilion, almost as though he had lived there in some previous incarnation. No doubt he spoke from personal experience of his rural cottage at Langford, Oxfordshire, which served him as a retreat from the pressures of London's West End or the sound stages and back lots at the Ealing Studios. All this permitted Pember to penetrate into the depths of Pliny's house and his soul, much as the modern visitor to the Ashmolean Museum may do by peeking through the holes Pember left open in the roof of the model. It is possible to look from the *zotheca* alcove through the main reception area, gaily painted, and out along the axis of the cryptoporticus affording an architectural vista to match the natural one of seashore and umbrella pines. Last Pember turned attention to the secluded bedchamber facing out on the gardens at the back of the site. He concentrated his creative ingenuity on this area he said epitomized "Pliny's horror of being caught unawares by the unwelcome visitor."[17] Pember had in mind an appropriately British prototype for it: the light wells he knew from the street frontages of London row houses. This shallow shaft of space, he claimed, would allow circulation of air without any sunshine penetrating into the bedroom that opened onto it. A staircase

within it would give access to the hypocaust heating system underneath, thus
isolating the upstairs resident from servants downstairs. In another instance of this
English aversion to intrusion, William Melmoth, the eighteenth-century translator
of Pliny, laid similar emphasis on the service backstairs at the Tuscan Villa that
would have increased privacy at a select dinner party.[18]

In the concluding paragraph of his 1982 letter to Maurice Culot, David Bigelman promised his correspondent a more extensive account of the Laurentine Villa
garden buildings, together with drawings in addition to those already prepared
(figs. 138–47). The drawings, though never published or exhibited, were in fact
made; the original draft of the Bigelman letter alludes to them. Heavily edited in
the version that appeared in the catalog, his remarks and the images that go with
them clearly show his profound understanding of Pliny. Particularly revealing in
this respect is the section of the letter devoted to the villa's purported three-stage
chronology. The draft reads: "Finally, I think that the pavilion at the northern

extremity of the property, because of its orientation, cannot be attributed to the second architect but to Pliny himself. It is too reminiscent of the experiments of Hadrian [at his villa] at Tivoli for it to have been conceived by someone from the circle of Apollodorus."[19] What Bigelman had in mind, of course, was the well-known *canopus* and the *Serapaeum* at the emperor Hadrian's villa at Tivoli. The complex consists of a water-filled elliptical area fronted by the *Serapaeum* building, with a wide facade and an elongated series of inner chambers narrowing toward the back. Bigelman's *amores mei* pavilion is modeled directly on this prototype, the implication being that Pliny, like Hadrian, relied on himself for the design rather than on a professional architect such as Apollodorus. Bigelman's building, however, faces onto the *gestatio* and xystus in the gardens instead of facing an elongated pool as at Tivoli. Otherwise the similarities are close and deliberate.

In an early Bigelman sketch the *amores mei* appears at the top of the page just below the compass rose and in two details down at the bottom left (fig. 184). One near the margin spells out the Latin garden spaces and their relation to the

184. Bigelman, Laurentine Villa, sketch site plan and sketch plan of *amores mei* pavilion (CCA, DR 1984:1636:4 verso)

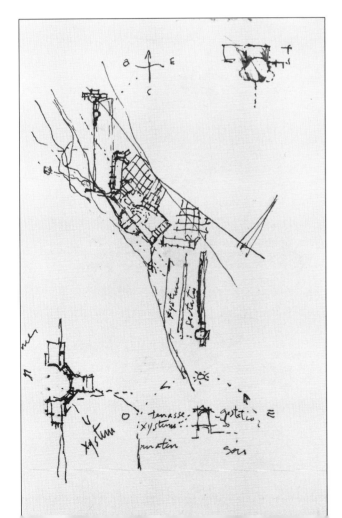

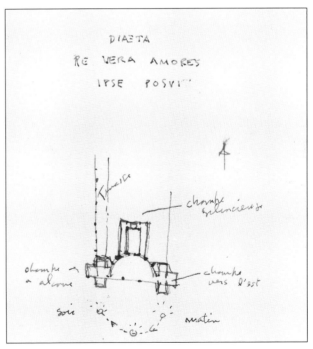

185. Bigelman, Laurentine Villa, sketch plan (CCA, DR 1984:1636:10 verso)

little building, planned in much the form it takes in the final suite of drawings (cf. figs. 139 and 141). Off to the right the arc of the sun's passage is hastily sketched over the pavilion, documenting Bigelman's extreme concern for orienting it. (This did not prevent him from becoming confused about the positions of *soir* and *matin* with reference to the east and west.) A subsequent page in the sketchbook entirely devoted to the *amores mei* catches Bigelman's mistake and corrects it (fig. 185). The plan's exact designation of the various rooms according to Pliny shows how attentively Bigelman had read the letter to Gallus, especially the passage about the *cubiculum* closed off from light and noise. Bigelman placed it in the extension at the back of the building, and he completely isolated his *chambre silencieuse* with a corridor that insulates it from all the rest. At the east and west ends of the entrance facade are small rooms, and between them is a semicircular loggia over-looking the garden. The open columnar porch receives the full warmth of the sun all day long, and it best represents to Bigelman's mind the probable appearance of the *heliocaminus*. In the light of Bigelman's assumptions regarding the peculiari-ties of this building, it is fitting to find the words *ipse posui* inscribed at the top of the page, indicating that it belongs to Pliny's own intervention in the construction of the villa. The analogy to Hadrian is largely speculative, of course, but it points out that the two ancient Romans had idiosyncrasies in common. Pliny's letters document his phobia about noise that might interrupt a fleeting train of thought.

The stately plan of Bigelman's *amores mei* pavilion corresponds to an equally assured final elevation (fig. 186), one of the architect's happiest moments of inspira-tion, though for some reason it was not included in the Laurentine exhibition and thus has never before been published. Bigelman prepared a perspective view complete with colonnades, flower beds, and a delightful Schinkelesque vine pergola stretching along the edge of the seawall. Over the parapet appears a tiny boat tacking past immense cliffs that fall right down to the water's edge. Bigelman's sparse, pointillist pen-and-ink technique helps to endow the scene with greater monumentality than it could have in reality. In comparison with the rest of the villa, too chockablock with artful asymmetry and recondite references to architecture of the past, the *amores mei* pavilion breathes a more relaxed, natural, and truly classic air. In keeping with its function, it seems to invite quiet contemplation in the way it overlooks an inspiring coastline. This architectural finishing touch, analogous to Pliny's epistolary flourish at the end of the letter to Gallus, suggests that Bigelman had discovered in himself a literary bent that made him an ideal interpreter of Pliny. Bigelman found in Pliny's concluding words a love of quiet study, of books, and of nature that they share and that the *amores mei* pavilion stands for. But Bigelman's subsequent efforts at restitution have failed to recapture the ideal mix-ture of fact and fantasy exemplified by Laurentinum. He finds the classroom an

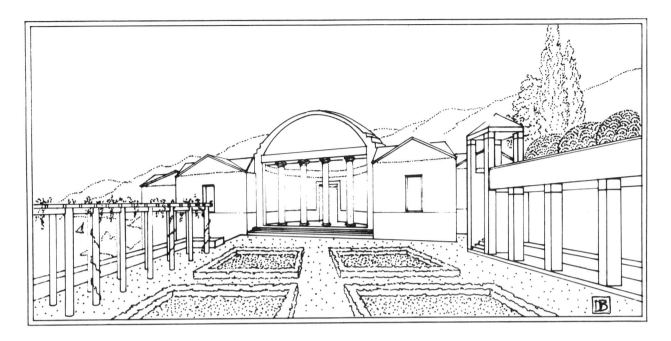

IN CAPITE XYSTI...DIAETA EST, AMORES MEI...IPSE POSUI.

186. Bigelman, Laurentine Villa, perspective of *amores mei* pavilion (CCA, DR 1984: 1635)

arid desert compared with the delights of that imaginary place. His students lack a love of literature, a passion for history, or even a studious disposition, and so he retires in upon himself.

Although Bigelman did not know it at the time, another participant in the Laurentine *concours d'émulation* has a similar interest in literature. During a period of harsh repression by the Argentine military dictators in the late 1970s, Justo Solsona spent his enforced leisure time in his own private school of architecture and in writing a book of short stories, partly inspired by autobiographical themes. Titled somewhat enigmatically *Letrógrafo,* the collection came out under the imprint of Summa, the publishing house responsible for the architectural magazine of the same name, to which Solsona and his partners over the years have contributed articles on their built work.[20] In the light of his publishing record, the brevity of Solsona's Laurentine manifesto is all the more puzzling. Five short paragraphs of text, handwritten directly underneath his perspective drawing, is all it amounts to (pl. 48). In common with Bigelman's wording, that of Solsona uses the first-person singular as if penned by a latter-day Pliny. As we have already seen (cf. chap. 6), the voice of the writer mimics a language unmistakably derived from the polemics of Le Corbusier and Aldo Rossi, but the Latin American accent gives a new twist to familiar concepts. Le Corbusier's *volumes assemblés sous la lumière* become entire gleaming glass buildings; Rossi's containers encase the villa remains Pliny inherited from his forefathers.

In essence, however, Solsona's highflown allusions to the masters of modern design boil down to a project couched in simple terms that evoke the sensuous delights of the place. A peculiarity of the ground plan (cf. fig. 132) receives a simple explanation. The long file of columns along the lower enclosure wall becomes compressed in width by the advance of the wall and the increasing girth of the columns themselves as they move from left to right. Solsona contemplates with perverse pleasure the nightmarish frisson visitors will experience when moving down his imaginary colonnade and being forced to squeeze between the shafts as they march along. His words in French speak poetically of the reflections off the glass and the water and the wavelike motion of the beds of violets in front of the cryptoporticus. The explanatory letter concludes: "Finalement, ma petite maison, placée sur une plate-forme et entourée entièrement par des murs de cristal transparent, d'où je jouis, en observant la mobilité immobile de la mer et le jardin des violettes."[21] The *maison* referred to is, of course, the *amores mei,* reformulated on the plan as though it were a Miesian glass house—a South American version of the Barcelona Pavilion—within whose walls partitions float about, creating both privacy and openness to the all-important views. If the somewhat obscure wording of the explanation and the small sectional drawings below it are to be taken at face value, then Pliny's ruined ancestral villa has turned into a dusty excavation hermetically sealed within glass block containers. Only the *amores mei* remains habitable. It provides a refuge from within which to survey an archaeological landscape symbolic of all that is past. At the same time, the motion of the sea and of the beds of violets ruffled by the north wind is a constant reminder of values that remain ever present.

In company with Léon Krier and Bernard Huet, Solsona ranks as one of the main author-architects of the present day to have taken an interest in Pliny. Solsona is the only one, however, who has turned his hand to fiction. His 1979 collection of short stories titled *Letrógrafo* alludes to a machine that corrects the author's bad penmanship—a reference to an automatic writing device, in effect, much in keeping with the surrealist aspects of the prose. In their disjointed story lines, their quick shifts of place or mood, their hints of social inequality, and their unclear but palpable sense of menace, they bear allegiance to the writings of Solsona's more famous countrymen, the late Jorge Luis Borges and Julio Cortazar. But Solsona adds a unique architectural element as he plays upon the realm of fiction versus the real world. In the story "Premonición del Plano," for example, an architect is commissioned to design a house for a young couple. In drawing up the plans he discovers a love triangle underneath the facade of an ideal marriage. When the wife finds out that her illicit affair has been revealed, she rips up the house plans to indicate that the liaison is over. Similarly, in the "Fascinación del Plano," an architect who wants to design an ideal city wanders by mistake into a slummy part of town. His life is suddenly threatened because he bears a coincidental resemblance to a known murderer. As in a Walt Disney animated cartoon, he extracts himself from the situation by literally designing his way out of danger. In the process of writing he enriches his art form with all kinds of unusual allusions to architecture, to various drafting instruments, to the colors and flow of the ink on paper, and so forth. Solsona's neo-Plinian epistle therefore is best seen as an abbreviated short story. Pliny exerted an influence such that the "Fascinación del Plano" of 1979 becomes a "fascinación del Plinio" three years later.[22]

Although Pliny's influence on Solsona has notably diminished since 1982 (see chap. 6), the exact opposite is true in the work of his much younger Canadian colleague Erik Marosi (b. 1953). At the time Solsona participated in the Laurentine *concours* as the eldest representative of his profession, Marosi was still pursuing a graduate degree in architecture. In the decade that has followed, however, Marosi's fixation with Pliny has continued to strengthen with time. After Marosi's previous studies at McGill University in his native Montreal (B. Arch., 1976) and subsequent job experience with the local firms of Arcop and Peter Rose, he enrolled in architecture school at Princeton in 1982 and received his master's degree two years later. During his first autumn in New Jersey he saw the Laurentine exhibition catalog, found a copy of Helen Tanzer's *The Villas of Pliny* in the Marquand Library, and enrolled in a course with the dean of Renaissance garden specialists in North America, David R. Coffin. All these events, coupled with his participation in the villa and garden design studio run by his then mentor, Michael Graves, prompted Marosi to attempt a Laurentine restitution of his own. Graves agreed to the topic. He had previously known and admired Krier's artistry when the two of them taught together at Princeton in 1977. By this somewhat circuitous route Krier entered Marosi's own Pantheon of "greats," where architects such as Lutyens, Asplund, Mackintosh, and Jože Plečnik already occupied niches.

During a 1986 interview Marosi stated that he had consciously chosen to emulate Krier's peninsular site plan as the parti, or starting point, for his own restitution. Realizing how Krier had gone about fragmenting Pliny's house into a whole quasi-urban community, Marosi determined to put the pieces back together. Much as Krier has done, he began by filling up sketchbook after sketchbook, red- instead of blue-bound ones in his case. In page after page of small and delicate drawings, Marosi sifted through the various influences at work upon him, not the least being that of Graves himself, as Marosi readily admits. Out of a very heterogeneous mixture emerged a quite original series of colored drawings on Mylar. Marosi presented this version in Graves's studio—the architect himself and Thomas Schumacher both sat on the jury. Marosi's former employer, Peter Rose, heard about the work in progress and mentioned it to the other members of the organizing committee for the 1983 Villas of Pliny exhibition, on which he sat. When the exhibition mounted by the Canadian Centre for Architecture opened in October of that year in the Montreal Museum of Fine Arts, it included Marosi's preliminary suite. Since it hung close to the set of Kriers that had been its inspiration, the similarities in overall plan between the two became quite obvious, but so did the differences, especially the more Gravesian look of the elevations.[23]

According to the early tracing-paper sketches Marosi prepared for his Laurentine Villa restitution, the site as well as the scattered disposition of buildings upon it markedly resembles Krier's arrangement (fig. 187; cf. fig. 156). Overall, at this preliminary stage Marosi thought in terms of a large number of structures surrounded by elaborate gardens. The cryptoporticus Marosi envisioned occupies the lower side of the headland at a distance from the main house and the three or four outbuildings adjacent to it. On the upper side a small rivulet in a ravine runs down to the open water, just as in Krier's site plan. This topographical derivativeness accounts for Marosi's lack of cohesion and conviction compared with Krier's intimate personal knowledge of the site at Sperlonga. But by the time Marosi finished his set of nine drawings for the jury, the plan had pulled all the disparate bits and pieces together into one main building (fig. 188). The principal point of

187. Marosi, Laurentine Villa, sketch site plans (collection of the artist)

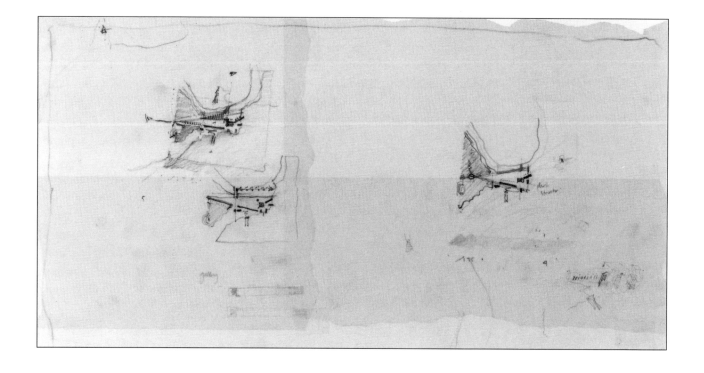

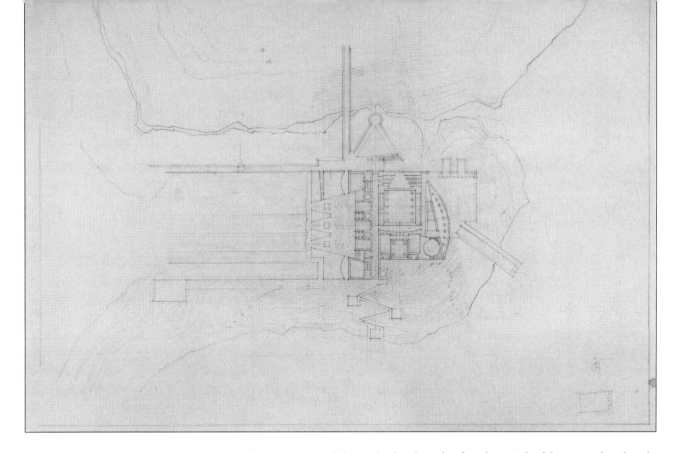

188. Marosi, Laurentine Villa, plan (collection of the artist)

access had swung around from the landward side where it had been in the sketch version and in Krier's design. Entry is now over a bridge spanning the ravine and leading into a triangular piazza. The shape of a keystone so prevalent in Graves's current work comes to mind as a possible inspiration. A long corridor then communicates directly with another triangular space, this time reminiscent of Marosi's favorite Michelangelo rare book room design for the Laurentian Library in Florence. (Marosi is probably unaware of the bibliophile Medicis' fondness for Pliny.) The cross section (fig. 189) corresponding to this part of the plan depicts this alcove as part of a rectangular courtyard seen as though the viewer's back is to the ravine. The ceremonial character of the space is stressed by the majestic scale. The walls round about are stratified into strips of blue-and-brown masonry, as in Schinkel's Orianda Villa, punctuated here and there with elliptical arches. These are supported by stubby columns like the ones that were going up at the exactly contemporary Environmental Education Center by Graves in the Statue of Liberty State Park near Jersey City.[24]

As if to underscore the Graves connection, the missing keystone motif in an inverted form figures prominently again in Marosi's side elevation (fig. 190). Here and elsewhere the preference for narrow, slitlike windows isolated amid vast expanses of blue-and-brown striped masonry contradicts the notion of a marine villa, open to the views and the ocean breezes. In this sense Marosi's elevation facing

the formal gardens is altogether more successful (fig. 191). Marosi worked hard to get the balance right between built and plant forms. He broke away from the brooding massiveness of the rest of the villa by introducing into the sketch version three small pavilions. These are probably intended as triclinia or as libraries, although the room designations are not clear at this or any later stage of the design's evolution. The bookish function recalls Graves's contemporary mission-style library that was under construction at San Juan Capistrano, California, consisting of numerous pavilions with plaster walls and red roofs. Marosi's finished version for presentation to the jury (fig. 192) bears out the favorable first impression obtained from the sketch. The three white pavilions with their red tiles tone down the villa's oppressive bluishness, to which Graves himself took exception at the time of the jury evaluation. Marosi's considerable gift for drafting also appears to best advantage in this view. He created a windswept impression through the hastily drawn in sky and the rooftop greenery, which seems to toss its head in a gust.

Returning to Montreal, Marosi did not abandon his Laurentine student designs as many architects might have done—far from it! He resumed work on his Pliny studies with a vengeance in the autumn of 1984. The year before at Princeton, in the sketch of the garden facade (cf. fig. 191), the background already hinted at a much more elaborate roofscape bursting with architectural pyrotechnics, which Marosi obviously thought better of submitting to his design jury. Twelve months later, when left on his own, the tendencies to elaboration exerted themselves strongly in a series of a dozen or more sketches, one of them dated November

189. Marosi, Laurentine Villa, cross section (collection of the artist)

190. Marosi, Laurentine Villa, elevation of side facade (collection of the artist)

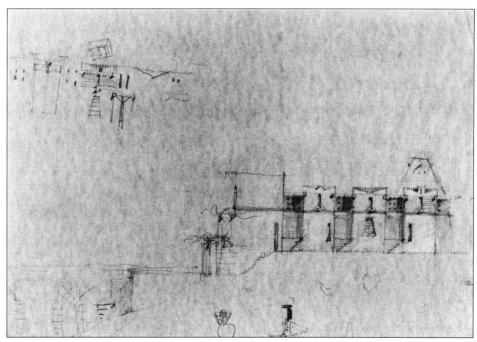

191. Marosi, Laurentine Villa, sketch elevations of main and garden facades (collection of the artist)

1984 (fig. 193). Barely legible marginalia refer to the villa's principal doorway flanked by Pliny's (not very private) apartment on the left and a corresponding guest suite on the right. The whole facade is now overshadowed by a huge pyramidal centerpiece rising up behind. With swags dangling from around the top, it looks like a neoclassical mausoleum project such as Graves might have designed had he been Etienne-Louis Boullée. The triangular shape above echoes a proliferation of triangular missing keystone motifs below. In other versions the skyline sprouts obelisks; in still others the central pyramid inverts itself and turns into an open funnel-shaped interior courtyard where everything that was up is down. Pliny's Laurentinum serves as the excuse for an enormous number of inversions and geometric manipulations of a few set themes as the young architect experiments, seeking to master them. Throughout the unwieldy masses a funereal quality prevails in place of the life-giving theme so central to the Laurentine Villa restitution from the beginning.

At about the same moment these changes to the elevation get under way, Marosi's Laurentine ground plan undergoes a set of revisions whose aim is clarification and restraint rather than bombastic excess. Two tracing-paper ground plans dated 6 December 1984 pick up where the Princeton plans left off (fig. 194). The general disposition remains the same, but for the first time an entirely new circular courtyard replaces the earlier rectangles and inverted cones. Historically and philologically, the clock turns back to the Villa Madama in the Renaissance, on which Marosi could have heard David Coffin lecture at Princeton. A matter of a month later, in January 1985, Marosi had resolved any doubts in his mind and had produced a startling symmetrical plan, close to his original parti (cf. figs. 187 and 195), closer to Krier, and closest of all to the Sangallesque Villa Madama schemes that

192. Marosi, Laurentine Villa, elevation of garden facade (collection of the artist)

193. (*Opposite, top*) Marosi, Laurentine Villa, sketch elevations (collection of the artist)

194. (*Opposite, left*) Marosi, Laurentine Villa, sketch plans (collection of the artist)

195. (*Opposite, right*) Marosi, Laurentine Villa, sketch site plan (collection of the artist)

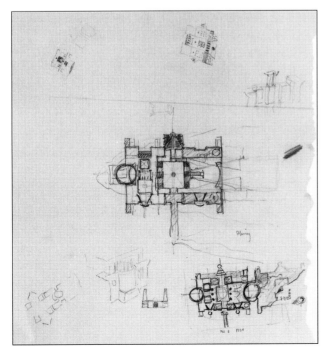

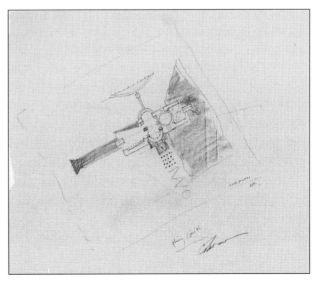

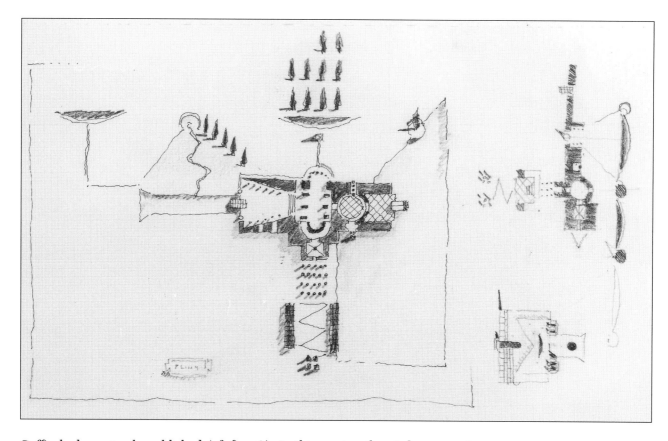

196. Marosi, Laurentine Villa, sketch site plans and elevations (collection of the artist)

Coffin had previously published (cf. fig. 18). In this version the viaduct over the ravine disappears in favor of the more wavy access route also seen in some of the early plans. A reflecting pool on the main axis aligns itself with a keystone-shaped forecourt preceding the grouping of courtyards, in which use is made of the apsidal passageways the Sangallos had placed around the transept of Saint Peter's before Michelangelo removed them. Based on this hasty sketch, Marosi produced a more coherent pair of plans on a page he drew about the same time (fig. 196). In this instance the arms of the sea around Krier's peninsular site dry up, leaving flattened ponds and sinuous rivulets that feed the reflecting pool and the fountains in the courtyard, emptying near the shoreline. These watery elements are set amid the loveliest Plinian-style gardens in recent memory. In contrast to the lightness of the landscape gardening elements, checkerboard patterns on the plan indicate some heavy superstructure of the type seen in a small elevation sketch over in the bottom right corner.

A year later, in January 1986, Marosi inverted the orientation of his plan on the page while further reinforcing its Renaissance characteristics (fig. 197). An abundance of tiny fruit trees and cypresses enhance the Italian feeling, and the flights of steps over to the right explicitly recall the Villa Madama forecourt, as does the *O*-shaped courtyard beyond. (A *D*-shaped one is added in for good measure.) The new relationship to garden rather than seashore in all three villa schemes just considered probably had to do with Marosi's current involvement in developing designs for the Canadian Centre for Architecture in Montreal. His contribution to the planning, in association with Peter Rose and the CCA director, Phyllis Lambert, began in earnest early in 1985. In fact the Marosi sketchbooks for the period frequently have schemes for Pliny's villa and for the CCA all on the same page, showing how the ideas for one influenced the other. This was a perfectly fitting outcome to a process that had begun when the institution's maiden exhibition in Montreal, sponsored by Phyllis Lambert, displayed Pliny's villa restitutions, including the one by Marosi. On that occasion it was Melvin Charney who designed the installation (fig. 126) and who then went on brilliantly to design the garden for the CCA. So one can argue on several counts that when the history of the CCA's design comes to be written, the influence of Pliny's villas will play a more significant part than has hitherto been remarked.[25]

197. Marosi, Laurentine Villa, sketch site plan and elevation (collection of the artist)

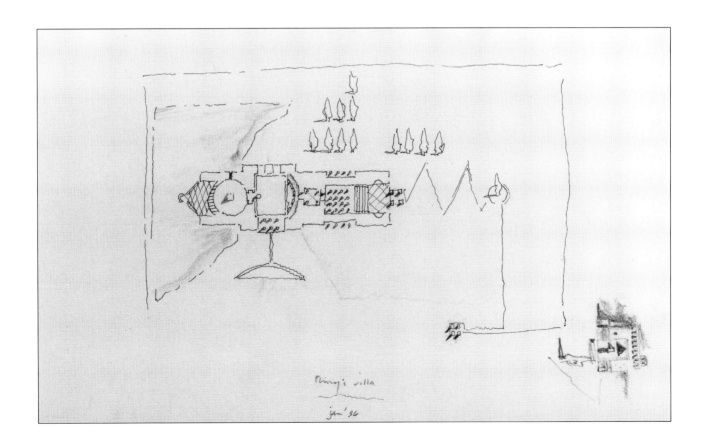

Two years after drawing the last of his Laurentine plans, Marosi sliced off the central section of his latest 1986 version—cypresses, *D*-shaped atrium, and all—and turned it into a separate house. In association with Martin Troy, Marosi submitted the new design to a competition sponsored by *Domus* magazine for the *casa più bella del mondo*. The two competitors won an honorable mention. In the process they transformed the relative lightness of the Laurentine Villa into the heaviness of their new house, crowned by a massively sturdy tower and a Venetian-style "Carpaccio" chimney to match. Not content with such ephemeral villa plans on paper, Marosi set about making furniture designs with Pliny in mind. He built a wooden model for a *secrétaire à la Pline* whose striated bands of color, battered forms, and massiveness recall the polychromy, geometry, and solidity of his Laurentine restitution as a whole.[26]

At present Marosi continues with plans and furniture designs for the Laurentine Villa, but they have taken an unexpected turn toward the neomodernist. In rare spare moments Marosi has given additional thought to the Laurentine Villa as recently as 1992. By then the villa had lost most of its classical overtones in preference to a more abstract language, in line with recent developments in Marosi's stylistic interests and active practice (fig. 198). Classical elements have not been entirely uprooted. A wall slashing across the site refers to Hadrian's Wall in the north of England. It runs adjacent to the rectangular house at an oblique angle, creating an abstract composition in its own right. Among so many overt references to posterity, the last vestiges of antiquity linger on in the centrally placed open courtyard and the separate study on the right, distinctly suggestive of Pliny's *amores mei* pavilion. A similar dining pavilion discreetly set off to the left recalls Pliny's *stibadium*. There is surely some reason why these long-repressed references to Pliny's private realm surface in Marosi's work at this particular time.

Perhaps the explanation for Marosi's volte-face is that in 1989 he took the same logical next step as Manfred Sundermann had done and proposed to undertake the restitution of Pliny's Tuscan Villa. His bid for the Canadian Rome Prize proved unsuccessful; no prize was awarded that year. Had he received it, there seems little doubt that Marosi would have pursued some of the more serene and meditative aspects expressed in this recent villa scheme. As its inscription attests, Marosi has transformed the Laurentine and Tuscan villa restitutions into the design of what he calls a "House for Me." The simple phrase conveys in a nutshell the whole appeal that Pliny has exerted for nineteen hundred years on those architects who have fallen under the spell of his writing. He enunciates their innermost need for a carefree place in the country to pursue their art. He encourages them to dream and to excel. If ever living proof were sought of Pliny's tenacious grip on artistic creativity, surely this Marosi design provides it. For each individual, of course, the exact circumstances vary—a Rome Prize competition, a publication, a lecture

198. Marosi, "House for Me," plan and aerial perspective (collection of the artist)

illustration, an international *concours d'émulation,* or simply a chance to while away some time after long hours over the drafting table. Whatever the case, the personal rewards derived from such a grand tradition of emulation remain the same as they always have been and always will be: in all architecture, perhaps, no subject could be more congenial than an ideal country house without budgetary limits. Lacking archaeological remains, the elusive villas of Pliny encourage freedom of the imagination and the joys of restitution.

Appendixes

Appendix 1
Pliny's Letter to Gallus

Book 2, epistle 17, as translated by John Boyle, fifth earl of Orrery, *The Letters of Pliny
the Younger, with Observations on Each Letter,* 2 vols. (London, 1751), 1:162–69.

You wonder why I am so infinitely fond of my Laurentinum, or, if you had rather
call it so, my Laurens. I dare say your wonder will cease when I make you acquainted
with the beauties of the villa, the situation of the place, and the large extent of the
shore upon which it stands.

The distance is seventeen miles from Rome: a distance which allows us, after we
have finished the business of the day, to return thither from town, with the setting
sun. We are not confined to one road; for both the Laurentine and the Ostian way will
bring us home. If you go the Laurentine, you must quit the high road at the fourteenth
stone: if the Ostian, at the eleventh. Each of these roads is sandy, and therefore a little
tedious and heavy in a wheeled carriage, but on horseback extremely short and pleasant.
The prospects on every side are finely diversified; sometimes your view is limited by
woods; then again is opened and extended by spacious meadows. Here, you see flocks
of sheep; there, studs of horses and herds of cattle; all driven down from the mountains
by the inclemency of the winter, and growing fat and sleek by the pasturage, and the
warmth of the spring.

The house itself is made for use, not for parade. In the front you enter a courtyard,
plain and void of ornament, but handsome. This leads to a little neat court in the shape
of the letter *O*, surrounded by galleries, an absolute shelter against all storms; being
well defended, both by the transparent windows of the house, and by the projecting
roof above. Overagainst the middle portico is a large cheerful court, leading to a very
handsome dining room, which projects towards the seashore; and the walls of it are
gently washed by the waves of the sea, whenever the south-westerly wind drives them
in upon the land. Every side of the room has either folding doors, or windows as large
as doors; so that from the sides and from the front you have the prospect, as it were,
of three different oceans. Behind is a quadrangle, a portico, and a lesser court; then
again a portico, and then a vestibule, beyond which woods are seen, and at a greater
distance mountains. On the left hand of the dining room, a little farther from the
shore, is a very large parlor: within that a smaller withdrawing room, which has one
window looking to the east, another to the west. From the western window you have
a prospect of the sea, more distant indeed but more agreeable. There is an angle

formed between the dining room and parlor that collects the rays and augments the heat of the warmest sun. Here I have my winter apartments: and here is the place of exercise for my servants. Not a breath of wind is stirring here, except now and then a blast, which brings a cloud upon us; but it clears up again before the warmth is gone off from the place. Adjoining to this angle is a room in an elliptic form: a shape that allows us from the several windows to enjoy the benefit of the sun during the whole course of the day; and the walls of it are so contrived as to hold books and be a kind of library for such volumes as are rather designed for amusement than study. Next to this, a passage only intervening, is a bedchamber: the passage is raised and boarded in such a manner that the heat it receives is most equally dispensed and distributed throughout every part of it. The remaining part of this side of the house is destined for servants and freedmen: but some of the apartments are so neatly fitted up that they may be filled upon occasion by guests of a much bigger rank. On the other side is a most elegant bedchamber, or a moderate sized eating room, enlivened both by the sun, and by the sea. After this, you enter into another bedchamber with a lobby before it. The height makes it cool in summer; the thick walls make it warm in winter; for it is absolutely withdrawn from the inclemencies of every wind. There is another bedchamber and lobby joined to it by a partition wall. Then you come to the baths.

The cold bath is very wide and spacious. On the opposite walls are fixed two bathing cisterns that jet [*sic*] out into the room and are made large enough to swim in. Contiguous to which are the chambers for the use of the bath, particularly the room where the different oils are kept, another for the stoves, another for the furnace; then two little baths which are rather neat than sumptuous: and to these is joined, by an exquisite piece of workmanship, the hot bath; where, as you swim, you have a full prospect of the sea.

At no great distance is the tennis court, so situated as never to be annoyed by the heat, and only to be visited by the setting sun. At the end of the tennis court rises a tower containing two rooms at the top of it and two again under them; besides a banqueting room from whence there is a view of a very wide ocean, a very extensive continent, and numberless beautiful villas interspersed upon the shore. Answerable to this is another turret, containing on the top one single room where we enjoy both the rising and the setting sun. Underneath is a very large store room for fruit and a granary, and under these again a dining room from whence, even when the sea is most tempestuous, we only hear the roaring of it, and that but languidly and at a distance. It looks upon the garden. The whole is encompassed with box; and, where that is wanting, with rosemary: for box, when sheltered by buildings, will flourish very well, but withers immediately if exposed to wind and weather; or ever so distantly affected by the moist dews from the sea. This place for exercise surrounds a delicate shady vineyard, the paths of which are easy and soft, even to the naked feet.

The garden is filled with mulberry and fig trees, the soil being propitious to both those kinds of trees but scarce to any other. A dining room, too remote to view the ocean, commands an object no less agreeable, the prospect of the garden: and at the back of the dining room are two apartments, whose windows look upon the vestibule of the house; and upon a fruitery and kitchen garden. From hence you enter into a covered gallery, large enough to appear a public work. The gallery has a double row of windows on both sides; in the lower row are several which look towards the sea; and one on each side towards the garden; in the upper row there are fewer: in calm days, when there is not a breath of air stirring, we open all the windows: but in windy weather we take the advantage of opening that side only which is entirely free from the hurricane. Before the gallery lies a terrace, perfumed with violets. The building not only retains the heat of the sun, and increases it by reflection, but defends and protects us from the northern blasts; and as the front is always warm, the back part, in like manner, is equally cool. It is so contrived that we are entirely sheltered from the violent heats of the south west; and indeed let the wind blow from what corner it will, the influence and power of it are broken and destroyed by the position of the gallery: and therefore we find it a very pleasant room in winter, and much more so in summer: for then the shadow of the building is thrown upon the terrace in the fore-noon; and in the afternoon we can walk under the shade of it in the place of exercise, or in that part of the garden next to it: the shade lengthening and decreasing according to the length or decrease of the day. But the gallery itself is never cooler than when the sun shines perpendicularly upon the roof of it. Add to this, that by opening the windows we have a thorough draught of the west wind, which prevents all bad effects arising from the stagnation of unwholesome air.

At the end of the terrace adjoining the gallery is a little garden apartment, which I own is my delight. In truth it is my mistress: I built it; and in it is a particular kind of hothouse, which looks on one side towards the terrace, on the other towards the sea; but on both sides has the advantage of the sun. A double door opens into another room, and one of the windows has a full view of the gallery. On the side next the sea, overagainst the middle wall, is an elegant little closet; separated only by transparent windows, and a curtain, which can be opened or shut at pleasure from the room just mentioned. It holds a bed and two chairs; the feet of the bed stand towards the sea, the back towards the house, and one side of it towards some distant woods. So many different views, seen from so many different windows, diversify and yet blend the prospect. Adjoining to this cabinet is my own constant bedchamber: where I am never disturbed by the discourse of my servants, the murmurs of the sea, nor the violence of a storm. Neither lightning nor daylight break in upon me till my windows are opened. The reason of so perfect and undisturbed a calm here arises from a large void space which is left between the walls of the bedchamber and of the garden; so that all sound is drowned in the intervening vacancy. Close to the bedchamber is a little stove, placed so near a small window of communication that it lets out or retains the heat just as we think fit. From hence we pass through a lobby into another room, which stands in such a position as to receive the sun, though obliquely, from day-break till past noon. When I shut myself up in this apartment, I seem to be enclosed at a great distance from my own house. The chief delight I take here is during the feasts of Saturn, at a time when all the rest of the house is filled with clamors of the festival; for then I never interrupt the diversions of my domestics, nor do they break in upon my studies.

But amidst all these conveniences and all this pleasure we want running water.

However, we have wells, or rather springs at command: for such is the wonderful nature of the ground, that in any part of the shore, take off the surface of the earth where you will, water immediately bubbles up and presents itself; and it is so perfectly pure as not to have the least briny taste, though so near the sea. The neighboring woods yield us great plenty of fuel, and Ostia furnishes every kind of provision. A frugal man can be very well contented with what a small village affords; especially when it is so near as to be only separated from us by one house. There are three inns in this little town, in each of which there is a bath; a very great convenience, in case my bath at home is not ready heated and prepared; which may happen either by my too sudden arrival, or my too short stay. A great many little houses, here and there joined in clusters, or separately scattered along the coast, seem to entertain us with a prospect of several cities. If you go upon the water, or if you walk upon the shore, the landscape is the same: the strand itself is sometimes softened by a long calm, but much oftener hardened by the tumult and conflict of the waves. I must own that our ocean does not abound with the choicest kind of fish: however, it produces excellent soles and prawns. But as to inland plenty, my house is never without it, especially milk; for the cattle are continually coming from their pastures to seek water and shade near this place.

Now tell me, do I appear to act reasonably in fixing my habitation, and taking infinite delight in such a retreat? If you are not too much wedded to the city, you will be impatient to retire hither also. I wish you may; that amidst so many pleasing circumstances which attend my villa, it might still boast of a superior recommendation in the happiness of your company. Adieu.

APPENDIX 2

Pliny's Letter to Apollinaris

(Book 5, epistle 6, as translated by John Boyle, fifth earl of Orrery, *The Letters of Pliny the Younger, with Observations on Each Letter,* 2 vols. (London, 1751), 1:378–88.

I am much delighted with the care and anxiety you have expressed in persuading me not to pass the summer, as I intended, in Tuscany, merely because you imagine the place unhealthy. The seashore of Tuscany is certainly moist and unwholesome. But my lands lie at a distance from the ocean, and are placed under the healthiest of our mountains, the Apennines: and therefore that you may lay aside all your anxiety for me, attend to the temperature of the climate, the situation of the country, and the sweetness of my particular dwelling. I shall give you the description with no less pleasure than you will hear it.

The air in the winter is sharp and frosty: myrtles, olives, and such plants as require a constant warmth will not grow there. The laurel generally thrives and sometimes produces a very beautiful green, although now and then it is killed, but not more frequently than with us at Rome. The heat in summer is very moderate. There is always some air stirring abroad, but oftener gentle than stormy. To this I attribute the number of our old men. Here you see the grandfathers and great grandfathers of those who are now young men. You hear old stories and the speeches of our ancestors. So that, were you to come hither, you would think yourself in another age.

The face of the country is extremely beautiful: imagine to yourself an amphitheatre of immense circumference, such as could be formed only by the hand of nature. A wide extended plain is surrounded by mountains whose summits are covered with tall ancient woods, stocked with game for all kinds of hunting. The descent is planted with underwoods, among which are frequently little risings of a rich and deep soil where a stone, if sought for, is scarce to be found: in fertility they yield not to the finest vales and produce as good crops of corn, although not so early in the year. Below these, on the side of the mountain, is a continued range of vineyards that extend themselves without interruption, far and near; at the foot of which is a sort of border of shrubs. From thence you have meadows and open fields. The arable grounds require large oxen and the strongest ploughs. The earth is so tough and rises in such large clods when it is first broken up, that it cannot be reduced till it has been ploughed nine times. The meadows glitter with flowers and produce the trefoil and other kinds of grass, always soft and tender, and appearing always new; for they are excellently well watered with never-failing springs; yet where these springs are in greatest confluence they make no marshes; the declivity of the land discharging into the Tiber all the water that it does not drink in.

The Tiber runs through the middle of our lands; is navigable, and supplies the city from hence with all kinds of grain, but only in winter and spring; for in summer it shrinks to nothing, leaving the bare name of a great river to almost an empty channel. In the autumn it rises to its usual height.

You would be much delighted were you to take a prospect of this place from a neighboring mountain as you could scarce believe you were looking upon a real country, but a landscape painting drawn with all the beauties imaginable; with so charming a representation and such a variety of agreeable objects will your eyes be regaled, which ever way they turn.

My house, although built at the foot of a hill, has a view as if it stood upon the brow of it. The ascent is so gradual and easy, that you find yourself on the top almost before you perceive yourself ascending. Behind it, but at a distance, is the Apennine mountain range, from whence it is refreshed with continual breezes, the weather never so calm or still; and yet they are not too cutting or immoderate, but broken and weakened by the very distance. The largest part of the house lies to the south and enjoys the sun all the afternoon; but something earlier in the winter than in the summer. In the front of it is a portico, pretty large and of a proportionable length, in which there are several apartments, and the court is laid out after the manner of the ancients.

Before the portico is a terrace, adorned with various figures, and bounded with an edging of box. Below this is a gravel walk; on each side of which, a little upon the descent, are figures of diverse animals cut in box. Upon a level plot stands an acanthus bed, so soft that it is almost liquid. Round the acanthus is a walk bounded by a close hedge of evergreens, cut into a variety of shapes: on the other side is a ring for taking the air on horseback in the shape of the circus, which goes round the box hedge, that is cut into different shapes; and a row of dwarf trees that are always kept sheared. The whole is encompassed with a wall, so covered with box that no part of it can be seen. On the outside is a lawn, as beautiful by nature as what I have been describing is by art. Farther on, the prospect is terminated by meadows and many other fields, and little coppices of wood. From the extremity of the portico projects a large dining room, from the doors of which you look to the end of the terrace; and from the windows you view the meadows and a large extent of the country. From the portico you look upon the side of the terrace, and that part of the house which stands most forward; as also upon the wood, and the tops of the trees in the adjoining race course. Almost opposite to the middle of the portico is a summer house which surrounds a small court shaded by four plane trees; in the midst of which a marble fountain gently plays upon the roots of those trees, and upon the grass plots under them. In this summer house is a bedchamber, where neither light, noise, nor sound can enter; and close to it a supper room, for my particular friends. Another portico overlooks this little court and enjoys all the same views with the former. There is another bedchamber, shaded and adorned by the verdure and gloom of the neighboring plane tree; the outside is of carved work in marble, as high as the balcony. Above is a painting of trees, and birds sitting amidst the branches, equally beautiful with the marble; at the foot of which is a small fountain from whence the water running through several little pipes into a basin makes a most agreeable murmur. In the corner of the portico is a very spacious bedchamber, facing the dining room, with windows both to the terrace and to the meadows; and before it a piece of water which delights at once our ears and eyes, being near and in the view of the front windows; and falling from a considerable height into a marble cistern, where it breaks and foams. This bedchamber is very warm in winter, the sun during that season being full upon it. Adjoining to it is a stove, whose warm steams, when the weather is cloudy, supply the heat of the sun: from thence you pass through a cheerful undressing chamber into a cold bathroom, which is darkened and provided with a bathing cistern of a convenient size. If this be not large enough to swim in, or if you choose a warmer bath, in the outward court there is a basin with a well adjoining to it, from whence you may be supplied with cold water, in case the warmer bath should be hotter than you desire it. Adjoining to the cold bath is another of a middle tempera- ture, and more exposed to the sun, but not so much as the hot bath, because that is built farther out. You have three staircases to go down to it; two of them quite open to the sun; the third less exposed, although full as light. Over the undressing room is a tennis court, which is accommodated to several sorts of exercise, by means of several circles which are made in it. Not far from the baths is a staircase that leads into a close gallery, at the entrance of which are three apartments: one looks into the little court, where the four plane trees are; another into the meadow; and the third has a view of several vineyards: so that each has a different prospect and looks towards a different point of the heavens. At the upper end of the gallery is a bedchamber, taken out of the gallery itself. It has a prospect of the race course, the vineyard, and the mountains. To this adjoins a bedchamber which is open to the sun, especially in winter. From hence there is another apartment between the race course and the dwelling house. All this makes the front facade.

On the south side is a close gallery of a considerable height above the ground; from whence the vineyards appear so near that you seem almost to touch them. In the middle of it a large dining room receives a very wholesome air from the valleys of the Apennine mountains: in the back facade, from the largest windows and the folding doors, you have a view of the vineyards through the gallery. On that side of the dining room, which has no windows, is a private staircase, which we make use of for serving up an entertainment when I sup there: the gallery ends in a bedchamber, beautified by the prospect both of the gallery itself and of the vineyards.

Underneath is another gallery, much like a subterraneous passage. In summer it is perfectly cool, and having sufficient air within itself, neither wants nor admits any from without. After both these galleries, at the end of the dining room, is an open portico cool in the forepart of the day, but exposed to the sun in the afternoon. Through this you go into two different apartments, one of which contains four, the other three chambers; all which enjoy, in their turns, both the sunshine and the shade.

This disposition of the several parts of the house is extremely delightful; although it equals in no degree the beauty of the race course, which is a large open area presenting itself entire, at one view, to the eyes of the beholder. It is set round with plane trees, which are covered with ivy; and as their tops flourish by their own beauty, so, towards the bottom, their verdure is borrowed from the ivy that runs over the trunk and the branches, and spreading itself from one tree to another joins them together. The vacancy between the bodies of the trees is filled up with box; which is again surrounded by a laurel hedge, vying in shade with the plane trees. This straight boundary of the race course changes its figure at the end into a semi-circle; which is set round and covered with cypress trees, composing a thicker and more gloomy shade than the former hedge. The inner circles (for there are many of them) enjoy the clearest daylight. They are filled with plenty of roses, and relieve you from the chilliness of the shade, with the agreeable warmth of the sun.

When you are arrived at the end of all these winding alleys, you come out into a straight walk; nay, not into one but into several; divided in some places by grass plots, in others by box trees cut into a thousand shapes; some of which are letters forming my name; and others the name of my gardener. In these are mixed, alternately, small pyramids and apple trees; and now and then, in the midst of a plot, improved with all imaginable art, you meet on a sudden with a spot of ground, wild and uncultivated, as if transplanted hither on purpose. The middle space is adorned on both sides with dwarf plane trees. Beyond these again is an acanthus bed, that waves and bends under your hand; and then again various figures and various names. At the upper end is a couch made of white marble, over which a vine, supported by four small pillars of Carystian marble, forms an arbor. From the couch several pipes spout forth water, as if forced out by the weight of those who lie down. It falls first into a stone cistern, and from thence into a marble basin, and is so managed by pipes under ground that it keeps the basin always full without ever running over. When I sup here, the more substantial dishes are placed upon the border of the basin, whilst the lesser float in the water in the shape of little boats and birds. Over against this is a fountain, which throws up water and receives it back again. The apertures that swallow it and return it communicate with each other.

Opposite to the marble couch stands a bedchamber which gives an ornament to that couch equal to what it receives from it. This room is beautified with marble; the doors project and are surrounded with greens. The windows, both above and below, are shaded on every side with the same. Within this chamber is a little closet that appears to belong to another room. Here is a bed and windows on every side which let in but a gloomy sort of light, being obscured by the shade of a most luxuriant vine, which ascends and covers the whole building from the bottom to the very roof. You may lie here as in a grove, only more secure from rain. Here also rises a fountain, which immediately disappears. In many places of the walks and alleys are marble seats, disposed at convenient distances; upon which, when you are tired with walking, you may rest yourself with as much ease as in the chamber. Near these seats are little fountains. In every part of the race course you hear the murmur of water, conveyed through pipes by the hand of the artificer, in such a manner as best pleased his fancy. This serves to water my greens, sometimes in one part, sometimes in another, and sometimes in all parts at once. I should have ended before now, for fear of seeming tedious, had I not been determined thus to walk over every corner with you in my letter: nor did I apprehend you would be tired in reading what would not tire you in seeing; especially as you may rest, and, by laying down my epistle, relieve yourself as often as you please. Besides, I was willing to indulge myself in the description of what I love; for I am particularly fond of places which I have either laid out myself, or have finished when begun by others. In a word, (for why should not I unbosom to you my thoughts, whether right or wrong?) I always look upon it as the chief duty of a writer, to keep a close eye to his title, and often ask himself what he has proposed to treat of; well knowing, while he confines himself to his subject, he cannot seem long; but if he deviates in the least, and launches out into any foreign matter, he must appear exceedingly tedious. You see how many lines are employed by Homer and Virgil, the one in describing the arms of Aeneas, the other of Achilles; yet neither of these poets are too prolix, because each fulfills his original intention. You see in what manner Aratus has searched out and numbered the smallest stars; yet he preserves himself from the character of too voluminous an author, for he never rambles but keeps close to his work. In like manner, (to compare small things with great) whilst I was endeavoring to place before your eyes a complete description of my feat, if I have never deviated from the subject, nor related what was foreign to my purpose, it is not the description of my house but my house itself, that is large.

But to return where I begun, lest I should be justly condemned by my own law if I continue longer in this digression; you now see the reasons why I prefer my seat in Tuscany to those I have at Tusculum, Tibur, and Praeneste; for, besides what I have already told you, the repose I enjoy here is more quiet and undisturbed than anywhere else. No summons to the bar; no clients at my gate; all is calm and still; which added to the healthiness of the place, the clearness of the sky, and the softness of the air, makes me enjoy the greatest vigor, both of body and mind. The one is kept in exercise by hunting, the other by study. Besides, my family are never in better health than here. To this very day (in a lucky moment be it spoken) I have not lost one of all the retinue I brought with me. May the Gods continue this happiness to me, and this glory to the place itself. Adieu.

APPENDIX 3

Thomas Wright's Description of His Villa

Thomas Wright, "Mr. Wright's Description of His Villa at Byer's Green," *Gentleman's Magazine* 63, pt. 1 (1793): 213–16.

You say you should be very glad to read a description of a place that renders all the charms of London so insipid. I really wish to answer this; but I confess I do not know very well how, especially to one who has so often said he can have no clear notion of the happiness of a retired life, or of any provincial pleasures. But surely something must be said to so very kind a friend who seems to share in all my satisfactions.

My place is distant from the metropolis nearly 260 miles; and if you come by Piersbridge you must turn off at the two-mile stone from Castle Auckland, and two miles more of very irregular road will bring you to my gates.

Here, if you look round, you will find my *villula* or *villulet,* for I cannot well call it a villa from its miniature, situated as in a vast amphitheatre, bounded by high hills on every side, through which a beautiful river winds, at about 20 miles from the sea; the descent from, and elevation to, my house being nearly equal, which makes it very beautiful, healthful, and not too much exposed.

The spring, indeed, and the autumn winds, are here sometimes very severe, but the summer and winter ones more mild and temperate. Many old people here live to the end of the century, and some of my own family have reached that period.

The house stands in the centre of a plantation of my own rearing, mostly of forest trees and flowering shrubs of every kind, both foreign and domestic, with a small but pleasing terrace before it considerably elevated above the rest of the garden and rich with various evergreens and flowers. Behind it, in the other front, is a small grass plot with a forest walk well bordered with various kinds of shrubs and trees, affording both a cool and pleasing shelter from almost every wind and on each side, towards the offices, are two corresponding courts, communicating with two small kitchen gardens, one for salad herbs, the other for roots etc. Thirty-six fruit trees of various kinds are disposed upon the walls and round the house, which not only have a pleasant effect, but prove very beneficial in their season.

The offices are detached from the body of the house, and effectually hid by plantations full grown, with Chinese and other seats everywhere disposed to take in several large and pleasing views; some of which are well clothed with wood, and others very extensive. Adjoining to the two courts are two Roman *suggestia;* and between these, but less elevated, is a small *praetorium* joining to the house. This overlooks all the finest part of the country, and also the river Were which runs before it, with the cathedral church of Durham, a noble Gothic building, as the principal point of view. On this side of my house I have a prospect, from my dining room windows, of upwards of 500 beautiful inclosures in a most picturesque situation, truly pastoral, in all the scenes of agriculture. I can truly say,

> Here the ploughman near at hand
> Whistles o'er the furrow'd land,
> And the milkmaid singeth blithe,
> And the mower whets his scythe,
> And every shepherd tells his tale
> Under the hawthorn in the dale.

In the village front is an open view without the appearance of any inclosures, the lawn extending a full half mile long, and near a furlong wide, all of green turf, in beautiful verdure most part of the year. There is a bowling green before the house, and in the centre of the town; the whole being nearly in the proportion of a Roman circus: and here frequently are both horse and foot races. Many other sports and games are also exhibited here annually on the 29th of June, in imitation of those of Rome, or the Olympiad, probably as relics of the former, who in neighborhood of this place had once a station called *Vinovium.*

Near to this village is also a manifest Roman circus, all good ground and two miles in compass; which, as being in the neighborhood of the camp, is supposed to be that of Albinus, his principal camp being at Alclunum, now Auckland, and the undoubted Binovium of Ptolemy. This (circus) I procured to be restored in the year 1778, by a subscription of the neighboring gentlemen, and it is judged to be the finest piece of race ground in the North of England.

The body of the building is but small, consisting only of a principal and rustic floor; the rustic or foundation part is formed into a parlor, kitchen, staircase, pantry, cellar, and servants' room. In the parlor are two alcoves, the one for books, etc. the other for a bed. In this small room is also an elegant museum in the shape of a pyramid; the bottom part is a scrutoire with commode drawers, and the upper part is full of the works of the most eminent English poets, with their heads in mezzotint on the inside of its folding doors. Before the window is a large library table full of fine prints and curious books, together of very great value, and not easily estimated. In the alcove also is a library of many books, chiefly of history and sciences. On each side, in the podgio part, are stoles for cloths and linen. Here likewise is a curious cedar cabinet full of drawings and original mss, some of them inestimable, and several of them ready for publishing. These, with many more already made public, are the works and labors of upwards of thirty years of my retired study, and most of them in this place.

In the adjacent kitchen are likewise two familiar alcoves, answering to those in the parlor; in one of which is a folding bed, and in the other a commodious dresser, with all things necessary for serving up a dinner. The entry on the side, as well as to the parlor, is covered with an arcade or portico of four arches each, which connects both courts with the two front parts of the garden, one way leading to the terrace, the other to the forest walk and *praetorium.*

The principal story is entered by a flight of steps from the outside, with an half space from the terrace which serves to dine upon in summer, having stone seats on each side and an abacus or balustrade, which answers very well both for a sideboard and dumbwaiter. Here I can most pleasantly enjoy a view of the town, the Roman camp, and the evening fun.

My first room is a small vestibule, adorned with medallions of the twelve Caesars; and through this, on one side, you enter the drawing room and, on the other, the staircase. Right forward is my dining room, and over the door this motto, transposed, in Greek characters, to render it more difficult to read:

Mihi vivam quod superest aevi.

The staircase is ornamented with my own works, particularly a large scheme of the universe, the visible creation, the sun, moon and systems of the planets and comets etc. In the drawing room are all the faculties of human knowledge represented by a curious collection of prints, disposed in twenty-seven large compositions, 500 being selected for that purpose and elegantly framed. At one end of this room, parted off from the other with two Doric pillars, is a Roman *triclinium;* the sofa is composed of six large cushions; in all 16 parts; mostly used for holding books and easier reading. In the other end is a handsome but plain chimneypiece, in the tablet of which Vulcan is represented forging the arms of Aeneas, with Venus sitting by him. In the ceiling of this part is the system of the sun, decorated with the representation of the four seasons, and other ancient historical figures. That of the sofa part is the *sedes beatorum,* or supreme heaven, with the hours and times disposed around it. In the cove of both parts are represented, as on medallions, all the human passions after Le Brun. On each side of my *triclinium,* in two tablets, and facing each other, are the following mottos from Lord Lansdowne:

Early and vain into the world I came,
Big with false hopes, and eager after fame,
Till looking round me, ere the race began,
Madmen and giddy fools were all that ran;
Reclaim'd by time, I from the lists retire,
And thank the Gods—who my retreat inspire.
    Happy the man, of mortals happiest he,
Whose quiet mind from vain desires is free,
Whom neither hopes deceive, nor fears torment,
But lives at peace, within himself content;
How sweet the morn! how gentle is the night!
How calm the evening! and the noon how bright!

The dining room is elegantly fitted up with a crimson embossed paper, and some remarkable good paintings, particularly one by Old Wyks, and two small ones on copper. Here is one of myself, a half-length, with an orrery before; another of the moon's rising in a Milton's evening; the fellow of it, a Stonehenge with the *aurora borealis;* likewise a sun and moon's eclipse; three night views of the last comets; morning, noon, and night, three good paintings on plate glass and several meteoric scenes etc.; most of them well framed, and regularly disposed. The chimneypiece is well carved in stone, with a chaplet of oakleaves and acorns in the tablet, and boys, in *basso relievo,* on each side, represent the arts and sciences. On the sideboard table is painted, in perspective distortion, Charles the Fifth with his secretary Maximilian.

The original building was only designed for a retirement for study; but now too small *cubicula,* as wings, are added to it; the one designed as a bedchamber, the other as a laboratory for the purposes of mechanical and other experimental philosophy. The one window of the new apartments views the summer setting sun, and the other the winter rising one; and the other windows the reverse.

Here I have perfect tranquility, though in a village, having no house nearer than a hundred yards.

I have one seat in my dining room where I can imagine myself in the midst of an American forest, well wooded on all sides, and mixed with beautiful inclosures, and an Indian town on each side my gates which are adorned with yew trees. There are two weeping willows which are trimmed every year, and constantly throw out new branches like the *polypus,* and so thick and flexible as to represent the Egyptian god Acanthus pouring out so many streams of water, beautifully bending to the ground. In almost every part of my garden I have a retreat from bad weather, and shelter from every wind, and, at the same time, commanding most pleasing views, one of my village, another of an extensive park, and also a provincial one terminated by the finest hill in the county at the distance of twenty miles.

Plenty of fuel is to be had from the adjoining common; and good salmon is caught frequently within half a mile of my house.

When I indulge myself with poetic ideas I can naturally conceive myself with an Olympus before me, a Mount Hemus on one side, and a Parnassus on the other.

Now, notwithstanding your astonishment at my love of a retired life, tell me if I have not just reason to exult a little in what I feel in such a delightful situation, and to give up as much of my time as I can preserve to myself, centered in such pleasing circumstances in which no human joy is wanting?

If all mankind would endeavor to cultivate such objects as are in their own power and be content with their private station and situation, every human being would soon have its share of well-earned happiness. But those who are attached to the pleasures of the town, I fear, can have no just idea of the calm and serene sensations of such a life.

Besides all this, I have in agitation to erect a Gothic tower on one of the highest hills in the country, and have been several years preparing materials for it; when that is done you may expect to hear a farther account of my amusements.

Chronological Table of Known
Laurentine and Tuscan Villa Restitutions

(Asterisk means restitution is illustrated in this book)

Date	Designer	Laurentine (L) or Tuscan (T)	First Published Reference
1615	Vincenzo Scamozzi	L°	Scamozzi, *Idea dell'architettura* (Venice, 1615)
ca. 1620	Giovanni Ambrogio Magenta	L	Lancisi, *Dissertatio de Plinianae Villae* (Rome, 1714)
1699	Jean-François Félibien des Avaux	L° T°	Félibien, *Plans* (Paris, 1699)
ca. 1700	Francesco Ignazio Lazzari	T°	
1728	Robert Castell	L° T°	Castell, *Villas of the Ancients* (London, 1728)
1751	John Boyle, earl of Orrery	T° (*stibadium* only)	Pliny, *Letters*, Orrery ed. (London, 1751)
1760	Friedrich August Krubsacius	L°	*Das Neueste aus der Anmuthigen Gelehrsamkeit* 6–7 (1760)
1762	Friedrich August Krubsacius	T°	*Das Neueste aus der Anmuthigen Gelehrsamkeit* 11–12 (1762)
ca. 1770	Edward Stevens	L°	*Royal Academy Exhibition Catalogue* (London, 1771)
ca. 1775	William Newton	L° T°	
ca. 1779	Stanislas Kostka Potocki	L°	
1796	Pedro José Marquez	L° T°	Marquez, *Ville di Plinio* (Rome, 1796)
1818	Pascal Lepage	L°	
1818	Amable Macquet	L°	Vaudoyer, *Grands prix* (Paris, 1834)
1818	Achille Normand	L°	Vaudoyer, *Grands prix* (Paris, 1834)
1827	Aloys Ludwig Hirt	L° T°	Hirt, *Die Geschichte der Baukunst bei den Alten* (Berlin, 1827)
1832	Friedrich Wilhelm Ludwig Stier	L° T°	*Allgemeine Bauzeitung* 7 (1842) *Allgemeine Bauzeitung* 8 (1843)
1838	Louis-Pierre Haudebourt	L°	Haudebourt, *Laurentin* (Paris, 1838)
1840	Luigi Canina	L°	Canina, *Architettura antica* (Rome, 1840)
1841	Karl Friedrich Schinkel	L° T°	Schinkel, *Architektonisches Album* (Berlin, 1841) Schinkel, *Architektonisches Album* (Berlin, 1841)
1843	Charles Robert Cockerell	L	*Athenaeum*, no. 798 (1843)
1852	Jules Bouchet	L°	Bouchet, *Laurentin* (Paris, 1852)

Date	Designer	Laurentine (L) or Tuscan (T)	First Published Reference
1853	Jules Bouchet	T	*Explication des ouvrages de peinture . . . des artistes vivants* (Paris, 1853)
ca. 1855	Anonymous student "villa" design, ASL	L°	
1860	Gustav Meyer	T	Meyer, *Lehrbuch der schönen Gartenkunst* (Berlin, 1860)
ca. 1860	Anonymous student *casa* design, ASL	L°	
ca. 1864	J. W. Loring, student design, Columbia University	L	
1864	J. G. S. Jr., student design, Columbia University	L	
1889	James Cowan	L	*Pliny, Epistularum,* Cowan ed. (London, 1889)
1891	Hermann Winnefeld	L°	*Jahrbuch des Kaiserlich Deutschen Archäologischen Institut* 6 (1891)
		T°	*Jahrbuch des Kaiserlich Deutschen Archäologischen Institut* 6 (1891)
1895	Herbert Magoun	L	*Transactions of the American Philosophical Society* 26 (1895)
1914	Marie Luise Gothein	T	*Geschichte der Gartenkunst* (Jena, 1914)
1921	Helen Tanzer	L	Tanzer, *Villas of Pliny* (New York, 1924)
1921	Anonymous student design, RIBA	L	*Architectural Review* 56 (1924)
ca. 1931	Guido Carafa	L	*Mostra del giardino Italiano* (Florence, 1931)
1943	Albert van Buren	L	*Rendiconti della Pontificia Accademia Romana di Archaeologia* 20 (1943–44)
1947	Clifford Pember	L°	*Illustrated London News,* no. 5653 (1947)
1981	Jean-Pierre Adam	L°	Pinon and Culot, *Laurentine* (Paris, 1982)
1981	David Bigelman	L°	Pinon and Culot, *Laurentine* (Paris, 1982)
1981	Paolo Farina	L°	Pinon and Culot, *Laurentine* (Paris, 1982)
1981	Philippe Fraisse and Jean-Pierre Braun	L°	Pinon and Culot, *Laurentine* (Paris, 1982)
1981	Bernard Huet	L°	Pinon and Culot, *Laurentine* (Paris, 1982)
1981	Manuel Iñiguez and Alberto Ustarroz	L°	Pinon and Culot, *Laurentine* (Paris, 1982)

Date	Designer	Laurentine (L) or Tuscan (T)	First Published Reference
1981	Léon Krier	L°	Pinon and Culot, *Laurentine* (Paris, 1982)
1981	Fernando Montes	L°	Pinon and Culot, *Laurentine* (Paris, 1982)
1981	Serge Santelli	L°	Pinon and Culot, *Laurentine* (Paris, 1982)
1981	Justo Solsona	L°	Pinon and Culot, *Laurentine* (Paris, 1982)
1981	Manfred Sundermann	L°	Pinon and Culot, *Laurentine* (Paris, 1982)
1981	Jean-Jacques Treuttel, Jean-Claude Garcias, and Jérôme Treuttel	L°	Pinon and Culot, *Laurentine* (Paris, 1982)
1981	Patrick Weber and Didier Laroche	L°	Pinon and Culot, *Laurentine* (Paris, 1982)
1983	Erik Marosi, student design, Princeton University	L°	*Fifth Column* 4 (1984)
1984	Eugenia Salza Prina Ricotti	L° T (*stibadium* only)	*Ancient Roman Villa Gardens: The Tenth Dumbarton Oaks Symposium* (Washington, D.C., 1987)
1984	Manfred Sundermann	T°	*Deutsche Akademie Villa Massimo in Rom, 1983–84* (Rome, 1984)
1984	Richard Peckham, Dan Pratt, and Christopher Pickell, student designs, Rensselaer Polytechnic Institute	L	
1985	Anonymous student design, McGill University	L	
1985	Anonymous student design, Syracuse University	L	
1985	Anonymous student design, University of Toronto	L	
1993	Reinhard Förtsch	L (*hortus* only) T	*Archäologischer Kommentar zu den Villenbriefen des jüngeren Plinius* (1993)

ABBREVIATIONS

ADAG	State Archives, Warsaw
AN	Archives Nationales, Paris
AMO	Ashmolean Museum, Oxford
ASL	Accademia Nazionale di San Luca, Rome
BM	British Museum, London (British Library unless otherwise noted)
BNW	Biblioteka Narodowa, Warsaw
BSGCDC	Biblioteca "Storti Guerri," Città di Castello
BGCCDC	Biblioteca "G. Carducci," Città di Castello
CCA	Centre Canadien d'Architecture/Canadian Centre for Architecture, Montreal
DO	Dumbarton Oaks, Garden Library, Washington, D.C.
EBA	Ecole Nationale Supérieure des Beaux-Arts, Paris
IFA	Institut Français d'Architecture, Paris
RIBA	Royal Institute of British Architects, Drawings Collection or British Architectural Library, London
SA	Schinkel Archive, Nationalgalerie, Staatliche Museen zu Berlin
SL	Sächsische Landesbibliothek, Dresden
SM	Sir John Soane's Museum, London
TUB	Technische Universität, Berlin, Plansammlung der Universitätsbibliothek

Notes

Introduction: "Comum Tuae Meaeque Deliciae"

1. Caius Caecilius Secundus Pliny, *The Letters of Pliny the Younger, with Observations on Each Letter*, trans. John Boyle, fifth earl of Orrery, 2 vols. (London, 1751), 1:7. It is not generally known, I believe, that the engraving in Orrery's book (illustrated as my fig. 1) provided the inspiration for Angelica Kauffmann's 1785 painting of the same scene now in the Princeton University Art Gallery.

2. Paolo Giovio, *Descriptio Larii Lacus* (Venice, 1559), p. xi. I have referred to the edition printed by Zilletti. The relevant letters by Giovio have been extracted in Matteo Gianoncelli's *L'antico museo di Paolo Giovio in Borgovico* (Como, 1977). The same subject is treated in Paul Ortwin Rave, "Das Museo Giovio zu Como," *Römische Forschungen des Bibliotheca Hertziana* 16 (1961): 275–84. Rave (p. 277), however, misidentified the map depicted in my fig. 2 as from Giovio's *Descriptio*. I owe the correct identification to Margarete Kühn and to the assistance of Nancy L. Romero, head of rare books at the University of Illinois Library at Urbana-Champaign. The anonymous *Descrizione del museo del Giovio* (Venice, 1558) was kindly brought to my attention by George L. Gorse. There is a full and curious account of Pliny and Giovio on Lake Como in Gilbert Laing Meason, *On the Landscape Architecture of the Great Painters of Italy* (London, 1828), pp. 28, 31.

3. See Eckard Lefèvre, "Plinius Studien IV: Die Naturauffassung in den Beschreibungen der Quelle am *Lacus Larius* . . . ," *Gymnasium* 95 (1988): 236–69. For the brief commentary of Pliny the Elder on the spring see his *Natural History*, bk. 2, chap. 106.

4. Pliny, *Letters*, Orrery, ed., 2:272–73. Orrery's criticism of the villas (p. 275), is immediately qualified by the observation that their situation must have been "extremely beautiful." His mention of Chiswick Villa is on 1:175.

5. See Xavier Jacques and J. van Ooteghem, "Index de Pline le jeune," *Mémoires de l'Académie Royale de Belgique, Classe de Lettres* 58 (1965): 904. The authors count no fewer than sixteen references to Cicero in the writings of Pliny—more than to any other Latin author. For Anne-Marie Guillemin, *Pline et la vie littéraire de son temps* (Paris, 1929), p. 114, there is no question that Pliny's letter to Mustius emulates Cicero's letter to Atticus. For a discussion of Mustius see note 7 below.

6. See the article on *ekphrasis* by G. Downey in *Reallexikon für Antike und Christentum* 4 (1959). He makes no specific mention of Pliny, nor does Henry Maguire in "Truth and Convention in Byzantine Descriptions of Works of Art," *Dumbarton Oaks Papers* 28 (1974): 112–40, and idem, *Art and Eloquence in Byzantium* (Princeton, N.J., 1981), p. 22.

7. Jean-François Félibien des Avaux, *Recueil historique de la vie et des ouvrages des plus célèbres architectes*, 2d ed. (Paris, 1696), pp. 102–3, writes a highly speculative life of Mustius based on the Pliny correspondence.

8. Vitruvius *De architectura*, bk. 4, chap. 1, discusses the Doric and Ionic orders in terms of different genders and their appropriateness to the temples dedicated to various male and female gods. John Onions, *Bearers of Meaning: The Classical Orders in Antiquity, the Middle Ages, and the Renaissance* (Princeton, N.J., 1988), pp. 36–39, argues convincingly that the proper system of "decorum" for the use of the orders was derived by Vitruvius from the three Ciceronian types of orations.

Chapter One

1. A. N. Sherwin-White, *The Letters of Pliny: A Historical and Social Commentary* (Oxford, 1966), pp. 186, 321, speculates on the dates and true identities of the recipients of the letters to Gallus and Apollinaris.

2. On the matter of the interpretation of *villula* see Albert W. van Buren, "Laurentinum Plinii Minoris," *Rendiconti della Pontificia Accademia Romana di Archaeologia* 20 (1943–44): 165–92, esp. p. 191. Alexander G. McKay, *Houses, Villas, and Palaces in the Roman World* (Ithaca, N.Y., 1975), p. 115, speaks of Pliny's "fantastic" villas, and James S. Ackerman, *The Villa: Form and Ideology of Country Houses* (Princeton, N.J., 1990), p. 29, refers to their "lavishness."

3. Plutarch, *Lucullus* 39. 3–5, translated and quoted by A. R. Littlewood, "Ancient Literary Evidence for the Pleasure Gardens of Roman Country Villas," in *Ancient Roman Villa Gardens: The Tenth Dumbarton Oaks Colloquium on the History of Landscape Architecture* (Washington, D.C., 1987), pp. 7–30; see esp. p. 11.

4. Pliny the Elder, *Natural History,* bk. 35, chap. 36, sec. 65.

5. See Eckard Lefèvre, "Plinius Studien II: Diana und Minerva. Die beiden Jagd-Billette an Tacitus," *Gymnasium* 85 (1978): 37–47, and esp. p. 44, which touches on Pliny's preference for pendant pairs of letters.

6. Lucius Junius Moderatus Columella, *De re rustica.*

7. I have previously discussed these ideas in an article, "Four Cardinal Points of a Villa," *ARQ/ Architecture Québec* 15 (October 1983): 16–22.

8. Andrea Palladio, *I quattro libri dell'architettura* (Venice, 1570), bk. 2, chap. 2. I am using the translation in Ackerman, *Villa,* p. 106. Hugh Honour and John Fleming, *The Visual Arts: A History* (Englewood Cliffs, N.J., 1982), p. 378, draws a parallel between Palladio's words and those of Pliny.

9. The ecclesiastical overtones of the secular cupola over the Villa La Rotonda are brought out in Wolfgang Lotz, "La Rotonda: Edificio civile con cupola," *Bollettino del Centro Internazionale di Studi di Architettura "Andrea Palladio"* 4 (1962): 69–73. This has been included in Lotz's collected and translated essays as "The Rotonda: A Secular Building with a Dome," in *Studies in Italian Renaissance Architecture* (Cambridge, Mass., 1981), pp. 190–96. Details on the colorful life of Paolo Almerico based on documentary evidence are to be found in Giangiorgio Zorzi, *Le ville e i teatri di Andrea Palladio* (Vicenza, 1969). Palladio, *Quattro libri,* bk. 2, chap. 16, alludes briefly to Pliny.

10. Schinkel's letter is quoted in full in Alfred von Wolzogen, *Als Schinkels Nachlass,* 4 vols. (Berlin, 1862–64), 3:336–41. See also Karl Friedrich Schinkel, *Entwurf zu dem Kaiserlichen Palast Orianda in der Krimm . . . ,* 4th ed. (Berlin, 1873).

11. German editions available to Schinkel speculate on whether Pliny meant glass or translucent stone. See the Johann Mathias Gesner edition of Pliny's letters (Leipzig, 1739), p. 80, and Aloys Hirt's translation in *Die Geschichte der Baukunst bei den Alten* (Berlin, 1821–27), p. 296, which Schinkel almost certainly used because of his friendship with Hirt.

12. Details on the life and works of George Browne and an exhaustive bibliography are provided by J. Douglas Stewart's entry in *Dictionary of Canadian Biography,* 12 vols. and index (Toronto, 1966–91), 11:117–20.

13. Letter of 15 August 1848 to his sister, Margaret Green, as quoted in J. K. Johnson, *Affectionately Yours* (Toronto, 1969), p. 58. With special reference to Hales's Cottages and Bellevue see Margaret Angus, *The Old Stones of Kingston* (Toronto, 1966), pp. 84–87. Jennifer McKendry also kindly gave me a copy of the 1981 abstract she prepared of all the documents then available relating to Bellevue.

14. Possible links between Bellevue and the publication of Downing's book were brought to my attention by Arthur Channing Downs in a letter of 11 April 1989.

15. Littlewood, "Ancient Literary Evidence," p. 23, discusses Pliny's constitutionals measured in number of laps around the hippodrome.

16. Ackerman, *Villa,* p. 35, quotes as his source Juvenal, *Satires* 3.160.

17. Francesco Petrarca, *Letters from Petrarch,* trans. Morris Bishop (Bloomington, Ind., 1966), p. 287, letter of 6 January 1371 to Matteo Longo, archdeacon of Liège. Petrarch's love of Cicero but unfamiliarity with Pliny is well documented.

18. Eve Borsook, *Companion Guide to Florence* (London, 1966), p. 343, quotes Vieri as writing, "I enjoy Pliny's letters, these are my real delight."

19. See Ludwig Heydenreich, "Federigo da Montefeltro as Building Patron: Some Remarks on the Ducal Palace of Urbino," in *Studies in Renaissance and Baroque Art Presented to Anthony Blunt*

on His Sixtieth Birthday (London, 1967), pp. 5–6; and idem with Wolfgang Lotz, *Architecture in Italy, 1400–1600* (Harmondsworth, Eng., 1974), p. 343, n. 18.

20. A recent interpretation of the *studiolo* similar to my own may be found in Luciano Cheles, *The Studiolo of Urbino: An Iconographic Investigation* (University Park, Pa., 1986), pp. 22–23. Cheles adopts an opinion midway between the pro-Plinian one of Heydenreich (see n. 19 above) and the anti-Plinian ones of others.

21. Whitehall figures in Rosamond Randal Beirne's *William Buckland, 1734–74, Architect of Virginia and Maryland* (Baltimore, 1958). Drawings of the house, said to be in Buckland's hand, were published by its restorer, Charles Scarlett, in his "Governor Horatio Sharpe's Whitehall," *Maryland Historical Magazine* 46 (1951): 8–26. Sharpe has been the subject of Matilde Ridout Edgar's *A Colonial Governor in Maryland: Horatio Sharpe and His Times, 1733–1773* (London, 1912). Unfortunately none of these sources give proper references. A well-illustrated recent account is by Susan Stiles Dowell, "Whitehall: Representing the Height of Colonial Architecture," *Southern Accents* 9, no. 6 (1986): 87–95.

22. Howard Colvin and John Newman, eds., *Of Building: Roger North's Writings on Architecture* (Oxford, 1981), p. 62. Sharpe's letter to his brother dated 10 December 1768, now in the manuscript division of the Library of Congress, is referred to by Scarlett, "Sharpe's Whitehall," p. 22.

23. *Archives of Maryland XIV. Correspondence of Governor Horatio Sharpe (1761–71)*, ed. William Hand Browne (Baltimore, 1895), p. 142, letter of Caecilius Calvert dated 29 February 1764; p. 402 for the letter of 15 June 1767; p. 550 for Sharpe's long letter of self-justification of 30 October 1768—as unusually long as is Pliny's letter to Apollinaris.

24. Scarlett, "Sharpe's Whitehall," p. 22.

25. *The Papers of Thomas Jefferson*, ed. Julian P. Boyd, vol. 10 (Princeton, N.J., 1954), p. 447, letter of 12 October 1786.

26. For Jefferson's architectural books, including the one by Castell, see William B. O'Neal, *Jefferson's Fine Arts Library* (Charlottesville, Va., 1976). Jefferson's ownership of the Orrery edition is confirmed by E. Millicent Sowerby, comp., *Catalogue of the Library of Thomas Jefferson*, 5 vols. (Washington, D.C., 1952–59), 5:7–8.

27. Ackerman, *Villa*, p. 189, quoting from a letter of 23 February 1816. On p. 201 Ackerman suggests the derivation of the place-name Monticello from Palladio, as I did in my "Four Cardinal Points," p. 19.

28. Ackerman, *Villa*, p. 55.

29. On this point see ibid., p. 53, and Eckard Lefèvre, "Plinius Studien I: Römische Baugesinnung und Landschaftsauffassung in der Villenbriefen (2, 17; 5, 6)," *Gymnasium* 84 (1977): 539.

30. Lefèvre, "Plinius Studien I," p. 529. The specific passage from Statius *Silvae* 2.74–76 reads: "Each chamber has its own delight, its own particular sea, and . . . each window commands a different landscape." By comparing this text with Pliny's, Anne-Marie Guillemin, *Pline et la vie littéraire de son temps* (Paris, 1929), pp. 125–26, comes to the conclusion that Pliny knew and imitated these lines from Statius. Without drawing the same conclusion, Bettina Bergmann compares Statius with Pliny in her essay "Painted Perspectives of a Villa Visit: Landscape as Status and Metaphor," in *Roman Art in the Private Sphere: New Perspectives on the Architecture and Decor of the Domus, Villa, and Insula*, ed. Elaine K. Gazda (Ann Arbor, Mich., 1991), pp. 49–70.

31. Christoph Luitpold Frommel, *Die Farnesina und Peruzzis architektonisches Frühwerk* (Berlin, 1961), p. 117. See also Ingrid D. Rowland, "Render unto Caesar the Things Which Are Caesar's: Humanism and the Arts in the Patronage of Agostino Chigi," *Renaissance Quarterly* 39 (1968): 673–729.

32. Rowland, "Patronage Agostino Chigi," p. 720, translates and quotes from the panegyric written by Girolamo Borgia in honor of Chigi, just as Pliny praised the emperor Trajan in his *Panegyricus*.

33. David R. Coffin, *The Villa in the Life of Renaissance Rome* (Princeton, N.J., 1979), pp. 87–91, gives the building history of the Farnesina, publishes early drawings relating to it, and discusses the lavish entertainments Agostino Chigi gave there.

34. Through the kind offices of the late Felix Gilbert I was shown a manuscript by Ingrid D.

Rowland prepared for *Studi e Testi*. In it she includes the transcription of the letter dated 30 January 1500 sent by Agostino Chigi from Rome to his father Mariano (Vatican, Cod. Chigi R. V. c., fols. 33–34). I am grateful to her for granting me access to her transcription ahead of publication. Isa Bella Barsali, *Baldassare Peruzzi e le ville senesi del cinquecento* (San Quirico d'Orcia, 1977), pp. 38–63, discusses and illustrates the Villa Le Volte.

35. Ackerman, *Villa*, fig. 1.20, implies a link between the wings of the Farnesina and Roman prototypes. This implication may be incorrect, as was the case on an earlier occasion when Ackerman used the Ca' Brusà at Lovolo to prove a similar point, only to retract the suggestion when Renato Cevese demonstrated that the wings there had been added later (see James S. Ackerman, review of Renato Cevese, *Ville della provincia di Vicenza*, in *Journal of the Society of Architectural Historians* 32 (1973): 73–74.

36. Emmanuel-Pierre Rodocanachi, like a true Frenchman, delights in recounting the gastronomic delicacies on Agostino Chigi's banquet table. See *La première renaissance: Rome au temps de Jules II et Léon X* (Paris, 1912), pp. 231–32.

37. Coffin, *Villa*, p. 77 and fig. 44, shows that the same trick was played slightly earlier in the loggia frescoes at the Villa Belvedere, and again at a later date at the Villa Lante in Bagnaia (p. 346 and fig. 222).

38. Martin Kubelik, Christian Goedicke, and Klaus Slusallek, "Thermoluminescence Dating in Architectural History: The Chronology of Palladio's Villa Rotonda," *Journal of the Society of Architectural Historians* 45 (1986): 396–407, sheds additional light on Scamozzi's intervention in the Villa Rotonda.

39. Vincenzo Scamozzi, *L'idea dell'architettura universale*, 2 vols. (Venice, 1615), 1:272 and the woodcut illustration on the page opposite.

40. Camillo Semensato, "La Rocca Pisani dello Scamozzi," *Arte Veneta* 16 (1962): 98–109, remarks perceptively that the villa was probably used only on rare occasions, hence its unspoiled state of preservation. Certainly in winter it would be uninhabitable on so exposed a hilltop. It is the perfect house for a summer evening's soiree.

41. See David Morton, "Eclectic Revivals: Laurentian and Tuscan Houses, Livermore, California," *Progressive Architecture* 62 (October 1981): 98–101. The houses measure 1,700 and 1,900 square feet, respectively, including two-car garages that project prominently forward on the street side. See also Thomas Gordon Smith, *Classical Architecture: Rule and Invention* (Layton, Utah, 1988), pp. 114–17.

42. These and other details come from a broadsheet printed by Smith that he kindly sent to me. See also his *Classical Architecture*, pp. 122–25. Smith complained in a letter to me of 18 July 1983 that the antique color scheme of the Laurentine house had already been changed without his approval. For another point of view and good illustrations, see Sally Woodbridge, "Vest Pocket Villa: Thomas Gordon Smith House, Richmond, California," *Progressive Architecture* 66 (March 1985): 86–90.

43. See Lefèvre, "Plinius Studien I," p. 537, on this point, though I do not think he has taken the liquid analogy to its natural conclusion.

44. Ibid., p. 532.

45. The letter, which is in the Biblioteca Oliveriana, Pesaro, MS 374, vol. 2, fols. 91–96, is transcribed in full in Tilman Falk, "Studien zur Topographie und Geschichte der Villa Giulia in Rom," *Römisches Jahrbuch für Kunstgeschichte* 13 (1971): 171–73.

46. Vasari's own autobiography provides revealing insights into the various roles played by the talented triumvirate of designers. Similarly, his life of Taddeo Zuccaro documents Vasari's design of the papal farmstead at Monte San Savino, as well as the participation of the painters Zuccaro and Stefano Vetroni in the decoration of the Villa Giulia.

47. Coffin, *Villa*, p. 163, discusses the Plinian resemblance, cites a contemporary poem by Lelio Capilupi that further documents the plane trees' existence, and illustrates an engraving that shows the trees set into the pavement of the courtyard.

48. Vasari's life of Fra Giocondo states that Budé recorded the discovery of Pliny's letters by Fra Giocondo in a library in Paris and that these letters were then printed in an edition by Aldus Manutius. I presume Vasari is referring to Manutius's preface as his printed source.

49. Craig Hugh Smythe, "The Sunken Courts of the Villa Giulia and the Villa Imperiale," *Essays in Memory of Karl Lehman,* in *Marsyas,* suppl. 1 (1964): 303–13.

50. See Leon Satkowski on Ammannati in *The Macmillan Encyclopedia of Architects,* 4 vols. (New York, 1982), 1:77. Satkowski's entry on Vasari, ibid., 4:292, lists among his oeuvre the Monte San Savino and Villa Giulia projects.

51. John Coolidge, "The Villa Giulia: A Study of Central Italian Architecture in the Mid-Sixteenth Century," *Art Bulletin* 25 (1943): 177. Thanks to my correspondence with Professor Coolidge I was able to trace the Turpin Bannister drawings first published in his article. Coolidge does refer to Pliny's Laurentine Villa, but he draws no connection between the four plane trees at the Villa Giulia and those at the Tuscan Villa. The antique statues of nymphs that he alludes to may have included some of those noted by Pirro Ligorio as having been purchased for the villa. This point is touched on in Robert W. Gaston, "Ligorio on Rivers and Fountains: Prologomena to a Study of Naples XIII. B. 9," in *Pirro Ligorio, Artist and Antiquarian,* ed. Robert W. Gaston (Milan, 1988), p. 178.

52. David R. Coffin, "Some Aspects of the Villa Lante at Bagnaia," in *Arte in Europa: Scritti in storia dell'arte in onore di Edoardo Arslan* (Milan, 1966), pp. 569–75, first published the draft copy of the Farnese letter he had found in the Archivio di Stato in Parma. The discussion given then has subsequently been enlarged in idem, *Villa,* pp. 340–61.

53. Coffin, *Villa,* p. 347. I wonder also about the practical good sense of having two separate pavilions unless one was intended as a *foresteria,* or unless some allusion was being made to a pair of antique dwellings like Pliny's Comedy and Tragedy villas on Lake Como.

54. Claudia Lazzaro, *The Italian Renaissance Garden: From the Conventions of Planting, Design, and Ornament to the Grand Gardens of Sixteenth-Century Central Italy* (New Haven, Conn., 1990), pp. 257–58, draws attention to the words *cryptoporticus, hypoporticus,* and *porticus deambulatoriae,* which appear in the marginalia of the engraving and drawing by Giacomo Lauro and Giovanni Guerra that she publishes. She goes further than Coffin, *Villa,* in attaching Pliny's name to the inspiration behind the table fountain at the Villa Lante.

55. Johannes Sievens, *Karl Friedrich Schinkel Lebenswerk: Bauten für den Prinzen Karl von Preussen* (Berlin, 1942), p. 85, gives the basic chronology for the casino and archival photos of it before its postwar restoration.

56. I am indebted to Margarete Kühn for sending me a copy of the article by Martin Sperling, "Nicht Schloss, sondern Villa," from the 1987 Berlin exhibition catalog *Schloss Glienicke: Bewohner; Künstler; Parklandschaft,* pp. 27–31. A splendid painting by Freydanck of the view from the Persius *stibadium* with the domes and spires of Potsdam in the distance was published by Rand Carter, "Ludwig Persius and the Romantic Landscape of Potsdam," *Composicion Arquitectonica, Art and Architecture* 4 (October 1989): 115–60. The actual construction of the *stibadium* went on before 1840, according to the edited diary of Persius published by Eva Börsch-Supan as *Ludwig Persius: Das Tagebuch des Architekten Friedrich Wilhelms IV, 1840–45* (Munich, 1980).

Chapter Two

1. A. N. Sherwin-White, *The Letters of Pliny: A Historical and Social Commentary* (Oxford, 1966), supplies approximate dates for each letter where possible. Pliny (bk. 9, ep. 11) had heard from Rosianus Geminus that copies of his letters were available in bookshops as far afield as Lyons. The critical philological analysis of Pliny's letters falls outside the scope of this book; I have relied on the study now generally accepted as authoritative: Selatie Edgar Stout, *Plinius Epistulae: A Critical Edition* (Bloomington, Ind., 1962). For more on Stout see n. 38 below. Another key study is P. A. B. Mynors, *C. Plini Caecili Secundi epistularum libri decem* (Oxford, 1963).

2. Stout, *Plinius,* p. 6.

3. See Harriet McNeil Caplow on Michelozzo in *The Macmillan Encyclopedia of Architects,* 4 vols. (New York, 1982), 3:179–81. A recent monograph is by Miranda Ferrara and Francesco Quinterio, *Michelozzo di Bartolomeo* (Florence, 1984).

4. Guido Carocci, *I dintorni di Firenze*, 2d ed., 2 vols. (Florence, 1906–7), 1:119. The date Carocci gives for the purchase of the property, 1458, cannot be correct in the light of other evidence. The original owners were the Baldi family.

5. Giorgio Vasari, *Le vite dei più eccelenti pittori, scultori, ed architetti . . .* , ed. Gaetano Milanesi, 9 vols. (Florence, 1878–85), 2:442–43. I am using the English translation by A. B. Hinds.

6. James S. Ackerman, *The Villa: Form and Ideology of Country Houses* (Princeton, N.J., 1990), p. 73, quoting from Alison Brown, *Bartolomeo Scala, 1430–1497, Chancellor of Florence* (Princeton, N.J., 1979), pp. 17–18, who cites a letter datable, from its position in a sequence, to September or October 1455. The citation of the letter is Modena, Biblioteca Estense, MS Campori 2358 P.2.5, fol. 6 recto. Ackerman has previously published "The Medici Villa in Fiesole," in *Il se rendit en Italie: Etudes offertes à André Chastel* (Rome, 1987), pp. 49–56. Eve Borsook, *Companion Guide to Florence* (London, 1966), p. 345, had given the date for the villa as 1455 but had not specified her authority for the statement.

7. Brown, *Scala*, pp. 36, 268, discusses the manuscript "Dialogue of Consolation."

8. John R. Spencer, *Filarete's Treatise on Architecture*, 2 vols. (New Haven, Conn., 1965), 1: 318–22. John Onians, *Bearers of Meaning: The Classical Orders in Antiquity, the Middle Ages, and the Renaissance* (Princeton, N.J., 1988), p. 159, notes that the last book of Filarete was devoted to Medici projects when he decided to dedicate the manuscript now in Florence to Piero de' Medici.

9. See Angelo Maria Bandini, *Catalogus codicum latinorum Bibliothecae Mediceae Laurentinae . . .* , 4 vols. (Florence, 1774–84), vol. 3 passim. The helpful index in vol. 4, however, singles out all copies with an association to Giovanni de' Medici. William Roscoe, *The Life of Lorenzo de' Medici, Called the Magnificent*, 4th ed., 3 vols. (London, 1800), 1:65–66, cites some of these books, but his dates for the birth and death of Giovanni must be compared with the authoritative Vittorio Rossi, "L'indole e gli studi di Giovanni di Cosimo de' Medici," *Rendiconti della Reale Accademia dei Lincei: Rendiconti Morali*, ser. 5, 2A (1893): 38–60, 129–50, and especially 54–59 for Giovanni's purchases of manuscripts. For the reference to Rossi's writings I am indebted to Gaetano Pieraccini, *Le stirpe de' Medici di Cafaggiolo: Saggio de richerche dei caratteri biologici*, 3d ed., 3 vols. (Florence, 1986), 1:81.

10. Pieraccini, *Stirpe*, p. 83. A whole section, pp. 77–87, provides Giovanni's medical history.

11. Alluded to by Roscoe, *Life of Lorenzo*, 3:191, and by Borsook, *Guide to Florence*, p. 345, and quoted by David R. Coffin, *The Villa in the Life of Renaissance Rome* (Princeton, N.J., 1979), p. 294. The full anecdote is given by Teodoro degli Angeli (1495–1567), *Facezie e motti de' secoli XV e XVI*, in vol. 138 of *Scelta di curiosità letterarie inedite* (Bologna, 1874), p. 70. John V. Fleming of Princeton University kindly made this material available to me.

12. Quite apart from anything else, Cosimo's reply to his son ought to dispel any idea that Cosimo built the villa at Fiesole for Giovanni, as was maintained by Bernhard Patzak, *Palast und Villa in Toscana*, 2 vols. (Leipzig, 1913), 2:89. See also Ackerman, *Villa*, p. 73.

13. See Clara Bargellini and Pierre de la Ruffinière du Prey, "Sources for a Reconstruction of the Villa Medici, Fiesole," *Burlington Magazine* 111 (1969): 597–605, and especially fig. 37 for a reproduction of the painting by Biagio d'Antonio, now hanging in the Accademia di San Luca in Rome. The attribution to Biagio is generally accepted.

14. Detlef Heikamp, "Unbekannte Medici-Bildteppiche in Siena," *Pantheon* 37 (1979): 376–82; see especially fig. 1. The tapestry representation of the Villa Medici is very difficult to make out, as I was able to verify at the 1980 Council of Europe exhibition in Florence where it was on display. See *Palazzo Vecchio: Committenza e collezionismo Medicei* (Florence, 1980), p. 81.

15. David R. Wright, "The Villa Medici at Olmo a Castello: Its History and Iconography," Ph.D. diss., Princeton University, 1976), discusses the growing impact of tourism on villas.

16. Carocci, *Dintorni di Firenze*, 1:119–20.

17. *The Yale Edition of Horace Walpole's Correspondence*, ed. Wilmarth S. Lewis and Warren Hunting Smith, 48 vols. (New Haven, Conn., 1937–83), 24:190; see also 24:200, 305; 23:463–64, 468. Bargellini and du Prey, "Sources," p. 601, give these and other relevant quotations from the letters

of Horace Mann to Walpole, but owing to errors in the dating these passages should be checked against the published edition, which was not in print at the time our article appeared.

18. Vasari-Milanesi, *Vite*, 1:443, n. 1. This *viale* noted by Milanesi presumably corresponds to the "new road cut through the mountain" mentioned in a letter of 16 November 1776 from Horace Mann to Horace Walpole.

19. Bargellini and du Prey, "Sources," pp. 602, 605, go into Cecil Pinsent's alterations to the house and gardens, and p. 601, n. 22, discusses at length various routes of access to the villa. More recently, additional information has come to light on Pinsent in two articles: Erika Neubauer, "The Garden Architecture of Cecil Pinsent, 1884–1964," *Journal of Garden History* 3 (1983): 35–48; and Patrick Bowe, "Designs on the Tuscan Soil," *Country Life* 174 (July 1990): 90–95, who writes that Pinsent died a year earlier than stated by Neubauer. Plans, elevations, and sections dated 1924, documenting the work of Pinsent and Scott, were prepared by Norman J. Newton and appeared in an article by him, "Villa Medici at Fiesole," *Landscape Architecture* 27 (1927): 185–98.

20. More or less schematic and partial plans appear in Carl von Stegmann and Heinrich von Geymüller, *Die Architektur der Renaissance in Toscana*, 11 vols. (Munich, 1885–1908), 2:28–29, and in J. C. Shepherd and Geoffrey A. Jellicoe, *Italian Gardens of the Renaissance* (London, 1925). Newton's survey referred to in the previous note seems the most accurate of them all.

21. See Rossi, "Indole," p. 44, for the Alberti letter to Giovanni de' Medici published in Alberti's *Opera inedita et pauca separatim edita* (Florence, 1890).

22. Leon Battista Alberti, *On the Art of Building in Ten Books*, trans. Joseph Rykwert, Neil Leach, and Robert Tavernor (Cambridge, Mass., 1988), p. 385 (bk. 10, chap. 16).

23. Bargellini and du Prey, "Sources," p. 602, n. 29, for a reference of 1783 to the restoration of the chapel *a uso sacro*. The chapel in its present form and function is obviously eighteenth century in date and represents the work of Lady Orford and her heir and constant companion Giulio Mozzi. David R. Coffin remarked to me in conversation that the quasi-public placement of the chapel would be unusual by quattrocento standards.

24. Stegmann and Geymüller, *Architektur Toscana*, 2:29.

25. An illuminating discussion of quattrocento architects' preference for simple proportions related to musical intervals such as the octave is provided in Rudolf Wittkower, *Architectural Principles in the Age of Humanism*, 3d ed. (London, 1962).

26. The inscription is translated in Susan Horner and Joanna Horner, *Walks in Florence and Its Environs*, 2 vols. (London, 1884), 2:307, who relate that the owner at the time, the artist William Blundell Spence, discovered the two blocks of *pietra serena* in a cellar and reinstalled them near the eastern loggia. See also Patzak, *Palast und Villa*, 2:91, quoting from a 1776 letter of Angelo Maria Bandini, who had seen the inscription in the upper part of the villa.

27. Borsook, *Guide to Florence*, p. 346. Ackerman, *Villa*, p. 74, while stressing the absence of *all'antica* features in the Fiesole villa, claims it had "the first formal garden in the Renaissance to be conceived as an extension of the architecture."

28. The last record of Ginevra, the wife of Giovanni de' Medici, is a letter of 20 October 1476, written to her nephew Lorenzo from the villa at Trebbio. See Pieraccini, *Stirpe*, p. 88. Rossi, "Indole," p. 149, published Ginevra's will dated 25 April 1471. An inventory of 1482 listing Lorenzo's belongings at Fiesole is published in Philip Foster, *A Study of Lorenzo de' Medici's Villa at Poggio a Caiano*, 2 vols. (New York, 1978), 1:29. Foster also states on p. 211 that Lorenzo inherited Fiesole in 1469 when he came of age.

29. The translation is given in Roscoe, *Life of Lorenzo*, 2:190–91. For the Latin original, see Angelo Poliziano, *Angeli Politiani opera* (Basel, 1553), p. 135 (bk. 10, ep. 14). Ackerman, *Villa*, p. 77, n. 22, suggests the poem may date from either 1479 or 1483, years in which Poliziano is known to have been in residence at the Fiesole villa. Patzak, *Palast und Villa*, p. 89, supplied the year 1478, which is the date of the previous letter in the Poliziano collection but not necessarily of this letter. Patzak must be incorrect because the letter's concluding section refers to a wine tasting with Pico della Mirandola (1463–94), who would still have been very much below the drinking age at the time.

30. Foster, *Study of Poggio a Caiano*, 1:32, refers to a letter of 1475 requesting permission from Lorenzo de' Medici to see the Fiesole villa, so famous had it become as "a place well situated and created by human effort."

31. Ackerman, *Villa*, p. 77, quoting from Ficino's *Opera omnia* (Turin, 1959).

32. Roscoe, *Life of Lorenzo*, 2:183–85, translates Vieri's letter from the manuscript in the Laurentian Library. Foster, *Study of Poggio a Caiano*, 1:110, also quotes from it. He furthermore suggests that the arcaded podium or *basis villa* at Poggio a Caiano comes from Pliny's cryptoporticus.

33. The key source is Foster's *Study of Poggio a Caiano*, to which Ackerman, *Villa*, is indebted, as is the exhaustively illustrated book by Silvestro Bardazzi and Eugenio Cattellani, *La Villa Medicea di Poggio a Caiano*, 2 vols. (Prato, 1981).

34. Foster, *Study of Poggio a Caiano*, 1:117, and Ackerman, *Villa*, p. 79, who quotes the relevant passage from Alberti.

35. Quoted extensively in Roscoe, *Life of Lorenzo*, 2:186–87, where an English translation is provided: "Go on, Lorenzo, thou the muse's pride / Pierce the hard rock and scoop the mountain's side; / The distant streams shall hear thy potent call, / And the proud arch receive them as they fall. / Thence o'er the fields the genial waters lead, / That with luxuriant verdure crown the mead."

36. Philip Foster, "Lorenzo de' Medici's Cascina at Poggio a Caiano," *Mitteilungen des Kunsthistorischen Instituts in Florenz* 14 (1969–70): 47–56, first published Lorenzo's extraordinary model farm and dairy.

37. It is worth noting here that Giuliano da Sangallo provided a wooden model similar to Poggio a Caiano for the use of King Ferdinand I of Naples (see Ackerman, *Villa*, p. 290, n. 26, for a full bibliography). A connection of Poggio a Caiano and Lorenzo has also been drawn to Poggio Reale, the villa built outside Naples for Alfonso II in 1487 by the Florentine architect Giuliano da Maiano. The literature on this matter is extensive and is well summarized by Fritz-Eugen Keller, "Die Zeichnung Uffizi 363A von Baldassare Peruzzi und das Bad von Poggio Reale," *Architectura* 1 (1973): 22–35, and by George Hersey in the same issue (pp. 13–21). An apparently lost letter from Antonio Michiel described the extensive and possibly Pliny-inspired gardens. Keller intended to develop these links in an article on Pliny's villas, but he told me in 1987 that he had given up the idea, which is a pity. A recent addition to the literature is Linda Pellecchia, "Reconstructing the Greek House: Giuliano da Sangallo's Villa for the Medici in Florence," *Journal of the Society of Architectural Historians* 52 (1993): 323–28.

38. A useful compendium of all the early printed editions of Pliny's letters is given by Samuel Ball Platner, "Bibliography of the Younger Pliny," *Western Reserve University Bulletin* 1 (1895): 24–39. On the book collecting of Pope Leo X and his association with the younger Beroaldo, see William Roscoe, *The Life and Pontificate of Leo the Tenth*, 6 vols. (London, 1806). Stout, *Plinius*, pp. 367–68, gives the fascinating history of the purloined Corbie manuscript of Pliny's letters in the collection of Leo X. Stout, the great North American Pliny scholar of the early part of this century, was also dean of the University of Indiana and a dedicated bibliophile. This explains why the Lilly Library at Bloomington, Indiana, has one of the most extensive and complete holdings of Pliny incunables and other early printed editions. My thanks to the staff of the Lilly Library, especially Joel Silver, for making my visit there so pleasant and productive.

39. For a full transcription of the once-lost Raphael letter, see Philip Foster, "Raphael on the Villa Madama: The Text of a Lost Letter," *Römisches Jahrbuch für Kunstgeschichte* 11 (1967–68): 307–12, or Renato Lefevre, *Villa Madama* (Rome, 1973), pp. 52–60. I am grateful to James S. Ackerman for providing me with a typescript of a translation of the Raphael letter. Coffin, *Villa*, pp. 348–49, comments on Raphael's use of Latin sources and deals especially with the problem of the *D*- versus *O*-shaped courtyard described by Pliny.

40. Stout, *Plinius*, p. 76.

41. Christoph Luitpold Frommel, "Die Architektonische Planung der Villa Madama," *Römisches Jahrbuch für Kunstgeschichte* 15 (1975): 63, believes Leo X helped Giulio de' Medici pay for the Villa Madama with papal funds.

42. Lefevre, *Villa Madama,* p. 6. General agreement on the points in common between the Villa Madama and the Villa Medici, Fiesole, can be found in Christoph Luitpold Frommel, "La Villa Madame e la tipologia della villa romana nel rinascimento," *Bollettino del Centro Internazionale de Studi di Architettura "Andrea Palladio"* 11 (1969): 50, and in John Shearman, "A Functional Interpretation of Villa Madama," *Römisches Jahrbuch für Kunstgeschichte* 20 (1983): 316.

43. Shearman, "Functional Interpretation," pp. 318–23, has persuasively argued that the Villa Madama was altogether too big for purely private delectation. But it was ideally situated for a guest-house where those about to make a triumphal entry into Rome followed by a papal audience could rest and freshen up. It now serves such a guesthouse function for the Italian government.

44. Compare David R. Coffin, "The Plans of the Villa Madama," *Art Bulletin* 49 (1967): 111–22, who sees the drawings as post-Raphael, and Frommel, "Planung der Villa Madama," pp. 59–87, who sees them as pre-1520. Coffin, *Villa,* pp. 247–49, has been able to amplify his argument with the assistance of the Raphael letter.

45. Coffin, *Villa,* p. 247, first drew attention to the inscription and related it to Pliny. The most recent addition to the literature on this subject, G. Dewez, *Villa Madama: Memoria sul projetto di Raffaello* (Rome, 1990), provides a difficult-to-follow series of the author's drawings and his wooden model of 1984 that attempt to restitute the appearance of the Villa Madama based on the Uffizi drawings.

46. For the reconstruction of the inscription and its attribution to Antonio da Sangallo the Younger (1485–1546), see Frommel, "Planung der Villa Madama," pp. 74–75. Frommel would like to see this drawing later in the design process than I would, but in any event he places it before Raphael's death. My own inspection of the inscription on the verso, without benefit of ultraviolet light, has caused me to defer to Frommel, especially as concerns his reading of the word *Colunela.*

47. See the discussion of Harrison Boyd Ash, "I. Iuni Moderati Columellae Rei Rusticae Liber Decimus: De Cultu Hortorum: Text, Critical Apparatus, Translation," (Ph.D. diss., University of Pennsylvania, 1930), pp. 21–25. On the association copies of Columella in the Laurentian Library, see Bandini, *Catalogus Laurentinae,* 2:621, 623.

48. Coffin, "Villa Madama," p. 120, writes of "the possibility that there may have been a learned conceit behind the plans of the Villa Madama."

49. Coffin, *Villa,* p. 256, notes that Julius III visited the Villa Madama twice in 1550 before commencing his own Villa Giulia. Palladio studied both these villas, the only contemporary ones of which he is known to have left any record. See Howard Burns et al., *Andrea Palladio, 1508–1580: The Portico and the Farmyard* (London, 1975), pp. 88–89, 264–65, which discusses Palladio's drawing of the Villa Madama and an elevation for the circular courtyard attributed to Raphael's atelier. On p. 196 the connection is made between the 1554 visit of Palladio to the Villa Giulia and the nymphaeum at his Villa Barbaro, Maser (the similarity had already occurred to Vasari during Palladio's lifetime). Douglas Lewis, *The Drawings of Andrea Palladio* (Washington, D.C., 1981), pp. 55–56, has given the most detailed scrutiny to the physical state of Palladio's Villa Madama drawing, presumably to be associated with his 1541 trip to Rome.

50. Coffin, "Villa Madama," p. 111, cites the anecdote regarding the destruction of the Villa Madama as recorded by Paolo Giovio.

51. Most of these points have been made by Earl E. Rosenthal, *The Palace of Charles V in Granada* (Princeton, N.J., 1985), pp. 22, 162, but he does not follow up on the Raphael letter as the most likely link between Pliny's villas, on the one hand, and the Villa Madama and Granada palace on the other. Rosenthal, p. 252, muddies the waters somewhat by introducing as an alternative source the Teatro Marittimo at Hadrian's villa. Foster, "Raphael Letter," p. 309, discusses the copy of the letter Castiglione had in his possession by 1522.

52. The following are some notes regarding eighteenth- and nineteenth-century French and British student architects, for whom the Villa Madama became a sort of Mecca. The earliest record I have found was compiled by John Soane and Thomas Hardwick in 1778. See my article "Soane and Hardwick in Rome: A Neo-classical Partnership," *Architectural History* 15 (1972): 51–67. Unlike that of Soane

and Hardwick, the partnership of the Frenchmen Charles Percier and Pierre Fontaine, established in Rome in 1786, lasted their lifetimes. Their Villa Madama studies were published in their book *Choix des plus célèbres maisons de plaisance de Rome et de ses environs* (Paris, 1809). Adolphe Goujon visited the villa in 1833 and has left some of his measured drawings. Charles Rohault de Fleury came at least twice: once on an October morning in 1842 for only an hour, and the second time in mid-May 1858 for a more extensive stay. In 1826 Jules-Frédéric Bouchet produced some evocative watercolors of the villa, and he later went on to attempt a restitution of Pliny's Laurentinum (see chap. 3). This partial list of French material is based upon my research among the following drawings in the Académie d'Architecture in Paris: no. 132 (drawings by Goujon and Henri Labrouste); nos. 418, 425 (two albums by Rohault de Fleury); no. 9 (four drawings by Bouchet). I am most grateful to Mme de Vauchier for help in consulting this uncataloged collection. An additional cluster of French studies in the second half of the century forms the subject of n. 60 below.

53. On Cormier see Phyllis Lambert's entry in the *Macmillan Encyclopedia of Architects*, 4 vols. (New York, 1982), 1:452–53, and idem, "Architecture Where Cultures Meet," in *Ernest Cormier and the Université de Montréal*, ed. Isabelle Gournay (Montreal, 1990), pp. 17–29.

54. CCA, Cormier Archive, dossier marked "British School at Rome," contains the draft letter sent by Cormier to Evelyn Shaw in London, dated 1 July 1916. Similarly dated is the progress report with its attached "List of Work Done." On 2 November 1914, Shaw wrote to the director of the British School in Rome, Thomas Ashby, to expect the arrival of Cormier at the end of that year. This letter was kindly communicated to me by the archivist of the British School, Valerie Stott, during my stay there in June 1988. She also supplied me with references from three *Annual Reports to the Subscribers, Faculty of Archaeology, History, and Letters;* that is, those of 1914–15 (p. 3), 1915–16 (p. 3); and 1916–17 (p. 2). These reports note Cormier's arrival in January 1915, his activities during 1915–16, and his departure at Christmas 1916. The second of the three reports states: "In the course of his work Mr. Cormier has made many valuable discoveries and has been able to make much clearer the original plans [of the Villa Madama]. . . . It is to be hoped that his results may be published hereafter in our *Papers*." This never came to pass.

55. The history of the Villa Madama's acquisition, restoration, and partial enlargement by Bergès is carefully documented and illustrated in Lefevre, *Villa Madama*, pp. 213–30, without benefit of additional information provided by Cormier, whose involvement is not mentioned.

56. Snapshot-sized photographs are all that appear to survive of Cormier's rendered northwest facade elevation and his section along the main axis of the villa. A drawing of the northeast elevation, the one facing the Tiber, appears exhibited against a wall in a photo Cormier took of his apartment at 55 Via Flaminia. The references to these three images is CCA, Cormier Archive, no. 207, 3(RE)66 207, file marked "Villa Madama," and APO 1:P-6353. Cormier's daily progress on his drawings is recorded on three sheets in ARV-1/-D-1.

57. The Percier and Fontaine plate in question is in CCA, Cormier Archive, no. 336 xx, R/A/12. The plan, Cormier's own that is related to it, and two of his measured studies of the Villa Madama were exhibited by me at the Musée des Beaux-Arts de Montréal in the 1983 exhibition "The Villas of Pliny and Classical Architecture in Montreal."

58. Cormier's extensive textual notes and references to secondary sources are found in CCA, Cormier Archive, ARV-1/D-1, which lists the books he consulted for the Villa Madama project.

59. Fols. 2 and 3 recto of Cormier's "Memorandum Tablet" notebook in the CCA, Cormier Archive, ARV-1/-D-1, single out his reading of the 1873 Berlin edition of Gustave Meyer's *Lehrbuch der schönen Gartenkunst . . .* , with special reference to Pliny. Fol. 9 recto makes it clear that the notebook was in use while Cormier was in Rome. Meyer included his own restitution plan of the Tuscan Villa (see appendix 4).

60. Most of the tracings, photographs, and photostats mentioned here are contained in the CCA, Cormier Archive, no. 207, 3(RE)66. Other tracings are in no. 704, 5(RO) C4. The five lantern slides, however, are in P-4 and are still in the original box and wrappers supplied by the Milanese firm of C. Cappelli. The photographs sent from Paris relate to the illustrations of Bénard's Villa Madama

restitution of 1871 published in Hector D'Espouy, *Fragments d'architecture du Moyen Age et de la Renaissance d'après les relevés et restaurations des anciens pensionnaires de l'Académie de France à Rome,* 2 vols. (Paris 1897–1928), vol. 1, figs. 25–30. This book also illustrates samples from the Villa Madama studies by the French students Charles Questel, François-Philippe Boitte, and Pierre-Joseph Esquie, the grand prix recipient in 1882. Bénard's restitution drawings of the villa are illustrated in David van Zanten's contribution to *The Architecture of the Ecole des Beaux-Arts,* ed. Arthur Drexler (New York, 1976), pp. 291 ff. At an earlier date, while a student of David Coffin's, van Zanten himself had drawn the schematic plan of the Villa Madama, which is reproduced here as my fig. 18.

61. In Gournay, *Ernest Cormier,* p. 19 and figs. 1–2, Phyllis Lambert implies a connection between the Cormier house and the Villa Madama by discussing them on the same page and illustrating them side by side. The Cormier house is well illustrated in articles by Susan May Alsop, "Architectural Digest Visits: Pierre Trudeau," *Architectural Digest* 43 (January 1986): 106–13, and Geoffrey Simmins, "Ernest Cormier," *City and Country Home* 6 (December 1987): 50–64. In an exchange of letters and telephone calls with me in September 1990, Pierre Elliott Trudeau expressed himself as intrigued by the resemblances between the Villa Madama and the Cormier house.

Chapter Three

1. Rudolf Wittkower, *Art and Architecture in Italy, 1600 to 1750,* 2d ed. (Harmondsworth, Eng., 1965), p. 78; see also n. 18 below.

2. Alessandro Certini, *Vita di S. Crescentiano martire e protettore di Città di Castello* (Foligno, 1709), p. 17.

3. Francesco Ignazio Lazzari, *Serie de' vescovi e breve notizia del sito . . . governo, santi prelati . . . e persone nobile di Città di Castello* (Foligno, 1693), p. 8. The reference reads: "Plinio edificio . . . in luogo detto . . . Pliniano ora Pitigliano, una deliciosa villa." The book was reprinted at Bologna in 1975. The manuscript in DO is pressmarked F-3-4. It is within a vellum-bound folder bearing the bookplate of Mildred Bliss, which indicates a purchase in the 1950s according to what former DO director Elisabeth Blair McDougall told me in a midair conversation over Poland. The twenty-seven-folio text is titled "Discrizione della Pianta, e delle Altezze della Villa Pliniana, che C. Plinio Giuniore detto il Nipote haveva nel Territorio di Tiferno, hora Città di Castello." The similarly titled copy in the Biblioteca Comunale "G. Carducci" in Città di Castello is a neater paper-bound, thirty-two-folio version bearing the pressmarks MS 654 and VII. 6b. 44. In these two manuscripts, fols. 15 verso and 11 verso, respectively, refer to the Vatican colonnades. The manuscripts are virtually identical in content, but a significant passage added with a caret on fol. 7 of the DO version is included as an integral part of the text on fol. 6 verso of the Città di Castello version, perhaps indicating a later date. This hypothesis is strengthened by the eight generally less neat though twice as numerous illustrations in the DO version. The references to the *Serie* occur on fol. 13 verso and fol. 10 recto, respectively. Finally, a full manuscript of the *Serie* is to be found in the BSGCDC, pressmarked 62B.

4. BSGCDC, manuscript volume titled "Istoria genealogica de trenta tre famiglie di Città di Castello Abozzata da Me, Don Alessandro Certini." About midway through this unpaginated volume is the family tree of the Lazzari and biographical information on its members. The family tree erroneously gives Francesco Ignazio Lazzari's birth date as 1650, but the baptismal record of the cathedral of Città di Castello for the years 1630–36 (no. 3368 in Archivio Vescovile collection, also housed in the BSGCDC) gives the correct date as 26 December 1633. I owe the thorough search for this information to the knowledgeable assistance of the archivist and librarian of the BSGCDC, Beniamino Schivo.

5. Giovanni Muzi, *Memorie ecclesiastiche di Città di Castello,* 5 vols. (Città di Castello, 1842–43), 3:114, and 1:256–57 respectively. From Muzi's passing remarks comes the mistaken belief, reported in the current Touring Club d'Italia guidebook to Umbria, that Lazzari designed the entire facade of the cathedral in 1632, the year before his birth.

6. The DO manuscript speaks of the "Villa dei Pitigliano cioe Pliniano" (fol. 3 verso), and its mate in Città di Castello uses the same words on fol. 3 recto.

7. Florence, Palazzo Vecchio, *Mostra del giardino italiano,* ed. Alfredo Lensi and Ugo Ojetti (Florence, 1931), p. 62. It is described as being by an unknown seventeenth-century artist. The same gallery in the exhibition displayed the recent drawings of the Villa Medici at Fiesole by Norman Newton (see chap. 2) and a Laurentine Villa restitution by a living architect named Guido Carafa, whom I have not been able to trace. I owe this exhibition catalog reference to David R. Coffin and Jacques de Faramond. The latter I thank especially for putting me back on the track of the Lazzari drawing, which he owned in 1983 when I first saw his photograph of it.

8. After the drawing's sale by Jacques de Faramond to the New York City dealers Stubbs Books and Prints, it was advertised by them in 1988 and sold in the spring of that year. Nancy Rosen greatly assisted me in reaching the private collector who now owns the drawing.

9. DO, Lazzari MS, fol. 9 verso (the corresponding reference in the Città di Castello MS is fol. 7 recto). The passage reads, "I leave until the end Colle [Plinio] a community near Pitigliano . . . at which spot . . . exist all the conditions described by Pliny at his villa, and I affirm it would have been . . . where stands the present villa of Cavaliere Girolamo Brozzi."

10. The references to "qualche pezzo di muro" are DO, Lazzari MS, fol. 11 verso and fols. 8 verso and 9 recto in the Città di Castello MS. Fol. 5 in each manuscript refers to a pair of Priapus statuettes belonging to Lazzari's brother Alessandro, the rector of San Giovanni at Montione, in the grounds of which they had been unearthed. As a matter of interest, the Lazzari tradition of archaeology was continued by the local historian Giovanni Magherini Graziani, owner of the Villa Graziani, who probably had knowledge of the Lazzari manuscript and may even have owned one of the copies of it. Graziani's *Storia di Città di Castello* (Città di Castello, 1890), p. 115, n. 2, reports having seen Pliny-related ruins and inscriptions at the Colle Plinio site.

11. The association between Pliny and this site at Colle Plinio has been widely hinted at in the scholarly and even the popular literature. Geoffrey Bret Harte's curious book *The Villas of Pliny: A Study of the Pastimes of a Roman Gentleman* (Boston, 1928) has the interest of illustrating five antique portrait busts purporting to come from an excavation of Pliny's villa. At the time Harte wrote they were in the collections of Marchese Bufalini at Città di Castello and San Giustino.

12. Daniela Monacchi, "Colle Plinio: Relazione della campagna 1979," in *Villa e insediamenti rustici d'età romana in Umbria* (Perugia, 1983), pp. 11–44, made the 1979 excavation report. She acknowledges the Lazzari manuscript and the speculations of Giovanni Magherini Graziani. For information about more recent campaigns at Colle Plinio I have had to rely on the preliminary reports of the Soprintendenza's director of excavations, Laura Bonomi Ponsi. Brief articles by her appeared in the October 1987 issue of *Archeologia* and in the *Rassegna d'Arte Altotiberina* in late 1984. Most recently a number of photocopied documents were distributed in the context of the 1 April 1990 conference at San Giustino, " 'In Tuscis:' Ricerche sulla proprietà di Plinio il giovane nell'alta valle del Tevere." Most of this information and copies of clippings from the popular press were made available to me thanks to the kindness of the cultural services officer of San Giustino, Giovanna Pucci. She also accompanied me to see the artifacts from the Pliny dig now arranged—very appropriately, I might add—adjacent to the Villa Graziani at Celalba.

13. See Giuseppe Rocco Volpi, *Vetus Latium profanum et sacrum,* 11 vols. (Rome, 1704–45), 6:50. Published in Rome in 1734, this volume refers to Philipp Cluver's *Italia antica* (Leyden, 1634) and Lucas Holsten's *Annotationes in geographiam sacrum . . . Italiam antiquan Cluverii et thesaurum geographicum Ortelii* (Rome, 1666).

14. Fra Marcello is sometimes confused in the literature with his father the marchese Matteo Sacchetti. I thank their descendant, the present marchese Giulio Sacchetti, for sending me the correct information and for according me access to his family archives in Rome. Malcolm Campbell told me about the absence of Pliny imagery in any of Cortona's subjects painted for the Sacchetti brothers' villa.

15. The naturalist count Luigi Ferdinando Marsili's *Dissertatio de generatione fungorum* (Rome,

1714) contains Lancisi's twenty-seven-page contribution titled "Dissertatio de Plinianae villae ruderibus atque Ostiensis litoris incremento."

16. Lancisi, "Dissertatio," pp. xxiii–xxiv. Lancisi has relatively little to say about Pliny's villa. Nevertheless, his botanical description of the seacoast is the starting point for speculations about the alluvial buildup on the shore and its effect on plant life. Moreover, his fleeting eyewitness report on the excavated ruins is among the earliest quasi-archaeological evidence to have come down in relation to either of Pliny's villas.

17. Volpi, *Vetus Latium*, 6:52. Father Leonard Boyle, *prefetto* of the Vatican Library, aided my fruitless search for the elusive Sacchetti excavation report. Neither copy of the plan could be located by Pedro José Marquez when he searched for them in preparation for his Pliny book in the 1790s (see n. 28 below). I was not able to consult the Biblioteca Lancisiana, bequeathed by Dr. Lancisi to the Ospedale Santo Spirito in Rome, where some additional information might be found.

18. Lancisi, "Dissertatio," p. xxiii. In his day the Magenta plan was in the private library of Pope Clement XI Albani. For more on Magenta, see n. 1 above.

19. Useful studies on the significance of Lancisi's writings in the broader context are Giovanni Alberto Fabrici, *Ioannes Albertus Fabricii biblioteca latina nunc melius delecta*, 3 vols. (Leipzig, 1773–74), 2:416–17; Carlo Fea, *Relazione di un viaggio ad Ostia e alla villa di Plinio detta Laurentino* (Rome, 1802), pp. 66–78; and most recently, Pierre Pinon and Maurice Culot, eds., *La Laurentine et l'invention de la villa romaine* (Paris, 1982), p. 48, nn. 72, 74, and p. 70.

20. Dottoressa Ricotti graciously sent me her publications, including "La Villa Magna a Grotte de Piastra," in *Castelporziano I: Campagna di scavo e di restauro 1984* (Rome, 1985), pp. 53–66. Page 56 makes special reference to the Sacchetti dig.

21. For a full discussion of the *bolli* she found and the various styles of mosaic pavement, see Eugenia Salza Prina Ricotti, "Il Laurentino: Scavi del 1985," in *Castelporziano II: Campagna di scavo e di restauro, 1985–86* (Rome, 1986), pp. 45–56.

22. Eugenia Salza Prina Ricotti, "The Importance of Water in Roman Garden Triclinia," in *Ancient Roman Villa Gardens: The Tenth Dumbarton Oaks Colloquium on the History of Landscape Architecture* (Washington, D.C., 1987), pp. 137–84. See esp. pp. 182–84, where Ricotti sums up her earlier findings and postulates the reasons for the possible disappearance of Pliny's triclinium. But on this same point, see Thomas Ashby, *The Roman Campagna in Classical Times* (London, 1927), p. 211.

23. Rodolfo Amadeo Lanciani, *Wanderings in the Roman Campagna* (Boston, 1909), p. 306. On the merits of Lanciani as opposed to Canina, see Eugenia Salza Prina Ricotti, "La cosi detta Villa Magna il Laurentinum di Plinio il giovane," *Atti della Accademia Nazionale dei Lincei: Rendiconti* 39 (1984): 339–58.

24. Eugenia Salza Prina Ricotti, "Sul terrazzo odoroso di viole: La scoperta della villa di Plinio il giovane," *Archeo attualità del passato* 54 (August 1989): 34–43; see especially the final page. Ricotti, "Laurentino 1985," p. 56, had concluded in much the same way.

25. Pedro José Marquez, *Delle ville di Plinio il giovane* (Rome, 1796), pp. 31, 171, mentions Perez and Petit-Radel. Petit-Radel was brother of the architect Louis and canon of Couserans. He eventually published *Recherches sur les monuments cyclopéens ou pélagiques* (Paris, 1841), in which he mentioned his friendship with Marquez.

26. The biographical details of Marquez and his bibliography are given in Julio Orozco Muñoz, *Pedro José Marquez: Su vida y su obra* (Mexico City, 1941), and are somewhat amplified in Justino Fernández, "Pedro José Marquez en el recuerdo y en la critica," *Anales del Instituto de Investigaciones Esteticas* 32 (1963): 5–19. I am indebted to Clara Bargellini for making these publications available to me. Regarding Marquez and his Roman circle, see Pinon and Culot, *Laurentine*, p. 77, n. 12, and p. 113.

27. Marquez, *Ville di Plinio,* pp. 117–19.

28. Ibid., pp. 3–5, quotes Volpi (see nn. 13 and 17 above), and p. 32 goes into the search by Marquez for the Sacchetti excavation plan.

29. Ibid., pp. 6, 8, 15, and 41–42 for Marquez on *D* vs. *O*.

30. Ibid., p. 2.

31. Carlos Sambricio, *Silvestre Perez arquitecto de la ilustración* (San Sebastian, 1975), pp. 51–53, provides a chronology, and fig. 61 is reminiscent of the style of the Tuscan Villa vignette. The tireless efforts of Enrique Muga in San Sebastián finally turned up this publication for me. In Madrid the staff of the Accademia di San Fernando gave me access to Perez's drawings on very short notice.

32. Helen Tanzer, *The Villas of Pliny the Younger* (New York, 1924), pp. 118–21, is fond of Marquez's Tuscan Villa plan despite its discrepancies and prefers it to his Laurentine Villa scheme, which she discusses on pp. 60–62.

33. Sambricio, *Silvestre Perez,* p. 51, records the patronage of Azara and the Maecenas project of Perez without relating them.

34. Marquez, *Ville di Plinio,* p. 82.

35. Werner Oechslin, "Luigi Canina," in *Macmillan Encyclopedia of Architects,* 4 vols. (New York, 1982), 1:374. Oechslin writes a perceptive appreciation of Canina and notes that at the time of his death he received eulogies not only at home but abroad.

36. See Carroll L. V. Meeks, *Italian Architecture, 1750–1914* (New Haven, Conn., 1966), figs. 44, 46, and 48, which illustrates three Canina garden buildings at the Villa Borghese in Rome, each representing one of Canina's three fundamental styles.

37. Luigi Canina, *L'architettura romana descritta e dimonstrata coi monumenti,* atlas volume (Rome, 1840), pp. 786–94. Tanzer, *Villas of Pliny,* p. 75, agrees with Canina on the choice of the *D*-shaped courtyard.

38. Lanciani, *Wanderings,* p. 306.

39. Canina, *Architettura romana,* pp. 794–96.

40. Luigi Canina, *Gli edifici di Roma antica e sua campagna. . . . Edifici dei contorni della città,* 6 vols. (Rome, 1848–56), 5:208–10.

41. Canina, *Edifici di Roma,* 6:793–94.

42. See Tilman-François Suys and Louis-Pierre Haudebourt, *Le Palais Massimi à Rome* (Paris, 1818).

43. Désiré Raoul-Rochette and Jules-Frédéric Bouchet, *Pompéi* (Paris, 1828–30), and François Mazois, *Les ruines de Pompéi: Seconde partie. Habitations* (Paris, 1824). Apropos of this, Louis-Pierre Haudebourt, *Le Laurentin maison de campagne de Pline le jeune restituée d'après la description de Pline* (Paris, 1838), p. 22, wrote: "Je n'aurais pas osé me présenter dans la lice, si je n'avais pas sur mes devanciers l'avantage d'avoir vu Pompéi et étudié ses antiques maisons" (I would not have dared present myself in the lists had I not had the advantage over my predecessors of having seen Pompeii and studied its ancient houses).

44. Haudebourt, *Laurentin,* p. 61, mentions the excavation report by the librarian of Prince Agostino Chigi, Carlo Fea, in his *Relazione,* pp. 67–73, especially with reference to bricks discovered at the site. Fea's somewhat obsequious text—comparable to Lancisi's addressed to his patron Marcello Sacchetti—nevertheless recounts quite comprehensively various attempts to identify the Laurentine ruins.

45. Haudebourt, *Laurentin,* p. 216.

46. Ibid., pp. 66–67, 232. Haudebourt mentioned Odesius by name.

47. Ibid., p. 158. By calling himself a Gaul, Haudebourt becomes a veritable Dr. Who of the nineteenth century.

48. François Mazois, *Le Palais de Scaurus, ou Description d'une maison romaine . . .* (Paris, 1819).

49. Haudebourt, *Laurentin,* p. 98, n. 1. But he claims that de Sacy regarded the *D* solution as the most commonly accepted, which my study shows was demonstrably not the case up until the time of Haudebourt and Canina.

50. Ibid., p. 196.

51. Biographical details on the Haudebourts may be found in Michaud's nineteenth-century *Biographie universelle,* which is particularly rich on Mme Haudebourt-Lescot. In suggesting her as a possible influence on the painterly quality of *Le Laurentin,* I am nonetheless aware of the debt the book owes to the style and format of Mazois's publications.

52. See Donald Drew Egbert, *The Beaux-Arts Tradition in French Architecture Illustrated by the Grands Prix de Rome,* ed. David van Zanten (Princeton, N.J., 1980), p. 180, and the references to the 1824 Grand Prix de Rome competition in Neil Levine's contribution to *The Beaux-Arts and Nineteenth-Century French Architecture,* ed. Robin Middleton (Cambridge, Mass., 1982), pp. 67–123.

53. The 1850 Paris Salon included Bouchet's Laurentine plan, aerial perspective, elevation, cross section, atrium, and tablinum interiors, all of which reappear in presumably much the same form in Jules-Frédéric Bouchet, *Le Laurentin maison de campagne de Pline le consul* (Paris, 1852). But the plan described in the 1853 Salon *livret* as an "essai de restitution de la villa de Pline le consul, en Toscane" has so far not come to light. See the *livrets* of those years: *Explication des ouvrages de peinture, sculpture, architecture, gravure et lithographie des artistes vivants,* pp. 294, 282. I was able to ascertain that the Bouchet drawings in the Musée Vivenel in Compiègne do not relate to either of his Pliny villa restitutions.

54. Compare, for example, Bouchet, *Laurentin,* p. 21 (which, to be fair, calls Haudebourt *celui à qui je dois le plus*), with Haudebourt, *Laurentin,* p. 61.

55. Graham Smith, *The Casino of Pius IV* (Princeton, N.J., 1977), pp. 20–23. An analogy between the casino and the "Laurentina court" was drawn by Wolfgang Lotz in Ludwig Heydenreich and Wolfgang Lotz, *Architecture in Italy, 1400–1600* (Harmondsworth, Eng., 1974), p. 265, and p. 381, n. 8.

56. Bouchet, *Laurentin,* p. 20.

57. Johann Bernhard Fischer von Erlach's *Entwurf einer historischen Architektur* (Vienna, 1721) appears to be the first instance of an arrangement of architectural illustrations in this manner. Bouchet's Laurentine restitution plan had a certain influence in its own right. In a simplified form it was reproduced in conjunction with the discussion of the Laurentine and Tuscan villas in A. Ammann and Charles Garnier's *L'habitation humaine* (Paris, 1892), p. 569. Their passages on the Tuscan Villa (pp. 568–70) are without illustration.

58. This passage is quoted by Pinon and Culot, *Laurentine,* p. 67, to whom I owe the obscure reference to Johann Joachim Winckelmann's *Lettres familières,* ed. H. Jansen, 2 vols. (Amsterdam, 1781), 2:206. See especially Jansen's note to this letter. I have used the modern scholarly edition: Johann Joachim Winckelmann, *Briefe,* ed. Hans Diepolder and Walther Rehm, 4 vols. (Berlin, 1952–57), 3:344–49. The original letter is now presumed lost.

59. The document sent to Catherine of Russia by Clérisseau is quoted in full and illustrated with the relevant drawings in Thomas J. McCormick, *Charles-Louis Clérisseau and the Genesis of Neoclassicism* (Cambridge, Mass., 1990), pp. 179–90, 213–16. But McCormick does not mention the Winckelmann letter to Clérisseau (see previous note) concerning the Laurentine Villa, nor does he make any connection between it and the drawings for Catherine.

60. Winckelmann, *Briefe,* 2:170–71. The original letter of 28 July 1761, now in Zurich, refers to "Krusasius," whom the editors at first misidentify (p. 435) and then reidentify correctly as Krubsacius (p. 539).

61. Ibid., 2:177–81, letter no. 442, dated to late September 1761. See also Johann Joachim Winckelmann, *Geschichte der Kunst des Altertums* (Dresden, 1764), p. 313.

62. Rudolf Berliner, "Zeichnungen von Carlo und Filippo Marchionni: Ein Beitrag zur Kunst- und Kulturgeschichte Roms im 18. Jahrhundert," *Münchener Jahrbuch der Bildenden Kunst* 9–10 (1958–59): 267–396. Although a number of Carlo Marchionni's designs for the Albani villas in Rome and at Anzio are illustrated, none has an unmistakably Plinian iconography.

63. Johann Jacob Volkmann, *Historisch-kritische Nachrichten von Italien,* 2d ed., 3 vols. (Leipzig, 1777), 2:938, mentions Pliny villa restitutions in a passage about Ostia and on p. 885 compares the Villa Albani to the Laurentine Villa. A similar comparison occurs in Abbé Jérôme Richard's *Description historique et critique de l'Italie . . . ,* 2d ed., 6 vols. (Paris, 1769), 6:219–20, recording impressions of a visit in 1762 and twice referring to the Villa Albani's garden colonnade as a *xiste*—that is, a *xystus* as mentioned by Pliny. Both references were drawn to my attention by David R. Coffin, *Gardens and Gardening in Papal Rome* (Princeton, N.J., 1991), pp. 164–69. Professor Coffin wrote to me about his conviction that the Villa Albani was designed with the Plinian models in mind.

64. This letter of 2 April 1767 to Baron Philipp von Stosch and a subsequent one of 6 February

1768 to J. M. Francke are conflated by Carl Justi in *Winckelmann und seine Zeitgenossen*, 3d ed., 3 vols. (Leipzig, 1923), 3:400–401. See Winkelmann, *Briefe*, 3:244–46 and 365–67.

65. See Adolf Heinrich Borbein, "Klassische Archäologie in Berlin von 18. bis 20. Jahrhundert," in *Berlin und die Antike*, Aufsätze volume (Berlin, 1979), pp. 99–150, esp. 106–11.

66. I refer to the 1762 Leipzig first edition of the *Anmerkungen*, pp. 40, 47, in which mention is made of the cryptoporticus and of the vaulting of the Laurentine Villa. Winckelmann stated that he used the 1669 Johannes Veenhusius edition of Pliny published in Lyons, the town where the first edition ever recorded was mentioned in a Pliny letter as being on sale (bk. 9, ep. 11).

67. Aloys Ludwig Hirt, *Die Geschichte der Baukunst bei den Alten* (Berlin, 1821–27), p. 294. Hirt's pedimented Frederick the Great mausoleum is described in the Berlin Academy 1797 exhibition catalog as a "länglichen Tempel mit Pronaos . . . ganz um das Gebäude laufen [den] freye[n] Säulengänge[n]" (as quoted by Jutta von Simson, "Friderico Secundo Patria: Antikenrezeption in den Entwürfen zum Denkmal Friedrichs des Grossen in Berlin," in *Berlin und die Antike*, Aufsätze volume [Berlin, 1979], p. 381).

68. Hirt, *Geschichte*, p. 300.

69. Ibid., pp. 316–18.

70. Hirt's influence on the direction of German classicism is noted by David Watkin and Tilman Mellinghof, *German Architecture and the Classical Ideal, 1740–1840* (London, 1987), pp. 60–61.

71. Karl Friedrich Schinkel, *Architektonisches Album*, no. 7 (Berlin, 1841), p. 2. The editorial note is unsigned but may be by Schinkel. Tanzer, *Villas of Pliny*, p. 124, argues that Schinkel's Tuscan design owes much to Hirt's. I disagree with her except as regards the plan.

72. On Schinkel's reactions to Italy, see Gottfried Riemann, "Schinkel begegnet der Antike: Eindrücke 1803/04 in Italien," in *Karl Friedrich Schinkel und der Antike: Beiträge der Winckelmann Gesellschaft* 12 (1985): 7–10. The primary source material has been conveniently gathered together in the volume titled *Karl Friedrich Schinkel: Reisen nach Italien. Tagebücher. Briefe. Zeichnungen. Aquarelle* (Berlin, 1982).

73. The dated drawing by Schinkel (SA, S.175 M40ᶜ, no. 71) is a preparatory one of the Pliny *stibadium*, published as a color lithograph in Schinkel, *Architektonisches Album* (see fig. 182). The entire Pliny suite is discussed in the exhibition catalog *Karl Friedrich Schinkel, 1781–1841* (Berlin, 1982), pp. 348–53. A more recent catalog, Michael Snodin, ed., *Karl Friedrich Schinkel: A Universal Man* (New Haven, 1991), has less to say about the Pliny villa restitutions. See also Eva Börsch-Supan, "Friedrich Wilhelm IV und das antike Landhaus," in *Berlin und die Antike*, Aufsätze volume (Berlin, 1979), pp. 491–94, who places much of the initiative for the Pliny revival on the shoulders of the crown prince, the future Friedrich Wilhelm IV. Finally, a very useful register to the Pliny-related drawings in the Schinkel Archive can be found in Goerd Peschken, *Das Architektonische Lehrbuch* (Munich, 1979), pp. 173–77. Gottfried Riemann acted as my helpful guide through the intricacies of the Schinkel Archive.

74. In certain details my figure 42 is not as close to the color lithograph of 1841 (fig. 5) as is the drawing SA, S.175 M.XL., no. 84. I take this other drawing to be a slightly later and less expertly drawn copy of the one illustrated here. Peschken, *Lehrbuch*, p. 177, claims that the later drawing is part of a set prepared for the crown prince.

75. SA, S.178 M.XL., no. 68, is a slightly modified freehand plan at ground-floor level, which may be in the hand of the crown prince according to Peschken, *Lehrbuch*, p. 176.

76. Manfred Sundermann, interview with me at Munster, 8 July 1987, and idem, "Das Tuscum des Plinius," in *Deutsche Akademie Villa Massimo in Rom, 1983–1984* (Rome, 1984).

77. In fact the color lithograph (fig. 6) is closer to the copy of the plan in the Schinkel Archive, S.175 M.XL., no. 85. Not illustrated here, it was apparently one of those prepared for the crown prince. The main discrepancy is the inclusion in this version of two boats beached on the shoreline.

78. I have written on this particular casino type of plan in my *John Soane: The Making of an Architect* (Chicago, 1982), pp. 265–76, and more recently in "The Bombé Fronted Country House from Talman to Soane," *Studies in the History of Art* 25 (1989): 29–49.

79. A mate to this drawing is SA, S.175 M.XL.ᶜ, no. 75. It is virtually identical except for an application of gouache to the waves and a slight hesitancy in the depiction of the sailboat.

80. The Bigelman sketchbook in CCA, DR 1984:1636: 6 recto, contains sketches of three early Christian chapels next to San Gregorio Magno on the Celian Hill in Rome (see my fig. 143). See also my earlier remarks on Bigelman's possible sources—before I had seen this sketchbook—in "The Villas of Pliny: Reflections on the Exhibition by Its Guest Curator," *Fifth Column* 4 (1983–84): 21–24. Bigelman is the subject of a discussion in the conclusion and next to last chapter of this book.

Chapter Four

1. The best of the scant bibliography on Scamozzi is Franco Barbieri's monograph, *Vincenzo Scamozzi* (Vicenza, 1952), and the article on him by Douglas Lewis, "Vincenzo Scamozzi," in *Macmillan Encyclopedia of Architects,* 4 vols. (New York, 1982), 3:667–72. I have yet to see the very recent Cornell University doctoral dissertation written on Scamozzi under the supervision of Martin Kubelik.

2. See Tommaso Temanza, *Vite dei più celebri architetti, e scultori veneziani* (Venice, 1778), p. 472. Inigo Jones railed against the "ignorance and malice of Scamotzio against Paladio" in an undated remark written in the margin of Jones's copy of *I quattro libri dell'architettura,* preserved at Worchester College, Oxford (see bk. 3, chap. 17, p. 34). On Jones's ownership of *L'idea* (also in Worchester College) see John Harris and Gordon Higgott, *Inigo Jones: Complete Architectural Drawings* (New York, 1989), p. 72.

3. Vincenzo Scamozzi, *L'idea dell'architettura universale,* 2 vols. (Venice, 1615), pt. 1, bk. 3, chap. 12, pp. 261–68.

4. Ibid., pt. 1, bk. 3, chap. 22, p. 322.

5. Ibid., pt. 1, bk. 3, chap. 2, p. 224.

6. Barbieri, *Scamozzi,* p. 186. Helen Tanzer, *The Villas of Pliny the Younger* (New York, 1924), p. 50, points out some of the drawbacks to Scamozzi's restitution and tries to compensate for them by supplying a key to identifying the parts of the villa in the woodcut. See also Pierre Pinon and Maurice Culot, eds., *La Laurentine et l'invention de la villa romaine* (Paris, 1982), p. 104.

7. François Mazois, *Le Palais de Scaurus, ou Description d'une maison romaine . . .* (Paris, 1819), published Scamozzi's entire Laurentine text in an appendix. In the Italian translation published in Milan in 1825 under the title *Il Palazzo de Scauro, ossia Descrizione d'una casa romana . . . ,* the translator added the Pliny letter to Gallus in Italian (pp. 199–208).

8. See Robin Middleton, "Jean-François Félibien des Avaux," in *Macmillan Encyclopedia of Architects,* 4 vols. (New York, 1982), 2:50.

9. Jean-François Félibien des Avaux, *Recueil historique de la vie et des ouvrages des plus célèbres architectes,* 2d ed. (Paris, 1696), pp. 102–3.

10. Claude Le Peletier [or Le Pelletier], *Comes rusticus, ex optimus latinae linguae scriptoribus excerptus* (Paris, 1692). This small octavo volume came out in a second edition in 1708. Marianne Fischer, "Die frühen Rekonstruktionen der Landhäuser Plinius' des jüngeren" (Ph.d. diss., Freie Universität, Berlin, 1962), p. 157, no. 110, mentions consulting several copies of the *Comes rusticus* without finding any that included the engravings. She concludes, in part correctly no doubt, that Le Peletier distributed copies with Félibien's plates inside as gifts to friends. I have consulted the extra-illustrated copy in the National Agricultural Library, Beltsville, Maryland. The six plates here appear in a first state, later augmented by inscribed page references, a compass rose, and the like. Apparently the Bibliothèque Nationale in Paris also has an extra-illustrated copy. My thanks to Dr. Fischer and to the Freie Universität for providing a copy of her dissertation.

11. Henry Lemmonier, *Procès verbaux de l'Académie Royale d'Architecture, 1671–1793,* 10 vols. (Paris, 1911–29), 2:301–2 (meetings held 28 March and 25 April 1695).

12. Jean-François Félibien des Avaux, *Les plans et les descriptions de deux des plus belles maisons de campagne de Pline le consul . . .* (Paris, 1699), pp. 78–79 and plate opposite, for the commentary

on Scamozzi. Pinon and Culot, *Laurentine,* p. 106, illustrates the engraved version of Scamozzi's woodcut.

13. Félibien, *Plans,* p. 7.

14. Apart from the 1699 first edition, another edition of 1706 published in Amsterdam is recorded and illustrated in Tanzer, *Villas of Pliny,* pls. 6–7, 41–42, whereas a variant of it, in the collection of the Ecole Nationale Supérieure des Beaux-Arts, is illustrated in Pinon and Culot, *Laurentine,* pp. 106–8. The 1707 London edition is a scaled-down version but with all seven of the plates. The 1736 Paris and Amsterdam editions, bearing the new title *Délices de la maison de Toscane et la maison de Laurentin,* are sometimes erroneously connected with the name *Parfait* simply because a pamphlet titled *L'idée du peintre parfait* is bound in with them and the last word must have been stamped on the spine of some of the copies. The mistake originated with Johann Matthias Gesner's 1739 edition of Pliny's letters. It was subsequently repeated by Samuel Ball Platner, "Bibliography of the Younger Pliny," *Western Reserve University Bulletin* 1 (1895): 24–39, esp. pp. 33, 37, and by Tanzer, *Villas of Pliny,* p. 140.

15. Regarding possible sources for Félibien's Tuscan and Laurentine villas as well as their future influence, see Fischer, "Rekonstruktionen," pp. 77–90.

16. With special reference to the Académie des Inscriptions et Belles Lettres, see Joseph Rykwert, *The First Moderns: The Architects of the Eighteenth Century* (Cambridge, Mass., 1980), pp. 25–28.

17. André Félibien des Avaux, *Entretiens sur les vies et sur les ouvrages des plus excellents peintres anciens et modernes* (Paris, 1685), p. 321, as quoted by Wolfgang Herrmann, *The Theory of Claude Perrault* (London, 1973), p. 50. For a slightly different interpretation of the place of Félibien's theory in the debate between the ancients and the moderns, see Donald Drew Egbert, *The Beaux-Arts Tradition in French Architecture Illustrated by the Grands Prix de Rome,* ed. David van Zanten (Princeton, N.J., 1980), pp. 102–8.

18. Félibien, *Plans,* pp. 3–4, 84–85.

19. Bernard de Montfaucon, *L'antiquité expliquée et représentée en figures,* 15 vols. and 5 suppls. (Paris, 1719–24), 3:129. The passage translates: "He has succeeded as much as one can in such obscure matters." Kerry Downes, *Hawksmoor,* 2d ed. (Cambridge, Mass., 1980), p. 218, n. 4, and idem, *Hawksmoor* (London, 1969), p. 196 and fig. 175, suggests that Nicholas Hawksmoor's unexecuted 1724 design for a belvedere at Castle Howard is based either on the passage on Pliny in Montfaucon or directly on Félibien, a copy of whose book was in the Hawksmoor library at the time of its sale in 1740.

20. Robert Castell, *The Villas of the Ancients Illustrated* (London, 1728), unpaginated preface. A letter from William Aikman to Sir John Clerk of Penicuik dated 11 November 1727 describes the Vitruvius translation of Castell as "pretty far advanced . . . as Proposals are to come out this winter." In the same sentence Aikman wrote of Castell's villa book as if it were already in print. Clerk in turn wrote the poem "The Country Seat," in which he said, "Mark how the Plinian villa was disposed"; see John Fleming, *Robert Adam and His Circle in Edinburgh and Rome* (London, 1962), pp. 28–30, 328. One John Clerk subscribed to Castell's book, but it is not clear whether this is Sir John. Aikman was the favorite portraitist of Lord Burlington. On Burlington's relations with Castell apropos of Vitruvius, see n. 32 below. A number of sources indicate incorrectly that the Vitruvius translation was actually published; see Pinon and Culot, *Laurentine,* p. 110.

21. Castell, *Villas of the Ancients,* pp. 8, 11.

22. Ibid., p. 100.

23. Melvin Charney, "Of Temples and Sheds," *ARQ/Architecture Québec* 15 (1983): 12.

24. Castell, *Villas of the Ancients,* pls. opposite pp. 66, 67, and 78. The plan and cross section of the restitution of Varro's ornithon are pls. opposite pp. 70 and 71. The topic of the various aviary restitutions by Giacomo Lauro (1584–1637), Castell, Krubsacius, and others deserves detailed study. On Lauro, see the exhibition catalog by Elisabeth B. MacDougall et al., *Fons Sapientiae: Garden Fountains in Illustrated Books, Sixteenth–Eighteenth Centuries* (Washington, D.C., 1977), pp. 40, 80; and for Krubsacius see chapter 5 below.

25. Castell, *Villas of the Ancients*, p. 104.

26. Ibid., p. 6.

27. Fischer, "Rekonstruktionen," pp. 108–9, comments on the oriel and the bay window as possible inspirations for Castell. For a general consideration of the associated plan type see my article "The Bombé Fronted Country House from Talman to Soane," *Studies in the History of Art* 25 (1989): 29–49, though it does not refer specifically to Castell.

28. Tanzer, *Villas of Pliny*, p. 54.

29. John Foster, *Alumni Oxonienses*, ser. 1, 1–2 (1500–1714), records a Robert Castell of Deptford, aged seventeen. But an examination of the original matriculation book for 1673–1740, p. 97, shows that the age should be sixteen, place of birth "Dedford," and the date of matriculation 8 May. The kindness of the librarian of Lincoln College made the manuscript volume available to me at short notice. At the trial (see n. 30 below) Robert is referred to in the testimony as a "gentleman that lived in good figure." A certain Westbrook gave evidence as a character witness that he had been "Mr. Castell's neighbor for twenty years" (p. 430).

30. These are reported to be the parting words of Peter Ellam to Castell as recollected at the time of the trial. The testimony is contained in the two trials of Thomas Bambridge, Castell's jailer, held on 22 May 1729 and in 1730. Bambridge was never convicted. See *A Complete Collection of State Trials and Proceedings for High Treason . . .* , comp. T. B. Howell (London, 1813), 17:383–462, esp. pp. 411–16. Ellam was one of two brothers who subscribed to Castell's book and also stood surety for him in jail.

31. This quotation comes from the *Journal of the House of Commons*, 21:273–83, a report presented on 20 March 1729 by Oglethorpe on behalf of his committee. Page 277 refers specifically to Castell and is quoted in full by Robert Wright, *A Memoir of General James Oglethorpe . . . the Founder of Georgia, in America* (London, 1867), pp. 17, 22, who notes (p. 17) that on 5 July 1729 the residue of Castell's copies of the book was sold for the benefit of his widow and children. The press run must have been considerable, since it is not uncommon to find multiple copies in North American collections: three copies in Montreal alone, two copies at Yale University, and so forth. The printer may have been Thomas Heath, who was a subscriber and also a publisher of architectural books. A reduced reprinting minus the list of subscribers exists and is referred to as a "trade edition." See also John Archer, *The Literature of British Domestic Architecture, 1715–1842* (Cambridge, Mass., 1985), pp. 249–51. The chronology of Castell's death is less clearly established in John Thomas Smith, *The Streets of London: Anecdotes of Their More Celebrated Residents*, 2d ed. (London, 1861), pp. 282–83, which seems to have caused the confusion between 1728 and 1729 that still persists; e.g., Howard Colvin, *A Biographical Dictionary of British Architects, 1600–1840* (London, 1978), pp. 202–3.

32. The Castell connection with Burlington has been discussed by James Lees-Milne, *Earls of Creation* (London, 1962), pp. 144–56; Peter Willis in his essay "Lord Burlington and Landscape Design," in *Apollo of the Arts: Lord Burlington and His Circle*, exhibition catalog, Nottingham University Art Gallery (Nottingham, 1973), pp. 13–14; and Joseph Burke, *English Art, 1714–1800* (Oxford, 1976), p. 52. Most recently Eileen Harris, *British Architectural Books and Writers, 1556–1785* (Cambridge, 1990), pp. 149–54, discusses the production of Castell's book and illuminates Burlington's role in the abortive Vitruvius translation. She publishes the 1 June 1728 proposal for the Vitruvius in which Castell claimed to have had the "special favor" of consulting Burlington's Palladio and Pirro Ligorio drawings. On an earlier occasion, when advertising his villa book Castell had called himself "R.C. Architect," but he later dropped the title (p. 150).

33. Castell, *Villas of the Ancients*, pp. 116–17. In the same passage, Castell alluded to the similarity between the Chinese approach to gardening and European landscape paintings, presumably in the manner of Claude Lorraine.

34. The literature on Burlington, Kent, Ripa, and Castell is extensive despite the rarity of Ripa's engravings. Concerning the BM copy of Ripa bearing a Chiswick bookplate, see Basil Gray, "Lord Burlington and Father Ripa's Chinese Engravings," *British Museum Quarterly* 22 (1960): 40–43. The discussion is picked up in Rudolf Wittkower, "English Neo-Palladianism, the Landscape Garden,

China and the Enlightenment," in *Palladio and English Palladianism*, ed. Margot Wittkower (London, 1974), pp. 177–90, and Rykwert, *First Moderns*, pp. 249–50. John Harris recently cautioned me, however, on interpreting the presence of a Chiswick bookplate as absolute proof that the book had been in Lord Burlington's possession. To this information I may add that the CCA now holds the copy of Ripa extensively discussed by John Bury in his informative entry to the bookseller's catalog *Gardens and Landscapes*, ed. Hugh Pagan (London, 1977), pp. 51–53. This is no. 37 in the B. Weinreb series of architectural book catalogs. The same catalog contains an entry on Castell, pp. 12–13. James Ackerman, *The Villa: Form and Ideology of Country Houses* (Princeton, N.J., 1990), pp. 167–69, deals with the role of William Kent at the Chiswick and Twickenham gardens.

35. Castell, *Villas of the Ancients*, pp. 102–3.

36. Ibid., p. 116, and see also p. 71, where Castell acknowledged the adoption of the word *parterre* from French into English.

37. Ibid., pp. 42, 102.

38. William A. Brogden writes me from Aberdeen in Scotland about Switzer's magazine, which I have not seen. Daniel Malthus took Castell to task in the introduction to his translation of René-Louis de Girardin's *An Essay on Landscape: or, On the Means of Improving and Embellishing the Country Round Our Habitations* (London, 1783), pp. xix–xxvii. I owe this reference to Loudon; see n. 39 below.

39. I have referred to the 1835 edition of John Claudius Loudon's *Encyclopedia of Gardening*, pp. 17–22. Since most of the material in that edition is described by Loudon as "nearly all rewritten," I imagine the Pliny passages to be of 1830s vintage rather than from the previous decade. In fact the Loudon-edited *Garden Magazine* 4 (1830): 226–27 includes the Laurentine site plan of Castell. In response to the request from a correspondent, Loudon promised to publish the Tuscan counterpart, but *Garden Magazine* 7 (1831): 723 actually reproduces a reduced version of Castell's restitution of the villa after the writings of the agronomes Columella and Varro. I owe this information to Arthur Channing Downs.

40. My *John Soane: The Making of an Architect* (Chicago, 1982), p. 44, illustrates Newton's scheme for Saint Luke's Asylum. For Newton's sojourn in Rome see Lindsay Stainton's publication of the so-called Hayward's List, a manuscript in the BM, Department of Prints and Drawings, in *The Walpole Society* 49 (1983): 3–36. Newton was back in England by April 1767, when he wrote to Carrara in fluent Italian about procuring marble for a chimneypiece. See Damie Stillman, "Chimney-Pieces for the English Market: A Thriving Business in Late Eighteenth-Century Rome," *Art Bulletin* 59 (1977): 93–94.

41. William Newton, *The Architecture of M. Vitruvius Pollio*, ed. James Newton, 2 vols. (London, 1791), 1:iv–v. This and the passage concerning Castell are found in virtually identical form in idem, *The Architecture of M. Vitruvius Pollio* (London, 1771), p. v. Newton cited as his authority on Castell's Vitruvius translation the Leipzig publication of 1731, *Acta Erudita*.

42. Algernon Graves, *The Royal Academy of Arts: A Complete Dictionary of Contributors and Their Work from Its Foundation in 1769 to 1904*, 4 vols. (London, 1905), 3:357; and idem, *The Society of Artists of Great Britain, 1760–1791. The Free Society of Artists, 1761–1783. A Complete Dictionary of Contributors . . .* (London, 1907), p. 182. These drawings agree with pls. 57 and 59 in Newton, *Vitruvius* (1791). Neither engraving is included in the 1780 version of the book published in London in French as *Commentaires sur Vitruve éclaircis par des figures et propre à être joints aux différentes traductions de cet auteur. . . .*

43. RIBA, Drawings Collection, formerly numbered K9/16 recto. See *Catalogue of the Royal Institute of British Architects Drawings Collection*, vol. L–N (Farnborough, 1973), p. 144, where under item 104 the drawing in question and four others are mentioned in a summary way.

44. Newton, *Vitruvius* (1791), 2:144, n. 1.

45. Ibid., p. 133, n. 1. This demonstrates that Newton referred to a Latin text of the letters, such as Castell's, rather than to an English translation such as William Melmoth's, which would also have been available to him.

46. Ibid., p. 125, n. 1.

47. The only reference to Potocki in the literature on Pliny's villas is Fischer, "Rekonstruktionen," p. 21, who derives her information from Stanislas Lorentz, "Relazioni artistiche fra la Polonia et l'Italia nel secolo dell'illuminismo," *Palladio*, n.s., 6 (1956): 68–77. On Lorentz's fundamental contribution to the bibliography see n. 54 below.

48. The dating of David's portrait, in addition to much archival information, is the subject of Andrzej Ryszkiewicz, "Portrait équestre de Stanislas Kostka Potocki par Jacques-Louis David," *Bulletin du Musée National de Warsovie* 4 (1963): 77–95. Unfortunately, the key Potocki document for the period, a 214-page bound manuscript titled "Voyage en Italie," is still listed as missing from the ADAG, Archives Publiques de Potocki, no. 245.

49. ADAG, Archives Publiques de Potocki, no. 244, "Notes et Idées sur la Ville de Pline," p. 203, has the references to the Villa Sacchetti and, in somewhat garbled form, to vol. 2, p. 344, of Winckelmann. This manuscript is one item among six other writings all bound together in a green leather booklet. On the page immediately after the title page (p. 202) is written, "Notes et observations sur la lettre XVII du II Livre de Pline de jeune," and it is by this title that the manuscript is listed in the printed catalog of the archive by W. Semkowicz, *Przewodnik po zbiorze rekopisów wilanówskich* (Warsaw, 1961), p. 181. According to note 7 in Kazimierz Michałowski, "Stanisław Kostka Potocki jako archeolog," *Rosznik Historii Sztuki* (Wrocław), 1 (1956): 502–9, the "Notes" manuscript, or one similar to it, had been discovered by the Polish archaeologist Marie Bernhard and was to be published by her. But the ADAG consultation listing indicates she never saw the "Notes," nor could any publication on it by her be found in the literature, despite a search through the years 1956–65 conducted on my behalf by Grzegorz Grątkowski. I conclude, therefore, that the "Notes" are published here for the first time. The post-1800 dating is clear from p. 217, with its reference to Marquez (see also n. 50 below).

50. ADAG, Archives Publiques de Potocki, no. 244, "Notes et Idees sur la Ville de Pline," pp. 217–24. The Poles had recently been ruled by two Saxon absentee monarchs, and the contacts with Dresden remained strong under King Stanislas II August Poniatowski (r. 1764–95). This makes it all the more surprising that Potocki made no mention of Friedrich August Krubsacius, whose former pupil, Jan Chrystian Kamsetzer, became the Polish royal architect in 1773.

51. Ibid., pp. 219–22.

52. Ibid., p. 218.

53. Ibid., and Stanislas Kostka Potocki, *O sztuce u dawnych czyli: Winckelmann polski*, 4 vols. (Warsaw, 1815–18).

54. The following is a list of Stanislas Lorentz's principal publications in which mention of the Laurentine restitution drawings is made: "Domus Aurea Nerona i Willa Laurentina," *Meander* 1 (1946): 314–24; "Działalnosc Stanisław Kostki Potockiego w Dziedzinie Archiketury," *Rocznik Historii Sztuki* (Wrocław), 1 (1956): 450–501; and, with Andrzej Rottermund, *Neoclassicism in Poland* (Warsaw, 1986), pp. 12–13, 242, and see n. 49 above. It should also be noted that six of the drawings were included in the 1975 Rome Exhibition catalog, Palazzo Venezia, *Polonia: Arte e cultura dal Medioevo all'illuminismo* (Florence, 1975), pp. 259–67, with an introduction by Lorentz. In my view only one of the drawings, the site plan, specifically relates to the Laurentine Villa.

55. ADAG, Archives Publiques Potocki, no. 255. This separate booklet is fifty-two pages long and has been referred to and illustrated in the second of Lorentz's articles mentioned in the previous note.

56. See Palazzo Venezia, *Polonia: Arte e cultura*, p. 246, entries 239a and b, relating to a suite of *vedute*, or views, and renderings of Roman wall paintings from the Baths of Titus. Of course Brenna might have prepared these drawings well before meeting Potocki and independent of his patronage.

57. BNW, WAF 67, J. Rys. 5.018. The inscription on the drawing reads: "Cornice di Giove Statore. Giuseppe Manocchi Romano 1777." Other drawings that I exclude from the Pliny restitution are as follows: WAF 67, J. Rys. 5.014, J. Rys. 5.016. For an instance of Manocchi drawings in student architects' possession, see my entries for "Thomas Hardwick" in *Catalogue of the Royal Institute of British Architects Drawings Collection*, vol. G–K (Farnborough, 1973), pp. 89–95.

58. ADAG, Archives Publiques Potocki, no. 244, "Notes," p. 209, "Rien ne constate mieux la magnificence des . . . Empereurs."

59. Ibid., p. 218.

60. On Natolin see Tadeusz Stefan Jaroszewski, *Chrystian Piotr Aigner: Architekt warszawskiego klasycyzmu* (Warsaw, 1970), and Brian Knox, *The Architecture of Poland* (New York, 1971), p. 134.

61. BNW, WAF 67, J. Rys. 5.023, J. Rys. 5.025, J. Rys. 5.026; WAF 68, J. Rys. 5.027, J. Rys. 5.028, J. Rys. 5.029, J. Rys. 5.030, J. Rys. 5.031. As though it belonged to the Laurentine Villa set of drawings, the next to the last of those just enumerated has been included in the recent catalog of the North American traveling exhibition, *Master European Drawings from Polish Collections* (Washington, D.C., 1993), pp. 22–23.

62. See n. 57 above.

63. ADAG, Archives Publiques Potocki, no. 244, "Notes," p. 215. I have so far been unable to identify Orlandi.

64. Palazzo Venezia, *Polonia: Arte e cultura*, p. 14, introduction by Stanislas Lorentz.

Chapter Five

1. Henry Lemmonier, *Procès verbaux de l'Académie Royale d'Architecture, 1671–1793*, 10 vols. (Paris, 1911–29), 7:146, records the first use of the *prix d'émulation*. See Donald Drew Egbert, *The Beaux-Arts Tradition in French Architecture Illustrated by the Grands Prix de Rome*, ed. David van Zanten (Princeton, N.J., 1980), p. 27 on *prix d'émulation*, and nn. 51 and 53 on pp. 33–34 regarding their origin as well as the origin of Blondel's Ecole des Arts. See Kevin Harrington, "Jacques-François Blondel," in *Macmillan Encyclopedia of Architects*, 4 vols. (New York, 1982), 1:220–23, and idem, *Changing Ideas on Architecture in the Encyclopédie, 1750–1776* (Ann Arbor, Mich., 1985).

2. See Robin Middleton on Vaudoyer in *Macmillan Encyclopedia of Architects*, 4 vols. (New York, 1982), 4:300–301.

3. Jean-Nicolas-Louis Durand, *Recueil et parallèle des édifices de tout genre, anciens et modernes, remarquables par leur beauté, par leur grandeur ou par leur singularité, et dessinés sur une même échelle* (Paris, 1799–1801). I have referred to an 1842 Brussels edition.

4. Durand, *Recueil* (1842), pp. 146–47. For an illuminating discussion of Durand's sources of graphic inspiration, see Werner Szambien, *Jean-Nicolas-Louis Durand, 1760–1834: De l'imitation à la norme* (Paris, 1984), pp. 27–30 and pls. 20–23, including the engraving by Leroy in a 1770 version, as well as a similar plate engraved in the 1750s by Juste-Aurèle Meissonier.

5. Jean-Nicolas-Louis Durand, *Précis des leçons d'architecture données à l'Ecole Polytechnique*, 2 vols. (Paris, 1802–5). I am referring to a later, revised edition (Paris, 1817–19), 2:83–84, 94. For the translations of Pliny's letters, see pp. 84–93. This last page refers the reader back to the relevant plate in the *Recueil*. The translations are similar but not identical to those of Louis de Sacy, published in Paris in 1699, the same year the book by Félibien appeared.

6. Szambien, *Durand*, p. 24, notes that both architects proposed building a memorial to Leroy in 1803. In other respects this book overlooks the influence of Pliny on Durand, although an appendix (pp. 179–80) points out that the influence was clear enough to a contemporary reviewer of Durand's book, the architect Détournelle. Szambien also provides dates for and illustrations of Durand's country villas. On Durand in general and his teaching at the Ecole Polytechnique, see Egbert, *Beaux-Arts Tradition*, pp. 45–50.

7. The printed version of the *programme* can be consulted in Antoine-Laurent-Thomas Vaudoyer and Louis-Pierre Baltard, *Grands prix d'architecture: Projets couronnés par l'Académie Royale des Beaux-Arts de France* (Paris, 1834). The manuscript version from the minute book of the Ecole is quoted in full by Pierre Pinon and Maurice Culot, eds., *La Laurentine et l'invention de la villa romaine* (Paris, 1982), pp. 116–17, which also provides the biographical details about the three winning contestants.

8. Vaudoyer and Baltard, *Grands prix*, pls. 47–48 and 68–69, respectively. Helen Tanzer, *The*

Villas of Pliny the Younger (New York, 1924), pls. 13–16, reproduces all four engravings. Of the original drawings rolled up and hence badly damaged, I was able to study only Normand's finely executed *prix d'émulation*, thanks to the archivist of the EBA, Annie Jacques. The other schemes were being conserved.

9. Pinon and Culot, *Laurentine*, p. 121, reproduce the original Macquet drawing in the EBA, ink spill and all. The Grand Prix menagerie designs of Vaudoyer and Percier are discussed and reproduced in Jean-Marie Pérouse de Montclos, *"Les Prix de Rome": Concours de l'Académie Royale d'Architecture au XVIIIe siècle* (Paris, 1984), pp. 183–87.

10. Jules-Frédéric Bouchet, *Le Laurentin maison de campagne de Pline le consul* (Paris, 1852), p. 22, comments on Vaudoyer's overediting of Pliny's letter to Gallus. Bouchet reproduced Macquet's restitution (pl. 2) but misidentified it as the winner of the first prize in the *concours d'émulation*.

11. Eugène-Emmanuel Viollet-le-Duc, *Entretiens sur l'architecture*, 2 vols. (Paris, 1863–72). For a careful chronology of the lectures and their appearance in print as well as their content, see Robin Middleton, "Eugène-Emmanuel Viollet-le-Duc," in *Macmillan Encyclopedia of Architects*, 4 vols. (New York, 1982), 4:324–32.

12. Viollet-le-Duc, *Entretiens*, 1:163–64.

13. Ibid., 1:167. Pinon and Culot, *Laurentine*, p. 55, illustrate and briefly discuss Viollet-le-Duc's scheme of 1875 for a fictive villa of Mummius at Lavinium complete with a cryptoporticus like Pliny's at Laurentinum.

14. Ibid., 1:4, for the comment from the preface about the joys of peaceful study. Contemporary architect and Pliny enthusiast Bernard Huet (see chap. 6) recounts *l'affaire Viollet-le-Duc* without noting the irony of Pliny's appearance in Durand (see Huet's introduction to Szambien, *Durand*, p. 8).

15. CCA, Cormier Archive, Contenant 733, file marked "Ecole Polytechnique Correspondence," contains a bill of 3 May 1928 for three copies of Guadet's book. The file marked "Cours d'architecture Exames Ec. Polytechnique" contains a 19 July 1942 letter of thanks for the gift of two volumes of Choisy. Contenant 682 contains Cormier's diploma from the Ecole des Beaux-Arts. Cormier's personal copy of Guadet is also in the CCA.

16. I have referred to a later edition of Auguste Choisy, *Histoire de l'architecture*, 2 vols. (Paris, 1929) 1:595–96.

17. CCA, Cormier Archive, Contenant ARV-2/A-2, is a black ring binder containing sets of Cormier's mimeographed "Cours d'architecture" lecture notes of various dates. Interleaved with a mimeograph of pre-1940s date is a penciled sheet with thirty-two numbered references to the Laurentine Villa that exactly match the numbered legend of Winnefeld's restitution (see next note). I wish to thank the CCA's archivists Robert Desaulniers and Robert Fortier for their help in the fruitless search for Cormier's slides of the Pliny restitutions.

18. Hermann Winnefeld, "Tusci und Laurentinum des jüngeren Plinius," *Jahrbuch des Kaiserlich Deutschen Archäologischen Institut* 6 (1891): 201–17. James S. Ackerman, *The Villa: Form and Ideology of Country Houses* (Princeton, N.J., 1990), p. 52, calls the Winnefeld Laurentine restitution "as persuasive as any" and reproduces a redrawing of it.

19. *Royal Academy Exhibition Catalogue* (London, 1771), p. 18. Number 190 was the plan by Stevens and number 191 his elevation drawing.

20. For an illustration of a James Wyatt country house design similar to Stevens's Laurentinum and hung in the same Royal Academy exhibition, see John Harris, *Georgian Country Houses: The RIBA Drawings Series* (London, 1968), p. 32.

21. The drawing has been reproduced in John Soane, *Lectures on Architecture*, ed. Arthur T. Bolton (London, 1929), pl. 82, and p. 150 correctly identifies the artist as Stevens. But Pinon and Culot, *Laurentine*, p. 115, attach the name of Soane to the two drawings they illustrate, both of which are identified as representing the Scamozzi Laurentine restitution, whereas only the upper one does; the lower one is by Soane's draftsmen after Stevens.

22. The original letter from Chambers to Stevens came into Soane's hands (from Stevens's widow?)

and is in SM, Correspondence Cupboard I, Division 1, C (7), item 1. The letter is dated 5 August 1774, and I have transcribed it fully in my *John Soane's Architectural Education, 1753–80* (New York, 1977), pp. 370–73. See also my pp. 103–4 regarding Soane and Stevens.

23. SM, Architectural Library 31B, is Soane's copy of the Thomas Sandby manuscript lectures. The original is in RIBA, British Architectural Library. Lecture 5, pp. 40–41, and a prefatory list of illustrations identify the drawings of Laurentinum Sandby exhibited during this lecture. Soane, *Lectures*, p. 150, mentions that he knew Scamozzi's restitution from his *Idea* and from a later Italian version by Fossati.

24. The information comes from a manuscript letter from Sandby to Chambers dated 4 September 1769. An abstract is in the sale catalogs of the autograph dealers Maggs Brothers of London in the period 1925–28 (BM, Department of Prints and Drawings, Whitely Papers, for copies of clippings from catalogs). I do not know the present whereabouts of this letter. Chambers's lecture notes in the RIBA, British Architectural Library contain references to Pliny.

25. SM, Architectural Library, Sir John Soane's Case, shelf E, volume titled "Lectures on Architecture/Royal Academy/1815," p. 77 (lecture "read for the first time" on 2 March 1815). See also Soane, *Lectures*, p. 150.

26. Soane's copy of Castell is SM, Architectural Library 4B. Another copy on the same shelf may be the one he purchased at a bargain price on 8 July 1784 (Soane Notebooks, 12, p. 10). His ownership by about 1782 of an edition of Orrery's translation of Pliny is confirmed by a booklist in the contemporary notebook "Notes Italy and Italian Language," p. 289. A copy of the 1721 edition of the letters translated by Louis de Sacy is inscribed "John Soane 1798."

27. Soane, *Lectures*, pp. 151, 155. For Soane's statement on ancient Roman gardens as quoted here see SM, Architectural Library, Sir John Soane's Case, shelf E, volume titled "Lectures on Architecture/Royal Academy/1815–1833," p. 23 (lecture delivered 7 March 1815).

28. As quoted in *Athenaeum*, no. 798 (11 February 1843): 134. This fourth lecture was largely given over to villa architecture. Cockerell's biographer, David Watkin, kindly writes me that in his research he has come across no Laurentine restitution by Cockerell. Watkin's *The Life and Work of C. R. Cockerell, R. A.* (London, 1974), pp. 105–32, refers to Cockerell's lectures, to their surviving manuscripts, and to newspaper reports of the talks, but it makes no mention of the Pliny episode in 1843.

29. "Professor Cockerell's Lectures on Architecture at the Royal Academy," *Builder* 1 (1843): 27.

30. The "wonderful erudition" of Canina's plates is mentioned in the fourth lecture delivered on 30 January 1845 as reported in *Builder* 3 (1845): 66. Schinkel's works were also shown to the students on a later occasion (p. 73). In neither case, however, is it clear that Cockerell illustrated Pliny restitutions by these two architects.

31. RIBA, British Architectural Library, COC, 1/8-12 contains an incomplete set of lecture notes for the 1843 course, from which the reference to Pliny's villas is missing. For the opportunity to consult the original manuscript I thank Ruth Kamen of the British Architectural Library.

32. "Professor Smirke's Lectures on Architecture," *Builder* 20 (1864): 109–11 (15 February 1862 for the reference to Soane), and pp. 90–92 (8 February 1862 for the reference to the Laurentine Villa).

33. For the praise of Cockerell see George Aitchison, "Charles Robert Cockerell, R.A., Second President of the RIBA," *Royal Institute of British Architects Transactions*, n.s., 6 (1890): 255–61. See p. 261 especially on Cockerell as a lecturer and p. 258 on his lack of fondness for writing. Aitchison's own Royal Academy lecture on Pliny is reported in the *Builder* 58 (1890): 94–97, 135–36, which reproduced Castell's restitutions.

34. Albert E. Richardson, *Monumental Classic Architecture in Great Britain and Ireland during the Eighteenth and Nineteenth Centuries* (London, 1914) p. 42, records Richardson's admiration for Aitchison's lectures, particularly the "lecture on excellence in architecture."

35. Albert E. Richardson, "Laurentinum: The Winter Villa of C. Plinius Caecilius Secundus," *Architects' and Builders' Journal* 37 (1913): 388–90. It subsequently reappeared, unsigned this time, as "The Winter Villa of Pliny," *Architectural Review* 40 (1916): 56–59. Unfortunately, Simon Houfe's

entertaining biography of his grandfather, *Sir Albert Richardson: The Professor* (Luton, 1980), makes no reference to Sir Albert's writings on Pliny or to his attendance at Aitchison's lectures.

36. Aitchison, "Pliny," p. 96.

37. Richardson, "Laurentinum," p. 388.

38. *Illustrated London News*, no. 5653 (23 August 1947): 220–21. Michael Vickers, senior assistant keeper in the Department of Antiquities of the Ashmolean Museum, corresponded with me and generously gave me access to the museum's authority files regarding Pember's model. Among the interesting letters in it were those of Betty de Lisle Radice, the translator of Pliny, and Albert W. van Buren. Van Buren had previously produced his own restitution in article form as "Laurentinum Plinii Minoris," *Rendiconti della Pontificia Accademia Romana di Archaeologia* 20 (1943–44): 165–92. After reading Pember's article, van Buren wrote in 1947 requesting photos of the model. Then he had his restitution redrawn and republished it, along with general praise for Pember's solution, in another article titled "Pliny's Laurentine Villa," *Journal of Roman Studies* 38 (1948): 35–36. Van Buren's is a generally cautious yet very practical restitution. He makes much of a twin axial arrangement and draws heavily on the Villa of the Mysteries outside Pompeii for precedent.

39. See the Pember obituary in *Oxford Times*, no. 4936 (4 November 1955): 9, and also *Brasenose College Register, 1509–1909* (Oxford, 1909), p. 728. The copy of the register in Brasenose College has his birthdate of 21 October 1881 penciled in.

40. Brasenose College Archives, Oxford, Registrar's Department, letter from George Herbert Pember, dated 30 March 1909. I am grateful to the archivist of Brasenose, Elizabeth Boardman, for locating this letter and providing a copy. The senior Pember states in his letter that his son is currently working in Toronto, Ontario, but I am informed by my friends Robert Hill and Stephen Otto that no trace of Pember exists in the Toronto directories for that period.

41. After his Hollywood period Pember's obituary states that he returned to England to become "one of the leading British art directors of both stage and screen in the inter war years."

42. See Moritz Wiessner, *Die Akademie der Bildenden Künste zu Dresden von ihrer Gründung 1764 bis zum Tode von Hagedorns 1780* (Dresden, 1864), pp. 70–82, which dwells on the architecture curriculum at the academy, its headquarters buildings, its exhibitions, and so forth.

43. The portfolio protecting the drawings in the Sächsische Landesbibliothek is pressmarked "Forma max. qu. 2, Archaeol. 177." I thank Manfred Mühlner and Walter May for their assistance both during and since my visit to Dresden. I presume that this folio-sized collection of nine drawings is what is referred to in Christoph Gottlob Kayser's *Bücher Lexikon, 1750–1832*, 3:429, when it cites a 1776 Dresden folio by Krubsacius devoted to Pliny's villas. I know of no such published title of that type by Krubsacius.

44. It is calculated that 226 houses and the 4 main churches of Dresden were burned during the siege. See Paul Schumann, "Barock und Rococo: Studien zur Baugeschichte des 18. Jahrhunderts mit Besonderen Bezug auf Dresden," *Beiträge zur Kunstgeschichte*, n.s., 1 (1885): 72, and see also pp. 54–70 for the most detailed existing account of the life and times of Krubsacius. For a brief account of some of Krubsacius's literary endeavors, see Ernst H. Gombrich, *The Sense of Order: A Study in the Psychology of Decorative Art* (Ithaca, N.Y., 1979), pp. 25–26.

45. "Wahrscheinlicher Entwurf von des jüngern Plinius Landhause, Laurens gennant . . . ," *Das Neueste aus der Anmuthigen Gelehrsamkeit* 6–7 (1760): 382–94, 416–33, 503–15, 582–95.

46. The only copy of the separately bound booklet I have seen is in the collection of the New York Botanical Garden. I owe grateful thanks to Charles Long, the head librarian there, for making it available to me.

47. Krubsacius's contemporary biographer Heinrich Keller stressed the architect's early training in languages by his father. See Keller's *Nachrichten von allen in Dresden lebenden Künstlern* (Leipzig, 1788), p. 92. For Krubsacius on the low-lying houses of the ancients, see "Wahrscheinlicher Entwurf . . . Laurens," p. 387.

48. Schumann, "Barock," p. 73, assured readers of the existence of the Krubsacius drawings, and Tanzer, *Villas of Pliny*, p. 116, knew such drawings existed without having seen them.

49. Friedrich August Krubsacius, "Wahrscheinlicher Entwurf von des jüngern Plinius Landhause und Garten in der toscanischen Gegend . . . ," *Das Neueste aus der Anmuthigen Gelehrsamkeit* 11–12 (1762): 805–11, 812–30, 895–930.

50. The booklet version is titled *Wahrscheinlicher Entwurf von des jüngern Plinius Landhause und Garten in der toscanischen Gegend . . . durch Anmerkungen und Risse erkläret* (Leipzig, 1763) and like its predecessor was published by B. C. Breitkopf. The aerial view (my fig. 100) appears on the recto of an unnumbered page at the beginning, and the ground plan, reused directly from the previously published magazine article, appears on the verso. Based on my bibliographical research to date, the octavo volume in the BM seems to be the only surviving copy. Krubsacius, "Toscanischen Gegend," p. 806, discusses Félibien and by implication Laugier too. Wolfgang Herrmann, *Laugier and Eighteenth-Century French Theory* (London, 1962), p. 190, mentions an anonymous 1773 book review of Laugier attributed to Krubsacius.

51. Unfortunately, only the exhibitions of 1771 and 1772 are reviewed, and not until 1773 and 1778, pp. 130–61 and pp. 5–57, respectively. The reviews are unusually long and unusual also for their date in that they concentrate on architecture. Keller, *Nachrichten,* pp. 92–95, says the reviews were by Krubsacius. Krubsacius's illness toward the end of his life may account for the delays in the appearance of the reviews and for their ultimate cessation. See the previous note about a book review appearing in the same periodical in 1773 (pp. 287–94), which may be by Krubsacius.

52. Friedrich Wilhelm Ludwig Stier, *Hesperische Blätter: Nachgelassene Schriften von Wilhelm Stier* (Berlin, 1857), p. 132. Characteristically, this work was published after Stier's death. The section in question is undated, but its date can be narrowed down to late June or early July 1826 based on a reference to a three-day sirocco that blew in mid-June and prompted the group of friends to escape Rome for a breath of fresh air.

53. The watercolor has previously been discussed and illustrated in Pinon and Culot, *Laurentine,* pp. 140–41, and more extensively in the thorough study by Eva Börsch-Supan, *Berliner Baukunst nach Schinkel, 1840–70* (Berlin, 1977), fig. 142 and p. 687. See especially her section on pp. 89–96, "Das antike Landhaus." Her p. 227, n. 753, clarifies the artistic roots of this Stier drawing. Stier also figures prominently in the exhibition catalog *Berlin und die Antike,* 2 vols. (Berlin, 1979), 2:316–20, and throughout the essay by Rolf Bothe, "Berliner Architekten zwischen 1790–1870."

54. Anonymous exhibition review, "Die erste Versammlung deutscher Architekten in Leipzig während des 10, 11 und 12 September 1842," *Allgemeine Bauzeitung* 7 (1842): 378–88. On p. 387 the reviewer notes the twin Laurentine projects of Stier and Schinkel without passing judgment on either and then goes on to note that the Glienicke and Charlottenhof garden buildings must be understood against this Laurentine background.

55. Friedrich Wilhelm Ludwig Stier, *Architektonische Erfindungen von Wilhelm Stier,* ed. Hubert Stier, vol. 1, *Entwurf zu dem laurentinischen Landsitze des Plinius* (Berlin, 1867), and vol. 2, *Entwurf zu dem tuskischen Landsitze des Plinius* (Berlin, 1868). The first volume has a foreword by Hubert Stier dated October 1866, which gives an account of his father's work and promises a full biography to follow. It existed in manuscript, according to the informative entry by a descendant, Rudolf Stier, in the *Thieme-Becker Künstlerlexikon,* but it no longer survives among the Stier papers in the TUB. The text fascicles were published simultaneously with the engravings, which are much larger in format and were therefore bound separately. Copies of both text and images known to me are in the BM and the TUB.

56. Stier's approach to teaching as gleaned from his surviving lecture notes in the TUB has been discussed by Wolfram Hoepfner and Ernst Ludwig Schwandner in their contribution, "Archäologische Bauforschung," in the catalog *Berlin und die Antike,* 2:343–44.

57. Stier, *Architektonische Erfindungen,* 1:v, provides in Hubert Stier's words an impression of his father's love of artistic challenge for its own sake without thought of gain and with such attention to detail as to discourage any hope of actual employment.

58. Ibid., p. 1, section titled "Historische Notizen über die Entwürfe."

59. Börsch-Supan, *Berliner Baukunst,* p. 685, gives her opinion about Stier's dream schemes. She

also quotes from a revealing Stier letter to the diplomat Bunsen, his patron from their days together in Rome. When Stier mentioned the Crimea, did he have Schinkel's Orianda schemes in mind (see chap. 1)?

60. The Stier manuscript "Erläuterung zu dem Architektonischen Entwürfe von dem laurentischen Landsitz des jüngeren Plinius . . . ," is TUB, II M. 42A. I have been sent a typescript transcription of the original thanks to Dieter Radicke of the TUB. The manuscript version of the text should be consulted jointly with the ones published in the *Architektonische Erfindungen.* I have preferred using the manuscript because of its undoubted authenticity.

61. Ibid., p. 12 of the manuscript version.

62. Ibid., p. 10 (pavements), pp. 20–21 (vaulting and wooden ceilings), pp. 20, 24 (bay windows), p. 26 (roofing shapes), and p. 21 (stage and musicians' gallery). Cf. in the printed version pp. 27, 35–36, 35, 38, 40, and 35.

63. Ibid., p. 11 (painted animal stalls), pp. 18–19 (library), pp. 20–21 (*cubiculum politissimum*), p. 23 (*sphaeristerium*), p. 24 (*cenatio rimota a mari*), and p. 11 (Apollo Nonios). Cf. in the printed version pp. 28, 33–34, 35, 37, 38, and 28. On the allusions to classical statuary in Stier's restitution see *Berlin und die Antike,* 2:320.

64. Ibid., pp. 27–29, "Bauanlagen in Garten der Villa," and pp. 29–31, "der Garten der Villa." These long passages, with some of the most florid language in the manuscript, were drastically cut in the printed version, but some of the information was used elsewhere in the general observations on pp. 23–24.

65. Ibid., pp. 16–17; cf. p. 32 in the printed version. In manuscript the second passage reads, "Die Beschreibung ist hier augenscheinlich nach der Phantasie . . . sie ist rhetorische Form." In the printed version it reads, "Die Beschreibung ist hier wohl etwas rhetorische Form, aus der Phantasie geschrieben."

66. Joseph Egle, "Bericht über die Ausstellung zu Bamberg," *Allgemeine Bauzeitung* 8 (1843): 281–96. On the first and next to last of these pages, Egle refers to the Tuscan Villa and regrets that he has no more space to devote to it in his review.

67. The five surviving drawings in the TUB related to the Tuscan Villa are 7215–19. Of these, 7219 corresponds to pl. 1 in the *Architektonische Erfindungen,* vol. 2, 7215–16 relate to pl. 2, 7217 relates to pl. 3, and 7218 roughly corresponds to pl. 6. The seventh and last plate consisting of two cross sections is not found among the drawings. I have preferred to illustrate the drawings when possible because, being tinted, they reproduce better. Stier's *Architektonische Erfindungen,* 2:2, gives the genesis of the drawings. The engravings based on them appeared separately in atlas-sized format under the slightly variant title *Entwurf zur Wiederherstellung des tuskischen Landsitzes des Plinius* (Berlin, 1868), in accord with its companion volume of the previous year *Entwurf zur Wiederherstellung des laurentischen Landsitzes des Plinius.*

68. Stier, *Architektonische Erfindungen,* 2:43, 45, 46. The pagination is continuous from volume 1 and thus runs from 43 to 66. On the first of these pages Hubert Stier remarked on the greater play the letter to Apollinaris gives to "der Phantasie des Künstlers." Nevertheless, the prose of this subsection lacks the flourish of Wilhelm Stier's prose style and his sense of conviction. Börsch-Supan, *Berliner Baukunst,* figs. 137, 139, and p. 95, is the only source to illustrate and discuss Stier's Tuscan Villa restitution. Tanzer, *Villas of Pliny,* was unaware of the existence of this restitution, although Samuel Ball Platner, "Bibliography of Pliny the Younger," *Western Reserve University Bulletin* 1 (1895): 24–39, in his useful list of writings on Pliny, includes Stier's Laurentine Villa publication based on having seen the text portion. No complete copy of plates and text exists in North America to the best of my knowledge.

69. Stier, *Architektonische Erfindungen,* 2:44; cf. p. 18 of the "Ansichten" in the *Architektonische Erfindungen,* vol. 1, on the Italians' love of landscape that is synonymous with the choicest locations they select for villas. The manuscript "Erläuterung," p. 18, reads "Sind nicht die beliebtesten Orte für Landsitze . . . gleichzeitig auch die schönsten Gegenden Italiens?" This passage is omitted from the printed version.

70. Stier, *Architektonische Erfindungen,* vol. 1, "Ansichten," p. 21; cf. pp. 19 and 45 regarding the functional role the cryptoporticus plays in binding together the entire Tuscan Villa.

71. Ibid., pp. 20–21 (on asymmetry), 16–17 and 45, 48 (on Pliny's omission of certain villa functions).

72. Ibid., "Ansichten," p. 19, and pp. 45, 50, 53. References to Pompeii in the "Ansichten" far outnumber mentions of other sites. See, for example, pp. 15, 19, 21, and 23.

73. Ibid., pp. 50, 65.

74. Ibid., pp. 52, 55, 62.

75. Ibid., "Ansichten," pp. 15–17, regarding Stier's aims, and pp. 17, 21 for Stier's opinion on the relation between inner function and outer form.

76. Ibid., "Ansichten," p. 18.

77. Ibid., "Ansichten," pp. 15–19.

Chapter Six

1. A general discussion of the Concorso Clementino and some of its early competitions in particular is provided by the Museum of Art exhibition catalog *Architectural Fantasy and Reality: Drawings from the Accademia di San Luca in Rome Concorsi Clementini, 1700–1750* (University Park, Pa., 1981). The exhibition coordinator, Hellmut Hager, very kindly provided me with this catalog prepared by him and his students at Pennsylvania State University.

2. Both sets of drawings have been assigned consecutive numbers by the Accademia di San Luca and are illustrated in its comprehensive but very cursory catalog *I disegni di architettura dell'archivio storico dell'Accademia di San Luca,* 2 vols. (Rome, 1978), 2:13, and figs. 2289–93. Pierre Pinon and Maurice Culot, eds., *La Laurentine et l'invention de la villa romaine* (Paris, 1982), pp. 124–26, are unsure about the dates of these drawings, but they infer a date (p. 79, n. 61) sometime around the middle of the nineteenth century.

3. See Pinon and Culot, *Laurentine,* pp. 56–57, for a discussion of the Pompeian room in Paris and the one by Friedrich von Gärtner at Schloss Aschaffenburg.

4. Helen Tanzer, *The Villas of Pliny the Younger* (New York, 1924), pp. 83–87 and pls. 27–30.

5. The envois are the subject of the recent exhibition catalog published by the Ecole des Beaux-Arts, *Paris, Rome, Athènes: Le voyage en Grèce des architectes français aux XIXe et XXe siècles* (Paris, 1982).

6. See Pinon's essay "Invention de la maison romaine," in Pinon and Culot, *Laurentine,* and in the Ecole des Beaux-Arts exhibition catalog *Pompéi: Travaux et envois des architectes français au XIXe siècle* (Paris, 1981).

7. IFA, Archives Department, document of 1 June 1981.

8. Personal interview with Jean-Pierre Braun, 5 February 1987, Paris.

9. See the exhibition catalog *Parables and Other Allegories: The Work of Melvin Charney, 1975–1990* (Montreal, 1991), pp. 136–39, for Charney's own interpretation, and see also his earlier analysis in "Of Temples and Sheds," *ARQ/Architecture Québec* 15 (1983): 11–15. I have made some personal observations on Charney's installation in "The Villas of Pliny: Reflections on the Exhibition by Its Guest Curator," *Fifth Column* 4 (1983–84): 21–24.

10. IFA, Archives Department, letters of invitation and acceptance. The quoted passage reads in translation: "Pliny, ever young, awaits his next competition; it is the continuity of classicism that is at issue."

11. Personal interview with Jean-Pierre Adam, 1 April 1987, Château de Vincennes.

12. Pierre-Yves Balut, "Architectes et archéologues," in Pinon and Culot, *Laurentine,* pp. 244–45, writes of the Adam restitution, "C'est un néo- du XXe siècle."

13. Personal interview with Jean-Pierre Adam, 1 April 1987, Château de Vincennes. Pinon and Culot, *Laurentine,* pp. 58–59, discuss and illustrate Kerylos.

14. Jean-Pierre Adam, "La villa de Pline le jeune aux Laurentes," in Pinon and Culot, *Laurentine,* pp. 170–75, esp. p. 175.

15. IFA, Archives Department, letter of 12 August 1981.

16. Personal interviews with Jean-Pierre Braun and with Fraisse at the time of the round-table discussion at Paris on 18 June 1987.

17. IFA, Archives Department, letter of June 1982 from Jacques Martin to Maurice Culot regarding payment for the Alix drawing.

18. Philippe Fraise and Jean-Pierre Braun, "Un seul texte n'a jamais permis une restitution définitive," in Pinon and Culot, *Laurentine,* pp. 177–80.

19. Balut, "Architectes et archéologues," p. 218. Favorable comments on Fraisse and Braun's entry appeared in exhibition reviews by Pascale Beaudot, *Vie des Arts,* 28, no. 113 (1983): 70; Claudette Hould, *Vie des Arts* 28, no. 114 (1984): 24; and Odile Hénault, *Devoir,* 28 October 1983, p. 28. The Montreal *jeu de Pline* was specially designed for the education department of the Musée des Beaux-Arts de Montréal by Chantal Leveiller. Because the Fraisse and Braun restitution hung in the separate children's section along with the game, both Beaudot and Hould failed to see it and therefore incorrectly lamented its absence from the exhibition.

20. Biographical notice in the CCA archives. Copy in my possession.

21. Personal interview with Patrick Weber and Didier Laroche, 16 February 1987, Strasbourg.

22. Balut, "Architectes et archéologues," pp. 220, 245. And see the untitled essay by Patrick Weber and Didier Laroche in Pinon and Culot, *Laurentine,* pp. 204–5. This published version is slightly mistranscribed from the original document in IFA, Archives Department, and this accounts for some, though not all, of the non sequiturs in syntax.

23. Biographical notice in the CCA archives. Copy in my possession.

24. Personal interview with Treuttel, Garcias, and Treuttel, 3 April 1987, Paris.

25. Jean-Jacques Treuttel, Jean-Claude Garcias, and Jérôme Treuttel, "Otium cum dignitate, labor cum flagello," in Pinon and Culot, *Laurentine,* pp. 186–89; see p. 189, n. 5, for their reference to Viollet-le-Duc.

26. Personal interview with Fernando Montes, 3 April 1987, Paris. The passage quoted reads in translation: "I try by every possible means to supply something that resembles a scenario."

27. Fernando Montes, "Campus autiosus," in Pinon and Culot, *Laurentine,* pp. 207–11. The original title, according to the submission document of December 1981 in IFA, Archives Department, was "Campus autosius," which I believe to be the correct version. In French *autosite* means something that feeds upon itself.

28. In his biographical notice (copies in the CCA archives and in my possession), and in the March 1986 issue of *Architecture and Urbanism,* Montes with a straight face makes the Laurentine restitution scheme sound like a design for a real poor man's vacation center at Tréguenec in Brittany.

29. *Château Bordeaux,* ed. Jean Dethier (London, 1989), pp. 201–5, 226–31.

30. Personal interviews with Justo Solsona and Alberto Damp, 19 and 21 April 1988, Buenos Aires. A biographical notice and letter from Solsona are in the CCA archives, copies in my possession. For more on the work of Solsona's firm see Mario Gandelsonas and Kenneth Frampton, *Manteola Sanchez-Gomez Santos Solsona Viñoly* (Buenos Aires, 1978). I thank Professor Solsona for giving me a copy of this publication.

31. Justo Solsona, "Ils ont fini la villa," in Pinon and Culot, *Laurentine,* p. 206.

32. IFA, Archives Department, contains a 9 December 1981 typed *répartition des honoraires,* to which Farina's name is added in manuscript as if to indicate a late submission. On the list neither the name of Solsona nor those of Weber and Laroche appear. But, curiously, the names of Sefik Birkiye and Gilbert Busieau are included, though no restitution by them was ever exhibited at IFA. Details of Farina's activities before the competition are based on his biographical notice in the CCA archives (copy in my possession). Farina's involvement in the competition was the subject of a personal interview with him 14 April 1987, Milan.

33. Paolo Farina, "Puzzle City: Mailand," *Daidalos* 3 (15 March 1982): 81–91. It is worth noting that the entire issue is devoted to the theme of the labyrinth and that the gardens at Bomarzo, which are also included, interest Farina a good deal.

34. IFA, Archives Department, original Italian text by Farina. It has been translated as "Le jeu de Pline continue" for inclusion in Pinon and Culot, *Laurentine*, pp. 212–13.

35. Balut, "Architectes et archéologues," p. 221.

36. *Terza mostra internazionale de architettura: Progetto Venezia. Biennale di Venezia* (Milan, 1985), p. 142. For the existing Villa Farsetti see Joseph Rykwert, *The First Moderns: The Architects of the Eighteenth Century* (Cambridge, Mass., 1980), pp. 290–94, and more recently Margherita Azzi Visentini, *Il giardino veneto tra sette e ottocento e le sue fonti* (Milan, 1988), which I have not seen.

37. For some of Farina's recent work, see the issue of *Domus* for April 1984 and those of *Casa Vogue* for January 1985, pp. 98–101, and November 1986, pp. 176–79.

38. The Alcan Architecture Lecture Series press release for 1983 in my possession also mentions that from 1974 to 1977 Huet edited the influential magazine *Architecture d'Aujourd'hui*. Other biographical details are furnished on the dust jacket of a book published by Maurice Culot's Archives d'Architecture Moderne, titled *Anachroniques d'architecture* (Brussels, 1981). Especially interesting is the transcribed dialogue between Culot and Huet (pp. 161–79), in which frequent references are made to Krier.

39. Bernard Huet, "Relire Pline," in Pinon and Culot, *Laurentine*, pp. 165–69; see esp. p. 169 on the pleasures of reading Pliny and pp. 165–66 on the Laurentine restitutions of the past.

40. Ibid., pp. 240, 246, gives Balut's commentary on Huet.

41. Personal interview with Bernard Huet, 24 March 1987, Paris.

42. On the now completed Place Stalingrad project, see Odile Seyler, "Bernard Huet: Paris, Place Stalingrad," *Ottagono* 93 (December 1989): 60–73. I am grateful to Alessandra Ponte for bringing this article to my attention. See also Bernard Huet, "Place Stalingrad: A Project of Urban Reconstruction," *Composicion Arquitectonica, Art and Architecture* 9 (1992): 13–44.

43. Personal interview with Serge Santelli, 30 May 1990, Montreal.

44. Balut, "Architectes et archéologues," pp. 240–41.

45. IFA, Archives Department, file folder relating to this incident. Personal interview with Pierre-Yves Balut, 15 January 1987, Paris.

46. CCA archives, letter from David Bigelman of 27 September 1983 to Joanne Desilets, copy in my possession.

47. CCA, DR 1984: 1636, fols. 20 verso to 26 recto, contain the revealing original draft of Bigelman's letter later printed as "De David Bigelman à M. C. salut," in Pinon and Culot, *Laurentine*, pp. 201–2.

48. Ibid., fol. 23 verso.

49. Personal interview with David Bigelman, 30 January 1987, Paris, in the course of which Bigelman showed me his unfinished Palissy restitution as well as those preliminary drawings for the Laurentine Villa still in his possession. He gave me a photocopy of his underlined English translation of Bernard Palissy's *A Delectable Garden*, trans. and with an introduction by Helen Morgenthau Fox (Peekskill, N.Y., 1931).

50. IFA, Archives Department, letter to Pinon and Culot from Garay and José Linazasoro, signed by both architects.

51. CCA archives has a biographical notice for each architect, and copies are in my possession. Much of my information is based on a personal interview with the architects, 28 April 1987, in Pamplona, and on subsequent meetings with them, notably in May of the following summer, when I saw additional examples of their work. On that occasion they urged me not to miss seeing the Madrid Observatory when visiting that city. Léon Krier has been a frequent visitor to the San Sebastián school of architecture.

52. Manuel Iñiguez and Alberto Ustarroz, "Des pierres authentiques," in Pinon and Culot, *Lauren-*

tine, pp. 192–94. The original French version of the text, somewhat edited to improve the grammar for the printed book, is in IFA, Archives Department.

53. Balut, "Architectes et archéologues," pp. 241–42.

54. For the Lesaka town hall building and views of their medical center in the same Basque town, as well as drawings of their rejected university building, see Miguel Garay, "Manuel Iñiguez and Alberto Ustarroz: Projets et réalisations en Espagne," *Archives d'Architecture Moderne,* nos. 35–36 (1987): 78–99.

55. *Château Bordeaux,* pp. 195–99. The accompanying texts are written by the architects themselves and by Maurice Culot.

56. IFA, Archives Department, has letters on file in English from Sundermann to Culot written on 12 December 1981 and 30 January 1982 recording his initial failure to meet the deadline and his final submission. But a copy of a letter from Culot to him, dated 18 December 1981, indicates that Sundermann had, between his two letters, sent a partial submission that nevertheless arrived too late for the exhibition at the Académie d'Architecture. The IFA file on Sundermann is unusually full, reflecting his punctiliousness. If similar exchanges occurred with other architects, and I personally doubt it, then no record of them has been preserved or else communication was carried on largely by telephone. The CCA archives have a long biographical notice on Sundermann, a copy of which is in my possession. I conducted a personal interview with Manfred Sundermann on 8 July 1987 at Münster.

57. Manfred Sundermann, "La lettre est le plan," in Pinon and Culot, *Laurentine,* pp. 181–85.

58. Balut, "Architectes et archéologues," p. 241.

59. See Manfred Sundermann, "Villa Laurentium de Plinius," *Architectural Design* 57 (1987): 9–13. In the same issue, pp 14–15, is Sundermann's "Villa Tuscum de Plinius."

60. Manfred Sundermann, "Das Tuscum des Plinius," in *Deutsche Akademie Villa Massimo in Rome, 1983–1984* (Rome, 1984), n.p. The text is dated 25 January 1984. I thank the architect for giving me a copy. The passage quoted reads in translation: "Sketches are freer and not tied to a particular representational convention."

61. Sundermann, who grew up in Münster and now works there, is very proud of the city and knowledgeable about it. He took me on a tour of local monuments, including examples of the strong regional styles practiced in a number of historical periods.

62. The relationship of Krier both with Culot and with the polemical writings of Le Corbusier forms the subject of a study by Denise Jakal. See her "Politics in the Architecture of Léon Krier," *Architecture Research Criticism* 1 (1990): 4–11, and more recently "Léon Krier: The Architect and the City after the Reign of Modernism," *Queen's Quarterly* 99 (spring 1992): 105–24.

63. Personal interview with Léon Krier, 29–30 June 1987, London, and on several other occasions beforehand and subsequently, most recently on 29–31 October 1991.

64. Léon Krier, "L'amour des ruines ou les ruines de l'amour," in Pinon and Culot, *Laurentine,* pp. 151–52. Elsewhere in the essay (pp. 149–54) Krier mentions restitutions by Canina (cf. figs. 30 and 31); Fritz Krischen, author of *Weltwunder der Baukunst in Babylonien und Jonien* (Tübingen, 1956); Luigi Crema, author of the article "L'architettura romana," in *Enciclopedia classica* (Turin, 1959); Gustavo Giovannoni, coauthor of *L'urbanistica dall'antichià ad oggi* (Florence, 1943); and Italo Gismondi, whose writings I have so far been unable to trace. For a slightly different list of names see the version of Krier's article translated by Richard Becherer, "The Love of Ruins, or Ruins of Love," *Modulus* 16 (1983): 48–61. In conversation (see n. 63 above) Krier told me about his admiration for C. Weichardt's *Pompeji vor der Zerstörung Reconstruktionen der Tempel und ihrer Umgebung . . .* (Berlin, 1897) and J. B. Ward-Perkins's *Roman Imperial Architecture* (Harmondsworth, Eng., 1981).

65. These ideas have been expressed in Krier's lectures "L'amour des ruines" (Montreal, 27 October 1983) and, with respect to "modernist" values, "The City, the Citizen, and the State" (Kingston, Ontario, 30 October 1991).

66. On Rita Wolff see Maurice Culot, "Peintre de rêve," *Archives d'Architecture Moderne,* no. 31 (1986): 68, which illustrates Wolff's watercolor *Winter Night at Sperlonga* of 1980. The postcard

message Krier sent me in June 1984 reads in part, "En pleine province des barbares . . . les pirates aujourd'hui malheureusement occupent les terres." On an earlier occasion Culot wrote an editorial on Krier and the Laurentine *concours,* "Le démon de midi," *Archives d'Architecture Moderne,* no. 24 (1982). A reply by François Loyer is titled "La terre brûlé," *Archives d'Architecture Moderne,* no. 25 (1983): 2–10.

67. It was so engaging a drawing that someone spirited it away from IFA after the original series of drawings was complete and a colored illustration had been taken for inclusion in Pinon and Culot, *Laurentine,* p. 164. Krier told me that to complete the set he had to remake the drawing at the time he sent the rest of them to the CCA. Tiny differences distinguish the original drawing from Krier's later autograph version. At that time Krier wrote in retrospectively the date 10 October 1981. Some doubt therefore exists concerning the dates inscribed on the final series. But the dating "10 October 1981–1 March 1982," on the ground plan in the CCA, DR 1985:293 probably reflects the time it took to prepare the entire final series of drawings.

68. Krier shares his enthusiasm for Alix not only with Culot but also with Pierre-Yves Balut. In "Architectes et archéologues," pp. 233 and 246, Balut shows himself knowledgeable about comic books and popular movie epics such as *Spartacus.* The normally acerbic Balut could find little fault with Krier's utopian Laurentine restitution, which he describes as "nourricière de programmes futurs," or nursemaid to future architectural programs (p. 247). The only direct paraphrase of Martin by Krier comes in a sketchbook drawing of the Laurentine harbor lighthouse inscribed by Krier "d'après la griffe noir" in reference to *La griffe noir,* one of the Alix comic book adventures.

69. Krier, "Amour des ruines," p. 151.

70. I have previously discussed Krier's Platonism with respect to the Laurentine Villa in my article "La Laurentina di Léon Krier tra eidos e polis," *Eidos,* no. 9 (October 1991): 84–91, edited by Massimo Scolari. I have also collaborated with Joan Coutu and Denise Jakal on a small exhibition catalog for the Agnes Etherington Art Centre, *The Design Process of Léon Krier's Laurentine Villa Project* (Kingston, Ontario, 5 October–24 November 1991), which contains excellent essays on the chronology and significance of Krier's restitution by Coutu and Jakal, respectively.

71. Hannah Arendt, *The Human Condition,* 2d ed. (Garden City, N.Y., 1959). Krier mentioned Arendt as his "pillar" in a telephone conversation I had with him in December 1988.

72. Léon Krier in the foreword to *New Classicism,* ed. Andreas Papadakis (London, 1990). This foreword is a revised and expanded version of a seminal essay, "The Reconstruction of Vernacular Building and Classical Architecture," *Architects' Journal* 180, no. 37 (1984): 55–65, see especially p. 58. I am grateful to the architect for sending me a copy.

73. For illustrations of some of these tower retreats see *Léon Krier Drawings, 1967–1980* (Brussels, 1980), pl. 1 (house for Rita, 1969–74), pls. 2–3, 40 (house for Giovanni Mayer, 1974), pl. 80 (house for Massimo Scolari, 1978). See also *Léon Krier: Houses, Palaces, Cities,* ed. Demetri Porphyrios (London, 1984), front flyleaf ("Because," 1982), pp. 120–28 (Laurentine Villa, houses for Rita, Giovanni Mayer), back flyleaf (house for Mr. and Mrs. Stillman, 1982).

74. Léon Krier, "Léon Krier talks to Colin Davies," in *Léon Krier Drawings, 1967–1980* (Brussels, 1980), p. xvii.

Conclusion

1. Caius Caecilius Secundus Pliny, *The Letters of Pliny the Younger, with Observations on Each Letter,* trans. John Boyle, fifth earl of Orrery, 2 vols. (London, 1751), 1:387. The quotation is taken from Orrery's translation of Pliny's letter to Apollinaris.

2. Alexander G. McKay, *Houses, Villas and Palaces in the Roman World* (Ithaca, N.Y., 1975), p. 139, writes of the Roman villa: "There is an aversion to admitting sunlight into the interiors of houses and every conceivable device, venetian blinds, shutters, awnings, and curtains, is brought into play to fend off the rays." Regarding the influence of Hadrian's villa, see the forthcoming book about it by William McDonald and John Pinto, which was still in press when this note was being written.

3. Pliny, *Letters*, Orrery ed., 2:159, says of Pliny: "His eyes were impaired by continual study."

4. Jean-François Félibien des Avaux, *Les plans et les descriptions de deux des plus belles maisons de campagne de Pline le consul* (Paris, 1699), p. 4.

5. DO, Lazzari MS, fols. 25 recto to 26 verso, BGCCDC, Lazzari MS, fols. 20 verso to 22 recto.

6. Pliny, *Letters*, Orrery ed., 1:vi.

7. Ibid., 1:175. In light of Orrery's background and his kinship with Burlington, it would not be astonishing to find that Orrery carried the paradigm to its logical conclusion by adorning with Plinian pavilions the grounds of his own beloved Marston House in Somerset. After inheriting the house and property in 1731, Orrery carried out alterations that ceased only about the time of the publication of his Pliny edition in 1751. See Michael McGarvie, "Marston House: A Study of Its History and Architecture," *Somerset Archaeology and Natural History* 118 (1974): 15–24, which provides many details on Orrery's architectural undertakings but nothing that appears to link them directly with any of Pliny's building projects. Despite this lack of evidence, a recent book by Douglas D. C. Chambers, *The Planters of the English Landscape Garden: Botany, Trees, and the Georgics* (New Haven, Conn., 1993), p. 195, n. 2, sees Orrery's Marston as a sort of landlocked Laurentinum. Chambers kindly passed on to me the information that on 27 November 1731, two decades before publishing his translation of Pliny, Orrery wrote a letter in which Pliny's letter to Gallus is paraphrased. Orrery told his correspondent that when he settled at Marston he hoped to be able to extend hospitality of the sort proffered by the ancient Roman. The letter is among the Orrery Papers at Harvard University, MS Eng. 218. 2(1), letter 7, pp. 12–14. In Chambers's book figure 13 reproduces the same engraving as my figure 179, but the caption incorrectly places Pliny's *stibadium* at Laurentinum rather than at the Tuscan Villa.

8. Pliny, *Letters*, Orrery ed., 1:388.

9. Ibid., p. 393.

10. Ibid., 2:274 and 1:389, refers to the maps by Ortellius of Como and of Tuscany, respectively. The second reference also contains the quotation about the villas' disappearance. The Rev. Mr. John Duncombe, former chaplain to Orrery, edited the nobleman's *Letters from Italy in the Years 1754 and 1755*, 2d ed. (London, 1774). Duncombe's preface speaks of Orrery's "taste for architecture which had enabled him to design his own alterations to Marston House" (p. xxiii). The preface concludes with a long eulogy on Orrery, in which almost every aspect of his career and life is related to comparable events in the life of Pliny (pp. xxxv–xxxvii).

11. Eugenia Salza Prina Ricotti has written on this topic from the archaeological standpoint in her article "The Importance of Water in Roman Villa Gardens," in *Ancient Roman Villa Gardens: The Tenth Dumbarton Oaks Colloquium on the History of Landscape Architecture* (Washington, D.C., 1987), pp. 137–84, and figs. 1, 35. Ricotti includes her own restitution of the Laurentine Villa and the Tuscan Villa *stibadium*.

12. On the hippodrome garden at Sans Souci, see the article by Harri Günther in *The Oxford Companion to Gardens*, ed. Geoffrey Jellicoe, Susan Jellicoe, et al. (Oxford, 1986), p. 499. Günther has published the relevant plans and maps of the royal estate at Potsdam in *Peter Joseph Lenné: Gärten/Parke/Landschaften* (Anstalt, 1985), pp. 46–47. They are dated by him 1825–26 and have the faint outlines of the hippodrome garden penciled in. The printed map dated 1828 shows no hippodrome had as yet been laid out. Martin Sperlich, "Nicht Schloss, sondern Villa," in *Schloss Glienicke: Bewohner, Künstler, Parklandschaft* (Berlin, 1987), p. 30, claims that as early as 1825 Schinkel already cited Pliny in conjunction with Charlottenhof. Sperlich gives no source for this statement, but he means to allude to the quotation given by Harri Günther; see n. 14 below.

13. Günther, *Lenné*, pp. 48–50, reproduces and discusses no fewer than four maps of the Potsdam estate, which he dates 1835.

14. Ibid., p. 49, quoting from the text accompanying pls. 119–20 in Karl Friedrich Schinkel, *Architektonischer Entwürfe* (Potsdam, 1841–43). The text by Schinkel actually refers to the project illustrated in my figure 41.

15. The original Schinkel drawing for the lithograph is SA 175, MXL, no. 71, dated 1833. The Charlottenhof *stibadium* with marble columns was actually carried out, but the work dragged on until after Schinkel's death. In the diary of his pupil Ludwig Persius for May 1843 there is a reference to ongoing construction of the little building. See Eva Börsch-Supan, *Ludwig Persius: Das Tagebuch des Architekten Friedrich Wilhelms IV, 1840–1845* (Munich, 1980), pp. 61, 79, 82, 111, 148, 198. The last of these quotations mentions Charlottenhof in the same breath with Schinkel's Tuscan Villa restitution.

16. Clifford Pember, "The Country House of a Roman Man of Letters: The Lost Villa of the Younger Pliny," *Illustrated London News*, no. 5653 (1947): 220.

17. Ibid.

18. Caius Caecilius Secundus Pliny, *The Letters of Pliny the Consul: With Occasional Remarks,* trans. William Melmoth, 9th ed., 2 vols. (London, 1796), 1:263, translating from Pliny's letter to Apollinaris.

19. CCA, DR 1984:1636, fols. 24 recto to 25 verso. The letter is written in Bigelman's sketchbook. Pierre Pinon and Maurice Culot, eds., *La Laurentine et l'invention de la villa romaine* (Paris, 1982), p. 202, publish the final, much changed version of the same Bigelman letter. I have referred also to my personal interview with David Bigelman, 30 January 1987, Paris.

20. Justo Solsona, *Letrógrafo cuentos* (Buenos Aires, 1979). The author himself presented me with a copy of his now out-of-print collection of stories, for which I am most grateful.

21. Pinon and Culot, *Laurentine,* p. 206, give a full transcript of the text on the drawing.

22. Solsona, *Letrógrafo,* pp. 88–111 and 121–34, for the two stories in question. I am grateful to Dolores Gutierrez, formerly of Queen's University, for help with the translation and interpretation of Solsona's fiction.

23. Personal interviews with Erik Marosi, 29 September 1986, 8 October 1991, and 8 December 1992, Montreal.

24. See *Michael Graves Buildings and Projects, 1982–1989* (New York, 1990), especially pp. 24–33, where such projects as the Environmental Education Center are discussed. It is interesting in this connection that Susan Doubilet titled her discussion of the Center "Pliny's Villa: Environmental Education Center," *Progressive Architecture* 64 (August 1983): 88–93.

25. An essay by Larry Richards in *Canadian Centre for Architecture: Buildings and Gardens* (Montreal, 1983), pp. 128, 130, alludes to Marosi's contributions to the design and to the influence of Graves, but it makes no mention to the connection between the Montreal building and the restitutions of Pliny's villas.

26. According to a biographical notice of Marosi's in my collection, the *secrétaire* design became one of the finalists in the 1987 furniture design competition organized by *Progressive Architecture* magazine. Subsequently the model appeared in the exhibition catalog *Five Architects* of the Galérie John A. Schweitzer (Montreal, 6–30 April 1989).

BIBLIOGRAPHY

Ackerman, James S. *The Villa: Form and Ideology of Country Houses.* Princeton, N.J., 1990.

Aitchison, George. "Pliny the Younger's Laurentine and Tuscan Villas." *Builder* 58 (1890): 94–97, 135–36.

Balut, Pierre-Yves. "Architectes et archéologues." In *La Laurentine et l'invention de la villa romaine,* edited by Pierre Pinon and Maurice Culot, pp. 217–52. Paris, 1982.

Bandini, Angelo Maria. *Catalogus codicum latinorum Bibliothecae Mediceae Laurentinae.* 4 vols. Florence, 1774–84.

Barbieri, Franco. *Vincenzo Scamozzi.* Vicenza, 1952.

Bargellini, Clara, and Pierre de la Ruffinière du Prey. "Sources for a Reconstruction of the Villa Medici, Fiesole." *Burlington Magazine* 111 (1969): 597–605.

Berlin und die Antike. 2 vols. Berlin, 1979.

Börsch-Supan, Eva. *Berliner Baukunst nach Schinkel, 1840–70.* Berlin, 1977.

Borsook, Eve. *Companion Guide to Florence.* London, 1966.

Bouchet, Jules-Frédéric. *Le Laurentin maison de campagne de Pline le consul.* Paris, 1852.

Brown, Alison. *Bartolomeo Scala, 1430–1497, Chancellor of Florence.* Princeton, N.J., 1979.

Canina, Luigi. *L'architettura romana descritta e dimonstrata coi monumenti.* Atlas vol. Rome, 1840.

——— . *Gli edifici di Roma antica e sua campagna . . . Edifici dei contorni della città.* 6 vols. Rome, 1848–56.

Carocci, Guido. *I dintorni di Firenze.* 2d ed. 2 vols. Florence, 1906–07.

Castell, Robert. *The Villas of the Ancients Illustrated.* London, 1728.

Château Bordeaux. Edited by Jean Dethier. London, 1989.

Coffin, David R. "The Plans of the Villa Madama." *Art Bulletin* 49 (1967): 111–22.

——— . *The Villa in the Life of Renaissance Rome.* Princeton, N.J., 1979.

du Prey, Pierre de la Ruffinière. "Four Cardinal Points of a Villa." *ARQ/Architecture Québec* 15 (October 1983): 16–22.

Durand, Jean-Nicolas-Louis. *Précis des leçons d'architecture données à l'Ecole Polytechnique.* 2d ed. 2 vols. Paris, 1817–19.

——— . *Recueil et parallèle des édifices de tout genre, anciens et modernes . . . dessinés sur une même échelle.* Paris, 1799–1801.

Egbert, Donald Drew. *The Beaux-Arts Tradition in French Architecture Illustrated by the Grands Prix de Rome*. Edited by David van Zanten. Princeton, N.J., 1980.

Fea, Carlo. *Relazione di un viaggio ad Ostia e alla villa di Plinio detta Laurentino*. Rome, 1802.

Félibien des Avaux, Jean-François. *Les plans et les descriptions de deux des plus belles maisons de campagne de Pline le consul*. Paris, 1699.

Fischer, Marianne. "Die frühen Rekonstruktionen der Landhaüser Plinius' des jüngeren." Ph.D. diss., Freie Universität, Berlin, 1962.

Foster, Philip. "Raphael on the Villa Madama: The Text of a Lost Letter." *Römisches Jahrbuch für Kunstgeschichte* 11 (1967–68): 307–12.

———. *A Study of Lorenzo de' Medici's Villa at Poggio a Caiano*. 2 vols. New York, 1978.

Frommel, Christoph Luitpold. "Die Architektonische Planung der Villa Madama." *Römisches Jahrbuch für Kunstgeschichte* 15 (1975): 61–83.

Gournay, Isabelle, ed. *Ernest Cormier and the Université de Montréal*. Montreal, 1990.

Günther, Harri. *Peter Joseph Lenné: Gärten/Parke/Landschaften*. Anstalt, 1985.

Haudebourt, Louis-Pierre. *Le Laurentin maison de campagne de Pline le jeune restituée d'après la description de Pline*. Paris, 1838.

Hirt, Aloys Ludwig. *Die Geschichte der Baukunst bei den Alten*. Berlin, 1821–27.

Keller, Heinrich. *Nachrichten von allen in Dresden lebenden Künstlern*. Leipzig, 1788.

Krier, Léon. "Amour des ruines ou les ruines de l'amour." In *La Laurentine et l'invention de la villa romaine*, edited by Pierre Pinon and Maurice Culot, pp. 149–54. Paris, 1982.

Krubsacius, Friedrich August. "Wahrscheinlicher Entwurf von des jüngern Plinius Landhause, Laurens gennant. . . ." *Das Neueste aus der Anmuthigen Gelehrsamkeit* 6–7 (1760): 382–94, 416–33, 503–15, 582–95.

———. *Wahrscheinlicher Entwurf von des jüngern Plinius Landhause, Laurens gennant. . . .* Leipzig, 1760.

———. "Wahrscheinlicher Entwurf von des jüngern Plinius Landhause und Garten in der toscanischen Gegend. . . ." *Das Neueste aus der Anmuthigen Gelehrsamkeit* 11–12 (1762): 805–11, 812–30, 895–930.

———. *Wahrscheinlicher Entwurf von des jüngern Plinius Landhause und Garten in der toscanischen Gegend. . . .* Leipzig, 1763.

Lanciani, Rodolfo Amadeo. *Wanderings in the Roman Campagna*. Boston, 1909.

Lancisi, Giovanni Maria. "Dissertatio de Plinianae villae ruderibus atque Ostiensis litoris incremento." In *Dissertatio de generatione fungorum*, by Luigi Ferdinando Marsili. Rome, 1714.

Lefèvre, Eckard. "Plinius Studien I: Römische Baugesinnung und Landschaftsauffassung in der Villenbriefen (2, 17; 5, 6)." *Gymnasium* 84 (1977): 519–41.

Lefevre, Renato. *Villa Madama*. Rome, 1973.

Littlewood, A. R. "Ancient Literary Evidence for the Pleasure Gardens of Roman Country Villas." In *Ancient Roman Villa Gardens: The Tenth Dumbarton Oaks Colloquium on the History of Landscape Architecture,* edited by Elisabeth Blair Macdougall. Washington, D.C., 1987.

Marquez, Pedro José. *Delle ville di Plinio il giovane*. Rome, 1796.

Newton, William. *The Architecture of M. Vitruvius Pollio*. London, 1771.

———. *The Architecture of M. Vitruvius Pollio*. Edited by James Newton. 2 vols. London, 1791.

Palladio, Andrea. *I quattro libri dell'architettura*. Venice, 1570.

Patzak, Bernhard. *Palast und Villa in Toscana*. 2 vols. Leipzig, 1913.

Pember, Clifford. "The Country House of a Roman Man of Letters: The Lost Villa of the Younger Pliny." *Illustrated London News*, no. 5653 (1947): 220–21.

Peschken, Goerd. *Das Architektonische Lehrbuch*. Munich, 1979.

Pieraccini, Gaetano. *Le stirpe de' Medici di Cafaggiolo: Saggio de richerche dei caratteri biologici*. 3d ed. 3 vols. Florence, 1986.

Pinon, Pierre, and Maurice Culot. eds. *La Laurentine et l'invention de la villa romaine*. Paris, 1982.

Pliny, Caius Caecilius Secundus. *The Letters of Pliny the Younger, with Observations on Each Letter*. Translated by John Boyle, fifth earl of Orrery. 2 vols. London, 1751.

Polonia: Arte e cultura dal Medioevo all'illuminismo. Florence, 1975.

Richardson, Albert E. "Laurentinum: The Winter Villa of C. Plinius Caecilius Secundus." *Architects' and Builders' Journal* 37 (1913): 388–90.

Ricotti, Eugenia Salza Prina. "Il Laurentino: Scavi del 1985." In *Castelporziano II: Campagna di scavo e di restauro, 1985–86,* pp. 45–56. Rome, 1986.

Rome, Palazzo Venezia. *Polonia: Arte e cultura dal medioevo all'illuminismo*. Florence, 1975.

Roscoe, William. *The Life of Lorenzo de' Medici, Called the Magnificent*. 4th ed. 3 vols. London, 1800.

Rossi, Vittorio. "L'indole e gli studi di Giovanni di Cosimo de' Medici." *Rendiconti della Reale Accademia dei Lincei: Rendiconti Morali,* ser. 5, 2A (1893): 38–60, 129–50.

Rowland, Ingrid D. "Render unto Caesar the Things Which Are Caesar's: Humanism and the Arts in the Patronage of Agostino Chigi." *Renaissance Quarterly* 39 (1968): 673–729.

Rykwert, Joseph. *The First Moderns: The Architects of the Eighteenth Century*. Cambridge, Mass., 1980.

Sambricio, Carlos. *Silvestre Perez arquitecto de la ilustración*. San Sebastian, 1975.

Scamozzi, Vincenzo. *L'idea dell'architettura universale*. 2 vols. Venice, 1615.

Scarlett, Charles. "Governor Horatio Sharpe's Whitehall." *Maryland Historical Magazine* 46 (1951): 8–26.

Schinkel, Karl Friedrich. *Architektonisches Album*. No. 7. Berlin, 1841.

Schumann, Paul. "Barock und Rococo: Studien zur Baugeschichte des 18. Jahrhunderts mit besonderen Bezug auf Dresden." *Beiträge zur Kunstgeschichte*, n.s. 1 (1885).

Shearman, John. "A Functional Interpretation of Villa Madama." *Römisches Jahrbuch für Kunstgeschichte* 20 (1983): 315–27.

Smith, Thomas Gordon. *Classical Architecture: Rule and Invention*. Layton, Utah, 1988.

Soane, John. *Lectures on Architecture*. Edited by Arthur T. Bolton. London, 1929.

Solsona, Justo. *Letrógrafo cuentos*. Buenos Aires, 1979.

Stegmann, Carl von, and Heinrich von Geymüller. *Die Architektur der Renaissance in Toscana*. 11 vols. Munich, 1885–1908.

Stier, Friedrich Wilhelm Ludwig. *Architektonische Erfindungen von Wilhelm Stier*. Vol. 1, *Entwurf zu dem laurentinischen Landsitze des Plinius*. Edited by Hubert Stier. 1 vol. and atlas. Berlin, 1867.

———. *Architektonische Erfindungen von Wilhelm Stier*. Vol. 2, *Entwurf zu dem tuskischen Landsitze des Plinius*. Edited by Hubert Stier. 1 vol. and atlas. Berlin, 1868.

Stout, Selatie Edgar. *Plinius Epistulae: A Critical Edition*. Bloomington, Ind., 1962.

Szambien, Werner. *Jean-Nicolas-Louis Durand, 1760–1834: De l'imitation à la norme*. Paris, 1984.

Tanzer, Helen. *The Villas of Pliny the Younger*. New York, 1924.

Vasari, Giorgio. *Le vite dei più eccelenti pittori, scultori, ed architetti.* . . . Edited by Gaetano Milanesi. 9 vols. Florence, 1878–85.

Vaudoyer, Antoine-Laurent-Thomas, and Louis-Pierre Baltard. *Grands prix d'architecture: Projets couronnés par l'Académie Royale des Beaux-Arts de France*. Paris, 1834.

Viollet-le-Duc, Eugène-Emmanuel. *Entretiens sur l'architecture*. 2 vols. Paris, 1863–72.

Volpi, Giuseppe Rocco. *Vetus Latium profanum et sacrum*. 11 vols. Rome, 1704–45.

Winckelmann, Johann Joachim. *Briefe*. Edited by Hans Diepolder and Walther Rehm. 4 vols. Berlin, 1952–57.

Winnefeld, Hermann. "Tusci und Laurentinum des jüngeren Plinius." *Jahrbuch des Kaiserlich Deutschen Archäologischen Institut* 6 (1891): 201–17.

INDEX